V!VA
TRAVEL GUIDES

ECUADOR & THE GALÁPAGOS ISLANDS

Quito - Cuenca - Otavalo - Baños - Andes - Amazon - Coast

3rd Edition
August 2007

V!VA Travel Guides' Guarantee:
We guarantee our guidebook to be the most up-to-date printed
guidebook available. Visit www.vivatravelguides.com/guarantee/to learn more.

V!VA Travel Guide: Ecuador & the Galápagos Islands.

ISBN-10: 0-9791264-2-8
ISBN-13: 978-0-9791264-2-0

Copyright © 2007, Viva Publishing Network.
Voice: (970) 744-4244
Fax: (612) 605-5720
Website: www.vivatravelguides.com
Information: info@vivatravelguides.com

www.vivatravelguides.com

CONTENTS

QUITO   66

THE GALÁPAGOS ISLANDS   138

ABOUT V!VA TRAVEL GUIDES

V!VA Travel Guides is a new approach to travel guides. We have taken the travel guide and re-designed it from the ground up using the internet, geographic databases, community participation, and the latest in printing technology which allows us to print our guidebooks one at a time when they are ordered. Reversing the general progression, we have started with a website, gathered user ratings and reviews, and then compiled the community's favorites into a book. Every time you see the V!VA insignia you know that the location is a favorite of the V!VA Travel Community. For you, the reader, this means more accurate and up-to-date travel information and more ratings by travelers like yourself.

COMMUNITY AND FREE MEMBERSHIP:
The accuracy and quality of the information in this book is largely thanks to our online community of travelers. If you would like to join them go to www.vivatravelguides.com/members/ to get more information and to sign up for free.

YOUR OPINIONS, EXPERIENCES AND TRAVELS:
Did you love a place? Will you never return to another? Every destination in this guidebook is listed on our web site with space for user ratings and reviews. Share your experiences, help out other travelers and let the world know what you think.

UPDATES & REGISTERING:
We update our books at least twice a year. By purchasing this book you are entitled to one year of free electronic updates. Go to www.vivatravelguides.com/updates/ to register for your free updates. Feedback on our book to get a free ebook by registering your views at www.vivatravelguides.com/register.

CORRECTIONS & SUGGESTIONS:
We are committed to bringing you the most accurate and up-to-date information. However, places change, prices rise, businesses close down, and information, no matter how accurate it once was, inevitably changes. Thus we ask for your help: If you find an error in this book or something that has changed, go to www.vivatravelguides.com/corrections and report them (oh, and unlike the other guidebooks, we'll incorporate them into our information within a few days).

If you think we have missed something, or want to see something in our next book go to www.vivatravelguides.com/suggestions/ and let us know. As a small token of our thanks for correcting an error or submitting a suggestion we'll send you a coupon for 50 percent off any of our eBooks or 20 percent off any of our printed books.

COMING SOON ON WWW.VIVATRAVELGUIDES.COM
This is just the beginning. We're busy adding new features that our users have requested to our books and website. A few coming attractions are:
• Improved Community Functions: join groups, find travel partners, participate in forums.
• Write travel blogs and share travel photos from your trip
• And more!

HOW TO USE THIS BOOK

This book is a best-of Ecuador taken straight from our website. You can check out the website to read user reviews, rate your favorite hotels and restaurants and add in information you think we are missing. The book also features highlighted sections on haciendas, eco-tourism in Ecuador, and adventure travel. Use our helpful tear-out sheet, complete with emergency contact details and helpful numbers, whilst you are out and about in Ecuador.

ABOUT THE AUTHORS

Paula Newton is V!VA's operations expert. With an MBA and a background in New Media, Paula is the Editor-in-Chief and the organizing force behind the team. With an insatiable thirst for off-the-beaten-track travel, Paula has traveled extensively, especially in Europe and Asia, and has explored more than 25 countries. She currently lives in Quito.

Shortly after completing her degree in Print Journalism at the University of St. Thomas, St. Paul, Minnesota, Erin Helland moved to Ecuador to work for V!VA Travel Guides, writing and designing for both the web and the guidebooks. A native of South Dakota, Erin has always had a desire to see the world, studying in both England and Mexico. She hopes to combine her passions for design and travel in her career.

Caroline Bennett has long been melding passions for storytelling and wanderlust through writing and photographing across the globe. Proudly from Penobscot, Maine in the US, Caroline graduated cum laude from Colorado College in 2006 with a dual B.A. in Documenting International Culture & Society and Political Science/Latin American Studies. Several projects and a lively up-for-anything spirit have seen her through much of Latin America, Oceania, Southeast Asia and Europe.

Dr. Christopher Minster, PhD is a graduate of Penn State University, The University of Montana, and Ohio State. He is the resident V!VA Travel Guides expert on ruins, history and culture, as well as spooky things like haunted museums. He worked for the U.S. Peace Corps in Guatemala as a volunteer from 1991 to 1994 and has traveled extensively in Latin America. He currently resides in Quito.

Katie Tibbetts's sense of adventure has taken her around the globe. A native of Connecticut U.S.A., she received her Bachelor of Arts and Post Graduate Degree in English Literature from the University of Otago, Dunedin, New Zealand. Her passion for hiking, climbing and the great outdoors has taken her extensively through Australia, Europe and Ecuador. Katie was the editor of the second edition of this guidebook.

Dawn (Wohlfarth) Arteaga, researches and writes for the International Center for Journalists in Washington, D.C. Dawn lived in Ecuador for two years and was editor and writer of V!VA's first edition of V!VA Guides Ecuador (November, 2005) paving the way for the current guidebook. She holds a B.A. in Journalism and Spanish from American University, Washington D.C.

Many Thanks To:

Tania Morales and Paul Anthony, the programming masterminds who keep our parent website www.vivatravelguides.com running smoothly and always lend a hand to the not-always-computer-savvy staff. Also, **Christian Llaguno** who helped with painstakingly creating all of our maps and **Gabriela Freile** who updated the book's details, and the whole **Metamorf** team. Special thanks to **Kristi Mohrbacher** who got down and dirty in the jungle to improve our Amazon section. Also, thanks to all of our contributors, especially **Michelle Hopey, Karey Fuhs, Freddie Sumption and Chris Sacco.** Last but not least, thanks to **Jordan Barnes** and **Blessing Waung,** who spent many hours editing and proofreading this edition of the book and writing last minute additions.

◊ Cover Design: ◊ Cover Photo (Masked Booby): Suco Viteri ◊
◊ Cover Photo: "Cayambe." Caroline Bennett ◊
◊ Back Cover Photo (Cotopaxi): Suco Viteri◊ Title Page Photo: Caroline Bennett ◊

Get your writing published in our books, go to www.vivatravelguides.com

Ecuador Highlights

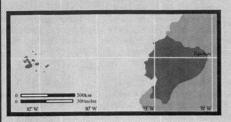

Mindo A hummingbird and butterfly paradise in this cloud forest biodiversity hotspot.

Canoa Long stretches of white sand, chilled Pacific surf and easy-going locals.

Cotopaxi National Park The perfect glacial-topped cone is one of the world's highest active volcanoes, with incredible views from the top.

Quilotoa Loop Mountainous stretch of patchwork hills, alive with indigenous farm life and breathtaking scenery.

Puyango petrified forest Rare dry tropical forest, far off the Gringo trail in the deep south.

Vilcabamba Great horseback riding, hiking or just relaxing in the "valley of eternal youth".

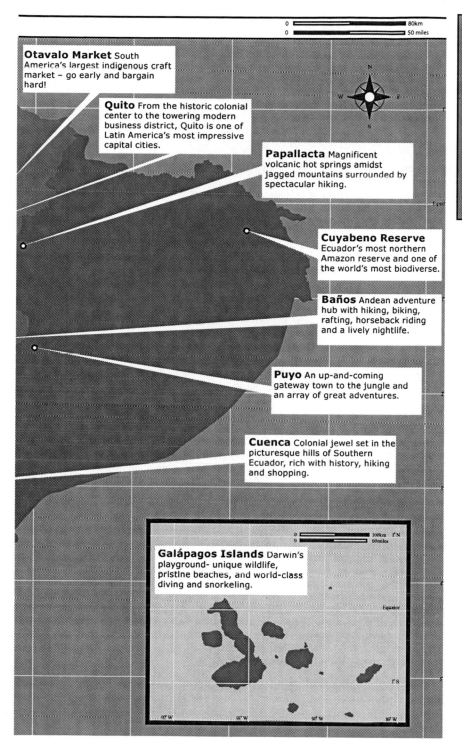

0 ▰▰▰▰▰▰▰ 80km
0 ▰▰▰▰▰▰▰ 50 miles

Otavalo Market South America's largest indigenous craft market – go early and bargain hard!

Quito From the historic colonial center to the towering modern business district, Quito is one of Latin America's most impressive capital cities.

Papallacta Magnificent volcanic hot springs amidst jagged mountains surrounded by spectacular hiking.

Cuyabeno Reserve Ecuador's most northern Amazon reserve and one of the world's most biodiverse.

Baños Andean adventure hub with hiking, biking, rafting, horseback riding and a lively nightlife.

Puyo An up-and-coming gateway town to the jungle and an array of great adventures.

Cuenca Colonial jewel set in the picturesque hills of Southern Ecuador, rich with history, hiking and shopping.

0 ▰▰▰▰▰▰▰ 100km
0 ▰▰▰▰▰▰▰ 60miles

Galápagos Islands Darwin's playground- unique wildlife, pristine beaches, and world-class diving and snorkeling.

Equator

92° W   91° W   90° W   89° W

REGIONS OF ECUADOR
QUITO (P. 66)

Quito, the bustling capital of Ecuador, is more than just a place to pass through *en-route* to other spectacular sites, such as the Galápagos, Otavalo or the Amazon basin. Most visitors to Quito are struck by how the modern and the traditional exist side by side: the city has everything from baroque cathedrals to TGI Friday's. The colonial city center, named by UNESCO as the first world heritage site because of its well-preserved, beautiful architecture, is a great place to take a stroll or even spend the night if you don't mind a little more noise. One downtown highlight is La Compañia church: the interior is one of the most striking in the world, as there is a vast amount of gold leaf covering all of the intricate woodwork on the walls and ceiling. You'll want to visit the Panecillo, a small hill near colonial Quito where an impressive statue of an angel overlooks the city: the view is fantastic.

The Mariscal district, beloved by international visitors, is where you'll find all of the *chévere* ("cool") places: nightclubs, bars, internet cafes, bookstores, and hip restaurants. Shoppers won't want to miss the indigenous artisan markets in and around El Ejido park: they're the best place to find a bargain south of Otavalo. Visitors of all ages will want to visit Quito's newest attraction, the Telefériqo, a gondola-style cable car that whisks visitors from downtown Quito to the top of Pichincha volcano, climbing several hundred meters in the process—the complex also features an amusement park, restaurants and shops.

Quito is the cultural and artistic heart of Ecuador—it is where you'll find all of the best museums, restaurants and upscale shops. If you're interested in culture, Quito has it in abundance. Visitors can see shows and concerts at the elegant and newly restored Teatro Sucre or catch the world-famous Jacchigua national folkloric ballet. No visit to Quito is complete without a stop at Mitad del Mundo, a small "village" for tourists about twenty minutes north of the city where the Equatorial Line is marked by an impressive monument. Take your photo with one foot in each hemisphere, then enjoy local cuisine at the restaurants in the complex as you listen to impromptu concerts by Andean bands.

THE GALÁPAGOS ISLANDS (P. 138)

If you've ever switched on the Discovery Channel, chances are you've heard of the Galápagos Islands—the archipelago is certainly Ecuador's most-hyped and most famous tourist destination, attracting thousands of visitors annually from around the world. These visitors are not disappointed: if anything, they find that the islands are even more special and unique than they had anticipated.

Santa Cruz, the likely port of entry for most Galápagos visitors, is home to the largest city in the islands, Puerto Ayora. It is also where you'll find the world-renowned Charles Darwin Research Station, where scientists continue Darwin's work on evolution and natural selection and protect imperiled Galápagos species. Remote Genovesa, known by its nickname "bird island," is home to large colonies of frigate birds, boobys, swallow-tailed gulls and more. San Cristobal is where you'll find Puerto Baquerizo Moreno, the capital of Galápagos Province, as well as several good beaches and Isla Lobos, one of the best places in the islands to snorkel or dive with sea lions. Española is the only nesting place in the world of the waved albatross, the largest bird found in the islands. Floreana is a good place to see flamingos and where you'll find The Devil's Crown, considered by many to be the best snorkeling site in the islands. Isabela, the largest island, boasts no less than five volcanoes, each of which is home to a different species of giant tortoise. Fernandina, the youngest island, is where you'll find the flightless cormorant, a remarkable bird endemic to Galápagos.

Whether you've come for history, science, the wildlife or just to relax, Galápagos is sure not to disappoint.

THE ANDES (P. 220)

The majestic Andes mountains bisect Ecuador along a north-south line, effectively dividing mainland Ecuador into three zones: the rainforest, the highlands, and the coast. The Andes region is home to several of the most interesting places to visit in Ecuador, including the country's most charming cities, one of the best markets in the Americas, several volcanoes and many opportunities for adventure travel, such as rafting and hiking.

No visit to Ecuador is complete without a trip to the famous indigenous crafts market at Otavalo, located just to the north of Quito. South of Quito, the mellow tourist town of Baños attracts visitors from around the world who want to test the thermal baths, which supposedly have divine healing powers, and enjoy the lively nightlife. Most travelers try to find time to fit in at least a day trip to Cotopaxi, one of the highest active volcanoes on earth. On a clear day, it can be seen towering over Quito. If remote is your thing, head to the Quilotoa Loop where you will find a spectactular crater lake and fine opportunities to observe less-touched rural life. Cuenca should not be missed with its well preserved colonial center and opportunities for hiking and shopping in the surrounding area. If you have the time, head very far south to Vilcabamba—you will quickly see why its inhabitants claim to live long lives—the pace of life is sublimely relaxed.

THE AMAZON BASIN (P. 300)

Much of the water that flows eastward through South America along the Amazon river and its tributaries originates in the mountains of Ecuador. The Ecuadorian Amazon basin is a fantastic place to visit—you can expect to see monkeys, birds, caimans, butterflies and more on a trip to the jungle. Most visitors to the rainforest take advantage of the services offered by the various jungle lodges, who arrange everything from transportation to guides to food. Other travelers go to the city of Tena, a ramshackle jungle city not too far from Quito, from where it is possible to set out to visit the rainforest. Puyo is up-and-coming as an alterntive jungle entry point. It is worth noting that if you want to see lots of wildlife, head deep into the primary rainforest to one of the outlying lodges.

THE COAST (P. 324)

Ecuador's Pacific coast is long, largely undeveloped (apart from major ports at Esmeraldas, Manta and Guayaquil), and dotted with many excellent beaches.

One of the routes to the beach goes via the small town of Mindo, located in the tropical cloud forest. Mindo is a prime destination for birdwatchers, who can expect to see hundreds of species in a very small area. Mindo is also known for rafting and adventure travel. Ecuador's biggest city, Guayaquil is located in the coastal region.

While the northern coastline is lined with greenery, the southern coast is typified by countless shrimp farms and drier scrubland. Banana plantations and swampy mangroves are found along pretty much the entire length of the coast. Coastal highlights include the beach towns of Esmeraldas province, such as Atacames which have good nightlife, but can get overrun at weekends and public holidays with *quiteños* escaping the city, the laid-back surfing town of Montañita, and the stretch of beach in between known as "La Ruta Del Sol"—the route of the sun. The portion of coast around the Machalilla national park is particularly stunning with many a pretty white-sand beach to laze on. Canoa's popularity has been increasing recently and it's not hard to see why, with its divine beach and relaxed atmosphere. If you're ready for some fun in the sun after shopping in the highlands or hiking through the jungle, then it's time to hit the beach. Don't forget the sunscreen!

INTRODUCTION

Ecuador is the smallest of the Andean countries, just smaller than Italy. With the Pacific Coast, the Andean Highlands and the Amazon Basin packed into its small surface area, plus the Galápagos Islands off the coast, it boasts a little of everything the continent has to offer - like South America in miniature, as the locals are fond of saying. Ecuador's diversity is its biggest draw. In the morning, you can plunge into the sparkling blue waters off one of the Galápagos Islands where playful sea lions will swim through your legs and hammerhead sharks will swim by without giving you a second glance. By early afternoon you can sip a cappuccino in the capital's historic colonial center and absorb the beauty of Spanish cathedrals built over the ruins of the Inca Empire set against the breathtaking backdrop of the Andes Mountains and volcanoes. At sunset, you could pull up to a remote jungle lodge in a dugout canoe, carved the same way Amazon tribes have been doing it for thousands of years, listening to toucans, parrots, and howler monkeys play out their nighttime opera in the dense forest all around you.

You may imagine that this diversity, the low cost of living and the abundance of cheap travel services, along with luxury travel options, would make Ecuador one of the most popular destinations in South America. However, the country is relatively undiscovered and there are plenty of opportunities for remote and adventure travel.

GEOGRAPHY

Provinces: 22 provinces: Azuay, Bolívar, Cañar, Carchi, Chimborazo, Cotopaxi, El Oro, Esmeraldas, Galápagos, Guayas, Imbabura, Loja, Los Ríos, Manabí, Morona-Santiago, Napo, Orellana, Pastaza, Pichincha, Sucumbíos, Tungurahua, Zamora-Chinchipe.
Highest point: Volcán Chimborazo 6,267 meters (20,561 ft)
Natural Resources: petroleum, fish, timber, hydropower.
Natural Disasters: earthquakes, landslides, volcanic activity, floods, periodic droughts.

FLORA & FAUNA

Nature lovers from around the world are drawn to the rain forests, cloud forests, deserts, islands, volcanoes and snow-capped peaks of Ecuador, one of the world's most bio-diverse nations. This tiny nation holds 46 different ecosystems. Many private and public organizations work to protect Ecuador's biodiversity, which includes 10 national parks, 14 natural reserves and several UNESCO Natural Heritage Sites. Most notable of these flora and fauna-rich areas are Ecuador's portion of the Amazon Rainforest and the enchanted Galápagos Islands. Ecuador is rich with flora. Ecuador has 2,725 orchid species growing in the wild in the Andes and 25,000 different species of trees in the northeastern Amazon Rainforest. Ecuadorian Amazonia is particularly rich in flora; the Andes sharply drop off into the Amazon River Basin, feeding rich nutrients right into the rainforest. The Andes Mountains feature cloud forests rich in orchids, bromeliads and tropical plants and trees. In total, the Andes have an estimated 8,200 plant species. Although the Galápagos Islands were volcanically formed and are largely barren, they are still home to over 600 native plant species and many more that have been introduced.The small country of Ecuador is home to more bird species than North America and Europe combined: a total of 18 percent of the world's birds and 15 percent of the world's endemic bird species call the country home. A million species of insects, 4,500 species of butterflies, 350 reptile species, 375 amphibian species, 800 fresh water fish species, 450 salt water fish species, and 1,550 mammal species crawl, climb, fly and swim around this bio-diverse country.

CLIMATE

Ecuador has two seasons: wet and dry, which come and go depending on which part of the country you are in. But, generally speaking, the temperature is dictated by altitude. Quito and the Andes have spring-like weather year-round. The Galápagos' weather varies between misty and cool and sunny and steamy. The Amazon Rainforest weather is generally either hot and humid or hot and rainy.

Ecuadorian History

PRE-INCA TIMES

Although the earliest evidence of man in Ecuador can be traced back to 10,000 BC, there are few concrete facts about the country's history before the invasion of the Inca in the middle of the 15th century. Research is ongoing, and the Museo Nacional del Banco Central has some fascinating artifacts that are laid out to chart the probable development of the country before the Incas, from the age of hunter-gatherers to the dawn of pottery and ceramics, agriculture and fixed settlements. By 1480, dominant indigenous groups included Imbayas, Shyris, Quitus, Puruhaes and Cañaris in the highlands, and the Caras, Manteños and Huancavilcas along the coast.

THE INCA INVASION

The Incas had dominated present-day Peru since the 11th-century, but it was not until the mid 15th-century that they began to expand into what is now Ecuador. Yapanqui led the invasion with his son Túpac Yapanqui. Native resistance was fierce, particularly in the north, but they eventually arranged peace terms with one dominant group in the south, the Cañaris. Túpac Yapanqui extended the empire further after the death of his father, establishing himself at Ingipirca before conquering the Quitu/Caras Indians in present-day Quito. He then built an impressive network of roads, stretching the length of his empire from Cusco in southern Peru north to Quito. Some of these roads survive today and are popular with hikers. Problems arose when Túpac Yapanqui died, setting off a war over succession between two of his sons, Huascar and Atahualpa. Huascar, Túpac's eldest son, was based at Cusco, while Atahualpa, Huascar's younger brother, governed his half of the empire from Quito. Both brothers were power-hungry, and soon after their father's death, civil war broke out. In 1532, Atahualpa secured victory over his brother and re-established his base in northern Peru.

THE SPANISH INVASION - THE CONQUEST

The Inca Ruler Atahualpa governed for less than a year before the Spanish arrived. The Spanish were led by Francisco Pizarro. Atahualpa—foolishly as it turns out—thought of Pizarro and his band as an innocent bunch of foreigners. He welcomed them into his empire and befriended them, only to be captured and held hostage by them. Fearing for his life, Atahualpa offered a huge ransom of gold and silver in return for his release. Pizarro accepted, then beheaded the leader anyway. Knowing that the Spanish were winning the battle for Quito, the Incas, led by General Rumiñahui, chose to destroy their city rather than leave it in the hands of the Conquistadors. Within one bloody year, hundreds of thousands of Incas had been slaughtered and the whole empire had fallen to the Spanish.

Pizarro founded his capital at Lima, Peru, while his lieutenants, Sebastian de Benalcázar and Diego de Almagro, founded San Francisco de Quito on the charred remains of the Inca city. Following a local legend of great riches in the lands to the east, Pizarro sent an expedition down into the Amazon Basin in 1540. Pizarro placed his brother in charge of the expedition, which departed from Quito. Having found nothing after several months, and running out of food, Gonzalo Pizarro sent Francisco de Orellana ahead to see what could be found. Orellana never returned. Instead he had floated down the entire Amazon River, through Brazil, out to the Atlantic Ocean. This marked the first crossing of the continent by a white man in a canoe, an event that is still celebrated in Ecuador today.

Meanwhile, the Spanish had been busy dividing up Ecuador's land among themselves. The *encomienda* system was established by the Spanish crown to reward *conquistadores*. Under this system landowners were granted huge tracts of land and could force the indigenous people who happened to occupy the land into slavery. In exchange for their back-breaking labor, the slaves were given room, board and religious instruction. The food was meager and the work so hard that many starved to death or died from diseases. As a result, the indigenous population decreased dramatically. About half of Ecuador's Indian population was forced to live like this for centuries.

Although the encomienda system was theoretically outlawed in the 17th century, in practice, the oppression of the indigenous population continued under various guises until 1964, when the Agrarian Reform Law was passed. Two sectors of the indigenous population escaped the encomienda system. Some were rounded up to live in specially constructed indigenous towns and forced to work in textiles or agriculture (it is for this reason that Otavalo became so famous for its weavings), or lived so deep in the Amazonian lowlands that they completely escaped all the implications of Spanish rule, both good and bad. One positive legacy of this troubled time is Ecuador's beautiful *haciendas*, elaborate country mansions built by the wealthy Spaniards. Today, many of these haciendas have been converted into some of Ecuador's most memorable and unique hotels.

INDEPENDENCE FROM SPAIN
The Spanish rule continued with relative peace until the late 18th-century, when *creole* (Spanish-born in the New World) leaders started to resent Spain for its constant interference and for demanding high taxes. The creoles began working toward independence. When Napoleon placed his brother Joseph on the throne of Spain in 1807, many creoles saw it as the opportunity for independence they had been waiting for. After a couple of failed attempts to defeat the Spanish armies, the first real victory was won at Guayaquil, which gained independence in October 1820. At this point an urgent request for backup was sent to the South American liberator, Simon Bolívar.

To help prevent the Spanish from regaining power, Bolívar swept into action, sending his best general, Antonio José de Sucre, to take command of the rebel army based in Quito. Sucre and his forces won the pivotal Battle of Pichincha on May 24, 1822, ending Spanish rule in Ecuador. Bolívar declared Quito the southern capital of a huge new nation, Gran Colombia, which included present-day Colombia, Ecuador and parts of Panama and Venezuela. His dream was to make the whole continent into a single, independent nation. However, his idea went down badly with the residents, and in 1830, the Quito representatives won independence for their own republic, calling it Ecuador because of its location on the equator.

CIVIL WAR AND COAST-SIERRA RIVALRY
New problems emerged between the conservative residents of the highlands, who were content with Spanish rule, and the liberal *costeños*, who wanted complete independence. To some extent this rivalry still continues, albeit in the form of lighthearted teasing; the coastal residents call the highlanders boring and backward, and the highlanders call their coastal counterparts *monos* (monkeys) and tease them for being loud and obnoxious. In the mid-1800s, different cities and areas attempted to declare their own various rules. Guayaquil gave itself over to Peruvian rule, and much of Ecuador was close to being taken over by Colombia. However, in 1861, Gabriel García Moreno, a fearless leader and devout Catholic, became president. The most significant legacy of his rule was to turn Ecuador into a Catholic republic and force his beliefs on all of its residents.

Those who rejected Catholicism were not granted official citizenship. Moreno was assassinated in the streets of Quito by political rivals in 1875. After Moreno's death, the equally fearsome, but liberal president, Eloy Alfaro, took over and immediately started undoing Moreno's work, secularizing the state and education. He came to a sticky end in 1911, when he was overthrown by the military; his body was dragged through the streets of Quito and publicly burned. This marked the beginning of a 50-year tug-of-war between the liberals and conservatives, which cost the country thousands of lives, numerous presidents (some of whom lasted only days) and almost half of its land, which Peru—taking advantage of Ecuador's weakened state—claimed as its own in 1948.

BANANAS AND OIL
Ecuador went through a relatively peaceful period in the 1950s and 1960s, helped by both the popular president, Galo Plaza Lasso, and the beginning of the banana boom, which created thousands of jobs and had a very positive impact on the economy. It was during this period

that the Agrarian Reform Law put a stop to the virtual slavery that the indigenous people had been subjected to since the 16th century. Unfortunately, in the 1960s, banana exportation was abruptly cut by a fungal disease that affected the country's entire crop, and caused Ecuador to go into a short period of economic decline.

This decline ended when large oil reserves were found in the Oriente in 1967 by Texaco, an international oil company. The Ecuadorian military, led by General Guillermo Rodríguez Lara, managed to block the swarms of money-hungry oil companies waiting to pounce on the land, and negotiated fair contracts for oil extraction. While the environment underwent some terrible damage, the economy began to prosper and money was pumped into education, health care, urbanization and transport. Even with the new oil money, Ecuador was unable to pay off its enormous debts, and foolish decisions by Lara to overcome this problem (such as raising taxes to absurd levels) resulted in his overthrow in 1976. Democracy was restored soon after.

DOLLARIZATION AND BEYOND
From 1979 until 1996, a string of governments attempted (and failed) to stabilize the delicate economy—which swung dramatically up and down due to fluctuating oil prices and severe debt—and to placate the indigenous people, who had started to rise up against the government through their new organization, the Confederación de Nacionalidades Indígenas del Ecuador.

In 1998, the situation worsened. Ecuador suffered its most severe economic crisis; the GDP shrank dramatically, inflation rose and banks collapsed. The citizens of Ecuador were furious with their leaders, whose corruption and ineptitude had contributed to the crisis. Roads were blockaded and virtually the whole country went on strike.

In 1999, then-President Jamil Mahuad decided nothing could be done to stop the national currency—the *sucre*—from failing completely, and he decided that the only answer was to change over to the US dollar. Although this move had the immediate desired effect of stabilizing the economy, it brought numerous other problems for the Ecuadorian people. The cost of living went up and poverty worsened. The indigenous population suffered the most. Thousands of protesters stormed Congress in the year 2000, backed by the military, and ousted Mahuad from office in just three hours. He was replaced immediately by his vice-president, Gustavo Noboa, under whom the economy slowly started to recover. On April 20, 2005, the 2002-elected president, Lucio Gutiérrez, was overthrown by popular protest and a vote in Congress, and was replaced by his vice president, Dr. Alfredo Palacio. In January 2007, Rafael Correa was sworn in as elected president.

POLITICS
Ecuador has been a constitutional republic with a democratic government since 1976. The government consists of three main branches: executive, headed by a president—currently Rafael Correa (since January 2007); legislative, made up of dozens of political parties that constantly come and go; and judicial.

Political instability has plagued Ecuador in recent years, and subsequently the country has witnessed a procession of incompetent and/or corrupt leaders. Eight different presidents have risen to and fallen from power in the last decade, and Ecuadorians are generally frustrated with their politicians, as is often demonstrated in street protests. In April 2005, popular protest against unconstitutional actions by former President Lucio Gutiérrez brought an early end to his term.

Then-Vice President, Dr. Alfredo Palacio, took over shortly after Congress voted to remove Gutiérrez from office. US-trained economist Rafael Correa was elected president in November 2006 and sworn in to replace Palacio as president in January of 2007.

ECONOMY

Ecuador's economy is based on exports from the banana, shrimp and other agriculture industries; money transfers from natives employed abroad; and petroleum production, which accounts for 40% of export earnings and one-third of the central government budget revenues. The economy went into a scary free-fall in the late 1990s, when the nation experienced natural disasters such as El Niño and the eruption of the volcano Pichincha, in combination with a sharp decline in world petroleum prices. Poverty worsened and the banking system collapsed. Bankers fled the country in 1999 without honoring their clients' accounts. When the sucre—the nation's currency—depreciated by about 70% in the same decade, then-President Jamil Mahuad made the wildly unpopular announcement that he would adopt the US dollar as the national currency. A coup in January 2000 ousted Mahuad. With few alternatives to save the struggling economy, Congress went on to approve the adoption of the dollar in March of that year. Since then the nation's economy has been relatively solid, though an estimated 41% of the population still lives below the poverty line.

Newly elected President Correa has not been quiet about his opposition to Free Trade Agreement talks with the US, and stated in his campaign that Ecuador will acknowledge its external debt—and only what it deemed to be "legitimate debt"—only after successfully funding domestic social programs. As of June 2007, the government has implemented income transfers to the poor and has announced plans to increase spending on health and education.

UNEMPLOYMENT: 10.6% (as of 2006)
UNDEREMPLOYMENT: 47% (as of 2006)
GDP PER CAPITA: $3,050 (as of 2006)
PUBLIC DEBT: 36% of GDP (as of 2006)
CHIEF AGRICULTURAL EXPORTS: flowers, bananas, coffee, cocoa, rice, potatoes, manioc (tapioca), plantains, sugarcane, cattle, sheep, pigs, beef, pork, dairy products, balsa wood, fish, shrimp.
EXPORT COMMODITIES: petroleum, bananas, cut flowers, shrimp.
MAIN INDUSTRIES: petroleum, food processing, textiles, wood products, chemicals.

POPULATION

The population of Ecuador is 13,755,680 (2007), with an annual population growth of 1.5% (2006). Ethnic groups include mestizo (mixed Amerindian and white) 65%, Amerindian 25%, Spanish, others 7% and black 3%.

LANGUAGES

Almost all Ecuadorians speak Spanish as either a first or second language. Amerindian languages come a close second, with many Ecuadorians speaking Quichua. English is taught from an early age in schools, but is not taught well. Most Ecuadorians understand much more English than one might imagine, but relatively few are fluent.

Ecuadorian Spanish is different in each region. On the coast, the Spanish is slurred and final syllables are dropped. In the Andes, the Spanish is slow and clear, making it one of the easiest places to learn the language. See the "Spanish Schools" section for more information.

RELIGION

Indigenous groups once practiced different religions across Ecuador, but the arrival of the Spanish wiped out much of this diversity. Using fear, intimidation and bribery, the country was almost completely converted to Catholicism. Today, even Amazon villages that have never seen a car have Catholic churches. Many rural villages that once practiced other religions still blend old traditions with the practice of Catholicism. Native religious celebrations are still occasionally held at Ingapirca, the most important Inca site in Ecuador. Other religions are beginning to gain a following in this strong Catholic culture, but remain less than 5% of the total.

CULTURE

Elements of *cultura* are everywhere you turn in Ecuador. From the gilded, glittering 19th-century theaters of Quito to the raucous parades and dancing in the streets of tiny Andean towns, Ecuadorians across the nation love to celebrate their heritage and traditions. Ecuador boasts a rainbow of cultures: the native inhabitants had a well-developed sense of cultural identity before the arrival of the Spanish, who added their own traditions to the mix. Later, Africans came to the region—primarily the coast—and brought with them their own unique culture. Today, Ecuador has even embraced international traditions, such as Halloween!

Ecuador's culture ranges from upscale (opera at Teatro Sucre in Quito) to low-key (cockfights in rural towns), and from very old (religious processions for Holy Week) to new (*chivas*—party buses with a loud band on top—driving through the modern streets of Quito). No matter what aspects of Ecuadorian culture you choose to explore, you can be sure that it will be colorful, boisterous and lots of fun. Ecuador takes art and music very seriously. The nation—Quito in particular—was a thriving artistic center during the colonial period, and the people of Ecuador developed a love for art that continues on today. Quito's museums and galleries should not be missed if you are an art aficionado. Music is also important to Ecuadorians: you won't go anywhere in Ecuador without seeing a small Andean band playing traditional tunes, hoping to sell a CD to tourists.

Keep your eyes and mind open: there are opportunities everywhere in Ecuador to sample local culture. The people of Ecuador are excited when a foreigner wants to participate in a town festival or other local celebration: let the locals be your guides and enjoy!

OSWALDO GUAYASAMÍN

Born in 1919 to humble, indigenous parents, Oswaldo Guayasamín would mature into Ecuador's most famous artist. His striking art portrays the humanity and suffering of the repressed classes and people of the Americas. Considered an expressionist, Guayasamín used bright colors, symbolism and images of pain and torment to create truly unique and memorable works.

By the time he was middle-aged, Guayasamín was being awarded numerous honors as an artist and humanitarian. His art has been exhibited in the USA, Italy, Spain, France, Brazil, the Soviet Union, Cuba, China and elsewhere abroad. Some of these exhibitions have been in prestigious locations such as the Palais de Luxembourg (Paris, 1992) and the L'Hermitage Museum (Sant Petersburg, 1982). In 1978 he was named to the Royal Academy of Fine Arts of Spain, and in 1979 he was named to the Academy of Italian Arts. The United Nations' Educational, Scientific and Cultural Organization gave him a prize for "an entire life of work for peace."

In spite of these lofty awards, Guaysamín never lost his contact with the common, repressed people of Ecuador, who adored him. Toward the end of his life, he began work on "la Capilla del Hombre," or "The Chapel of Man," dedicated to the races of Latin America, although he never lived to see it finished. He passed away in 1999, and the chapel has since been completed.

Guayasamín also never lost his artistic edge. Commissioned to do a series of murals for the Ecuadorian Congress in 1988, he painted 23 panels depicting the nation's history. One of the panels features a black-and-white painting of a horrid, skeletal face wearing a Nazi-style helmet with the letters CIA on it. The painting caused an international incident between Ecuador and the USA, although the artist held firm and the painting remains.

Today, Guayasamín is still very popular. His work is on display in his museum and at the Capilla del Hombre. If you go shopping in the Mariscal area, you're likely to see many knock-offs of his works for sale in a variety of mediums. Works are easy to spot: they are colorful and feature people with distinctive, twisted hands and faces.

Capilla del Hombre: Mariano Calvache and Lorenzo Chavez, Bellavista. Tuesday - Sunday, 10 a.m. – 5 p.m. Admission $3.
Guayasamin Museum: Monday - Friday, 9:30 a.m - 1 p.m, 3 - 6 p.m. José Bosmediano 543 and José Carbo, Tel: 593-2-244-6455.

500 YEARS OF ART

Ecuador has always been a nation of painters and artists. During the colonial era, Quito built a solid reputation as a center for religious art in the New World, and has never looked back. Today, Ecuador is still one of the best places in the world to appreciate and purchase beautiful works of art.

THE QUITO SCHOOL OF ART

Within a few years of arrival in Quito, the Catholic church began constructing houses of worship, from huge cathedrals to small chapels. These churches, emulating their European counterparts, featured elaborate, impressive interiors with hand-carved decorations and pillars, paintings and arches. Rather than importing artistic works such as crucifixes, paintings and statues of saints from Europe, the priests began training local artists to produce them. For the first hundred years or so, the copies of European art made by Ecuadorians were skilled and workmanlike, if uninspiring in nature. But then something happened that the priests did not foresee: the local artists began to develop their own techniques and styles. Their art became more visceral and detailed than the European works they copied. The crucifixes, which had previously portrayed a stoic Christ on the cross with a single wound over his heart, now were of a Christ in agony, his flesh shredded, his ribs showing, his skin flayed. Few who view crucifixes from this period can resist an involuntary shudder as they see Christ's pain and torment—the pain and torment of the conquered, enslaved native people who produced the crucifix.

The Quito school is also known for highly detailed statues. The saints and other religious figures that were depicted were made from finely carved local wood, painstakingly whittled into shape before being painted with incredible attention to detail. The cheeks of the saints were given a rosy glow, and fake glass eyes were included to improve the sense of realism. Some even had real hair, and many even had robes of fine local cloth. The Quito style of art became well-known in the region and in the world, and by the middle of the eighteenth century, there were more than 30 art guilds operating in Quito producing art full-time. With the advent of independence and the resulting loosening of the stranglehold on art and culture by the Catholic church, the Quito School of Art began exploring their roots, blending what they knew with their own culture. From this period come paintings of Christ wearing Andean clothes and even eating *cuy*—guinea pig!—at the last supper.

INDIGENOUS MOVEMENT

In the early 20th century, a new artistic movement swept the country: the Indigenous Movement. Inspired by the Quito School of Art, as well as by the suffering of native peoples in the Americas, artists from Ecuador began producing works which reflected the sorry state of native populations in South America. Artists such as Oswaldo Guayasamín, Eduardo Kingman and Camilo Egas gained worldwide fame with their portrayals of the trials and tribulations of native life, contact between natives and Spaniards, and pressures of modern life. Their works can be seen at the Guayasamín museum, the Casa de la Cultura and the Kingman museum. See the museums section for locations and hours.

TODAY'S ART SCENE IN ECUADOR

Today, Ecuador and Quito in particular is home to a vibrant art scene. There are several good art galleries in Quito that feature work by local artists. A good place to see local artists and their work is Ejido Park (across from the Hilton Colón) on Sunday morning, when dozens of local artists unpack their canvases for everyone to admire and purchase.

If you're interested in other forms of art, such as tapestries, check out the fancy boutiques on Amazonas and Juan León Mera. There are a few art galleries in Mitad del Mundo, but the paintings are a bit more touristy. There are several galleries (the term is used loosely: some "galleries" are converted family living rooms) in Otavalo: on market day, you can choose from a wide array of local art, mostly watercolors. Prices are reasonable, but bargain very hard—art dealers in Otavalo tend to jack up their initial prices much more than other merchants. You may find yourself paying less than half the original price for a piece of art if you bargain hard enough.

JULIO JARAMILLO

Born in Guayaquil in 1935, Julio Jaramillo would become the most famous Ecuadorian singer and a major cultural icon–sort of like an Ecuadorian Elvis Presley. Like Elvis, he became famous at a young age, and died young at the age of 42 in 1978. Because Ecuador was considered something of a musical backwater, he spent much of his career elsewhere–mainly Venezuela, Colombia, Mexico and Uruguay. Jaramillo recorded songs in several different genres, including *boleros, pasillos,* waltzes, *tangos* and *rancheras:* he is most famous for the boleros, which are commonly referred to as *corta-venas* or 'vein-cutters' in Ecuador because they are remarkably depressing. At the height of his career, he sold records from Mexico to Argentina and was greeted by huge crowds wherever he went. His most famous song was "*Nuestro Juramento,*" or "Our Oath." It became so famous that he was known as "Mr. Juramento" for most of his career. He returned to Ecuador in 1976. By then, he was very popular in native land and treated like royalty. When he died two years later, thousands of sorrowful fans filled the streets near his home. Today, he is still widely popular, particularly in his native Guayaquil: whenever someone plays a Jaramillo song on the jukebox in a bar–and every jukebox has at least one of his songs–the crowds go wild.

One local form of art that is popular with visitors is the *Tigua* painting. Tigua is a tiny town high in the Andes known for small, colorful paintings made on stretched sheepskin. The paintings usually feature tiny figures of Andeans about their daily life herding llamas, attending local fairs, etc. Some feature mythological elements, such as condors, faces in the mountains and volcanoes. Be sure to ask the vendor (who is often also the artist) about any element in the painting that you don't understand: often, there is an interesting story behind it. Tigua paintings are available almost everywhere–you're sure to see them in any market you visit.

MUSIC

Ecuadorians love music. On the streets, in homes, at parties, and on buses–if you're traveling in Ecuador, you're going to hear a wide variety of music. In tourist areas such as Otavalo or Baños, you're bound to encounter a native band (called a *grupo* or *conjunto*) composed of four to ten Ecuadorians, often dressed in native clothing, playing traditional songs on traditional instruments. The group is bound to have at least one guitarist, a drummer, and at least one musician producing a haunting melody on a pan-flute, a traditional Andean instrument composed of varying lengths of bamboo lashed together.

In towns like Baños, the groups make the rounds of the more expensive tourist restaurants, stopping by and playing three or four songs, then passing the hat for tips and selling CDs of their music. Some fancier places, such as haciendas that have been converted into hotels, have their own native bands that play for guests in the evening and during dinner (they'll probably have CDs, too). If you're lucky enough to get invited to a private party or make it to a local festival, you may see a *banda del pueblo.* These bands are composed of locals who get together on special occasions to play mostly traditional music. The instruments are often old and fairly beat up, and occasionally the musical talent is questionable, but whatever they may lack in skill or instruments they more than make up for in exuberance and volume.

Ecuadorians have diverse musical tastes when it comes to international music. If you spin the dial on a radio in Quito, you'll find different stations playing *salsa*, rap, Spanish oldies (always hugely popular), elevator music, pop, rock and everything in between. Some stations consider "music in English" to be its own genre, which means that the same station plays music that would never be played together in the states, like Britney Spears, Eminem, Korn and the Bee Gees.

International Spanish-language music is widely popular in Ecuador. Salsa, *merengue* and *cumbia*–all different forms of dance music from Latin America and the Caribbean–can be heard around the nation. Each is a different genre of music which requires different dance moves, but to the untrained ear they can be difficult to tell apart. If you plan on visiting a *sal-*

sateca (salsa dancing club) while in Ecuador (and you should, they're a lot of fun!) you may want to take a dance class or two first. The Mariscal area in Quito is full of dancing schools. Alternatively, try to check out a dance show if you can: they're hyped up by the tour companies for a reason. You should also check out what is happening at major cultural centers such as the Casa de la Cultura and Teatro Sucre, as they often have special events and shows.

DANCE, THEATER AND COMEDY

Live entertainment is popular in Quito, with dance shows, concerts, and comedy clubs. Prices are quite reasonable, and the quality is excellent. One popular option is a dance show. The most famous and prestigious dance group in Quito is *Jacchigua Ballet*, who have given performances in more than 150 cities around the world. Performances are held Wednesdays at 7:30 p.m. at Teatro Demetrio Aguilera Malta in the Casa de la Cultura (12 de Octubre and Patria, just outside the Ejido park). Tickets are sold by Metropolitan Touring. Their main office is at Ave. República de El Salvador N36-84 between Ave. Nacionas Unidas and Ave. Portugal, though they have several other offices scattered throughout Quito including ones on Amazonas, inside the Megamaxi shopping complex and in the Centro Histórico. For rates and more information, visit www.galapagosvoyage.com. Metropolitan's ballet information number is 593-2-2988-200. You can also purchase tickets at the theater itself on the day of the performance (it's cheaper to buy them at the theater, and ask for a student discount if you have a card).

Their main competition is Humanizarte Danza Andina. Performances are held at a newly constructed theatre inside the Humanizarte main office located at Leonidas Plaza N24-226 and Lizardo García. The theatre is hidden on a tiny, one-block street called Xaura, west of Tamayo between Lizardo García and Baquerizo Moreno. The Ballet Danza Tradicional Andina is performed every Wednesday at 7:30 p.m..

If you want to see a dance show but don't want to buy a ticket, one elegant Quito restaurant, *Rincón La Ronda* (Bello Horizonte 400 and Almagro, Tel: 593-2-254-0459), offers a traditional dance show every Sunday at 8 p.m. It is very popular with quiteños who wish to impress out-of-town guests, so make a reservation, especially if you're in a large group. There is no additional cost for the dance show if you eat dinner as you watch.

Quito's most important cultural center is the *Casa de la Cultura Ecuatoriana Benjamín Carrión*. Located on 12 de Octubre 400 and Patria (just inside the Ejido Park), it is a large complex of theaters, galleries and concert halls. In addition to hosting the world-famous Jacchigua Ballet every Wednesday, the Casa de la Cultura regularly hosts concerts, art and photo exhibits and special events. If you're coming to Quito, be sure to check out their web page, http://cce.org.ec, before you go. Call 593-2-290-2272 to get the scoop on current performances.

The venerable *Teatro Nacional Sucre*, first built between 1879 and 1886 and recently beautifully restored, is an elegant venue for high culture in Ecuador. The Sucre offers varied presentations, from Cuban pianists to Japanese violinists, jazz duets and Argentine tango singers. Check out their website, www.teatrosucre.com. The box office telephone number is 593-2-257-2823, and you can also purchase tickets and get more information at the Hilton Colón.

The Teatro Bolívar (Pasaje Espejo, between Guayaquil and Flores) is another old theater in Quito that features live performances. Check their web site (www.teatrobolivar.org) for more information, or give them a buzz at 593-2-258-2486 or 593-2-258-2487.

Quito's lone comedy club is *El Patio de Comedias* (18 de Septiembre E-426 and 9 de Octubre). It hosts performances Thursday through Sunday at 8 p.m. Their telephone number is 593-2-256-1902, call to find out who is slated to perform. Performances are in Spanish.

Holidays and Fiestas

January 1 - New Year's Day

January 6 - Three Kings Day (a.k.a. Epiphany)

February 12 - Anniversary of the Discovery of the Amazon River; Province Day (Galápagos)

February 27 - National Community Spirit Day

End of February or early March - Carnival

March or early April - Easter and Holy Week

May 1 - Labor Day: Processions fill the streets and plazas to honor workers nationwide

May 24 - Battle of Pichincha: Military and civilian parades show the nation's pride of the day in 1822 when the country's most important battle in the war for independence from Spain was fought

June - *Corpus Cristi*: Usually celebrated on the 9th Thursday after Easter

June 24 - Saint John the Baptist: Celebrations in Otavalo and the surrounding highland communities

June 29 - Saints Peter and Paul: Celebrations in Otavalo and the surrounding highland communities

July 24 - Simón Bolívar's Birthday

July 25 - Founder's Day, Guayaquil: Guayaquil's biggest 2-day party

August 10 - Quito Independence Day

September - Various harvest festivals throughout the country

September 1-15 - *Fiesta del Yamor*: An annual festival in the highland town of Otavalo

September 23-24 - Festival of the Virgin of Mercy

October 9 - Guayaquil Independence Day: Once again, Guayaquil combines holidays (Independence Day and Columbus Day) to ensure a multi-day festival

October 12 - Columbus Day, also known as *Día de la Raza* (Day of the Race)

November 1 - All Saints' Day

November 2 - All Soul's Day (a.k.a. "Day of the Dead"): All Soul's Day is a day during which families visit cemeteries to dance, drink, eat, and leave flowers and other offerings for deceased friends and relatives in a convivial ceremony designed to celebrate the lives of those who have past on

November 3 - Cuenca Independence Day

November 11 - Latacunga Independence Day and Festival of the Mama Negra

December 6 - Founder's Day, Quito; also known as *Fiestas de Quito*

December 24 - Christmas Eve

December 25 - Christmas Day

December 28-31 - Year's End Celebrations: Starting with the Day of the Innocents, the entire nation symbolically prepares to enter a new year by burning human effigies in the streets as Quiteños end a nearly month-long party

SPECIAL EVENTS IN ECUADOR

CARNIVAL

Carnival, which is celebrated each year in February or March the week before Lent, is Latin America's version of Mardi Gras. The celebrations that take place in Ecuador the four days preceding Ash Wednesday may not be as crazy as in some countries, but if you happen to be in the area during this holiday it is worth checking one out.

The main component of any carnival celebration in Ecuador is water, and lots of it. Beware, as a gringo, you are a very attractive target. If you are in a town with a huge celebration, you are sure to be drenched with water and silly string by hoards of children. It can be annoying, but try to accept that it is just their way of celebrating this holiday. If you prefer a dryer holiday weekend, head to Ambato, where water throwing is prohibited. Here there is a huge festival called the *Fiesta de las Flores y de las Frutas*. This event is filled with colorful parades, bullfights and handicraft exhibits.

Another town that has an impressive carnival celebration is the town of Guaranda, which is located in the central Andes. Usually this town is your average sleepy Ecuadorian town, nothing remarkable for a tourist. However, carnival transforms it into a four day non-stop party, filled with parades, music and fun. Also the locals tend to be very hospitable, many prepare large feasts and invite anyone on the street into their homes to celebrate with them.

CEREMONIA DE RESEÑA O VÍSPERAS

The Ceremonia de Reseña o Vísperas in Quito's Catedral is one of the oldest and rarest ceremonies in the Catholic Church. The centuries-old procession happens the Wednesday before Easter, *Miércoles Santo*, in only three churches in the world, and one of them is in Quito.

The procession, consisting of six priests and the Archbishop, represents the life, death and subsequent resurrection of Jesus Christ.

GOOD FRIDAY

One of the most grandiose events for Quito's religious community, the great procession of Good Friday follows the morning *Via Crucis* prayer on the final Friday of Holy Week, paying tribute to the moment when Pontius Pilate condemned Jesus to death. Tens of thousands—many donning purple robes and coned hoods reminiscent of the Ku Klux Klan but without the negative context—flock to the city's historic center, winding through the streets in a solemn mass. It's a colorful scene and unique to Quito, not to be missed from a high balcony or join the masses in walking through the streets.

The procession begins at midday and lasts until three, beginning and ending at the San Francisco church and making its way through El Centro. Traditional purple-hooded *cucuruchos* (representing penitents, many donning thorny headpieces, massive crosses and chains around their feet demonstrating their will to change) and robed *Verónicas* (also wearing purple dresses and black shrouds as they pay tribute to the women who wiped the sweat and blood from Jesus' face as he was carried on the cross) encircle a figure of Jesus and the *Virgen Dolorosa* (Virgin of Sorrow), further surrounded by the solemn masses.

The procession ends at three—the hour of Jesus' death—and is followed by a ceremony reconstructing the descent from the cross at six in the evening. Some Quito churches make quite an ordeal of this, with the priest recounting the story of the apostles performing the sepulcher of Christ from his pulpit. Finally, designated men remove the nails from the crucified Christ, passing the body along to a group of women who lay him to rest in a white tunic and flowers.

THE DAY OF THE DEAD

The Day of the Dead, traditionally celebrated between October 31 and November 2, is a much bigger holiday in Mexico and Central America than it is in Ecuador, but there are nevertheless places you can go to see it celebrated in Ecuador.

Day of the Dead is a time to remember loved ones who have passed away. Packing a picnic lunch, families will gather at cemeteries and basically hang out for much of the day, talking, eating, and performing routine maintenance on the grave site, such as changing old flowers for fresh ones. Outside the cemeteries, vendors sell *colada morada*, a purple, fruity beverage that is only available at that time of year. You can also get a *guagua de pan*, a doughy piece of bread baked in the shape of a person: it is vaguely sweet. There are also vendors selling flowers, religious pictures and posters and colorful decorations.

FIESTA DE LA MAMA NEGRA

The Fiesta of the Mama Negra, which takes place in the city of Latacunga, is one of the most fascinating cultural events in Ecuador. This public celebration of civic pride rivals Brazil's festivals as an emblematic melting pot of wildly divergent cultural traditions: Spanish, Incan, Aymaran, Mayan, African and most recently, gay.

The fiesta has its origins with the colonization of Latacunga by the Spanish for its rich mineral resources. The native inhabitants were forced to convert to Catholicism, but the conversion was not entirely pure, with the result that indigenous elements, such as a polytheistic belief in "spirits" became part of the new religion. The Spanish conquerors brought in additional populations from Bolivia, Guatemala, and ultimately, Africa as slaves. They too, brought their own beliefs and traditions to Latacunga.

What set the holiday in motion was the eruption of the Cotopaxi volcano in 1742. The citizens of the region petitioned the "Virgin of Mercy," who had been designated the patron of the volcano, and when Latacunga was spared, an annual celebration was set in place to honor her.

The festival was traditionally held during the last weekend in September, but was on the verge of dying out in the early 1960's when Cotopaxi Governor Virgilio Guerrero proposed saving it and making it coincide with Latacunga's official celebration of its founding on November 11th. The now-official holiday had the ironic effect of reviving interest in the traditional religious celebration of the "Virgin of Mercy," which also features the Mama Negra, but the larger and more colorful celebration is in November.

The event constitutes a parade of characters, such as the Angel of the Stars, the Moorish King, as well as Los Huacos, who represent Latacunga's pre-Columbian heritage, and the Camisonas, colorful transvestites, in a parade that attracts many, as well as dancers, musicians, and marching bands, all culminating in the arrival, on horseback, of the Mama Negra, the Black Mother, a combination of the Virgin with African deities. The Mama Negra, bearing dolls representing her "children," is elaborately costumed and from a container sprays milk and water on the parade goers.

Candy and wine containers are also tossed to the crowds, and restaurateurs all feature Latacunga's most famous contribution to Ecuadorian cuisine, *chugchucaras*—deep fried pork, pork rinds, popcorn, potatoes, maize and plantains.

FESTIVITIES OF QUITO

If you are in Quito during the last days of November and during the run up to December 6th, you can't help but notice the build up of a distinctly fiesta-ish atmosphere in the city. During these days, quiteños let their hair down to celebrate the Spanish founding of the city on the same date in 1534.

In late November, the festivities start with the election of the Queen of Quito. From this point on, the streets become filled with *chivas*—colorful open-top buses driving through the streets—

Get your writing published in our books, go to www.vivatravelguides.com

carrying as many as 50 people who may be dancing to the banda del pueblo which play on the top, drinking *canelazo*—a potent alcoholic drink with a sugarcane alcohol and cinnamon base. This happens night and day, with chivas getting booked weeks ahead of time for the early days of December.

For the ten days running up to and including December 6th, there are bull fights at the *Plaza de Toros*, the only time during the year when the bull ring is actually used for bull fighting. The fights are considered by most to be a high-class social event, and Quito's elite flock to the fights, dressed in their finest smart-casual wear, donning cowboy or panama hats to keep the sun off. Many also have *botas* (wineskins). Those who can't afford to go inside linger outside and in the surrounding streets in groups drinking beer and whiskey and dancing in makeshift discos.

Photo by Caroline Schiff

On the night of December 5th, the partying reaches a climax and street parties take over all of Quito. A good place to go is El Parque Carolina, as there will often be open-air concerts and fireworks. If street parties are your thing, head to Vancouver and Polonia (located behind the Petrocomerical gas station on Amazonas), where there is usually a DJ, decent music and plenty of dancing to be had. Needless to say, December 6th itself is usually a fairly quiet day, with many quiteños sleeping off hangovers.

NEW YEAR'S EVE

A New Year's Eve, or *Año Viejo*, spent in Ecuador provides a fascinating insight into local culture and folklore. During the buildup to the day itself, you will see effergies for sale in the streets, made from wood, paper, cloth and firecrackers. These effergies, also known as año viejos will usually represent political figures that are hated, such as G.W. Bush or Osama Bin Laden, locally-despised politicians, or icons from popular music or culture, from the old year. These figures are later burned on New Year's Eve itself to banish the bad and welcome in the new.

In Quito, Amazonas Avenue is the place to head early in the evening to check out the stalls and open-air entertainment. You may see effergies being burned, and you will certainly see fireworks. Outside of Quito, the coastal town of Salinas is a popular Ecuadorian New Year's Eve haunt.

Throughout the country, a popular pursuit is for men to dress up as women and beg for money. Also, outside of the main cities, especially on roads to the smaller countryside towns, you may come across children holding string across the roads. They are trying to stop the traffic with the aim of relieving you of your small change. In the countryside, many people light fires in the street, upon which they burn the effergies. This happens in Quito too, but more frequently in the suburbs.

Midnight itself tends to be a family affair, with a meal spent at home with relatives. A local tradition is to eat twelve grapes at the stroke of midnight, which is supposed to bring luck throughout the year. After dinner, younger people head off to clubs or parties to see in the New Year in style.

SOCIAL AND ENVIRONMENTAL ISSUES

There are a number of social and environmental challenges facing Ecuador today as the nation tries to balance conflicting requirements of repaying international debt, developing industry and keeping the poorest sectors of society alive. Three of the currently most pressing issues are:

OIL EXPLOITATION

Oil was discovered in Ecuador in the late 1960s and large-scale production began in the 1970s. Oil has been a huge boost to the nation's economy, however, development has not been sustainable, the effects have not been felt at community level and there have been negative consequences for both public health and the environment. Oil companies are a serious threat to the rainforest today. Even at lodges deep in the jungle, plumes of smoke coming from oil refineries smudge the otherwise untouched horizon. The Ecuadorian Amazon is one of the most bio-diverse regions on the planet, and the exploitation of oil has been particularly detrimental on the region's fragile ecosystems and vulnerable indigenous populations. Research has shown that oil has had an extremely destructive impact on the environment, with many gallons of crude oil and toxic waste spilled into the waterways of the Amazon each year. It is estimated that the extent of the damage in the Ecuadorian Amazon is far greater than that caused by the Exxon Valdez disaster in Alaska in 1989. Furthermore, oil production requires waste pits where carcinogenic "produced water" is dumped back into the Earth, a damaging process for which Chevron/Texaco has faced a billion-dollar lawsuit since 2003. Whilst few long-term studies have examined the effects of oil production on the health of local communities, investigations have proven an increase in miscarriages, cancers and leukemia local residents.

Additionally, the development of oil has not generally benefited the development of infrastructure and basic services for local indigenous populations. There have been instances of drilling on ancestral land, notably in 1999, when the government sold exploration rights in two areas of the jungle, known as Blocks 23 and 24, without consulting the indigenous communities to whom those areas were considered ancestral. Community groups demonstrated and local workers have held strikes with some limited success. Protests in Sucumbios and Orellana provinces in 2005 caused the state-owned oil company Petroecuador to halt production for several days. While consequences were dire on the economy, the local people gained some concessions in terms of health and infrastructure investment in these areas.

However, the general government response to the situation in the Oriente has not gone far enough to limit environmental damage, impacts on health of the local people or the negative consequences for community life. Experts argue for a more inclusive approach with Amazon communities, including partnerships between indigenous bodies and the oil companies. It is undeniable that a detailed environmental impact analysis, a plan to repair the destruction that has already taken place, and a series of environmental controls and planning for future development to minimize the impact are urgently needed.

SUSTAINABLE TOURISM

Ecuador suffered a severe economic crisis in the late 1990s and currently has a poverty rate of 41% (CIA Word Factbook, 2006), which has led to high levels of migration to cities and foreign countries. Tourism and travel is an important source of income for Ecuador, bringing in over $710 million of annual revenues to the country, contributing 1.8% to the GDP (World Tourism and Travel Council, 2007). The tourism and travel industry is expected to provide 361,000 jobs in 2007, representing 6.7% of total employment (WTTC, 2007). Thus, tourism has the ability to decrease poverty in Ecuador in a manner that is potentially less damaging to the environment and more sustainable than other revenue generating enterprises such as export agriculture and petroleum extraction.

Many of the tourist operations in the Andean region of Ecuador promote the beauty and indigenous culture of the area, yet only a handful classify themselves as ecological and try to meaningfully engage in conservation and community awareness. Key factors determining the success of pioneering Eco-Lodges are conservation and community development. Most tourist operations recognize the importance of sustainable practices but do not have sufficient technological or financial resources to engage in them.

One model for encouraging sustainability is through outreach by non-governmental organizations (NGOs). The Ecuadorian NGO Conservation and Development has implemented a program called Smart Voyager that is aimed at training and certifying operations in sustainable tourism. The Smart Voyager program increases the efficiency and profitability of tourism operations, which provides an economic incentive for the operations to become certified. Certification helps to ensure that growth in tourism has a positive impact on workers, communities, poverty and the environment. It also provides consumers with independent information on the environmental and social standards of an operation. Moreover, through workshops

and training sessions run in collaboration with C and D's partner Rainforest Alliance, tourism operators are able to share ideas and learn new methods of conserving the environment, promoting social programs and reducing poverty in their own areas.

There are a number of ways you can leave a positive mark on the places you visit: practicing responsible tourism and using companies that have received ecotourism certification are two of the most important measures to ensure the country and its people benefit from your travels as much as you do.

THE INDIGENOUS MOVEMENT IN ECUADOR

Over the past 20 or so years, a strong and largely united indigenous movement has been developing in Ecuador and it is considered to be among the most persuasive in Latin America. The indigenous population comprises approximately one-third of the population. Indigenous political groups wield significant power in Ecuador and some attributed the beginning of ex-president Lucio Gutiérrez's downfall in 2005 to the loss of support of his indigenous allies, caused by disagreement regarding IMF recommendations.

Lucio's power base was built on siding with indigenous Ecuadorians, unhappy with a government that appeared to be out of touch with the poor. When he turned his back on this base his power began to disintegrate. Prior to Lucio and illustrative of its power, in recent years, the indigenous movement has led several uprisings, in one instance even ousting a government. In the 1980s, the Amazonian and highland federation CONAIE (Confederation of Indigenous Nationalities of Ecuador) was formed, bringing together the 11 ethnic groups (approximately 3.5 million people) in Ecuador with a united purpose. This was no easy feat considering all the different needs of the ethnically and culturally diverse indigenous groups. The group focuses on high level key aims for all of its member groups such as human rights, consolidation of territory and education.

In 1990, thousands of indigenous people held a three week strike, the first major indigenous uprising against the government. This was the first time that such power had been wielded by these groups and came as a shock to the establishment. Roadblocks were placed in the Andes and a march took place in Quito to demand land rights and bilingual education. In the aftermath of the 1990 uprising, CONAIE began to gain real political influence as the indigenous people saw that it was possible to have a say and gain rights if they united in their goals. This led to a number of massive protests and finally in 1996, Pachakutik (the indigenous political party) was formed, to drive the rights of the people forward in the political arena.

A decade of unrest, lack of social reform and government corruption in the 1990s came to head in early 2000, as the indigenous people had been left in poverty. When demonstrating again in Quito, troops were called in to break up the demonstrations. Lucio Gutiérrez (at the time an army colonel) did not follow orders and instead, provided mobile army kitchens to support them and let the indigenous protesters overtake the congress building, declaring a "Parliament of the People." Gutiérrez worked with the indigenous people to unsuccessfully try to form a new government to replace ousted president Jamil Mahuad. Gutiérrez was arrested and imprisoned for six months and deputy Gustavo Noboa was installed as president. Despite the failure of the indigenous movement to form a new government, this was landmark news. Failure of the Noboa government to take notice led to further uprisings in January and February 2001. These united not only the indigenous groups but also the urban and rural poor, who had many of the same problems. Many marches were held in Quito. After stating he would not negotiate, Noboa was eventually forced to concede to end ten days of protests. This significantly weakened his political position, strengthening that of the indigenous movement and setting the scene for the election of Gutiérrez in 2002.

Following the ousting of Gutiérrez in April 2005, it is unclear what the future holds, however, it is certain that the indigenous movement wields significant power within Ecuadorian politics. The most recent notable indigenous uprising in Ecuador occurred in March 2006 in defiance of Alfredo Palacio's provisional government to sign a free trade agreement with the United States. Indigenous groups fear the Fair Trade Agreement will cripple small-scale

EMBASSIES AND CONSULATES

Argentina
Quito: Edificio Av. Amazonas 477 and Roca 8th Floor, Tel: 593-2-256-2292 / 593-2-252-7624, Fax: 593-2-256-8177, E-mail: embarge2@embargenti.int.ec / feecua@mrecic.gov.ar.
Guayaquil: Aguirre 104, Tel: 593-4-232-3574 / 253-0767 / 253-4666 / 253-4893.

Bolivia
Quito: Av. Eloy Alfaro 2432 and Fernando Ayarza, Tel: 593-2-224-4830, Fax: 593-2-224-4833, E-mail: embolivia-quito@rree.gov.bo.
Guayaquil: Urdesa, Cedros 100, Tel: 593-4-288-5789 / 288-5790 / 288-5791.

Brazil
Quito: Amazonas 1429 and Colón, Edificio España, 9th Floor, Tel: 593-2-256-3086, Fax: 593-2-250-4468.
Guayaquil: Km. 7.5 Vía Daule (Along Daule road), Tel: 593-4-226-1915.

Canada
Quito: 6 de Diciembre 2816 and Paul Rivet, Josueth Gonzales Building, Of. 4-N, Tel: 593-2-250-6162, Fax: 593-2-223-2114.
Guayaquil: General Córdova 812, Tel: 593-4-256-3580.

Chile
Quito: Juan Pablo Sanz 3617 and Amazonas, Edificio Xerox, 4th Floor, Tel: 593-2-246-6780, Fax: 593-2-244-4470.
In Guayaquil: Av. 9 de Octubre 100, Tel: 593-4-256-2995 / 256-4619 / 256-5151.

China
Quito: Atahualpa 349 and Amazonas, Tel: 593-2-243-3337, Fax: 593-2-244-4362.
Guayaquil: Santa Cecilia, Av. Central 840 and 7ma. (7th) Mz W S 6, Tel: 593-4-285-0611 / 285-0876 / 285-2108.

Colombia
Quito: Colón 133 and Amazonas, 7th Floor, Tel: 593-2-222-2486, Fax: 593-2-256-7766.
Guayaquil: Av. 9 de Octubre and Córdova, Tel: 593-4-256-8749 / 256-8752.

Costa Rica
Quito: Rumipamba 692 and República, 2nd Floor, Tel: 593-2-225-4945, Fax: 593-2-225-4087.
Guayaquil : New Kennedy (Nueva Kennedy) 7ma. (7th) Este B and D, Tel: 593-4-239-8871.

Cuba
Quito: Mercurio 365 between La Razón and El Vengador, Tel: 593-2-245-6936

Dominican Republic
Quito: Av. de los Shyris 1240 and Portugal, Edificio Albatros, 5th Floor, Tel: 593-2-243-4275 Fax: 593-2-243-4275 (ex. 72).

Finland
Guayaquil: Luis Urdaneta 206 and Córdova, Tel: 593-4-256-4268, Fax: 593-4-256-6291.

France
Quito: Leonidas Plaza 107 and Patria, Tel: 593-2-294-3800, Fax: 593-2-254-6118, E-mail: francie@uio.satnet.net, URL: www.ambafrance-equateur.org.
Consulate: Diego de Almagro 1550 and Pradera, Edificio Kingman, 2nd Floor, Tel: 593-2-254-3110 / 256-9883, Fax: 593-2-250-6468.
Guayaquil: Mascote and Hurtado, Tel: 593-4-232-8442.

Germany
Quito: Conjunto Citiplaza 14th Floor, Tel: 593-2-297-0821.
Guayaquil: Av. Las Monjas # 10 and Av. Carlos Julio Arosemena, Tel: 593-4-2206867 / 220-6868 / 220-6869.

Guatemala
Quito: República del Salvador 733 and Portugal, Gabriela 3 Building, 3rd Floor, Tel: 593-2-245-9700.

Honduras
Quito: Av. 12 de Octubre 1942 and Cordero, World Trade Center Building Torre A, 5th Floor, Of. 501, Tel: 593-2-222-0441, Fax: 593-2-222-0441.

Israel
Quito: Av. 12 de Octubre 1059 and Francisco Salazar, Plaza 2000 Building, 9th Floor, Tel: 593-2-223-7474, Fax: 593-2-223-8055.

Italy
Quito: Isla 111 and Humberto Albornoz, Tel: 593-2-256-1077, Fax: 593-2-250-2818, E-mail: ambital@ambitalquito.org.
Guayaquil: Baquerizo Moreno 1120, Tel: 593-4-231-2523 / 256-3136 / 256-3140.

Japan
Quito: Juan León Mera 130 and Patria, Corporación Financiera Nacional building, 7th Floor, Tel: 593-2-256-1899, Fax: 593-2-250-3670.

Lithuania
Quito: Pasaje Frederico Paredes 555 and 10 de Agosto, Tel: 593-2-243-9450, Fax: 593-4-241-2230 / 241-2707, E-mail: jbwalker@hoy.net.

Mexico
Quito: 6 de Diciembre N36-165 and Naciones Unidas, Tel: 593-2-292-3770, Fax: 593-2-244-8245, E-mail: embmxec2@uio.satnet.net.

Netherlands
Quito: Av. 12 de Octubre 1942 and Cordero, World Trade Center Building Torre A, 1st Floor, Tel: 593-2-222-9229, Fax: 593-2-256-7917, E-mail: ecuador@embajadadeholanda.com, URL: www.embajadadeholanda.com.

Panama
Quito: Alpallana 501 Francisco Flores, Tel: 593-2-256-6449, Fax: 593-2-252-5234.
Guayaquil: Aguirre 509, Tel: 593-4-251-2158.

Peru
Quito: Av. Rep. del Salvador 495 and Irlanda, Irlanda Building, Tel: 593-2-246-8410.
Guayaquil: Av. 9 de Octubre 411, Tel: 593-4-232-2738 / 593-4-232-5679

Russia
Quito: Reina Victoria 462 and Roca, Tel: 593-2-252-6361, Fax: 593-2-256-5531.

South Korea
Quito: Av. Naciones Unidas and República del Salvador, Citi Plaza Building, 8th Floor. Tel: 593-2-297-0625, Fax: 593-2-297-0630.
Guayaquil: Av. 9 de Octubre 203, Tel: 593-4-253-2495

Sweden
Quito: Alonso Jerves 134 and Orellana, Tel: 593-2-225-3910 / 250-9423 / 250-9514, Fax: 593-2-250-2593, E-mail: ecuanor@uio.satnet.net.
Guayaquil: Km. 6 1/2 Via Daule (Along Daule road), Tel: 593-2-225-4111 / 225-8666, Fax: 593-2-225-4159.

Switzerland
Quito: Juan Pablo Sanz 120 and Av. Amazonas, Xerox Building, 2nd Floor, Tel: 593-2-243-4948 / 243-4949, Fax: 244,9314.
Guayaquil: Av. 9 de Octubre 2105, Tel: 593-4-245-3607.

Spain
Quito: La Pinta 455 and Amazonas, Tel: 593-2-256-4373 / 256-4390 / 256-4377. Fax: 593-2-250-0826, E-mail: embespec@correo.mae.es.
Guayaquil: Urdesa, Circunvalación S 118, Tel: 593-4-288-1691.

Uruguay
Quito: 6 de Diciembre 2816 and Paul Rivet, Josueth Gonzalez Building, 9th Floor. Tel: 593-2-254-4228, Fax: 593-2-256-3763, Email: emburug1@emburuguay.int.ec.
Guayaquil: Junín 114 and Malecón, 5th floor, Office #9, Tel: 593-4-231-1058.

United Kingdom
Quito: Av. Naciones Unidas and República del Salvador, Citiplaza Building, 12 and 14th Floor. Tel: 593-2-297-0800 / 297-0801 Fax: 593-2-297-0809, URL: www.britembquito.org.ec.
Guayaquil:General Córdova 623 and Padre Solano, Tel: 593-4-256-0400.

United States of America
Quito: 12 de Octubre and Patria, Tel: 593-2-256-2890, Fax: 593-2-250-2052, URL: www.usis.org.ec

Venezuela
Quito: Ave. Amazonas 5546, Tel: 593-2-224-6526 / 226-8635 / 224-6676
Guayaquil: Chile 331, Tel: 593-4-232-0751 / 232-6566 / 232-6579 / 232-6600.

farmers in rural communities, especially those who produce rice, potatoes, beans, meat, cheese and maize. During the protests in late March, indigenous groups blocked the Panamericana north and south of Quito using burning tires and rubble. A state of emergency was declared in 5 central provinces: Cotopaxi, Cañar, Chimborazo, Imbabura and part of Pichincha. These protests follow on the heels of TLC negotiations with the United States (due to wrap up towards the end of June) and set the pace for political movements heading up to the October 2006 presidential elections.

Indigenous groups currently face the arduous task of taking a clear stand on primary issues facing their communities; free trade agreements, and water, agriculture and natural resource management are among the most polemic matters on the table. Recent protests to oil exploitation in the Amazon have been smaller but frequent as local residents urge ther government to leave oil in the ground in the environmentally sensitive area.

THE GALÁPAGOS FISHING WAR

There is constant tension in Galápagos between the two main industries in the islands: fishing and tourism. Those in the fishing industry are always pushing for ecologically questionable concessions from the government such as long-line fishing, long seasons for valuable species such as lobsters and sea cucumbers, and removal of protections on marine reserves.

The fishermen are quite short-sighted: catches are way down in recent years, yet they continue to push for longer seasons and larger catch limits. Worse still, there is a lot of illegal fishing in the Galápagos, both by foreign vessels and local boats. In particular, sharks are being hunted to near extinction: they are caught for their fins, which bring in a lucrative price in Asia. There is a ban on shark fishing, but Ecuador does not have the resources nor desire to enforce it.

The tourism operators in the islands favor stringent restrictions, as unchecked fishing is severely detrimental to the ecosystem. Most Galápagos life ultimately depends on the sea: many of the birds in the islands feed on fish, and if the marine ecosystem collapses, there will be no more boobies, frigates, or albatrosses for tourists to come and see. Therefore, tour operators are constantly pressuring the Ecuadorian government to enact and enforce strict rules for those who want to fish in Galápagos.

However, for now, the fishermen seem to have the upper hand. For years, fishing was the main industry in the islands, which were considered an unattractive place to live. The fishermen feel that any effort to limit the money they can make is a personal affront: they accuse the government of caring more about endangered Galápagos species than it does about them. Most of the residents of the islands are either fishermen themselves or have family members who fish. This is true of many of the park rangers, who are charged with enforcing the rules: they often accept bribes or look the other way if they catch family or friends doing something illegal.

The fishermen are very powerful in the islands: on more than one occasion, they have blockaded whole islands from tour vessels to protest a new ban or law, and once they even took over the Charles Darwin Research Station, held the scientists hostage, and threatened to kill Lonesome George, at the time thought to be the last remaining Pinta Island giant tortoise. Although the two sides seem beyond any sort of agreement, there are those who are working on compromises and new solutions: large tour operators Metropolitan Touring and Lindblad Expeditions support projects such as the "Teachers on Board" plan, in which schoolteachers from Galápagos spend time on cruise ships, learning about the islands from a tourism perspective. Metropolitan also has a project in which fishermen are paid to pick up trash off the islands. Perhaps in the future, fishing, wildlife and tourism will be able to coexist in these fragile islands.

ADDITIONAL BASIC FACTS
(CIA World Factbook)

Time Mainland = GMT minus 5; Galápagos = GMT minus 6
Electricity: Ecuador's electrical current is 110 volts 60 cycles, the same as North America, so adapters for North American equipment are not needed. However, plug converters are necessary in older buildings. Generally speaking, European electrical equipment such as portable computers and digital cameras will have variable power blocks that work on both 110-240v currents, so all you need is a plug adapter to use the appliance in Ecuador. Cheaper appliances such as hairdryers will probably require a power adapter (as well as a plug adapter) to make them suitable for 110v sockets.

TRANSPORTATION TO ECUADOR
BY PLANE
A number of airlines offer regular international flights to and from Ecuador. The high seasons, from the beginning of July to the beginning of September and December to mid-January, bring a bump in ticket price and extremely limited availability. Try to travel outside of these times, but if you can't, be sure to reserve your ticket well in advance. If you purchase your ticket in Ecuador, call the airline or travel agency where you purchased your ticket 72 hours before your flight to confirm, or you may be bumped from the flight. Ecuador recently raised its departure tax from Quito to $40.80, charged in cash after checking your bags and before going through migration. From Guayaquil the tax is $26.00.

BY LAND
While there is no road connecting Central to South America because of the zone of untamed rainforest between Colombia and Panama, many travelers make their way by bus once they are in Ecuador. This is entirely possible, perfectly safe and often cheaper than flying. Remember, though, South America is huge and multi-day bus rides are the norm if you are traveling through countries. Most major cities have international bus stations.

BORDER CROSSINGS
The three border crossings from Ecuador to Peru are at Huaqillas, Macará and La Balsa. The Huaquillas border and Macará are open 24 hours. La Balsa, south of Vilcabamba, is open from 6 a.m to 6 p.m. The border at Tulcán/Rumichaca is the best place to cross into or out of Colombia. The Ecuadorian town of Rumichaca is where the border patrol will stamp your passport and Tulcán is the border town 6 km away on the Colombian side. Tip: change money in a large Ecuadorian city before crossing any border. The money-changers at the border often pass false bills and will rip you off badly on the exchange rate.

VISA INFORMATION
NOTE: The following information was obtained from the Ecuadorian Embassy and Consulate General in the United States and should be confirmed with the Ecuadorian Embassy or Consulate in your own country. Visa policies and regulations change frequently, and can vary from one office to another. Sometimes the best sources are other travelers who have gone through the process themselves.

Most travelers to Ecuador will not have to think about procuring a visa before departure. When you arrive, the migration officials will stamp a tourist visa valid up to 90 days. If you plan to stay the entire 90 days, be sure to request the full visa limit as migration officials will sometimes give a visa for less time. They will also give you give you an embarkation card. Save this. You will need to present it when you leave the country. Your 90-day visa can be extended one month at a time, up to a total of six months. If you overstay your tourist visa, you will be charged a fine when you leave. The fine is less if you pay in Quito or Guayaquil at the migration police's headquarters where you will receive a 24, 48 or 72-hour visa for a fee.

Citizens of the following countries need to obtain a 12-X visa to visit Ecuador: Afghanistan, Algeria, Bangladesh, China, Costa Rica, Cuba, El Salvador, Guatemala, Honduras, India, Iraq, Iran, Jordan, North Korea, South Korea, Lebanon, Libya, Nigeria, Pakistan, Palestine, Syria, Sri Lanka, Sudan, Tunisia, Vietnam, Yemen and Members of the Sikh Sect.

If you want to work, study or just travel for more than 90 days, you may need to look into a different visa. There are two main types of visas: resident and non-resident (referred to as immigrant and non-immigrant on the Ecuadorian government website). Student visas, work visas, volunteer and religious work visas, cultural exchanges and tourist visas all fall under the category of non-resident and will set you back between $50 and $200.

The 12-IX, Tourism, Commercial activities, Sports, Health and Other Visa is valid for up to six months and allows you to change your visa status. If you are planning to stay for more than a year, and want to be able to work and have unlimited exit and entry status, you may want to look into a resident visa. Tourist visas can be extended up to 6 months per year, one month at a time after the 90-day time-limit has expired. Work visas are more complicated and are best arranged with your employer. Student visas are less complicated but are also best obtained with the help of your school or study program, which will undoubtedly have experience in jumping through the necessary bureaucratic hoops.

NOTE: All non-resident visas, except for the 12-X Transient, must be registered within the first 30 days of arrival. Failure to do so will result in a hefty $200 fine. Overstaying your visa will result in between a $200-$2,000 fine.

TRANSPORTATION WITHIN ECUADOR

BY PLANE
Ecuador's national airlines, TAME, Icaro and Aerogal offer daily service to 10 cities in Ecuador. These are also the only airlines that fly to the Galápagos Islands. Flying within Ecuador is not always cheap, considering the short distance from point-to-point, but it can save you hours of travel time. For example, a flight from Quito to Guayaquil takes about 35 minutes and costs around $99 roundtrip, while the bus takes over 10 hours (each way!) and costs about $24 roundtrip. A flight from Quito to Lago Agrio, the jump-off point to the Cuyabeno National Reserve in the Amazon, takes 25 minutes and costs $120 roundtrip as opposed to the 8-10 hour bus ride on shoddy roads that costs $16 roundtrip. Student and senior discounts may apply for both land and air travel, so be sure to ask. It is easiest to stop at a travel agency to book your flight, but be sure to call the airline to confirm a couple of days before you travel.

BY BUS
You will inevitably find yourself on a bus at some point during your time in Ecuador. It is the most common method of transportation for Ecuadorians as well as the cheapest and often the most convenient. Long-distance buses charge $1 per hour on average, slightly more for the Ejecutivo or First-Class buses. Buses in Quito cost 25 cents and fall under two categories: the regular buses and the trolleys or trams. The *Ecovia*, the *Trolle* and the *Metro Bus* system runs north and south and has extension routes that stretch out farther into the valleys and neighborhoods to the north and south. Other buses weave throughout the city and can be confusing for travelers, especially those not fluent in Spanish.

The best way to orient yourself on these buses is by reading the major destinations on the placards on the front window of the bus, and asking the driver and/or driver's assistant if they will be passing by your destination. The buses are numbered, but in no apparent order: it is best to ignore the numbers and focus on the placards. Bus drivers, especially in the sierra, are fearless. If you have a queasy stomach, sit near the front. Most long-distance buses are equipped with DVD players and TVs so you can enjoy Jean Claude Van Damme, Arnold Schwarzenegger, and many more action stars dubbed in Spanish as you speed around curvaceous two-lane mountain roads. Ecuadorian bus drivers tend to like action flicks, so don't get your hopes up for anything in the line of sappy dramas or romantic comedies.

By Train

The construction of a railway from the Sierra to the coast in 1873 was initiated by President Gabriel García Moreno. The 91 kilometers of rail service to the coast was essential to commerce and trade within the country. Today, travel by train is not the most extensive or efficient method of travel, but it is one of the most exhilarating. One such popular thrill ride is the *Nariz del Diablo* (the Devil's Nose) a series of switch back rails that go from downtown Riobamba to Alausi, where the scenery is stunning.

By Taxi

In Quito and Guayaquil, taxis will be an important way for you to get around. They are quite cheap, reliable and safe. There are a few rules and tips you need to familiarize yourself with first, however. In Quito (but not in Guayaquil), taxis are required to have a taximetro, or taxi meter, which measures how much the passenger must pay. Generally, the drivers keep it in the center of the dashboard, below the radio. Currently, the meters start at $.35 and go up from there. During the daytime, the taxis must use it if the passenger asks. Especially in the Mariscal (p. 93) or when dealing with foreigners, some less scrupulous taxis will hide it or claim that it doesn't work. Rule of thumb: once you flag down a cab, ask to see the *taximetro* before you get in. If the driver starts mumbling something about it being broken, wave him on and get the next cab.

There are some exceptions: taxis at the airport are not required to use the taximeter and negotiate directly with passengers. They'll hose you badly if they can, so if you don't have much stuff, cross the street and catch a cab there. Before you get in a cab from the airpot, you should agree on the price for your destination: it will go up if you're sitting in the back seat when you begin to negotiate. From the airport, expect to pay about $4-5 to the Mariscal, more for Old Town. At night after 9 p.m., Quito cabs are allowed to disconnect their taximetros and wheel and deal with passengers. Expect to pay about a dollar more than you would for the same trip in the daytime. Again, you should negotiate before you get in the cab: never simply get in and ask how much it was once you get to your destination. Although some lines stay open until 11 p.m., after 8 p.m. or so it is probably safest to travel in taxis, even for very short distances.

Hitchhiking

In a country full of pickup trucks, hitchhiking is a fairly common way to get around, especially in small towns where there is no established bus system. Some drivers, especially in the larger pickup trucks with seats and wooden walls to block the wind, will charge a small fee. You should always ask about price before hopping in Although hitchhiking is more common in Ecuador than in many other countries, it is still not guaranteed to be safe. Use common sense, especially if you are a woman or traveling alone.

By Car

The general philosophy of drivers in Ecuador is "I have the right of way." In practice, whoever is bigger goes first. As a result, you will hear lots of horns blaring, brakes screeching, insults flying and pedestrians running for their lives. That said, there are some advantages to renting a car while you are traveling in Ecuador. There are many spots that buses dare not venture and can only be reached by 4-wheel drive, on bicycle or by foot. In order to legally drive in Ecuador, you need an international driver's license used in conjunction with a driver's license from your home country. It's a good idea to also have healthy insurance coverage. Seven car rental companies operate in Ecuador; all charge between $25-90 a day.

ADVENTURE TRAVEL

Ecuador is a great destination for adventurous visitors itching to get off the tourist track. It features a fairly well developed infrastructure for activities like climbing, hiking, mountain biking, rafting, surfing, diving and bird-watching. Whether you decide to ramble out on your own or hook up with a local guide service, the logistics of planning excursions in Ecuador are simpler and the approach time shorter than in other, more remote areas of the world.

nber of excellent trips through the Andean páramo (grassland) which features 's of Ecuador's volcanic peaks. The most popular treks are the *Trek de Con-* s the often cloud-shrouded Antisana, Sincholagua and Cotopaxi Volcano; *ngapirca Trek* which takes you along an old Inca trail to Ecuador's most important ca site. For the intrepid trekker there are several multi-day Andes-to-Amazon hikes that take you from the grassy plains of the high altitude páramo, through cloud forest, and finally to lowland rainforest. During your descent, as you pass from one ecosystem to another, you'll see dramatic changes in the flora and fauna while you are peeling off layer after layer of clothing. Rainforest hikes are also possible, but it's a good idea to hire a local guide as it is easy to get lost. There are some great hikes from lodges along the Napo River in the Amazon.

RAFTING AND KAYAKING
Ecuador is considered one of the best destinations in the world for whitewater sports due to the steep drop-offs from snow-capped peaks to rich lowland areas connected by one of the highest concentrations of rushing rivers per square kilometer. In addition, its tropical location provides for year-round water sports. Whether you are interested in whitewater rafting or kayaking, Ecuador has the tours, isolated destinations and heart-racing rapids.

WHERE TO GO?
Tena is the biggest kayak and rafting destination in Ecuador; some say it offers the best kayaking rapids in Latin America. Many travelers choose to start in Quito and shop around the dozens of tour operators that base their operations in the capital before heading out. Santo Domingo also has a developed whitewater community, and offers warmer water than mountain rivers at higher altitudes. For something a bit more low key, head down to Baños and give rafting a go on the Pastaza River.

PACKING LIST
Swimsuit, tennis shoes or Teva-like sandals with secure ankle straps, T-shirt (quick drying

---

ECO-TOURISM IN ECUADOR
Eco-tourism in Ecuador has boomed in the last decade. There are many valid eco-lodges that have little to no negative effect on the environment and help you truly appreciate Ecuador's natural beauty. However, many hotels claim to be eco-lodges without following basic steps to guarantee ecological protection. All good eco-lodges should follow a few basic guidelines:

1. Minimal environmental impact should be the fundamental goal of every eco-operator. How a hotel or tour operator manages its impact will tell you immediately if it is truly ecologically minded. Ecologically responsible businesses recycle, conserve water and energy, manage waste properly (i.e., implement composting and gray water projects), and allow guests to choose whether or not to change linens or towels daily. These simple efforts make a huge difference in the long-term environmental impact of tourism.
2. Conservation may be practiced in many different ways. Habitat preservation is one of the principal forms of conservation. Habitats may be preserved by establishing private reserves, supporting established national parks and reserves, or funding native tree reforestation projects. Although protected areas may be visited by tourists, it is important to recognize that their primary purpose is preservation. Whenever visiting a protected area, your visit should be made with minimal impact.
3. Sustainability is vital to the long-term success of eco-tourism. The majority of products consumed at an eco-facility should be locally produced. Furthermore, construction should be done using local materials and methods, and local organic gardens should be the source of the majority of the food served. Ultimately, sustainability means a lifestyle that is in balance and that can be maintained indefinitely without depleting the earth's resources.
4. Community involvement is a crucial aspect of eco-tourism. Eco-tourism should generate revenue for the local economy without harming the environment. Ideally, the community should own the establishment. If this is not possible, the operation should at least employ local labor. Moreover, in addition to generating revenue and providing employment, eco-establishments should sponsor community development projects.
5. Environmental education teaches others to be ecologically responsible. Every guest should leave an eco-facility having learned something about environmental preservation and cultural sensitivity. This ensures the continued growth of environmental and cultural awareness.

material is best), easy-dry shorts or running tights, safety strap if wearing glasses, and water-proof cameras are all suggested. Don't forget a waterproof bag for anything you want to stay dry during your trip and a dry change of clothes for the trip back to Quito.

MOUNTAIN CLIMBING

Ecuador offers an incredible diversity of mountains to explore. Within one day's drive from Quito are several glaciated peaks which rise over 6,000 meters (20,000 feet). The highest Andean peaks in Ecuador are located primarily along the Avenue of the Volcanoes, a fertile central valley just south of Quito, which is buttressed by two mountain ranges, the Eastern and the Western Cordilleras. Some of the summits are young, cone-shaped volcanoes like Cotopaxi with technically straight-forward climbs offering the novice a chance to get near to or above high altitudes. Others are deeply eroded, older volcanoes with challenging rock and ice routes (such as the glorious ring of peaks on El Altar).

For your first few days in Ecuador, you should acclimate by ascending some of the smaller mountains, such as Iliniza Norte, Imbabura or Pichincha to avoid developing AMS (Acute Mountain Sickness) or the more severe Pulmonary Adenoma or Cerebral Adenoma. See the "Health" section for more information. These lower peaks are non-glaciated, easily accessible within a day's travel from Quito, and offer either hut facilities or nearby hostels that can be used as a climbing base. Once your body has adjusted to the altitude, you are ready to try one of Ecuador's four classic glaciated peaks: Chimborazo, Cotopaxi , Cayambe or Tungurahua. Although the standard routes are technically straightforward, people do die every year—primarily from avoidable mistakes. Novices should hire a guide. Experienced mountaineers can attempt the more remote and/or more difficult peaks of Antisana, El Altar and Iliniza Sur or the more challenging routes on other mountains.

As a relatively recent playground for climbers, Ecuador still provides many opportunities for ascents on new routes. There are three anomalous volcanoes (Reventador, Sumaco and Sangay) that do not belong to either of the Cordillera mountain ranges, but rather thrust up from dense jungle east of the Andes. These climbs have the added attraction of giving you a chance to test out your machete skills, as you must blaze trails through dense cloud forest or rainforest just to get to the base of these giants. Sangay is also noteworthy for its healthy population of woolly mountain tapirs.

V!VA Update: As of this edition, Tungurahua, Sangay and Reventador are highly active. We do not recommend that you try to climb them at this time. Check with your climbing outfitter and guides for up-to-the-minute information.

ENTRANCE FEES

Mainland park entrance fees generally run from $5-10, but Cotopaxi National Park is the only one that strictly enforces its entrance fee; all others are hit or miss.

CLIMBING HUTS (REFUGIOS)

There are huts at Cotopaxi (p. 254), Chimborazo (p. 265), Cayambe, the Ilinizas and Tungu-rahua. Almost all huts have bunks, stoves, pots/pans and toilets. Some even have electricity. The cost per night is around $10. The hut at Cotopaxi has a cellular telephone for weather information and emergencies: 593-9-963-8344. Plans to install cell phones at the other refuges have also been discussed as part of future improvements.

GUIDE SERVICES

Guide services in Ecuador are a classic example of "you get what you pay for," so we recommend avoiding the cheapest ones. There are many agencies and individuals who will take you up Cotopaxi for nickels, but they don't know the first thing about mountaineering, and they could put you in a dangerous situation. Equipment and climbing and hiking gear can be purchased or rented at reasonable prices in Quito, and with a bit more difficulty in Baños, or Riobamba. Helmets are an exception to this rule; if you have your own helmet, bring it.

PACKING LIST

Below are supplies you will need on a two-day non-technical climb up mountains such as Cotopaxi and Chimborazo. For the more technical climbs, specialized equipment is needed. For nearly all tours, the items listed under Equipment (below) are provided by the tour company. All equipment may be rented in Quito as well. Helmets are the exception to both of these statements, they are rarely provided and are also very difficult to rent.

Equipment: Mountaineering boots, crampons, ice axe, carabineers, climbing ropes, harness; and gaiters. Recommended personal gear: Water, headlamp, three sets of batteries, glacier glasses, lip balm, sunscreen, knife, two water bottles, two insulating layer tops: one thin, one thick, insulating layer bottoms, Gore-Tex type hooded coat, Gore-Tex type bottom, glove liners, Gore-Tex gloves, two pairs of socks, warm hat, camera—keep it in your inside pocket or it will freeze—extra change of clothes, shoes for around camp.

MOUNTAIN BIKING

Ecuador offers the cyclist seemingly endless back roads and trails to explore. The Incas, who were legendary road builders, and their living descendants have been carving scenic paths for centuries. Today, mountain bikes are used by rural communities as a major form of transportation in many areas. The Andes create a playground of huge vertical descents and lung-bursting climbs where the snow line and the equator meet. For most people the extreme cycling environment of the Andes is best enjoyed going downhill. Descents of 3,000 m (10,000 ft) in a single day can be obtained in several areas of the country. The world-class descent directly down the slopes of Cotopaxi Volcano, the technical descent down Pichincha Volcano, and trips that take riders from the heights of the Andes to the Amazon Basin are all highly recommended.

Biker-friendly buses and pickup truck taxis, plus readily available lodging and food in most rural areas, make cross-country, independent bicycle travel in Ecuador extremely appealing, but careful planning is essential. The lesser-traveled back roads make the best routes. Avoid the Pan-American Highway, and most other paved roads in Ecuador, as you will encounter reckless bus and truck drivers that are not used to seeing bicycles on the road. Most parts of Quito are extremely biker-unfriendly, and should be avoided. Not only will the traditional cobblestone roads throughout the city rattle your bones loose, but the city is often packed with bumper-to-bumper traffic. Cars will rarely give bikers the right-of-way. Bike rental is available in Quito and Baños, but quality varies widely, so check your bike carefully before heading out. Shocks and strong aluminum rims are essential as the high speed descents on potted terrain will otherwise lead to unwanted bent wheels.

Packing your bike up at home and bringing it with you on the plane is one alternative to rental. Be sure to bring a strong lock and always leave your bike locked in a secure location. Pack wisely and bring plenty of spare parts, including extra tubes and tires, and don't forget a first-aid kit as you'll probably be pedaling in remote areas.

HORSEBACK RIDING AND TOURS

Ecuador provides riding enthusiasts with a surprising range of excellent riding opportunities. You can ride high in the Andes through the páramo, grasslands and plains with snow capped volcanoes as a backdrop; through lowland tropical rain forest; or even through the many unique ecosystems of the Galápagos Islands. Ecuador's extensive hacienda system makes it possible to ride through quilted pasture land from one hacienda to another, many of which now operate as country inns and send riders out with scrumptious picnics.

Ecuador has a number of stables that rent good horses, and if you know where to look you can find pure Peruvian Pasos, Andalusians, and Arabs. Beginning riders are advised to hire the tough, mixed-blood "Criollo" horses. However, even healthy horses will generally look thin in the Sierra—at these altitudes the horses cannot afford to carry extra weight—so you will rarely find well-padded mounts.

RULES OF RIDING

Stable standards, ethics and horse-care policies vary tremendously in Ecuador. Horse owners and trainers change regularly, which means that training and care also changes. Common sense is therefore essential. When considering a horse for hire, follow these basic rules:

1. If a horse appears ill, lame or abused, REFUSE to ride it. Change horses or leave. Please let VivaTravelGuides.com know if you find inhumane conditions at any stables.

2. If you cannot control the horse or do not feel safe, it's best to change horses or to not ride. If you are on a trail when a problem arises, do not hesitate to dismount.

3. If the tack (saddle and bridle) looks ill-fitted, old, cracked, and/or damaged, ask to have it changed—a fall could ruin your entire trip.

4. Check the tack adjustments before getting on the horse. Is the girth band tight? Are the reins and stirrup leathers in good condition? Most importantly, take the time to set your stirrups for the right length. Stirrups that are too short will hurt your knees and can be dangerous, as can stirrups that are too long.

Western tack is typically used in Ecuador, although some stables offer English saddles. Western saddles are recommended as they are safer going up and down steep terrain and are generally more comfortable for long rides. Few stables offer riding helmets, so if you are planning on doing any serious riding bring your own helmet.

WHERE TO RIDE

There are many places in Ecuador that offer horseback riding. The central highlands have the best scenery, including snow-capped volcanoes, wide valleys and stark high-altitude grasslands known as páramos. It is also in the highlands where you'll find most of the best haciendas, which generally offer horses. Baños has a number of good riding trails nearby, although shop for horses carefully as there are many disreputable stables in the area.

WHEN TO RIDE

In Ecuador you can ride year-round, although some months are better than others for certain areas. The coastal areas and semi-tropical Baños have a tendency to be muggy. In the Sierra north of Quito, the month of May can be rather wet. During the rest of the year, it typically rains only in the late afternoons and by this time the horses are back in the stables and you are fireside enjoying a pre-dinner cocktail.

BIRDWATCHING IN ECUADOR

Ecuador is a popular destination for bird watching. With upward of 1,500 species, it boasts as many species as in Europe and North America put together. Ecuador's top birding spots are in the Oriente region, with over 600 species, and the Galápagos (p. 117) with many endemic species. However, there are other regions that birders may wish to explore, including the bird-rich cloud forest area surrounding Mindo (p. 325), and many unusual species can also be found in the páramo region. Because Ecuador is small and has a decent infrastructure, it is possible to access many of these areas fairly easily. It is recommended to hire the services of local guides for the best birding experiences, as they have good local knowledge and know exactly where to look in the undergrowth to locate that rare bird. Don't forget your binoculars!

BIRDWATCHING IN THE AMAZON

To spot the widest variety of species of birds in the Amazon (p. 300), it is worth heading there during the transitions between the dry and wet months. The worst time is during the dry months (December, January and August). Species to be spotted in the Amazon include the Rufousheaded Woodpecker, Fiery Topaz, Harpy Eagle and Zigzag Heron, as well as various species of Tanagers, Toucans, Parrots, Antbirds and more. The best birdwatching opportunities in the Amazon region are found by staying at a jungle lodge, and there are many to choose from. Be sure to select one with an observation tower: these are built around the tall Kapok Trees and allow climbing above the forrest canopy to spot a great variety of species.

Sacha Lodge is unique for its 40-meter tower, from which it is possible to spot many species. From the tower, a wild cacophony greets you as you spot a wide variety of colorful birds, including parrots and macaws. Sacha boasts that it is possible for a guide to spot as many as 80 species in a morning from this tower. With 500 recorded species in the area, this could be true. For an alternative birding experience, take a motorized canoe for one and a half hours to the Yasuní Parrot Lick. Here, in a colorful spectacle, several species of parrots gather in the early morning to eat the exposed, salty clay, which is vital for their digestion.

The Kapawi Lodge is another alternative for great birding. In a stay of ten days, it is possible for a keen and dedicated spotter to see up to an astounding 400 species. The building of the lodge was one of the biggest community-based projects in Ecuador and there is a push to provide genuine ecotourism. River islands close to Kapawi are home to Horned Scream-ers, Orinoco Geese and Muscovy Ducks. Other birds around here include Brown Jacamars, Plumbeous Antbird, Buckley's Forest Falcon and the Blue-winged Parrotlet, to name just a few. It is possible to observe species here that cannot be found at other lodges.

At La Selva, native birding experts are hired to assist those interested in birdwatching. While their English is not great, their birding skills more than make up for this. Close to the lodge it is possible to see many varieties of birds just by walking around. However, for a great view, La Selva offers an observation tree tower. La Selva is also close to parrot salt licks, and it is a great place for spotting the Cocha Antshrike and the Zigzag Heron.

Birdwatching in the Galápagos

Where else could birdwatching be easier? Even for an amateur, it is possible to spot most of the species with little effort or patience. The coastline is quite biologically diverse, allowing visitors to view a large cross-section of Galápagos bird life. A typical shoreline might contain sandy and rocky beach, mangroves and saline tidal pools. There are countless opportunities for observing the life rituals of these birds including courtship and nurturing of the young.

The most famous of the Galápagos Islands for bird-watching is probably Tower Island (Gen-ovesa). This remote northern island was never colonized by many land animals, which left it almost completely open to birds. If you visit Tower, you can expect to see a wide variety of birds including boobies, frigates, gulls and the short-eared owl. Red-footed boobies and frig-ates nest at one of the visitor sites, so you may get the opportunity to view chicks.

It's doubtful that you would leave the Galápagos without observing all three types of boo-by—blue footed, red footed and masked (also referred to as Nazca). Blue-footed boobies are famous for their intriguing courtship dance which you may be lucky enough to see. Frigate birds are common. They spend a lot of time offshore, and often there will be two or three in flight accompanying your boat. If you are keen to see the Waved Albatross, visit the islands between April and December, during the other months you may be disappointed. An unfor-gettable sight is watching the albatross make its way to the cliffs at the southern end of the island in order to launch their large, heavy body into the air. The Waved Albatross can only be seen on Española Island, so plan your trip accordingly.

The Galápagos Penguin is one of the smallest species of penguins and is unusual in that it lives north of the equator. If you are lucky, you may spot penguins fishing underwater, whilst while snorkeling—don't forget your underwater camera! Flightless Cormorants are found on some islands. It is interesting to observe them stretching out on the rocks to dry after swim-ming. Great Flamingos are a bright pink stark contrast to the volcanic backdrop of the islands and can be found inhabiting the lagoons that are found slightly inland on several islands. The Mockingbirds found on the islands are arguably the tamest creatures of all. They'll land on you and clamour to get into your water bottle. Last but not least, and famed for inspiring Darwin's theory of evolution, the thirteen varieties of Darwin Finches can be spotted on the islands.

BIRDWATCHING IN THE CLOUD FOREST AND SURROUNDING AREAS

In the subtropical cloud forest regions, the humid conditions and high biodiversity create a birdwatcher's paradise. Of particular note, the town of Mindo has been designated an Important Bird Area since 1997, the first area in South America to be attributed this honor. The Mindo-Nambillo protected forest supports over 350 species of birds, over 50 of which are endemic to the area. The Mindo area is home to more than 500 species of birds. Some of the more spectacular ones include the Golden-headed Quetzal, Yellow-collared Chlorophonia, Choco Toucan, Club-winged Manakin and Cock-of-the-Rock. Mindo is a two hour drive from Quito and the best months for birdwatching are September through to January. There are many lodges to choose from in the Mindo area. It is worth heading a bit further out, 29km from Mindo, to the Bellavista Cloud Forest Reserve, where 263 species have reportedly been observed. Unusually, the Tanager Finch has been spotted here—Bellavista is the only known place in Ecuador where this species resides.

Alternatively, if interested in observing the birds of the lowland forests, head west of Mindo to Santo Domingo (p. 331), 2-3 hours drive from Quito. However, this is for keen birdwatchers only, as there is not a lot else to see or do in Santo Domingo. It is however, worth a stay in Tinalandia close by as more than 270 species of birds have been spotted, including the Long-wattled Umbrella bird, the Golden-winged Manakin and the Glistening-green Tanager. The area surrounding Tinalandia is considered by ornithologists and botanists to be one of the most biodiverse areas in the world. There are opportunities to bird just walking around the grounds, and those staying for a while can take trips to see birds such as Torrent Duck and Black Phoebe. Another option, 50km from Santo Domingo, is the Rio Palenque Science Center, located on the Palenque River. This reserve has 360 species of bird and it is possible to see a variety of species, including Yellow-tailed Oriole, Ecuadorian Trogon, Northern Barred-Woodcreeper, Orange-billed sparrow and species of hawks and kites. The center has a capacity for 26 guests.

BIRDWATCHING IN THE PÁRAMO

Above the Cloud Forest region sits the Páramo, the barren zone above the treeline from 3100 m to 4700 m. Birds here are easy to spot due to the lack of vegetation. Ecuador's national symbol, the Andean Condor can be found here, along with the Tawny Antpitta and the Andean Snipe. Condors can also be spotted on the road to Papallacta from Quito. Areas of Páramo worth visiting include the national parks of El Ángel, Cajas and the highland areas of Cotacatchi-Cayapas and Cayambe-Coca. The Cajas National Park is home to 125 species, including the Condor and the Violet-tailed Metaltail, an endemic hummingbird. The Cotapaxi National Park is also a good place for Páramo birding, with 90 species of birds to be found, including the Black-chested Hawk-eagle, the Andean Coot, the Andean Lapwing and the Páramo Pipit. Other birds that make their home in the páramo include the Rufous-bellied Seed Snipe and the Stout-billed Cinclodes.

TRAVEL TIPS FOR ECUADOR

Travel means different things to different people. Why are you traveling? Some travel for business, some for pleasure. Some are low-budget backpackers, some have money to burn. Some travelers have special needs such as handicap access or child-friendly facilities. In order to provide you with the best service possible, our writers here at V!VA Travel Guides have included this section on Ecuador Travel Tips and advice. In it, you'll find all of the travel tips, advice and suggestions that you'll need to custom-fit your trip to best suit your needs. Are you a woman traveling alone? If so, you'll want to check out our page on tips for women travelers (p. 58). Traveling with kids? You'll want to see our section on Ecuador travel for families (p. 59). Gay/lesbian? Don't go without first looking at out Gay/Lesbian travel tips page (p. 58). Senior citizens will also find useful advice, as will handicapped travelers (p. 58).

Planning on taking some photos while in Ecuador? Photographers will want to take a look at our Photography in Ecuador page (p. 56).

So, how much is this trip going to cost you? We can help you lower your costs and get the most for your buck. Ecuador has excellent travel options for all sorts of budgets: no matter how much you can afford to spend, you'll find many good, fun, healthy options. On a tight budget? If you intend to spend less than $30/day in Ecuador, check out our tips for budget travelers (p. 59). Not counting every dime but still want to save some money? Visit our page about budgeting tips for mid-range travelers if you're planning on spending $30-70 per day (p. 60). Have bags of cash lying around? If you want to have the best trip possible and money is not a consideration, have the butler turn the page to our tips for luxury travelers section (p. 61).

STUDYING SPANISH

Ecuador's excellent selection of Spanish schools is unmatched in South America. Prices are low, averaging $3-8 an hour for individual classes. Most schools also arrange homestays with a local family, and some offer excursions, salsa dancing or cooking classes as part of the package.

Although Quito has the biggest choice of Spanish schools, you can also sign up for classes in numerous other towns and cities in Ecuador. Baños, Otavalo and Cuenca are all popular places to take classes. Some Quito schools allow you the option to take classes in the jungle or on the beach too.

VOLUNTEERING AND WORKING

Ecuador has seen an explosion in voluntourism recently. There are a huge choice of organizations, both in and out of Ecuador, that can set you up with voluntary work. Popular options are working with children (generally teaching English at a school or helping out at an orphanage) or ecology-based projects such as reforestation, research or conservation projects.

Some organizations offer free accommodation and food in return for your labor, while others charge a small fee. If you're planning to stay for a while (generally a month or longer) the price goes down. If you are in Quito, check with the South American Explorers Club, which can give you up-to-date information on organizations that offer volunteer work.

There are also numerous possibilities for working in Ecuador, although this is more difficult to arrange from home. Your best bet is to turn up and see what you can find. There are vacancies year-round for English teachers in Quito and Guayaquil (less so in other cities) and most of the teachers we spoke to had no problems finding a job, even with little experience.

The best way to find work is to print off a few copies of your resume/CV and visit a few language schools in person. Chances are you'll be hired on the spot. Pay ranges from $3 to $8 per hour. Schools that teach business English pay the best, but tend to require certification such as CELTA or International TESOL. Some bilingual high schools require native English speakers (with the relevant experience and qualifications) to teach English as well as other

ALL IN THE FAMILY

Cold electric showers, rice and potato dinners, and drinking games with drunken uncles. Red, rare, raw, and dripping with the unrefined realities of everyday living in a foreign country. Stripped bare and without the travel brochure bombast and tour guide diplomacy, the country conjures the images of a lackluster life that's—gasp—dishearteningly similar to the one we left behind. No ad-agency adjectives or airbrushed photos of models riding bareback on deserted beaches; a homestay in Quito promises the willing traveler a very different spread.

While living with an Ecuadorian family, one can expect wild encounters with the ordinary activities of every-day-life. You will have the rare opportunity to eat, sleep, live and breathe Ecuador. There are no class five rapids to write home about and no survival stories of hairy encounters with wild beasts. A homestay will not boast five-star accommodation, gourmet spreads or National Geographic-type natives. Monthly rent doesn't cover snorkeling with endangered turtles or bungee jumping in National Parks—in fact, you'll be lucky to get red meat and a green vegetable once a week. What a homestay does provide, however, is a wild adventure into the heart and soul of a country, its natural rhythms and the heartbeat of its people. It is a rare opportunity to drop the accoutrements of an outsider and don the apparel of an insider. Living with a family is about delighting in the strange and bizarre occurrences that inevitably accompany the uncut, unrefined, realities of family life.

subjects. Private schools generally hire in September and their pay is probably the best you will find as a foreign teacher in Ecuador.

Your second best bet is to get a job in the tourism industry, such as travel agency or hotel work. Pay is not as good as the top-end English schools but pay often includes accommodation and food so you can live rather cheaply. For these jobs you need a good level of Spanish. If you want to work in business, it may be worth checking out the notice boards in the Mariscal as there are often vacancies for jobs in the flower and oil industries. Again, your chances will be far better if you have a good level of Spanish and English.

LIVING IN ECUADOR

Many travelers passing through Ecuador fall in love with the country and decide to stay for an extended period of time. According to the US Embassy, about 10,000 Americans live and work in Ecuador. Undoubtedly, there are countless Europeans who make this beautiful country their home too. Quito has a large expatriate community and lots of options for furnished apartments, jobs for English speakers and volunteer projects. Expect to pay $90-350 a month per person for an apartment. $90/month will get you a small apartment in the Centro Histórico or Guápulo that will be furnished with the bare necessities. On the other end of the scale, $350/month (per person) can get you a luxury apartment in the north of Quito or in one of the valleys like Cumbayá with beautiful furnishings and often a common pool, hot tub and terrace with mountain views.

Outside of Quito, the prices drop by almost half for apartments, but it will be harder to find a furnished place. For apartment listings local newspapers, such as El Comercio, are an ex-

Have a great travel story? Tell it at www.vivatravelguides.com

cellent source, though you will have to be able to read Spanish, or know someone who does. Another great option for travelers looking to stay a bit longer is living with a family. Many families in Quito (and around Ecuador) offer rooms in their homes as an alternative source of income, or for inter-cultural exchange. Prices for homestays vary drastically, ranging from $100-450/month, and usually include 2-3 meals/day.

If you plan to stay in Ecuador longer than six months, you will need to look into getting a non-resident or resident visa. See our visa section for more information. Many people enjoy the options for work in Ecuador. Salaries are somewhat low for the cost of living. Expect to earn between $400-1,000 in Quito, much less outside of the city. For more information, see our work/volunteering section. For retirees interested in stretching their retirement savings the extra inch, Ecuador is an excellent place to live. Property is fairly easy to purchase and makes for a relatively safe investment. Be sure to get a good lawyer and/or real estate agent, though. It is not possible to buy land in the Galápagos Islands due to strict restrictions protecting the flora and fauna in the national park.

LODGING

Accommodation in Ecuador is wide-ranging, and caters to everyone from penny-pinching backpackers to those with money to burn. All across the country, in rural areas, small towns and cities, you will find hostels which cater to the budget market. Some have dorm rooms, which cost as little as $2 per night (up to $8 per night in Quito) per person. Many *hostales* have private rooms as well, with shared or private baths. Most towns also feature *hoteles*, which tend to cost from $10 up to the low $100s—generally speaking, you get what you pay for. International four and five-star hotel chains exist only in Quito and Guayaquil.

ECO-LODGES

In recent years there has been a proliferation of eco-lodges across Ecuador, basically environmentally-friendly hotels often set in large, protected areas of land. In theory, they use the money they get from tourism to help conserve their particular plot of land. Many also work with local communities to improve schools, build paths and improve the quality of life for the locals. While there are many legitimate eco-lodges around, there are also plenty of fakes that think they can boost their popularity simply by tacking 'eco' onto their name. One place we visited claimed to be an eco-lodge because it had a papaya tree! Have a look at our guide to eco-tourism to find out some of the basic principles that lodges should abide by in order to use this title.

RAINFOREST LODGES

The Amazon Rainforest Basin, or *el oriente*, is a popular visitor destination, and a number of jungle lodges have sprung up in recent years. Most of them are located by Tena, Puerto Francisco de Orellana (Coca), or Nueva Loja (Lago Agrio) which are transportation hubs in Ecuador's eastern lowlands. Although each is quite unique, activities and basic features do not vary much. Location is the first consideration. The lodges near Tena are more easily accessible than those near Coca or Lago Agrio, but have significantly less wildlife. Getting from Quito to Tena is a relatively easy six-hour bus ride, whereas the buses from Quito to Coca or Lago Agrio take at least 10 hours. There are also flights to all major launching points in the jungle in and out of Quito. Flights to both Coca and Lago Agrio take about 30 minutes and cost $120 round trip. Another consideration is comfort. If your idea of a vacation includes a pool, a buffet table and hammocks, there are jungle lodges that will provide that. If you are more interested in animals and birds than comfort, you should check out the more remote lodges. Still other lodges offer a closer look at local jungle communities, which can also be fascinating. See our Amazon section for a list of jungle lodges in Ecuador's *Oriente*.

HACIENDAS

Ecuador is a country with a rich colonial past. In colonial times, the mountainous countryside was divided up among rich landowners who ruled Indian villages like medieval dukes. The landowners usually built a hacienda, a sort of rural mansion, as a place to live and oversee the work done on their lands. The system was in place for centuries, and the Ecuadorian country-side is dotted with old haciendas in varying states of upkeep. In the last few years, many of the most picturesque old haciendas have been converted into hotels and guesthouses. The area to the north of Quito, near Otavalo, is particularly known for excellent converted haciendas. The spacious rooms, beautiful gardens and centuries of history have proved irresistible to thousands of travelers every year. The best haciendas have not lost their rural charm: they still feel like a home, and friendly staff members make guests comfortable.

Haciendas are not meant for the backpacker crowd, as it is hard to reach many of the best ones without private transportation. In addition, prices are significantly higher than the hostels and smaller hotels. However, travelers willing to spend a little more should make a point of visiting at least one hacienda while in Ecuador. Each is unique and memorable, and value for the money spent for a hacienda stay is usually quite good. Ecuadorian haciendas have much in common. Most of them offer horseback riding, mountain biking and gardens where guests can wander and relax. Many also have an on-site restaurant. Some of the haciendas can host and help plan special events such as conferences and weddings. The least expensive haciendas run at about $30-40/room per night, whereas the more expensive ones can cost over $200/person per night. Most of them fall into the mid-range of about $70-90/night. Guests can often negotiate discounts for large groups or extended stays.

FOOD AND DRINK IN ECUADOR

Ecuador is known for its wonderful exotic fruits, high quality fish and seafood and the countless varieties of Andean corn and potatoes. Across the country you'll find a broad spectrum of national and regional dishes, including lemon-marinated shrimp, toasted corn and pastries stuffed with spiced meats. If you're feeling courageous, put your culinary bravery to the test with roasted *cuy* (guinea pig) or cow-stomach stew, *guatita*. If you're looking to stretch your buck take advantage of set dishes, an Ecuadorian institution in many restaurants. Lunches, *almuerzos*, and dinners, *meriendas*, usually give you soup, a main course, juice and dessert for between $1.50 and $3. Dishes sold on the street are also quite cheap, but hygiene is often questionable. A good rule to follow is the locals rule: if the place is frequented by many locals, the food probably merits joining the crowd.

Ají, hot sauce made from a spicy red pepper grown in the Ecuadorian rainforest, complements the regular diet of rice, potatoes, and meat. Most Ecuadorian restaurants and homes have their own version of ají. Some versions of the homemade ají are basically tomato sauce, while others are incredibly spicy (Spanish: *picante*) so be sure to sample a bit before smothering your food. If you don't see a little bowl of ají on your table, just ask, they're sure to have it. In addition to ají, a mound of rice, a small salad and potatoes or *patacones* (squashed, fried green plantains) accompany basic dishes. On the coast and in the Amazon, potatoes are often supplemented or replaced by *menestras* (beans or lentils) or yuca.

Soups are without a doubt Ecuador's specialty. The first course of most lunches and dinners is a savory soup, rich with grains, vegetables and chicken or beef. *Locro* soup, made with cheese, avocado and potato, sounds a bit odd, but is actually quite tasty. *Chupe de pescado*, a fish and vegetable soup with coastal origins, is becoming popular throughout the country. Bolder diners can try *yaguar locro*, a potato soup made with sprinklings of cow blood. Those ready to throw their inhibitions completely to the wind should dip their spoon into *caldo de patas*, a broth containing chunks of boiled cow hooves, considered a delicacy by locals and believed by hopeful men to increase virility.

Brave travelers will want to try cuy, a traditional dish that dates back to before the days of the Inca. It is generally fried or cooked over an open fire. There is not a lot of meat on a guinea pig, which tastes like a cross between chicken and pork. If you want to try cuy, your best bet is to check out a traditional Ecuadorian restaurant in Quito such as Mama Clorindas, or look for one in an indigenous area like Otavalo. You can also find them on the grill on the main street in Baños. Other classic dishes include: *seco de pollo* (stewed chicken accompanied by rice and avocado slices); *lomo salteado* (thin beef steak covered with onions and tomatoes); and *seco de chivo* (goat stew served with a mound of rice).

Have a great travel story? Tell it at www.vivatravelguides.com

INTERNATIONAL CUISINE

If after your share of guinea pig you find yourself hankering for a familiar burger, burrito or pizza, don't panic. The major cities feature (for better or worse) the ever-present American fast food chains such as Pizza Hut, Taco Bell, McDonalds and KFC as well as some higher-quality American chains like T.G.I. Fridays, Applebee's and Tony Roma's. As an up-and-coming cosmopolitan city, Quito also offers a good selection of international cuisine. If you fancy Argentine steak, Italian pasta, Japanese sushi or French fondue you won't be disappointed. Expect prices lower than those in the United States or Europe but higher than local cuisine. Chinese, Mexican, Cuban, Arabic, Indian and vegetarian meals are available in Quito at reasonable prices.

SEAFOOD

Seafood is popular and plentiful throughout Ecuador. Lobster dinners can be enjoyed along the coast and in major cities for low prices. In Esmeraldas on the northern coast, try the delicious *encocados*, seafood dishes prepared in coconut milk. The signature dish of the country, however, is *ceviche*, a cold soup featuring seafood marinated in a broth of tomato, lime and onions —Ecuador's answer to sushi. Unlike sushi however, Ecuadorian ceviche is always dished up with popcorn! Ceviche can be made with fish (*de pescado*), shrimp (*de camarones*), shellfish (*de concha*), squid (*de calamari*) or all of the above (*mixta*). Exercise caution though, as improperly prepared ceviche—especially *de concha*—has become one of the primary vectors for cholera and other nasty bacteria. Most restaurants are aware of this and act accordingly, but choose your dining establishment wisely. Note that in general, the seafood in Ecuadorian ceviche has been cooked through before preparation. In other countries such as Peru, the seafood in ceviche is not cooked: the acidic juice of the limes "cooks" the seafood.

VEGETARIAN/VEGAN CUISINE

Vegetarians will be pleasantly surprised by the wide selection of vegetarian options in popular tourist destinations like Quito and Baños. However, in smaller towns, you will often be stuck eating some combination of rice, oily salads and eggs. Strict vegans will have a tough time finding acceptable food in Ecuador. Vegans should plan on doing a lot of grocery , as restaurants in Ecuador don't really understand the concept of a meal without some sort of animal product: most vegetarian options include milk, eggs or cheese.

DRINKS

With the mouthwatering exotic fruits of Ecuador come delicious fruit juices (*jugos*) including *naranjilla* (a tangy orange fruit), *tomate de arbol* (a fruity tomato with a kick), *mora* (blackberry), *guanabana* (an almost milky, sweet, white fruit), *maracuya* (passionfruit) and *papaya*. If you're staying in a home with an Ecuadorian family, chances are good you'll be treated to a fresh glass with breakfast every day. Most restaurants offer a variety of juices as well: ask for what's fresh. Bottled and canned fizzy drinks (including Coca Cola, Sprite and Fanta) are widely available throughout the country, as are teas and coffees. Ecuador produces good coffee, but, surprisingly, most Ecuadorians seem to prefer instant over brewed coffee. If you are willing to pay slightly more, you can usually find a well-brewed cappuccino in the bigger cities and most popular tourist haunts.

Chicha is a traditional concoction found throughout the Andes and Amazon, made from fermented *maiz* (corn), rice or yuca (manioc). In some rural parts of Ecuador the fermentation process is augmented by human saliva: Chicha makers (traditionally women) chew the ingredients and spit them back in the pot to brew! However, this practice is generally only still common in remote parts of the rainforest, so if you're offered chicha in the highlands, don't worry. Not to be missed is the Andean drink of choice: *canelazo* (or *canelito*), a popular fiesta drink similar to a hot toddy made of boiled water, sugar cane alcohol, lemon, sugar and cinnamon.

Good wine from Chile and Argentina is widely available. The cheapest way to enjoy it is in the form of a *cartón* (yes, a box!) from the local supermarket. The quality is not the best and you won't get the glorious sound of a popping cork, but you'll pay only half the price. If your palate is a bit more finicky, fine wines from Chile, France, Spain and Italy are also available. Most bars serve local beers of decent quality and very good value. The most popular brand is *Pilsener*, which comes in a large bottle. If you are a fan of Cuba Libres, Daiquiris or Piña Coladas, the local rum is great, as well as quite cheap. Use common sense, as with everything, and stick to bottled water rather than over tap water. Remember that tap water is frequently used in ice, so request your beverages "*sin hielo*" (without ice) in restaurants.

COMMON SENSE AT THE TABLE: A FEW TIPS

Allow yourself some time to adjust intestinally; eat cautiously the first few days and then slowly begin to venture out on a culinary limb. Staying healthy is not only about avoiding germs, but also about acclimating to new ones. Many Ecuadorians complain about traveling to the States and getting sick from US food or water, so it goes both ways!

Bottled water is very easily purchased at any corner store for a reasonable price: do not drink tap water. Contrary to popular belief, food, rather than water, is usually the culprit of intestinal problems. Eating well-cooked, piping hot food is possibly the best way to avoid problems. Avoid uncooked and under-cooked foods. Salads should especially be avoided at first. Fruits that must be peeled before being eaten, such as bananas, pineapples, and oranges are usually a safe bet. See Health for more information.

SHOPPING

Shopping is a varied experience in Ecuador. From dusty, noisy animal markets to craft markets, to sterile, glossy malls, there is something for everyone here. Ecuador produces an interesting array of products that can be purchased as souvenirs. Arts and crafts (in Spanish, *artesanía*) such as weavings, wood carvings, rugs, toys and clothes can be picked up all over Ecuador. Prices are reasonable and bargaining is encouraged.

WHAT TO BUY?

Special to Ecuador and of note, so-called "Panama" hats are produced in Ecuador. Despite their name, their origin is in Ecuador. Good quality hats can be rolled up and will spring back into shape. Beware the hats available in Otavalo market, cheap does not equate to a bargain! Vegetable ivory or *tagua* items are a nice buy and can be both cheap and small—helpful for getting them home. An unusual and colorful purchase is a bread dough ornament. It is possible to buy bread dough fridge magnets, nativity and Christmas decorations (available year-round) and other figures such as llamas for a cheap price in Calderón, just north of Quito. The Otavalo region is known for its excellent quality textiles which are sold daily in its famous market. Good quality, cheap leather goods are also a good bet in Ecuador.If you plan on picking up some souvenirs in the enchanted islands, it's a good idea to choose carefully: avoid purchasing items that appear to have been made from endangered plant or animal species.

WHAT NOT TO BUY?

It is not possible to export animal products out of Ecuador, and in fact it is not usually permissible to import them to most countries either. Thus avoid products manufactured from animals, endangered or otherwise. This includes insects and feathers. Take care with antiques, it is difficult to export these too.

WHERE TO BUY?

For artesanía, Otavalo is the most famous and possibly the best place to bargain for good quality products, such as weavings, woodwork and jewelry. It is possible to pick up Panama hats all over Ecuador, but Montecristi and Cuenca arguably hold the best stock. For bread dough ornaments, head to the small town of Calderón, located just to the north of Quito.

HOW TO BUY?

Bargaining is the name of the game in Ecuador in the markets and often in the craft shops too. Indeed, in the markets there are no prices on display. You need to bargain prices with the stall holder. Wait until the seller suggests a price, and then offer to pay half to two-thirds of that price and take it from there. To find out the lowest price that a vendor will accept, ask "*el último?*" It is worth checking out prices on a few different stalls with similar products before entering into bargaining, to get a good idea of value. Also recommended is to buy a lot of things at the same stall. Sellers will often discount prices for those buying in bulk. Stalls away from the main arteries of markets will often have better bargains than those near strategic corners. Most importantly, don't pass up that unique sweater for the sake of a dollar. That dollar will mean more to the stall holder than to you, and you will surely regret it when you get home.

QUITO MALLS

At the opposite end of the scale, Quito's malls are shiny, slick and expensive. Wealthy quiteños just love wandering around them in the evenings and weekends. Many recognizable brand names can be found here, such as Bally, Liz Clairborne, Nine West and Diesel. In each mall there are huge food courts where familiar fast food restaurants such as KFC and Taco Bells coexist with chains catering to more traditional tastes. Groceries and other supermarket goods can be picked up in the ubiquitous Supermaxi supermarket chain. There are stores to be found in the El Jardin, CCI, El Bosque and El Recreo malls.

The main malls in Quito are listed here:
Quicentro is possibly Quito's premier mall. It is located at Av. Naciones Unidas and 6 de Diciembre.
The **El Jardin** mall can be found at Amazonas and Republica.
Centro Comercial Inaquito (known as CCI) is at Amazonas and Naciones Unidas.
El Bosque, Quito's first mall, built in the 1980s is situated in the north of the city at on the Occidental avenue and Carvajal.
In the south of the city, the **El Recreo** mall, popular with Quito's less affluent, is found on Avenida Maldonado. The trole stops right outside.

MARKETS

OTAVALO MARKET

Colorful and buzzing, Otavalo Market is the biggest indigenous market in South America. It is held daily, but the most important day is Saturday. The market is based in Plaza de los Ponchos and extends far into the local streets on a Saturday. During the rest of the week, the market is pretty much confined to the plaza, but you'll still find a variety of fine products, less stalls and gringos to contend with, and a more relaxed atmosphere. It is often possible to barter for better prices on days other than Saturday due to the smaller number of buyers. For a unique cultural experience visit the animal market on the outskirts of Otavalo, located in a field. It is also held on Saturday mornings and starts in the wee hours. This is not for late-risers—if you get there after 9:30 a.m. there will be little left to see. For a few hours the field is a throng of pigs, sheep, goats, cows, chicken and bartering, along with a rather unsavory-looking selection of food stalls. It you want to visit the animal market it is probably best to stay overnight in one of the many Otavalo hotels to avoid a very early start.

SAQUISILÍ MARKET

At Saquisili, about 2.5 hours from Quito the market kicks off at 7 a.m. on Thursday mornings and is pretty much over by 2 p.m. This is one of the largest markets in the Ecuadorian highlands and vendors travel from miles around to display their wares. It is possible to get a bus from Quito, or there are tours available. Alternatively, stay nearby overnight in one of the hotels in Latacunga. As well as being a food market, there are a wide variety of arts and crafts on sale. There is also an animal market a short walk from the main market, best visited before 10 a.m.

COTACATCHI LEATHER TOWN

The leather-making town of Cotacatchi is worth a stop. Cotacatchi is about 11 km from Otavalo and is renowned for its leather goods. Market day is Sunday, but if you can't get there on a Sunday it is not a big deal because on 10 de Agosto street it is possible to pick up all variety of good quality leather items all week long. Products available include jackets, shoes and boots, bags, wallets and belts. This street is also is the centerpiece of the Sunday leather market.

Photo by Caroline Bennett

INTRO & INFO

SAN ANTONIO DE IBARRA

Also near Otavalo is the small town of San Antonio de Ibarra. This village, located about mid-way between Otavalo and Ibarra, is known for woodcarvings. There is no market *per se*, but there are several shops that sell a variety of intricately carved wooden items, such as bowls, religious figures, boxes, chess sets, flowers and much, much more. The gallery of Luís Potosí is located on the main square and in general probably has the best items, although there are little treasures to be found in each of the shops. As usual, bargaining is the norm: never pay the first price offered, even in the fancier galleries. Check out hotels in Otavalo or Ibarra as an overnight stay is recommended.

MERCADO ARTESANAL LA MARISCAL

In Quito, visit Mercado Artesanal La Mariscal at Reina Victoria and Jorge Washington to pick up arts and crafts. Panama hats can be purchased here, along with woodwork, weaving, jewelry and tagua items. In the center of the Mariscal, the market is very accessible and is open between 10 a.m. and 6 p.m. daily.

PARQUE EL EJIDO MARKET

Opposite the Hotel Hilton Colon in Parque El Ejido a small market is held on Saturday and Sunday mornings. Paintings are the main focus here, and if this is your interest, it is worth a visit.

MERCADO SANTA CLARA

For a taste of the real Ecuador in Quito, stop at Mercado Santa Clara at Versalles and Ramirez Davalos. This is just hopping distance from the conveniently-named "Santa Clara" trole stop on 10 de Agosto. On the ground floor, sellers vie for your attention to sell you a mysterious-looking selection of fruits and vegetables, many of which don't have English translations. If your stomach can handle it, upstairs is the meat and fish market. It is better to visit before 2 p.m. as the market starts to wind down after that. You can also find some basic artesanía here, such as fine hand-made baskets.

TRAVELER RESOURCES
THE SOUTH AMERICAN EXPLORERS' CLUB

The Quito branch of the South American Explorers' Club has recently experienced something of a renaissance, thanks to new management of the day-to-day running of the club. It is a lively hub, has a lot to offer to both travelers and ex-pats and is a great place to meet people. For trav-

Have a great travel story? Tell it at www.vivatravelguides.com

elers, the club is an excellent source for maps, guidebooks and generally up-to-date safety and travel information. Regular weeknight events include pub quizzes, yoga classes and Thursday night presentations. The club also organizes good value excursions regularly to the beach or hiking. Club members get discounts on all of this, plus cheaper deals in many bars, restaurants and tour agencies in Ecuador. Washington 311 and Leónidas Plaza, near the American Embassy. Tel: 593-2-222-5228, E-mail: quitoclub@saexplorers.org, URL: www.saexplorers.org.

Health and Safety

While traveling in Ecuador, it is important to feel safe and at ease and not focus on all the potential diseases you could contract. To do this effectively, follow our preparation guidelines and you should be fine. However, should you have a medical emergency, remember that after Cuba, Ecuador has the best private health care system in Latin America and while it may cut into your budget, you will be well taken care of. Pharmacies in Ecuador are conveniently located and common. As with most Latin American countries, if you tell the pharmacist your symptoms, he/she will often be able to recommend what you need, helping to avoid a costly visit to the doctor. Reliable national chains are Fybeca and Pharmacys.

Minor Health Problems

Altitude Sickness

When traveling in the Ecuadorian Andes it is important to rest the first few days and drink lots of bottled water. Should you feel a severe headache, drowsiness, confusion, dry cough, and/or breathlessness, drink lots of water and rest. If the symptoms continue, you may want to move to a lower altitude. Aspirin is locally recommended for mild symptoms. Anyone planning to hike at high altitudes is advised to relax in a high altitude city such as Quito for a few days before any physical exertion.

Note that altitude sickness, locally called *soroche*, can come on suddenly if you experience a sudden change of altitude. You may get it if you ride the Telefériqo to the top of the mountain or take a bus to the refuge at Cotopaxi, even if you've been in Quito or another highland city for a while. Even native quiteños have been known to occasionally pass out at the top of the Telefériqo, so take care!

Sunburn/Heat Exhaustion

Ecuador straddles the equator; therefore, even at high altitudes, where cool breezes constantly blow and snow can accumulate, the sun is incredibly strong. Apply sunscreen with at least an SPF 30 every few hours you are outside. The sun in Galápagos and on the coast is particularly strong and unprepared visitors get badly burned regularly. If you get a severe sunburn, treat it with a cream and stay out of the sun for a while. To avoid overheating, wear a hat and sunglasses and drink lots of water. Overweight people are more susceptible to sun stroke. The symptoms of heat exhaustion are profuse sweating, weakness, exhaustion, muscle cramps, rapid pulse and vomiting. If you experience heat stroke, go to a cool, shaded area until your body temperature normalizes and drink lots of water. If the symptoms continue, consult a doctor.

Motion Sickness

Even the hardiest of travelers can be hit by motion sickness on the buses in the Andes and boats in the Galápagos. Sit near the front of the bus or stay above deck on the boat and focus on the horizon. If you are prone to motion sickness, eat light, non-greasy food before traveling and avoid drinking too much, particularly alcohol. If you're prone to motion sickness, over-the-counter medications such as *Dramamine* can prevent it: in Ecuador, go to a pharmacy and ask for *Mareol*, a liquid medicine similar to Dramamine. If you suffer from severe motion sickness, you may want to get a prescription for something stronger, like a patch.

Traveler's Diarrhea

This is probably the most common disease for travelers. There is no vaccine to protect you from traveler's diarrhea; it is avoided by eating sensibly. Contrary to popular belief, it is usually transmitted by food, not contaminated water. Eat only steaming hot food that has been cooked all the way through in clean establishments. Avoid raw lettuce and fruit that cannot be peeled, like strawberries. Vegetables are usually safer than meat. An inexpensive vegetable wash (known as vitalín) can be purchased at any supermarket and is a good way to ensure clean fruit and vegetables if you are cooking your own meals.

Make sure any milk you drink has been boiled. Avoid ice cream that could have melted and been refrozen, such as anything for sale in the street. *Helado de paila* does not contain milk and is safer. If you do get diarrhea, the best way is to let it run its course while staying hydrated with clear soups, lemon tea, Gatorade and soda that has gone flat. Bananas are also a good source of potassium and help stop diarrhea. If you need to travel and can't afford to let the illness run its course, any pharmacy will give you something that will make you comfortable enough for a bus trip. If the diarrhea persists for more than five days, see a doctor.

MORE SERIOUS HEALTH PROBLEMS

HEPATITIS
If you are planning to live in Ecuador for more than six months or work in a hospital, it may a good idea to get a vaccination against hepatitis. A hepatitis vaccination is not considered necessary for short-term travelers. Avoid situations where you could be subject to being punctured by a dirty needle. One of our writers was on a local bus on the coast where a nurse was giving out free measles shots while the bus was in motion. Needless to say, it is a good idea to stay away from any sort of questionable injection. It is also not a good idea to get a piercing while traveling, especially at the popular outdoor markets.

MALARIA
Most doctors around the world will tell you that if you travel anywhere in Ecuador, you must take pills to prevent malaria. This is not true. Malaria is only found on the Pacific Coast (but not in the Galápagos Islands) and in the Amazon Rainforest. If you are only traveling in the Andes and to the Galápagos, you run no risk of contracting malaria.

However, if you plan to spend a lot of time along the Pacific Coast or in the Amazon Rainforest, it is a good idea to take proper measures to prevent the disease. Mosquitoes carrying malaria are evening and nighttime biters.

If you are planning to go to the Amazon Rainforest for a couple of days, you may want to ask the staff of the lodge for recommendations. Many areas of the Amazon are relatively mosquito-free because black-water rivers are inhospitable breeding grounds to mosquitoes. Thoroughly apply insect repellent with at least 30% DEET. Applying to your hair is good way to make the scent stay on your body longer. Sleep under a mosquito net. Wear light-colored clothes and avoid shiny jewelry. Also avoid using scented soaps or perfumes.

RABIES
There are stray dogs throughout Ecuador that are usually harmless. However, many homeowners train guard dogs to attack trespassers. On long hikes in rural areas, always carry a walking stick to defend yourself if a dog starts to attack. In case you are attacked by a dog, rabies vaccinations are readily available in Quito and other major cities.

TYPHOID
An oral capsule or injection should be taken before travel if you are planning to travel in Ecuador or South America for an extended period of time (six months or more). The injection needs boosting every three years.

YELLOW FEVER
This mosquito-born disease is endemic to Ecuador and many other parts of South America. Talk to your doctor before taking the vaccine, as it is not recommended for people with certain allergies, pregnant women and other special cases. The vaccine is good for ten years.

SAFETY

As is true in most Latin American countries, travelers tend to stand out in Ecuador. There is a good chance you will stand a head taller than the crowds on rural buses throughout the country, and people will notice that you're foreign. As a result, travelers are easy targets for petty crime. While crime in Ecuador is rarely violent and many travelers have escaped sketchy situations by yelling and running away, good street sense and awareness must be exercised. In crowds, always hold your bag close to your body and in front of you where you can see it. Most thieves work in teams: one will distract you while the other slashes your bag or picks your pocket. If you are approached by a suspicious person asking for money or the time, just walk away quickly. Don't let yourself get cornered.

Distribute important documents into at least two stashes. Keep your passport, at least one credit card and most of your cash well protected under your clothes: either in a money belt, in-sewn pocket or other contraption. Keep a wallet or coin purse within easy reach (but NOT in a hip pocket) with a small amount of money and perhaps a second credit card for daily food and shopping so that you don't have to reach into your main reserve when you aren't in a comfortable space.

In most cities in Ecuador, the dodgy neighborhoods are easy to identify; they are around bus stations and major outdoor markets. Lodging is usually slightly cheaper in these areas, but for a dollar or two more a night, you can get a substantial upgrade worth the piece of mind. Researching the perfect spot beforehand is the best way to avoid being stuck in a neighborhood that makes you uncomfortable.

PHONE AND MAIL SERVICES

POSTAL SERVICES
SENDING MAIL AND PACKAGES:
Sending packages over two kilograms (5 lbs.) is very expensive: $25 and up. Packages under this weight limit cost up to $10 to mail and may take 8-10 business days to most North American destinations, longer to other parts of the world. Mailing letters and postcards usually costs upwards of $2. Mail service from Ecuador to other parts of the world is reliable. Don't close your packages before you get to the post office, though; the staff is required to check the contents before the envelope or box is mailed. It is technically prohibited to mail jewelry, cash or other valuables, so use some discretion when choosing to mail something.

Quito has branches of international postal companies like DHL and FedEx. This is the best way to send express mail. However, for regular packages, stick to the national service, DHL and FedEx are easily triple the national post office price. You can also send packages with major airlines like American Airlines (go to their main office on Patria and Amazonas in Quito).

RECEIVING MAIL AND PACKAGES:
If you plan to receive letters or small packages (under two kg), they will be delivered directly to your residence, hotel, guesthouse etc. Any boxes bigger than two kg must be picked up at a local post office. Any large package can be extremely difficult to retrieve from the main post office; you almost always have to pay high taxes on the package and the delays can take months. Given this possibility of delay, tell your friends and family back home to avoid mailing you large packages.

PHONE SERVICES
CALLS FROM/WITHIN ECUADOR
Public phone booths are widespread and fairly user-friendly. Most mini-markets and pharmacies sell cards to use in the booths. Choose from Porta and Telefonica MoviStar and then use the corresponding telephone. Alternatively, at most you can just pay in cash after the call. Rates are not cheap (between 15-99 cents a minute) and vary depending on if you are calling a landline, a cell phone or an international number. Cards are sold in denominations of $3, $6 and $10.

If you need to make an international phone call, your best bet is to use a phone booth in an internet café in Quito, Guayaquil, Baños, or any other city with a lot of tourist traffic. Internet cafes take advantage of their internet connection to make cheap international calls from 10-30 cents a minute around the word. Andinatel, the national phone company, often has offices with booths from which you can make international calls. The rates are much higher than in the internet cafés, but the connection is often better.

CELL PHONES
Cell phones are very popular but can be very expensive. The three major providers, Telefonica MoviStar, Porta and Alegro, all have pre-paid and monthly plans. Rates, depending on your plan, are roughly $0.10-0.50/minute to other cell phones and almost double for calls to land-lines. Text messages run from 1-6 cents per message. There is no charge for incoming calls.If you have a cell pjone in the USA or Europe and want to bring it with you, the conversion costs are high. It is usually a better idea to buy a cell phone in Ecuador. If you're just staying for a while, the best option is to pick up a cheap phone and top it up with phone cards.

CALLING ECUADOR FROM ABROAD
To call Ecuador from another country dial 00 (011 from the US) + 593 (Ecuador's country code) + the city code (Quito and surrounding area is 2, Guayaquil and surrounding area is 4) + the seven digit number. If you are only given six digits, add 2 to the beginning of the six digits. The national phone company recently decided it would be a good idea to have longer phone numbers and stuck a 2 at the beginning of every number nationwide. Numbers created recently begin with 3.

Rates to call Ecaudor from abroad vary widely depending on your home country. Pre-paid phone cards are usually the best way to go: they can be found online or in grocery stores in Hispanic or international neighborhoods. If you're buying a phone card at a corner store, buy several and keep track of which ones let you talk the longest. Some are a good deal, and some will rip you off badly. Rates will sometimes be higher to call a cell phone. Also, check that your phone card does not have a high connection fee or your time will be up before you know it.

MONEY AND COSTS
While Ecuador is not as cheap as it was before converting to the US dollar, it is still quite affordable for most travelers. See our Tips for Travelers section for detailed guidelines for budget, mid-range and luxury travelers.

If you're prepared to rough it you should be able to get by on $20-25 per day by staying in hostel dorms, eating the set meal at restaurants and traveling on buses. If you are traveling in a group, you can cut daily costs down to $15 per person. If you have a little more money at your disposal you can live a modest, yet comfortable lifestyle on about $30-50 per day while staying at low-end hotels or hostels, eating out three times a day, and still have some cash left over to enjoy the nightlife or splurge on the odd day trip such as rafting or hiking. On the other hand, if money is no object you can travel very comfortably using private transportation and have a lot of fun eating out (Quito offers some world-class restaurants, many of which are located in stunning colonial buildings), touring the Galápagos and Oriente in style and shopping to your heart's content at Ecuador's many craft markets.

BANKS AND ATMS
Travelers in Ecuador should have no problem withdrawing money from local banks using a debit or credit card with VISA, Mastercard, Cirrus or Maestro representation. Travelers' checks can be difficult to exchange, even in major cities, so it's a good idea to always have an emergency stash of cash. Most travelers find it best to bring a combination of cash, credit or debit cards and travelers' checks. There are several banks in Ecuador that can help with international transfers and wiring money. The easiest way to access money is via the ATM. Always use ATMs located inside banks or malls with a guard nearby. There have been several reports of theft from outdoor ATMs.

ATM WARNINGS AND ADVICE

The bank in your home country will likely charge a hefty amount for each time you use an ATM in Ecuador - even if you are just looking at your balance, so be sure to check with your home bank before going nuts. Also, at times the bank will not get a good connection to your home bank and will tell you that you have insufficient funds. Sometimes this is true, but often it is not, so before making an expensive and frustrating international call you your home bank, try another ATM or wait a day. In general, however, using ATMs are the easiest way to stay supplied with cash in Ecuador. If your country does not have the US dollar, an exchange rate fee will also be charged to your account as the ATMs in Ecuador only deal in dollars.

NOTE: Be warned that criminals sometimes target foreigners at ATMs. Be very careful after dark or in very busy or very deserted areas. If someone is standing too close to you, he or she may be trying to look over your shoulder at your PIN code. When in doubt, walk away and use another machine later. Some ATMs in tourist areas, such as Quito Mariscal, are manned by security guards.

TRAVELERS' CHECKS

It is a good idea to come with an emergency stash of travelers' checks. Most hotels accept traveler's checks (American Express is best, VISA is not always accepted) even in remote areas where you have to travel for hours to reach a bank. While hotels may accept them, you are likely to have a difficult time trying to cash travelers checks at a bank in exchange for dollars. Always bring your actual passport and even then it might be difficult. Banco de Guayaquil is your best bet for cashing such checks, but be prepared to pay a higher-than-average exchange fee.

WIRE TRANSFERS

Money Grams and Western Union wires are fairly common in Ecuador, as they form alliances with local banks around the country. Fees vary and tend to be high, so this option is best for emergencies.

CREDIT CARDS

All international hotels and most higher-priced hotels and restaurants accept Visa and Master Card. Many also accept Diners Club and American Express cards. Beware: an extra 10% is often added to your total bill if you pay with a credit card. Depending on the price, you may be better served withdrawing the cash from an ATM and stashing the credit cards. In general, most Ecuadorian shops do not accept credit cards: some exceptions are mall stores and high-end gift and artesanía stores.

BANCO DEL PACÍFICO

This is a smaller bank, with only a few branches in Quito, but one of the few that will exchange travelers' checks. There is a $5 charge for the exchange and they only exchange checks up to $200. The ATM accepts Cirrus and Maestro debit cards and will charge you $1.50 in addition to whatever your home bank charges for international withdrawals.

Branches in Quito:

This branch is open from Monday - Friday, 8:30 a.m. - 4 p.m. and Saturdays from 9 a.m. - 2 p.m. (but doesn't exchange traveler's checks on Saturdays) Av. Naciones Unidas E7-95 and Los Shyris, Tel: 593-2-298-2000 (west of Quicentro).

Open from Monday - Friday, 8:30 a.m. - 4 p.m. and Saturdays from 9 a.m. - 2 p.m. Av. Amazonas 720 and Veintimilla, Phone: 593-2-252-1586.

Monday - Friday, 10 a.m. - 5 p.m. and Saturdays from 10 a.m.-4 p.m. Centro Comercial El Bosque (large mall in the north of the city on Occidental)

BANCO DE GUAYAQUIL
This bank cashes travelers' checks at a rate of $3 for checks up to $300 in value. For checks higher than $300, a 1% commission is charged. The ATM accepts all VISA and American Express cards for cash withdrawals. There is a $1.50 charge for using the ATM.

Branches in Quito:
Open Monday - Friday, 8:30 a.m. - 4:30 p.m. (ATM 24 hours but inside) Av. Colón and Reina Victoria, Tel: 593-2-256-6800.

Open Monday - Friday, 8:30 a.m. - 5 p.m. (only open until 4 p.m. for cashing travelers checks, ATM is 24 hours and is outside, not protected) Av. Amazonas and Veintimilla, Tel: 593-2-256-4324.

BANCO DEL PICHINCHA
The Banco del Pichincha is probably the bank that you will notice the most around Quito. Unfortunately, they don't cash travelers' checks, but the ATM accepts all Visa, Cirrus and Plus cards and is fairly reliable—although we have had some reports of problems. Only the branches in the malls are open on Saturdays and the rest are open roughly from 9 a.m. - 5 p.m. The malls that have branches are: Quicentro, CCI, El Jardín, El Recreo and El Bosque.

BUSINESS HOURS
Banks vary their hours but are generally open from Monday - Friday, 9 a.m. to 4:30 p.m., around the country. Hours for money and travelers' check exchange are often different. See our Banks and ATM and Money and Costs sections for more information.

Restaurants often shut down between meals. Breakfast is generally served from 8 a.m. to 10 a.m.; lunch from 12 p.m. to 3 p.m. and dinner from 6 p.m. to 10 p.m. In smaller towns, dinner will end earlier. In Quito, Guayaquil and cities with high tourist traffic, it is not uncommon to eat at 10 p.m. Restaurants, especially in small towns, are often closed on Sundays and public holidays. In Quito and Guayaquil, the international chains always stay open on these days. Hotels are a good option when restaurants are closed; they are almost always prepared to serve food.

ETIQUETTE AND DRESS
Ecuadorians are polite: when entering a store, or restaurants or even browsing goods at an outdoor market, its expected to greet the staff with a *buenos dias, buenas tardes* or *buenas noches*, depending on the time of day and to say *gracias* or *hasta luego* when you leave. Greetings involving women are a kiss on the right cheek and between two men, a handshake. In a business meeting and when meeting an indigenous person, a handshake is sufficient for women.

HOW TO DRESS:
Ecuadorians tend to be better dressed than most North Americans and Europeans. So if you are wearing old, tattered travel clothes and flip flops, you will invariably get some stares. That said, Ecuadorians are infinitely patient with the ways of the gringo traveler and will treat you respectfully regardless of how raggedy your outfit—as long as you aren't trying to get into a nice restaurant, bar or club dressed like a bum.

In the Andes, people tend to cover up a lot more than on the coast: partially because it is much colder and partially because the culture tends to be a bit more conservative. You will rarely see an Andino wearing shorts off the futbol field, and flip flops are an oddity. Men should never plan to travel bare-chested in the Andes. Likewise, women should never wear just a sports bra or swimsuit around town. If blending in is important to you, wear pants more often than shorts, don't fly in a t-shirt and shorts, don't wear flip flops; and when going out at night, men should wear collared shirts (no hats!) and women should wear clean, stylish clothes—pants are fine. Dress outside of cities and at the beach is much more casual, but the same basic principles apply.

FOOD MANNERS:

Like all countries, there is a certain way to eat all typical meals: like tossing popcorn and fried banana chips into ceviche soup, for example. Table manners are more relaxed, though, so don't worry too much about them. Tables at casual, crowded restaurants are often shared; so don't be surprised. When you get up to leave or join someone's table, it is appropriate to say "*buen provecho*"—bon appétit.

ETIQUETTE WHEN VISITING SOMEONE'S HOME:

If visiting someone's home for a party or meal, it is polite to bring a small gift like a cake for dessert or a bottle of wine. Bigger gifts can be overwhelming and the host may feel like he or she needs to give you something in return, so stick with something small. Ecuadorians are incredibly generous by nature and will want to feel one ahead in gift exchanges, so try not to overwhelm your host with expensive presents.

If you are staying with your host for an extended period of time, offer to help out with groceries and bring fresh flowers. A memento from your hometown like a photo, post card or small book will be appreciated. Also remember that, unless you are staying with one of Ecuador's handful of insanely rich families, your visit will probably be something of a financial strain. You can make it less so by taking short showers—hot water is expensive—and minimizing electricity use—also extremely expensive. Phone calls to cell phones should never be made from land lines—they cost up to $1/minute. Phone service and internet service in general tends to be very pricey, so try not to run up your host's bill.

RESPONSIBLE TOURISM

Tourism is a vital source of income to Ecuador and one that will long outlast the petroleum industry. Support this struggling nation by encouraging local industries. Eat at local restaurants and stay at locally-owned hotels as opposed to international chains. There is a wide selection of comfortable, clean and reasonably priced hotels all over the country, owned and operated by Ecuadorians. V!VA Travel Guides usually mentions if the owners are foreign, so choose wisely. Use water and electricity carefully. When city officials cut down on the community's supply, travelers are usually given preference, so don't abuse the privilege.

BEGGARS

Don't give money or candy to children begging. You are just encouraging this destructive cycle by financing parents willing to send their little ones out onto the streets to work. Many disabled adults and senior citizens also beg; you can decide if you want to help them out or not, most Ecuadorians do.

ENVIRONMENTAL AWARENESS

An eco-tourism movement is slowly but surely making its way through Ecuador. The habits of throwing trash out bus windows and littering in general are deeply engrained in Ecuadorian collective consciousness. Be responsible by not participating in these bad habits and make a point of leaving camping areas, nature walks, picnics, etc. cleaner than you left them. Ecuadorian cities have started putting up "Do Not Litter" signs, but there is a long way to go. Consider staying at an eco-lodge or volunteering for an organization working to educate the community and preserve the environment. See our eco-tourism page, eco-travel links and eco-lodge page for more information.

PHOTOGRAPHY

Anyone with even a passing interest in photography will love Ecuador: it is probably one of the most scenic countries in the world, with several places—Galápagos, the Otavalo market, the waterfalls near Baños, to name but a few—being truly exceptional and unique places to take photos. Take care with your cameras: they are one of the most-stolen items that visitors bring.

For any camera, make sure you have extra batteries: they can be difficult to find in Ecuador unless they're a common type like AA. If you use filters, it is a good idea to bring them, as lighting and weather conditions in Ecuador can often be extreme. Talk to an expert at the local photo shop about filters if you don't know much about them: tell him or her that you'll be going to a place with very strong sunlight. A waterproof camera bag is a must, as is camera cleaning equipment.

If you use print film, it is possible to purchase it fairly easily in Ecuador. Common 35mm film is easy to find. The best prices are usually at the little photo developing shops that you'll find almost everywhere. Prices for decent 100, 200, and 400 speed film are a little bit higher than in the States, but the quality is the same and the convenience factor probably makes it worth it to purchase film in Ecuador, especially when you consider that you won't have to pass your film through several x-ray machines as you go through airport security. Specialized film, such as 160 speed film for portraits, black-and-white film or any film that is not 35mm, may be difficult to find. If you run out and you're at a tourist destination such as Mitad del Mundo, film will be easy to find but more expensive.

It is possible to develop your print film in Ecuador, but many visitors complain about quality. Stories of lost photos, botched developing and scratched negatives are common enough for concern. Black-and-white processing is nearly impossible. Of the various developing chains in Ecuador, "Ecuacolor" seems to have the most satisfied customers. There are several Ecuacolor branches in Quito, and they are easily identified by their bright yellow color scheme. You will find branches in most of the malls. Ask about special deals: most photo places offer daily specials such as two rolls for the price of one, a free new roll of film with developing, etc.

If you use a digital camera, be sure to have more than one memory chip: you'll take a lot of photos, and downloading them to a disc or computer may be challenging outside of the larger cities. If your chip is full, internet cafés may be able to put all of your photos on a disc for you for a minimal price. Many of the high-end tourist places, such as the nicer hotels and Galápagos cruise ships, also offer this service. Before you go, be absolutely sure to bring all appropriate cables, chargers and other accessories: do not expect any computer places to have them. A spare battery or two is also a good idea, as you may be away from a wall socket for a while.

If you use a video camcorder, bring as many tapes or mini DVDs as you think you're going to need, as it may be hard to find them in Ecuador in rural areas. Assume that you will not be able to download the tapes onto any disc or DVD until you get home, although some of the better internet cafés might be able to do it.

Underwater photography: the Galápagos is a fantastic place to take underwater photos, as the water is often clear, there are many opportunities to dive and snorkel, and there are endemic species of marine life found nowhere else in the world. Plan on bringing all of your own equipment, though: dive shops in the Galápagos tend to be very basic and probably won't be able to lend you any gear.

It is a good idea to bring along one or two disposable cameras. If you're going out with friends to dance and drink, they're perfect: small, handy and replaceable if stolen. Disposable cameras are available in the larger cities and in photo shops, but they're more expensive than they are in the States: a decent one with flash will cost you around $15-20 in Ecuador. Semiwaterproof cameras are also a good idea: they're fun to bring on rafting trips and while snorkeling in Galápagos (tip: get close or the picture won't work). Disposable water cameras are available in Quito, but a little bit expensive.

Cultural note: Some Ecuadorians are uncomfortable having their photo taken, particularly the indigenous people commonly found in the highlands and rainforests. It is always polite to ask before you take someone's photo. In common tourist places like Otavalo and Baños, locals (particularly children) sometimes dress up for the express purpose of letting visitors take their picture: in this case, they'll expect to be paid. Again, the best way is to ask first. If the photo is worth fifty cents or a dollar to you, go ahead. One good way to get photos in Otavalo is to make a purchase first at a particular stall: the local's attitude toward a photo may change very quickly if you're a paying customer! Powerful zoom lenses can also let you take some excellent photos of people without making them uncomfortable. If you're taking a general photo, such as a market street, it is not necessary to ask anyone first.

Also, be careful when taking photos near any sort of official or military installation: it may be illegal to take photos in certain areas. If there is a soldier or policeman nearby, it is best to ask first if photography is permitted.

SPECIAL GROUPS

WOMEN TRAVELERS

Machismo is alive and well in Ecuador. Ecuadorian men endlessly call out to women in public. Ignore the comments and they won't go any further.

Women travelers interested in meeting men will run into more complications, however. "*Gringueros*," or Ecuadorian men who habitually prowl the tourist scene, have quite a reputation throughout the country. Be careful and don't expect to be friends with an Ecuadorian man, there will almost always be ulterior motives.

In general, women should have no problems with safety, even if traveling alone throughout the country. Be smart, though: take cabs after dark and don't go to a club or bar alone. See our section on Safety in Ecuador for more information.

GAY AND LESBIAN TRAVELERS

Ecuador, like most Latin American countries, has well-defined, stereotypical roles for men and women; men like to be seen as strong, macho figures and the women as dependent homemakers. That is not always practiced, and the younger generation is rapidly changing that image. However, the image does not lend to open acceptance of homosexuality.

Politically, Ecuador is fairly accepting of homosexual citizens. On August 10, 1998, the Ecuadorian constitution was reformed to: "recognize the equality of all before the law without discrimination against age, sex, ethnic origin, color, religion, political affiliation, economic position, sexual orientation, state of health, incapacity, or difference of any kind." Before this, citizens could be arrested for any action which offended "public morality." For example: patronizing a gay bar.

In practice, Ecuador has a long way to go on the road to acceptance. The coast tends to be more liberal. Guayaquil has a fairly active gay scene. Quito also hosts a growing gay scene, but is fighting the very conservative Catholic culture of the sierra. There is widespread bias to homosexuality. "*Maricon*"—a negative term for gay man—is a common insult for a man acting at all effeminate.

Gay and lesbian travelers will be surprised on New Year's and other holidays such as Latacunga's Mama Negra festival in September, when men cross-dress as women to ask for money, join in parades and act generally goofy. Unfortunately, this is seen more as a joke than a widespread acceptance of sexual alternatives. See http://quito.queercity.info/ for a guide to the gay scene and general information about gay and lesbian travel in Ecuador.

DISABLED TRAVELERS

Unfortunately, Ecuador has extremely undeveloped infrastructure for disabled travelers, especially those on a tight budget. The internationally-owned hotels in Quito and Guayaquil are recommended for disabled travelers, but are still not perfect. Sidewalks are often cobblestone with a generous helping of potholes and cracks. Much of the activity for travelers in Ecuador is active: hiking, biking, etc. and is not conducive to wheelchairs. Even the Galápagos, which is the most developed tourist destination in Ecuador, requires a certain level of agility to get on and off the boat and to explore each different island.

SENIOR TRAVELERS

Active, adventurous senior travelers will be delighted with travel in Ecuador and will be pleasantly surprised with the level of respect and consideration they will be greeted with. Older citizens are greatly respected in Ecuador; most live with their children. Nursing homes and care facilities are all but nonexistent and considered a shameful and embarrassing gringo practice.

Many travelers wait a lifetime to visit the world's most diverse cageless zoo: the Galápagos Islands. As a result, many of the travelers to the Galápagos Islands are active senior citizens. The activities in the Galápagos do require someone with a certain level of stamina and agility—many of the hikes require wet landings where you wade onto the beach and climbing around rocks on your walks. However, there are a number of tour operators and cruise boats that will cater their itinerary to your specific needs, so be sure to ask before booking your cruise.

Travelers over 65 are eligible to discounts throughout the country on buses, planes and tourist attractions like museums and national parks, so be sure to ask if it applies to you.

TRAVELERS WITH CHILDREN

Children under 12 will often get discounts on buses, planes, and hotels when traveling throughout Ecuador, so be sure to ask before paying full price. On Quito city buses and trolleys, children up to age 16 pay only 12 cents. Ecuadorian children are generally treated with extra special attention, and travelers with children will be greeted with friendly care and interest.

ECUADOR TIPS FOR BUDGET TRAVELERS

Great news for budget travelers! Ecuador is one of the best countries in the world to visit if you're watching your cash flow. In a nation where the average monthly income is about $250/month, essentials such as food, lodging and transportation are reasonably priced wherever you go. Every place in Ecuador worth seeing—Baños, Quito, Cuenca, the coast and the jungle to name a few—has budget options such as hostels and cheap food. Even Ecuador's top destination, Galápagos, might not necessarily be impossible, if you know where to look. As a backpacker, your biggest expenses will be food, lodging and transportation. And just because you're on a tight budget doesn't mean you can't enjoy some pre-arranged trips and tours, which can be quite reasonable.

ECUADOR SECURITY TIPS FOR BUDGET TRAVELERS

Ecuador is a poor country, and budget travelers are particularly at risk: many professional criminals in touristy areas specifically target them. Many mid-range and luxury travelers are insulated from street crime because they're traveling with reputable travel agencies which Keep an eye on your luggage at all times, and take care to hide your valuables when staying in cheap hostels. Internet cafés are particularly perilous: thieves wait and watch, hoping to see a poorly attended backpack or purse they can walk off with. Always remember that if you're a foreigner with luggage, you'll be considered a target, whether you have anything of value or not. Put a small padlock on the zipper of your backpack when you travel.

ECUADOR TOUR TIPS FOR BUDGET TRAVELERS

If you're on a super-tight budget, chances are you won't be able to afford a long, extended tour. There may be some exceptions, however. If you want to take a big-ticket tour, like a visit to a jungle lodge or even Galápagos, you can consider going last-minute. Travel agencies in Quito often have last-minute deals to lodges and Galápagos cruises. If the lodge or cruise has not filled up two or three days before a scheduled tour, they'll often dramatically cut their prices, sometimes by as much as half. Obviously, this option is more likely in low tourist seasons. Sometimes, you can do a web search and find last-minute deals, too. In addition to last-minute deals, you may want to look into day trips such as horseback riding, whitewater rafting or mountain biking. These day trips can cost anywhere from $35-80 or so, and if you go with a reputable company you're sure to have a good time.

Have a great travel story? Tell it at www.vivatravelguides.com

ECUADOR LODGING TIPS FOR BUDGET TRAVELERS

Every major or minor tourist destination in Ecuador has at least one or two hostales that cater to the budget traveler set. In some, you can find decent, dorm-style lodging for as little as $4/night or less, a price to warm the heart of the most tightfisted backpacker. Many of the better hostels accept reservations via the internet or by phone: V!VA Travel Guides is a good place to begin your search. In many hostels, the most inexpensive lodging option is a bunk room. Bring a padlock to secure your belongings while you explore. Most of the better hostel dorm rooms have small lockers for guests to keep their things.

ECUADOR FOOD TIPS FOR BUDGET TRAVELERS

Ecuador has great food if you're on a tight budget: a true budget traveler can get by on as little as $5/day for food. If you don't need a sit-down meal, check out the local fruit and vegetable market. Bargain with the little old ladies selling produce: you can often get deals like five avocados for a buck. Many markets have food stands featuring ceviches, hornado or other local specialties: you'll be rolling the dice somewhat in terms of health, but the food is tasty and the price is right. Some even have seafood like fried fish, which you can try if you're feeling really brave and/or have good health insurance.

If you've had one too many bouts of the runs and don't want to eat street or market food, ask a local to recommend a cheap restaurant offering *almuerzos ejecutivos* (executive lunches). These are places that cater to Ecuadorians leaving their offices for lunch, and for anywhere from one to three dollars, you'll get a full meal. Note: vegetarians should not consider this an option, as 99% of almuerzos ejecutivos have meat.

Many of the larger cities have supermarkets such as Supermaxi and Santa Maria. These are good places to shop for food because they have much more selection than the little tienda on the corner, although surprisingly, the price might not be much better. If you want a jar of peanut butter or similar uncommon item, the *supermercados* are your only option.

Another hint is to familiarize yourself with local foods. Try an *empanada*—in Ecuador, empanadas are pastries, folded-over with chicken, beef or cheese inside, then baked or deep-fried. Yummy and cheap, you can find them in most bakeries for under a dollar each, and there are bakeries everywhere. One is a snack, two are a meal.

ECUADOR TRANSPORTATION TIPS FOR BUDGET TRAVELERS

If you want to get around Ecuador on the cheap, take a bus. They're fairly comfortable and many have DVD players for longer trips, which can be a blessing or a curse depending on what the bus attendant decides to pop in (they showed "Leprechaun 3" on a recent trip, which was painfully bad). Within cities, try to master the public transportation system. Quito in particular has a pretty good one, largely based upon the Trole and the Ecovia, two parallel transportation lines that run north-south on either side of the city. Taxis are inexpensive and safe. If you're lost, lugging a lot of stuff or returning from a night out, don't hesitate to flag one down. See our taxis in Ecuador section for tips on how to deal with Ecuador's clever cabbies.

ECUADOR TIPS FOR MID-RANGE TRAVELERS

Great news! Ecuador is a fabulous place for mid-range ($30-75 daily budget) travelers. Of all of our three categories, you'll be the ones who get the most bang for your buck: while tightwad backpackers are stuck in hostels and well-heeled luxury travelers are staying at the Marriott—which is gorgeous, but frankly, the rooms are the same in Ecuador as they are in Paris and any other place in the world—you'll be enjoying Ecuador's cozy, charming mid-range hotels, which consist of everything from converted colonial homes and haciendas to bed and breakfasts and adventurous eco-lodges.

ECUADOR SECURITY TIPS FOR MID-RANGE TRAVELERS

Mid-range travelers are not considered to be as much at risk for theft or other security problems as budget travelers are. But in a country like Ecuador, where there is a lot of crime and unemployment, any visitor should be extra careful. If you're traveling by bus, lock your packs or suitcases if you can. If you're with a reputable travel agency, you can relax when it comes to your things: if they tell you it's okay to leave your things on the bus on a trip, such as a shopping visit to Otavalo, then you can. When staying at hotels, lock valuables in the security safe or at reception but don't worry much—theft of valuables by hotel staff or outsiders is very rare although not unheard of. See our security section for more general tips.

ECUADOR TOUR TIPS FOR MID-RANGE TRAVELERS
The best part about booking a trip through a tour agency is not having to deal with pesky matters like airport transfers, worrying about the security of your luggage and not having an emergency number to call when you need it. Many mid-range travelers arrive to Ecuador with a tour already booked: if you're going to take a tour, booking before you go is definitely preferable. Reputable agencies such as Metropolitan or Lindblad are more expensive, but your satisfaction is almost assured. If you want to save a little money, you may want to look for a newer, up-and-coming agency looking to win a good reputation.

ECUADOR FOOD TIPS FOR MID-RANGE TRAVELERS
The restaurants in Ecuador are excellent, safe and reasonably priced. Almost all of them should be within your price range, especially if you save a little money here and there, on breakfast and lunch, in order to splurge on dinner. In Quito, which is considered expensive by the rest of Ecuador, dinner at a very nice restaurant such as a steakhouse will cost you $15-20/person, all inclusive. Be sure to check out fancy restaurants offering Ecuadorian cuisine. Avoid street food.

ECUADOR LODGING TIPS FOR MID-RANGE TRAVELERS
The best part about being a mid-range traveler is the variety and quality of options in your price range. In every Ecuador city and tourist destination, you'll find attractive, clean mid-range hotels with a lot of charm and personality. Most have an array of two-to-three star perks: free breakfast, travel info desk, adventures such as mountain biking or horseback riding, cable TV, private bathrooms, 24-hour hot water and more. Some even have spas, swimming pools, free internet and free airport pickups!

One huge bonus that mid-range travelers enjoy over budget travelers in Ecuador is internet presence of hotels: most of the best mid-range hotels have a website or at least an e-mail address so that you can make reservations. Some of the sites are better than others, but most offer at least basic contact information, rates and location. If you're emailing back and forth to a hotel before your trip, you can even negotiate the price a little, especially if you're coming out of season (September-November and February-May) or if you're going to stay more than one night.

ECUADOR TRANSPORTATION TIPS FOR MID-RANGE TRAVELERS
As mid-range travelers, you'll have more options than budget travelers, but unless you're with a tour company, buses are still probably your best option. Even if you can afford a rental car, it's a bad idea. Quito and Guayaquil are terrible cities to drive in—there are no street signs, one-way streets are not always labeled, and there are some truly bizarre traffic rules, such as: it is legal to turn left on red if no one is coming. Guayaquil is worse than Quito. After a few minutes on the road in Guayaquil, you will wonder who left the asylum door open and let all of the lunatics out. Even when you're not in the city, there are no road signs, so you may come upon an intersection in a remote location with no indication of which way you need to go. Roads are bad, and breakdowns, flat tires and other automotive problems are very common. As an option, buses are pretty easy and comfortable and allow you to rest between adventures. An even more comfortable option is a tour, which are pretty affordable in Ecuador. In cities, take taxis because they're safe and cheap. See our taxis in Ecuador section for tips on dealing with cabbies.

ECUADOR TIPS FOR LUXURY TRAVELERS
Great news! Hotels, restaurants, visitor sites, and travel agencies in Ecuador have the professionalism, attention to detail and elegance that the first-class traveler has come to expect. In the major cities, internationally renowned hotels such as the Hilton and the Marriott have modern, attractive

branches. In the Galápagos, some of the finest cruise ships in the world, luxuriously outfitted and staffed with the best guides Galápagos has to offer, await you. Even some of the remote jungle lodges, often uncomfortable and rustic, now have fine dining, air conditioning, and other amenities which allow you to visit the Amazon without having to sacrifice any comfort.

ECUADOR FOOD TIPS FOR LUXURY TRAVELERS
Upper-end travelers will greatly enjoy the quality of food in Ecuador's finest restaurants. In the larger cities, such as Quito, Cuenca and Guayaquil, there are world-class restaurants that boast fine cuisine and excellent service. Some of the cruise ships in Galápagos offer fine dining as well: Metropolitan's M/N Santa Cruz offers lobster thermidor and filet mignon. The best news is the price: even in the finest restaurants, it is uncommon to pay more than $60 or so for a dinner for two (not counting alcohol). Remember, when calculating price for a meal in Ecuador, add 22%: 10% for service (making a tip optional) and 12% for taxes. Outside of the cities and cruise ships, fine international cuisine is difficult to find, but that's not all bad: it gives you an excuse to sample Ecuador's fine traditional plates. Nearly everywhere you go, there will be a local restaurant or two that is a cut above the rest: your guide or tour agency will see to it that you find your way into them for a good meal.

ECUADOR TOUR TIPS FOR LUXURY TRAVELERS
If you can afford them, there are a variety of tour options available in Ecuador. The most famous part of Ecuador, is, of course, the Galápagos, and there are numerous tour operators who specialize in nothing but the islands. When booking a Galápagos tour, one thing to bear in mind is the luxury/comfort level of the vessel: there are many ships working the islands, and some of them are much more luxurious than others. Another thing to consider is guide quality: an exceptional guide can make all the difference in the world on a Galápagos trip: the more expensive ships generally pay their guides better, which in turn attracts the best guides.

There are many other tours and trips available in Ecuador: don't simply spend a couple of days in Quito, fly to Galápagos and assume you've seen all there is of the country. There are many fascinating places and sites in Ecuador—do some research and figure out which ones are the best for you to see. Tour agencies commonly offer trips to favorite places like Baños, Otavalo, Cuenca and the jungle. Their prices are a little bit higher than they would be if you did them by yourself, but you pay for convenience. Backpackers will want to save money by taking a local bus for a day trip to Otavalo, but if you have a little bit more money, having the travel agency van pick you up and drop you off at your hotel is probably worth it.

ECUADOR SECURITY TIPS FOR LUXURY TRAVELERS
Luxury travelers to Ecuador need not worry too much about security. Ecuador's top hotels are known for honest employees, and guides and tour operators will help protect you from street crime. The only real risks you'll face will come from pickpockets and other opportunistic thieves: follow some basic security precautions as outlined in our safety in Ecuador section and you'll be fine. Remember, however, that Ecuador is a very poor country, and even the most honest hotel worker, guide or person on the street might not be able to resist an item of obvious great value. Non-essential items such as valuable jewelry, fancy clothes and sunglasses might prove to be too much of a temptation for some of the people you meet. It is best to leave such things somewhere they'll be safe and come to Ecuador with less valuable replacements such as a cheap watch or sunglasses. One obvious exception to this rule is cameras: Ecuador is one of the best places in the world to take photos and you'll want your best camera.

ECUADOR LODGING TIPS FOR LUXURY TRAVELERS
First-class travelers will find a wide array of lodging options in Ecuador. There are super-deluxe hotels in every major Ecuadorian city: Quito, Cuenca and Guayaquil. These are modern, five-star hotels that have every imaginable luxury: room service, in-room internet, mints on the pillows, you name it. Chances are you've booked a tour, and you may have your hotel already selected for you. If not, or if you have some flexibility, you may want to consider some options: many of the upper mid-range hotels are cheaper and more charming than the large luxury

chains. If you can choose, say, between a large international chain and an elegant converted seventeenth century hacienda, you may want to choose the latter if you're interested in history and want a more memorable experience. Speaking of haciendas, you'll definitely want to check out one of the converted haciendas to the north of Quito: they're truly unique and memorable and offer first-class service. See our haciendas in Ecuador section for more information.

ECUADOR TRANSPORTATION TIPS FOR LUXURY TRAVELERS
No buses or cars for you, luxury travelers! If money is no object, you'll definitely want to arrange a very complete tour that includes all transfers and trips. Buses in Ecuador are convenient, comfortable and cheap, but they can be somewhat limiting and dealing with them will take up valuable time: if you can afford it, going with a tour is definitely the way to go. If you're traveling to the rainforest you may have the option of overland or air travel to Coca or Lago Agrio. The overland trip is interesting but long and somewhat grueling, as the roads are terrible. Flying will also change a ten-hour trip to forty-five minutes: big difference.

ECUADOR PACKING LIST
The difficult thing about packing for Ecuador is that you have to be prepared for every type of climate if you are going to travel extensively throughout the country. The easy thing is that everything you need can easily be purchased in Quito, Guayaquil and other tourist cities. Climbing and camping gear is a little more expensive, but sunglasses, hats, hand-knit items like hats, gloves, sweaters and other basic supplies are plentiful and cheap. We have divided the packing list into regional lists and included extra sections for backpackers and adventure travel.

Some basic things to consider: the voltage in Ecuador is the same as in the United States, 110 volts 60 cycles. However, many older buildings require a converter for plugs with three prongs. A small medical kit and extra personal supplies like tampons are a good idea as they can be hard to find outside of Quito and Guayaquil.

The seasons on the coast and in the Amazon Basin are divided between wet and dry. December to July is sunny and dry on the coast, while the rest of the year is foggy and cooler. November to March in the Amazon is the driest part of the year and some lodges are unreachable by boat during this time. The weather in the Andes is unpredictable, so be prepared for hot, cool, wet and dry on any given day. Sunglasses and sunscreen are a must throughout the country, as is bug repellant. Malaria is only found on the coast (but not in the Galápagos) and in the Amazon Rainforest Basin.

Take extra safety precautions. Petty theft is commonplace, especially in Quito and Guayaquil, but it can easily be avoided. Leave copies of important documents like your passport, credit cards and the numbers from your travelers' checks, if you are using them, in a separate part of your luggage. It's also a good idea to store important information, including the international phone number for your credit cards online somewhere easy to access and remember like in an e-mail account. Traveler's insurance is an excellent idea, especially if you are bringing expensive camera equipment or electronics that you want to feel comfortable using frequently. Keep all important documents, credit cards and most of your cash inside your clothing and a separate wallet or coin purse within easy reach for small purchases and meals.

ADVENTURE SPORTS PACKING LIST
RIVER RAFTING
Swimsuit; tennis shoes or Teva-like sandals with secure ankle straps; t-shirt (quick drying material is best); easy-dry shorts or running tights; safety strap if wearing glasses; waterproof camera; plastic bags for anything you want to stay dry; dry clothes for after the trip and lots of adrenaline.

MOUNTAIN CLIMBING
Below are supplies you will need on a two day non-technical climb up mountains such as Cotopaxi and Chimborazo. For the more technical climbs, more specialized equipment is needed. For nearly all tours, the items listed under "Equipment" are provided by the tour

company. All equipment may be rented in Quito as well. Helmets are the exception to both of these statements, they are rarely provided and are also very difficult to rent.

Equipment: Mountaineering boots; crampons; ice axe; carabineers; climbing ropes; harness and gaiters. **Personal:** Food; water; headlamp; 3 sets of batteries; glacier glasses; lip balm; sunscreen; knife; 2 water bottles; two thick insulating layer tops; one thin, one thick; insulating layer bottoms; Gore-Tex type hooded coat; Gore-Tex type bottom; glove liners; Gore-Tex Gloves; 2 pairs of socks; warm hat; camera—keep it in your inside pocket, it'll freeze; extra change of clothes and shoes for around camp.

ANDES PACKING LIST

Because of the rapid change in seasons, bring lots of layers of fast-drying clothes. Fleece and other synthetic fabrics are perfect. Hiking boots and comfortable sandals are also essential. Hiking in the páramo, or high grassland, requires rubber boots, which cost only around $5 in any part of Ecuador.

GALAPAGOS PACKING LIST

CLOTHES

There is no dress code on most boats or in island towns, so pack casual, yet comfortable clothing. Bring lightweight, breathable items for day hikes and a sweater or jacket for cool evenings on the boat. Terrain on some islands is rough and rocky, so bring comfortable sneakers or hiking boots with good traction. Tevas, Chacos or any other types of sandal with a security strap are great for beach sites and less rugged trails. On the boat, you will keep your shoes in a communal bin and either walk barefoot or in flip-flops.

LUGGAGE

If you are on a cruise tour, it is a good idea to pack as lightly and compactly as possible, since there is only a finite amount of space in your cabin and on board. Backpacks are the most portable through all of the required land-water transfers, but suitcases and duffel bags are fine. Your boat will send representatives from the crew to meet you at the airport, collect your bags, deliver them to the boat, and ultimately place them in your cabin. So if you have bulky or awkward pieces of luggage, the burden of transporting them will fall upon the helpful and gracious members of the crew. Because you will have day excursions on the islands, it is essential that you bring a daypack or fanny pack so that you can have water, sun protection, photographic equipment, raingear and any other items you may need with you at all times.

SWIMMING/SNORKELING GEAR

If you like the water, you will have a number of opportunities to swim, snorkel or scuba dive in the Galápagos, oftentimes more than once a day. As such, you should bring more than one swimsuit, a towel (some boats may provide beach towels but others will not), and beach attire (a sarong or beach wrap is perfect for women). Because you can get cold and sunburned very easily in Galapagos waters, it is also a good idea to bring a lightweight neoprene wetsuit or dive skin, if you have one, or some other quick-dry outfit (that you don't mind wearing in the ocean), like long underwear or sport clothes. You can rent wetsuits in Quito, Guayaquil, Puerto Ayora or sometimes directly on your boat for a reasonable daily price. Many boats have their own snorkeling equipment, which is complementary or available for rent, but the quality and maintenance may be sub-par and the sizes available may be limited. If you are on a boat with scuba diving capability, you will probably have more luck, but you should still bring your own if you have it.

SCUBA DIVING EQUIPMENT

If you plan on scuba-diving and have your own equipment, bring it. You will need at least a 6mm wetsuit, boots, gloves and possibly a hood, in addition to a regulator, BCD, computer, weight belt, fins and mask. All of the dive shops will include equipment in the price of their packages, but the quality and size availability varies from place to place. Some dive shops replace their equipment every year, keep a variety of sizes and styles and maintain their gear in stellar condition. Others have older, worn-out equipment—a sticky regulator, a leaky BCD, ill-fitting apparel, etc.—that is still usable but less desirable for many recreational divers. The conditions in the Galápagos can be challenging for many divers, so if you are at all nervous about your abilities, ease some of your worries by bringing your own gear.

PHOTOGRAPHY

The Galápagos are an excellent place—even for novices—to take magazine-quality photographs and to make exciting home-videos. Because much of the wildlife in the Galápagos is stationary and close to the trails, you can get very good results with digital, manual and even point-and-shoot cameras. Although you probably don't need anything larger than a hand-held lens, you can get some very good close-up results if you bring a zoom lens. You should also bring an underwater casing for your camera (if you have one) or an underwater camera. Although capturing the underwater landscape and bigger creatures is best with a video-camera or a camera with a strobe, the smaller digital cameras with flash are great for macro shots of fish, eels, or coral.

EXTRAS

Keep in mind that facilities for recharging batteries on boats are limited (some have 110-V outlets), so it is a good idea to invest in some long-life batteries or bring along a lot of spares. It is also a good rule to bring twice as much film or memory than you think you will need. If you know you will be making a stop in Puerto Ayora during your cruise, you can plan to download photos from your memory card onto a CD at any of the internet cafes in town.

In summary, a basic packing list of the essentials in Galápagos: Sunhat; sunglasses; sandals (for the boat); sneakers (for dry landings and rocky shores); Teva-style sandals (for wet landings); swimsuit; umbrella (for sun protection during island hikes or the occasional downpour); high factor, waterproof sunscreen; flashlight or head lamp; water bottle; plastic ziploc bags to keep things from getting wet; snorkel and mask if you aren't renting; beach towel and bath towel; wind resistant jacket; light sweater or sweatshirt; twice as much film or memory cards as you think you will need; extra batteries; underwater camera; and motion sickness pills. The water can be very cold so you may want to bring a dive skin or wet suit.

AMAZON RAINFOREST PACKING LIST

Rubber boots are a must and are almost always provided at the lodge or through your tour company, up to size 10 (US), or can be purchased in advance. Also bring: insect repellent (with DEET); malaria pills; antihistamine tablets and an epi-pen for people with serious allergies to stings; binoculars (invaluable in the rainforest—it's worth spending a bit of extra money to get a good pair—8 x 40 are excellent for poor light conditions under the forest canopy); plastic bags for keeping your clothes dry; swimming suit; lightweight, quick-drying clothes; at least one long-sleeved shirt; one pair of loose-fitting pants (no jeans); a light sweater (it gets surprisingly chilly in the rainforest, especially on boat trips); poncho that fits over you and your pack (the cheap plastic knee-length type coats are better than Gore-tex, which will soak right through in a real rainforest deluge); bandana; at least one pair of socks per day—or more; Teva-like sandals or sneakers for around camp; and ziploc bags for food, books, maps and anything else you hope to keep dry. All clothes (undergarments included) should be loose fitting to help keep you cool and to reduce your chances of being bitten by chiggers.

BACKPACKERS' PACKING LIST

Ecuador is an excellent country for travelers willing to rough it. Public buses are plentiful and inexpensive; dorm beds range from $2-5 per person per night around the country, including in the more expensive capital Quito; and fixed meals provide cheap nutriment. As for a restaurant or cafe's "desayuno," "almuerzo" or "merienda" (breakfast, lunch or dinner) and you will find yourself with more food than you usually eat for $1.50-3 around Ecuador. While this is not to be considered an authoritative packing list, here are a few items that we have found handy when backpacking around Ecuador: Flashlight; clothesline; mosquito net; Swiss Army Knife or Leatherman (don't forget to put it in your checked luggage!); watch with alarm clock; toilet paper; plastic bags for separating dirty and clean clothes and shoes; needle and thread; biodegradable soap; notebooks and pens/pencils; hat; and poncho. Anitbacterial hand gel is less wasteful than wet wipes. Tents and sleeping bags can be easily rented and you will find that camping is often the same price as a budget hostel.

Have a great travel story? Tell it at www.vivatravelguides.com

QUITO

This rapidly growing capital city has a past stretching back to times before the Incas made Quito the second capital of their empire. Only the mountains that cradle the city remain unchanged; the Centro Histórico features colonial architecture the Spanish constructed over the charred remains of the Incan city.

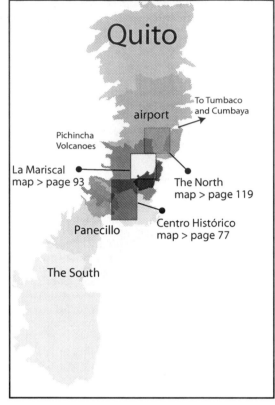

Just north of the Centro Histórico, towering concrete and glass structures host the business and tourist center of the city. Travelers worldwide are drawn to Quito for its developed tourist infrastructure, international cuisine, spectacular setting, adventure travel opportunities and the gentle, generous culture. Quito makes a good base for travel around Ecuador: most travel agencies have an office here and transportation by land and air is plentiful and inexpensive, depending on the time of year.

QUITO WEATHER AND GEOGRAPHY

Quito is set in a long, shallow valley at an elevation of 2,800 m (9,200 ft) above sea level. Surrounded by green Andes peaks, Quito's weather is spring-like year-round. Temperatures drop drastically after sunset (6:30 p.m. year-round). The sun is incredibly strong, so be smart about sunscreen, hats and sunglasses. Also, because of the city's altitude, allow yourself at least one day to relax and acclimate. Drink lots of bottled water and don't plan too much physical activity the first day or two.

QUITO'S SECTORS

Divided into different neighborhoods (sectores), most tourists spend their time in the Mariscal (p. 93), or the area north of Parque el Ejido and south of Avenida Orellana. The Mariscal has the highest concentration of travel agencies, hostels, international restaurants and inexpensive bars, but there are a couple of other neighborhoods that are worth devoting some time to—be sure to branch out. The Centro Histórico (p. 77), for example, hosts a diverse and rich colonial history with some beautiful plazas, churches, museums and pedestrian walkways. Other good neighborhoods include Guápulo (p. 117), La Floresta (p. 113) and the North part of Quito (p. 119). Quito was originally contained within the limits of what is now called the Centro Histórico. Today it is about 35 kilometers long from north to south (21 miles) and on average 8 kilometers (about five miles) wide east to west.

QUITO HIGHLIGHTS

If you have a limited period of time in Quito, don't miss a tour of the Centro Histórico at night, or the weekend market at Parque el Ejido, especially if you can't make it to the market in Otavalo. If you have more time, be sure to take a trip to the Panecillo and its resident religious icon, where you'll encounter excellent views of the city; the Teleférigo and Vulcano Park are the newest additions to Quito's tourist industry and offers a spectacular gondola ride up to the Pichincha volcanoes, the western wall of the city. Some museums not to miss while in Quito are Guayasamín's Capilla del Hombre and the Museo Nacional del Banco Central del Ecuador.

WHEN TO GO

Quito has two seasons: spring with rain, and spring with sun. Quito's location, about 40 kilometers south of the equator and at an altitude of 2,800 meters above sea level, makes for startling temperature changes in a 24-hour period. The city gets downright cool when the sun is down (from 6:30 p.m.- 6 a.m. every day of the year) and when it rains. When the sun is out, however, you will find yourself stripped down to the bare minimum. Consequently, wearing layers is fundamental to being comfortable in Quito. Pants, a light T-shirt or tank top layered with a long-sleeve shirt and jacket or sweater should be fine most of the year. Travelers coming from colder climates will be amused at the winter garb of most quiteños from September-April, which often includes jackets, scarves, gloves and hats. Winter is a strong word, but during these months, afternoon storms are common and tend to drop the temperature to around 50 degrees Fahrenheit (10 degrees Celsius). During sunny days, the temperatures can rise up to 85 degrees Fahrenheit (30 degrees Celsius).

HOLIDAYS AND FIESTAS

Fiestas de Quito, celebrating Quito's Independence Day, are technically on December 6, but really end up taking the entire week leading before. Quiteños celebrate by drag racing colorfully painted, open-air buses called *chivas,* complete with beverage service and live music. They also hold beauty pageants for the 'Queen of Quito,' along with dozens of live concerts, bullfights and massive competitions of 'Cuarenta,' Ecuador's national card game. Other festivals unique to Quito take place mainly during the month of August, leading up to El Día del Patrimonio, the day the Centro Histórico was named a UNESCO Historical Landmark. These celebrations consist of outdoor concerts, theater and other cultural events.

HISTORY

PRE-INCA CIVILIZATION

Considering its location 2,850 meters (9,300 feet) above the sea, it is astonishing that Quito was inhabited at all before modern transportation and cultivation technology, but the first signs of inhabitants in the area date back nearly 10,000 years with the Quitu (who gave the city its name), Cara, Shyri and Puruhá groups. Due to its central location, Quito was a permanent commercial trading center, or *tianguez,* for the Coast, Sierra and Amazon Basin regions. The merchants and mindalaes traded products like salt, cotton and shells from the coast for cinnamon, medicinal herbs and precious metals from the Amazon Basin. The sierra produced and traded potatoes, corn and other agricultural products endemic to the area.

INCA RULE

Little is known about Quito's first inhabitants, apart from the fact that in the late 15th century, they put up an extremely strong front against the Incas. After at least a decade of fighting, however, Quito fell to Inca rule under Huayna Capac, who built a road south to his preferred capital in Cusco. Upon Huayna Capac's death, the empire was divided in two and bequeathed to his sons, Huascar and Atahualpa. Huascar ruled from Cusco, while Atahualpa made Quito the northern capital of the Inca Empire. Unfortunately, there are no remaining Inca structures left in Quito. Shortly after the Spanish invaded the region and beheaded Atahualpa, his lead general, Rumiñahui, razed the city, rather than surrender to the Spanish. If you're keen to see some Inca ruins head south to Ingapirca, Ecuador's most famous archaeological site.

SPANISH RULE

Just 30 years after the Inca wars, the Spanish arrived, led by Francisco Pizarro. Their decisive victory is a fascinating and tragic part of history, and a source of bitterness for many present-day quiteños. A series of unfortunate decisions by the Inca leader Atahualpa, coupled with the shrewd deception of Pizarro, eventually enabled the Spanish to overtake the Inca army, which was estimated at over 5,000, with only a few hundred men. For a memento of this historic battle, just stop by almost any local outdoor market, where you can pick up Inca versus Spanish chess sets, complete with llamas on the Inca side and horses on the Spanish side.

Today, the Centro Histórico (p. 77) has the best display of colonial Quito, with many original structures dating back to the mid- to late-1500s and built on Inca foundations. The Plaza San Francisco, for example, has a beautiful monastery and plaza built in the same spot that the pre-Inca tribes held their tianguez. The Spanish introduced many changes to the indigenous population; among them, violent and obligatory conversion to Catholicism as well as an oppressive feudal system. The new system placed social status on race. Spanish were on the top rung of society, then the *mestizo*, or mixed population, followed by the indigenous groups and the African slaves the Spanish brought with them.

The Catholic Church, faithful to the Spanish Crown, dominated economically and socially during the Colonial Period until the beginning of the 19th century, when a common desire for liberation began to brew in Quito. On August 10, 1809—still celebrated today as Ecuador's Independence Day—the first cry for independence was proclaimed in Quito. Thirteen years later, rebellious forces under the command of José Antonio de Sucre defeated the Spanish in the decisive battle of Pichincha. Ecuador was part of liberator Simón Bolívar's Gran Colombia, along with parts of Panama, Venezuela and Colombia until 1830. The first constitutional government was headed by Juan José Flores that same year. For more details on the political history of Ecuador, see our History of Ecuador section.

LODGING IN QUITO

From a mattress on the floor to a suite at a high-end international chain, Quito has a hotel to meet everyone's needs. The prices tend to be a little higher than in other parts of the country, but so is the overall quality. There are some basic things to look for in a hotel in Quito. With cool evenings year-round, hot water and thick blankets are a necessity. Location is also important and will greatly impact the kind of experience you have. There is a good variety of hotels in every neighborhood, so if you want a non-touristy experience, it is worth it to venture out of the Mariscal area. If you are willing to spend a little more money on lodging, consider staying at one of Quito's many independently-run hotels. They offer similar services as international chains at lower prices, and you get a hotel with much more personality. Also, many hotels have rooms with beautiful views of the Pichincha volcanoes or city skylines at no extra charge, so it never hurts to ask. Quito is a large city with much to see and do. If you stay for more than a day or two, ask for a discount on your room. Bargaining is always appropriate.

TOUR OPERATORS IN QUITO

A popular spot on any traveler's itinerary, Quito boasts more than its fair share of travel operators with the majority clustered around the Mariscal. Many places can organize day trips in, around and outside the of city. Some can also organize longer trips through the Andes and to the jungle or the coast. If you're lucky (and if you have a flexible travel itinerary) you might be able to take advantage of last minute deals to the Galápagos and other exciting places around Ecuador.

ADVENTURE PLANET ECUADOR

Adventure Planet Ecudaor offers tours all over Quito and the Galápagos Islands. Their tours range from biking to hiking to trekking through the jungle to climbing the Andes. They have decades of experience in showing Quito off to natives and tourists alike. Club Los Chillos Portal 2 No. 42, Quito, Tel: 593-2-287-1105, Fax: 593-2-287-1605, Cell: 593-9-811-2154, E-mail: info@adventureplanet-ecuador.com, URL: www.adventureplanet-ecuador.com.

COLUMBUS TRAVEL LTD.
Columbus Travel Ltd. is an Ecuador-based company under Norwegian management. They specialize in tours of the Galápagos, the Andes Sierra and Peru and the Amazon jungle. Calle Leonidas Plaza 353 and Roca, La Mariscal, Quito, Tel: 593-2-223-6688, Fax: 593-2-250-4977, E-mail: info@columbusecuador.com.

ECUADOR EXPERIENCE
Ecuador Experience is a tour operator based in Quito. Their tours specialize in birdwatching due to the great number and variety of species throughout the country. Guides speak French, Spanish, English and German. The tours can be modified to suit travellers' needs. Ulloa 3045 and Moncayo, Quito, Tel: 593-2-243-5692, Cell: 593-9-812-3023, E-mail: ecuadorexperience@yahoo.fr, URL: www.ecuadorexperience.com.

ECUADOR TIERRA VIVA TRAVEL COMPANY
Tierra Viva Travel Company specializes in ecotourism. Their tours stay off the beaten path a bit (something that's easy to do in Ecuador) and visit mostly small communities, national parks and nature reserves. It's most definitely not the company for the five-star tourist, but for a more nature-loving patron. Contact: Peter Rodriguez. Diaz de la Madrid 612 and Diego Utreras, Quito, Tel: 593-2-223-9786, E-mail: peter@ecuador-tierra-viva.com.

EQTOURING
Eqtouring has been traveling Ecuador and the Galápagos as an independent company for the past five years. They specialize in luxury Galápagos cruises and multi-day tours of the Amazon Basin. Panamericana Norte, Jardines de Carcelén A34, Quito, Tel: 593-2-248-6685, Cell: 593-9-944-3139, E-mail: info@eqtouring.com, URL: www.eqtouring.com

FLASH TRAVEL
Flash Travel is a tour company over 10 years old. They offer day tours in Quito, the Upper Andes, the Amazon Wildlife Center, Machalilla, and a rafting, climbing and biking tour. They also have mutli-day tours covering a multitude of sites in Ecuador. Avenida Cristóbal Colon E4-175, Torres de la Colón Building, Apartment 612, Quito, Tel: 593-2-290-6050, Fax: 593-2-290-6051, URL: www.ecuadoor.com.

GALAECO
Galaeco hosts ecotours in every major part of Ecuador. They do single-day and multi-day tours of the Galápagos, the coast, the Andes and in the rainforest. Joaquin Pinto E4-358 and Av. Amazonas, Salgado Building, 2nd floor, Office 203, Quito, Tel: 593-2-255-3098 / 593-2-290-6626, Cell: 593-9-580-0830, E-mail: info@galaeco.com, URL: www.galaeco.com.

Enter photo competitions at www.vivatravelguides.com

GALASAM TOURS

Galasam Tours specialize in Galápagos cruises but have much to offer the land-bound tourist. They have tours all over Ecuador's extremely diverse terrain including Quito, Cuenca, Baños and also of Ecuador's national parks. Contact: Christian Samán. Cordero 1342 and Amazonas, Quito, Tel: 593-4-230-4488, E-mail: christian@galasam.com, URL: www.galápagos-islands.com.

GEO REISEN TOURS

Geo Reisen Tours specializes in personal-tours to fit individual or group needs in the the Galápagos and in the varried landscape of mainland Ecuador. Yugoeslavia No. 265 and Azuay, Edificio Arion, PB, Quito, Tel: 593-2-292-0583, Cell: 593-9-601-9995, E-mail: info@georeisentours.com, URL: www.georeisentours.com.

GOLONDRINA TURISMO

With tour operaters speaking English, Spanish, French, Italian and Dutch, Golondrina Turismo is a great company for the international traveler. They have tours in every area of Ecuador as well as the ever-popular Galápagos cruises and a special tour of the Indian markets. Contact: Ruben. Juan León Mera N 22-37 and Carrión, Quito, Tel: 593-2-252-8616/252-8570, E-mail: golondri@uio.satnet.net, URL: www.adventuregalapagos.com.

GRAYLINE

One of the world's leading tour companies, Grayline offers a multitude of tours around Ecuador. They host one-day and multi-day tours of the big cities in Ecuador as well as circuit packages covering several different areas over several days. Santa María E4-125 and Francisco Pizarro, 5th floor, Tel: 1-800-GRAY-LINE, E-mail: info@graylineecuador.com, URL: www.graylineecuador.com.

GREENPACIFIC S.A.

GreenPacific has tour guides who speak English, Spanish, French, German, Italian and Dutch. They have tours in all the major cities in Ecuador as well as in the jungle and Galápagos boat tours. They also offer Spanish classes and volunteer programs. Mariscal Foch E4-167 and Amazonas, Quito, Tel: 593-2-254-5210, E-mail: info@greenpacific.com, URL: www.greenpacific.com.

GUANGUILTAGUA EXPEDITIONS

Professional tour guide with ten years' experience offers customized overland tours of any length throughout mainland Ecuador. They're flexible and can provide quotes for any type of tour from backpacking through luxury tours. You advise what your interests are for your day trip, short trip or longer tour, and they will provide an itinerary and quote. Dates to suit you. Cell: 593-9-971-2169, E-mail: info@guanguiltagua.com, URL: www.guanguiltagua.com.

GULLIVER TRAVEL

Gulliver Travel provides an array of different tour types in Ecuador: everything from biki
ing and horseback riding. Their web site is user-friendly with a special section for last minu__
for that on-the-go traveler. Contact: Max, Juan Leon Mera and Jose Calama, Quito, Cell: 593-9-946-
2265, Fax: 593-2-252-9297, E-mail: gulliverexpeditions@yahoo.com, URL: www.gulliver.com.ec.

JARIBÚ ADVENTURES

Ecuador is a great destination for adventurous visitors itching to get off the tourist track. It
features a fairly well developed infrastructure for activities like climbing, hiking, mountain
biking, rafting, surfing, diving and bird-watching. Whether you decide to ramble out on your
own or hook up with a local guide service, the logistics of planning excursions in Ecuador are
simpler and the approach time shorter than in other, more remote areas of the world. Av.
Amazonas 477 and Roca, Office 1016, Quito, Tel: 593-2-256-3551/256-4315, Cell: 593-9-966-
1745, E-mail: info@jaribuadventures.com.

KEMPERY TOURS

Kempery Tours has a main office in Quito, as well as satellite offices in the Andes and in the
Galápagos Islands. Operating for over a decade, Kempery offers a vast array of tours, like
trips to markets like Otavalo, treks to Cotopaxi and extensive land tours throughout Ecuador.
Kempery is owned and operated by Swiss transplants to Ecuador, and the staff are all Ecuadorian natives. French, German, Swiss and English are spoken. Kempery Ramíres Dávalos
117 and Amazonas, Edif. Tourismundial, Office 101, Quito, Tel: 593-2-250-5600, Fax: 593-2-
222-6715, E-mail: kempery@kempery.com, URL: www.kempery.com.

LAKE & MOUNTAIN TRAVEL AGENCY AND TOUR OPERATOR

Lake & Mountain offers many different tour types in Ecuador and the Galápagos. They
have tours involving biking, hiking, birdwatching and rafting and even an Ecuador Explorer tour that lasts 14 days, traveling around the country. Abdón Calderón E 10-14
and Shyris Avenue, Quito, Tel: 593-2-246-3904 / 593-2-229-5277 / 593-2-259-4008,
Cell: 593-9-834-8963/258-5323, Fax: 593-2-246-3904, E- Mail: lakem@uio.satnet.net,
URL: www.lakeandmountainecuador.com.

NAUTICA GALÁPAGOS CIA LTD.

Natutica specializes in boat tours and island tours of the Galápagos, but also has a wide-range
of land tours including the mountains and the jungle. They also have a spot on their web site
for last minute deals. 18 de Septiembre 413 and Av. Amazonas, Alamo Building, Office 502,
Quito, Tel: 593-2-290-6371, Fax: 593-2-250-3608, Cell: 593-9-981-5500, E-mail: info@nau-
ticagalapagos.com, nautica@interactive.net.ec.

SPRING TRAVEL ECUADOR

Spring Travel offers tours of Ecuador's coast, mountains, jungles and the Galápagos. They
offer hotel packages for any traveler's budget. They also have a Spanish school. Av. Amazonas
and Naciones Unidas, Unicornio Torre Empresarial, 10th floor, Office 1002, Quito, Tel: 593-
2-225-6351, E-mail: info@springtravelecuador.com.

SUN & SNOW EXPEDITIONS

Sun & Snow Expeditions is a tour company specializing in mountain climbing in the Andes.
Their Ecuadorian tours last anywhere for 12 to 20 days hiking everything from Cotopaxi to
the Sangay Volcano or an hacienda tour around the country. Calama E8-07 and Almagro,
Quito, Tel: 593-2-290-7236, Cell: 593-9-961-6119, E-mail: info@andeanchallenge.com.

TREK ECUADOR

Trek Ecuador gives personally-designed tours of the Amazon, Andes, coast and Galápagos.
Cell: 593-9-190-1138, E-mail: info@trekecuador.com, URL: www.trekecuador.com.

Enter photo competitions at www.vivatravelguides.com

QUITO

ZENITH TRAVEL

With over 15 years experience in Ecuador, Peru and the Galápagos, Zenith Travel offers expertise in the area of budget travel, without a sacrifice of quality. Juan León Mera 453 and Roca, Edif. Chiriboga #202, Quito, Tel: 593-2-252-9993, Cell: 593-9-955-5951, E-mail: info@zenithecuador.com, URL: www.zenithecuador.com.

STUDYING SPANISH

Quito is a major hub for travelers who want to study Spanish. Most schools offer homestays, excursions and even other types of classes like cooking classes and salsa lessons. Rates range from around $4/hour to $10/hour. If that is out of your budget, many schools will hire you as an English teacher and either give you a discount on your Spanish lessons or let you take classes for free. Price also depends on class size. Classes are rarely less than one week and run as long as several months in length.

QUITO ANTIGUO SPANISH SCHOOL ($2.50-3/HOUR)

Quito Antiguo Spanish School is one of the cheapest in Quito. Located in Quito's Centro Histórico, this school offers less extra features than other schools in Quito, but is well-located for strolls around the colonial neighborhoods in the area. Programs outside of Quito (Coast, Oriente, Indigenous Markets, Baños) can be organized. Packages for 5 days/4 nights cost around $300 and include 20 hours of Spanish, transport and excursions. Homestays can be arranged. Volunteer opportunities through the school, such as working with street children, are also available. Discounts are given for long-term commitments, so don't be afraid to negotiate the price. Caspicara Spanish School is run by the same director. (Plaza San Francisco, Sucre Oe6, 2nd floor, Tel: 593-2-957-023, E-mail: spanishauthentic@yahoo.es). Venezuela 1129 and Olmeda, Centro Histórico, Tel: 593-2-957-023, E-mail: quitoantiguo@yahoo.es.

BERACA SPANISH SCHOOL ($2.50-4.50/HOUR)

Beraca Spanish School offers lots of opportunities to absorb Ecuadorian culture as you learn the language with such included services as: airport pick-up, help with lodging, daytrips with teachers, multiple levels of study and flexible schedules. South American Explorers Club members receive a 10% discount. Av. Amazonas N24-66 and Pinto, Second Floor, Mariscal, Tel: 593-2-290-6642, E-mail: beraca@interactive.net.ec, URL: www.beraca.net.

APF LANGUAGES ($4-5/HOUR)

APF Languages offers flexible schedules, experienced teachers and services and facilities above and beyond what the price suggests. Along with a Spanish conversation club, dance and cooking classes, two free hours of internet each week, videos and documentaries in Spanish, information on travel and volunteer opportunities around Ecuador, the two large houses in Quito are comfortable and full of homey touches. Groups have the chance to study at an Andean hacienda or in the Amazon Rainforest. Mercurio 345 and La Razón, North of Quito, Tel: 593-2-226-5618, E-mail: info@apf-languages.com, URL: www.apf-languages.com.

CRISTÓBAL COLÓN SPANISH LANGUAGE SCHOOL ($4.50-5/HOUR)

Private classes at Cristóbal Colón are reasonably priced. No registration fee is necessary, just pay as you go. The library offers a selection of materials and you can change teachers every week to practice a variety of accents and teaching styles. There are several ways you can get discounts at this language school, including working in the office, staying at the hostel next door and printing out a brochure from their web site. Extra services offered include excursions, English teacher placements around Quito and host family accommodation. Salsa classes, cooking classes, internet facilities and city excursions with your teachers are all included. Colon and Versailles (one block from 10 de Agosto) Mariscal, Tel: 593-2-250-6508, Fax: 593-2-222-2964, E-mail: info@colonspanishschool.com, URL: www.colonspanishschool.com.

> **V!VA Member Review-Cristobal Colon Spanish Language School**
> *I was looking for somewhere really cheap to study Spanish and found this school. It has great teachers and a good course which helped me to improve my Spanish considerably. It also has a warm and friendly atmosphere which made it easy to meet other students. 27 April 2007. Australia.*

CENTRO DE ESPAÑOL VIDA VERDE ($4-6/HOUR)

Classes at Centro De Español Vida Verde are different from other Spanish schools in Quito because a small portion of the profits go to conservation and development projects around Ecuador. Class schedules are flexible and include such extras as excursions with your teacher, airport pickup, help with lodging, including homestays if you are interested, and all class materials. All teachers have a minimum of five years experience and most have degrees in

Enter photo competitions at www.vivatravelguides.com

education. The school now also runs Casa Vida Verde, a fully furnished residential hostal in a quiet neighborhood close to Parque Metropolitano. Wilson N23100 and Leonodis Plaza, La Mariscal, Tel: 593-2-222-6635, Fax: 593-2-256-3110, E-mail: info@vidaverde.com, URL: www.vidaverde.com.

ACADEMIA DE ESPAÑOL GUAYASAMÍN ($4-6/HOUR)

Academia de Español Guayasamín offers class from $4-6/hour depending on group size. Teachers have from 7-16 years experience and are all native speakers. All materials are included in the price along with salsa classes, city excursions, volunteer opportunities and help with accommodation. Class schedules are flexible. Programs are also offered on the coast and in the Amazon Rainforest. Calama and 6 de Diciembre, La Mariscal, Tel: 593-2-254-4210, E-mail: info@guayasaminschool.com, URL: www.guayasaminschool.com.

SIMÓN BOLÍVAR SPANISH SCHOOL ($4.50-8/HOUR)

Located on a quiet street in the east of La Mariscal, Simón Bolívar Spanish School offers lots of extra services like free internet, airport pickup, city tours, two salsa classes per week, classes on culture, economy and other Ecuadorian subjects, cooking classes and most importantly, teachers with lots of experience. Flexible schedules and small class sizes are also a plus. There are equivalent branches in Cuenca, on the coast, just south of Puerto López and in the Amazon Rainforest. Homestays can be arranged for $120/week with all meals included. Leónidas Plaza and Foch, Mariscal, Tel: 593-2-250-4977, Fax: 593-2-223-6688, E-mail: info@simonbolivar.com, URL: www.ecuadorschools.com.

APU INTY SPANISH SCHOOL ($4-6/HOUR)

Although there are tons of Spanish schools to choose from while staying in Quito, it is the little things that make the difference. With a variety of "extras," Apu Inty stands apart from the pack. The school offers amenities such as free wireless internet, coffee and tea. Once a week, on Wednesday evenings, students join local Ecuadorian students for a "Conversation Club" at a local restaurant or bar. This, coupled with the school's weekly Spanish movie night and dancing classes, is a surefire way to learn Spanish quickly. Xaura 159 and Foch, Tel: 593-2-222-1541, E-mail: info@apuintyspanishschool.com, URL: www.apuintyspanishschool.com.

RUMIÑAHUI SPANISH SCHOOL ($5/HOUR)

The Rumiñahui Spanish School offers as many benefits as you can hope for at $5/hour: one-on-one classes, all books, free salsa lessons, homestay recommendations, volunteer work opportunities, free coffee and tea and a diploma from the Ecuadorian Ministry of Education at the end of your course. South American Explorers Club members receive a ten percent discount. 10 de Agosto 1893 and Carrión, 2nd floor, Office 201, Mariscal, Tel: 593-2-256-2664, E-mail: rumieducacion@yahoo.com.es, URL: www.rumieducacion.com.

BIPO & TONI'S ACADEMIA DE ESPAÑOL ($5-8/HOUR)

Bipo & Toni's Academia de Español is a well-established Spanish school offering private classes and classes in small groups from $5-8/hour depending on the package and group size. Typical activities like city and market tours, certificates from the Ministry of Education, and help with accommodation at a host family's home or hotel are all included. They do a good job of customizing your classes and schedules. Set in a quiet neighborhood in La Floresta, the facilities are clean and spacious and offer a great way to meet other travelers. You can also arrange for Spanish classes from their office in Switzerland. There is a five percent discount for early bookings. Leonodis Plaza between Veintimilla and Carrión, La Floresta, Tel: 593-2-255-6614, Fax: 593-2-254-7090, E-mail: info@bipo.net, URL: www.academia.bipo.net.

THE SECRET GARDEN ($6/HOUR)

Set in a converted colonial building in Quito's Centro Histórico district, the Secret Garden Hostel's main selling points are the stunning view over the colonial district from the roof terrace restaurant/bar and the friendly, laid-back atmosphere. The Secret Garden can arrange Spanish lessons, taken on the roof terrace. If you take a course of 40 hours, you get a free three-course meal. Dinner is a particularly sociable occasion. There's a small book exchange and reference library, and the friendly staff can help with travel arrangements and recommend several good hostels to visit on your travels around Ecuador. José Anteparra, between Los Rios and Vicente León, San Blas, Tel: 593-2-295-6704, E-mail: hola@secretgardenquito.com, URL: www.secretgardenquito.com.

LA LENGUA ($120/20 HOURS)

La Lengua's flexible, one-to-one Spanish lessons provide a solid introduction to the Spanish language and Latin American culture. Tours and volunteering options are offered. Students determine the number of classes they want to take, but the school runs classes Monday through Friday, 8:30 a.m. - 5:30 p.m., with a break of 20 minutes in the morning and in the afternoon. Saturday and Sunday lessons are available on request. Colón 1001 and Juan León Mera, 8th floor, Tel/Fax: 593-2-250-1271, E-mail: lalengua@hoy.net, URL: www.la-lengua.com.

MITAD DEL MUNDO ($7/CLASS + $30 REGISTRATION FEE)

Mitad del Mundo offers both individual and group courses. The school is located in the center of modern Quito, close to the major banks, shopping malls, travel agencies and restaurants. Founded in 1990 by a select group of professionals dedicated to the teaching of Spanish to foreigners, the school's principal objective has been to disseminate Ecuadorian culture through the teaching of the Spanish language under the highest professional standards. The school is recognized by the Ministry of Education and the German Ministry of Education, and supported by the Bildungsurlaub certificate. Courses are available throughout the year. Av. Patria 640 and 9 de Octubre. Edificio Patria (12th floor) Office 1204, Tel: 593-2-256-7875, E-mail: mitmund1@mitadmundo.com.ec, URL:www.mitadmundo.com.ec.

Enter photo competitions at www.vivatravelguides.com

QUITO

SOUTH AMERICAN LANGUAGE CENTER ($8/HOUR)

The South American Language Center has been operating from La Mariscal for about 14 years. It is a bit pricey, but with the price comes one-on-one classes, help with homestay arrangements, salsa lessons, cooking classes and tours around Quito. Courses can last anywhere between a week to 8 weeks and go for four hours a day up to seven hours. There are video, multimedia and listening labs and the price includes books, an ID card, and a diploma from the Ecuadorian Ministry of Education at the end of the course. Amazonas N26 and Santa Maria (just north of Colón), Mariscal, Tel: 593-2-254-4715, E-mail: info@southamerican.edu.ec, URL: www.southamerican.edu.ec.

AMAZONAS LANGUAGE SCHOOL ($8/HOUR)

Amazonas Language School features private Spanish classes. Because the school is paired up with a travel agency, students have the advantage of learning about the country and language as they travel. Founded in 1989, the school is well-established and all teachers have degrees in language and literature along with a minimum of six years teaching experience. There are various options for study around Ecuador including classes in Quito, The Galápagos Islands and the Amazon Jungle. English, French and German language classes are also offered. Jorge Washington and Amazonas Mariscal, Tel: 593-2-250-4654, E-mail: info@eduamazonas.com, URL: www.eduamazonas.com.

ECOLE IDIOMAS ($8/HOUR)

This Spanish school is smack in the middle of La Mariscal. Ecole Idiomas offers Spanish lessons and homestays with an emphasis on volunteer work in Quito. Volunteer options are generally full-time and can be activities like working at a day care center, nursing home or nature center outside of Quito. There is also volunteer work available in the Galápagos. This is one of the more expensive Spanish schools in the city, with prices at about $8 per hour. Included in this price is a weekly salsa lesson, all class materials, help with travel plans and 24-hour luggage storage. There are several packages involving home stays and classes that are worth taking a look at. Lizardo García E6-15 and Juan León Mera, Tel: 593-2-223-1592, Fax: 592-2-252-0850, E-mail: info@ecoletravel-ecuador.com, URL: www.ecole-idiomas.com.

LENGUATEC

A new addition among Quito Spanish schools, LenguaTec specializes in custom-designed language instruction based on small, intensive and personalized English and Spanish classes. The school utilizes bilingual professional instructors, whose friendly manner facilitates open dialogue between students. Placement exams ensure that students are placed at the appropriate level. Luxemburgo 219 and Hola, Tel: 593-2-246-0237, Cell: 593-9-822-5001 / 593-9-631-3074, E-mail: administration@lenguatec.com, URL: www.lenguatec.com.

ANDEAN STUDY PROGRAMS

Andean Study Programs specializes in study abroad programs for American and European Universities. If a university has a specific program in mind, the company will take that idea, compile an itinerary to complement it, and arrange the proper accommodations and activities. For example, if you want a biology-focused program, the company will organize Galápagos and Amazon trips for you. The process is very convenient for schools and students alike! Foch 721 and Amazonas, E-mail: info@andeanstudy.com, URL: www.andeanstudy.com.

INSTITUTO SUPERIOR DE ESPANOL

Established in 1988, the Instituto Superior de Espanol is a great choice for tourists to pick up the language while staying in Ecuador. With six entirely different locations to choose from, the school is easily accessible, not to mention well-organized. Flexibility is key when choosing a Spanish school in Ecuador. At the Instituto, students can fulfill their needs with either individual or group lessons. Additionally, an interesting option is to pick up Spanish while exploring the Galápagos Islands. The teachers are unversity trained, and accompany students on optional excursions. According to past students, Eugenio Cordova (the director), is an excellent resource while in Ecuador. Homestays can also be arranged. Quito: Darquea Terán 1650 and Av. 10 de Agosto, Otavalo: Sucre 1110 and Morales, Galápagos: Puerto Ayora, Santa

Cruz, Tel: Quito: 593-2-222-3242, Otavalo: 593-6-292-2 414, Fax: Quito: 593-2-222-1628, Otavalo: 593-6-292-2415, E-mail: superior@ecnet.ec, URL: www.instituto-superior.net.

ANDEAN GLOBAL STUDIES

Andean Global Studies, which is based in Quito, offers a wide variety of Spanish study programs that are sure to suit any student's needs. These programs include a Spanish immersion program, a medical Spanish program and a program that mixes Spanish study and volunteer work. Their Quito facilities are conveniently located near the Quicentro Shopping Mall and have multiple classrooms, a cafeteria and a recreation room. If language study in Quito is not quite what you are looking for, Andean Global Studies also offers programs in Manta, Baños and Cuenca. The school also helps organize trips around Ecuador for its students to places such as Papallacta, Baños, Otavalo and the Saquisilí Animal Market. El Norte 222 and El Sol, Tel: 593-2-226-5618, E-mail: info@andeanglobalstudies.org.

ACADEMIA LATINOAMERICANA DE ESPAÑOL

The key to learning and understanding a language lies in your experience and the degree that you are able to delve into the culture. At Academia Latinoamericana de Español, you will find yourself swiftly learning Spanish amidst friendly Ecuadorians and the mix of Spanish and indigenous history that defines Quito. Regardless of your level of proficiency, students will find a program that suits their needs, goals and learning styles. Classes are 60 minutes in length for four hours a day. The maximum number of students per class is four and students will learn using the four language skills: listening, grammar, oral and written comprehension. Students will be well taken care of in their homestay by native, middle-class families who live no further than a ten-minute bus ride from the school. Calle Noruega 156 and 6 de Diciembre, Tel: 593-2-225-0946, E-mail: info@latinoschools.com, URL: www.latinoschools.com.

CENTRO HISTÓRICO

The Centro Histórico is an extensive colonial center built over the ashes of what was a major part of the Inca empire until the Inca general Rumiñahui razed it to the ground rather than surrender to the Spanish conquistadors. Named a World Heritage Site by the United Nations in

1978, Quito's Centro Histórico will transport you back and forth between centuries as you meander down its cobblestone streets and pedestrian walkways, passing by vendors selling everything from *choclo* (Andean corn) to DVDs. At the beginning of the 20th century, Quito fit within the boundaries of the Old Town. Today, it is just a small slice of Quito, but undoubtedly the sector richest in history. Some of Ecuador's most famous battles and executions took place in the plazas that now peacefully bustle with tourists, beggars, protesters and locals out for a stroll. Some of Quito's best bars and restaurants are in this area. Veer off from the guided tour and spend some quality time in the plazas and side streets that feature exquisite colonial architecture and winding pathways which open up into lovely courtyards.

Photo by Evan Centanni

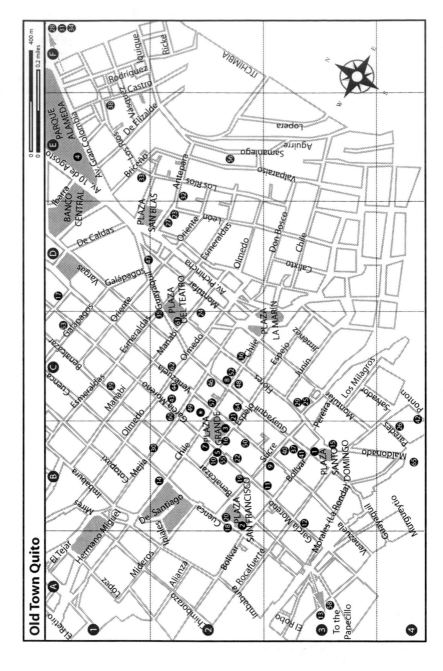

Old Town Quito

CITY PLAZAS   ⊗
1. (B3) PLAZA SANTO DOMINGO
2. (B2) SAN FRANCISCO PLAZA
3. (B2) PLAZA GRANDE (DE LA INDEPENDENCIA)

PARKS   ⬥
4. (E1) PARQUE LA ALAMEDA

MUSEUMS AND MONUMENTS   ⓘ
5. (B2) MUSEO ALBERTO MENA CAAMAÑO
6.*(C2) EL PALACIO ARZOBISPAL
7. (B2) PALACIO DEL GOBIERNO
8. (C2) SAN AGUSTÍN
9. (B3) MUSEO CASA DE SUCRE
10. (B2) CENTRO CULTURAL METROPOLITANO
11. (B3) CASA MUSEO MARÍA AUGUSTA URRUTIA
12. (B3) MUSEO DE LA CIUDAD
13. (A3) EL PANECILLO

CHURCHES AND CATHEDRALS   ⬥
14. (B2) IGLESIA DE LA MERCED
15. (B3) IGLESIA Y MUSEO DE SANTO DOMINGO
16. (B2) IGLESIA DE LA CATEDRAL
17. (D1) LA BASÍLICA DEL VOTO NACIONAL
18. (B2) MONASTERIO DE SAN FRANCISCO
19. (B2) LA COMPAÑÍA

SHOPPING   ⊞
20. (B2) TIANGUEZ GIFT SHOP & CAFÉ

INFORMATION AND ACTIVITES   ⓘ
21. (C2) TOURIST INFORMATION CENTER
22. (B2) HORSE DRAWN CARRIAGE TOURS

LODGING   ⊖
23. (D2) HOSTAL BELMONT
24. (C2) HOTEL DE LA CASONA
25. (C3) HOSTAL RESIDENCIAL MONTÚFAR
26. (B4) LA POSADA COLONIAL
27. (D2) HOSTAL OASIS
28. (F1) CASA BAMBÚ
29. (C3) HOTEL HUASI CONTINENTAL
30. (B2) HOTEL CATEDRAL INTERNACIONAL
31. (F1) HOSTAL 'LOS CHASQUIS'
32. (E2) THE SECRET GARDEN
33. (E1) CHICAGO HOSTEL AND PUB
34. (F1) L'AUBERGE INN HOSTAL
35. (C2) HOTEL INTERNACIONAL PLAZA DEL TEATRO
36. (C2) HOTEL VIENA INTERNACIONAL
37. (B3) PUERTA DEL SOL
38. (E1) HOSTEL REVOLUTION
39 (C1).- VILLA COLONNA BED & BREAKFAST
40 (B2).- HOTEL SAN FRANCISCO
41 (B3).- HOTEL REAL AUDIENCIA
42 (C4).- GRAND HOTEL

43. (C2) PATIO ANDALUZ
44. (C2) HOTEL EL RELICARIO DEL CARMEN

RESTAURANTS   ⑪
45.*(C2) BAR TEMPLO
46. (C2) HELADERÍA SAN AGUSTIN
47. (D1) CAFETERÍA Y FRUTERÍA COLONIAL
48. (C2) CARAVANA
49. (C2) CAFE MIRADOR VISTA HERMOSA
50. (B2) CAFETERIA CARMITA
51.*(C2) CAFÉ DE FRAILE
52. (C2) CAFETO COFFEE HOUSE
53. (C1) LA CASA DE LA PEÑA
54.*(C2) HASTA LA VUELTA SEÑOR
55. (B2) EL BUHO CAFÉ BAR
56. (E2) CAFÉ MOSAICO
57. (C2) LA CUEVA DEL OSO
58. (A4) PIM'S
59.*(C2) MEA CULPA
60. (C2) EL PATIO TRATTORIA
61. (C2) THEATRUM RESTAURANT

INTERNET CAFES   @
62.*(C2) PAPAYA NET
63.*(C2) KANTUÑ@ NET
64. (C2) STOP 'N' SURF

TRANSPORT   ⊡
65. (B4) CUMANDÁ BUS TERMINAL

* ARE LOCATED AT THE POINT MARKED
WITH AN ASTERISK ON THE MAP

QUITO

SAFETY

Once considered dangerous, the Centro has drastically changed over the last five years, thanks mainly to the current mayor, Paco Moncayo. Sidewalk vendors are banned, many of the facades have been repainted, and the Trole and Ecovía have cut down on bus traffic and fumes. Most importantly, the police are a strong presence deterring pickpockets and other criminals. As with all places, be cautious and discreet, as the streets do quickly fill with people.

THINGS TO SEE & DO

Quito's Centro Histórico takes you back to the era of the Spanish Empire, with its beautiful colonial buildings and elaborate churches. There are also several interesting museums in this area that house colonial and indigenous art, military memorabilia and relics that chart the country's checkered history from pre-Inca times to the present.

CITY PLAZAS

PLAZA SANTO DOMINGO (GUAYAQUIL & BOLÍVAR)

Towards the south of the city, the wide open Plaza Santo Domingo is dominated by the Iglesia de Santo Domingo on the southeastern edge, and statue of marshal Mariscal Sucre in the centre, his arm outstretched to the Pichincha Volcanoes where he led the winning battle for Ecuador's independence in 1822. Being slightly out of the way of the main attractions in the Centro Histórico, many tourists miss the plaza altogether. This is a shame, as its certainly worth at least a quick detour, especially on weekends when hundreds of *quiteños* congregate here to be entertained by storytellers, jugglers, acrobats and magicians. Unfortunately this area is a prime target for muggers in the evenings. If you want to see the domes of the church lit up, it's advisable to go with a group of people or get a taxi to take you there and wait for you.

PLAZA SAN FRANCISCO (CUENCA & BOLÍVAR)

Backed by the magnificent white edifice of the Monastery of San Francisco and behind it the towering peak of Volcán Pichincha, the cobbled Plaza de San Francisco is one of Quito's oldest and most impressive sights. Located where the palace of the Inca ruler Atahualpa's son, Auqui Francisco Tupatauchi, once stood, the plaza was used for centuries by indigenous groups as a trading center, or *tianguez*. The plaza and church that you can visit today were built between 1536 and 1580. Built on a slight incline, it also affords fine views over the rooftops of southern Quito, and it is easy to pass an hour or two taking in the view and watching the ever present throng of strolling quiteño families, wide-eyed tourists, shoe-cleaning kids and thousands of pigeons passing you by. The Café Tianguez in the northern corner of the square is a good place to park yourself for this purpose, as it just happens to offer comfortable seating and good coffee. It's expensive by Quito standards, but you pay for the location.

PLAZA DE LA INDEPENDENCIA (GARCÍA MORENO & CHILE)

Slap bang in the middle of the Centro Histórico, you'll probably find yourself in the majestic Plaza de la Independencia (Plaza Grande) even when you're not looking for it. It's as much a local hangout as a tourist hot spot, and is always buzzing with life, regardless of the time or the weather. You could comfortably spend half a day here, exploring the attractions around the edges of the Plaza. On the southwestern side is the 19th century Iglesia de la Cathedral, and opposite it, the Palacio Arzobispal (Archbishop's Palace). The building on the northwestern side of the plaza above the row of arched, hole-in-the-wall shops is the Palacio del Gobierno (Presidential Palace). On the corner between the presidential palace and the cathedral is the Centro Cultural Metropolitano, and inside it the Museo Alberto Meno Caamaño.

PARKS

PARQUE LA ALAMEDA

Between the Centro Histórico and the modern part of Quito to the north, the small triangular Parque Alameda is the closest open space to the Centro Histórico, and therefore one of the busiest in the city. The grassy banks of the boating lake are particularly popular with picnicking families during the weekends, while other spaces are taken up with various ball games and smooching teenage couples escaping their parents for the day. Scores of food vendors make their way around the park with carts of ice cream, hot dogs, candy and the like. In the middle of the park is the Quito Observatory, which is open to the public on weekdays and still houses a German telescope, reputedly once among the most advanced in the world—it can no longer claim this title. The park is fine during the day, but don't hang around after dusk.

MUSEUMS AND MONUMENTS
MUSEO ALBERTO MENA CAAMAÑO
Hidden up some stairs at the back of the Centro Cultural Metropolitano with no signs in sight, this museum can be tricky to find. Formerly known as the Antiguo Cuartel de la Real Audiencia thanks to its former function as *cuartel* (army barracks), the museum underwent a large-scale expansion and refurbishment in 2002 and was subsequently renamed after its biggest donor, Alberto Mena Caamaño. He bequeathed his impressive collection of painting and sculpture to the museum in the 1950s, most of which is colonial art from the 16th and 17th centuries, attributed to well known artists from the Quito School, including Miguel de Santiago and Joaquín Pinto. However, there are several more modern works as well. Open Tuesday - Sunday, 9 a.m. - 5 p.m. Closed Monday. Centro Cultural Metropolitano, García Moreno and Espejo (Plaza de la Independencia), Tel: 593-2-258-4363, Fax: 593-2-258-4363, E-mail: info@centrocultural-quito.com, URL: www.centrocultural-quito.com.

EL PALACIO ARZOBISPAL (THE ARCHBISHOP'S PALACE)
Opposite the cathedral in the Plaza Grande, the former Palacio Arzobispal (Archbishop's Palace) now houses a row of shops, ranging from delicatessens to clothes stores. During the last few years, the central courtyard of the palace with its whitewashed walls and wooden balconies has been converted into a food court offering everything from a quick burger to first class dining. One of Quito's most famous restaurants, Mea Culpa overlooks the plaza from its first floor location, and is a great place for a splurge (for more information on the eateries inside the palace, see restaurant reviews). On Friday evenings, locals pour into the courtyard to watch the free performances of dancing and singing. Avenida Chile and García Moreno.

PALACIO DEL GOBIERNO (PRESIDENTIAL PALACE)
The building on the northwestern side of the Plaza Grande above the row of arched, hole-in-the-wall shops is the Palacio del Gobierno. Only the entrance area is open to the public. It's worth a peek, although there's nothing particularly outstanding about it apart from a mural by one of Ecuador's most famous artists, Guayasamín. You can get a glimpse of it in the stairwell behind the guards. It illustrates Francisco de Orellana's celebrated descent of the Amazon. It's open only when the president is not in residence. Open Monday - Friday, 9 a.m. - noon and 3 p.m. - 5 p.m. Avenida Chile between Venezuela and García Moreno.

SAN AGUSTÍN - MUSEUM AND MONASTERY (ENTRANCE: $1)
Just a couple of blocks down Guayaquil from the Plaza de la Independencia, the San Agustín Monastery and Museum is a nice stop if you are touring churches in the Centro Histórico. Admission is only $1. Venezuela 573 and Sucre, Tel: 593-2-295-1001, URL: www.quito.gov.ec/turismo/t_museo_h_agustin.htm.

MUSEO CASA DE SUCRE (ENTRANCE: $0.25-1)
The Casa de Sucre, or Sucre residence, is a museum located in the old home of Mariscal José Antonio de Sucre, one of the greatest heroes of Ecuadorian independence. The ground floor houses an impressive array of weapons and military relics, some of which belonged to Sucre himself. The second floor has been restored to what it might have looked like in Sucre's time. Venezuela No. 573 and Sucre, Tel: 593-2-295-2860.

CENTRO CULTURAL METROPOLITANO
Tuesday to Sunday 9:00 a.m. - 5:00 p.m. Closed Monday. García Moreno and Espejo (Plaza de la Independencia), Tel: 593-2-258-4363, Fax: 593-2-2584362, E-mail: info@centrocultural-quito.com, URL: www.centrocultural-quito.com.

QUITO

CASA MUSEO MARÍA AUGUSTA URRUTIA

Once the home of Quito's best known philanthropist, this museum is now dedicated to María Augusta's life and work: helping Quito's street children—for whom she was always, famously, making ice cream. The downstairs rooms are set up like a museum, with portraits of María Augusta and her family, some of her personal diaries and letters and numerous appliances used in the house throughout her life, such as an early refrigerator and washing machine. Some of the upstairs rooms have been preserved pretty much as they were when she died in 1987, offering a more detailed and somewhat personal insight into the way she lived; the comb she used each morning, what she ate for breakfast and the clothes she wore, giving a good impression of how upper class quiteños lived in the mid 1900s. María Augusta was a collector of art, and there are some interesting paintings and sculptures around the house, from colonial to contemporary. In particular, she was a great fan of painter Victor Mideros, and the house features what is probably the biggest collection of his work in the city. Open Tuesday - Sunday, 10 a.m. - 6 a.m. Closed Monday. García Moreno N2-60, between Sucre and Bolívar, Tel: 593-2-285-0103, E-mail: cmmau@fmjd.org, URL: www.casamuseomaurrutia.org.ec.

MUSEO DE LA CIUDAD

Housed in a spacious and attractively restored old hospital building just east of Plaza de Santo Domingo, the Museo de la Ciudad is certainly worth a visit, and a good starting point if you are new to Quito and unfamiliar with its history. Two floors of models, interactive displays and memorabilia—from horse-drawn carriages to 17th century pots and pans—map out Quito's checkered past, century-by-century, in clear, uncluttered displays. Beside each one is a written explanation in Spanish; if you don't read Spanish, a guided tour is recommended, and these are available in English, French, German, Italian and Spanish for an extra $4. Another draw of the museum is the central courtyard, offering a welcome respite from the bustle of Quito's city center, and fantastic views over southern Quito and the Panecillo. The well-priced café looks onto the courtyard, and is open to the general public as well as museum-visitors. Open Tuesday - Sunday, 9 a.m. - 5:30 p.m. Garcia Moreno 572 and Rocafuerte, Tel: 593-2-228-3882, E-mail: museociu@museociudadquito.gov.ec, URL: www.museociudadquito.gov.ec.

EL PANECILLO (ENTRANCE: $1)

El Panecillo, or to use the Inca name, Yavirac, is a lush green hill visible from many different points in Quito. La Virgen del Panecillo, the winged virgin sitting atop the hill is essentially the main religious symbol of Quito. As a result, when visiting the monument, guides tend to quote scriptures as opposed to emphasizing historical or structural facts. The view is incredible, especially on a clear day, so even if aren't interested in listening to a recital of Revelations 12, you will enjoy the trip. The best way to get there is by cab. From the Centro Histórico, you shouldn't pay much more than $5. Alternatively, you can arrange a tour that includes a trip to the Panecillo at any travel agency. The bus that goes up to the Panecillo is the southern stop for green bus to Mitad del Mundo. Be careful at the bottom of the hill on the roads leading up the Panecillo as there have been reports of mugging. It's open Monday - Sunday, 9 a.m. - 6 a.m. Palestina, General Melchor Aymerich, Cima del Panecillo.

CHURCHES AND CATHEDRALS

IGLESIA DE LA MERCED

With its plain white exterior, handsome bell tower (the highest in Colonial Quito) and tiled domes, the church of La Merced is a good example of the Moorish influences in Spanish architecture in the late 18th century, and a pleasure to stumble upon while exploring the back-streets of Colonial Quito. The rather conservative-looking exterior, however, does little to prepare you for what is inside: a sea of pink and white plasterwork covering every surface providing the backdrop for surely some of the most imaginative and dramatic paintings in Quito. Bleeding, neon-lit, representations of Jesus occupy shiny gold side chapels around the edge. Not to everyone's taste, but certainly worth a look if you're passing by. Open daily, 7 a.m. - noon, 2 p.m. - 7 p.m. Chile and Cuenca.

IGLESIA Y MUSEO DE SANTO DOMINGO (MUSEUM: $0.25-1.50)

The Iglesia de Santo Domingo may at first seem like one of those churches that is far more impressive from the outside. However, step into its dimly lit, moody interior and you'll find some surprising treasures. There are numerous paintings from the Quito School hanging in its side chapels, one of which also houses the church's showpiece: a statue of the *virgen de Rosario*, given by King Charles V of Spain. Unfortunately, the tower, which gives great views over Quito, is now unsafe to climb and will be closed for the foreseeable future until funds are raised to restore it. The museum is also worth a visit, housing an interesting collection of 16th and 17th century religious art around an intimate courtyard. The entrance is about 15 meters to the left of the main church door. Museum open Monday - Friday, 9 a.m. - noon and 1:30 p.m. - 5 p.m. Church open 7 a.m.-12:30 p.m. and 5 p.m. - 7:30 p.m. Flores 150 between Rocafuerte and Pereira.

IGLESIA DE LA CATEDRAL
On the southwestern side of the Plaza de la Independencia (Plaza Grande) is the Iglesia de la Cathedral. It is unusual in Ecuador, in that it is refreshingly free of the head-to-toe decoration that adorns most churches, although it does feature several interesting paintings by artists of the Quito School. Although it is considered relatively austere by Ecuadorian standards, the 16th century cathedral is probably the most important church in Ecuador, and the location for state funerals of the country's political and cultural heroes. It is here that Quito's liberator, Mariscal Sucre, is buried. Open Monday - Friday, 10 a.m. - 4 p.m., Saturday, 10 a.m. - 2 p.m. Plaza de la Independencia.

LA BASÍLICA DEL VOTO NACIONAL (ENTRANCE: $2)
A relatively new addition to the Quito skyline (and now one of its most striking landmarks) is the Basílica del Voto Nacional, or simply the Basílica. Consecrated in 1988 (though still technically unfinished) the church stands on a steep hill to the northeast of the Centro Histórico and can be seen from almost everywhere in the city, particularly at night when it is illuminated, beacon-like, in bright greens and blues. The highlight of a visit here is undoubtedly the climb up the tower, which offers several vantage points along the way. The first flight of stone stairs leads to a balcony where you can look down on the nave, its stone arches mottled in the bright colors of the stained glass windows. The second flight leads up to a southern viewpoint with a telescope, offering a close-up inspection of some of the old towns other landmarks, including the Virgen perched on the Panecillo. From here you have to negotiate a tenuous-looking (though perfectly safe) causeway and exposed iron ladder to get to the top. Anyone fearful of heights, would be well-advised to stick to the first floor, as the climb up may be a bit daunting if you suffer from even the slightest vertigo. If you can manage it, however, you will be rewarded with excellent views that, on a clear day, stretch for miles over both the new and old parts of the city—something even the Panecillo can't claim. Open daily, 9 a.m - 5 p.m. Carchi and Venezuela.

The Basilica del Voto Nacional may not have the splendid gold or fresco-clad interior of other churches in Quito, but it's a favorite with daring travellers, who scale its grey and rough-hewn heights for the best views of Ecuador's capital. The journey begins at a wheel-shaped window of radiant stained-glass roses in the clerestory, the mezzanine that overlooks the church's main body. Corkscrew stairs lead to views of the Basilica's gargoyles, which on closer inspection are ominous models of Ecuador's fauna, including condors, monkeys and jaguars. In defiance of all notions of occupational health and safety, a trembling gang-plank and iron ladder deliver hot and dirty climbers to their final destination—the rose-bud encrusted bell tower.

Most clang the Basilica's four bells before enjoying their reward—90-meter high views that soar from the statuesque Virgin of Quito south of the city's colonial Old Town over faded terraces and modern skyscrapers to the far northern suburbs, a 360-degree spectacle offered by no other location.
- excerpt, V!VA List Latin America 2007, Kathleen Fisher, Australia.

QUITO

MONASTERIO DE SAN FRANCISCO
The bored-looking stone chap in the northern corner of the Plaza de San Francisco is Franciscan missionary Joedco Ricke, who set to work in the Monastery de San Francisco soon after the foundation of Quito in 1534. It took his team 70 years to complete, but it remains Quito's largest colonial structure, although much of it has been destroyed and rebuilt over the years. However, its gold interior retains its grand and imposing feel, and it's certainly worth a visit, especially since admission is free. Some of the Monastery's most precious and delicate relics have been re-housed in the Museo Franciscano. Open Monday - Saturday, 9 a.m. - 6 p.m., Sunday, 9 a.m. - 1 p.m. Cuenca 477 and Sucre in La Plaza de San Francisco. Tel: 593-2-228-1124/593-2-228 2545

LA COMPAÑÍA (ENTRANCE: $1)
Carved entirely out of volcanic stone, the ornate Baroque façade of this Jesuit church is probably the most exquisitely executed in Quito. From the arresting outside, walk inside and you'll be awed by the sculptured interior, shimmering beneath fifty kilograms of gold leaf. A stunning display of art and architecture, appointed with a community of cherubs, angels and saints, keeps the eyes busy as the feet shuffle between the skyward stretching Corinthian pillars, soaring arches and carefully decorated cornices. Jesuits began work on the church in 1605, but the structure wasn't complete until 1765 (a lucky coincidence considering the Spanish expelled the order just two years later). Today, some of the most important, and impressive artifacts to grace the interior are housed in the vaults of the Banco Central; one such piece is the emerald-framed painting of the Virgin Dolorosa. Monday - Saturday, 10 a.m. - 1 p.m., Monday - Friday 2 p.m. - 5 p.m. Calle García Moreno, one block south of Plaza de la Independencia. Free tours on the first Sunday of each month, 1:30-4:30 p.m.

SHOPPING
TIANGUEZ GIFT SHOP
The Tianguez Gift Shop supports the entrepreneurial spirit of Ecuador. There are handmade crafts from around 350 groups and individuals in the country; from Panama Hats (which unlike their name suggests, are made in Southern Ecuador) to blow guns, pre-Columbian ceramics, tapestries and Tigua paintings. Those noble souls who aspire to pay fair prices to the original artists will find the prices here higher than most outdoor markets, however the variety and quality is exceptional. Open daily 9:30 a.m. - 6:30 p.m. Plaza de San Francisco, below the church, Tel: 593-2-295-4326, E-mail: tianguez@andinanet.net, URL: www.sinchisacha.org.

INFORMATION AND ACTIVITIES
TOURIST INFORMATION CENTER
These are excellent spots to pick up detailed maps, get tour information and shop for overpriced crafts. The staff will help orient you, give directions, maps, and recommend restaurants, information on churches and museums, transportation information and even make your flight confirmations. The main center has one computer which they let tourists use for free, though they discourage lingering by not offering you a chair. Open Monday - Saturday, 9 a.m. - 6 p.m., Sunday, 9 a.m. - 4 p.m. Venezuela and Espejo, diagonal from the Cathedral on the Plaza Grande. There is also a kiosk of Plaza San Francisco, Espejo and Benalcázar.

HORSEDRAWN CARRIAGE TOURS
What better way to enjoy the colonial center of Quito than in the preferred method of transportation of a century ago, a horse and cart! Quito's colonial founders would be surprised to hop into one of these carriages as soon as the MP3 player starts bumping, the headlights flick on and the high-tech brakes kick in. The tour is about 15 minutes long and runs from the Plaza de la Independencia (Plaza Grande) to the Plaza de San Francisco and back. Go after dark when the cathedrals are lit up, traffic is less horrendous, and the cool breeze will require snuggling to stay warm. Open Monday - Wednesday, 4 p.m. - 10:30 p.m., Thursday - Friday 4:30 p.m. - midnight, Saturday, noon - midnight, Sunday, 11 a.m. - 11 p.m. García Moreno between Espejo and Sucre.

CENTRO HISTÓRICO HOTELS

The hotels in the Centro Histórico are rapidly being renovated and becoming more popular as Quito tries to reestablish the Centro as the main tourist hub. There is still work to be done, and most hotels are based in the newer parts of Quito.

BUDGET

HOSTAL BELMONT ($3-4/PERSON)

This is one of the cheapest places in Old Quito, at around $3 per person for a room with shared bathroom. This hostal is in desperate need of a paint job and most of the rooms are tiny, dark and damp. However, before you completely rule it out, check out a couple of rooms, some are better than others. The family that runs the place is friendly and lets guests use the kitchen and TV room. There are discounts for extended stays and many travelers take advantage of this, so be sure to negotiate if you are planning a longer trip in Quito. Price per person, including tax, is $3 for shared bathroom and $4 with a private bath. Anteparra 413 and Vicente Leon, Tel: 593-2-295-6235, E-mail: hbelmonte@waccom.net.ec.

HOSTAL MONTÚFAR ($4/PERSON)

This place is an excellent value for your money, especially for single travelers. The rooms are clean and safe, although very run-down, and the mattresses are a bit saggy. Some rooms are much better—bigger and with more light—than others, so ask to see a few before settling in. All have color television and private bathrooms with hot water. Be careful when leaving the hotel, and don't walk back late at night. The management can call you a taxi if you plan to leave after dark. Sucre 160 and Flores, Centro Histórico, Tel: 593-2-228-4644.

HOSTAL OASIS ($4-5/PERSON)

Owned by the same family that runs the big Chinese restaurant downstairs, Hostal Oasis is brand new and spotlessly clean, with modern bathrooms and 24-hour hot water. The rooms are spartan with just a bed, chair and nightstand. The best rooms overlook the street; they are light and airy and provide excellent people-watching. If you're not put off by the likelihood that you'll probably be the only person there, Hostal Oasis is a great value choice, especially if you're traveling alone. Anteparra E3-34 and Pedro Fermín Caballos, Tel: 593-2-316-0664.

CASA BAMBU ($4-7/PERSON, MONTHLY RENTALS: $100-150)

Casa Bambu is one of Quito's best value options, with clean dorm rooms at $4/person and private rooms at $7. This small hotel is full of character and homey touches. The lounges are spacious and full of comfy couches, flowering plants, a collection of books, games and DVDs and several outdoor patios provide excellent views of Quito. We recommend you take a cab when you first arrive, the hotel is located up a steep hill not conducive to luggage. It's just a block from several main bus lines, so transportation isn't a problem once you stash the heavy stuff. Solano 17 58 and Av. Colombia (up a steep hill from the southernmost corner of Parque el Ejido), Tel: 593-2-222-6738.

HOTEL HUASI CONTINENTAL ($4.50-9/PERSON)

This is a friendly, secure hotel in a dodgy area. The rooms are clean, but some are pretty small, and offer good value for your money. Some rooms come with TV and private bath, some with TV and shared bath and some with neither. The restaurant is open for breakfast and lunch. If you are traveling with a group, you can make arrangements to have dinner served as well. Because the area is not the best, be careful with valuables, especially when leaving the hotel. They offer a safe-deposit for guests. Discounts are given for groups of two people or more, so be sure to negotiate a bit. Calle Flores 332 and Sucre, Tel: 593-2-295-7327, Fax: 593-2-295-6335.

HOSTEL REVOLUTION QUITO (ROOMS: $5-14)

Hostel Revolution Quito is a cool new hostel in Historical Quito. Created by and for backpackers who want to socialize, take in the historical sights and culture, exchange info and go out and have a great time. Great location in a renovated colonial-type house with wooden floors and decorative plaster ceilings. Facilities include great bar, lounge, shared kitchen, new bathrooms, rooftop terrace with great views and internet. Los Rios N13-11 and Julio Castro, Tel: 593-2-254-6458, URL: www.hostelrevolutionquito.com.

> *V!VA Member Review-Hostel Revolution Quito*
> *Excellent value. Everything new, owner Matt will go out of his way to help. Highly recommend it. Fun place, with bar, net, etc. 16 March 2007. Germany.*

GRAND HOTEL ($4.50-16.50/PERSON)

This family-run hotel is popular with backpackers and justly so: the staff bend over backwards to help their guests and offer personal service. The rooms are all spotlessly clean—although a few are in dire need of a paint job—and simply, but adequately, furnished. There is a living room downstairs with a TV, big sofas and chairs as well as a kitchen for guests to use.

There are plans for a roof terrace restaurant which will offer great views over the center of Quito and the Panecillo; but that probably won't take place for a couple of years. Rocafuerte 1001 and Pontón (Loma Grande), Tel: 593-2-228-0192, Fax: 593-2-295-8044, E-mail: grand-hotelquito1@hotmail.com, URL: www.geocities.com/grandhotelquito.

HOSTAL LOS CHASQUIS ($6/PERSON)

A run-down hotel in a busy neighborhood between La Mariscal and El Centro. The price is reasonable at $6/person, but the facilities don't offer any of the same style, personality and comfort of nearby hotels like Casa Bambu and L'Auberge Inn. Av. 12 de Octubre 338 and Tarqui, Tel: 593-2-222-4768, Fax: 593-9-798-5156.

HOTEL DE LA CASONA ($6/PERSON)

This hotel is situated right behind the northbound trolley stop, Plaza del Teatro. It boasts 22 rooms overlooking a quiet courtyard. All rooms have private bathrooms and some have televisions. There is a nice atmosphere, thanks to a friendly staff and a lack of international travelers. The hotel is very popular with Ecuadorians. A basic breakfast is provided in the somewhat spartan courtyard and the restaurant also churns out a good 60 fixed lunch menus daily. Manabí 255 and Flores, Plaza del Teatro, Tel: 593-2-257-0626.

HOTEL CATEDRAL INTERNACIONAL ($6-7/PERSON)

Apparently named due to its proximity to the cathedral, this hotel is on a busy street right in the center of the Centro Histórico. Its approximately 20 rooms are set around a leafy court-yard and all have private bathrooms and color televisions. There is a good restaurant down-stairs which is open from 8 a.m. - 21:30. Breakfast is not included in the price. Mejía 638, between Cuenca and Benalcázar, Tel: 593-2-299509527, Fax: 593-2-255-7890.

LA POSADA COLONIAL ($6-8/PERSON)

Set on a quiet street just east of Plaza Santo Domingo, this friendly hotel is spotlessly clean, and a great value for groups and single travelers alike. There's no restaurant, but there is a kitchen that guests can use. The staff is also good at recommending cheap eateries nearby. Some of the light, airy rooms have great views of the Panecillo—sensational at night. Paredes 188 and Rocafuerte, Tel: 593-2-228-2859, E-mail: giamm5@yahoo.com.

CHICAGO HOSTEL AND PUB ($6-9/PERSON)

A solid budget option located in Centro Histórico, just two blocks from the Secret Garden Hostal, and just a stone's throw away from historical sites like the Basílica and Plaza San Blas. Accommodation is simple but comfortable, and guests can enjoy the modern facilities infused with colonial warmth and charm. A communal kitchen is a great place to whip up a meal and chat with fellow travelers, but on nice days you may want to head up to the terrace, where you can catch some great city views while flipping burgers on the BBQ. The cheerful staff creates a welcoming family atmosphere. Rooms with shared bathrooms are cheaper. Calle Los Rios 1730-A and Briceno, San Blas, Tel: 593-2-228-0224, E-mail: chicagohostel_ecuador@hotmail.com, URL: www.chicagohostelquitoecuador.htmlplanet.com.

HOTEL INTERNACIONAL PLAZA DEL TEATRO ($7-10/PERSON)

This is a perfectly serviceable hotel ideally located for visiting Quito's Centro Histórico. The rooms, which all have private bathrooms and television, are clean and modern. Some have views over the Plaza del Teatro. However, these tend to be quite noisy so if you want quiet, ask for one in the back. The restaurant is open for breakfast and lunch. It has a very popular fixed lunch and is therefore packed between about noon and 2 p.m. Calle Guayaquil 8-75 and Esmeraldas (Esquina), Centro Histórico, Tel: 593-2-295-9462, Fax: 593-2-251-9462.

THE SECRET GARDEN ($7-20/PERSON)

Set in a converted colonial building in Quito's Centro Histórico district, the Secret Garden is a top VTG favorite. Its main selling points are the stunning view over the colonial district from the roof terrace restaurant/bar, and the friendly, laid-back atmosphere. Dinner is a particularly sociable occasion—there is a set menu option (always with a vegetarian alternative) and everyone eats together at a long table. The rooms are slightly more expensive than other hostels in the area, but it's worth it for the incredibly comfortable mattresses and real duvets. The Secret Garden can also arrange Spanish lessons—taken on the roof terrace. If you take a course of 40 hours, you get a free three-course meal. There are also regular day-trips to Cotopaxi from the hostel. Dinner is served daily at 7:30 p.m. and reservations are essential by 5 p.m. José Anteparra E4-60 and Los Rios, Tel: 593-2-295-6704, 593-2-316-0949, E-mail: hola@secretgardenquito.com, URL: www.secretgardenquito.com.

L'AUBERGE INN HOSTAL ($7-27/PERSON)

L'Auberge Inn Hostal (literally 'Inn Inn Inn' in French, English and Spanish) is located between the Centro Histórico and La Mariscal. Its a bit of an oasis in a fairly dumpy, trafficky area with its tranquil garden, delicious pizza parlor, and comfy lounge complete with games, a pool table and a fireplace. The rooms are basic, but clean. Most look out onto the common garden. The rooms with shared bath also share a threadbare carpet but are fine otherwise. If you make a reservation for L'Auberge at the information desk when you arrive at the airport, transportation is free to the hotel. Otherwise it is $6. Colombia 1138 and Yaguachi, Tel: 593-2-255-2912, Fax: 593-2-256-9886, E-mail: auberge@uio.satnet.net, URL: www.ioda.net/auberge-inn.

PUERTA DEL SOL (ROOMS: $10-18)

This hotel has clearly seen better days. It is not worth the starting price of $10 for a single. The rooms are large, but dark and musty. Many of the bathrooms need a makeover. However, it is very secure, centrally located and the owners are friendly enough. All rooms have televisions and private baths. Calle Guayaquil between Sucre and Bolívar, Tel: 593-2-228-4046.

HOTEL VIENA INTERNACIONAL ($12/PERSON)

This hotel is popular with Ecuadorian and foreign visitors alike. Though set in an old, colonial building, the interior is modern and clean. Rooms are fairly standard and look out onto the central patio. Some, however, are quite dark. All have private bathrooms with new, fully functioning fittings. The hotel is centrally located and provides a good launching point to seeing the major sights of Quito's historic center. The staff are friendly and willing to answer any queries. Calle Flores 600 and Chile Esquina (corner), Tel: 593-2-295-4860, E-mail: vienaint@interactive.net.ec.

CASA ORIENTE ($120/MONTH)

Casa Oriente is located between the Centro Histórico and La Mariscal about four blocks east of the southernmost end of 12 de Octubre on Yaguachi. Despite being a somewhat nondescript building, the inside is charming and homey. A common patio on the top floor offers excellent views, a big picnic table and common kitchen for residents. Designed for travelers planning extended stays in Quito—the owner won't rent out a room for less than a week—Casa Oriente is an excellent place to meet travelers from around the world. The rooms are basic. There is no refrigerator or oven, but a gas stove, sink and a few cabinets complete the kitchen. The mattresses are all good and linens are provided. Residents can use the computers after the cafe is closed to the public—until around midnight. Several pool tables, a ping-pong table, some arcade games and board games also make Casa Oriente a great home away from home.Yaguachi and Llona (about three blocks east of the southernmost end of 12 de Octubre on Yaguachi), Tel: 593-2-254-6457, Fax: 593-9-892-1496, E-mail: agrodelicias@yahoo.es.

Mid Range
Hotel San Francisco (Rooms: $22-60)
The Hotel San Francisco is an attractive colonial building right in the middle of Quito's Centro Histórico. It's tastefully decorated, spacious rooms have recently been renovated. There is a quiet interior courtyard overflowing with plants and black and white photos of 19th century Quito covering the walls. The friendly staff are always willing to help with travel advice and are on hand to answer questions from guests. The spa includes a sauna, steam room and jacuzzi. It is modern and clean and is available for guests' use at no extra charge. This hotel is great value for your money. Sucre 217 and Guayaquil (corner), Tel: 593-2-228-7758, Fax: 593-2-295-1241, E-mail: hotel@sanfranciscodequito.com.ec, URL: www.uio-guided.com/hsfquito.

Hotel Real Audiencia ($20-27/person)
Set just off the Plaza Santo Domingo, the Real Audiencia Hotel offers dusty but decent rooms and discounts for Ecuadorians. Transportation can be arranged from the airport for just $3 more than the regular room rate. Make arrangements with the hotel in advance. The highlight is the top-floor restaurant and bar with large windows looking out onto the Plaza Santo Domingo. The hotel makes an effort to work with the city to protect the historic buildings in the area, of which the hotel is one. Bolívar 220 Oe-3-18 and Guayaquil, Tel: 593-2-295-2711, E-mail: hotel@realaudiencia.com, URL: www.realaudiencia.com.

Luxury
Hotel El Relicario del Carmen (Rooms: $70-120)
A historic house dating back to 1705, El Relicario del Carmen has reopened its doors as a hotel with 18 comfortable rooms. It is beautifully renovated, with great emphasis on the original details and has many comforts, including a central air conditioning system. All the furniture is handmade by recognized Ecuadorian artisans and many original paintings decorate public and private areas. It is located a block away from the Plaza de la Independencia and very close to many historic monuments of Quito. There is also an exclusive dining room and coffee shop. Venezuela 1041 and Olmedo, Tel: 593-2-228 9120, 593-2-228-5917, Fax: 593-2-226 5764, E-mail: info@hotelrelicariocarmen.com, URL: www.hotelrelicariodelcarmen.com.

Patio Andaluz (Rooms: $80-100)
Patio Andaluz is located in the heart of the Centro Histórico in a 400+ year-old house that was once owned by the first president of Ecuador, Juan José Flores. The hotel was renovated in December 2003 but retains its classic colonial style. It is a harmonious combination of colonial Quito and modern luxuries you will appreciate. The rooms are beautiful, with hardwood floors and views onto the courtyard. Play chess on handcrafted tables overlooking the courtyard, relax in the hammocks, read magazines and books in English and Spanish in the peaceful Guayasamín Lounge, or spend your free time in the sauna and fitness room. Some guests have complained about the lack of ventilation as the only windows look out onto an indoor courtyard. There is also an on-site restaurant and gift shop with local artesian crafts. Ask about package deals, including all your meals and Centro tours, including featured museums. Av. García Moreno N6-52 between Olmedo and Mejía, Tel: 593-2-228-0830, Fax: 593-2-228-8690, E-mail: cialcotel@hotelpatioandaluz.com, URL: www.hotelpatioandaluz.com.

Villa Colonna Bed and Breakfast (Rooms: $150-200)
This boutique bed and breakfast offers six beautiful suites with fireplaces, large bathrooms, and a tasteful decor, as well as wireless internet connection, e-mail and cell phones with a

complimentary phone card included. Walking distance from all major attractions in this area. The gourmet breakfast is a marvelous array of fresh international flavors from tropical Ecuador. Benalcazar 1128 and Esmeraldas, Tel: 593-2-295-5805, Fax: 593-2-295-5805, E-mail: info@villacolonna.ec, URL: www.villacolonna.ec.

HOTEL PLAZA GRANDE (ROOMS: $500-$2000)
Located in the heart of Quito's Old Town and just 20 minutes from the Mariscal Sucre airport, Hotel Plaza Grande is surrounded by fascinating historical sights, including the presidential palace. This luxury hotel offers 15 suites including Royal, Plaza View and Presidential. All rooms have air conditioning, VIP treatment and many additional premium amenities. Other services include 24 hour room service, spa and fitness facilities and meeting facilities. Fine dining is available at three restaurants as well as a variety of entertainment. Prices do not include tax and service. Calle García Moreno N5-16 y Chile. Tel: 593-2-256-6497, Fax: 593-2-251-0800, E-mail: contactus@plazagrandequito.com, URL: www.plazagrandequito.com.

CENTRO HISTÓRICO RESTAURANTS, CAFÉS AND BARS
The Centro Histórico offers everything from elegant restaurants with live music every night, dress codes and waiters in tuxedos to diners where a lunch is $1. In the last few years, several international restaurants have opened, especially in the area around the Plaza de la Independencia (Plaza Grande).

BUDGET
CAFETERÍA Y FRUTERÍA COLONIAL (ENTREES: $1-1.40)
Proof that there are Ecuadorian hippies outside of Montañita, Cafetería y Frutería Colonial is more psychedelic than colonial. The café is just north of the Plaza del Teatro. This café will be a breath of fresh air for vegetarians tired of oily lettuce and rice for every meal. Vegetarian dishes are from $1 -1.40. The menu also features a selection of sandwiches, breakfast platters and let's not forget, incense! Open daily, 7 a.m. - 5:30 p.m., Guayaquil 11-32 and Oriente.

CAFETO (ENTREES: $1-5)
A prime spot to grab a cup of java and people watch, Cafeto Coffee House is also probably one of the only real coffee shops in the area—it even has its own coffee philosophy. Reasonable prices and great music only add to the already delicious atmosphere. Highly recommended. Monday - Saturday, 7 a.m. - 8 p.m., Sunday, 7 a.m. - 1 p.m. Chile 930 and Guayaquil, E-mail: quito@elcafeto.com, URL: www.elcafeto.com.

CARAVANA (ENTREES: $2-3)
The fanciest fast-food restaurant for miles, Caravana is basically a glorified stand set in a lovely colonial courtyard with a small fountain. The elegant atmosphere makes you forget you're eating a $2 combo meal. This is quick, cheap food in a spot with great atmosphere. Carvana offers chicken platters and burger combos and instant Nescafé. Centro Comercial la Internacional, Guayaquil and Chile.

BAR TEMPLO (ENTREES: $1-6)
Bar Templo has windows looking out onto one of Quito's most famous plazas and a dark, cozy atmosphere inside. The atmosphere doesn't receive a full five stars because of the strange use of office-style chairs at the tables. With a wide range in food from traditional dishes from $1-1.50 to filet mignon for $5.50 and an extensive mixed drinks selection; you are bound to find something of interest here. Try the blended juices, which come in many creative combinations and a glass so tall you will have to stretch to reach the straw. The service leaves much to be desired, although they are certainly friendly. The staff is mostly young college students who seem more interested in chatting at the bar than attending customers. Sit back and relax—the atmosphere and drink selection make it all worthwhile. Open daily, 9 a.m. - 11 p.m. Chile 422 and Venezuela, Tel: 593-2-251-2532.

CAFÉ DE FRAILE (ENTREES: $3-5)

Café de Fraile is in the Edificio Arzobispal right in the Plaza de la Independencia. You can't beat the intimate setting. There is courtyard seating on the second floor balcony. The setting and dress is casual. The food at Café de Fraile is really nothing more than small, overpriced and not especially tasty appetizers and sandwiches to accompany a cocktail. Chile 422 and Venezuela.

HELADERÍA SAN AGUSTIN (ENTREES: $3-5)

Featuring the delicious *helados de paila*, *ceviche*, traditional food and pastries, the Heladería San Agustín has been making the same excellent dishes for about 146 years and has never used preservatives or artificial coloring. You can't leave without trying the helado de paila (ice cream that tastes more like sorbet). Heladería San Agustín has been in the same family for six generations—since 1858. The owner is almost always on-site and will happily recommend her favorite dishes or tell you some of Quito's history, as seen from the doorway of this classic cafe. Monday - Friday, 9 a.m. - 6 p.m., Saturday, 9 a.m. - 4 p.m., Sunday, 10 a.m. - 3 p.m. Guayaquil 153 and Mejía, Tel: 593-2-228-5082, E-mail: artemaniaandres@yahoo.com.

CAFETERÍA CARMITA (ENTREES; $3-6)

A cafeteria you could easily walk by without a second glance, Cafetería Carmita has a little more than meets the eye, but not much. For one, it has been around for over 30 years. It seems older, with fading photos of Quito and Guayaquil from the early 20th century. It has traditional dishes and desserts from around Ecuador at decent prices. The hygiene of the food is questionable, but it's definitely authentic. For a very traditional platter of *mote* (white Andean corn) with your choice of meat, *pillo* (lard) or *chicharron* (fried pork skin) this is the spot for you. There are also Chilean empanadas with either chicken or meat and sandwiches all for right around $1. Monday - Saturday, 7:30 a.m. - 7:30 p.m. Venezuela 737 and Espejo (just southwest of the Plaza de la Independencia), Tel: 593-2-221-8695.

MID-RANGE
TIANGUEZ CAFÉ (ENTREES: $4-8)
Tianguez features some of the best traditional Ecuadorian dishes. This is a great spot to try out some of the dishes you might hesitate to eat otherwise because of sanitary concerns. Try the Plato Típico, with mote, *maduro frito* (fried plantain), *llapingacho* (a type of cheesy potato pancake), fresh avocado, lettuce and tomato and your choice of chicken or *fritada* (fried pork bits). Set right in the Plaza de San Francisco, this is the perfect spot to try out some traditional Ecuadorian dishes in one of the most traditional colonial plazas in the old town. Its also a great place to relax, sip a cappuccino and people watch. The restaurant—which is also connected to a small gift shop/museum in a cave-like structure underneath the church—is named after the Nahuatl word for market. Before the Spanish arrived, the plaza was used as a market for tribes from all over Ecuador. When the Spanish constructed the church between 1536 and 1580 over the ruins of an Inca palace, the market continued for centuries more. Today, besides the items for sale at the Tianguez café and gift shop, pretty much the only wares for purchase are shoe shines and newspapers. Open daily, 9:30 a.m. - 6:30 p.m. Plaza de San Francisco, under the church, Tel: 593-2-295-4326, 593-2-252-7240, E-mail: tianguez@andinanet.net.

LA CASA DE LA PEÑA (ENTREES: $5-10)
Located in a 400-year-old building, La Casa de la Peña is full of quiteño culture, history and views. Diagonal from the Basílica and with views from the many patios, Casa de la Peña features rotating art and poetry exhibits, live music and poetry readings on Thursday-Saturday nights and holidays. Try the *canelazo*, a typical hot alcoholic beverage served in a wooden pitcher. There is also a wide selection of coffees, drinks, appetizers and sandwiches. There are comfy couches, a fireplace and blankets to stay warm in this drafty old gem of a house and cultural center. Thursday - Saturday, 8 p.m. - 1 a.m. García Moreno 17-13 and Galápagos, Tel: 593-9-972-1652, E-mail: theatrum@andinanet.com.

CAFÉ MIRADOR/VISTA HERMOSA (ENTREES: $5-12)
Two restaurants in one: one with romantic roof terrace seating and a spectacular 360-degree view of Quito. Enjoy a warm canelazo or hot wine while gazing out over the colonial building tops of El Centro. A simple but slightly pricey (you pay for the locale) menu features several Ecuadorian plates, pizza and a full bar list. Mejía 453 and Garcia Moreno, Tel: 593-2-295-1401.

EL BUHO CAFÉ BAR (ENTREES: $6-12)
Set in the Centro Cultural Metropolitano with views onto the enclosed courtyard, El Buho provides a fun, relaxing break from the rigors of sightseeing. After your meal, don't miss a view of the Plaza de la Independencia and surrounding area from the roof of the museum. Just climb the stairs by the entrance to El Buho to the third floor. El Buho has a wide variety of international and local favorites, from BBQ ribs to empanadas. Happy Hour drinks are two-for-one from Monday - Wednesday, 4 p.m. - 9 p.m. Open Monday - Wednesday, 11 a.m. - 6 p.m., Thursday - Saturday, 11 a.m. - 10 p.m., Sunday, 11 a.m. - 5 p.m. García Moreno and Pasaje Espejo, Tel: 593-2-228-9877.

CAFÉ MOSAICO (ENTREES: $7-18)
Ecuador goes international in this lively, well-appointed cafe and restaurant perched high above the city. Besides the atmosphere, Cafe Mosaico offers an extensive menu: from American sandwiches and burgers to more elaborate dishes from Greece (the feta cheese is authentic!) and Ecuador, this place has the inter-continental cuisine pretty much covered. And don't forget to try the New York cheesecake (if there's room, that is). Originally from New York City, the owners clearly packed their stylish city instincts and gastronomical intuition. At night, the clink of wine glasses mingles with mealtime chatter, while the city lights shimmer in the valley below. Open daily, 11 a.m. - 11 p.m. Manuel Samaniego N8-95 and Anteparra, on Ichimbia, Tel: 593-2-254-2871, Fax: 593-2-254-2871, E-mail: info@cafemosaico.com.ec, URL: www.cafemosaic.com.ec.

QUITO

HASTA LA VUELTA SEÑOR (ENTREES: $7-10)

Set in the Mediterranean courtyard of Edificio Arzobisbal facing the cathedral in the Plaza de la Independencia, the location is ideal and the atmosphere is warm and inviting. Hasta la Vuelta features traditional quiteño dishes. You can definitely find a slightly less sanitary version of the same fare for a much cheaper price in dozens of cafes in this same area. The atmosphere is what makes this restaurant special. Monday - Saturday, 12:30 p.m. - 11 p.m., Sunday, 12:30 p.m. - 4 p.m.. Venezuela and Mejía, Piso 3, Tel: 593-2-258-0887.

> ### V!VA Member Review-Hasta la Vuelta Señor
>
> As a native Ecuadorian now living on the States, I am always craving authentic Ecuadorian food. Problem is, I've grown accustomed to the food safety levels of the US. This place offers both, in addition to a very attractive setting in a colonial house that takes you back to the 1600s. 25 April 2007. Ecuador.

TOP-END

LA CUEVA DEL OSO (ENTREES: $8-12)

This is a beautiful spot to spend an elegant evening, with live music every night and a wide selection of local and international dishes. Dress is semi-formal. Monday - Saturday, 12:30 p.m. - midnight, Sunday, noon - 4 p.m. Chile Oe3-66 and Venezuela, Tel: 593-2-258-3826.

PIM'S (ENTREES: $8-14)

Pim's at the Panecillo provides an elegant view of the city from the inside and out. Despite their spacious two-level dining area inside and outdoor seating (with space heaters), reservations are highly recommended—especially for weekends. With an extensive menu that starts with a page of Quichua vocabulary translated into Spanish and English, you may be surprised that the most recommended dish is the hamburger! There are five different steak preparations, seafood, pork, salads and a few traditional dishes. On Sundays there is only an all-day buffet for $12.50. Monday - Saturday, noon - midnight, Sunday, noon - 6 p.m. Gral. Aymerich S/N, Cima del Panecillo, Tel: 593-9-820-1416, E-mail: panecillo@andinanet.net.

PATIO ANDALUZ RESTAURANT (ENTREES: $8-15)

The Patio Andaluz Restaurant is set in the enclosed courtyard of a lovely 400-year-old colonial building that was renovated in December 2003. It is a breath of fresh air in the middle of the bustling Old Town. The restaurant serves breakfast, lunch and dinner and features Ecuadorian classics. There is also international cuisine, though, and you are sure to find something to suit your palette on their extensive menu. Open daily, 7 a.m. - 11 p.m. Av. García Moreno N6-52 between Olmedo and Mejía, Tel: 593-2-288-0830, Fax: 593-2-228-8690.

MEA CULPA (ENTREES: $10-16)

A lovely and spacious restaurant with a wide selection of Mediterranean food, featuring seafood and an extensive *tapas* menu. A sign at the entrance warns all that dress is semi-formal. Monday - Friday, 12:30 p.m. - 3:30 p.m., 7 p.m. - 11 p.m., Saturday, 7 p.m. - 11 p.m. Chile and Venezuela, inside Edificio Arzobispal on the northern side of the Plaza de la Independencia (Plaza Grande), go up the first staircase on your left within the front hallway.

EL PATIO TRATTORIA (ENTREES: $10-16)

A pleasant Italian restaurant, café and bar right in the heart of Old Town, within the Casa del Cadisán on the second floor. You will feel like you are miles away from the chaos on the streets below as you sip Italian wine in this new restaurant right next to the tourism center. Save room for the tiramisu. Monday, 8 p.m. - midnight, Tuesday - Saturday, noon - midnight, Sunday, noon - 5 p.m. García Moreno 1201 and Calle de Mejía, 2nd Floor, Tel: 593-2-228-8140, Fax: 593-2-295-2519.

THEATRUM RESTAURANT (ENTREES: $14-16)

Located on the second floor of the historic Teatro Nacional Sucre, the Theatrum Restaurant is a must-see while in the Centro Histórico. With its soaring ceilings and muted décor, it is a fancy atmosphere befitting an equally posh menu. And with offerings such as baby Ecuadorian banana with warm chocolate soup and rabbit risotto, travelers are infused with a feeling of international cuisine made with Ecuadorian ingredients. Don't be afraid to splurge when it comes to Theatrum. The restaurant even offers free transportation when you make a lunch or dinner reservation online, so be sure to take advantage of this offer. Monday - Friday and Sundays, 12:30 p.m. - 4 p.m. and 7 p.m. - 11:30 p.m., Saturday, 7 p.m. - 11:30 p.m. Calle Manabí between Guayaquil and Flores, Tel: 593-2-257-1011, 593-2-228-9669, E-mail: reservas@theatrum.com.ec, URL: www.theatrum.com.ec.

CENTRO HISTÓRICO INTERNET CAFÉS

Stroll down a cobblestone street surrounded by colonial houses and 400-year-old churches and monuments, then sit in a modern internet café waving to family and friends on the other side of the world through a web camera. Seems surreal, but it's entirely possible in Quito's historic center.

PAPAYA NET ($1/HOUR)

Like its mother branch in La Mariscal, this Papaya Net offers luscious desserts, sandwiches and coffees to fuel you through all your E-mail and international call sessions..Palacio Arzobispal, Plaza de la Independencia. Open Monday-Friday, 8 a.m.-11:30 p.m.; Saturday, Sunday 9:30 a.m.-11:30 p.m.

KANTUÑ@ NET ($1/HOUR)

Kantuñ@ Net is a decent internet cafe with a small extra charge for use of web cameras, along with drinks and snacks and phone booths for international calls. Monday - Friday, 8:30 a.m. - 8:30 p.m., weekends, 9:30 p.m. - 11 p.m. Venezuela and Chile, Palacio de Arzobispal, Tel: 593-2-258-9800, E-mail: kantu_net@yahoo.com.

STOP 'N' SURF ($1/HOUR)

Stop 'n' Surf is a great, if slightly expensive, internet cafe in the Centro Histórico. Snacks and coffee are sold on the premises. Be aware that it's almost double for use of web cameras and headphones. Open daily, 10 a.m. - 7 p.m. Espejo OE 2-40 and Guayaquil (Pasaje Espejo), Tel: 593-2-228-3066, E-mail: info@stopnsurf.net, URL: www.stopnsurf.net.

LA MARISCAL

The Mariscal Sucre area, or "Gringolandia" as it has become known, is the main tourist hub of Quito. It runs from Parque El Ejido in the South up to Avenida Orellana in the North, and is centered around the road Juan León Mera. Most of Quito's budget accommodation is located here, as well as every tourist service you could possibly want.

A five-minute walk through this area will take you past countless restaurants featuring every imaginable cuisine. It is also home to Quito's most popular bars and clubs which stay open until dawn, as well as numerous internet cafés and other services such as banks, laundromats and mini-marts. Here, you will also find Quito's best English bookstores, LibriMundi and Confederate Books.

Most Quito travel agencies also have their home offices here, so it's a good place to find a tour, whether you're after an international airline ticket, a week's cruise in the Galápagos or a mountain biking trip. Quality and prices vary, so shop around.

QUITO

La Mariscal

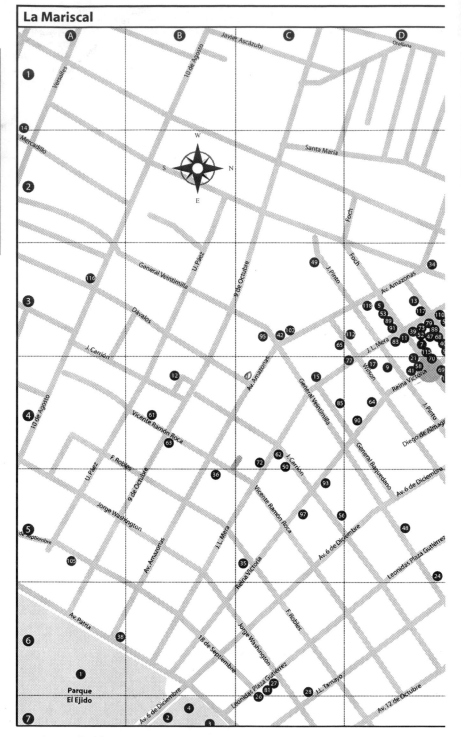

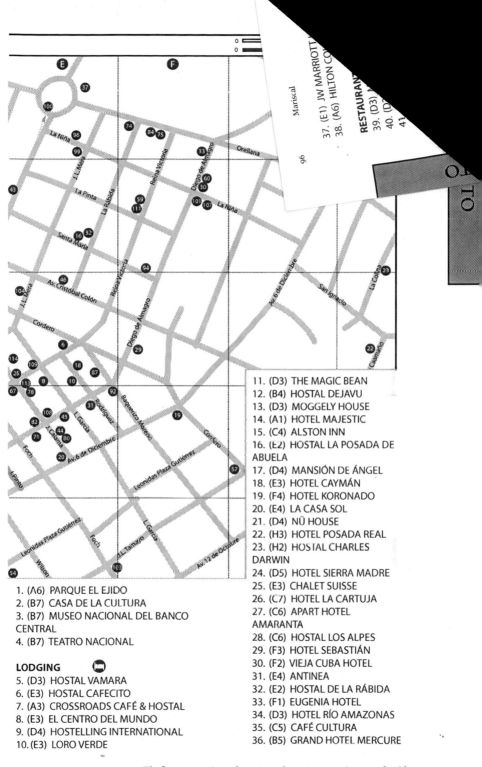

11. (D3) THE MAGIC BEAN
12. (B4) HOSTAL DEJAVU
13. (D3) MOGGELY HOUSE
14. (A1) HOTEL MAJESTIC
15. (C4) ALSTON INN
16. (E2) HOSTAL LA POSADA DE ABUELA
17. (D4) MANSIÓN DE ÁNGEL
18. (E3) HOTEL CAYMÁN
19. (F4) HOTEL KORONADO
20. (E4) LA CASA SOL
21. (D4) NÜ HOUSE
22. (H3) HOTEL POSADA REAL
23. (H2) HOSTAL CHARLES DARWIN
24. (D5) HOTEL SIERRA MADRE
25. (E3) CHALET SUISSE
26. (C7) HOTEL LA CARTUJA
27. (C6) APART HOTEL AMARANTA
28. (C6) HOSTAL LOS ALPES
29. (F3) HOTEL SEBASTIÁN
30. (F2) VIEJA CUBA HOTEL
31. (E4) ANTINEA
32. (E2) HOSTAL DE LA RÁBIDA
33. (F1) EUGENIA HOTEL
34. (D3) HOTEL RÍO AMAZONAS
35. (C5) CAFÉ CULTURA
36. (B5) GRAND HOTEL MERCURE

1. (A6) PARQUE EL EJIDO
2. (B7) CASA DE LA CULTURA
3. (B7) MUSEO NACIONAL DEL BANCO CENTRAL
4. (B7) TEATRO NACIONAL

LODGING

5. (D3) HOSTAL VAMARA
6. (E3) HOSTAL CAFECITO
7. (A3) CROSSROADS CAFÉ & HOSTAL
8. (E3) EL CENTRO DEL MUNDO
9. (D4) HOSTELLING INTERNATIONAL
10. (E3) LORO VERDE

HOTEL QUITO
LÓN QUITO

🍴

MI VIEJO ARRABAL
) ADAM'S RIB
(D4) XOCOA
42. (C3) LA TERRAZA DEL TÁRTARO
43. (E2) COLUMBUS
44. (E4) SHORTON GRILL
45. (E4) EL RINCÓN DEL GAUCHO
46. (E3) COLUMBIA STEAK HOUSE
47. (D3) SIAM
48. (D5) CHURRASCARÍA TROPEIRO
49. (C3) CAFÉ COLIBRÍ
50. (C4) CAFÉ GALLETTI
51. (D3) CAFÉ SUTRA
52. (D3) TEXAS RANCH
53. (D3) MANGO TREE CAFÉ
54. (E5) CAFÉ LIBRO
55. (G1) RINCÓN ECUATORIANO CHILENO
56. (C5) CHIFA MAYFLOWER
57. (G4) CASA CHINA
58. (D4) Q
59. (F2) LA BODEGUITA DE CUBA
60. (F2) ORISHA
61. (B4) MESÓN EUROPEO RESTAURANTE
62. (C4) EL ANTOJO
63. (B4) RINCÓN DE FRANCIA
64. (D4) RAJ TANDOORI
65. (C3) KALLARI
66. (G1) RINCÓN DE LA RONDA
67. (E4) MAMA CLORINDA
68. (D3) MONGOS
69. (D4) COFFEE TREE
70. (D4) LATITUD
71. (E4) G-SPOT BURGERS
72. (C4) FRIED BANANAS
73. (D3) SUTRA LOUNGE
74. (F1) CREPES AND WAFFLES
75. (F1) METRO CAFÉ
76. (D3) THE MAGIC BEAN (see 11)
77. (D4) EL ESPAÑOL
78. (E4) LA BOCA DEL LOBO
79. (D3) ZÓCALO
80. (C5) CAFÉ CULTURA (see 35)
81. (C6) SERRANO'S BAR AND GRILL
82. (E4) RISTORANTE PIZZERÍA MILANO
83. (D3) PIZZAIOLO
84. (F1) SPAGHETTI
85. (C4) LE ARCATE
86. (E4) INDOCHINE
87. (E3) CARMINE

88. (D3) SHOGUN
89. (D3) RED HOT CHILI PEPPERS
90. (D4) TEX MEX
91. (D3) EL MARIACHI TACO FACTORY
92. (E4) ALADIN
93. (C5) EL ARABE
94. (F2) DAMASCO
95. (C3) EL HORNERO
96. (E1) TURTLE'S HEAD
97. (C5) REINA VICTORIA PUB
98. (D3) MULLIGAN'S NEW
99. (E1) CEVICHERÍA MARISQUERÍA LOS SIETE MARES
100. (E1) JOCAY MARISQUERÍA
101. (F2) MANOLO CEVICHERÍA
102. (C3) LAS REDES
103. (E5) MARE NOSTRUM
104. (E3) CHANDANI TANDOORI
105. (A5) COSTA VASCA
106. (D4) DRAGONFLY
107. (F2) LA POSADA DE MÁRQUEZ

NIGHTLIFE 🍸
108. (E4) BUNGALOW
109. (E3) BOGARÍN
110. (D3) NO BAR
111. (F2) VARADERO
112. (D3) PATATU´S
113. (E3) AGUIJÓN
114. (E3) STRAWBERRY FIELDS FOREVER
115. (D3) CHELSEA

INTERNET CAFES @
116. (A3) JAVA NET
117. (D3) PAPAYA NET
118. (D3) AMAZONAS NET

THINGS TO SEE & DO
PARQUE EL EJIDO
On the southern edge of the new town, the big, grassy Parque El Ejido is fairly empty on weekdays, but fills up on weekends with families and their picnics—although with the scores of fútbol-playing youth that also frequent the park, it doesn't make for very relaxing picnicking. Most tourists come for the Saturday and Sunday handicrafts market, which stretches around the semicircular path at the northern end of the park. It has a good selection of stuff, with vendors from all over the country coming to sell their wares. Prices are slightly higher here than in the larger markets such as Otavalo, but lower than in the shops and other markets in Quito during the week.

MUSEO NACIONAL DEL BANCO CENTRAL DEL ECUADOR
If you only visit one museum in Ecuador, make it this one. Even if you're not an avid museum visitor, it's easy to spend an hour or two getting lost in the maze of exhibits, from ancient artifacts to contemporary paintings. There are five main sections in the museum: Perhaps the best known is the Sala Arqueología, which features artifacts from all over the country stretching back to pre-Columbian times. Some of the home exhibits taken from ancient tribes—tools, decorated plates and furniture, etc.—are particularly interesting if you have visited or plan to visit any of Ecuador's indigenous communities, where they still use similar objects and imagery today. Other areas are the Sala de Oro, which has a good collection of gold objects from before colonization, The Sala de Arte Colonial, the Sala de Arte Republicano and the Sala de Arte Contemporáneo, each with a good cross-section of work from its respective period. All five areas are very well laid out, with explanations in English and Spanish accompanying each display. At $1.50 for as long as you want to stay, there's really no excuse to miss it. Tuesday to Friday, 9 a.m. - 5 p.m., weekends and holidays, 10 a.m. - 4 p.m. 12 de Octubre and Patria, Tel: 593-2-222-3259.

LODGING
BUDGET
HOSTAL VAMARA (DORM: $4, ROOMS: $7-10)
Hostal Vamara is well-located in La Mariscal and one of the cheapest places to score a dorm bed. It's best for people who want a place to drop their backpack and be gone most of the day and night. There's no restaurant, bar or café, though the lounge has a hammock and a chair, but nothing that would make you want to hang around for longer than necessary. Mattresses are saggy, but rooms are clean and there's a nice balcony is off the dorm room. Mariscal Foch 753 and Amazonas, Tel: 593-2-222-6425.

EL CAFECITO (DORM: $6, ROOMS: $9-14)
A comfortable, reasonably-priced hotel in the Mariscal. Hostal Cafecito is Canadian-owned and the candle-lit coffee shop downstairs is a great spot to meet other travelers and locals. Nice café, but few choices of things to eat. Great for a few visits, the sweets and drinks, but not for the long run. Luis Cordero 11-24 and Reina Victoria, Tel: 593-2-223-4862, E-mail: quito@cafecito.net.

CROSSROADS CAFE AND HOSTAL (DORM: $5-6, ROOMS: $12-15)
A pretty standard budget hotel: clean and airy with friendly common areas, and lots of information on tours and hotels in other parts of Ecuador. A modest terrace with hammocks and a fireplace boasts great views of Pichincha, and inside there is free wireless internet, a big screen projector for movies and sporting events, laundry service and service for international phone calls. Rooms are reasonably priced (cheaper than The Magic Bean across the street) and offer standard services like a common kitchen, restaurant/bar and a 24-hour reception desk. There is also a small parking lot and bicycle rental, as well as information on rafting, kayaking and tour bookings. Foch E5-23 and Juan León Mera, Tel: 593-2-223-4735, E-mail: info@crossroadshostal.com, URL: www.crossroadshostal.com.

EL CENTRO DEL MUNDO (DORM: $5, ROOMS: $8)
While this hotel is one of the cheapest in the Mariscal and is well-located, there have been several negative reports of inappropriate behavior of the staff, especially during their fa-

mous free rum and coke nights. L García 569 (E7-22), between Diego de Almagro and Reina Victoria, Tel: 593-2-222-9050.

HOSTAL DEJAVU ($8-10/PERSON)

Hostal Dejavu is a friendly budget spot, with breakfast included in the price and lots of information on tours and travel in the area. Prices vary depending on availability, so feel free to negotiate, especially if traveling in a group. The entrance is through the downstairs café. 9 de Octubre and Carrión, Tel: 593-2-222-4483, Fax: 593-9-810-4414, URL: www.hostaldejavu.com.

HOSTELLING INTERNATIONAL (ROOMS: $8-15)

While located in a convenient section of the Mariscal, the only reason to stay at Hostelling International in Quito is if you have the HI discount card, don't mind roughing it and are on a budget. Private rooms, even with the discount, aren't a great deal and the hotel is run down, old and lacking personality. You can find dorm rooms less than 2 blocks away that are the same price without the discount and much better. Joaquín Pinto 325 and Reina Victoria, Tel: 593-2-250-8221, Fax: 593-2-254-3995, E-mail: quito@hihostels.com.ec, URL: www.hihostels.com/ecuador.

LORO VERDE ($9/PERSON)

The Loro Verde is a great spot to meet other travelers. It is well-located, on a street with more hotels than anything else in the heart of the Mariscal. The per person price is $9—a good deal for a private room—especially if you are traveling alone. The atmosphere is clean and cheerful and the service is good. Juan Rodríguez 241 and Reina Victoria, Tel: 593-2-222-6163.

HOSTAL TUTAMANDA AND SPANISH SCHOOL (ROOMS: $10)

Tutamanda Bed and Breakfast Hostel and Spanish courses provides good, cheap and cheerful accommodation. You will be personally attended like a king by your hosts, Jose and Boris, who will help you with the best of advice to make your stay and studies of the Spanish language in Ecuador a memorable experience. Make great savings by staying at Hostal Tutamanda and taking Spanish courses next door at Cristobal Colon Spanish School. Av. Colon 2088 and Versalles, Tel: 593-2-250-6508, Fax: 593-2-222-2964, E-mail: info@tutamandahostel.com, URL: www.tutamandahostel.com.

HOTEL MAJESTIC (ROOMS: $11-30)

Hotel Majestic is a family owned and operated business with more than 18 years of experience in making travelers feel welcome. Offering 40 rooms with private bathrooms, color TV, a mini-bar as well as a downstairs bar, restaurant and cafeteria, Hotel Majestic has all the amenities of a larger hotel. Prices include a continental breakfast, transportation from the airport and one hour of internet. Rooms are also available to rent per month, and discounts for SAE members and group rates are available. Mercadillo 366 and Versalles, Tel: 593-2-254-3182, Fax: 593-2-250-4207, E-mail: info@majesticquito.com, URL: www.majesticquito.com.

MID-RANGE
ALSTON INN (ROOMS: $15-40)
An older hotel smack-dab in the middle of the touristy part of the Mariscal, Alston Inn has a smokey, sad lobby and nicer, but by no means luxurious, rooms. The price includes breakfast, but seems a bit pricey considering the excellent alternatives in the area. If you are running low on cash, this can be a good alternative as they accept all credit cards at no extra charge. The book exchange costs $1 for as many exchanges as you want. Juan León Mera N23-41 and Veintimilla, Tel: 593-2-222-2721, Fax: 593-2-250-8956, E-mail: alston@interactive.net.ec, URL: www.angelfire.com/de/alston.

HOTEL CAYMAN (ROOMS: $19-40)
A good mid-range hotel in a small house in the heart of La Mariscal. Juan Rodríguez 270 and Reina Victoria, Tel: 593-2-256-7616, E-mail: hcayman@uio.satnet.net, URL: www.hotelcaymanquito.com.

V!VA Member Review-Hotel Cayman
I would definitely go back there, I stayed in many hotels during my visit to South America, and this was one of the best ones... Helpful and friendly staff, right in the heart of the city and a nice common room with a chimney! Nice big garden! Comfortable beds and spotless rooms! 16 May 2006.

HOSTAL QUITO-ANTIGUO (ROOMS: $20-60)
Looks can be deceiving, especially when it comes to Hostal Quito-Antiguo. Located only blocks away from the main hustle and bustle of La Mariscal, Hostal Quito-Antiguo is unremarkable. From the outside, you can hardly distinguish the entryway from the rest of the street. However, the rooms are neat, and the staff is eager to serve. As an added bonus, each room has its own private bathroom. Beware though—as it is located close to the party scene, the hostel's inhabitants may be subject to drunken revelers' singing or yelling, especially on the weekends. Joaquin Pinto and Juan León Mera, Tel: 593-2-254-7333 / 593-2-290-5552, E-mail: uioantig@uio.satnet.net, URL: www.quitoantiguo.com.ec.

THE MAGIC BEAN HOTEL (ROOMS: $22-32)
At $8 for a dorm bed, this hostal is not the best value in town. However, dorm rooms (which sleep three or four people) are clean, the beds are comfortable and there are big lockers in each room for you to store your stuff. There's also a great restaurant/café below, sometimes home to live music. The central location is convenient for the Mariscal's best bars, clubs and restaurants—although it can get a bit noisy at night when music from numerous locations filters through the windows until well into the early hours. Foch 681 (E5-08) and Juan León Mera, Tel: 593-2-256-6181, E-mail: magic@ecuadorexplorer.com, URL: www.ecuadorexplorer.com/magic/home.

QUITO

HOSTAL CHARLES DARWIN (ROOMS: $26-38)

A fine mid-range hotel in a quiet residential area between the north of Quito and the Mariscal, between 6 de Diciembre and Av. Coruña, close to some of the larger hotels. Rooms are simple, but clean and good value. The inner garden is a nice place to escape the hustle and bustle of the city. Breakfast is included in the price, and every room has cable TV and a private bathroom. There is shared internet for guests. The friendly staff will also help with private transportation to and from the airport at an extra cost. English spoken. La Colina 304 and Orellana, Tel: 593-2-223-4323/290-4049, Fax: 593-2-252-9384, E-mail: chdarwin@ecuanex.net.ec.

HOTEL POSADA REAL (ROOMS: $27-45)

A clean, well-maintained hotel with a friendly staff, Hotel Posada Real is a good choice if you're looking to stay in the new city. Besides comfortable rooms, the hotel offers 24-hour hot water, cable TV, on-site laundry services, and an organic restaurant—and the price includes a fairly extensive breakfast. Placido Caamano 213 (N26-19) between Av. Colon and San Ignacio, Tel: 593-2-255-2511, Fax: 593-2-222-4162, E-mail: hposreal@vio.satnet.net.

HOSTAL LA POSADA DE ABUELA (ROOMS: $29-50)

Located in the heart of Quito's Mariscal district, this charming hostal has a warm, friendly atmosphere where guests are treated like family. The place is decidedly cozy and boasts clean, comfortable and secure accommodations. All rooms have private baths, cable TV, and some have fireplaces and private balconies. The friendly staff, pleasant rooms and relaxed ambiance combine to provide guests with a markedly enjoyable experience. Sit and relax in the cafeteria, grab a drink at the bar or arrange a night tour of the city. Santa Maria 235 and Rábida, Tel: 593-2-222-5334, E-mail: posabuel@uio.satnet.net, URL: www.posabuela.com.ec.

LA CASA SOL (ROOMS: $30-60)

A quaint, homey hostel on a side street away from most of the noise in the Mariscal, La Casa Sol has comfortable rooms, a couple of cozy sitting areas including one with cable TV, a book exchange, a fireplace and a peaceful central courtyard. With a strong emphasis on native culture, decorations create a uniquely Ecuadorian atmosphere. Cultural events held on the last Friday of every month add to this. The 24-hour café boasts the best coffee in Ecuador. José Calama 127 and Av. 6 de Diciembre, Tel: 593-2-223-0798 / 593-2-222-3383, E-mail: info@lacasasol.com.

HOTEL LA CARTUJA (ROOMS: $33-65)

Hotel La Cartuja is a pleasant retreat from the bustle of the Mariscal. Set in a quiet neighborhood east of 6 de Diciembre, La Cartuja is spacious, clean and pleasant. There are hardwood floors, cheerful decorations and sunny yellow walls. Ask for a room with a view of the garden. The large courtyard garden is a great place to relax and soak up some rays. Many major attractions are within walking distance. Internet and breakfast are included in the price. Leonidas Plaza 170 and 18 de Septiembre, Tel: 593-2-252-3721, E-mail: info@hotelacartuja.com, URL: www.hotelacartuja.com.

CHALET SUISSE (ROOMS: $35-65)

A decent mid-range hotel in the Mariscal, somewhat lacking in personality and charm that other area hotels of the same price boast. There are 50 rooms and a banquet space for large groups. Breakfast is included in the price, as is a welcome cocktail. Calama N24-191 and Reina Victoria, Tel: 593-2-256-2700, Fax: 593-2-256-3966.

APART HOTEL AMARANTA (ROOMS: $35, SUITES: $50-220)

Set in a quiet and safe residential neighborhood in Quito, the hotel offers luxurious apartment suites, each with a private kitchen, living room, dining area, separate bedroom and private bathroom, as well as cable TV. There are also two penthouses, each one with four bedrooms and four baths, boasting spectacular views of the city skyline and Pichincha Volcano, and suited for 8-10 people. Other services include massages, an 80-person conference room, and Serrano's Bar and Grill. Leonidas Plaza N20-32, Tel: 593-2-254-3619, Fax: 593-2-254-3619, E-mail: reservations@aparthotelamaranta.com, URL: www.aparthotelamaranta.com.

HOTEL SIERRA MADRE (ROOMS: $37-55)

In a quiet neighborhood in the heart of Quito is your home-away-from-home in Ecuador. There was a time in Quito when people of vision built elegant homes that became history. At Sierra Madre, you relive this era in an immaculately restored Spanish villa. Veintimilla 464 (E9-33) between Plaza and Tamayo, Tel: 593-2-224-950 / 593-2-250-5688, Fax: 593-2-250-5715, E-mail: booking@hotelsierramadre.com, URL: www.hotelsierramadre.com.

HOSTAL LOS ALPES (ROOMS: $40-50 + TAX)

This average hotel in the Mariscal prides itself on its antiques and charm. It isn't the best value for your money. Tamayo 233 y J. Washington, Tel: 593-2-256-1110, Fax: 593-2-256-1128, E-mail: alpes@uio.satnet.net

HOTEL SEBASTIÁN (ROOMS: $40-70)

An elegant, spacious hotel perfect for business travelers. There are group discounts and ample meeting areas with capability for up to 800 people as well as catering services, a business center and a free parking garage with space for up to 150 vehicles. Rooms are clean and comfortable and the restaurant downstairs provides 24-hour room service. Diego de Almagro 822, Phone: 593-2-222-2300, Fax: 593-2-252-0738, E-mail: hotelsebastian@hotelsebastian.com.

VIEJA CUBA (ROOMS: $40-85)

Vieja Cuba is full of character and class. Rooms are spotless and sunny. Conveniently located in a corner house in La Mariscal, each room is slightly different and personality radiates from every corner. The owners are an Ecuadorian/Cuban couple and also own the Cuban restaurant downstairs. Diego de Almagro 1212 and La Niña, Tel: 593-2-290-6729, Fax: 593-2-252-0738, E-mail: viejacuba@andinanet.net, viejacuba@hotmail.com.

ANTINEA APART-HOTEL (ROOMS: $41-96)

A charming, quiet and unique French *hotel de charme* located in the heart of Quito. Antinea's rooms and furnished apartments are decorated with good taste and class and are a home-away-from-home for leisure and business travelers alike. Antinea is located close to the city's best restaurants, bars and shops and is situated only 15 minutes from both Quito's historic center and the airport. Juan Rodríguez E8-20 and Diego de Almagro, Tel: 593-2-250-6838, Fax: 593-2-250-4404, E-mail: hotelant@uio.satnet.net.

HOTEL LA RÁBIDA (ROOMS: $42-64)

This small, Italian-owned boutique hotel has a clean, colonial feel with friendly service, great food and lots of personal touches that make it unique. Hostal de La Rábida is an old traditional house recently restored into a first-class South American boutique hotel. La Rábida 227 (N26-33), near Santa María, Tel: 593-2-222-1720, E-mail: larabida@uio.satnet.net, URL: www.hotelrabida.com.

Find more reviews from travelers at www.vivatravelguides.com

EUGENIA HOTEL (ROOMS: $50-55)

From the outside, this multistory hotel looks like any other generic, cookie-cutter hotel. Once you step inside, though, the explosion of fresh flowers, colorful paintings, natural light and cheerful decoration sets Eugenia Hotel apart. Rooms come with a double bed or two twin beds and all have cable TV. A slow, internet-equipped computer downstairs offers all guests one hour free per night. Diego de Almagro 1245 and Orellana, Tel: 593-2-252-4895, Fax: 593-2-290-2550, E-mail: eugeniahotel@hotmail.com, URL: www.eugeniahotel.com.

HOTEL RÍO AMAZONAS (ROOMS: $60-80)

Conveniently located on the corner of Amazonas and Cordero, this multistory beast of a hotel offers good service and clean facilities. For the price, however, you can find hotels with much more personality in the same area. This hotel is perfect travelers looking for a sterile, generic place. Cordero E4-375 and Av. Amazonas (large glass building on the corner), Tel: 593-2-255-6666, Fax: 593-2-255-6670, E-mail: amazonas@hotelrioamazonas.com.

CAFÉ CULTURA (ROOMS: $79-109)

Café Cultura has a lovely lobby with a roaring fireplace and lush couches. The restaurant and café is also excellent, if a bit pricey. Rooms too, while exquisitely hand-painted, are small and overpriced. The best rooms are in the back with garden access. The newly added third floor rooms should be avoided: they are noisy and exceptionally small. Calle Robles and Calle Reina Victoria, Tel: 593-2-250-4078 / 593-2-255-8858 / 593-2-256-4956, Fax: 593-2-222-4271, E-mail: info@cafecultura.com, URL: www.cafecultura.com.

LUXURY
GRAND HOTEL MERCURE ALAMEDA (ROOMS: $79-129)

In the middle of the Mariscal, the modern Mercure is convenient for local eateries and is a reliable option. Rooms are well-appointed with comfortable beds and are a reasonable size. The hotel has plenty of services, including a casino that is popular with travelers and Ecuadorians alike. Breakfast is a generous buffet affair and there are other eating options for later in the day, including a coffee shop and deli. When you're done with eating, you can work off the calories in the hotel's fitness center. Roca 653 and Av. Amazonas, Tel: 593-2-299-4000, Fax: 593-2-256-5759, E-mail: reservas@grandhotelmercure-alameda.com.ec, URL: www.accorhotels.com.

NÜ HOUSE (ROOMS: $89-99)

Walking into this new "boutique hotel" makes you feel like you could be in a trendy high-class hotel, anywhere. Shiny lifts take you to rooms and suites with modern décor, flat-screen TVs and mini-bars. This place screams posh, down to the fancy shampoos and loofahs in marble-tiled bathrooms. You can also check out its sister restaurant and club, Q Café and The Loft. Hotel guests get 10% discount at each. Foch E6-12 and Reina Victoria, Tel: 593-2-255-7845, URL: www.nuhousehotels.com.

JW MARRIOTT HOTEL QUITO (ROOMS: $120-200)

The newest of Quito's luxury international hotels, the JW Marriott Quito is a gigantic, modern pyramid in the northern end of the Mariscal. It boasts spacious, sunny, elegantly decorated rooms with excellent city and mountain views, two good restaurants, a tropical pool area that will make you forget you are in the middle of a polluted city and spacious, relaxing common areas including an indoor waterfall. Each of the over 250 rooms has a safe, cable TV, data port, mini-bar and some have in-room hot tubs. Av. Orellana 1172 and Av. Amazonas, Tel: 593-2-297-2000, Fax: 593-2-297-2050, URL: www.marriott.com.

HILTON COLÓN ECUADOR (ROOMS: $150-800)

The Hilton Colón is one of Quito's older international luxury chains and it is beginning to show its age, but is nonetheless a beautiful hotel with extensive amenities and great city views. Located in the southern end of La Mariscal right in front of Parque el Ejido, the Hilton Colón is a blockish concrete structure. Services include a small but modern gym and heated outdoor pool. Two restaurants downstairs offer ample buffets and spacious seating areas. Av. Patria and Av. Amazonas, Tel: 593-2-256-1333, Fax: 593-2-256-3903, E-mail: sales.quito@hilton.com, URL: www.hiltoncolon.com.

RESTAURANTS

Finding a place to eat is no problem in Quito—it's deciding where to go that can be a challenge. Whether you're in the mood for a hearty steak, spicy sushi or traditional Ecuadorian fare, this city is prepared to appease your gastronomical cravings. Prices listed are for the range of main dishes, unless otherwise indicated.

ARGENTINE/STEAK RESTAURANTS

ADAM'S RIB (ENTREES: $5-7)

A casual, reasonably priced steak restaurant in the Mariscal. It has more of a bar feeling with the main deco being blaring TVs, but the place is a popular hub for cheap, big portions. Try the baked beans. Service is Ecuador-style (slow), so be prepared to sit back and relax. Calama 329 and Reina Victoria, Tel: 593-2-256-3196.

COLUMBUS (ENTREES: $7-11)

Columbus is the biggest steakhouse chain in Ecuador, with several locations in Quito. Prices are reasonable and the quality is consistent throughout the different branches. A salad bar and great parilladas (small, personal grill with a selection of meats and sausages) are highlights. Av. Amazonas 1539 y Santa María, Tel: 593-2-254-0780, Daily noon - 24:00.

COLUMBIA STEAK HOUSE (ENTREES: $8-10)

Colon 1262 y La Rábida, Tel: 593-2-255-1857, Daily 8 a.m - 11.30 p.m.

LA TERRAZA DEL TÁRTARO (ENTREES: $7-18)

An elegant steak and seafood restaurant with a great view of the city and a fireplace. Reservations are recommended, as the restaurant tends to fill up at night. Main dishes average around $7-10; the most expensive is a seafood platter at $18, but it's worth it. General Veintimilla 1106 and Av. Amazonas, Tel: 593-2-252-7987.

EL RINCÓN DEL GAUCHO (ENTREES: $8-12)

This Argentinean steakhouse has huge portions of excellent steak cooked on a charcoal grill on the premises. Try the *parillada*—a selection of steak, chicken and sausage to share in a group served on a mini grill that keeps your meat warm. The service is great, and there's a good wine selection. Plan to spend $8-12 per person. Diego de Almagro 422, Tel: 593-2-254-7846.

ASIAN

SIAM (ENTREES: $6-20)

A delectable Asian infusion, tasty Thai and Sushi are the highlights here. Though one may question the authenticity of some ethnic dishes, food is good for the area and the atmosphere is cozy and romantic. Look for daily deals, often for two and great for a date. Delicious fruit drinks—try the Siam juice. Calama E5-10 and Juan León Mera, Tel: 593-223-9404.

INDOCHINE (ENTREES: $6)

Indochine opened in Spring 2007, bringing Vietnamese food to Quito through this real gem of a restaurant. The owner is part-Vietnamese and the food is very authentic. The restaurant combines delicately flavored, mouth-watering food with friendly service. For a real taste of Vietnam, slurp on the "Pho", or try anything from Summer Rolls to Coconut Curry Chicken, all bring a delicious taste of Vietnam to your palate. Finish up with a round of Stuffed Fried Bananas, flambéed at your table. Jose Calama E8-29 y Diego de Almagro.

BRAZILIAN

CHURRASCARÍA TROPEIRO (BUFFET: $12.80)

A Brazilian buffet restaurant with the classic Brazilian spread of delicious meats, fruit and salad. For

$12.80 per person, enjoy the salad bar, and as much as you can eat of 10 different cuts of meat and desserts. There are a few more options on weekends. Veintimilla E8-153, Tel: 593-2-254-8012.

CAFÉ/BARS

CAFÉ COLIBRÍ (BREAKFAST: $1.20-3.50. LUNCH: $2.50-6)

Café Colibrí is a relaxed, tranquil café with an outdoor seating area and a small hummingbird garden. German-owned, it features German/Ecuadorian food along with typical café fare. Prices range from about $2.50-6 and value is excellent. Pinto 619, Tel: 593-2-256-4011.

XOCOA (DRINKS: $1.50-4)

A sweets lover's dream, nestled in the corner of the ever-happening Foch Plaza, but secluded enough to enjoy a mug of rich creamy chocolate away from it all. Menu features a wide variety of drinkable chocolate treats, cakes, pies, milkshakes and delicious gelato-style ice cream. There's wine and beer too, if you're still in the mood. Foch and Reina Victoria.

CAFÉ GALLETTI (SNACKS & COFFEE: $2-5)

This quiet, Mediterranean coffee and sandwich shop set in a two-story colonial house is a perfect place to sit and read or relax with some friends. Carrión 560 between Juan León Mera and Reina Victoria, Tel: 593-2-252-7361, 593-2-282-7129, E-mail: galletti@interactive.net.ec.

CAFÉ LIBRO (COFFEE & SNACKS: $2-6)

One of the few remaining hip coffee shops in the Mariscal area that yet to be discovered by the masses. There are live music performances, rotating art exhibits and a book exchange. Food is mostly drinks: coffee and other drinkables, appetizers and sandwiches. Leonidas Plaza N23-56, Monday - Friday, 5 p.m. - 1 a.m., Saturday, 3 p.m. - midnight, Sunday, closed.

CAFÉ SUTRA (ENTREES: $3-6)

Café Sutra is one of Mariscal's hippest restaurant/cafés and quickly fills up, especially on weekends. There is a wide variety of appetizers and meals in addition to a lengthy drinks and coffee menu. Food is mostly mid-Eastern with excellent hummus and other flavorful specialties. Calama 380 and Juan León Mera, Tel: 593-2-250-9106, Tel: 593-2-290-5883.

THE COFFEE TREE (ENTREES: $3-8)

THE spot for people watching, pre-game drinks or a late night bite on the always hopping Foch Plaza. A slew of outdoor tables are always full of a mixed gringo/Ecuadorian crowd. Drinks are reasonably priced for the area, food from an eclectic menu is decent and the service is not too shabby. Foch and Reina Victoria, Tel: 593-2-252-6957.

MANGO TREE CAFÉ (ENTREES: $4-5)

Mango Tree Café is a favorite among travelers. It has a very tranquil atmosphere, great for relaxing and enjoying a snack, sandwich, lunch or coffee. Foch 721, Tel: 593-2-222-6847.

SUZETTE (ENTREES: $4-8)

Craving a crepe? Take a pit stop at Suzette, a creperie that offers every kind of crepe you could ever want. They have ham and cheese or nutella crepes, but also shrimp or curry crepes for a twist. Crepes run for about $5. The restaurant, with its sunny disposition, is a good place to warm up, especially if the Quito weather brings rain for the day. Foch and Reina Victoria, Tel: 593-2-290-8124, E-mail: suzette.ecuador@gmail.com.

GRAIN DE CAFÉ (ENTREES: $4.50-8)

For a mix of French-influenced food and a casual atmosphere, Grain de Café is an excellent option. The restaurant offers vegetarian dishes, a great-value set lunch and a huge selection of imported drinks (Tequila shots, $2.65). With a book exchange, English films, coffee under $1 and a helpful owner, this restaurant is a great place to meet, greet and relax. Baquedano 332 and Reina Victoria, Tel: 593-2-256-5975.

DRAGONFLY (ENTREES: $5-6)

This self-dubbed "cocktail garden" is a color shock, to say the least. Neon green booths divert from the fact that the rest of the restaurant is relatively plain. The food, however, is relatively inexpensive compared to other restaurants in the area. Although the newer bar is in the shadow of its popular (and loud) neighbor Coffee Tree, it is worth a try for the friendly staff and extensive cocktail choices. Foch and Reina Victoria, Tel: 593-2-905-472.

Q (ENTREES: $8-12)

Sleek is the word that encapsulates Q. The restaurant, bar and lounge are part of the swanky Nü House hotel complex, which also includes The Loft disco. The restaurant, with its fluid setup and fusion food, is a perfect meeting point for groups. The menu gets pretty expensive, with dishes typically running around $10 per plate. As for the cocktails—every staple is on the menu. A nice touch is the alcove in the back, where you can be seated near an LCD screen and a modern display of wine bottles. Foch E6-12 and Reina Victoria, Tel: 593-2-255-7840.

CHILEAN

RINCÓN ECUATORIANO CHILENO (ENTREES: $2.50-5)

The Rincón Ecuatoriano Chileno is an inexpensive restaurant to try out Chilean specialties in the Mariscal. The T-bone steak might just be the cheapest in Quito. There is a wide selection of steaks, chicken and fish, but no real vegetarian dishes to speak of. 6 de Diciembre N28-30, Tel: 593-2-222-5498.

CHINESE (CHIFA)

CASA CHINA (ENTREES: $4-8)

Cordero 613 (E9-242) and Tamayo, Tel: 593-2-252-2115, Monday Friday 11:00 -15:30 and 18:30 22:30; Saturday 11:00 16:00 and 18:30-22:00; Sunday closed.

CHIFA MAYFLOWER (ENTREES: $3-6)

Your standard Ecuadorian-Chinese restaurant with heaping helpings of greasy rice, noodles, veggies and more. This is a cheap and filling option, and a popular one among Ecuadorians. Try the vegetarian chulafan. Jeronimo Carrión, Tel: 593-2-254-0510, URL: www.mayflower.com.ec.

CUBAN

LA BODEGUITA DE CUBA (ENTREES: $5-7)

A classy restaurant/bar, this place serves excellent food, accompanied by live Cuban music most nights. On Thursday to Saturday nights, it stays open until 2 a.m., when different live bands play to a packed room. Drinks are fairly expensive at $4 a throw. The next door Varadero is run by the same owners and also has live music on Thursdays, Fridays and Saturdays, it tends to appeal to a more mature clientele. The $5 cover charge after 9 p.m. includes a free drink (usually a *caipirinha* or *cuba libre*). Reina Victoria 1721, Tel: 593-2-254-2476.

ORISHA (ENTREES: $12-15)

Serving Afro-Cuban food in the north of the Mariscal. Prices are high, but the portions are large and full of flavor. There are no vegetarian dishes. Orisha is only open for dinner from 7 p.m. - 10 p.m. daily. Diego de Almagro 1212, Tel: 593-2-290-6729.

ECUADORIAN/TRADITIONAL FOOD

MESON EUROPEO RESTAURANTE (ENTREES: $1.80)

A great local lunch dive with outdoor seating and pleasant, Mediterranean decor. One of the best lunch spots in Quito, the lunch is $1.80 and includes a small appetizer like a tamale or small salad, a soup and a 'plato fuerte' with meat (you can request vegetarian), rice and plantains, juice and a small dessert. Vicente Ramón Roca 818 y 9 de Octubre, Tel: 593-2-223-6724, Monday - Friday 11:30 - 16:00.

EL ANTOJO (ENTREES: $2-3)

A simple lunch spot with self-service, Antojo (The Craving) is cheap, fast and delicious. It features

QUITO

classic Ecuadorian dishes. Try the *llapingacho* platter (cheesy potato pancakes with a sausage, egg over easy and a lettuce and beet salad) or the *churrasco* (grilled beef with a fried egg, sweet grilled onions, rice and beans). Desserts are also good, with fresh fruit salads mixed with ice cream, whipped cream, or both. Juan León Mera and Jerónimo Carrión, Tel: 593-2-250-0143.

KALLARI (ENTREES: $3-7.50)
Kallari is a community-owned coffee shop, restaurant and crafts shop owned by an association of Quichua communities in the Napo province. Organic coffee, organic chocolate brownies and hot chocolate accompany tasty snacks and meals. One of the best features is the cultural dinner: if you have a group of six people, you can reserve a private 3-course typical Amazonian meal along with a 15-minute presentation of Quichua language, culture, crafts and their traditional manufacturing methods. The price is $7.50 per person. Wilson E4-266 and Juan León Mera, Tel: 593-2-223-6009, URL: www.kallari.com/coffee.html.

RINCÓN LA RONDA (ENTREES: $5-8)
La Ronda serves traditional Ecuadorian food in an elegant atmosphere. It is very popular with Ecuadorians, especially among older members of the middle class. The food is quite good, although prices are steep for Quito. Every Sunday evening, they offer a performance by a traditional Ecuadorian ballet troupe—the performance is free for those dining there. Bello Horizonte E8-45 and Diego de Almagro.

MAMA CLORINDA (ENTREES: $5-15)
This is a sanitary place to try out some dishes you may hesitate to in other places, like *cuy*— roasted guinea pig. It's also large with two levels, and good for large groups. Vegetarians have two options: the llapingacho platter with cheesy potato pancakes, salad and veggies, or *locro de queso*, a creamy cheesy soup. Reina Victoria 1144, Tel: 593-2-254-2523.

FRENCH/SWISS
LA CREPERIE (ENTREES: $4-6)
This cozy restaurant in the Mariscal specializes in French food, particularly crepes. It is a bit pricey for Quito, but in reality a value compared to French restaurants in other countries. The food is very good, but the service is not always great. Calama 362, Tel: 593-2-222-6780.

INTERNATIONAL
G-SPOT BURGERS (ENTREES: $1-4)
G-SPOT Burgers grew so popular as part of the former Soul Bar, that when the Californian owners sold it in Spring 2006, they decided to open up a separate haven just for the now famous burgers. A variety of fresh burgers are available along with philly cheesesteaks, corn dogs and chili dogs. And don't forget the *papas fritas* (french fries) for only a buck. Bright and colorfully decorated by a grafitti artist, the inside is airy and open with plenty of table space. Open Tuesday - Saturday, 11 a.m - 3 a.m., and Sunday and Monday, noon - midnight. Diego de Almagro and Jose Calama.

CHANDANI TANDOORI (ENTREES: $2.50-3)
Long-established in Quito, Chandani Tandoori serves up tasty Indian curries from a mild *masala* right through the curry spectrum up to *madras* and *vindaloo*. Beware of the *phall*, the hottest option on the menu. The restaurant looks a little dingy, but step inside and you'll find that the food is great value. You pick your curry sauce, opt for vegetarian or chicken, and then choose between rice and naan. A good and cheap lunch menu includes *bhaji* or *pakora*, plus a reduced choice of chicken or vegetarian curries with rice and a juice for $2.50, but the normal menu is also available all day. Monday - Saturday, 11 a.m. - 10:15 p.m. Sometimes open on Sundays too. Juan León Mera Nº 1312, between Luis Cordero and Avenida Colón.

RAJ TANDOORI (ENTREES: $2.50-3)
This newer sister restaurant to Chandani Tandoori serves the exact same menu—mouth-watering curries with sauces ranging from mild and spicy through to sauces that will make your

nose run, served vegetarian style, or with chicken and either rice or naan. Try a curry served with a Brahma beer. They also offer the $2.50 lunch menu including curry, rice, pakora or bhaji and juice for $2.50. Reina Victoria and Wilson. Monday - Saturday, 11:00 a.m. - 10:15 p.m. Sometimes open on Sundays too.

MONGOS (ENTREES: $2.99-8; COCKTAILS: $1)
Right in the heart of the Mariscal, the Mongolian barbeque has quickly become a firm favorite with travelers and Ecuadorians alike. Go for the *todo lo que puede comer* or "all you can eat" option, for $4.99 (vegetarian $2.99). For this price you also get a soup or salad starter thrown in. While you're waiting for the starter, mix and match with the wide array of vegetables, choose chicken or beef and make a salsa from the wide variety of options available. For those not feeling creative, there are also meals on the menu. Cocktails are a bargain at a dollar a pop. It's worth being patient with the somewhat sullen staff for the excellent value food. Calama and Juan León Mera.

FRIED BANANAS (ENTREES: $3-6)
A cozy restaurant in La Mariscal with prices much lower than one would expect given the elegant atmosphere. Featuring a variety of seafood, steak, salads and excellent service. Try the seafood salad. Juan León Mera 539 and Jerónimo Carrión.

SUTRA LOUNGE (ENTREES: $3-6)
A slightly quieter version of the wildly popular Café Sutra, Sutra Lounge has a similar minimalist atmosphere and a great menu full of delicious snacks, meals and drinks. Cozy couches and pillows on the floor provide comfy seating areas along with tables and lots of candle-lit decor. Juan León Mera and Calama.

THE MAGIC BEAN (ENTREES: $3-7)
From the "have a nice day" sign by the bar to the huge pancakes served for breakfast, there's nothing Ecuadorian about this place. But unless you're seeking an authentic dining experience, you're unlikely to be disappointed. The cozy patio café is always packed with travelers and a great place to meet people, and all the dishes on the mind-boggling huge menu are excellent. Foch 681 and Juan León Mera, Tel: 593-2-256-6181, E-mail: magic@ecuadorexplorer.com, URL: www.ccuadorexplorer.com/magic/home.

CREPES AND WAFFLES (ENTREES: $3-8)
A Colombian chain with excellent value and good-sized portions. The waffles are not meant to be breakfast, but rather dessert: they're piled high with ice cream, whipped cream, nutella, fruit and more. Crepes are served with sweet or salty fillings and are full of flavor. The salads are gigantic and delicious. The atmosphere is casual, almost diner-style, which attracts a gringo and classy Ecuadorian crowd. We've listed the main restaurant in La Mariscal, but there is also a branch in the North of Quito in the popular Quicentro mall. Orellana 461, Tel: 593-250-0658.

EL ESPAÑOL (ENTREES: $4-6)
A sandwich shop with several locations around Quito, El Español has excellent imported cheeses, olives and meats (available on sandwiches and separately). There is not usually much seating; food is generally meant to go. Juan León Mera, Tel: 593-2-255-3995.

ZÓCALO (ENTREES: $6-8)
A perfect meeting place for big groups, Zócalo is funky and fresh with a colorful atmosphere. Look up to see the unique colored water jugs hanging from the ceiling. The restaurant has a simple menu, with fusion food galore. There are always special promotions going on, be sure to ask your waiter. The restaurant is often crowded, too, so avoid peak hours or prepare to wait a little! Calama E5-10 and Juan León Mera, Tel: 593-2-223-3929.

LA BOCA DEL LOBO (ENTREES: $6-10)
A cozy, gay-friendly restaurant/bar with creative, candle-lit decoration. The scene picks up

on weekends with crowds often hanging around the bar until 3 a.m. The menu is a bit random, with a page or two of stuffed mushroom appetizers, melted cheese platters and other odd starter dishes followed by steaks and chicken dishes. The drink menu is fairly extensive, and martinis are probably the best in Quito. . Calama 285, Tel: 593-223-4083.

GRUYERE DE FONDUE (ENTREES: $6-12)

Gruyere de Fondue, one of the orange canopied restaurants in the always-happening Foch plaza, is a perfect place to try the melting pot experience. Try traditional cheese and chocolate fondues at one of the few cozy tables, all with color-coordinated earth-toned cloths. As is true at any good fondue place, Gruyere has an extensive wine list to complement your order. Foch and Reina Victoria, Tel: 593-2-223-1461, E-mail: mechebarragan@hotmail.com.

SERRANO'S BAR AND GRILL (ENTREES: $6-25)

Offering excellent cuts of meat, fresh seafood and an incredibly well-stocked bar, Serrano's Bar and Grill has something for everyone. The laidback atmosphere is contrasted with creations to tantilize your taste buds. Lobster, seabass, and shrimp compliment the various cuts of fine beef and chicken. Leonidas Plaza N20-32, Tel: 593-2-254-3619, Fax: 593-2-254-3619, E-mail: reservations@aparthotelamaranta.com, URL: www.aparthotelamaranta.com/serranos.html.

METRO CAFÉ (ENTREES: $8-10)

Stepping into Metro Café is one step out of Ecuador. From oversized posters of famous American and British musicians, modern decor and a very Americanized menu down to brownies à la mode and cheesecake, Metro Café is perfect for the tourist who needs a taste of home without succumbing to McDonalds. Orellana and Rábida Esq., Tel: 593-2-222-4485, Open daily, 24 hours.

CAFÉ CULTURA (ENTREES: $8-10)

Café Cultura is a beautiful restaurant worth a visit, even if you aren't staying in the hotel. The atmosphere is the main attraction: the hotel and restaurant are located in what was once the French Cultural Center. The original style of this colonial home has been preserved and the interior is beautiful. There are a wide variety of international cuisine options. Calle Robles 513 and Calle Reina Victoria, Tel: 593-2-256-4956, URL: www.cafecultura.com.

AZUCA (ENTREES: $7-15)

Azuca, the freshest addition to Plaza El Quinde, is blatantly noticeable from the second you walk down Foch. This self-dubbed Latin Bistro serves an eclectic mix of seafood and meat dishes. The "aphrodisiac rice," is something you should try! The privacy of the booths in the back is a welcome hiding spot from the masses. Foch E6-11 and Reina Victoria, Tel: 593-2-290-7164.

ITALIAN
FOCCACIA (ENTREES: $5-9)

At Foccacia, two things immediately hit you: the smell of fresh baked bread and the sunny, California-esque atmosphere. With the acoustic music softly playing in the background, it's the perfect place to pick up some pasta or pizza with friends. And of course, some bread for dipping in oil and vinegar. Prices are normal for the Mariscal, but the atmosphere makes this restaurant a steal. Reina Victoria E6-43 and Foch, Tel: 593-2-255-5172.

SPAGHETTI (ENTREES: $5-10)

Spaghetti is an average Italian restaurant. There is a wide selection of dishes: both vegetarian and non; however, the dishes don't have much flavor. Prices are average and the ambiance is elegant. There is also a Spagetti's in Cumbaya and in the mall on América and Naciones Unidas, Plaza las Americas. Av. Orellana 1171, Tel: 593-2-255-2570.

CARMINE (ENTREES: $7.90-15)

Hip and modern, Carmine is in the northern sector of the Mariscal. Dishes include tasty pastas, seafood and meat cooked Mediterranean style. Owner and chef Bill Carmine translates the menu board and describes dishes in English for those with only a smattering of Spanish. The servings are generous and with the trendy décor and ambient vibes, you could be forgiven for believing yourself in New York City. Last entry at 11 p.m. Monday to Saturday, however, but service continues until you're done. Baquerizo 533, Tel: 593-2-222-5531.

MEXICAN
RED HOT CHILI PEPPERS (ENTREES: $4-7)
This is a great Tex-Mex restaurant with the best fajitas in Quito and possibly the best margaritas in Ecuador. The flavors and portions are American-style—that is, full of taste and huge portions for reasonable prices! All dishes can be served vegetarian. Foch 713, Tel: 593-2-255-7575.

TEX MEX (ENTREES: $6-8)
Tex Mex is a large Mexican restaurant in the Mariscal with a selection of typical Mexican dishes. Plan to spend at least $6-8 per person. Credit cards are accepted, but with a $20 minimum. Reina Victoria 847, Tel: 593-2-252-7689.

MIDDLE-EASTERN
ALADDIN (ENTREES: $2-5)
Aladdin is popular for its spacious outdoor seating, cozy indoor couches, late hours, tasty hookahs, and of course, its cheap and delicious Middle Eastern food. The Iranian owner has lived in Ecuador for over 20 years and has established this Mariscal institution well. Try the falafel platter. Diego del Almagro and Baquerizo Moreno.

PIZZA
TOMATO (SLICE: $1)
The spot for a $1 slice of good pizza from the takeaway window, conveniently located in a busy intersection of the pedestrian-ruled Mariscal. Good for eating in, too, with a cozy atmosphere and tables that look out at the street through large open windows. A wide variety of tasty pies at reasonable prices. Juan León Mera and Calama, Tel: 593-2-290-6201.

EL HORNERO (ENTREES: $4-7)
An Ecuadorian pizza chain with inexpensive, wood-oven pizza, El Hornero has interesting pizza toppings typical of Quito, like choclo (Andean corn). General Veintimilla 1149, Tel: 593-2-254-2518.

PUBS
TURTLE'S HEAD (ENTREES: $5-8)
An excellent Scottish-owned pub in Quito's Mariscal district, and the only spot in Quito to get home-brewed beer. Three varieties of micro-brews are for sale from the on-site brewery. The Turtle's Head also has great hamburgers and snacks, along with pool, darts, foosball and at times live music. The pub has a very British ambiance,enhanced by cartoon strips from the adult comic Viz. La Niña 626 and Amazonas, Tel: 593-2-256-5544.

REINA VICTORIA PUB (ENTREES: $5-8)
Can't last another day without your beloved fish and chips? Then Reina Victoria Pub is your spot. With classic British platters and a lively ex-pat crowd, this pub is getting up there in years and is a bit pricey for the fare, but a perfect spot for British travellers. Reina Victoria and Roca, Tel: 593-2-222-6369.

MULLIGAN'S (ENTREES: $8-10)
Looking for good food, good drinks and a great time? Head to Mulligan's, a lively Irish pub with cold beer and a chilled atmosphere. The menu is extensive and includes kid and vegetarian friendly options. Calama and Juan León Mera.

SEAFOOD
CEVICHERÍA MARISQUERÍA LOS SIETE MARES (ENTREES: $2-4)
Cevichería Marisquería Los Siete Mares has excellent ceviche, other seafood soups and lunch

platters in a variety of combinations. Don't forget to fill up a basket with popcorn and *chifles* (fried plantain chips) to dunk in your soup of choice. Juan León Mera and La Niña.

JOCAY MARISQUERÍA (ENTREES: $2.50-5.50)

Jocay Marisquería is an inexpensive seafood restaurant with a wide selection. Try the *ceviche jocay*, the specialty of the house. Amazonas 4739 and Jose Arizaga, Tel: 593-2-224-4177.

LOS CEBICHES DE LA RUMIÑAHUI (ENTREES: $4-7)

This is a good chain and a great place to try out the national seafood soup: ceviche. There are several locations around Quito. Real Audiencia N59-121, Tel: 593-2-259-9888.

EL ATRIO (ENTREES: $6-12)

A ritzy new place in a great location looking over the hip Foch Plaza, made to look like a church with waiters that dress like clergy. An international menu features decorative plates of savory-sweet flavor infusions, with tasty meats and seafood accented with fruity salsas. A wide variety of well selected imported wines make for the perfect accompaniment to succulent dishes. A little pricier than surrounding restaurants but you pay for what you get. Reina Victoria and Foch, Tel: 593-2-252-0581 Cell: 593-9-802-4750, E-mail: atrio_uio@yahoo.com.

LAS REDES

Located in the middle of the gringo district, it's easy to mistake Las Redes for a tourist trap. This is not the case, however, as the restaurant is better than expected and full of locals. The restaurant itself is somewhat cramped, and it tends to fill up, especially at lunchtime. The specialty of the house is *mariscada*, a heaping plate of fish, clams, crab legs, squid, you name it: it's as if some fisherman emptied a net right into the frying pan without really looking to see what he had caught. The prices are quite steep by Mariscal standards, but the service is good too. Amazonas 845 and Veintimilla, Tel: 593-2-252-5691.

MARE NOSTRUM (ENTREES: $6-10)

Mare Nostrum has delicious seafood dishes in an elegant setting right in the Mariscal. Foch 172 y Tamayo, Tel: 592-2-252-8686, Daily 12:00 - 22:00.

SPANISH

COSTA VASCA (ENTREES: $7-14)

Spanish restaurant in the Mariscal with a wide selection of classic Spanish dishes. Vegetarian dishes include a variety of salads and *tortilla española*—a potato omelet. 18 de Septiembre 553, Tel: 593-2-252-3827.

LA PAELLA VALENCIANA (ENTREES: $10-20)

This Spanish restaurant has excellent *paella*. With a variety of options for different types of paella, you really don't need to look any farther on the menu. Set in an elegant atmosphere, Service tends to be fairly slow and prices are expensive for Quito, but it is worth it. One paella feeds 2-3 people. There are no vegetarian dishes. Open Tuesday - Sunday, lunch and dinner. Diego de Almagro 1727 and República, Tel: 593-2-222-8681.

LATITUD (ENTREES: $12.99)

Latitud is also known as "*tapas, quesos y vinos*" and is popular with both gringos and Ecuador's elite. The deal is this: all you can eat or drink, for $12.99. The tapas are dubious at times, but with flowing vino, no one cares. Noon - 1.30 a.m. Reina Victoria N24-151 and Calama, Tel: 593-2-254-6086.

VEGETARIAN (SEE INTERNATIONAL)

LA POSADA DE MARQUEZ (ENTREES: $2.25)

A cozy lunch spot towards the north of the Mariscal—one block from Orellana—La Posada de Marquez offers creative vegetarian menus for the fixed price of $2.25. La Niña 275 and Diego de Almagro.

MARISCAL BARS AND NIGHTLIFE

Technically all bars in the Mariscal area must close by 2 a.m. but many stay open later if they can. The official opening times are quoted below, but some "clubs," stay open 6 or 7 a.m.

PATATU'S BAR (BEERS: $1.50)

At Patatu's, drinks are 2-for-1 during happy hour and at selected intervals throughout the night. Cover charge is $3 on Friday and Saturday, including a free drink (two if you go before 10 p.m.). There is also a free pool table and foosball. Good mix of music and great meeting place. Wilson, between Juan León Mera and Amazonas, Tel: 593-2-250-5233, Fax: 593-2-250-5233, E-Mail: alfonsoaguilar@barpatatus.com, URL: www.barpatatus.com.

NO BAR (WEEKEND COVER: $3)

Hot, sweaty and crowded, this place appeals almost exclusively to the very young and the very drunk. The music is a mix of Latin and western chart cheese. It could be anywhere in the world, but if you want to dance the night away and forget you're in Ecuador, it might be the place for you. It's less crowded on Tuesdays and Wednesdays. Calama and Juan León Mera.

STRAWBERRY FIELDS FOREVER (DRINKS: $3-5)

If you love the Beatles, you'll love Strawberry Fields. This relatively new bar is tucked away next to No Bar. Take a seat in the cozy alcove in the back, and rock out to the playlist, which also includes other bands inspired by the famous foursome. Drinks are named after the best of the Beatles, from their signature *Strawberry Fields Margarita* to the eclectic *Octupus's Garden*. Check out the Yellow Submarine-themed restroom! Calama E5-23 and Juan León Mera.

AGUIJÓN (COVER: $4)

A local favorite among hipsters and trendsetters but maintains a down-to-earth, chilled out vibe (and a cheaper cover) than some of its dressier neighbors. A wide variety of music keeps an eclectic crowd dancing to ever-changing beats of salsa, hip-hop, jazz, reggaeton and Top 20. The place is bit tricky to find, look for the white and red entrance and sign with a scorpion emblem. Calama E735 and Reina Victoria, Tel: 593-2-256-9014.

CHELSEA (COCKTAILS: $4)

If you want to get your night started off right, head over to Chelsea, a trendy newcomer on Foch Plaza. The decor is oddly reminiscent of what you might find in a bar off the Champs de Elysees in Paris, and techno or classic rock are accompanied by old-school music videos on the big screen. Plush, red velvet seats, mirrors everywhere, dim lighting and no fewer than three flat screen TVs. Mariscal Foch and Reina Victoria.

VARADERO (COVER: $4)

Varadero's long, skinny bar stretches the length of the room, giving the impression that the bar is always packed full. The tiny dance floor is almost always at least half-occupied by a live band playing Cuban dance tunes. Cover is cheap for the area—$4 includes a free drink, usually a cuba libre or a caipirinha. Reina Victoria 1721 and Pinta, Tel: 593-2-254-2575.

MACONDO (DRINKS: $4.50-6)

The new age décor, with padded white walls and Warholesque pictures on the ceiling, makes visiting Macondo worth the cash you're bound to shell out hanging out there. Popular with well-heeled locals, just sitting at the bar will make you forget you're in Ecuador. Macondo has SKYY bottles lining the bar and Grey Goose paraphernalia decorating the walls. Calama 368 and Juan León Mera, Tel: 593-2-222-7563, URL: www.macondoquito.com.

LA BUNGA (COVER: $5)

Ever-popular with the young locals, if you like ska or alternative, this will quickly become your dance club of choice. Not only will you hear rock, the club tends to throw in local salsa and merengue mixes. Check it out on a Saturday night, when the college crew comes out to play. Av. Orellana and Yanez Pinzón, Tel: 593-9-823-6500 / 593-9-604-0887.

QUITO

KAFEINA (COVER: $5)
Kafeina, is a hotspot among the young adult crowd. If you come here, dress up, as it is a place where people are constantly checking each other out. The cover charge, which is usually $5, includes one drink. In addition to a hip crowd, there are often events, live concerts and different DJs. Calama 368 and Juan León Mera, Tel: 593-2-222-7563.

ÑUCANCHI PEÑA (COVER: $5-8)
This bar/club is open from Thursday - Saturday and has live music each night. Located west of the Mariscal just two blocks south of Central University, you are pretty much guaranteed a tourist-free crowd. The music is usually local bands and Andean tunes. There is lots of space to let loose. Thursdays are free for ladies. Av. Universitaria 496 and Armero, Tel: 593-2-254-0967.

SESERIBÓ (COVER: $7)
Seseribó is the perfect place to go for Latin music and dancing. As Quito's premiere *salsateca*, the club charges a $7 cover, and drinks are more expensive than other places in La Mariscal. But for the atmosphere and music, there's no better place to go. Tuesday and Thursday evenings are lively, as the professional salsa dancers show up. Calle Veintimilla 325 and 12 de Octubre, Tel: 593-2-256-3598, E-mail: seseribo18@hotmail.com.

PAPILLON DISCO
Although it's new, Papillon Disco is already a huge hit in Quito. Perhaps it's because there is no cover charge, or because the music is an eclectic mix of pop and techno. Either way, it's always happening. Revelers of all ages turn out to hit the dance floor. Pinezon and Colón.

THE LOFT
Next to sister hotel Nü House and just as posh, this exclusive goth-modern bar is a hip spot for hotel guests, well-heeled tourists and quiteño trendsetters. DJs keep the place live most nights as guests sip fancy cocktails and cognac in VIP nooks under chandeliers. Foch and Reina Victoria, Tel: 593-2-255-7850, Cell: 593-8-476-8435, E-mail: reservas@theloftquito.com.

BUNGALOW 6
Bungalow 6 is sure to keep revelers happy. This is a hipster paradise, with funky artwork lacing the walls inside and out, dim lighting and comfortable seating. Cocktails are the specialty, and a mix from chilled out tunes to booty shakin' music completes the Bungalow experience. Corner of Calama y Diego de Almagro. Open at night, days vary; always open on the weekend.

BOGARÍN
A popular spot to get down with some music and have a few drinks. Reina Victoria N24-217 y Lizardo García, Tel: 593-2-255-5057, Tuesday - Saturday 19:00 - 01:00.

INTERNET CAFES
JAVA NET ($.70/HOUR)
Java has flat-screen monitors, a broadband connection, web cameras and phone booths for international calls. Monday-Saturday, 8:30 a.m. - 10 a.m., closed Sunday. 10 de Agosto and Ramirez Dávalos, Tel: 593-2-254-9829,

AMAZONAS NET ($.80/HOUR)
One of the biggest internet cafés in the Mariscal, Amazonas Net offers two stories of fast computers and cheap international phone calls. The Korean owner serves Korean food too! Amazonas and Foch, Tel: 593-2-290-8464, Open daily 7 a.m. - midnight.

PAPAYANET ($1/HOUR)
This is the hub for travelers and expatriates alike. Its atmosphere has been drawing in travelers for years. The coffee is great and the chocolate desserts are delicious. Open daily, 7 a.m. - 1 a.m. Calama and Juan León Mera, Tel: 593-2-255-6574,

LA FLORESTA

The region of Quito east of La Mariscal, La Floresta is more residential but nonetheless offers a wide variety of budget to luxury hotels and many of Quito's best restaurants, cafés and bars. The hub is on 12 de Octubre and Cordero with the World Trade Center, the Swissotel and The Radisson Hotel all in one small block.

THINGS TO SEE & DO

OCHO Y MEDIO - INDIE MOVIE THEATER ($4/TICKET)

Quito's only independent movie theater is a real gem. Located east of the Swissotel in the La Floresta neighborhood, the artsy film spot has four comfy rooms to view flicks and is teamed up with the trendy and delicious Este Café in front. Indie films from around the globe in a host of languages (with Spanish subtitles), and the occasional live theater, music or dance show. Villadolid N24-353 and Vizcaya, Tel: 593-2-246-9170, E-mail: info@octaedro.org.ec, URL: www.ochoymedio.net.

> *V!VA Member Review-Ocho y Medio*
> *Great indie flicks from all over the world, and a chill café to mix and mingle with an artsy-intellectual crowd. Go check it out, but don't tell your friends because I love this spot and don't want the place to get crowded! 27 March 2007. USA*

LODGING

Hotels in La Floresta range from cozy bunkhouses at $4/person, to room prices starting at $230 at the Swissotel, Quito's most expensive hotel. It is just a short walk from La Mariscal, but the feeling is a world away. You will run into less tourists and will avoid the nightly noise and chaos as well.

BUDGET

CASA DE ELIZA ($5/PERSON)

A V!VA favorite, Casa de Eliza not only has a great family atmosphere with all shared rooms and bath, a cozy lounge and terrace patio, but the profits go to an excellent preservation project in a cloud forest near the Colombian border. Somehow, Casa de Eliza has managed to keep the room rates to a bargain while purchasing over 1,600 hectares of land, where volunteers conduct research projects, help with environmental education, permaculture and eco-tourism. The hostal also provides day trips to tourist hot-spots outside of Quito along with city tours and private transportation. Isabel la Catolica N 24-679, near Av. Coruña east of 12 de Octubre, Tel: 593-2-222-6602, E-mail: manteca@uio.satnet.net, URL: www.ecuadorexplorer.com/golondrinas.

CASONA DE MARIO

Hostal La Casona de Mario is a quaint home with a spacious garden, two community kitchens and two comfortable lounges. All bathrooms are shared and rooms are spacious and clean with lots of natural light—most have private balconies. The internet café a few doors down gives guests a 10% discount on internet and international phone calls. Andalucía 213 and Galacia—2 blocks east of 12 de Octubre, Tel: 593-2-226-0129, Fax: 593-2-223-0129, E-mail: lacasona@punto.net.ec.

ALEIDA'S HOSTAL (ROOMS: $10-15)

Aleida's Hostal has recently opened in the laid-back neighborhood of La Floresta. It is a restored private residence with great views of Quito and a pretty garden where you can drink complimentary coffee. The staff speaks English and can help to arrange trips and/or tours to several locations in Quito and the surrounding areas. Rooms range from $10 for a shared bathroom, $15 for a private bathroom and $20 for a suite. Discounts of 10% are given for groups of over ten people and stays longer than one week. Andalucia No 559 and Salazar, Tel: 593-2-223-4570, E-mail: info@aleidashostal.com.ec, URL: www.aleidashostal.com.ec.

QUITO

QUITO

HOTEL FOLKLORE (ROOMS: $20-40)
Hotel Folklore is a colorfully decorated, intimate hotel. The rooms include a private bath and a home-cooked breakfast served every morning in their pleasant dining room. You're even welcome to use the kitchen to whip up a specialty from your home country! It is located close enough to Mariscal area to be close to the action, but far enough to be quiet. Madrid 868 and Pontevedra, Tel: 593-2-255-4621, Cell: 593-9-616-5711, Fax: 593-2-322-6966, E-mail: info@ folklorehotel.com, URL: www.folklorehotel.com.

MID-RANGE
HOSTAL SUR (ROOMS: $25-45 + TAX)
A larger house in a quiet neighborhood in La Floresta with comfortable, if slightly overpriced rooms. The rooms are basic, no frills, all with private baths and cable television. The service is one of the major perks of this family-run hotel. The staff are friendly, helpful and have working relationships with travel agencies nearby if you want to plan day trips or overnights while you are there. Use of internet in the common room is $1/hour. Francisco Salazar 134 E10 and Tamayo (corner), Tel: 593-2-255-8086, E-mail: info@hostalsur.com, URL: www.hostalsur.com.

LUXURY
HOTEL QUITO (ROOMS: $57-80 + TAX)
Hotel Quito is a large luxury hotel in La Floresta. It has some of the best views over Quito and the valleys to the east of Quito of any hotel and offers full services one would expect of an international chain at a much lower price. The exterior is somewhat obtrusive and outdated, but inside, the hotel feels spacious, comfortable and clean. The pool is a highlight; it is outdoors and, along with the hotel and rooftop restaurant, offers excellent views of the valleys east of Quito. In addition to the pool, there are tennis courts, playing fields, walking trails and more. Most rooms feature a balcony with a view, an internet connection, cable TV, room service and more. The rooftop restaurant, El Techo del Mundo, is a definite benefit, and worth a visit even if you aren't staying at the hotel. Hotel Quito is a great launching point to Guápulo, a popular neighborhood of Quito with an excellent nightlife. Gonzales Suarez N27-142, Tel: 593-2-254-4600, E-mail: reservaciones@hotelquito.com.ec.

HOTEL SANTA BARBARA (ROOMS: $54-79)
The Santa Barbara hotel is set in a beautiful old colonial house surrounded by a pretty garden, conveniently located in the La Floresta neighborhood. The hotel offers 16 tastefully decorated, well-appointed rooms with private bathrooms, cable TV and international calling facilities. There is a restaurant attached to the hotel, which serves up delicious Italian and international dishes. Av. 12 de Octubre N26-15 and Coruña, Tel: 593-2-222-5121 / 593-2-256-4382, Fax: 593-2-222-5121 / 593-2-256-4382, E-mail: mail@hotel-santabarbara.com, URL: www.hotel-santabarbara.com.

RADISSON ROYAL QUITO HOTEL (ROOMS: $80-160 + TAX)

The Radisson Royal Quito is a luxury hotel connected to the World Trade Center and centrally located in Quito's most exclusive financial and residential area. At only 15 minutes from the Mariscal Sucre Airport, Radisson Royal Quito Hotel is an elegant boutique hotel providing top-quality service and amenities sure to please business and leisure travellers alike. Cordero 444 and Av. 12 de Octubre, Tel: 593-2-223-3333, Fax: 593-2-223-5777, E-mail: reservas@radisson.com.ec, URL: www.radisson.com/quitoec.

SWISSOTEL (ROOMS: $230-500 + TAX)

Undoubtedly one of Quito's most elegant hotels, the Swissotel has full facilities, including a lovely outdoor pool and spa area, several exquisite restaurants and views of Quito. Most of the rooms are spacious suites catering mostly to business customers and travelers willing to spend almost double that of other high-end hotels in Quito. If you need to ask how much it costs, you probably can't afford to stay here! Av. 12 de Octubre 1820 and Cordero, Tel: 593-2-256-7600, 593-2-256-7128, E-mail: janetc@swissotel.com.

RESTAURANTS

Restaurants in La Floresta are some of the nicest and priciest in Quito, catering to Quito's privileged and discerning international travelers. Unlike the busier Mariscal section of town, La Floresta is set in a quiet, residential area away from Quito's traffic and pedestrian packed streets. This is a pleasant area to spend a night sipping drinks and chatting with friends over a delicious meal. Be prepared to spend a little more, but it's worth it.

ASIAN
HAPPY PANDA (ENTREES: $10-15)

An elegant Chinese restaurant near the Swissotel, Happy Panda is probably the closest in flavor to Chinese restaurants in the United States. The prices are high for Quito, but there is a good selection and vegetarians will be happy with the options offered in comparison to most Ecuadorian restaurants. Isabel la Catolica N94-464, Tel: 593-2-254-7322.

SAKE (ENTREES: $10-20)

It's hard to say which is better at Sake: the excellent Japanese cuisine or the view of Quito. A huge picture window up on a hill overlooks the city as you munch on fresh maki, sashimi, cooked platters, huge salads and flavorful soups. The service is excellent. Prices are relatively expensive, but the value for your money is good. Couples looking for an intimate date will not be disappointed. Large groups desiring a private room are easily accommodated as well. Paul Rivet N30-166, Tel: 593-2-254-5879.

TANOSHI (ENTREES: $10-20)

One of Quito's first sushi restaurants, Tanoshi has excellent quality sushi in the lower level of the Swissotel. Prices are high, but about on par for sushi in the area. Av. 12 de Oct. 1820 (in Swissotel), Tel: 593-2-256-7600.

CAFÉS/BARS
NARANJILLA MECÁNICA (ENTREES: $3-7)

With multidimensional floors, swinging metal tables and red velvet chairs, and one room carpeted from floor to ceiling in shag, this place is the essence of cool. Edgy contemporary art changes periodically and the bar/restaurant occasionally hosts local artists and live bands. Quito's hippest gather most nights for good food and better cocktails from a unique comic book-style menu. There's even a trendy Dutch fashion shop upstairs. JL Tamayo and General Veintimilla, Tel: 593-2-252-6468.

ECUADORIAN/LATIN AMERICAN
BARLOVENTO (ENTREES: $6-10)

Barlovento is an elegant sitting to try typical dishes like *fritada* (fried pork), *empanadas de morocho* and rich soups. 12 de Octubre N27-09 and Orellana, Tel: 593-2-222-4683.

EL RANCHO DE JUANCHO (ENTREES: $5-8)

El Rancho de Juancho is a Colombian restaurant with a casual ambiance and reasonable prices. There aren't many vegetarian dishes, but there is a wide selection of other options. Whymper 358, Tel: 593-2-245-0960.

EL POBRE DIABLO (ENTREES: $8-12)

A well-decorated place with great music, popular with artsy intellectuals and local bohemian types. Live music lights the place up most Thursday and Saturday nights, with jazz and soft Cuban beats on other nights. Food's a notch pricier than local norms, but dishes are good and the atmosphere more than makes up for the extra cents. Av. Isabela Católica and Francisco Galavis, Tel: 593-2-223-5194, E-mail: eventos@elpobrediablo.com, URL: www.elpobrediablo.com.

RESTAURANTE LA CHOZA (ENTREES: $10-12)

La Choza has all the classic Ecuadorian and Quiteño dishes. It is easy to construct a vegetarian dish with *llapingachos* (cheesy potato pancakes), *mote*, *tostado* (different preparations of Andean corn), cheese-filled empanadas and more. There are also several meat and fish dishes which are excellent. Plan to spend about $10-12 per person. 12 de Octubre N24-551 and Cordero, Tel: 593-2-250-7901.

FRENCH
CHEZ JEROME RESTAURANT (ENTREES: $12-18)

The most newly French cuisine in town. Combining a bit of the Ecuadorian culture with the most classical French cuisine. In a remarkable and magical location and a very comfortable ambiance, as well as decent prices. Whymper N30-96 and Coruña, Tel: 593-2-623-4067, E-mail: jeromari@uio.satnet.net.

STEAK
HUNTERS (ENTREES: $3-9)

An Ecuadorian restaurant that looks suspiciously like the American Hooter's Restaurant, Hunters offers several preparations of steaks along with seafood and Ecuadorian specialties like empanadas, *ceviche* (cold seafood soup), fritada and more. 12 de Octubre 2517, Tel: 593-2-223-4994.

ITALIAN
LA BRICIOLA (ENTREES: $6-8)

This Italian-owned restaurant in a quiet neighborhood in La Floresta is an V!VA favorite and a great value for your money. The service is friendly, the food is delicious and the prices are very reasonable. There aren't many vegetarian dishes, only salads and plain pasta dishes. Toledo 1255 and Luis Cordero, Tel: 593-2-254-7138.

> *V!VA Member Review-La Briciola*
> *I'm Italian and I can assure you, this is a place where you will really eat some good Italian food, prices are fair and the ambient is very warm and comfortable. 8 August 2006. Italy.*

FELLINI (ENTREES: $18-25)

Tastefully designed and laid out, Fellini has a wide variety of the usual Italian options but also has numerous seafood varieties of pasta dishes. There are also some decent Mediterranean options. The wine list is excellent, including a great Argentinian Malbec. Vegetarians can tuck into the spinach *risotto*, while the more carnivorous will be happy with any of the tasty meat mains. Whymper N29-58, Tel: 593-2-254-5112.

LE ARCATE

Le Arcate has the best traditional Italian pizzas in Quito. You have dozens of different pizza choices and each one is completely delectable. Run by an Italian, Le Arcate also has very reasonable prices. General Baquedana 358, Tel: 593-2-223-7659.

PAVAROTTI (ENTREES: $15-30)

Just across the street from the Swissotel, Pavarotti offers fairly standard Italian fare for prices similar to other Italian restaurants in Quito. The menu includes meat and chicken options and various pasta dishes including plates such as pasta with gorgonzola sauce, a rarity in Ecuador. The service is good and the waiters are happy to make suggestions to aid your choice. 12 de Octubre N24-551, Tel: 593-2-256-6668.

INTERNATIONAL

TIBIDABO (ENTREES: $5-10)

Tibidabo is a great international restaurant, with a cozy and elegant atmosphere including a private room. Along with the typical Ecuadorian fare, the restaurant features an extensive wine list. General Salazar 934, Tel: 593-2-223-7334, E-mail: tibidabo@itnet.ec.

SWISSOTEL

This is probably the best hotel restaurant in Quito with a wide selection of international dishes in an elegant atmosphere. Service is attentive. Prices are high for Quito. Av. 12 de Octubre, Tel: 593-2-222-6780.

TECHO DEL MUNDO

The 'Roof of the World' Restaurant connected to the Hotel Quito, is arguably the restaurant with the best views of Quito and Guápulo. Huge picture windows surround the top-floor restaurant and provide excellent atmosphere. The buffets, which are offered almost all day, are excellent and offer a wide selection of Ecuadorian favorites. There are also a la carte dishes all day. Gonzales Suarez N27-142, Tel: 593-2-254-4600, URL: www.hotelquito.com.ec.

GUÁPULO

Guápulo is a small section of Quito behind the Hotel Quito on Av. 12 de Octubre and Orellana. Walk down the stairs behind the hotel, and you will find yourself in the neighborhood of Guápulo with small bars and restaurants on every corner. From here, you can catch an excellent view of the valley and the Sanctuary of El Guápulo. Guápulo offers the perk of being close to the big city while staying in a neighborhood full of charm that has a small-town feel.

Most people feel a million miles away from Quito's new city, when Guápulo is really only one mile (2 km) up-and-over the hill. This enchanting village is reminiscent of an old Italian village, with steep cobblestoned streets, stucco houses built into the mountain side and stunning views. This part of Quito is considered the artistic district, where many artists take up shop. From painters to musicians, many things in town reflect this bohemian spirit, including the restaurants and bars.

MUSEUMS

MUSEO "FRAY ANTONIO RODRÍGUEZ" DE GUAPULO

Museo "Fray Antonio Rodríguez" de Guapulo is housed inside the Inglesia de Guapulo. A history lesson, along with a tour of the Iglesia de Guapulo, can be arranged. Small religious momentums can be purchased in museum shop, from posters of The Last Supper to silver rosaries. Compared to other religious paraphernalia in town, the prices are cheap and the variety is plenty. Open Monday - Saturday, 9 a.m. - 1 p.m. and 2 p.m. - 6 p.m. Entrance fee: $1.50 for adults, $1 for students and 50 cents for children. Tel: 593-2-256-5652 / 593-2-254-1858.

IGLESIA DE GUÁPULO

Santuario Franciscano "Nuestra Señora de Guápulo," is the centerpiece of Guápulo. Often referred to as the most beautiful church in all of Quito, this grandiose 17th century sanctuary houses exquisite art by some of Quito's most historically recognized sculptors and painters, including Juan Bautista Menacho, who designed and carved the side altar and pulpit. Intricately detailed, these carvings are now considered a masterpiece of colonial art. Situated on a small plateau overlooking the Tumbaco valley, the views from the church are spectacular, with rolling hills spanning what seems like forever, and the towering trees of the fresh-smelling, nearby eucalyptus forest. With such a peaceful setting and gorgeous church, it's no wonder that Iglesia de Guápulo is also the venue for many affluent quiteño weddings. In fact, competition is pretty fierce for a spot at this lovely location, so if you have plans to get hitched, it pays to inquire ahead. Especially moving are the beautiful, well-kept church gardens, making this a special place for any wedding. Tel: 593-2-295-3078.

RESTAURANTS/BARS

MIRADOR DE GUÁPULO

Mirador de Guápulo specializes in traditional Ecuadorian dishes like *fritada* (fried pork platter), *sanduches de pernil* (pulled pork sandwiches), *empanadas* (turnovers) and much more. Try the Tabla de Guápulo, which is a large platter with steak skewers, sausage and other meat off the grill. It's more than enough food for two, especially if accompanied with one of their large salads. There is live music Wednesday - Sunday evenings starting around 8 p.m. As a part of the Sinchi Sacha Foundation, the Mirador de Guápulo highlights traditional Ecuadorian food, culture, music and artifacts along with the museum in the same building. Even if you aren't interested in learning anything new, Mirador de Guápulo is a beautiful spot you shouldn't miss, with excellent views and rooftop seating with space heaters. Rafael León Larrea and Pasaje Stubel, Tel: 593-2-256-0364.

PIZZERÍA ANANKE

A small converted bungalow that feels more like a hipster's home than a restaurant, Pizzería Ananke has a stunning view of Guapulo from its upstairs outdoor patio. This artsy dive specializes in homemade wood-oven pizzas and calzones. Cheap and good, the menu also includes an array of appetizers and a thorough mixed-drink selection, including a fresh watermelon vodka cocktail, and of course, beers are on hand. Local live music weekly. Call for weekly schedule. Camino de Orellana 781, Tel: 593-2-255-1421. Open Monday - Saturday, 6 p.m. - 2:30 a.m.

V!VA Member Review-Pizzería Ananke
Perhaps my fave spot in Quito—a great place to meet up with friends and a beautiful view over Guapulo. Live music some nights and the atmosphere radiates chill. 27 April 2007. USA

LODGING

LA CASA DE GUÁPULO

La Casa de Guápulo is a quaint adobe house in the heart of Guápulo with great views and a cozy café with outdoor patio for enjoying breakfast. As with all things in Guápulo, transportation is the hardest thing, so take a cab after dark or when you are carrying luggage. This is also one of the biggest perks, as you are close to the big city while staying in a neighborhood full of charm and small-town feel. Leonidas Plaza Lasso 257 and Calvario, Tel: 593-2-222-0473, E-mail: casaguapulo@yahoo.fr.

Northern Quito - the "New Town"

The area north of La Mariscal and before the dropoff into the valleys is generally referred to as *el Norte*. Here you will find two of Quito's most beautiful parks—*Parque Carolina* and *Parque Metropolitano*—as well as some of the nicest restaurants, hotels, malls, office buildings and neighborhoods. In stark contrast with the Centro Histórico, the North is very modern and developed with a strong American influence.

Parque Carolina

Almost 2 km in length, Parque Carolina is toward the north of the new town, sandwiched between residential and commercial districts. It is the number one choice for sports enthusiasts, with facilities such as a *fútbol* pitch, basketball and tennis courts, volleyball nets, several skating areas and some of the few cycling lanes in the city.

A boating lake and children's playground make it a super popular weekend destination for families. Though the park can get crowded, it's probably your best chance at finding a private patch of grass in the city center.

Parque Metropolitano

This is Quito's biggest park, and one of the biggest city parks in Latin America. Set up on a hill overlooking Quito on one side and the valleys outside of Quito on the other, Parque Metropolitano is a maze of forest paths, roads, sports fields and picnic areas. Most of the trees are eucalyptus, which produce a heavenly odor year round. There are a couple of access roads to the park; the main one is Diego Noboa just up the hill from the Olympic soccer stadium. Open daily, 8 a.m. - 7 p.m.

Multicines CCI Movie Theater ($4/person, discounts on tuesdays)

Multicines CCI is an older movie theater in the small mall CCI on Amazonas and Naciones Unidas. CineMark, just up the street, is much nicer, but sometimes Multicines has movies that CineMark doesn't. Another advantage is that on Tuesdays, tickets are two for the price of one. Av. Amazonas and Naciones Unidas, Tel: 593-2-255-5616, URL: www.multicines.com.ec.

Museo Guayasamín y la Capilla del Hombre (entrance: $3)

Once the home and studio of Ecuador's most famous modern artist, Oswaldo Guayasamín, this spacious museum in the residential neighborhood *Bellavista* now houses an extensive collection of the artist's own work, from the beginning of his "career" at the age of seven, up until his death in 1999. The museum is also home to some of the artist's extensive collection of archaeological, colonial and contemporary art, which he bequeathed to the city of Quito shortly before he died.

Guayasamín's most ambitious work, however, is housed in the *Capilla del Hombre*, or "man's chapel," just up the hill from the museum. Unfortunately, it is unfinished (the artist was still working on it when he died), but contains some powerful imagery that reflects his own grim view of Latin American history since the arrival of the Spanish. The standard price for entrance to each site is $3—if you visit both on one day, you get a discount. Museum open Monday - Friday, 10 a.m. - 5 p.m.; Chapel open Tuesday - Sunday, 10 a.m. - 5 p.m., Calle José Bosmediano 543, at José Carbo; Tel: 593-2-245-2938.

CineMark Movie Theater ($4/person, discounts on wednesdays)

CineMark is Quito's nicest and most modern movie theater, located in the north part of town on Naciones Unidas and América in the mall, Plaza de las Americas. Tel: 593-2-226-2026, URL: www.cinemark.com.ec.

Northern Quito

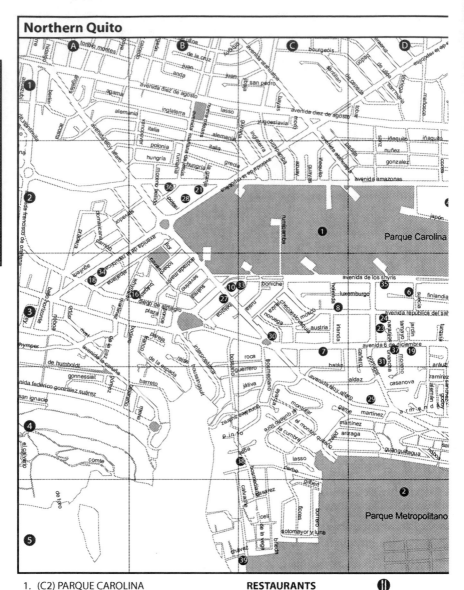

1. (C2) PARQUE CAROLINA
2. (D5) PARQUE METROPOLITANO
3. (E1) CINEMARK MOVIE THEATER
4. (D2) MULTICINES CCI MOVIE THEATER

LODGING

5. (F4) CASA VIDA VERDE
6. (D3) HOTEL FINLANDIA
7. (C3) HOTEL AKROS
8. (C3) HOTEL DANN CARLTON
9. (E3) FOUR POINTS SHERATON QUITO

RESTAURANTS

10. (B3) EL CHACAL PARRILLA
11. (E3) BUSTERS
12. (E3) FRUTERIA MONSERRAT
13. (E3) SUSHI ITTO
14. (E1) KANPAI
15. (F2) LAS CONCHITAS ASADAS
16. (B3) FRIED GREEN TOMATOES
17. (H3)COCOVICHE
18. (A3) LA PAELLA VALENCIANA
19. (D3) RESTAURANTE MI COCINA
20. (E3) PUERTO CAMARÓN

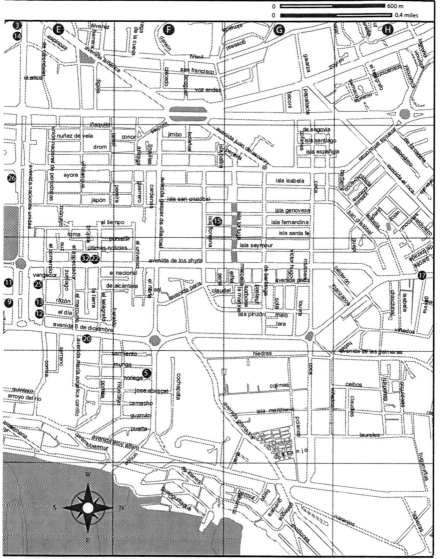

21. (B2) RACLETTE
22. (E3) SWISS CORNER
23. (D3) MISTER BAGEL
24. (D3) CACTUS COFFEE & SALAD BAR
25. (E3) T.G.I. FRIDAY'S
26. (E2) TONY ROMA'S
27. (B3) CAPULETO DELI CAFE
28. (B2) BOCATTO DA FLORENTINO
29. (D4) IL RISOTTO RISTORANTE ITALIANO
30. (C3) CANANAS
31. (D3) LA GUARIDA DEL COYOTE
32. (E3) HAMBURGUESAS DE RUSTY

33. (E3) LA BULERÍA

NIGHTLIFE
34. (A3) BLUES

INTERNET CAFES
35. (D3) PC MANIA
36. (B2) CHECK CENTER
37. (D3) CAFÉNET CITY

MUSEUMS AND MONUMENTS
38. (C4) MUSEO GUAYASAMIN
39. (C5) CAPILLA DEL HOMBRE

QUITO

LODGING

The hotels in the north of Quito cater to international business travelers for their spacious facilities, luxurious rooms and proximity to the airport. If you're looking to stay a bit longer in the city, the North is also a good place to find shared housing, homestays and private apartments. Prices vary, so be sure to scout out a few options before settling down.

CASA VIDA VERDE (ROOMS: $7-15, $100-250/MONTH)

Casa Vida Verde is an attractive, fully-furnished residential hostel, created to provide a safe and comfortable residence for foreign students, workers and tourists who seek both independence and the opportunity to socialize with others. Nightly and long-term stays available. Both English and Spanish are spoken. The hostel has a great view of Quito and the mountains from the rooftop terrace, as well as a huge kitchen with all essential items. All bills are included in the cost of a room. Gonzalo Noriego N39-221 and Gaspar de Villaroel, Tel: 593-2-226-0471, E-mail: info@vidaverde.com, URL: www.hosteltimes.com.

HOTEL FINLANDIA (ROOMS: $33-73 + TAX)

Hotel Finlandia is located about ten minutes from the airport, close to the city's financial district and popular tourist destinations. Friendly and modern, this hotel has 25 smartly styled and comfortable rooms with amenities like mini-fridges and cable TV. The cozy atmosphere, surounding gardens and welcoming staff are a pleasant complement to any international trip, whether you're just passing through on business or about to embark on an adventure in Ecuador. The hotel also has a restaurant, La Tuka, and offers 24-hour reception, city tours and wireless internet. Calle Finlandia 227 and Suecia, Tel: 593-2-224-4287, E-mail: info@hotelfinlandia.com.ec, URL: www.hotelfinlandia.com.ec.

HOTEL AKROS (ROOMS: $70-120 + TAX)

Not the most attractive from outside, Hotel Akros is an aging luxury hotel in the north of Quito. Rooms are well-appointed and include all the amenities one would expect from a luxury class hotel. The staff is warm and welcoming, always prepared to lend a hand with bags or to answer questions about the city. Av. 6 de Diciembre N34-120, Tel: 593-2-243-0600, Fax: 593-2-243-1727, E-mail: www.hotelakros.com/akros.

FOUR POINTS SHERATON QUITO (ROOMS: $80-110 + TAX)

A beautiful, multistory luxury hotel in the northern part of Quito right across from the popular mall, Quicentro. Prices are reasonable for the services offered and plenty of extras are included. There's a spa and gym, but no pool. Avenida Naciones Unidas and República de El Salvador, Tel: 593-2-297-0002, Fax: 593-2-243-3906.

HOTEL DANN CARLTON (ROOMS: $80-120 + TAX)

Hotel Dann Carlton Quito is a Colombian chain offering luxury standards and catering to business travelers. Prices tend to be a bit lower than other international chains, and special

rates are given to businesses. It is located a block from the Parque Carolina and closer to the airport than Mariscal hotels in a quiet neighborhood in the north of Quito. Av. República del Salvador N34-377 and Irlanda, Tel: 593-2-224-9008, Fax: 593-2-224-0952, E-mail: dannquito@punto.net.ec, URL: www.danncarltonquito.com.

RESTAURANTS

The restaurants in the north of Quito tend toward international cuisine and fast food. With three of Quito's larger malls, El Jardín (at Amazonas and República), CCI (Amazonas and Naciones Unidas) and Quicentro (6 de Diciembre and Naciones Unidas), food courts are wildly popular—you will be hard-pressed to find a seat on weekends. There are also several nicer restaurants along Portugal from Eloy Alfaro down to Shyris. The crowds are less touristy at these spots, but that doesn't mean the prices are any less than they are in restaurants in the Mariscal.

ARGENTINE/STEAKS
EL CHACAL PARRILLA (ENTREES: $5-8)
While not offering an incredible ambiance—they somehow managed to squeeze in two huge, loud TVs—this steak restaurant has possibly Quito's best steak. The value is excellent—about $6.50 for a huge filet. For those with smaller appetites, half portions of all the steaks are available at exactly half the price. Try the *picaña,* which comes with two delicious slabs of steak, a salad and garnishes. The *sanduche de lomo*—steak sandwich—is also highly recommended. Vegetarians won't be thrilled with the options: the only items for vegetarians are a salad of lettuce, onions and tomatoes and a baked potato. Av. de los Shyris 344, Tel: 593-2-246-3792.

ASIAN
KANPAI (ENTREES: $15-20)
Kanpai is set in one of Quito's newer malls in the north on Av. América and Naciones Unidas. The atmosphere is great and the sushi is even better. In addition to sushi, Kanpai offers Asian fusion. Try Kanpai's specialty sushi platters, many of which are original combinations. Plaza de las Americas Local M26, Tel: 593-2-331-7806.

ECUADORIAN/SEAFOOD
LAS CONCHITAS ASADAS (ENTREES: $3-5)
Las Conchitas Asadas is an inexpensive seafood restaurant with a casual atmosphere and big portions in the north of Quito. Isla Floreana 510 and Fernandina, Tel: 593-2-246-5444.

EL CEBICHE (ENTREES: $4-18)
El Cebiche is an elegant ceviche and seafood restaurant just south of the mall El Jardín. Prices are reasonable for seafood and service is excellent. Amazonas N24-28, Tel: 593-2-250-4593.

PUERTO CAMARON (ENTREES: $7-9)
Puerto Camaron is a small restaurant in the north of Quito, just past the Olympic stadium with a limited selection of seafood and chicken dishes. The service is great. There are no real vegetarian dishes. 6 de Diciembre N38-08 (Centro Comercial Olímpico), Tel: 593-2-225-213.

RESTAURANTE MI COCINA (ENTREES: $5-18)
A semi-elegant restaurant in the north of Quito a couple of blocks from the Parque Carolina, Restaurante Mi Cocina offers typical Ecuadorian cuisine like *empanadas* and *fritada.* There is outdoor seating and plenty of indoor tables for big groups. Try the *chocolate caliente* (hot chocolate). It's made from real chocolate and served with the traditional slice of *queso fresco* (flavorless cheese). 6 de Diciembre and Julio Moreno, Tel: 593-2-224-1210.

FRENCH/SWISS
RACLETTE (ENTREES: $3-9)
A fondue restaurant in a quiet neighborhood just north of the popular mall, Quicentro. The atmosphere is elegant and the prices are moderately expensive. Mall El Jardín, Patio de Comidas, Tel: 593-2-298-0266.

SWISS CORNER (ENTREES: $4-10)
This just may be the best bakery in Quito. The restaurant specializes in rich, creamy and slightly heavy Swiss food. We recommend the breakfasts and brunches. Shyris 2137, Tel: 593-2-246-8007.

INTERNATIONAL
BUSTERS
Little sister to the Turtle's Head, Busters sits opposite the swanky Quicentro mall. The bar is cozy and the same home-brewed beers are served as in the Turtle's Head. Regular bar snacks are offered, along with burgers and sandwiches and the staff is friendly. The fare is a little pricy by Ecuadorian standards, but the location is a great spot to meet and sink a few beers with local expats after shopping in the mall. Open daily, lunchtime 'til late. Naciones Unidas E9-138 and Av. República de El Salvador (close to the corner).

MISTER BAGEL
Mister Bagel is a great breakfast and lunch spot not only because it has the best bagels in Quito, but also one of the biggest book exchanges. With any purchase, you can exchange an unlimited number of books, contingent on the approval of one of the employees. Try the *ají* bagel, made with the famous Ecuadorian hot pepper, as well as any of their excellent juices. Av. Portugal 546 and 6 de Diciembre, Tel: 593-2-225-3885, E-mail: hgillis@pi.pro.ec.

CYRANO BAKERY
While there are hundreds of bakeries in Quito, one of the best fresh baked bread shops in town is Cyrano Bakery. Cyrano offers up more of a gourmet selection than other shops. Savory breads such as whole grain, yucca, quinoa, garlic or herbal foccacia are only some of the bread loaf and roll varieties available. Cyrano also serves up traditional, no preservative added cinnamon rolls and sweet orange rolls. A selection of scrumptious party-pleasing sized cakes and pies are also on hand, as are small individual pieces of cake and delicious fruit turnovers. Portugal E9-59 Av. de Los Shyris in the Quicentro Shopping Center, Tel: 593-02-2243-507, 593-02-225-9314.

CACTUS COFFEE AND SALAD BAR (ENTREES: $4-7)
Owned by an Ecuadorian who spent about a decade in California, the menu is a fusion of the best of Ecuador's fresh fruits and vegetables with California's best recipes. The restaurant in the north of Quito is much smaller than the original Cactus, about 30 minutes away in the Cumbayá valley. Featuring American Tex-Mex staples like wraps, quesadillas and grilled steak and fish as well as large, Californian salads, Cactus will give you a true taste of America at almost American prices. Monday - Saturday, 8 a.m. - 7 p.m., Sunday closed. República de El Salvador, Tel: 593-2-243-7759, E-mail: pilarmed@andinanet.net.

HAMBURGUESAS DE RUSTY (ENTREES: $4-8)
As far as hamburger joints in Quito, this is probably the best around. Owned by a Californian transplant, Rusty, it has been a fixture in Quito since the 80s. Rusty serves up all the fare you would expect from a diner: hamburgers, french fries, onion rings, milk shakes, even root beer! Sometimes you will find Rusty at the till taking orders—he is hard to miss with his handlebar mustache. It is a bit on the pricey side for Quito: a simple meal costs around $5, but if you really need your greasy food fix it is a great place to go. No vegetarian options. Av. De Los Shyris, a couple blocks north of Naciones Unidas.

T.G.I. FRIDAY'S (ENTREES: $8-10)
Friday's is wildly popular among quiteños and has a slightly more formal reputation than it does in the United States, partially because the people in Quito that can afford it have more money than the average citizen. Offering a wide selection of grilled meats, chicken, salads, fried food, huge scrumptious desserts and a gigantic drink menu, Friday's offers all-American food. Happy hour from 4 p.m. - 8 p.m. on weekdays, offering drinks and appetizers at two for the price of one. Quicentro Shopping, Tel: 593-2-226-4638.

ZAZÚ (ENTREES: $12-16)

Offering a modern interpretation of Peruvian cuisine, the tables at this sleek restaurant are filled nightly with diplomats, oil expats and quiteño high society. Stand out appetizers include thinly sliced octopus served with a creamy olive dip, and crispy mushroom and artichoke *empanadas* encased in wonton-style wrappers. There are plenty of main dishes to choose from for meat-eaters, including tender New Zealand lamb chops, but the house specialty is seafood. The wine list is complete by Ecuadorian standards, and several inexpensive bottles are available (starting around $16), all the way up to special occasion purchases (there is a reserve wine list with bottles for $400). There is a very large bar area with lounge chairs, limiting the number of tables available to diners—call ahead to reserve if you want to be sure to find a seat at one of the ten or so tables. Mariano Aguilera 331, Tel: 593-2-254-3559.

TONY ROMA'S (ENTREES: $18-22)

An all-American steak house with the best rack of rib in Quito and a delicious selection of different sauces to spread on your meat. This is a great place for someone craving a non-Ecuadorian experience: the atmosphere, food and prices are all 100% American. Plan to spend about $20 per person. Av. Amazonas, Tel: 593-2-226-5383.

ITALIAN
CAPULETO DELI CAFÉ (ENTREES: $5-10)

A lovely Italian restaurant and deli with a large garden patio with ample seating and a strange family of parakeets. Prices are on the expensive side, but the food is full of flavor and the portions are generous, making this place worth the splurge for a change. Monday - Saturday, 9 a.m. - 12 a.m., Sunday, 9 a.m. - 10 p.m. Av. Eloy Alfaro N23-544, Tel: 593-2-255-0611, E-mail: clan8cap@interactive.net.ec.

IL RISOTTO (ENTREES: $8-16)

For an authentic Italian banquet and elegant atmosphere with stunning city views, Il Risotto is your spot. The friendly, Italian owners create a pleasant service atmosphere and the buffet will make anyone start to drool. There is outdoor seating on a small balcony in the back. Eloy Alfaro N34-447 and Portugal, Tel: 593-2-224-6850, E-mail: risotto@interactive.net.ec.

MEXICAN
CANANAS (ENTREES: $3-8)

Cananas is a small, elegant Tex-Mex restaurant with reasonable prices and good-sized portions. It features a full breakfast menu, drink menu and Tex-Mex classics like *chimichangas*, hearty steaks and big salads. Try the *almuerzo*—fixed lunch—which, at $3.25, offers a fresh, delicious three-course meal. Eloy Alfaro 2045 and 6 de Diciembre, on the north side of Eloy Alfaro just west of 6 de Diciembre, Tel: 593-2-244-9546.

LA GUARIDA DEL COYOTE (ENTREES: $3-9)

This is an average Mexican restaurant with a couple of branches around Quito. The food is not as flavorful as one might expect of Mexican, and the value is not great considering the smallish portion sizes. All platters can be prepared vegetarian. Portugal E11-37, Tel: 593-2-246-7882.

SPANISH
LA BULERIA

Spanish food prepared by a world-renowned Spanish chef right across from Parque Carolina. There is a great variety of Spanish specialties, from the excellent paprika steak to popular *paella*. There are no vegetarian dishes. Av. de los Shyris N32-302, Tel: 593-2-245-4137.

NIGHTLIFE
BLUES (COVER: $10)

A home away from home for privileged Ecuadorians, Blues is another of the bars that has club status, meaning it can stay open late—it's often open until 4 or 5 a.m. It is particularly popular on Tuesdays and weekend nights, when the well-heeled clientele sip expensive imported spirits in dimly-lit corners or flaunt their designer labels on the dance floor. Music is an eclectic mix of Techno, Euro-cheese and 80s pop, punctuated with popular Latin-Caribbean tunes. Republica and Eloy Alfaro.

INTERNET CAFÉS

There are a plethora of internet cafes in Quito. In the northern neighborhoods, internet cafés tend to be a bit more spread out and slightly more expensive than those in the Mariscal. You can still find great service and speed though.

PC MANIA ($1/HOUR, $0.75/HOUR FOR MEMBERS)

PC Mania is spacious, well-located and reasonably priced. In addition to a broadband connection, there is a cafe, telephone booths for making international calls, copy machines and fax capabilities. Open Monday - Thursday, 8 a.m. - 11 p.m. Shyris N35-18 and Portugal (just across the street from Parque Carolina north of the grandstands), Tel: 593-2-243-6964, E-mail: damilee@yahoo.com.

CHECK CENTER ($1/HOUR)

The Check Center is a fairly large internet cafe with instant coffee and imported candies and treats. It is located in Quito's north, just south of the large mall, El Jardín, on Amazonas Avenue. Dress lightly, as the computers are crammed together and there's not much ventilation. Open Monday - Saturday, 7 a.m. - 12 a.m., Sunday, 8 a.m. - 11 p.m. Amazonas N31-98 and Mariana de Jesús (on the corner just south of the mall, El Jardín), Tel: 593-2-256-8382.

CAFÉNET CITY ($1.20/HOUR, $1.40/HOUR WITH A WEBCAM)

Cafénet City is expensive, small and the computers are slow. But if you're desperate for an e-mail check, it's an option. It is located in the north of Quito just south of Megamaxi. Monday - Friday, 9 a.m. - 9 p.m., Weekends, 10 a.m. - 8 p.m. Av. 6 de Diciembre N35-126, Tel: 593-2-227-1133, E-mail: sualmey@hotmail.com.

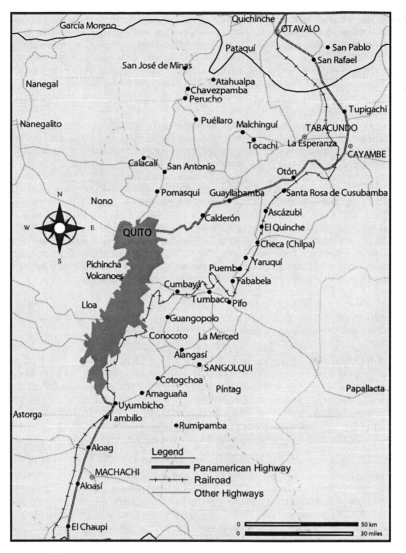

Around Quito

Many travelers choose to stay in Quito and take short day trips to nearby towns like Mitad del Mundo and Papallacta to enjoy monuments, hot springs, mountain hikes and more. Buses run regularly and are very inexpensive. Travel agencies are useful for arranging day trip activities like rafting, biking and climbing, but for basic day trips to nearby towns, you are better off planning it yourself as the tour agencies tend to inflate the prices.

Among the top destinations under two hours from Quito are: Cotopaxi National Park, the relaxing hot springs at Papallacta, the monument to the equator at Mitad del Mundo (along with the real equator 100 meters away) and the Pululahua crater just north of the equator. Just 1.5 hours from Quito by car and 2.5 by bus, Mindo, is one of the most ecologically-aware towns in Ecuador with several private reserves ideal for birdwatching, butterfly-spotting, hiking, river tubing and cliff diving into icy waterfalls.

Help other travelers. Publish your favorite places at www.vivatravelguides.com

Popular tourist destinations that are a little too far for a day trip, but under four hours from Quito, and therefore great weekend or overnight trips are: Otavalo, where you can shop for home-woven wool and alpaca goods along with other famous indigenous items at the market (best on Saturday but bustling all week) and Baños, with excellent biking, hiking, spa treatments and international food. Haciendas are also popular destinations just outside of Quito and provide a glimpse into Ecuadorian culture as well as its spectacular landscapes.

HIKING AROUND QUITO

Few large cities can top Quito when it comes to nearby hiking and climbing opportunities. Just 65 km (40 miles) from the capital, dozens of volcanoes and mountains jut forth from the rich tapestry of cultivated fields and high-altitude grasslands that extend north and south across the 400 km (249 mile) long "Avenue of the Volcanoes."

Some favorite day-hikes among Quito's outdoors community include Fuya Fuya, Pasachoa, Papallacta and Rucu Pichincha. None of these require any technical skills and, since they are day-hikes, you won't need much more than a good pair of boots. Hikes and non-technical climbs that can be done in a long day (mostly because of the drive) include Iliniza Norte, Imbabura, Rumiñahui and Sincholagua. If you are out to tackle snowcapped volcanoes, Cayambe and Cotopaxi await just 60 km (37 miles) north and south of Quito, respectively. Summiting either of these two glaciated beauties requires an overnight stay and, unless you are an expert, the help of one of Quito's numerous guiding companies.

The peaks within striking distance of Quito are numerous enough that you could easily spend a lifetime of vacations exploring them, and the breadth of hiking and climbing prospects are bound to satisfy regardless of your level of experience.

HORSEBACK RIDING AROUND QUITO

If your legs just aren't up to a massive hike or trek, another great way to enjoy the stunning scenery that unfolds just outside of Quito is from the back of a horse. A number of larger tour agencies, and smaller private companies offer horseback riding trips for all ages and skill levels. Single and multi-day trips are available, depending on how long you (and your bum) want to spend in the saddle. Three providers to check out are Ilalo Expeditions, the Green Horse Ranch and the Horse Riding in the Andes Association.

HORSE RIDING IN THE ANDES ASSOCIATION

An association of local riders headed up by the gregarious José Enriquez, Horse Riding in the Andes offers a number of spectacular horseback riding trips in the stunning highlands east of Quito, near Píntag. Trips range in length from short one-day trips to more extensive three and four-day treks, which involve camping or spending a night or two in cabins. If you're keen to see something other than city streets, there is really no better way than from the back of a horse. One of the highlights of longer rides is galloping into Reserva Ecológica Antisana, where lucky riders can spot condors soaring over head. All guides are experienced riders well-versed in local sites and sounds. José has lived in Canada for many years and speaks fluent English. Prices for trips include food and transport. For more information contact José Enriquez. Tel: 593-2-266-0995, Cell: 593-9-404-5458.

GREEN HORSE RANCH

The Green Horse Ranch is a German-operated horse ranch, located at the bottom of a volcanic crater, just outside of Quito. In operation since 1995, the ranch specializes in trail-rides throughout the Western Andes. Astrid Müller, owner of the ranch, has lived in Ecuador since 1990, after realizing her childhood-dream of working with horses. The knowledgeable international and local staff has life-long riding experience, and is happy to go that extra length to make your holiday as enjoyable as possible. Trips venture into the heart of the Ecuadorian Andes. Due to the remoteness of the area, overnight stops are mainly basic, though always carefully chosen, cozy and nice. Tel: 593-2-237-4847, E-mail: ranch@accessinter.net.

ILALO EXPEDITIONS

Ilalo Expeditions is a tour operator specializing in tailor made horseback riding tours on Peruvian Paso horses. The company offers a unique opportunity to experience the high parámo and surrounding landscapes. Los Ciruelos Oe 494 and Diego de Vásquez, Tel: 593-2-248-4219, E-mail: info@ilaloexpeditions.com, URL: www.ilaloexpeditions.com.

VALLE DE LOS CHILLOS

Sitting in a lush, sunbathed valley just a quick bus ride southeast of Quito is Valle de los Chillos, a popular weekend retreat for quiteños. Significantly warmer and more laid-back than the city, this area is perfect for anyone looking to relax and unwind without having to venture far from Quito. The largest town, Sangolquí, has a few accommodation options, as well as a Spanish school. The lively Sunday market is a good place to pick up fresh fruits and vegetables, and interact with the locals without bumping elbows with other tourists. Northeast of Sangolquí, but still in the Valle de los Chillos, are El Tingo and La Merced thermal pools, if you're up for a steamy soak. Llaló, located just 4 kilometers past La Merced, offers privately owned pools, which are cleaner and less-packed. To reach the pools catch one of the La Merced buses from La Marín. Anyone hoping to get out and about in the hills around Quito should make their way towards Alangasí and Píntag; the road forks from here and veers right towards the base of Sincholagua Volcano, or left towards Laguna La Mica near the base of Antisana volcano. The Reserva Ecológica Antisana, located near the similarly-named volcano, is a prime spot for hiking, trekking, horseback riding and condor-watching. Spread across the south end of Valle de Los Chillos is the Refugio de Vida Silvestre Pasochoa (Bosque Protector Pasochoa), managed by Fundación Natura, Pasochoa protects a rare tract of humid Andean forest, home to nearly 120 bird species and 50 different species of trees. This is a prime picnic spot and perfect place for families or anyone up for a little R&R (or some acclimatizing hikes) outside the city.

POSADA DE LOS VOLCANES ($12-25/PERSON)

Set in the quiet Andean town of Sangolquí, 30 minutes away from Quito, this beautiful colonial residence has been renovated to reveal spacious rooms spread across two stories and each with a private bathroom. The hostel offers a relaxing atmosphere and restaurant specializing in traditional Ecuadorian fare. Situated outside the fast-paced streets of Quito, the town and its hostel make the perfect destination for slightly more authentic cultural immersion in the Ecuadorian Andes. 356 Eloy Alfaro St. and Mercado St. Main Square, Contact: Rodrigo Cevallos, Tel: 593-2-233-0104 / 593-2-522-1061, E-mail: info@ecuadorhostel.net, URL: www.ecuadorhostel.net.

LIVE SPANISH IN ECUADOR (FROM $299/WEEK)

Located in Sangolquí, just 30 minutes outside of Quito, this school offers a little something different from its city-slicker cousins, in terms of both atmosphere and environment. Live aSpanish in Ecuador offers three different programs: Spanish & Fun (all-inclusive program), Spanish for Couples and Spanish 4 Me (individual lessons). All packages include airport pick-up, lodging, full board, a day trip and one salsa and/or cooking lesson per week. The Spanish & Fun program includes visits to major Ecuadorian tourist attractions. Flexible schedules are available and there are discounts for groups. Also ask about volunteer opportunities. As if the programs weren't evidence enough, the school has been the Spanish Extension provider for one of the top European tour operators in Latin America for four years. 368 García Moreno, Tel: 593-9-612-1603, E-mail: contact@latinsacademy.com URL: www.latinsacademy.com.

CUMBAYÁ

Little more than a decade ago, Cumbayá consisted mostly of open pastures and country cottages where Quito's elite escaped the hustle of the capital. Though the farms and rolling fields have been largely displaced by upscale suburbs and open-air shopping malls, the city has maintained some of its rustic charm and a decidedly slower pace than Quito. Cumbayá sits at the edge of the Valley of Tumbaco, some 20 kilometers east and several hundred meters below the capital. Its location in an inter-Andean valley provides for a climate that is both warmer and considerably drier than Quito's.

Cumbayá has none of the cultural attractions of Quito, but it is a good place to kick around and relax if you are worn out from the rigors of more sophisticated pursuits. The area around the old town plaza is certainly worth a stroll on the weekend. Literally dozens of eateries, including a good sushi bar, and shops have been established within the last three years.

A five-minute walk from the plaza towards *los reservorios* (go up Francisco de Orellana and then right on Chimborazo) will bring you to another appealing collection of stores anchored by Corfu, a café that serves up some of the best ice cream and pastries in all of Ecuador. For those that want to do more than peruse shops and sip cappuccinos, there is a brand-new bicycle and hiking path that stretches 20 kilometers along old railroad tracks from Cumbayá to the village of Puembo. The official name of the trail is "La ruta ecológica metropolitana 'Chaquiñán,'" and it begins on Avenida Francisco de Orellana approximately 200 meters up the road from the old town plaza.

Getting To Cumbayá

Green buses for Cumbayá depart from a bus station just above the Ecovia Terminal on Rio Coca. These same buses pick up passengers at the southeast corner of Eloy Alfaro and Via Interoceanica (frequently referred to as Los Granados) before heading to the valley. If you have your own vehicle, you can also drive to Cumbayá on a winding road that begins just north of Hotel Quito and follows Avenida de los Conquistadores through Guápulo and over a narrow bridge spanning the Machángara River Canyon. Recently, the Municipality of Quito completed a two-kilometer long tunnel connecting Quito with Cumbayá, cutting journey times. The tunnel enters Quito at La Plaza de Argentina on Avenida 6 de Diciembre and Diego del Almagro.

Around Cumbayá

Like Quito, Cumbayá has two centers, a new one and an old one, located just a few kilometers apart. The new city center consists of two strips of chain stores, including a Supermaxi and Fybeca, that parallel the Via Interoceanica. At the end of these outdoor malls there is a roundabout that gives way to the University of San Francisco de Quito, a small and well-respected liberal arts college that caters to Quito's upper class, the old town and Tumbaco. If you continue right off the roundabout on the highway you will eventually end up in Tumbaco. If you go straight and down the hill on Via Interoceanica, you will wind up in the original town. To get to the town plaza, just after the stop light and bus stop, go about a half a kilometer north on Manabí. The plaza has been recently renovated and boasts a wide assortment of good restaurants and high-end shops.

Restaurants

Spaghetti

Spaghetti serves moderately priced Italian cuisine in a polished dining area that includes a bar and outdoor patio. It has ample space to accomodate large groups. 610 Franciso de Orellana, Plaza Cumbayá, Tel: 593-2-289-3286.

Yappa

Yappa serves international and Ecuadorian cuisine in an elegantly decorated setting. It is priced above most other local restaurants, and it is usually not crowded. Corner of Pampite and Chimborazo, Tel: 593-2-289-2169.

Pekin Cantonese Cuisine

Pekin serves excellent Chinese and Cantonese dishes at reasonable prices. It's a bit hard to find but you'll be happy that you made the effort. Garcia Moreno, behind the Catholic church, Tel: 593-2-289-4913, E-mail: rpekin@uiosatnet.net.

EL SITIO
El Sitio is an upscale bar and grill that serves up an array of international cuisine. It's a little pricey, but the atmosphere and food make up for it. Francisco de Orellana 571, Tel: 593-2-204-0732, E-mail: railimsa@hotmail.com.

CACTUS COFFEE AND SALAD BAR
Cactus offers a menu full of healthy options that easily go down the hatch. Its upstairs patio is a great place to have lunch or just sip a coffee while reading a good book. Via Interoceánica and Diego Robles, Tel: 593-2-289-2740.

NOE SUSHI BAR
NOE is an excellent sushi bar located adjacent to Cumbayá's newly renovated plaza. The food, service, and atmosphere are first class, but expect to pay for it. As well as delicious sushi, NOE serves up good steaks and other international fare. Manabi and Francisco de Orellana, Plaza Cumbayá, Tel: 593-2-289-6858.

CEUCE
This is an exelent fusion cuisine restaurant. It is located in Cumbayá and in Mall El Jardín. It has great sushi but they also serve other types of food. Remember to try the famous salmon lasagna and the Kani Kama roll! The restaurant has a nice, classy atmosphere with a modern look. It is a bit expensive but worth it. Mall El Jardín and Cumbayá Plaza, Tel: 593-2-289-4020.

LA MARMITE
A beautiful Swiss-French restaurant with incredible views of the valley and Quito, La Marmite is worth a daytrip from Quito for its gourmet cuisine, tranquil setting and hiking trails. Open Friday - Sunday and holidays for lunch and drinks into the evening. Large groups can make reservations with a week's notice during the week. About 34 kilometers on the way to Quinche, Tel: 593-2-246-5666 / 593-2-279-0017, E-mail: marmite@uio.satnet.net.

CHECA
About 35 minutes from Quito on the road to El Quinche, Checa will undoubtedly become more developed when Quito's new airport opens in the area (estimated opening date, roughly 2010). Until then, Checa offers pleasant views of the valleys to the north of Quito and Quito in the distance.

PAPALLACTA
Papallacta is dusty little town known for its great hot springs and fresh trout, about one kilometer off the main road about an hour and a half east of Quito on the road to Tena. For $7 per day, soak in the well-maintained pools of varying degrees of heat from mountain-river cold to steamy hot. There is a spa to the right of the main entrance to the pools. There are a handful of hotels and small restaurants in the area ranging from $5-$15 per night. To have 24-hour access to the pools in the spa, you can stay in cozy cabañas on the grounds for around $50 each for two people sharing.

GETTING TO PAPALLACTA
Take the Via Interoceánica to Cumbaya and then follow the highway towards Baeza through the towns of Tumbaco and Pifo. All but the last few kilometers of the road have been paved, so the trip is smooth, allowing you to enjoy the beauty of the dramatic landscape along the two-hour ascent. To reach Papallacta on public transportation, take any bus going to Baeza, Tena or Lago Agrio, and get off just before you reach the village (you will see a sign on the left for Termas de Papallacta).

If you are traveling by private car, turn onto an unpaved path before the town of Papallacta off of the highway from Quito–Baeza. There is a large sign and small bus stop. The road from the highway to the entrance to the hot springs is about 2 km long. If you are taking public transportation, you will have to walk or hitchhike this stretch.

Help other travelers. Publish your favorite places at www.vivatravelguides.com

QUITO

PISCINAS TERMALES JAMANCO
Smaller, cheaper pools in a cow pasture just down the hill from the main Papallacta pools, definitely of a lesser quality. Second stop on the right as you walk up the dirt road toward Termas Papallacta.

HIKING IN PAPALLACTA
There is a rewarding three-hour hike through *páramo* and patches of cloud forest just behind the Termas de Papallacta Resort.

GETTING TO THE HIKING TRAIL
From the information/environmental education center, follow a well-marked trail for about 10 minutes until you reach a wooden bridge that takes you onto a small island. Continue up the trail for a few minutes to a fork. Go right for about 15 minutes until the forks meet again at another bridge. Walk another 100 meters up to a dirt road and concrete bridge. Here you will see another gate. Go in and follow the trail until you reach a patch of cloud forest.

About 20 minutes from the gate, you will come to an intersection of trails. Take the trail that goes east and then north into the cloud forest. Continue north for about half an hour until you reach yet another intersection. Here you can either go left on the main trail or continue straight north on a secondary trail for about 40 minutes until you reach a waterfall tumbling down the east slope of the valley. If you choose to go north in search of the waterfall, you will have to feel out the route as you go, which can be difficult because it's not well-trodden. The roundtrip takes about three hours.

You will find the public hot springs and an ample and safe parking area at the end of the road. On the hill just to the right of the entrance to the springs is a visitor information and environmental education center where you will have to pay a small entrance fee to access the trail.

LODGING
LA CHOZA DE DON WILSON HOSTERÍA
A simple hostel and restaurant looking out over Papallacta town at the corner fork between the road to Termas de Papallacta and the main drag to Papallacta town. A bit rough around the edges, but a good location for both exploring the hot pools and Papallacta town. A decent restaurant overlooks Papallacta and has a $3.50 set menu, including trout plates. Tel: 593-6-232-0627.

HOSTERÍA LA PAMPA (ROOMS: $10-45)
A nice mid-range alternative to staying up the road at the pricey Termas de Papallacta, the complex is a cute, smaller version of its neighbor up the hill. Double rooms and a small bunkhouse share private pools (though some are still under construction), a Jacuzzi and a small restaurant with pretty views and set meals featuring fresh trout ($3.50). The super-friendly owner will be happy to tell you about other activities in the area. Tel: 593-6-232-0624, URL: www.hosteltrail.com/papallacta.

HOSTAL Y RESTAURANTE ANTIZANA
A pink three-story house just before Papallacta complex offering cheap rooms and every style trucha (trout) you could dream up. Simple rooms, but prime location. Tel: 593-6-232-0626, Cell: 593-8-401-1530.

TERMAS DE PAPALLACTA (ROOMS: $65-205)
Located just 40 miles east of Quito, the Termas de Papallacta Spa, Resort and Convention Center is quite literally a world unto its own. For a city escape, make the trip to this inviting retreat perched high in the Andes. Stay at the hotel or in one of the cabins and enjoy the mountain-view hot pools day and night. When you've had enough poolside relaxation, dry off and head to one of the resort's other pamper-yourself facilities. You can choose to revitalize your body with a variety of therapies, massages, and tailor-made treatments—their

exclusive "Thermal Club" is a great opportunity to really relax and revamp. The area is also home to an abundance of flora and fauna, which can be explored via a number of walking trails. Guided ecological tours are available. As if the pools themselves weren't draw enough, the resort also has an on-site restaurant, where you can soak your senses in the flavors of international and national delicacies. Thanks to its beauty and promise of a relaxing get-away, this place is packed on weekends and during holidays: be sure to reserve early. The most economical way to stay at the Termas de Papallacta is to share one of the six or eight-person cabins. Bring your own group of six or eight, however: there is no dormitory-style lodging here. Quito office: Foch E7-38 and Reina Victoria, Tel: 593-2-256-8989 / 2593-2-50-4787 / 593-2-250-3487, Fax: 593-2-254-9794, E-mail: termasuio@termaspapallacta.com, URL: www.termaspapallacta.com.

MITAD DEL MUNDO

Just half an hour north of Quito, you'll find the Mitad del Mundo (the middle of the world), a monument marking the location of the equator. In actuality, the monument called Mitad del Mundo was inaccurately reported as the equator line by a group of international explorers in the 19th century. The original monument is worth a visit for its three-story museum (entrance: $3) which goes into great detail on all of Ecuador's indigenous tribes' typical dress, food and customs. Ask for a guide, they almost always have someone that speaks at least passable English, and it's difficult to understand the exhibits otherwise. The area around the monument has become something of a downtown Disney with touristy shops, a main plaza with occasional performances and lots of cafés and restaurants.

Photo by Freyja Ellis

Today anyone with access to a GPS can tell the line is about 100 meters off. There is a small sign at the actual equator now in an outdoor museum dedicated to experiments and a 45-minute tour for $2. The entrance is off the main highway less than a block north of the entrance to the small town of Mitad del Mundo.

PULULAHUA VOLCANIC CRATER

Pululahua is a volcanic crater just north of the equator. Set at an elevation of 3,356 m (11,010 ft) it offers spectacular views of a patchwork golden and green farms and forests. Hikes, horseback riding and relaxing are the main activities at this now dormant 3 km-wide crater. The last eruption was about 2,400 years ago. The weather is sunny and warm most of the year, but clouds can move in quickly, so come with layers. The only food and lodging on Pulalahua is the luxurious and relaxing El Crater Restaurant and Hotel. However, many tour operators based out of Quito offer day trips and activities in the area.

GETTING THERE

You need a private vehicle to reach the crater, which is about 15 minutes up from the main highway just north of Mitad del Mundo, the equator, and about 25 km (15 miles) north of Quito. The road is mostly unpaved, so a four-wheel drive is recommended.

LODGING AND RESTAURANTS

Options for eating and sleeping are few, but this place seems to prefer quality over quantity.

HOSTEL PULULAHUA (ROOMS: $3-8)

This new eco-resort, located in the 3,500-year old extinct Pululahua volcano crater is just ten minutes from Mitad del Mundo and is a lush outdoor oasis less than an hour from Quito. It's perfect for any nature lovers wanting an immediate release from the noisy and crowded city scene. The crater is located inside a geobotanical reserve and with various microclimates for wild flowers and orchids to grow and is home to a large variety of birds and native animals. The eco-resort includes three types of accommodations, private cabañas with private bathrooms and hot showers, several camping sites with use of bathrooms, a grill and wood, and there are also several comfortable rooms in the main house. All meals are made from fresh organic foods, with all vegetables grown on-site in the organic garden. With dozens of trails for hiking the botanical reserve and crater, the resort also offers guided horseback trips and bicycle rentals. An outdoor Jacuzzi is the perfect way to soak up the gorgeous scenery and relax after a long day of tramping in the forest, bird watching or horseback riding. The resort also organizes agricultural volunteer programs at the 16-student children's community school. Laundry is available on-site, as is transportation to and from Quito. In addition to the main lodge, there are also brand new cabañas and campsites available, one of the only places around to set up your tent. Tel: 593-2-252-5353, E-mail: pululahua@yahoo.com, friendsweb1@hotmail.com.

EL CRATER HOTEL (SUITES: $90)

A small, all-suites hotel with space for 24 people, El Crater Hotel feels more like a modern luxury spa than a hotel. The open, fresh rooms are decorated with minimalist décor using oversized picture windows and soft tones. The *vistas* are the main attraction: each suite has two spectacular views. When lying in bed, you look out over the edge of the Pululahua Volcano Crater. When you lounge on the plush couch, you look out over the mountains on the other side of the volcano. The suites are all one room with a divider between sitting area and the bed. The sitting area features a comfy leather couch and ergonomic leather chair, a picture window and a plasma screen connected to a DVD player—a selection of DVDs is found in the reception. The hotel is designed for complete relaxation. You can request aromatherapy treatments and personal massages in your suite. The hotel can arrange for personal guides to take you around the many hikes in the area. An orchid garden is in process and guests are invited to help out. Mirador de Pululahua 25 km (15 miles) north of Quito, Tel: 593-2-243-9254, E-mail: mb@elcrater.com, URL: www.elcrater.com.

EL CRATER RESTAURANT (ENTREES: $8-15)

A visit to this restaurant can easily be a vacation highlight. It offers one of the most spectacular views of any restaurant in Ecuador. Perched literally on the edge of the spectacular crater, Pululahua, the view will blow you away. The food comes in a very close second. The theme is contemporary Ecuadorian cuisine with excellent steaks, trout and other traditional dishes. Be sure to walk around the crater after you've eaten your fill of tasty Ecuadorian food. Mirador del Pululahua, Mitad del Mundo, Tel: 593-2-243-9254, E-mail: mb@elcrater.com, URL: www.elcrater.com.

PASOCHOA VOLCANO

Pasochoa's lushly vegetated crater and slopes make for an unforgettable day hike. In recent years, because of its beautiful setting and convenient location just 30 kilometers south of Quito, Pasochoa (elevation: 4,199 m, 13,766 ft) has become one of the most popular hiking excursions anywhere around the capital. The mountain can be climbed from every side but the west face, which is steep and composed of terrible rock. The two most easily accessible routes are via the Refugio de Vida Silvestre (Pasochoa Forest Reserve) or the Central Hidroeléctrica, which provides easier access to the peak but a much less picturesque ascent.

GETTING THERE FROM QUITO
Regardless of the route you ultimately choose, you need to travel south out of Quito on the Pan American Highway. There is a frequent bus service from the Plaza La Marín to Amaguaña. In bus or car, the trip takes about 1.5 hours.

HIKING THE REFUGIO DE VIDA SILVESTRE ROUTE
To get to the reserve, travel to Amaguaña and then take a left on to a cobblestone road just across from the main entrance to the town. Drive about 100 meters up to a church with a double bell tower, which is visible from the highway, and make a right. Follow the road for approximately six kilometers up to the reserve's main entrance. There is a fee of $2 for Ecuadorians and residents and $7 for foreigners. This fee gets you in and buys you a good map of the reserve's trail system. It's also possible to camp for $2 per person. About 100 meters up the hill from the caretaker's house and parking lot, there is an environmental education center. A number of trails ranging in difficulty and duration begin here. Sometimes there are also naturalist guides available to accompany you on the shorter walks.

To reach the summit, or most often just the cliff an hour short of the summit, you should follow the relatively well marked "green" trail for about two hours through a bamboo forest, a splendid stretch of cloudforest, and a pine grove until you reach the páramo. From here, follow the footpaths to the left of the crater for one to one and a half hours until you come to a steep rock cliff. At this point you are at approximately 3,950 meters. It's possible, but not recommended, to continue up the cliff and onto the peak because it's steep and the rock is unstable.

HIKING THE HYDROELECTRIC PLANT ROUTE
If you choose to seek the peak via the Hydroelectric Plant, you should hire a truck in Amaguaña. If you have your own vehicle, go left after the Repsol gas station located about three kilometers before Amaguaña. Follow this road for about five kilometers past Hacienda Cuendina and continue on until you reach the Hydroelectric Plant.

From there, continue on foot for 40 minutes until you reach the Comuna Pasochoa, where you need to turn left and cross a stream. Follow the trail through a small pine grove until you reach a gated pasture, where you may find bulls grazing. Beware: they have been known to charge. Walk south across this pasture and a second one to a dirt road. Go left and follow this road for about 150 meters and then turn right. Follow this larger road for about half an hour until you reach another gate. After the gate, go left again and climb to the top of the ridge and follow it. From this point, you should be able to discern a safe route without too much trouble. It should take you between one and two hours to reach the summit depending on your level of acclimatization. The very last stretch of the hike is over bare rock.

Note that getting back from the peak, if you don't have a car waiting at the Hydroelectric Plant, may require a 10-kilometer hump down to the Repsol station. There is very little traffic on the road, so hitching a ride is often not an option.

PICHINCHA VOLCANOES
Guagua and Rucu Pichincha, 4,776 m (15,670 ft) and 4,627 m (15,180 ft) respectively, are two volcanoes located about 10 km (6 miles) west of Quito. Guagua, which means "baby" in the Quichua language, is higher than its neighbor and currently active—it covered the Ecuadorian capital with ash in 1999. Rucu, meaning "old," is slightly lower and closer to Quito. Rucu is inactive.

RUCU PICHINCHA (VIA THE TELEFÉRIQO)
Climbing Rucu Pichincha used to require hiring a truck or making along, and sometimes dangerous, three-hour slog though eucalyptus forest and sponge grass up to Cruz Loma. Fortunately, the Municipality recently completed a gondola (Telefériqo in Spanish) that makes these less appealing options unnecessary. The gondola departs from a station on Avenida Occidental and Avenida La Gasca and costs $4 per person.

QUITO

HIKING RUCU PICHINCHA
The hike from Cruz Loma to Rucu's peak consists of a 2.5-hour walk along a grassy ridge that steadily rises towards a rocky base beneath the summit. Once you reach the rock, you can either go right and traverse the cliff until you reach a sandy slope that leads to the summit or go straight up the rock. Both of these routes require an additional 1.5 hours. The second option should not be attempted by inexperienced climbers unless they are accompanied by a guide equipped with ropes and harnesses.

GUGUA PICHINCHA
Guagua Pichincha is best accessed from Lloa, a village located south of the two volcanoes. Take a bus or cab south on Avenida Mariscal Jose Antonio de Sucre to Calle Angamarca, where you will find transportation to Lloa. You could also hire a cab to take you all the way to Lloa and even to the refuge, which is just an hour's walk from the crater.

HIKING GUAGUA PICHINCHA
If you decide to hike all the way from the village to the crater, head west out of town and follow a meandering road up to the refuge. It takes between five and six hours of steady walking. From the refuge, there is a clear trail to the crater. It was once possible to walk down into the crater; however since the eruption of Guagua Pichincha in 1999 and the possibility of renewed emissions of noxious volcanic gases, this is not recommended.

LODGING AROUND QUITO
SAN JORGE ECO-LODGE AND BIOLOGICAL RESERVE (ROOMS: $13-40)
San Jorge is a very historic hacienda—it was once owned by Ecuadorian president Eloy Alfaro—on the outskirts of Quito. It gets its name from the 375-acre San Jorge botanical reserve where it is located. There are a variety of rooms available, from singles to suites. It is a typical converted hacienda, with the wide hallways, elegant rooms, beautiful gardens and fine dining that the hacienda visitor has come to expect. It also has all the modern luxuries: game rooms, sauna, pool, steam room and hot tub are available in addition to conference facilities. San Jorge does special events: the dining room can seat 250 guests. San Jorge provides more activities than most converted haciendas do. There are the usual horseback rides and bike trips, but San Jorge also offers bird watching, a trip/class about shamanism in Ecuador, tours of the botanical reserve and more. There is also an acclimatization center for those who wish to do high-altitude hiking or mountain climbing. E-mail: info@eco-lodgesanjorge.com, URL: www.eco-lodgesanjorge.com.

HACIENDA LA ALEGRÍA ($45-120/PERSON)
Situated an hour south of Quito on the slopes of Corazón ("heart") volcano, Hacienda La Alegría is in the heart of the "avenue of the volcanoes." On a clear day, you can see not only Corazón, but also four other volcanoes from the courtyard. Still a working organic farm (guests can participate in farm-related activities such as cow milking, etc. if they wish), La Alegría specializes in horses. A variety of tours are offered, including a one-day trip (without lodging) for $75, a two-day overnight for $190, and longer multi-day trips for a variety of prices (one example is the "avenue of the volcanoes" trip, which is six days, five nights and costs $960). All meals are included. Although La Alegría's horseback excursions are more expensive than those you can find in a town like Baños, they take excellent care of their horses. La Alegría also offers hiking, mountain biking and excursions to the nearby cloud forest. In addition, La Alegría hosts an annual summer camp for Ecuadorian children. Simple bed and breakfast costs $45 per person, and full room and board is $120/person, with a horseback ride included. La Alegría only has space for 18 guests, so if you wish to visit, you may want to make reservations ahead of time. Tel: 593-9-980-252, 593-2-246-2319, E-mail: info@alegriafarm.com, URL: www.haciendalaalegria.com.

LA CARRIONA (ROOMS: $70-120)
Located a mere half hour south of Quito, La Carriona is a traditional, 200-year-old hacienda convenient to the Pasochoa Reserve and Cotopaxi National Park. The 25 rooms and

eight junior suites are elegant and ample, with large windows for guests to enjoy the view of the gardens. Facilities include a conference area, sauna, steam room, hot tub, pool, tennis court and soccer field. There is even a small bullring, and bullfights can be arranged with advance notice. Breakfast is included. Tel: 593-2-233-1974, E-mail: info@lacarriona.com, URL: www.lacarriona.com.

CASA IZABELLA (ROOMS: $70-100)
Beautiful bed and breakfast with swimming pool, sauna, tennis courts, gourmet meals, operated by Martha and Hugo Perez. Martha lived in Washington D.C. for 30 years, working at the Ecuadorian Embassy. Tel: 593-2-279-0005, E-mail: ishvara108@hotmail.com, URL: www.casaizabella.com.

MOUNTAIN VIEWS INN (ROOMS: $100-130)
A luxury retreat offering first class services and facilities, and spectacular surroundings, Mountain Views Inn is a lavish way to escape the city and pamper yourself with fresh air, spring-like weather, and organic food. Located just minutes from the incredible Chi Chi Canyon (a mini version of the Grand Canyon), and set alongside a gurgling river, the grounds are private and peaceful, accommodating only 16 people. Recently renovated, the inn is modern and manicured, inside and out. Suites are comfortable and cozy, and decked out in contemporary art and appliances. Splurge and go for the honeymoon suite, which offers amenities including a whirlpool and fireplace. In the morning, head to the colonial style dining room and enjoy a continental breakfast served with your choice of fresh juices. When you've eaten your fill, grab your swim gear and head to the outdoor pool, or lace up your walking shoes and explore the wooded grounds; MVI can organize adventure travel packages, such as horseback riding, bird watching, river rafting or mountain biking. After a long day, curl up in front of the fireplace or unwind with a movie in the home theater. A bit off the beaten path, Mountain Views Inn is worth a peek, even for just a night or two. Tel: 1-800-327-3573, E-mail: reservations@mountainviewsinn.com, URL: www.mountainviewsinn.com.

HACIENDA CHILLO-JIJÓN ($194-245/PERSON)
Hacienda Chillo-Jijón is one of the most elegant haciendas in Ecuador. Built in 1730, it served in part as a textile mill for a good portion of its history. It is conveniently located very close to Quito. Highly exclusive, Chillo-Jijón is not open to the public and is only available by advance reservation. There are ten suites available, for a maximum of twenty guests at once, and each suite is unique and extravagant. Chillo-Jijón has the feel of a European palace: four-poster beds, wide hallways, portraits on the walls, ornate hand-carved furniture, etc. There is a restaurant at the hacienda. Chillo-Jijón has tennis courts, horseback riding, and a 24 acre enclosed garden in which guests can wander and relax. It is also ten minutes from an 18-hole golf course. All of Chillo-Jijón's bookings are done through an affiliated travel agency, Alternative Promotions, and anyone wishing to stay there should contact the agency. Chillo-Jijón is one of the more expensive haciendas: posted rates are $245 per person per night all inclusive: food, hikes, etc. Lodging only with no meals included is $194 per night. E-mail: AltProm@hacienda-ecuador.com, URL:www.hacienda-ecuador.com.

SANTA MARTHA ANIMAL RESCUE RESERVE
Right south of Quito is the town of Tambillo, where the animal rescue ranch is located. You have to catch one of the white pick up truck/taxis at the intersection of Tambillo and the Pan American highway, near the train tracks. But boy, is it worth it! You'll climb the mountain to the yellow and green gate on the left, at the top of the mountain. There are no signs, but the taxis know it as the "zoo." Once you enter the gate, you'll see the ranch below you, a group of white buildings. Go to the main house and ask for a tour. Wear hiking boots, as the animals are spread all over the hill. They've got so many different species which have mainly been rescued from traveling circuses all over South America, such as lions, tigers, bears, monkeys, etc. Once having hiked around (it takes about an hour), please give your volunteer guide a donation. It costs $4,000 a month just to feed the animals, and it's all by donations. URL: www.santamartharescue.org.

HIGHLIGHTS IN THE GALÁPAGOS ISLANDS

1. WILDLIFE. (p. 169) Visitors to the Galápagos do not come for the great beaches, delicious food, or lavish accommodations—although these are a plus—they come to see the world's most amazing cage-less zoo. Travelers in the Galápagos can observe (without binoculars) the unique and often unusual characteristics and behavior of species not found anywhere else in the world.

2. DIVING. (p. 196) The Galápagos is consistently ranked among the best overall dive sites in the world. Because of the combination of cool and warm water ocean currents and a high level of ecosystem protection, the variety and abundance of Galápagos fish and marine mammal species is astounding.

3. PUERTO AYORA. (p. 194) The majority of land tours, scuba diving tours and adventure tours originate and/or are based in Puerto Ayora. Travelers with more time than money can often save up to 50 percent by booking a last-minute cruise in this quaint port town. Puerto Ayora has a wealth of hotels, restaurants, bars, stores, tour agencies, dive shops, internet cafés and phone cabinas.

4. CRUISE TOURS. (p. 154) The most popular way to see the islands is a boat tour through the archipelago. These boats become the visitor's home for the duration of the tour, and all activities occur onboard these ships.

5. VISITOR SITES. (p. 187) Travelers in the Galápagos will be amazed by the number and variation of visitor sites throughout the archipelago. There are over 50 accessible visitor sites in the Galápagos National Park territory. Each offers its own unique history, landscape, vegetative characteristics, and faunal features. When taken in tandem, visitors can begin to understand the complex evolutionary process that has shaped island biogeography. Read on to see each visitor site listed along with a map including island wildlife, paths, fauna and dive sites.

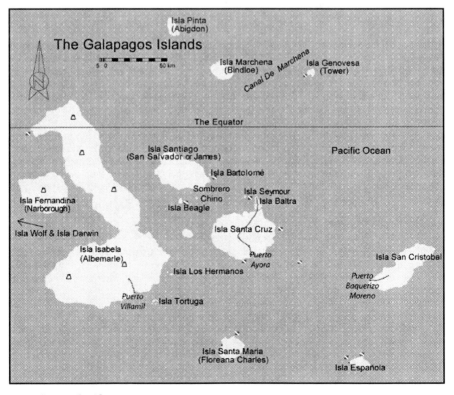

GALÁPAGOS ISLANDS

In the two-hour flight across the thousand kilometers of Pacific Ocean from the Ecuadorian mainland to the Galápagos archipelago, visitors can expect to be transported to an environment reminiscent of prehistoric times. Elegant folds and fans of solidified lava, imposing towers of solid rock, and vast expanses of white, red and green sand provide a Spartan, hauntingly beautiful landscape. Slate black marine iguanas crawl up the rocky substrate from their marine play place, announcing their presence with a primordial release of salt from their nostrils. Land tortoises—or *galápagos*, the Spanish word for the domed saddle resembling the tortoise's shell—slowly lumber their massive physique from slimy bog to grassy clearing.

The Galápagos Islands, made famous for inspiring biologist Charles Darwin's theory of evolution through natural selection, provide tourists the opportunity to observe—without the aid of binoculars—the unique and often unusual characteristics and behavior of island bird, reptile, mammal and fish species found nowhere else in the world. Nearly one in four species is endemic, found only in the Galápagos. And because many of the animals in the Galápagos have no natural predators, both land and sea animals remain "ecologically naïve," virtually fearless and unaffected by visitors.

On land, you will find yourself sidestepping over lounging sea lions, darting lava lizards and scuttling Sally Lightfoot crabs. Bird enthusiasts have the unexpected opportunity to observe both penguins and flamingos as well as blue-footed, red-footed and masked boobies flying, nesting and fishing.

In part due to the dynamic collision of three ocean currents at the Galápagos, there is an unbelievable abundance of sea life. As a result, visitors can observe large, charismatic marine biota—like dolphins, sharks, sea turtles and the occasional fin or sperm whale—as well as colorful reef fish and echinoderms (sea stars, brittle stars and sea cucumbers) found only in the waters surrounding the archipelago. Another highlight is snorkeling mask-to-whiskers with playful sea lion pups. Galápagos is one of the world's premier scuba diving sites.

If you are a passive traveler envisioning long naps on the beach and spacious accommodations, you best not spend the money on a Galápagos trip. Instead, expect to be visually and intellectually stimulated (if not physically challenged) by the unique beauty, natural history and evolutionary processes witnessed on each island. Should you choose to spend some time on land rather than sea, however, there are a number of Galápagos hotels to choose from.

WHEN TO GO TO THE GALÁPAGOS

Although the archipelago nestles the equator, distinct rainy and dry seasons—and distinct high and low-tourist seasons—create better times than others to visit the Galápagos Islands.

RAINY SEASON

The months of June to December tend to be characterized by cool *garúa* (mist) and temperatures averaging 72 degrees Fahrenheit. This time of year the sea is at its roughest (but not overwhelming), water temperatures are lowest (so bring or rent a wetsuit), and island landscapes are most barren (but still beautiful). Fortunately, the rain brings wet richness to the highlands, making them velvety green and flowery.

DRY SEASON

From January to May, the climate is more typically tropical: hot air temperatures, wide stretches of blue sky, and occasional—but brief—downpours. Be careful of the strong sun—because many of the islands are covered in black (bare) lava rock, you may find yourself baking and burning.

In the transition months, you will most likely experience climatic characteristics from the two extremes: from November to January, air temperature start to rise while water temperatures remain cool, and from April to June, fresh breezes and cooling water temperatures offset the heat.

Find more reviews from travelers at www.vivatravelguides.com

TOURIST SEASONS

Interestingly enough, the low tourist season coincides with these comfortable transition months. According to TAME, the major Ecuadorian airline servicing Galápagos, the low tourist season is from May 1 to June 14 and from September 15 to October 31. During these times, boat availability is higher, airline fares are lower and tour prices are most economical. In addition, tourists on a budget (with the freedom of extra time) have the greatest possibility of finding a deal: travel agencies and/or yacht representatives in Quito, Guayaquil or the main island port of Puerto Ayora are more likely to offer last-minute, discounted packages so that they can fill their boats to capacity. Also, visitors to the Galápagos during these times have more freedom to schedule non-cruise activities—like day trips to highland sites, scuba excursions or local beach visits—because they will not have to fight with other tourists for spaces.

During the high season months, however, this strategy is bound to lead to frustration. From June 15 to September 14 and November 1 to April 30, demand for cruises is so high that attempting to book at the last minute will most likely result in waiting time (sometimes up to a month in June or July) and the emptying of your pocketbook (tours are generally more expensive in the high season). Flights will cost more, and hotel and restaurant owners might raise their prices as well. Because so many cruise yachts are running during these months, you may also have to share the island trails with as many as five other tour groups. Despite the geographic isolation of the archipelago and the exclusivity of this type of trip, you will not be alone: in fact, you will probably be surprised by how many other tourists are there when you are. These things being said, all tourist services and facilities are up and running during the high season, so you have the maximum number of options at these times.

Finally, if you are a novice naturalist, keep in mind that migration of bird and sea mammals coincides with the changing seasons. If you are desperate to see the albatross or humpback whales, for example, plan to visit while these animals make their stops in the Galápagos (April-December for the albatross, June-September for the whales).

GALÁPAGOS BUDGETING AND COSTS

Even if you have already paid for your tour or set aside a reasonable budget for independent travel, the Galápagos, its National Park Service and its souvenir designers are going to hit you up for more cash. As soon as you land in Baltra, you will wait in line to pay the national park fee. The cost for foreigners is $110 (payable only in cash), and if you happen to have an Ecuadorian visa and censo, the cost is discounted to $25. Despite the Ecuadorian government's history of corruption, the majority of this income (over 95%) actually goes to the maintenance and conservation of the Galápagos National Park (although none of it goes to the Charles Darwin Research Station). You can also get a Galápagos National Park stamp in your passport, but park authorities ask that you wait until your return flight.

If you are going on a Galápagos Islands cruise tour, most of your expenses have been included in the packaged price. You will, however, have to pay for soda, beer, cocktails and any extra activity not included in the tour itinerary, like scuba expeditions. It is also customary to tip the crew and your naturalist guide at the end of your trip. This is always a delicate subject, since tips are generally meant to be a reflection of services rendered and not an obligation. Some people recommend giving the crew between $20 and $50 per week, and giving the guide as much as half of that amount. Others suggest tipping as much as $10 per day, which amounts to a pretty serious percentage of the total cost of the tour. Each boat has its own system for accepting tips—two envelopes, a communal tip-box, the honor system—but the crew, not the tourist, is responsible for dividing the tip money among the individual members. If any of the crew members was exceptional, feel free to give them an individual display of gratitude, monetary or verbal.

When you are in Puerto Ayora, the potential for spending money is high. The price of food and souvenirs is comparable to U.S. prices, and transportation costs can get very high if you have to take taxis everywhere, especially if you are alone. Tourist items—camera, batteries, film, sunscreen, etc.—are two to three times more expensive in the Galápagos than in the United States, or even on the mainland, so stock up before you come.

Nicer hotels, restaurants, gift shops and tour centers accept major credit cards, but they often charge up to 20 percent for use of this service. There is one bank in Puerto Ayora, the Banco del Pacífico, which gives cash advances on MasterCard, changes travelers' checks (with a minimal surcharge), and has a MasterCard and Cirrus-compatible ATM machine. The bank is open Monday to Friday (8-3:30 p.m.) and Saturday (9:30-12:30 p.m.). Another ATM is at Proinsular supermarket. There are also some stores on Avenida Charles Darwin that will change your travelers' checks for you. Make sure before you come that you will have the ability to withdraw money; otherwise, bring more cash than you think you will need—small bills are preferred. You are more likely to spend all of your cash than have it stolen!

HEALTH AND SAFETY

Touring the Galápagos will be a mentally and physically exhausting vacation if done right. The potentially long flights, extended periods of time on a moving boat, and drastic changes between land and sea temperatures can all take their toll on the body. Plus, cruise boats have very close quarters, which allow for the ultra-rapid spread of viruses. As such, it is a good idea to bring a variety of over-the-counter medicines, especially a nasal decongestant, cough drops and pain-killers.

If you know you get seasick, you should get a prescription for a motion-sickness patch or bring plenty of non-drowsy Dramamine, especially if you are visiting during the wet season, when the seas are roughest. You can also purchase an inexpensive sea-sickness medication on the mainland or in Puerto Ayora, called Mareol. Some boats may have Mareol reserves if you need them, since it is in everyone's best interest that you do not get sick. Although there are mosquitoes in Galápagos, they are not carriers of malaria or dengue fever, so you don't have to worry about getting any vaccinations for tropical diseases.

Medical facilities and pharmacies on Puerto Ayora are decent. The town's hospital offers basic medical services, but it is not very modern or well-stocked. The hyperbaric chamber/clinic offers 24-hour care for diving emergencies and serious burns. Although Dr. Gabriel Idrovo and Dr. Ramiro Lopez specialize in hyperbaric medicine, they also provide general medical consultations during their regular office hours (9:30-1:30 p.m and 3:30-7:30 p.m.). Since it is a private facility that counts on only a small percentage of its funding from local scuba diving operators, they may ask tourists that use the clinic to give a small contribution in addition to the $20-30 consultation fee.

TRANSPORTATION

Transportation on the Galápagos is mainly based on boats and planes. The only islands in the archipelago with cars are Santa Cruz, San Cristobal, Floreana and Isabela. Transportation to the islands from mainland Ecuador is only by plane. Ecuadorian airlines have a monopoly on the market and all flights to the islands leave from Quito or Guayaquil. Once you are on the islands, most visitor sites are a reached by boat.

TRANSPORTATION TO/FROM THE GALÁPAGOS ISLANDS

Flights to the main Galápagos airport on Baltra depart from Quito and most stop en-route in Guayaquil. The Quito-Guayaquil flight lasts about 40 minutes, and the Guayaquil-Baltra flight takes 1.5 hours. Since the archipelago is one hour behind mainland Ecuador, passengers leaving Quito in the morning will land before noon. For a significant portion of the flight, passengers travel over international waters, so they can make use of complimentary alcoholic beverages and duty-free items.

Two airlines, TAME and Aerogal, service the Galápagos Islands. TAME operates daily flights to the Baltra island airport and flies from Quito to San Cristóbal via Guayaquil on Mondays, Wednesdays and Saturdays. Aerogal flies from Quito to Baltra every day except Saturday and

GALÁPAGOS

from Quito to San Cristóbal on Mondays, Thursdays and Sundays. During the high season, flights on both airlines cost around $400. During the low season, flight prices are reduced. Children get a 50 percent discount, and infants get a 90 percent discount.

Even though there is usually some availability on flights to the Galápagos, it is a good idea to make independent flight reservations at least a few days in advance. Travel agencies will block seats for their all-inclusive tours, but then release them on the day of the flight if there are cancellations or unsold tour spaces. So if you are desperate to get to (or return from) the Enchanted Islands, you should be able to find spaces last-minute, especially during low-season.

Since flight prices are fixed, you can change the date of your ticket after purchasing it without penalty. This policy can come in handy if you—like many other tourists—get caught up in the small-town charm of Puerto Ayora and decide to extend your stay: just stop by the TAME office on Charles Darwin Avenue anytime before your flight to make alternative arrangements. Furthermore, if you decide after sun-bathing for a week that you want to spend more time in coastal climes, you can easily change your final destination to Guayaquil. This requires simply checking your luggage to Guayaquil; no ticket change is needed.

TRANSPORTATION TO/FROM PUERTO AYORA

After you de-plane in Baltra, you will either meet the naturalist guide leading your pre-arranged tour or you will head off individually to Puerto Ayora. If you have an organized cruise tour, you will go with your guide and boat-mates on a five-minute TAME or Aerogal bus ride to the *muelle*, or dock, where your boat is anchored. If you have arranged a day-tour from Puerto Ayora, you will take a similar bus-ride to the *canal*, or channel, where you will meet a ferry, take a five-minute trip to Santa Cruz and board an already-waiting tour bus.

If you are on your own and heading to Puerto Ayora, follow the day-tour groups: you can ride the same TAME or Aerogal bus to the canal (for free) and take the same ferry to Santa Cruz (80 cents, one way). Once you get across the channel to Santa Cruz, you can either catch a taxi (about $15 per truck, so try to share) or public bus ($3) to take you the final leg to Puerto Ayora. Ideally, the ferries and buses are scheduled to coincide with flights landing and taking off, so you should not have to wait long.

AROUND PUERTO AYORA

Puerto Ayora consists of one main thoroughfare, so local transportation needs are generally satisfied by your own two feet. Many of the local residents have bicycles for getting around, but unless you are planning to visit Puerto Ayora's surrounding residential neighborhoods, you should not require one. Bicycling is a fun way to get to know the town, though, if you are stuck for things to do or want to act like a local.

Bicycles are also a good way to travel to visitor sites on Santa Cruz within a two or three-hour radius (which are most visitor sites), but expect some physical challenge pedaling through the highlands. Rentals start at $10 per day; tours with a guide and/or support vehicle are also available. Transportation within the bay—either to the Playa de los Alemanes and Las Grietas or to the boats anchored there—is by water-taxi (50 cents, one-way).

If you organize a day-trip with an agency either as part of a package tour or separately, that agency will coordinate all transportation logistics for you: all you have to do is show up at an agreed-upon location in town.

If you want to visit the non-National Park sites on your own (i.e. without a guide and other tourists), you will have to arrange your own transportation. You can contract a taxi to take you anywhere on Santa Cruz (the price for which is negotiable and should be arranged ahead of time, but you should expect to pay about $10/hour). This can often result in an inexpensive, interesting and personalized experience, since the taxi drivers will undoubtedly serve as your tour guide for the day and give you a resident's perspective.

Around the Galápagos Islands

Inter-island transportation is relatively straightforward, but island hopping on your own can be tricky. You can travel between Baltra or Santa Cruz and the other main islands of San Cristóbal and Isabela either by plane, ferry or private boat (lancha). However, itineraries and prices often change.

The small airline, EMETEBE, flies a five-passenger plane between the main islands every day, if there are passengers. Tickets can be purchased at any of the airports or at the EMETEBE office near the port supermarket in Puerto Ayora (hours: 7:15-10:45 a.m., 2-6 p.m, Tel: 593-5-252-6177. The flight costs $65 one-way/$130 round-trip and lasts about 30 minutes.

Ingala operates a passenger ferry between Santa Cruz and San Cristóbal two times a week. Service between Santa Cruz and Isabela and between Floreana and Isabela is less frequent—about twice a month and once a month, respectively. Schedules often change, so inquire about the most up-to-date details at the Ingala office or at the *Cámara de Turismo* (Chamber of Tourism) office in Puerto Ayora. Ferries usually depart from the main pier in Puerto Ayora at noon on Tuesdays and Fridays, arriving in San Cristóbal at about 4 p.m. Return trips are Mondays and Thursdays at the same time. Tickets can be purchased at the Ingala office in Puerto Ayora from 9-11 a.m. on the day of departure. Fares are $50 one-way.

If you are in a hurry or cannot find space on the ferry, you can contract a private boat in any of the port towns. Private transportation will be more expensive. Prices are negotiable, but you should expect to pay between $80 and $100 one-way to either San Cristóbal or Isabela. However, it will be faster and most certainly guided, since local boat-owners love to share their knowledge with tourists. Feel free to ask around the harbors: you are bound to find someone to take you wherever you need to go. The *capitanía*, or port captain, should also be able to tell you which boats are going to these islands and their expected departure times.

Eco-tourism

Since the Galápagos Islands currently receive over 100,000 visitors each year, protective measures managing visitation and use of the islands and surrounding marine ecosystem have been implemented in order to sustain their ecological integrity. About nine-tenths of the archipelago has been set aside for conservation and scientific research. Specifically, 97 percent of the 7,800 km total land area of the archipelago has been protected as the Galápagos National Park (GNP). Since 1959, it has been managed by the Galápagos National Park Service, a specialized governmental arm of the national forestry, protected areas and wildlife agencies created in 1968. Legal protection was extended to the water in 1986 with the declaration of the islands' adjacent seascape as the Galápagos Marine Resource Reserve. Since the passing of the Special Law of the Galápagos in 1998, the area extending 40 miles beyond island territory has also been protected, patrolled and managed by the Galápagos National Park Service.

The importance of preserving the ecological dynamics of the Galápagos Islands has also been prioritized and supported on the international scale. The Galápagos were declared the world's first Natural World Heritage Site in 1978 and a UNESCO Biosphere Reserve in 1984. The Galápagos Marine Resources Reserve is now the second largest marine reserve in the world, after the Great Barrier Reef National Park in Australia.

For residents of the Galápagos, ecosystem management implies social and economic management as well. Population size on the four colonized islands—Santa Cruz, Isabela, San Cristobal and Floreana—is controlled through strict migration policies regulating the number of permanent residents and limiting the stay of temporary residents (tourists, volunteers and workers from mainland Ecuador and abroad) to six months. Furthermore, mandates for protection of the Galápagos Marine Resource Reserve place limits on the size, number and location of fish captured by local artisanal fishermen. Unfortunately, despite progressive legislation and a participatory political framework, the impacts from human populations and illegal fishing—especially sea cucumber and shark-fin harvesting for lucrative Asian markets—continue to be significant challenges to conservation.

For visitors, regulations pertaining to island conservation mean that visitation to the islands' National Park territory is limited to about 50 sites, available only during daylight hours (6 a.m.-6 p.m.) and subject to park rules and guidelines. Furthermore, in order to localize and monitor tourist impact at visitor sites, navigable and day cruise ships may not deviate from the itineraries specifically approved for them by the National Park Service. Park rangers and naturalist guides will insist that tourists refrain from eating, drinking alcoholic beverages, smoking on the islands, touching, feeding, chasing, and/or photographing animals with flash, removing any item—living or dead—from the islands and venturing off the trail or away from the tour group. Water-skiing and jet-skiing are prohibited due to their considerable environmental impacts, and recreational fishing is restricted to those boats that have legally purchased catch permits from operational artisanal fishermen. Do not be disappointed if you cannot partake in these tourist activities.

By following the guidelines established by the GNP, visitors will promote a standard of nature tourism that maintains the majestic appearance and wildlife abundance—as well as the overall ecological integrity—of the sites visited, which are among the most spectacular within the archipelago. Furthermore, visitors serve as an important link in the conservation strategy of the Galápagos: tourism promotes income generation in an environmentally benign way and generates sustainable ecological consciousness and understanding. Educating tourists about natural history and the interconnectedness of humans and the environment in the Galápagos spreads a localized message of conservation that can be promoted on a larger scale. The challenge to tourists is to adapt their Galápagos experience to their own lifestyles by continuing to support conservation initiatives financially and communicating their impressions to others.

GALÁPAGOS WORK AND VOLUNTEER OPPORTUNITIES

Since Puerto Ayora is a magnet for English-speaking tourists, there are a variety of tour operators looking for people who have language capacities (Spanish-English) and will work for cheap. Many travelers have found work in exchange for courses, dives or accommodation. Although migration policies are strict and usually limit tourist visas to six months, there are project-based opportunities that may allow you to stay for a longer period of time.

You will soon realize after talking to people in Puerto Ayora that a significant number of foreigners have come to Galápagos as volunteers or short-term residents, have fallen in love (either with the laid-back lifestyle, the beautiful terrain or the good-looking residents), and have stayed, although this is much less common and more difficult now.

The easiest way to get a job or volunteer position in the Galápagos, especially if you are a certified diver and speak English, is to contact scuba diving operators directly. Many dive centers will accept volunteers as office contacts and helpers in exchange for certification courses. If you already have your Divemaster or instructor certifications, you may be able to find temporary work in the Galápagos, although most places train locals—instead of relying on outside help—to work as guides in their dive shops.

Students of environmental science and/or conservation may have luck finding volunteer or research opportunities with the Charles Darwin Research Station, but the application process is rigorous and competitive. CDRS is usually looking for well-qualified volunteers, usually graduate students, that can give at least six months of their time. You can apply directly through the Charles Darwin Foundation website (www.darwinfoundation.org) or by contacting scientists collaborating with the station, a list of which is included in its annual publication.

If you have some teaching qualifications, you may be able to find a job teaching English on the islands. Most schools work with specific work-abroad or study-abroad organizations, like World Teach, AmeriSpan or the Alliance Abroad Group, but qualified teachers may find opportunities with specific schools, like the Galápagos Academic Institute for the Arts and Sciences (GAIAS).

TOURS

There are basically three kinds of tours in the Galápagos: 1) yacht cruises, or "navigable tours," around the archipelago, land-based, or 2) "combination tours," to sites near the islands' main towns, and 3) adventure tours, which can run the gamut and are usually sponsored by private entities, hotels or individuals as alternatives to the other tours. We have also included a section on avoiding problems and frustrations—which outlines some useful tips that may just save your vacation and thousands of dollars!

Navigable Galápagos tours are organized so that all visitor activities take place from an autonomous tourist vessel: tourists visit the island sites, eat their meals and sleep on their boat. This is the most popular option, because it allows tourists to visit a wide range of islands in the archipelago and because it is the most promoted by tour agencies.

Combination tours are organized in conjunction with hotels in Puerto Ayora on Santa Cruz and to a lesser extent, Puerto Baquerizo Moreno (San Cristóbal). Combination tours based in Puerto Ayora venture to various visitor sites on the island of Santa Cruz, on other central islands, and in the water, returning to the same hotel each night. Many day tours are thematic, like surfing tours and scuba diving tours, but most can be arranged according to the visitors' interests, combining local sites, nearby island sites and dive sites.

Galápagos Adventure tours are still in their infancy and include activities like kayaking, hiking, horseback riding, mountain biking, scuba diving, snorkeling and wildlife viewing, to name a few. These are generally promoted by individuals among the local population and are more flexible than their more expensive counterparts—organized tours arranged internationally.

LAND-BASED GALÁPAGOS TOURS

Combination tours, or land-based tours, are similar to navigable tours in that they combine visits to land and marine sites in the archipelago. The major difference is that combination tours include lodging on land and are limited to sites within a finite radius of the hub town, either Puerto Ayora or Puerto Baquerizo Moreno. These tours are based in certain hotels, which have partnerships with various tour agencies, dive centers and transportation services.

Package tours may offer any combination of trips to local visitor sites. You can book individually (with one or a few companies) or you can book a weekly tour package comprised of a series of day trips, which can include land sites, snorkeling/dive sites, surf sites or all three.

PRICES

Daily tours to island sites range in price from $30 to $115 per person per day when booked individually, depending on the services provided by the tour company and the site visited. Daily tours to dive sites have less variable prices: most dive centers charge a standard $100 to $120 per person per day, according to the site. The price of combination tour packages range from $800 to $1000 per week, including guided trips, hotel and meals. You can arrange these types of trips from your home country or from the mainland, following the same guidelines outlined for navigable tours.

The following companies offer land-based tours and/or lodging:

- Aventour, contact Marcelo, E-mail: marcelo@ecuadoradventure.ec.
- Galacruises, contact Luce, E-mail: info@galacruises.com.
- Red Mangrove Inn, E-mail: info@redmangroveinn.com.
- Galápagos Safari Camp, contact Stephanie, E-mail: info@galapagossafaricamp.com.

LAND DAY TRIPS

A typical island day trip begins at dawn, with a walk to the dock or a bus trip to the canal, where you meet the boat that will take you to your destination. You spend a short time—two hours maximum—in a slow boat to Bartolome, sailing to the pre-determined visitor site.

Find more reviews from travelers at www.vivatravelguides.com

GALÁPAGOS

Once there, you will spend the majority of the day touring the island with a naturalist guide, eating lunch, and (if available at the island site) swimming and snorkeling from the beach. You return to Puerto Ayora via the same route in the early afternoon.

There are plenty of day-trip operators in Puerto Ayora (fewer in Puerto Baquerizo Moreno) who will accept reservations until the day preceding the excursion. Day boats can vary in quality and comfort, but since most island sites are close and you spend a relatively longer time on-site, it is probably more important to shop for day trips by destination. Most day trip destinations from Puerto Ayora include visitor sites on the central islands of Santa Cruz, Santa Fé, North Seymour, South Plazas and Bartolomé. Different boats visit different islands on different days, so plan accordingly.

DIVE DAY TRIPS

Most dive centers utilize the same general framework for the day dive tour and charge the same prices. Day scuba diving packages include two submerges at one dive site, full equipment (6 mm wet suit, mask and snorkel, hood, gloves, boots, fins, weight belt, regulator and BCD), snack and hot beverage between dives and lunch.

Like most day trips, you will probably wake up early, meet at the dive center, and take pre-arranged transportation across the island to the canal, where you will board your boat. The trip lasts all day, since it requires navigation time (30 to 100 minutes to and from the site), dive time (45 to 60 minutes per tank, depending on individual breathing rates) and surface interval (30 to 60 minutes). Divemasters will often have long secondary regulators, so that individual divers running low on air can buddy-up with the Divemaster and stay underwater longer. You will return to Puerto Ayora in the early afternoon to process your dive, look at your amazing underwater photos and/or grab a beer with your new diver friends by the early afternoon.

The most common dive sites from Puerto Ayora are Gordon Rocks, Cousin's Rock, North Seymour, Daphne Minor and Academy Bay. Dive sites are chosen by the scuba center a few days before the trip and change daily. If you have organized dives within a packaged tour, you must dive with the scuba center contracted by your tour at the sites chosen by that center on the corresponding days of your tour.

Beware: because dive centers cannot predict which sites they will visit on a particular date, they will probably give you a list of all potential dive sites. Chances are you will not visit every site, just the most popular and interesting ones. Understand that a typical scuba diving day tour provides two dives at one site. Although some sites (North Seymour, in particular) have two distinct descent points (and thus two different dive possibilities), most do not. As a result, you have two opportunities to explore the same site, providing a second-chance to see any missed highlights, instead of getting to know two different sites.

LAND-BASED VERSUS CRUISE TOURS

There are certain benefits associated with land-based tours, the most important of which is the comfort of stationary hotel accommodations versus mobile staterooms. You are not limited to on-board facilities and services, gaining access to a wider variety of port town restaurants, nightlife and shops. Finally, your community and associated social outlets extend to town visitors and residents, not just the other passengers on your boat.

There are downsides to land-based tours relative to navigable tours. A considerable time is spent sailing back and forth to visitor sites. You are limited to visiting the close, central islands. Only one (versus two) site is visited per day, and there is no chance of visiting sites either very early or late in the day.

GALÁPAGOS ADVENTURE TOURS

Adventure tours basically encompass all tours not covered by the other two categories. These tours are usually self-styled and formulated in conjunction with a local individual, small company or hotel and often include activities like kayaking, hiking, wildlife viewing, mountain biking, horseback riding, scuba diving and/or camping.

Although the infrastructure for this type of tour is still in its initial stages, you will probably witness a boom in the coming years: entrepreneurs and tourism sector employees looking to venture into unexplored niches in the informal economy and generate income that stays in the islands (as opposed to foreign tour companies) have been developing creative tour opportunities. Since most residents of the major towns know their islands inside-and-out, the extreme version of this unofficial touring is to contract a local guide or taxi driver to take you on an individual tour. This is often a surprisingly informative, unique and cost-effective option for Spanish speakers.

GALÁPAGOS HOTELS

While most Galápagos visitors prefer to spend their time cruising around by boat, booking a hotel on mainland is a great way to relax and experience the simple joys of island life. Those with slightly shaky sea legs can spend their whole trip on shore, while the more adventurous sea monkeys can opt to extend a day or two after their cruise. Despite the hype of cruise boat tours, there is as much to do on land as in the water and the island inhabitants (human, that is) are just as welcoming as the highly touted animals. Like the boats, Galápagos hotels and resorts cover just about every price range; from backpacker-on-a-budget hostels to mint-on-your-pillow resorts.

Should you start to feel a little landlocked, most of the high-end places can help you book day tours and sea excursions, including cruise tours. There are four main Galápagos Islands that offer accommodation: Santa Cruz, Isabela, San Cristóbal and Floreana. A bustling tour hub, Santa Fe's Puerto Ayora offers the greatest variety of hotels and hostels, as well as a

wide range of restaurants. During high season (June 15 to September 14 and September 15 to October 31), it pays to book ahead of time, as the islands swell with tourists and it may be harder to find a room of your choice.

CRUISE TOURS

The most popular way to see the islands is by boat. These ships become the visitors' homes for the duration of their tour, and all activities (eating, sleeping, relaxing, partying, sharing in the customary welcome and good-bye toasts, etc.) take place onboard. Due to the increasing popularity of the Galápagos, nearly 75 tourist vessels are now available for cruises, ranging from small but charming sailboats, to elegant, custom-designed motor yachts and luxurious, mid-sized cruise ships.

ITINERARIES AND LANDINGS

Boat tours combine land and marine visits at each visitor site. Tourists usually visit two different land sites and one or two snorkeling sites (depending on the island) on each day of the tour. Visitors are transported by *panga* (dinghy or zodiac) from their yacht to the island's sandy or rocky beach according to what are known as wet and dry landings. Wet landings require that you wade to a sandy shore in up to knee-deep water, while dry landings are made along rocky outcroppings and require a bit of agile grace to avoid turning a dry landing into a wet one—watch out for slippery algae! Once on the island, visitors follow their naturalist guide along marked trails, periodically stopping to bird-watch, check out a scenic vista or snap photos.

GUIDES

Each boat is required to have one or more naturalist guides—each guide is responsible for up to 16 passengers—who is in charge of providing daily island briefings, natural history information on flora and fauna of the islands and suggestions for island conservation. There are over 200 certified naturalist guides in the Galápagos (not all work concurrently), who are qualified with a level I, II or III according to their educational background.

Generally speaking, level I guides have their high school diploma; level II guides have a bachelor's degree and some foreign language training; and level III guides have an advanced degree or specific training in the biological sciences and fluency in a foreign language. Unfortunately, these are fairly arbitrary designations that do not take into account years of experience in Galápagos, naturalist behavior or group facilitation style.

Guides can make or break a tour, so it is prudent to ask for additional recommendations and/or qualifications that clarify the ranking of the guide assigned to your cruise. Unfortunately, since most guides are hired on a tour-to-tour basis (some have semi-permanent placements on boats), visitors have very little control over guide selection.

CHOOSING A GALÁPAGOS CRUISE

The most important things to consider when deciding on a cruise are your expectations for price, boat quality, trip length and itineraries. In the Galápagos, the adage, "you get what you pay for" tends to be true. Accordingly, the tourist vessels in the Galápagos Islands are regularly inspected and categorized according to a set of fixed standards, including facilities, amenities, construction, maintenance and safety. Because new tourist boats occasionally arrive in the Galápagos, antiquated boats stop running tours, and Galápagos boats are periodically renovated or rebuilt, the class system is dynamic: tourist boats can move up, down, or straddle the line between two categories in the class hierarchy according to specifications set in a particular period of time.

BOAT CATEGORIES

Generally speaking, there are five categories of cruise yachts: luxury, first class, tourist superior class, tourist class and economy. V!VA Travel Guides includes a sixth, superior first class, to highlight the cruise boats between luxury and first class in the price spectrum.

Luxury yachts are the most expensive, since they have the most lavish accommodations, the most professional crews, the highest quality food, and the most in-demand (level II or III) naturalist guides. Yachts receiving this designation have at a minimum: air conditioning, hot water, ocean-view cabins with private facilities and spacious social areas (dining room, living room, sundecks). Luxury yachts also have a wealth of extravagant extras—swimming pool, jacuzzi, on-board medical facilities, gift shops and more. They also tend to be bigger and more stable (all of the large cruise ships fall into this category) and have the best cruise itineraries i.e. they visit more outlying islands.

Eight-day luxury cruise tours cost between $2,500 and $4,000, or around $315 to $500 per day. Four and five-day tours aboard the luxury yachts are not very common, but they do exist. Four day tours range in price from about $1300 to $2200, while five day tours cost from $1500 to $2800. These prices do not include airfare, national park fees or onboard beverages.

The superior first class category is not always recognized as an autonomous category, since it overlaps luxury and first class in terms of price and service. This designation encompasses the upper echelon of the first class category: boats with elegant furnishings, spaciousness and a slightly higher price tag. Eight-day cruises generally cost between $2000 and $3000, or $250 to $375 per day.

First class cruise yachts have spacious, comfortable and handsome accommodations, very experienced crews, gourmet food, and some of the most knowledgeable naturalist guides. Yachts in this category also have air conditioning, hot water, ocean-view cabins with private facilities and spacious social areas. Although first class yachts have unique, distinctive features that contribute to an extra-pleasurable experience, they lack the extravagant perks that would catapult them into the superior first class or luxury class. These boats can range in size, but most are well-designed, stable and fast. As such, many make trips to outlying islands in their itineraries. Prices for eight-day tours aboard these yachts range from $1500 to $2400, or about $200 to $300 per day. Four and five-day tours are more common on first class cruise boats, and they range in price from around $800 to $1250 for four days or $1000 to $1600 for five days. Again, these are cruise prices only and do not include airfare, national park fees or beverages.

Boats in the mid-range categories—tourist superior and tourist classes—tend to be slightly smaller (capacity of eight to twenty passengers), less private and less adorned. Yachts receiving a tourist superior designation have air conditioning and hot water (although it may not be fully functional), double cabins with private facilities that they may be below deck or with access to the outside and moderately spacious social areas. These boats have good quality food, a highly-trained crew, a level II or III naturalist guide and a good cruise itinerary. Prices range from $1000 to $1450 for an eight-day tour, or $125 to $180 daily. Four and five-day tours aboard tourist superior yachts are very common and are often your only last-minute option. Four-day tours cost about $650 to $800. Five-day tours cost about $700 to $1000.

Tourist class boats may or may not have air conditioning and hot water, double cabins with private or shared facilities, and small social areas. The food is average; the yacht crew is competent; the naturalist guide has a I or II certification; and the itinerary is decent. Cruise tours range in price from $800 to $980 for eight days, or $100 to $125 per day. Four-day tours ($450 to $650) and five-day tours ($550 to $700) are also very common on tourist class yachts.

Economy class boats are the least expensive, and as such, offer the lowest level of service. Conditions can even be cramped and primitive. These yachts usually do not have air conditioning or hot water (or any water at all), double, triple or quad cabins with private or shared facilities and small social areas. The food, crew, naturalist guide and itinerary are all decent, but pale in comparison to the higher category yachts. These yachts offer budget travelers and last-minute shoppers (these boats generally always have availability) an opportunity to experience the wonder of Galápagos. Unless you have a thriving spirit of adventure and zero claustrophobia, it is worth spending a few hundred extra dollars to travel comfortably. Economy class boat tours cost between $550 and $720 for eight days, or $70 to $90 per day. Four-day tours cost around $300 to $400, and five-day tours are about $375 to $500. Shorter itineraries are almost always offered in this class (and may just coincide with the maximum length of time you can tolerate the sub-par conditions!).

TRIP LENGTH

Because park rules limit the number of boats visiting each island, each boat carries a fixed trip length and itinerary. Voyages vary in length from four to fifteen days, although most cruises are excursions lasting four, five or eight days. You can get a taste of the Galápagos in four days, but since each island has its own unique characteristics, you will see a broader variety of plants and animals with each additional day's visit. Besides, since the first and last days of the tour include a morning flight, a four-day tour yields only two full days and two half-days in the islands. Because of travel time required on each end of the trip, an eight-day trip is recommended.

TRIP ITINERARIES

Generally, four-day tours wind through the northern islands; five-day tours follow the southern route; and eight-day tours offer both. Sometimes, eight-day tours are simply a combination of a four and five-day tour, resulting in a mid-tour transition day when new passengers arrive and other passengers leave. This results in one lost visitor excursion, since you will probably spend the afternoon at a beach near Baltra while they coordinate the shuffle, so try to avoid this. Fewer tours go to the western islands of Fernandina, Isabela, Darwin and Wolf, due to distance, fuel and price constraints. If visiting these islands is a priority, your choices are probably limited to a first class tour, luxury tour (the most expensive) or a charter. Most of the mid-range boats visit the same set of islands on different days, so boat quality and price are often more important considerations than itinerary when booking a trip.

WHERE TO BOOK YOUR GALÁPAGOS CRUISE
FROM ABROAD
Most visitors arrange their tours before arriving on the islands. Since the Galápagos are becoming ever more popular and high season tours sometimes fill up over a year in advance, arranging your tour early is often the only guarantee that you will get what you want. You can do this through a travel agency in your home country, but understand that while the process may be more efficient, you will pay more (commission cost, package fees, national taxes, etc.) and have fewer options (only those boats partnered with your home agency—usually the top-end boats). Many of the first class and luxury boats focus promotion on pre-arranged tours with foreign groups, making them unavailable to independent (or budget) travelers. If you want a more luxurious tour, you may get the best information and service from a travel agency in your home country.

ON THE MAINLAND
You can also arrange tours (from luxury to economy) in Guayaquil or Quito, either through the boats' city offices or through any number of travel agencies. During the low season, you may find a well-priced tour with openings leaving in only a few days, but expect to have to wait a month or more for availability during the high season. If you have a few extra travel days in one of the big cities, go to a number of different agencies to inquire about tour availability and prices. This methodology may result in one of a few fortuitous occurrences: you happen upon a cancellation, a tour looking to fill spaces on departures leaving right away may offer you a last-minute bargain (especially in the low season), or you find a travel agent who works directly with boat owners and offers you the at-cost (no commission) tour price.

ON THE ISLANDS
During the low season, some visitors opt to organize their Galápagos tour from the main island town of Puerto Ayora. Tour agencies based in Puerto Ayora will sometimes offer last-minute deals on cruises, which can save you up to 50 percent. Flying to the Galápagos and arranging a tour is not uncommon, but it may take several days—sometimes a week or more—to plan. If you have substantial travel time and a limited budget, you may save some money by staying in a cheap hostel in Puerto Ayora—all the while visiting local attractions—and waiting for a good deal. Finding boats in the high season is exponentially more difficult, but with a little bit of patience and luck, savvy bargaining skills and flexible expectations, you are bound to find a cruise tour in a reasonable amount of time.

SPECIAL GALÁPAGOS CRUISES
Tour boat companies—in conjunction with private agencies—sometimes offer special tours for families, scuba divers, photographers, students and scientists. Most of the time, these tours are coordinated by private organizations, which charter a boat to meet their special needs, and thus are not available to individual tourists. This mostly applies to photographic, student or research expeditions. If you have a special interest in the Galápagos that cannot be stimulated within the realm of the general tour, your best option is to organize a charter (six months to a year in advance) with others that have the same interest.

Family tours are not uncommon in the Galápagos. A few boats—especially the bigger cruise ships—will have special family promotions in order to attract younger visitors. Although the Galápagos vacation is more meaningful for visitors who can understand the evolutionary dynamics of island biogeography, students of all ages can learn important lessons from a Galápagos tour. If you want to bring young children, it is worthwhile to look for a family tour—other families will be present with playmates for your children, and your guides will have some experience with younger visitors.

Special scuba tours are the most common and accessible to individual tourists. A large percentage of the cruise boats have naturalist guides or crew members who are certified Divemasters and have scuba equipment onboard. If the general tour you book has scuba capabilities, you can either pre-arrange a set number of immersions, which you pay for as part of your entire package, or organize and pay for your dives onboard and on an individual basis. Depending on your tour itinerary (and your group's affinity for the water), you may be able to see as many interesting marine features and creatures snorkeling as scuba diving.

Extreme diving aficionados also have the option of booking a live-aboard scuba tour to the outlying islands of Darwin and Wolf. These trips organize two to three daily immersions in some of the archipelago's most amazing (and remote) dive sites along the route. Live-aboard scuba diving tours in the Galápagos do not incorporate on-land excursions, instead focusing entirely on cultivating the marine experience. You will, however, get interesting views of rarer island sites while you are navigating.

TOUR COMPANIES

AIDA MARÍA/GALÁPAGOSTOURS
This company is one of the longest-running tour companies in the archipelago, operating for over 30 years. Aida Maria has a large fleet of Galápagos touring boats: different sizes and offerings for different budgets—with multi-sport and diving tours, you're sure to find an Aida Maria tour to occupy you during your time in the Galápagos. They also offer one of the best surfing tour packages in the islands, claiming to take surfers to secret spots open year-round. Their website offers a decent FAQ answering common questions about the islands and what to pack before leaving the mainland. Amazonas N2331 and Veintimilla, Quito, Tel: 593-2-254-6028/254-8329, URL: www.galapagostours.net.

ANDANDO TOURS
This German-owned company has a long history in the Galápagos. The present owner's father sailed to the islands from Germany in 1930 and began one of the first charter boat services in the Galápagos. Fiddi Angermeyer has taken over and expanded his father's original business, adding overland and Amazonian tours (available to book on their website or through the Quito office). Andando Tours emphasis remains on the Galápagos: they own and operate 6 vessels equipped to cruise around the stunningly diverse islands. Check out the well-designed website to choose the cruising vessel that's right for your trip. Mariana de Jesús E7-113 and Pradera, Quito, Tel: 593-2-323-7186/323-7330/323-7857, Fax: 593-2-323-8309, E-mail: info@angermeyercruises.com, info@andandotours.com, URL: www.andandotours.com.

GALAKIWI
Southern Exposure Tours, in association with Galakiwi, bring you a wild and unforgettable Galápagos Islands experience. The Galápagos Islands are known worldwide for their fearless wildlife, but no amount of hype can prepare you for such a close encounter with nature. Here you can amaze at giant 200 kg tortoises lumbering through cactus forests, enjoy the entertaining courtship display of the blue footed boobies and Magnificent frigate birds, or snorkel with penguins, sea lions, and sea turtles, close up and personal. E-mail: galakiwi@yahoo.com.au, URL: www.galakiwi.com.

GALÁPAGOS TRAVEL LINE
Galápagos Travel Line specialize in offering four, five or eight day cruises in the Galápagos Islands for both individual passengers as well as for larger groups of travelers. They also offer charters for families, incentive groups and associations. They offer jungle tours in the upper Amazon rainforest in Ecuador as well as land tours through the beautiful landscape of the Ecuadorian Andes. Their staff of professional guides and drivers will give you a warm welcome to Ecuador. Carlos Tobar E6-101, 3rd floor-D, Quito, Tel: 593-2-323-8772, Fax: 593-2-323-8773, E-mail: info@galapagostraveline.com, URL: www.galapagostraveline.com.

GALASAM GALÁPAGOS TOURS
Galasam offers a range of accomodation from economy class to the budget-minded or student-traveler, to the first class and luxury yachts for those seeking additional comforts. 9 de Octubre 424 and Cordova, Quito, Tel: 593-4-230-4488, E-mail: christian@galasam.com, URL: www.galapagos-islands.com.

GOLONDRINA TURISMO

Golondrina has 14 cruise boats in all five categories of ship, to meet anyone's budget. They can also take you to great diving sites for new, intermediate and experienced divers. Juan León Mera N22-37 and Carrión, Quito, Tel: 593-2-252-8616/252-8570, Fax: 593-2-222-8954, E-mail: golondri@uio.satnet.net, URL: www.adventuregalapagos.com.

GUIDE2GALÁPAGOS

Guide2Galápagos is a multi-national company specializing in Galápagos cruises—offering up-to-date information, competetive prices and personalized attention on the internet. Pinto E4-366 and Amazonas, Quito, Tel: 593-2-255-0176 593-2-255-0180, Fax: 593-2-256-0426, E-mail: info@guide2galapagos.com, URL: guide2galapagos.com.

SCUBA IGUANA GALÁPAGOS

Scuba Iguana is the most efficient, detail-oriented, and professional dive operation in Puerto Ayora. Gear and equipment is available in all sizes, well-maintained, and replaced annually, so you will never feel uncomfortable due to poorly fitting gear or malfunctioning equipment. Pre- and post-dive periods are restful and relaxing on Scuba Iguana's spacious and cushy boat, but don't expect too much down-time, since the boat's twin engines get you to your dive location in record time. Safety is also a priority: all new divers must complete a check dive and receive an extensive safety briefing. Avenue Charles Darwin, Puerto Ayora, Tel: 593-5-252-6497, E-mail: info@scubaiguana.com, URL: www.scubaiguana.com.

SANDAES TOURS

Sandaes specializes in Galápagos tours. They own yachts of differing sizes and prices, so you're sure to find the perfect boat for your Galapogas experience. Diving tours are also available, so if you're interested in underwater life, don't pass up this opportunity to explore one of the "Seven Underwater Wonders of the World." Sandaes has other offerings throughout Ecuador, including jungle and overland trips. Their jungle tours are especially interesting, as visitors stay at beautiful haciendas in the rainforest, complete with gourmet food, outdoor activities and an opportunity to interact with knowledgeable indigenous guides. Joaquin Pinto St. E4-286 and Amazonas Ave. Saldaña Building, 6th Floor Office A, Ecuador, Tel: 593-2-252-2590, Fax: 593-2-290-6697.

TRANSCORD REISEN TOURS

Transcord Reisen Tours offers luxury and tourist class yacht tours of the Galápagos. Scuba diving is available on several of these yachts, although these tours are not recommended for the beginner diver. Special deals are available on their website, so take a look before you make a reservation. A German-owned operation, Transcord also leads tours in other locations in Ecuador, such as Quito and the Amazon. These tours generally last one week and can be combined with horseback riding, trekking, or mountain climbing. The Galápagos tours appear to be your best bet with Transcord, despite the plethora of other options. Ave. República de El Salvador 112 and Shyris Edif Onix, Quito, Tel: 593-2-246-7441, Fax: 593-2-246-7443, E-mail: transcor@transcord.com, URL: www.transcord.com.ec.

AVOIDING PROBLEMS AND FRUSTRATIONS

Since there is always the possibility that things will go wrong on vacation and the potential for rough sailing in the Galápagos does exist, it is impossible to make a comprehensive section on how to avoid any negative situation. However, we've tried to cover the basics and address the most common problems that travelers face in the Islands.

In order to better guarantee you will get what you pay for, especially if you are booking from abroad, make sure the agency you are using gives you a detailed contract outlining payment schedules and refund policies and that it—or its Ecuadorian counterpart—is registered with the government with a specific RUC-number. It is also a good idea to do your homework: search for information published in written or electronic form and ask for references.

Many tourists with combination tours have complained that the hotel, dive center or day-tour company associated with their package offers a sub-standard service relative to what is provided by others in Puerto Ayora. By organizing your trip outside of the tour context, you can avoid feeling locked in to any aspect of your vacation that may prove to be dissatisfactory. However, you should recognize that seeking out the perfect set of options will require more time, even though the services and accommodations are generally concentrated on one street in Puerto Ayora. It may also take a bit more money, although you will have the benefit of not paying for things you don't want.

People have also criticized economy-class cruise tours for bottom-of-the-barrel services and accommodations, so if you are not willing to chance it, pay the few hundred extra dollars for a nicer, more comfortable medium-class boat. This is a small upgrade, considering the total price of the trip.

Even people traveling on more expensive boats have reported problems—anything from sinking ships to sexual harassment. The most common complaints are last-minute boat changes (which the fine-print of the contract allows), overbooking and/or last-minute cancellations, changes in the itinerary, a poor crew, mechanical trouble and general dissatisfaction with the quality of the experience relative to the price of the trip.

If you experience problems once you are on your trip, register your complaints with the port captain at the capitania or at the *Cámara de Turismo* (Chamber of Tourism: infocptg@cap-turgal.org.ec) in Puerto Ayora. They will take your reports seriously and make sure the problems are not repeated on subsequent tours.

GALÁPAGOS ISLANDS CRUISE BOATS

The following is a comprehensive list of the ships that currently offer cruise tours in the Galápagos Islands. They are organized according to class: luxury, superior first class, first class, tourist superior, tourist and economy. Since the classification system is dynamic, boats may change their categorization as they improve (or diminish) the quality of services provided.

LUXURY CLASS CRUISES

Luxury yachts are the most expensive, since they have the most lavish accommodations, the most professional crew, the highest quality food, and the most in-demand (level II or III) naturalist guides. All yachts receiving this designation have air conditioning, hot water, double ocean-view cabins with private facilities and spacious social areas (dining room, living room, sundecks). They also tend to be bigger and more stable (all of the cruise ships fall into this category) and have the best cruise itineraries (i.e. they visit more outlying islands).

PRICES

Eight-day luxury cruise tours cost between $2,500 and $4,000, or around $315 to $500 per day. Four and five-day tours aboard the luxury yachts are not very common, but they do exist. Four-day tours range in price from about $1,300 to $2,200, while five-day tours cost from $1,500 to $2,800. Prices do not include airfare, national park fees or onboard beverages.

THE ATHALA

The Athala is a new luxury-class ship owned and operated by Huagan Cruises and Columbus Travel. It features eight nicely furnished double cabins, each with private bath, air conditioning, hot water and closet. The ship itself has a bar area, Jacuzzi, library, TV/DVD, and observation deck in addition to the dining area. The food is quite good and the staff and guides are very competent and professional. It is possible to combine a trip on the Athala with a short stay in Puerto Ayora. Beginning in April 2007, the Athala will be replaced by the Athala II, a new ship currently under construction. URL: www.haugancruises.com.

ANAHI

Owned and operated by Galápagos Catamarans, the Anahi is a luxury motor catamaran that began service in July 2006. New and comfortable, the Anahi prides itself on taking visitors to more remote islands that other cruises do not visit. The Anahi has eight air-conditioned cabins, each of which features hot water and large windows that look out over the water. Two of the cabins are suites and the twin beds can be converted into a double. The deck is spacious and pleasant, and there is a bar/lounge area there as well. The Anahi has excellent food and service and prides itself on knowledgeable naturalist guides. URL: www.galapagoscatamarans.com/OurCatamarans/MCANAHI/tabid/314/Default.aspx.

M/V EVOLUTION

The M/V Evolution, with a capacity for 32 passengers, has 15 total twin and double cabins and two suites, each beautifully furnished with private facilities, hot water, air conditioning and more. The Evolution caters to individual passengers seeking rest, relaxation, and lavish accommodations, as well as families or charters. A few important extras—most notably an open-air dining area, small heated pool, multimedia room and infirmary—set this cruise experience apart in measures of comfort. It also has ample deck space for your sunbathing habit and a boutique for your shopping habit. The design of the boat is reminiscent of the 1920s, but charming details and deluxe amenities provide modern-day comforts. Cruises depart from San Cristóbal on Sundays. Owner: Quasar Nautica.

THE INTEGRITY

The Integrity is a modern 141' motor yacht that began operations in mid-2005. Nine cabins, accommodating 16 passengers on the main deck, are equipped with lower twin, queen, or king beds, picture windows, private bath, individual climate control, a stocked refrigerator, satellite telephone, and an entertainment center with television, CD/DVD, VHS and LCD monitor. Meals are served at tables of four to six not far from a galley designed for gourmet chefs. On the covered top deck, you'll find a spa, a bar, barbecue and comfortable chaise lounges where you can relax, enjoy a beverage, or nap in the gentle breezes. With its huge, state-of-the-art stabilizers and vibration control, the Integrity will carry you through Darwin's Islands more smoothly and comfortably than on any other yacht. It also has diving/NITROX equipment available.

ISABELA II

The 40-guest Isabela II, with 20 spacious cabins with outside view, private bathrooms, hot water and air conditioning, offers an elegant yet relaxed atmosphere for experiencing the Galápagos adventure. It has three public decks with a bar-salon, dining room, sundeck and jacuzzi. It also has one of the most complete reference libraries, with a large selection of books on Ecuador and the Galápagos, nature and conservation videos, and nightly multimedia presentations. This is an outstanding vessel for whale and dolphin watching programs. Four-day, five-day, and eight-day cruises depart on Tuesdays and Fridays. Itineraries include islands covering the extremities of the archipelago: North Seymour, Española, Floreana, Santa Cruz, Genovesa, Isabela, Fernandina, Santiago and Bartolomé. Owner: Metropolitan Touring.

V!VA Member Review~Isabela II
The Isabella II and its crew over delivered for pretty much all of the 23 people on a four-night, five-day cruise last week. The crew and naturalists are wonderful. Food and hospitality were outstanding. Highly recommended. 14 March 2007. Los Angeles, CA.

ISLANDER

A Galápagos cruise on the 47-passenger Islander is one of the finest expedition-style experiences in the Galápagos Islands. Twenty-four comfortable cabins have outside views, private facilities and climate controls. Social areas include a lounge with bar, a conference room with facilities for films, slide-shows and lectures, a library and a covered deck with tables and

GALÁPAGOS

chairs. The ship is well-equipped with snorkeling gear, wet suits, a spa, guest e-mail station, video microscope, hydrophone, and Splash-Cam. A physician, a video chronicler and an undersea specialist are onboard at all times.

POLARIS

Traveling aboard the 80-passenger Polaris is a total experience in expeditionary cruising. The ship is large enough to operate comfortably in remote environments like the Galápagos, yet small enough to enter ports and narrow inlets inaccessible to bigger ships. Cabins are equipped with lower berths, private facilities and air-conditioning. Spacious social areas include: a sunny observation lounge with bar, piano, and facilities for films, slide shows and lectures, a library with an exceptional collection of books, a covered deck with chairs and tables, and a dining room with wrap-around views of the sea. There are also a number of luxurious perks: an open bridge with satellite communication equipment, a souvenir shop, a gym with sauna, a hospital with doctor onboard and a glass-bottom boat.

GALÁPAGOS EXPLORER II

The Galápagos Explorer II is a 100-passenger cruise ship with 50 ultra-elegant suites, each with television, VCR, mini-bar and satellite communication, in addition to the standard private facilities, hot water and air conditioning. It is one of the fastest, most modern and most luxurious tourist vessels in the Galápagos, blending comfort, adventure and environmental preservation. Social areas—including sundecks, a bar and lounge and a library—offer the amenities of a world class cruise liner. Tours depart from San Cristóbal on Wednesdays and from Santa Cruz on Saturdays. Their itineraries also include Española, Genovesa, Bartolomé, Santiago, Isabela and Fernandina.

ALTA

The ketch-rigged motor sailor, Alta, has capacity for 16 passengers in eight double cabins complete with private bath, hot walk-in shower, and air conditioning. She is an elegant yacht that provides the special charm of a sailing ship with the speed and stability of a motor yacht. The Alta is one of the most charming yachts in the Galápagos, offering its passengers exclusivity and uniqueness. Snorkeling and scuba-diving equipment is also available. Tours leave on Sundays and have a comprehensive itinerary, including the outlying Genovesa, Fernandina, and Isabela and central and southern islands. Owner: Quasar Nautica.

GALÁPAGOS LEGEND

The 90-passenger expedition ship, Galápagos Legend, is the fastest ship in the archipelago, offers the most extensive itineraries, and provides the most luxurious—if not surreal—Galápagos cruise experience. Spacious cabins and social areas provide the ultimate in relaxation and enjoyment. Deluxe amenities, including numerous sun terraces, a swimming pool, an outdoor bar area, a music lounge and a well-stocked library, will make you want to stay onboard and forget about blue-footed boobies and hammerhead sharks. Tours depart on Mondays and Thursdays and hit an impressive list of islands: Santa Cruz, Española, San Cristóbal, Bartolomé, Isabela, Fernandina, Santiago and Rábida. Owner: Klein Tours.

LAMMER LAW

The Lammer Law is a 16-passenger trimaran offering incredible space and comfort for naturalist and diving cruises. Attractive and functional, with an artful combination of stability, grace, and speed, the Lammer Law is perfect for the dedicated diver, enthusiastic nature-lover, or deluxe traveler. Also, since it has capacity for 18 passengers in nine cabins—replete with private facilities, hot water, and air-conditioning—and only carries 16 (the maximum number allowed per guide), the Lammer Law provides a welcome amount of privacy and comfort that many other private yachts cannot. It also has spacious dining and salon communal areas. Cruise tours depart on Saturdays and hit North Seymour, Genovesa, Fernandina, Isabela, Santiago, Bartolomé, Española and South Plazas. Owner: Quasar Nautica.

THE PARRANDA

The Parranda is an elegant, spacious 125-foot motor yacht with capacity for 16 passengers in eight double cabins. Facilities include a salon, galley and dining room. With its remarkable stability and speed, the Parranda is targeted at travelers who want to experience the Galápagos in comfort and refinement. Expeditions depart on Sundays and include in their itineraries the islands of Santa Cruz, Genovesa, Fernandina, Isabela, Santiago, Bartolomé, Española and South Plazas. Owner: Quasar Nautica.

THE SANTA CRUZ

The Santa Cruz, a 90-passenger cruise ship, is one of the only vessels exclusively designed for exploring the Galápagos. The 47 cabins are relatively spacious and well-maintained, each equipped with private facilities, hot water, and air conditioning. Comfort is a priority on the Santa Cruz, which has three decks filled with lounge chairs, a solarium, Jacuzzi, reading room and well-stocked bar and lounge. Added amenities for supreme enjoyment include exercise equipment on the sundeck (so you can run on the treadmill and whale-watch at the same time) and a glass-bottom boat. The Santa Cruz has gained worldwide recognition for its excellent standards, including superb service, expert crew, the most knowledgeable multilingual naturalist guides and menus that feature the very best Ecuadorian and international cuisine. Snorkeling equipment is provided complimentary. Four-day, five-day, and eight-day cruises depart on Mondays and Thursdays and follow a comprehensive itinerary to Isabela and Fernandina, as well as central and southern islands. Owner: Metropolitan Touring.

ECLIPSE

If it's space you're looking for, the Eclipse is your ship. This luxury ship boasts itself as the most uncrowded vessel of its size in the Galápagos. The Eclipse has a capacity for 48 passengers, housed in four suites, eight staterooms, 13 doubles and two singles. All rooms are very large and have a private bathrooom with hot shower and are fully air-conditioned. Dining Eclipse-style is alfresco, with the dining area seated around the 20-foot (six-meter) pool. Other amenities include a library/video room, an on-board shop and an observation deck. Tours of the islands are broken down into groups of no more than 12, divided between the four naturalists on-board. The Eclipse runs eight-day cruises, departing on Saturdays from Santa Cruz.

GALÁPAGOS AGGRESSOR I

The 100-foot dive boat Galápagos Aggressor I, also known as Jesus del Gran Poder, was specially designed for cruising the Galápagos archipelago in style. It has accommodations for 14 passengers in seven luxurious staterooms, each with two berths, private facilities, individual climate control, a cassette-stereo system and a port window offering great views and natural light. Social areas include: a comfortable salon area featuring a complete entertainment center with large-screen television, VCR, stereo system, CD-player and well-stocked library; a bright dining area; two spacious sundecks with chairs and chaise lounges; Jacuzzi; and upper sundeck with built-in seating. The bright and spacious dining area has three tables and chairs, where expertly prepared meals are served. Although the Galápagos Aggressor I offers lavish accommodations and comfortable furnishings, its specialty is providing unforgettable scuba-diving experiences. A large dive-deck, with individual storage lockers, a carpeted camera table, and freshwater showers, makes snorkeling or diving from the boat simple and convenient. Eight-day tours depart on Thursdays.

SUPERIOR FIRST CLASS

Superior First Class includes boats that have an extra special touch of elegance and refinement but lack the extravagant amenities associated with Luxury Class boats. We have included four boats in this category.

PRICES

Eight-day cruises generally cost between $2,000 and $3,000, or $250 to $375 per day.

ARCHIPEL I AND II

The motor catamaran, Archipel I, has nine double cabins for 16 passengers, each with outside view, private facilities, hot water and air conditioning. The Archipel II is newer (built in 2004) and has a layout almost identical to the Archipel I. Elegant facilities and modern details—including an ample bar/lounge, library, television, DVD, E-mail service, water purifier and onboard snorkeling and diving equipment—enhance the stylish design of the catamaran. An elastic observation deck and spacious sundeck provide comfortable, social areas for relaxing or searching the horizon for marine life. Five and eight-day cruises visiting northern and southern islands are available beginning Mondays and Thursdays. Owner: Galacruises Expeditions.

CORAL I

The Coral I is a spacious motor yacht with standard (bunk-style), superior (twin double), and deluxe cabins, all of which have outside access, carpeted floors, handsome wooden furnishings, private bathroom, hot water and air conditioning. Although it can accommodate up to 30 passengers, the Coral I carries only 20, which provides for a generous amount of privacy and personal space. Additional comforts include two ample sundecks, an interior buffet dining area, two indoor social areas, a well-stocked bar, television and VCR, stereo system and library. Dark teakwood and bronze interiors provide a touch of modernity and exclusivity to an already unique Galápagos tour. Since the Coral I also contracts two naturalist guides (one per 10 passengers) and a large crew, services are professional and extremely personalized. Snorkeling equipment is available onboard. Four-day, five-day and eight-day cruises depart on Wednesdays and Sundays and follow a comprehensive itinerary spanning the extremes of the archipelago and hitting up the outlying Isabela, Fernandina and San Cristóbal. Owner: Klein Tours.

CORAL II

The Coral II is a three-deck, 26-passenger fedship, which like her twin yacht, provides privacy, personal attention, and comfortable accommodations. Decorated in the same dark teakwood and sparkling bronze, the Coral II adds a touch of refinement to an open and spacious design, complete with ample social areas, large picture windows, and an expansive observation deck. The Coral II carries either 20 or 26 passengers and sails in tandem with its sister ship, the Coral I. Snorkeling equipment is also available. Four-day, five-day, and eight-day cruises depart on Wednesdays and Sundays and follow a comprehensive itinerary spanning the extremes of the archipelago and hitting up the outlying Isabela, Fernandina and San Cristóbal. Owner: Klein Tours.

THE XPEDITION

The Xpedition, one of the few mid-sized cruise ships catering to the Galápagos, has capacity for 92 passengers distributed in cabins on four decks, each equipped with private facilities, hot water, air-conditioning, phone, 20" television set and hair dryer. The Xpedition offers visitors a typical cruise experience—complete with a restaurant, grill, bar and lounge and activity coordinator all bearing the name of a Darwinian artifact—amidst an atypical environment. Owner: Islas Galápagos.

FIRST CLASS

First class cruise yachts have spacious, comfortable, and handsome accommodations, very experienced crews, gourmet food, and some of the most knowledgeable naturalist guides. Although first class yachts have unique, distinctive features that contribute to an extra-pleasurable experience, they lack the extravagant perks that would catapult them into the superior first class or luxury class.

PRICES

Prices for eight-day tours aboard these yachts range from $1,500 to $2,400, or about $200 to $300 per day. Four-and five-day tours are more common on first class cruise boats, and they range in price from about $800 to $1250 for four days or $1000 to $1600 for five days.

CACHALOTE

The ketch-rigged motor sailor Cachalote has capacity for 16 passengers in eight handsome double bunk cabins decorated in dark teakwood. Each cabin has two porthole windows, private bath, hot water and air conditioning. Other amenities include a large dining room, salon, bar and three ample wooden decks. The Cachalote was rebuilt and refurbished in 2002 to provide more space and to add modern touches to its Victorian style. The attractive design of the Cachalote, its professional crew, and excellent cuisine produces an ambience that enhances the character of the Enchanted Islands. Snorkeling and scuba-diving equipment is available for a price. Eight-day cruises depart on Wednesdays for central, southern and western islands. Owner: Enchanted Expeditions.

CRUZ DEL SUR

The Cruz del Sur, a 16-passenger motor yacht, has eight double-bunk cabins equipped with private facilities, hot water, air-conditioning and views of the sea. It has a spacious interior, complete with comfortable lounge, communal dining area, as well as ample outdoor space in the sun and shade. Four-, five-, and eight-day cruises depart from San Cristóbal on Mondays and visit the standard central and southern islands. Owner: Galasam.

DEEP BLUE

The Deep Blue combines spaciousness, comfort and service in their ultra-modern motor yacht that began its operations in Galápagos in mid-2003. It can accommodate 16 passengers in nine double cabins, with two lower twin berths or one double bed, private bathroom, hot water and individual climate control options. Added amenities include a guest room, a small library, cell phone communication, television and VCR, a large sundeck, a covered back deck, and an immense dining, buffet and bar area. The Deep Blue has excellent scuba-diving capabilities, with a large diving platform and air compressor. Five-day and eight-day tours depart from San Cristóbal on Mondays and include northern, central and southern islands in the itineraries. Owner: Sandaes.

DAPHNE

The Daphne is a 16-passenger motor yacht with eight fully-equipped double-occupancy cabins. Other amenities include a restaurant/bar, a small library, television and VCR, and solarium. The Daphne has received worldwide acclaim for its ecological and diving cruises, which expertly combine first-class service, a top-notch crew, and exquisite menus featuring the best in Ecuadorian and international cuisine. Snorkeling equipment is complimentary and scuba-diving equipment is available for a price. Four-day, five-day, and eight-day cruises depart on Wednesdays and Sundays and hit northern, central and southern island visitor sites.

EDEN

The 16-passenger Eden is equipped with eight spacious double cabins, each with private bath, hot water and air conditioning. Her elegant interior and refined details—complemented by a library, television, VCR and full bar—provide a touch of class to enhance the cruise itinerary, which spans the north-south gradient of the archipelago. An ample sundeck and accessible upper deck provide added comfort to an already luxurious trip. Snorkeling equipment is available free of charge. Four-, five-, and eight-day cruises depart on Wednesdays and Saturdays and include in their itineraries northern, central and southern islands. Owner: Aida María Travel.

ERIC

The Eric, in conjunction with her sisters, Letty and Flamingo I, were custom-designed for cruising the Galápagos archipelago. She can accommodate 20 passengers in 10 double cabins on three decks — seven with two twin lower beds and three with one double bed — each equipped with private bathroom, hot water, air-conditioning, intercom system, and hair

GALÁPAGOS

GALÁPAGOS

dryer. An ample dining space, a sundeck stocked with lounge chairs, and a conference area with television, VCR, stereo system, video collection, and library add comfort, relaxation, and modernity. Crew members provide dedicated and professional service, and naturalist guides — one per ten passengers — offer extensive and personalized information. Trips depart from San Cristóbal on Sundays and offer weeklong, comprehensive itineraries that span the entire archipelago, including western islands. Snorkeling equipment, sea kayaks, and beach towels are provided at no extra cost. Owner: Ecoventura.

ESTRELLA DEL MAR
The Estrella del Mar is a well-designed motor yacht with capacity for 16 passengers. Double cabins have private bathroom, hot water, air conditioning and views of the sea. The Estrella del Mar also has comfortable lounge and dining areas with plush booth seating. Ample sundecks are well-stocked with cushioned lounge chairs. Four-, five-, and eight-day cruise tours begin on Wednesdays and Sundays and include the standard central and southern island visitor sites in their itineraries. Owner: Galasam.

FLAMINGO I
The Flamingo I, like her sisters Eric and Letty, was custom-designed for cruising the Galápagos archipelago. She can accommodate 20 passengers in 10 double cabins on three decks—seven with two twin lower beds and three with one double bed—each equipped with private bathroom, hot water, air-conditioning, intercom system and hair dryer. An ample dining space, a sundeck stocked with lounge chairs and a conference area with television, VCR, stereo system, video collection, and library add comfort, relaxation and modernity. Crew members provide dedicated and professional service, and naturalist guides—one per ten passengers—offer extensive and personalized information. Trips depart from San Cristóbal on Sundays and offer weeklong, comprehensive itineraries that span the entire archipelago, including western islands. Snorkeling equipment, sea kayaks and beach towels are provided at no extra cost. Owner: Ecoventura.

GALÁPAGOS ADVENTURE I
The motor yacht Galápagos Adventure I combines a spacious design, fast cruising speed, and modern décor to produce a comfortable, unforgettable Galápagos experience. It has eleven single, double and triple bunk cabins, accommodating 22 passengers, each with private facilities, hot water, air conditioning and teakwood furnishings. It also has ample social areas: a sunny and shady deck-space stocked with lounge chairs, a carpeted interior lounge with panoramic views, stereo system, television, VCR and an elegant communal dining hall. It also has scuba-diving capabilities. Four-day, five-day, and eight-day cruises depart on Tuesdays and Fridays to island visitor sites in the north, center and south. Owner: Ninfa Tours.

LETTY
The Letty, like her sisters Eric and Flamingo I, was custom-designed for cruising the Galápagos archipelago. She can accommodate 20 passengers in 10 double cabins on three decks—seven with two twin lower beds and three with one double bed—each equipped with private bathroom, hot water, air-conditioning, intercom system, and hair dryer. An ample dining space, a sundeck stocked with lounge chairs, and a conference area with television, VCR, stereo system, video collection, and library add comfort, relaxation, and modernity. Crew members provide dedicated and professional service, and naturalist guides—one per 10 passengers—offer extensive and personalized information. Trips depart from San Cristóbal on Sundays and offer weeklong, comprehensive itineraries that span the entire archipelago, including western islands. Snorkeling equipment, sea kayaks, and beach towels are provided at no extra cost. Owner: Ecoventura.

MILLENIUM
The Millenium is a prestigious yet comfortable motor catamaran with capacity for 16 passengers. It has six spacious double cabins with a private balcony view, each of which have private facilities with bathtub, hot water and air conditioning. Two suites have Jacuzzis. It

also has ample social areas with views of the sea: a plush salon, communal dining room, well-stocked bar and four solaria. Four-, five- and eight-day tours depart from San Cristóbal or Santa Cruz on Thursdays and Sundays. The itinerary covers northern, central and southern islands. Owner: Galasam.

MISTRAL
The Mistral, a 74-foot motor yacht, can accommodate 12 passengers in six cabins, each with private bathroom, hot water and air conditioning. It also has a main salon, dining room and scuba-diving capabilities. Mistral is ideal for the more adventurous traveler or diver, who prefers the familiar atmosphere of a smaller boat. Cruises depart on Saturdays and make stops on North Seymour, Genovesa, Fernandina, Isabela, Santiago, Bartolomé, Española and South Plazas. Owner: Quasar Nautica.

MONTSERRAT
The Montserrat is a 75-foot motor yacht with capacity for 16 passengers in eight double cabins. Spacious cabins are equipped with double beds and upper berths or twin lower berths, private facilities, hot water and air conditioning. Social spaces include: a comfortable lounge area with television, VCR, and bar, communal dining room and sundeck. Excursions depart on Thursdays and Sundays from San Cristóbal and Santa Cruz, respectively.

NEMO
The Nemo is an ultra-modern catamaran sailor ideal for cruising with family or friends. It can accommodate 12 passengers in six double cabins, each with private bathroom, hot water and air conditioning. Spacious sundecks, an ample lounge area and an expansive dining room provide extreme comfort. Sea kayaks and snorkeling and diving equipment are also available. Four-day, five-day, and eight-day cruises offering a standard itinerary through central and southern islands depart from Baltra on Wednesdays and Sundays. Owner: Latin Tour.

REINA SYLVIA
The motor yacht Reina Sylvia offers elegance and style to individuals and charters, and carries the mystique of having been built to host to Queen Sylvia of Norway. Eight double cabins—equipped with private bath, hot water, air conditioning, oversized upper and lower berths, locker, drawers and vanity—provide spacious accommodations for 16 passengers. An upper-deck owner's suite, with a king-sized bed, and scuba-diving capabilities are also available for chartered cruises. Snorkeling equipment can be rented for a small fee. The Reina Sylvia boasts one of the most comprehensive itineraries, with visits to the outlying islands of Isabela, Fernandina, and Genovesa, as well as central and southern sites. Cruises depart from Baltra on Saturdays or Sundays. Owner: Transcord.

SAGITTA
The Sagitta is an impressive three-mast sailing ship with a handsome interior design, excellent naturalist guide and friendly crew. It accommodates 16 passengers in 10 spacious bunk cabins on two decks, each with private facilities, hot water and air conditioning. It has a large dining room, comfortable conference room, well-stocked library and deck salons. Excursions begin on Wednesdays. Owner: Andando Tours.

SKY DANCER
The Sky Dancer is an immense motor yacht that provides elegance, refinement and comfort to 16 passengers. It has four Master staterooms, with one queen bed or two twin beds, and four Deluxe staterooms with two twin beds and a panoramic view. All accommodations are equipped with private facilities, hot water, air-conditioning, and wardrobe. Snorkeling and scuba-diving equipment is also available. Eight-day cruises depart from Baltra on Sundays and make visits to outlying islands in the west. Owner: Ecoventura.

THE BEAGLE

The Beagle is a 105-foot steel-hulled schooner with enough space to comfortably accommodate 12 passengers in its six double cabins, each with private bathroom, hot water, and air-conditioning. Snorkeling equipment can be rented for a small charge. Eight-day cruises depart from Baltra on Tuesdays and include in their itinerary the outlying islands of Genovesa and Isabela as well as the standard central and southern island visitor sites. Owner: Andando Tours.

TIP TOP II

The Tip Top II is a modern steel-hulled motor yacht with a capacity for 16 passengers in eight double cabins—four below and four above deck—and one single cabin. Each double cabin has two twin beds, private facilities, hot water and air conditioning. It also has ample social spaces: a carpeted interior salon with fully-equipped bar, television, VCR and full sound system, as well as a plush dining room area, an extensive covered deck (perfect for relaxing or dancing the night away), open top-deck for star-gazing and diving platform. All crew members aboard the Tip Top II will provide top-notch, professional and personalized services, catering to your every need. They may even organize for you a special birthday celebration. You will not be lacking in comfort, refinement or attention. Common areas are well-decorated and clean; food is well-prepared and varied; and navigational equipment is well-maintained and modern. Scuba-diving facilities are available for two or more passengers. Cruises depart on Fridays for northern, central and southern islands. Owner: Rolf Wittmer.

TIP TOP III

The Tip Top III is the slightly more spacious equivalent of her sister ship, the Tip Top II. It too has capacity for 16 passengers, but in 10 double cabins with two lower twin beds, private facilities, hot water and air conditioning. It also has ample social spaces: a carpeted interior salon with fully-equipped bar, television, VCR, and full sound system, a plush dining room area, an extensive covered deck (perfect for relaxing or dancing the night away), open top-deck for star-gazing and diving platform. The crew is also extremely professional and attentive; the food is excellent and varied; and the navigational and safety equipment is well-maintained and modern. Scuba-diving facilities are available for two or more passengers. Cruises depart on Fridays for northern, central and southern islands. Owner: Rolf Wittmer.

DIAMANTE

The 12-passenger Diamante is a brigantine schooner motor sailor with six double cabins, each with private facilities, hot water and air conditioning. It also has a bright and airy deckhouse, with a main salon handsomely decorated in mahogany and dark teakwood and 360-degree visibility. Other pleasurable features are a small dining area behind the pilothouse and an outdoor poop-deck where guests can wine, dine and take in the beautiful natural surroundings. Snorkeling equipment is complimentary, and chartered tours can request scuba diving equipment. Cruises depart on Wednesdays and Saturdays for northern, central and southern islands. Owner: Andando Tours.

BELUGA

The Beluga is a deluxe, 110-foot, steel-hulled motor yacht, which accommodates 16 passengers in eight double staterooms, each with private bathroom, hot water, and air-conditioning. It is very spacious, with lots of deck space, a sundeck, a dining room, a bar, and a galley. The crew is well-trained and professional and takes very good care of their guests onboard and ashore. Snorkeling and scuba-diving equipment is also available. Tours depart on Fridays and hit Isabela, Fernandina, central and southern islands on their itineraries. Owner: Enchanted Expeditions

SAN JOSE

The San Jose is a large, stable and extremely comfortable motor yacht accommodating 16 passengers. The eight spacious double cabins on main and upper decks are equipped with two lower twin berths, outside access and windows on both sides of the stateroom, private facilities, hot water and climate control. Social areas are also extremely ample and comfortable. The indoor lounge has television, DVD, VCR, video collection and stereo system; the dining area has three communal tables (with propeller detailing); and the covered observation deck is well-stocked with plush lounge chairs. Besides offering a considerable amount of privacy and relaxation, the San Jose can also boast one of the most accommodating and professional crews in the archipelago as well as a genius chef who can prepare unforgettable seafood and vegetarian dishes. Snorkeling equipment is available free of charge. The San Jose is mostly available for group and scuba-diving charters, but it also offers four-day, five-day and eight-day cruise tours leaving Mondays and Fridays.

TOURIST SUPERIOR CLASS
Tourist Superior Class is generally affordable and has comfortable ammenities like A/C and private baths. Boats in this class are not as fancy—you won't have as much space and extra luxuries like gourmet food, cushioned lounge chairs, etc.—but all your basic needs will be well taken care of.

PRICES
Prices fo from $1,000 to $1,450 for an eight-day tour, or $125 to $180 daily. Four and five-day tours aboard tourist superior yachts are common, and are often your only last-minute option. Four-day tours cost about $650 to $800. Five-day tours cost about $700 to $1000.

SPONDYLUS
The Spondylus is a hand-crafted yacht that boasts a unique style in the Galápagos. It has nine fully air-conditioned double cabins with lower beds, each with private facilities with hot and cold water. There is a daily buffet with a variety of cuisines, a bar and a spacious sundeck. They offer four, five or eight-day cruises that go ashore twice daily to explore the islands, snorkel and enjoy the company of the animals. Owner: Kem Pery Tours, URL: www.kempery.com.

AHMARA
The Ahmara is a catamaran built by Philippe Jeantot, the champion around-the-world sailor. With capacity for eight passengers, this sailboat provides a private and comfortable atmosphere perfect for experiencing the thrill of navigating under sails. Elegant cabins have wood-paneled double beds, private facilities and hot water, and the indoor lounge provides a full bar and excellent onboard cuisine. The Ahmara also features modern navigation equipment, high performance, stability and scuba-diving capacity. Snorkeling equipment is provided free of charge. Eight-day cruise tours depart on Sundays and hit up the standard central and southern islands.

FREE ENTERPRISE
The Free Enterprise is a 20-passenger sailing yacht with style, comfort and charm. Ten double cabins, with twin upper and lower berths or double beds, are equipped with private bathroom, hot water and air conditioning. Social areas are limited but comfortable, with communal dining room, bar/lounge and some deck space. Snorkeling and scuba-diving equipment is also available for a price. Four-day, five-day and eight-day depart on Tuesdays and Saturdays.

Find more reviews from travelers at www.vivatravelguides.com

AIDA MARIA

The 16-passenger Aida Maria was designed to combine style, comfort and efficiency. Eight double bunk cabins—each with outside access—are minimalist, yet classy and equipped with private bath, hot shower and air conditioning. Ample dining and social areas—most notably an expansive external sundeck—provide plenty of space for passengers to make themselves at home. Television, VCR, stereo and library facilities, as well as plenty of onboard snorkeling and diving gear, add to the visitor experience. Five and eight-day cruises visiting the standard combination of central and southern islands leave on Sundays and Thursdays. Owner: Aida María Travel.

AMAZONIA

The Amazonia, also known as the Nemo II, is a large catamaran specially designed to take up to 14 passengers in seven double cabins. The ingeniously designed salon, cockpit and unique interior make this catamaran an exceptional cruising boat. It is also equipped for scuba-diving. Five-day and eight-day cruises depart on Wednesdays and Sundays.

AMIGO I

The Amigo I is a 16-passenger motor yacht with eight double cabins, each equipped with private bath and hot water. A small external sundeck provides extra comfort during weeklong excursions, beginning Fridays. The Amigo provides an adequate visitor experience for a reasonable price, offering seniors, students and groups special discounts. It also has complimentary snorkeling equipment and scuba-diving capabilities. Four-day, five-day and eight-day cruises depart on Mondays and Fridays and visit central and southern islands, including San Cristóbal. Owner: Isgal.

ANGELITO I

The Angelito I is a comfortable, 16-passenger motor yacht with eight double bunk cabins, each with private bath, hot water, air conditioning and outside access. Frill-less yet efficient, the Angelito I counts on a professional crew, attentive service and excellent food. Social areas are roomy, but communal, so it provides the perfect atmosphere for groups (to which special rates are offered, as well as to seniors and students) or for making new acquaintances. Snorkeling equipment is provided free of charge. Eight-day cruises depart on Sundays and include visits to northern, central and southern islands in their itineraries. Owner: Cometa Travel.

ANGELIQUE

The Angelique is a stylish sailing yacht with capacity for 16 passengers in eight double-bunk cabins, each equipped with private facilities, hot water and air conditioning. Although social spaces are limited and décor a bit outdated, the Angelique adds a few modern touches—television, VCR, small bar, library—to the colonial, pirate-ship ambience. Snorkeling equipment is available free of charge. In the spirit of swashbuckling adventure, the Angelique also spans the archipelago with her itinerary, hitting northern, central and southern islands.

DARWIN

The 16-passenger motor yacht, Darwin, has eight spacious double cabins, each with private bath, hot water and air conditioning. It also has plenty of comfortable social areas: a plush dining room, serving excellent food, living room area, bar and sundeck. Snorkeling equipment is also provided. Four-day, five-day and eight-day cruises depart on Wednesdays and Sundays, visiting northern, central and southern island sites. Owner: Vigaltravel.

ENCANTADA

The Encantada is a charming, candy-apple red, 10-passenger sailing boat, which offers style and adventure to their mostly scuba-diving clientele. It has five fully-equipped double bunk cabins, a small conference room with television and VCR, a sundeck an internal and an exterior dining room, and scuba-diving equipment. Its three bathrooms and three showers are shared. Four-day, five-day and eight-day cruises depart on Wednesdays and Sundays to northern, central and southern islands, including a visit to San Cristóbal. Owner: Scuba Galápagos.

FRAGATA

The Fragata, a 16-passenger motor yacht with eight fully-equipped double cabins, is outfitted to provide comfortable cruising, fine dining and attentive service. Recently rebuilt, the Fragata combines modern style with spaciousness and comfort. It also contracts experienced naturalist guides, maintains a professional crew and has diving capabilities. Snorkeling equipment is also provided free of charge. Four-day, five-day and eight-day cruise tours depart on Mondays and Fridays, stopping at visitor sites in northern, central and southern islands. Owner: Tierra Verde.

GUANTANAMERA

The Guantanamera is a poorly-designed, top-heavy motor yacht that can provide weak-stomached passengers hours of discomfort in rough seas. It has capacity for 16 passengers, distributed among two below-deck matrimonial suites. Each mid-sized, simple cabin is equipped with private bathroom, hot water and oftentimes frigid air conditioning, which passengers must adapt to since they cannot control it from their staterooms. External deck space is fairly ample, with a few front-facing lounge chairs providing excellent sunbathing and dolphin-watching opportunities and a covered conference area with tables and chairs. Unfortunately, this is the limit of the social space: the indoor lounge consists of two cushioned benches directly in front of the television/video and minimalist library facilities, while the dining/bar area includes three cramped, but plush, booths and a hallway doubling as a buffet area. Furthermore, the open-air conference area, while it provides excellent salsa-dancing space, is half-occupied by scuba-diving equipment and a noisy, often distracting, place to hear island briefings. Crew members are friendly and competent, and the cook is a master, especially with seafood. The Guantanamera has sophisticated scuba-diving capabilities. Four-day, five-day and eight-day cruises depart on Thursdays and Sundays, making stops at visitor sites in northern, central and southern islands. Owner: Aida María Travel.

LIBERTY

The motor yacht Liberty can accommodate 16 passengers in eight double cabins, each with private bathroom, hot water and air conditioning. All social areas—including dining room, living room and small shaded deck—have views of the sea. The Liberty was designed for travelers who want to enjoy ecotourism and diving in comfort. Cruise tours begin in San Cristóbal on Mondays and pass through southern islands, Puerto Villamil on Isabela, the central islands and Bartolomé. Owner: Galasam.

> *V!VA Member Review-Liberty*
> *I had a beautiful trip on Board Estrella del Mar 2 (Liberty). My cabin was very comfortable, lower beds, good air conditioning and hot water. The guide was excellent, he had a lot of knowledge. I would take a repeat trip on this boat. 27 March 2007. USA.*

SEA CLOUD

The Sea Cloud, like her sister ship Rachel III, is an eight-passenger, ketch-rigged motor sailor with an attractive design and elegant interior. It has four double cabins, each with double lower and single upper berths, private bathrooms, hot water, air conditioning and teak furnishings. Facilities include a dining room/salon, television and VCR, stereo system and swim ladder. It is a beautiful and comfortable yacht for passengers who seek a small group and more personalized experience, such as a family charter. Four-day, five-day and eight-day cruises depart on Wednesdays and Saturdays, and follow a standard itinerary through central and southern islands. Owner: Andando Tours.

GALÁPAGOS ADVENTURE II

The 16-passenger motor yacht Galápagos Adventure II combines comfort, speed and affordability to produce a unique "Galápagos adventure." Nine cabins on three decks have private bathrooms and hot water. Open-air deck spaces and interior lounge areas provide a significant amount of comfort and space for a tourist-class vessel. Four-day, five-day and eight-day cruises depart on Tuesdays and Fridays and visit central and southern islands. Owner: Ninfa Tours.

Find more reviews from travelers at www.vivatravelguides.com

FLOREANA

The Floreana is a motor yacht that accommodates 16 passengers in eight double cabins containing private facilities and hot water. Amenities include comfortable bar and lounge areas, equipped with television and VHS, sundeck, and indoor and outdoor dining areas. Quality and complete snorkeling gear is available. Four-day, five-day and eight-day tours depart on Thursdays and Sundays and pass through the main islands in the archipelago. Owner: UniGalápagos.

RACHEL III

The Rachel III, like her sister ship Sea Cloud, is an eight-passenger ketch-rigged motor sailor with an attractive design and elegant interior. It has four double cabins, each with double lower and single upper berths, private bathrooms, hot water, air-conditioning and teak furnishings. Facilities include a dining room/salon, television and VCR, stereo system and swim ladder. It is a beautiful and comfortable yacht for passengers who seek a small group and more personalized experience, such as a family charter. Four-day, five-day and eight-day cruises depart on Wednesdays and Saturdays and follow a standard itinerary through central and southern islands. Owner: Andando Tours.

LOBO DEL MAR III

The Lobo del Mar III is a sixteen-passenger motor yacht with eight double cabins, located below deck and on the upper deck. Accommodations are clean and spacious, with two lower twin berths, private facilities, hot water and air conditioning. It has a variety of comfortable social areas: a covered upper observation deck with six cushioned lounge chairs, an extensive wooden-paneled lounge/bar with television, VCR, and comfortable benches, and a communal dining area with plush booths. The naturalist guide and crew are extremely friendly, accommodating and professional, and they will go out of their way to provide an action-packed, detail-oriented and personalized experience. Four-day, five-day and eight-day cruises depart on Wednesdays and Sundays and offer site visits to northern, central and southern island destinations. Owner: Lobo del Mar.

SAMBA

The Samba is a 78-foot motor sailor with relatively spacious accommodations and shady and open-air observation decks. It can accommodate 14 passengers in seven double cabins, six with private bathrooms and air-conditioning and one with exterior shower and air-conditioning. It also features a stabilizing sail, which will enable a healthy and comfortable sailing experience. Snorkeling and scuba-diving equipment is available for a price. Eight-day cruises depart from Baltra on Tuesdays and follow an itinerary featuring Isabela, Fernandina, and the standard central and southern visitor sites. Owner: Andando Tours.

TOURIST CLASS

The Tourist Class offers lower prices, but not the bottom of the barrel. Boats in this category have few frills, basic accommodations and limited public (and private) space. Facilities are often shared. These boats often cater to backpackers, younger people or budget travelers. As such, tours tend to be fairly laid-back, and crew members and guides may substitute professionalism for camaraderie—an often welcome exchange for those adventure-seekers prioritizing fun over fancy.

PRICES

Cruise tours range in price from $800 to $980 for eight days, or $100 to $125 per day. Four-day tours ($450-$650) and five-day tours ($550 to $700) are also very common on tourist class yachts.

PELIKANO

The 16-passenger Pelikano is one of the more comfortable, lower-priced yachts, with eight double cabins, each with private bathroom and showers. Cabins are frill-less and small—although all have easy access to the eating area—and social space is limited to the dining room and upper deck, causing conditions to feel a bit cramped. If you are friendly, adventurous and on a strict budget, the Pelikano is one of your better options. Snorkeling equipment is provided, and scuba-diving is an option. Four-day, five-day and eight-day cruises depart on Sundays and Wednesdays. Owner: Pelikano.

MERAK

The Merak is a small sailboat that makes up for its limited lounging space and privacy with charm and character. It has four double cabins, accommodating eight passengers, and two shared bathrooms. Social areas include a communal dining area and outdoor solarium. The Merak caters to small groups looking for the intimacy of their own sailboat at a reasonable price. Four-day, five-day and eight-day cruises depart on Thursdays and Sundays. Owner: Sarvaltours.

RUMBA

The Rumba, a small, 10-passenger motorized yacht, is a cozy yet elegant option for budget travelers or small groups. It has five double bunk cabins, three on the main deck, and two on the upper deck, each with private bath and ventilation. It also has an ample sundeck, bar, lounge with television and VCR and a small library. It provides the professionalism and quality services of a larger vessel without sacrificing the friendly, personalized service of a private yacht. Five and eight-day cruises with a standard itinerary hitting central and southern islands depart on Sundays and Thursdays.

SEA MAN

The Sea Man is an excellent selection for visitors looking for a reasonably-priced diving tour in the Galápagos. It has a capacity for 16 passengers in eight double cabins, each with private bath. It also has a large dive platform, diving equipment and an experienced crew. The upper deck provides a great space to star-gaze, sun-bathe in lounge chairs or talk about the next dive. Four-day, five-day and eight-day cruises depart on Mondays and Thursdays and visit northern, central and southern island sites. Owner: Galacruises Expeditions.

SULIDAE

The Sulidae is a small but attractive motor sailor with a capacity for 12 passengers. It has six double cabins with private bathroom, a dining room and a galley. Snorkeling equipment is provided, and scuba-diving is available. Most of the dives offered by the Sulidae are more appropriate for advanced divers. The Sulidae has an interesting history. About 100 years old, the ship began its life as a cargo ship in the Baltic sea before heading to Guayaquil in the 1920's and to the Galápagos from there (don't worry: it's been renovated since its days hauling cargo). Passengers who have booked their trip on the Sulidae are generally very pleased with the service, crew and food. Being as old as it is, you miss out on a bit of comfort, but Sulidae visitors will tell you it makes up in charm what it lacks in roominess. Four-day, five-day, and eight-day cruises depart on Tuesdays and Fridays to the standard central and southern islands. Owner: Galaextur.

YOLITA

The Yolita is a small motor yacht with a capacity for 12 passengers. It has four double cabins with private toilet and sink, two double cabins with shared toilet and sink and shared showers located outside of the cabins. It also has a salon, dining room and complimentary snorkeling equipment. It has scuba diving capacity for those that are dive certified. Four-day, five-day and eight-day cruises depart on Thursdays and Sundays and visit the standard central and southern islands. Owner: Galasam.

GABY I

NOTE: This ship has been refurbished and renamed; it is now called Friendship and has moved to the Tourist Superior Class. The Gaby I is a standard motor yacht built to accommodate 16 passengers in eight double bunk cabins, each equipped with private bath and hot water. Other amenities include a comfortable dining area, a small, covered deck space, and bar. Tours depart on Tuesdays and include the standard central and southern islands in their itineraries. Owner: Galápagos Discovery.

ECONOMY CLASS

It's luck of the draw with these boats, the cheapest of the cruise boats in the Galápagos Islands. Many travelers who choose boats in this class leave wishing they had spent the extra couple of hundred dollars for a boat in a higher class. A few lucky travelers have a great time, though, and save a bundle. With a little research and our reviews, you should be able to avoid the lemons and get the best for your money.

PRICES

Economy class boat tours cost between $550 and $720 for eight days, or $70 to $90 per day. Four-day tours cost around $300 to $400, and five-day tours are about $375 to $500. Shortest itineraries are almost always offered in this class (and may just coincide with the maximum length of time you can tolerate the sub-par conditions!).

ANTARTIDA II

The small motor yacht Antartida II has capacity for 10 passengers in its five double cabins, each with private bathroom. Other amenities include a bar, dining lounge and small aft deck. Four-day, five-day, and eight-day cruises depart on Thursdays and Sundays and visit the standard combination of central and southern islands. Owner: Galasam.

CORMORANT II

The Cormorant II is a small yacht with capacity for 10 passengers in its five double cabins. Its facilities are basic and accommodations are rustic, and it has very little social space. It does, however, have scuba facilities, so if you want to dive for bottom-of-the-barrel prices you can work out a tour with the Cormorant II. Snorkeling and diving equipment is available for a price. Four-day, five-day and eight-day tours depart on Thursdays and Sundays and visit the standard combination of central and southern islands. Owner: Galaeco.

GOLONDRINA I

The Golondrina I is another option for visitors that do not require privacy or lavishness. With capacity for eight passengers in four double bunk cabins with two shared bathrooms, the Golondrina I provides basic comforts and facilities. For a small yacht, it does have a sizable sundeck and dining room and offers scuba-diving options. Owner: Tierra Verde.

FLAMINGO

The 10-passenger Flamingo, not to be confused with the first class Flamingo I, offers your typical economy-class amenities: five tiny double bunk cabins, which are all below deck, a small bar and dining room, a sundeck that also serves as the upper deck (or roof) of the boat and absolutely no public space. Privacy is at a minimum, but the experience is improved with complimentary snorkeling equipment (and hopefully the chance to use it, spending much of your time in the water instead of on the boat). Four-day, five-day and eight-day cruises depart on Tuesdays and Fridays.

> *V!VA Member Review-Flamingo*
> *Our guide, cook, and crew were excellent, professional, and friendly. Our guide was extremely knowledgeable and coordinated activities to maximize our experience (like visiting a lava flow at 6 a.m. so we didn't roast). Overall, I would recommend this ship to anyone heading to the Galápagos Islands. 12 April 2007. USA*

POSEIDON

The Poseidon, with its long body and covered deck spaces, is a motor yacht reminiscent of a riverboat casino. It has capacity for ten passengers in five double bunk cabins, each with private bath. It may be small and a bit unattractive, but accommodations are livable and snorkeling and diving opportunities are available for a price. Four-day, five-day, and eight-

GALÁPAGOS

day cruises depart on Wednesdays and Saturdays and visit the stand
islands. Owner: Golden Ray Travel.

GALÁPAGOS WILDLIFE GUIDE

As spectacular as the waters, islands and beaches of Galápagos ar
what visitors have come to see: the animals. Because the archipe
man until relatively recently, the endemic species of Galápagos nev
as animals and birds did in every other corner of the globe. In ot
the islands see the lumbering hairless monkeys that smell like sun
them as something predatory or dangerous! For this reason, you can get very close to them
before they spook and run away.

Some animals are more skittish than others: migratory birds such as flamingos and many
shore birds will not let you get too close, because they've encountered mankind in other parts
of the world. Other animals, like marine iguanas, barely seem to notice you at all. Many care-
less travelers have accidentally stepped on them: they can blend right in with the black lava
rocks! The sea lions will let you get fairly close, as will most of the sea and land birds, but
watch out! Get too close, and a sea lion or booby won't be afriad to give you a good nip!

The Galápagos wildlife can be divided into several categories. There are several species of
Galápagos reptiles, including the giant tortoises, marine iguanas and land iguanas. There are
very few native mammals in Galápagos, the most noteworthy of which is the Galápagos Sea
Lion. There are many birds in Galápagos, which are easily divided into categories. Land birds
are those that generally are seen inland, or who feed on land. Some endemic Galápagos land
birds include the Galápagos Hawk and the different Darwin's finches. Shore birds may nest
farther inland, but they are most commonly seen along the shoreline and in tidal pools and
mangroves where they feed. One endemic Galápagos shore bird is the Lava Heron. Sea birds
nest on land but feed exclusively on fish, squid and other marine life. The marine life in Galápagos is most impressive, and the snorkeling and diving in the islands are world-class. There
are many different fish, sharks and rays that are easily spotted and identified.

SEA BIRDS

Bird life is everywhere in Galápagos, and the marine species are particularly fun to watch
and identify. Because of the cold-water currents that cruise through the archipelago there is
an unusual abundance of marine life, which in turn supports large colonies of different avian
species.

Some species of sea birds are endemic to the Galápagos Islands. The three most noteworthy
are the Flightless Cormorant, the Waved Albatross and the Galápagos Penguin. The Flightless Cormorant is a marvel of evolution. Cormorants are common all around the world, but
the Galápagos variety found that there were few predators on the islands from which they
needed to flee. Their wings became unnecessary, and the Galápagos Cormorant no longer
flies, although in other senses it looks and acts like any other cormorant. The Galápagos Penguin is the one of the smallest penguins and the only one to live in the northern hemisphere
(good trivia question!). If you're lucky enough to get to Española during certain months of the
year, you'll get to see the rare Waved Albatross, a species not only unique to the Galápagos
but also to Española Island. These large, ungainly birds (which look vaguely like a duck on
steroids) travel great distances during the months of January, February and March, returning
from across the world to mate on Española.

The two varieties of Frigatebird (the Magnificent and Great subspecies) wheel overhead,
robbing boobies of their hard-won catch. The brown pelican crashes into the water, bobbing
up with a beakfull of water: flopping fish can be seen inside as he slowly lets the water out.
The Swallow-tailed Gull looks at you from her rocky perch, black eyes inscrutable. A Red-
billed Tropicbird sails gracefully past, long white tail streaming.

y other sea birds in the islands. Shearwaters and petrels can be seen skimmes, if you look for them. There are plovers and terns, and other species of gull ot endemic to the islands. A knowledgeable guide should be able to point out most e species to you as you spot them.

BLUE-FOOTED BOOBY

The Blue-footed Booby (*Sula nebouxii excisa, piquero de patas azules*) is most easily identified, as its name suggests, by its bright blue feet. It has brown upper plumage and white lower plumage, with wings that are a slightly darker brown than the rest of the body. Juveniles are completely brown and receive their coloration after about one year.

Photo by Caroline Bennett

Males are slightly smaller than females and perform an elaborate, intensely entertaining mating dance to attract their female partner. The male begins by lifting up his enormous clown-feet one-by-one, and then stops in a distinctive pose, beak raised skyward, announcing his manhood with a loud whistle, pointing out his tail, and opening his wings. This is accompanied by a love-offering of sticks and twigs. Females join in the mating dance, following the same movements, but respond with a guttural honk. Beyond their distinguishing sounds, the females also have larger eye pupils.

Breeding can take place at any time of the year when the food supply is abundant. Up to three eggs are laid in a "guano ring," or nested circle of booby dung. When food is scarce, the oldest sibling will push younger siblings out of the guano ring in an act of "cainism." This form of natural selection is effective, because young outside of the ring are refused care and ultimately perish.

The young take two to six years to mature, at which time they will return to their island birthplace to mate. Meanwhile, they travel among the islands feeding on fish, which are caught in a graceful plunge dive. Watching the boobies fish—either from the air or underwater—is a major highlight in the Galápagos. Blue-footed boobies are best viewed in coastal waters at the visitor sites of Punta Suarez (Española), North Seymour and Punta Pitt (San Cristóbal).

RED-FOOTED BOOBY

The Red-footed Booby (*Sula sula websteri, piquero de patas rojas*) can be easily identified by its distinctive red feet, blue-gray bill, pinkish facial skin and brown outer plumage. It is also the smallest of the three booby species in the Galápagos and nests in tree-tops and ledges, instead of on the ground. Courtship among red-footed boobies is similar to the blue-footed variety, but it is performed in the trees. Unlike the blue-footed booby, the red-footed booby lays a single egg on a platform of twigs and guano. The egg is then incubated by both parents for 45 days. The chick is dependent on its parents for food for about a year. The red-footed booby feeds exclusively on fish, which are caught far away from land near deep-ocean bajos, or submarine volcanoes. Red-footed boobies are most frequently viewed at Genovesa and Punta Pitt (San Cristóbal).

NAZCA BOOBY

The Nazca Booby (*Sula dactylatra granti, piquero de Nazca*), formerly known as the masked booby, is alabaster white with a black tail and black ends to the primary feathers on the wing. Some black skin at the base of the bill serves as an unequivocal Zorro-mask (hence the original name). The Nazca booby is also the largest of the three booby species in the Galápagos. As with other boobies, the Nazca booby feeds entirely on fish and follows the same courtship ritual, although a bit less elaborate. Males and females look alike, so the best way to distinguish them is by their sounds: the males whistle and females quack. Nazca boobies are commonly seen at Punta Suarez (Española), Punta Pitt (San Cristóbal), Daphne Major and Genovesa.

FRIGATEBIRD

The Magnificent Frigatebird (Fregata magnificens, fragata real) is the larger of the two species of frigatebirds found in the Galápagos, by about 50 cm. Male magnificent frigatebirds can be also be distinguished from the other species, the great frigatebird, by the purple sheen cast on his jet-black feathers and blue circles around the eyes. Females are slightly larger than males and also entirely black, except for her white breast and shoulders. Immature frigatebirds have a white head and neck and a pale beak.

Male frigatebirds are most recognizable by their red skin flaps, which they can inflate to football-sized balloons in about 25 minutes as a way to attract females. Males construct nests out of twigs in low trees or shrubs and wait in the nests with their pouches inflamed until a female arrives to copulate. Frigatebirds spend much of their time offshore, but return to island havens to mate, nest and rear their young.

Since frigatebirds do not secrete enough oils to waterproof their feathers, they cannot swim, even though they are sea birds. As such, they often steal food from other birds, especially the excellent blue-footed booby fishermen, or force them to regurgitate the food. Often times, frigatebirds will raise their young near blue-footed booby colonies so that they have a food source nearby and readily available. Because of this behavior, frigatebirds are considered kleptoparasites or pirates. Magnificent frigatebirds can be found on North Seymour, Punta Pitt (San Cristóbal) and Genovesa.

The Great Frigatebird (fregata menor, fragata común) is a bit smaller than the magnificent frigatebird and has a green sheen to its black feathers. It also has the same courtship and kleptoparasitistic behaviors. Great frigatebirds can be found on North Seymour, Punta Suarez (Española) and Punta Espinosa (Fernandina).

THE WAVED ALBATROSS

The Waved Albatross (Diomedea irrorata, albátros) is the largest bird that breeds in Galápagos, with a wingspan of almost 2.5 meters. It has brown upper parts and wings with gray, waved bars (hence its name), a white neck, a cream-colored nape and a handsome yellow beak. Males are a bit larger and have a thicker eyebrow than females. There are about 12,000 monogamous pairs of waved albatrosses that fly back and forth from the Ecuadorian coast and northern Peru to their only breeding ground in Galápagos: Punta Suarez (Española).

The males return first to the Galápagos in late March or early April and wait for the arrival of their mates, at which time they begin an elaborate courting ritual: pairs dance with each other in an awkward waddle, move their necks up and down in rhythm, clack and encircle their bills, and raise their bills skyward with an abrupt guttural release, reminiscent of a cow's moo. Albatrosses perform this unforgettable courtship display before, during, and after they lay their eggs, so you can witness it from mid-April to as late as November.

Albatrosses are expert flyers, but they require a significant amount of space and energy to get airborne. Often, you can see them (especially juveniles) jump off nearby cliffs and catch offshore winds as a method for getting their massive physiques in flight. Albatrosses usually live with their pairs for 45 to 50 years, sometimes up to 70 years.

GALÁPAGOS

FLIGHTLESS CORMORANT

The Flightless Cormorant (*Nannopterum harrisi, cormoran*) is unmistakably recognized by the stubby vestigial appendages that serve as completely useless wings. Although they cannot fly, they are excellent swimmers that feed on small fish, eels and octopus. Adults have black upper feathers and brown under feathers, but they—like the juveniles—look completely black when wet. They also have short black legs, large, black webbed feet, brilliant turquoise eyes and a hooked, black bill. Although the cormorant is a common bird around the world, flightless ones are only found on Galápagos.

Like many other sea birds, flightless cormorants have an elaborate courtship display: pairs begin with an aquatic dance, followed by an unusual "snake necking" embrace, where necks are intertwined in a snake-like spiral, swimming back and forth, a continuation of the dance on land, and a final presentation of a seaweed nest to the female by the male. Most females lay their eggs between May and October, which are incubated for about a month and reared for about nine months by both pairs. If, however, food supplies run low, the female may leave this male to care for the chick while she looks for another, more apt, mate. Flightless cormorants can be seen in Punta Espinosa (Fernandina) and the western visitor sites of Isabela.

GALÁPAGOS PENGUIN

The endemic Galápagos Penguin (*Sphensicus mendiculus, pinguino*) is the only species of penguin found north of the equatorial line that breeds in the tropics. At only 35 cm tall, the Galápagos penguin is also one of the world's smallest penguins. Adults have black outer feathers, white under feathers, an irregular black band across the breast, and a distinctive white stripe passing from the eye to the throat. There are only about 1,000 monogamous pairs of Galápagos penguins, which can breed at any time of year when resources are plentiful and water temperatures are cool. They will lay one or two eggs in shady holes or caves nestled along the shoreline. Pairs will take turns incubating the egg, for a period of about 40 days. Chicks can fend for themselves after two months, but often stay in swimming groups with the adults. Galápagos penguins can best be seen at Punta Espinosa (Fernandina), at various west coast Isabela visitor sites, Bartolomé, and Floreana.

BROWN PELICAN

The endemic Brown Pelican (*Pelecanus occidentalis urinator, pelícano*) is an unmistakable bird with a large, heavy body and enormous, deep bill. Mating adult pelicans have a striking white head and maroon neck; when they do not have their breeding plumage, their necks are gray. Brown pelicans breed individually or in small colonies, making their nests in mangroves or small bushes on virtually all islands in the archipelago. The female lays three large eggs, usually during the colder months of May to July, which are then incubated by both parents for about one month (if they are not eaten by the Galápagos Hawk). They feed mainly on large fish, which they catch by plunging in the ocean (a graceless but effective dive), filling their pouches with sea water, returning to land, and finally filtering out the food out by draining the pouch head-down. Since food is thus delivered in one large package, competition among the young tends to get pretty fierce (and provides an interesting site to see). Brown pelicans are common in the central islands and Bartolomé.

RED-BILLED TROPICBIRD

The Red-billed Tropicbird (*Phaethon aethereus, ave tropical*) is a spectacularly elegant, solitary bird with white feathers, black barring on the back, black primary feathers and bright red bill. Its most distinguishing characteristic, however, is its long white tail, which can reach up to a half-meter in length.

During the breeding season, which varies in the archipelago, the red-billed tropicbird performs a courtship flight characterized by a shrill, "nee-nee-nee" call. The female lays a single egg in a fissure of a cliff, which is then incubated by both parents for about six weeks. Red-billed tropicbirds are best seen off the cliffs of South Plaza, Daphne Major and Genovesa.

SWALLOW-TAILED GULL

The endemic Swallow-tailed Gull (*Larus furcatus, gaviota de cola bifurcada*) is the only nocturnal gull in the world. Adults have a distinctive black head with a red ring around the eye, black bill with a gray tip, white, forked tail and red, webbed feet. They often have white spots on their back, which resemble guano and help them to camouflage with their rocky cliff habitat. Immature gulls are white with dark brown spots on their backs and a black band on their tails.

Swallow-tailed gulls nest in small colonies on islands concentrated in the eastern archipelago, breeding all times of year. Their courtship ritual involves mutual preening, head-tossing, and regurgitation of food by the male. The young have a recognizably harsh call, consisting of an initial scream that displays their red gape and tongue, an uncharacteristic rattle and a final clicking noise, which may also be used for echo-location during night feeding. The most common places to encounter swallow-tailed gulls are Genovesa and South Plaza.

SHORE BIRDS

One of the best places in all of Galápagos to see birds is right along the shoreline. Many of the most interesting species in Galápagos are wading shore birds who feast on small fish, crabs, snails, small marine iguanas and other creatures that live in the mangroves and tidal pools of the islands. Since most of the visitor sites in Galápagos involve a transfer from the cruise boat to the island, usually by means of a zodiac or panga, visitors to the islands have a good chance of seeing one or more shore birds.

Herons and Egrets are commonly seen hunting in tidal pools and in mangroves. The Great Blue Heron may be known to visitors from North America: it's the same species that can be seen in northern lakes and rivers. Egrets tend to prefer inland ponds and grasslands, but can often be seen along the ocean shoreline as well. Look carefully for Lava Herons and Striated Herons: their coloration makes them sometimes difficult to spot against the grayish rocks. If you're lucky, you'll catch a glimpse of the elusive Yellow-Crowned Night Heron or the Black-Crowned Night Heron.

Flamingos are common visitors to the islands, where they flock to a limited number of salty, brackish lagoons that are the perfect home for the small shrimp that they like to eat. The American Oystercatcher, with its distinctive red-rimmed eyes, long orange bill and black-and-white plumage pattern, is a common sight in tidal pools along some of the most popular beaches and visitors sites in the islands. Although they're commonly spotted, it's rare to get too close to one: they're very shy. The Ruddy Turnstone is a common sight along the coast. A smallish shore bird with white, balck and brown markings, it also has orange legs.

The Whimbrel is easily identified by its curved beak, which is slightly curved at the end for poking around in small nooks and cracks in tidal pools. Like the Oystercatcher, it is a very shy bird and it's difficult to get a good look at one. Other shore birds include sandpipers, phalaropes and more.

AMERICAN OYSTERCATCHER

The American Oystercatcher (*Haematopus palliatus*) is a distinctive shorebird found up and down the eastern coast of North America, the Gulf of Mexico and the western coast of South America. They are a common sight in Galápagos, where they can be seen on the coast poking around tidal pools and along rocky shores. Some ornithologists consider the Galápagos American Oystercatcher to be an endemic subspecies, known as Haematopus palliatus Galapagensis. The American Oystercatcher is easily identified by its red-rimmed eyes, black head, white body, greyish-black wings and white legs. Its most distinctive feature, however, is certainly its long, thick, bright orange beak which looks from afar like a large plastic drinking straw. As you might imagine, the preferred food of the American Oystercatcher is shellfish. Using its sturdy beak, an American Oystercatcher can pry apart an oyster, clam or mussel. It then snips the muscle that holds the shells together and eats the oyster at its leisure. Their long beak allows them to poke into small nooks in lava-formed tidal pools that are too deep for other predators. American Oystercatchers are shy and will dart or fly away if closely approached.

RUDDY TURNSTONE

The Ruddy Turnstone (*Arenaria interpres*) is a stocky, smallish shorebird found all over the world, including on every island in Galápagos. Built roughly like a pigeon but a little bigger, the Ruddy Turnstone has a white breast with a blackish-brown "collar" which extends back to the mottled brown wings, speckled with black and white. It has reddish-orange feet and legs. Its medium-sized beak is black and pointed. In mating season, the ruddy turnstone changes colors: the black and white of the breast and collar sharpen, and the brown wing feathers become brighter. The legs and feet turn from orange to dazzling red.

Ruddy Turnstones are common sights around Galápagos. They have a hugely varied diet, including small fish, crustaceans, carrion, insects, garbage, other birds' eggs and even occasionally coconut. They prefer rocky shores and tidal pools where they dart quickly about, searching for morsels. They get their name from their tendency to flip over stones with their beaks to see if there isn't something delicious hiding underneath. They nest in a shallow, scraped-out hole in the ground. Shy by Galápagos standards, it is difficult to get within twenty feet (seven meters) of them before they scurry away or fly off.

GREATER FLAMINGO

The Greater Flamingo (*Phoenicopterus ruber, flamenco*) receives its characteristic pink color from the carotenoid (carotene) pigments consumed in its diet of crustaceans and shrimp larvae. Legs are gray or flesh-colored; feet are webbed for swimming; primary feathers are black; and bills are pink with a black tip. Young flamingos are pale white until about three months, when they find food and become a richer pink color.

This species of flamingo is thought to have arrived from the Bahamas during a one-time strange and intense tropical storm. Since they did not have the flying capacity to return, they made their homes in the brackish water (a mix of salt and fresh water) lagoons of the archipelago. Around July and August, the male flamingos perform their courting ritual: they join in fixed lines, moving and swaying together in a sensual, flamenco-like dance. Monogamous pairs will lay their eggs in cone-shaped, mud nests nearly 25 cm high, which have a 28-day incubation period before hatching in September and October. Chicks are born with a straight bill, but it starts to curve after about three weeks. There are currently about 500-600 flamingos on the various islands, which can live up to 20 or 30 years. They are most commonly found at Punta Cormorant (Floreana), Puerto Villamil (Isabela) and Las Bachas Beach (Santa Cruz).

HERONS AND EGRETS

Herons and egrets (*Order Ciconiiformes*) are shore birds distinguished by their long, pointed beaks, long necks and long, slender legs. They fly slowly and awkwardly, with their heads generally hunched forward. They are seen all over Galápagos, anywhere there is shallow water full of the small fish that is their preferred diet.

Galápagos is home to three species of egrets: the Great Egret, the Snowy Egret and the Cattle Egret. They are easily distinguished from the herons by their bright white coloration. The Great Egret is quite large, approximately the size of a Great Blue Heron, whereas the Snowy and Cattle Egrets are much smaller. The best way to tell the Snowy Egrets and Cattle Egrets apart is the color of the beak: the Snowy Egret has a black beak, and the Cattle Egret has a yellow one. Egrets are seen throughout the islands, from the ocean seaside to highland ponds and grassy fields. The Cattle Egret is, of course, often seen with cattle and other livestock. It is thought to arrived to Galápagos in the 1960s, when cattle ranching was introduced to the islands.

There are five different species of heron in Galápagos. The Great Blue Heron is the largest, and is easily identified by its white head with a black stripe. The Lava Heron is smaller, and an almost uniform ash-gray which allows it to blend in with the lava rocks which make up the tidal pools where it likes to hunt. The Striated Heron is often confused with the Lava Heron, as they are of a similar size and coloring, but the Striated Heron has a black crown and striated feathers on the wings. The Yellow-Crowned Night Heron is larger than the Lava and

Striated Herons and is easily identified by the yellow feathers on its head and a distinctive white stripe under the eye. The Black-Crowned Night Heron is a medium-sized heron with a white body and a black "cloak" that covers the top of its head and back.

All of the varieties of heron are common throughout Galápagos. They can be spotted in shallow waters where they feed on fish and even occasionally young marine iguanas. They tend to prefer mangroves and tidal pools. Herons tend to mostly ignore visitors if you don't make any sudden movements. If you creep up on a heron you can often get quite close.

YELLOW-CROWNED NIGHT HERON
The distinctive Yellow-crowned Night Heron (*Nycticorax violaceus*) can be easily identified by its yellow crown and a white stripe under its eye. They are gangly birds, with heads that seem a little too large for their bodies. During the day, they can often be seen poking around rocky shorelines. They are more active at night and sometimes even come into the towns to feed near streetlights.

Yellow-Crowned Night Herons can be found all over North America and in Northern South America. The ones in Galápagos are considered by some scientists to be a sub-species.
The Yellow-Crowned Night Heron mostly feeds on crabs, which it snatches off the rocks and downs in one big gulp. They're also known to eat shellfish, snails, fish and small reptiles. It nests in branches and mangroves that hang over water.

LAVA HERON
The Lava Heron (*Butorides sundevalli*) is very similar in appearance to the Striated Heron: they're the same size and shape, and have roughly the same coloration. You can tell them apart easily, however: the Striated Heron has a black crown and dappled wings, whereas the Lava Heron is a uniform gray color. Some experts believe that the heron has adapted to blend in easily with the lava rocks of Galápagos. During mating season, male Lava Herons develop brightly colored feet and his beak turns a glossy black. The Lava Heron is also called the Galápagos Heron because it is endemic to the islands.

The Lava Heron perches on rocks or branches in mangroves, tidal pools and along any shore where small crabs and fish can be found. It waits, still as a stone, before suddenly lunging forward to snap up its prey. They are very efficient hunters and fishers: some Lava Herons have been observed catching up to three small crabs per minute. Lava Herons are less shy than its cousins, the Striated and Great Blue Herons: if you move slowly, you can get quite close to them before they spook and fly off.

STRIATED HERON
The Striated Heron (Butorides striatus), also known in some parts of the world as the Little Heron, is a fairly common sight in Galápagos tidal pools, mangroves, ponds and rocky shores. Similar in size to a Lava Heron, the Striated Heron is also rocky gray in color. They can be easily differentiated, however. The Lava Heron's coloring is uniform, whereas the Striated Heron has a black crown and dappled wing feathers.

Striated Herons are common around the world, from Japan to South America, Africa and Russia. They usually perch on a branch or rock near the water's edge, head back, waiting for a small fish or crustaceans to swim by. They then lunge forward, trapping their prey in their sharp beak and quickly gobbling it. The Striated Heron is a clever bird, occasionally dropping a leaf into the water and snapping up fish that come to look at it.

GREAT BLUE HERON
Yes, the Great Blue Herons that you've seen back home in the USA and Canada are the same as the ones here in Galápagos. The Great Blue Heron (*Ardea herodias*) is a large, majestic bird that is relatively common in the United States and Canada, as well as Mexico and the West Indies. They can be found in South America as well. Great Blue Herons living in Canada

GALÁPAGOS

and the northern United States migrate south to spend the winter, but they can be seen year-round in Galápagos. They are considered a non-endangered species.

The Great Blue Heron is a shore bird, and can often be seen wading in tidal pools looking for small fish. They have also been known to eat reptiles, turtles and even rodents. Great Blue Herons nest in colonies of several nests, occasionally with or near other heron species. They tend to fish alone, however, stalking their prey both during daytime and at night. Males can be identified by the small patch of feathers sticking out of the back of their heads.

In Galápagos, Great Blue Herons can be found anywhere there are small fish in shallow water: look for them in tide pools, mangroves and sandy shores with some tree cover. The tidal pools near Cerro Brujo (San Cristobal) are a good place to look for them. In general, you won't see any along exposed stretches of beach or inland. If you move slowly, you may be able to get rather close for a good photo.

Reptiles

Reptiles dominate the animal scene in the Galápagos, due to their ability to cross long distances (i.e. from the mainland to the archipelago) without food or water. Giant tortoises and large land iguanas play the ecological role of larger mammals on the mainland. There are 22 species of Galápagos reptiles, 20 of which are endemic to the archipelago. Only five of the most common—Galápagos Giant tortoises, green sea turtles, lava lizards, land iguanas and marine iguanas—are described here.

Galápagos Giant Tortoise

The Galápagos Giant Tortoise (*Geochelone elephantophus, tortuga gigante*) is the namesake of the archipelago. The word "galápagos" refers to an old Spanish saddle very similar in shape to the shell of one of two major types of tortoises: saddleback tortoises and dome-shaped tortoises. The saddleback tortoises have long necks, are smaller in stature, and live in low areas with little vegetation. Dome-shaped tortoises live in the highlands of the larger islands.

Males have longer tails and are bigger than the females. Within these two categories fall 11 subspecies (once 14) of Galápagos giant tortoise, each having evolved differently due to habitat isolation.

Photo by Richard Blanchette

The Galápagos giant tortoise is most well-known for its immense size: it can grow to over 1.5 meters in length and up to 250 kg in weight. No one knows how long they can live, but growth ring approximations on their shells indicate a life span of at least 150 years. The rate of growth is controlled by the availability of food, their food of choice extending to over fifty species of plants, including poison apple, guava and cactus pads, among others.

Female tortoises reach sexual maturity between 25 and 30 years of age, at which time they will migrate to the lowlands, locate a suitably earthy area, dig a shallow pit, and deposit between two and 16 ping-pong ball-sized eggs. They will cover the eggs with mud and urine and leave the eggs incubating for 120 to 140 days. The distance traveled by female tortoises to lay their eggs is the greatest distance any tortoise will travel in its lifetime; males only move 4-5 km/year and can often stay for days in their mud holes without moving.

The most famous Galápagos giant tortoise is Lonesome George, the last of the Pinto island subspecies and a charismatic (and not very sexually promiscuous) representative of the plight of the tortoises due to human activity. Because tortoise populations have been drastically reduced from predation by introduced species, the Charles Darwin Research Station has spearheaded a very successful captive breeding and reintroduction program. The easiest places to see Galápagos giant tortoises (both types) are at the Charles Darwin Research Station and in the Santa Cruz highlands.

Update: In Spring 2007 another male turtle was found of the Pinto island subspecies, meaning Lonesome George finally has a companion. Who knows, perhaps someday a mate will even be found for poor old George.

LAVA LIZARD
There are seven endemic species of Lava Lizard (genus Microlophus, lagarto de lava) in the Galápagos. They are easily recognizable by their small size (up to 30 cm in length) and interesting coloring. Males and females of all species are wildly different. Males are up to three times heavier than females, have more patterned skin, and have a clearly visible black or yellow throat. Females, on the other hand, are smaller and have a bright red or orange throat. Lava lizards can be seen darting about on most islands of the archipelago (often under your feet—watch out!). All lava lizards also perform a characteristic "push-up" behavior to show territorial aggression or courtship tendencies; interestingly enough, this display is a vivid example of character divergence among species, since each of the islands' populations (even ones harboring the same species) have a slightly different display pattern. Lava lizards are omnivorous and feed primarily on small insects, arthropods, and plant material. Activity is closely dependent on daily temperature fluctuations, so you will probably see most lava lizards during the cool morning and mid-afternoon hours.

GREEN SEA TURTLE
The only marine turtle to breed in the Galápagos is the Green Sea Turtle (Chelonia mydas agassisi, tortuga verde), which has a hard, dark green to black shell and can weigh up to 150 kg. Unlike the giant tortoise, the female is larger than the male, since she is responsible for swimming while the male mounts and copulates.

Peak mating season is November to January, when both males and females will choose various partners with which to mate. You can often see a mating couple bobbing offshore or swimming near the surface of the water, while other males wait patiently for their turn.

The female then goes ashore to prepare her nest, a large "body pit" with a smaller flask-shaped pit inside where the eggs are laid. She may come ashore as many as eight times at two week intervals, each time depositing 70 to 80 eggs. The small hatchlings emerge after a three-month incubation period, only to be confronted immediately with the reality of their delectability; only about one percent will survive predation by crabs, birds, sharks, or introduced cats, dogs, or donkeys. Green sea turtles are fairly common throughout the islands, but common nesting spots are Las Bachas (Santa Cruz), Bartolomé, and Gardner Bay (Española).

LAND IGUANA
There are two endemic species of land iguana in the Galápagos archipelago: the more common Land Iguana (Conolophus subcristats, iguana terrestre) and the island-specific Santa Fé Land Iguana (Conolophus pallidus, iguana terrestre de Santa Fé). Both species look very similar, with pale to dark yellow coloring, but the Santa Fé land iguana is paler, has a more pronounced crest, and is covered with distinctive military camouflage. There are also select examples of land and marine iguanas hybridizing, the result of which is a land-loving iguana

GALÁPAGOS

with dark skin, light-colored bands, a small spinal crest and webbed feet. During the period of reproduction (the end of the year), males take on a brilliant red color to attract the females and become extremely territorial. After a somewhat violent copulation, the females will then lay six to eight eggs in underground nests, usually between January and March. The eggs are incubated for about 45 to 50 days, after which time young iguanas face the formidable challenge of surviving natural and introduced predators (especially the Galápagos Hawk). It is estimated that 70 percent of young land iguanas survive. The average life span is 45 years.

Land iguanas have a fairly limited home range of about 100 m2, which means that they feed in a small area, mostly on pads and fruit from the opuntia cactus, and thus can be affected by localized climatic changes. They are most common at Cerro Dragon (Santa Cruz), South Plaza and North Seymour. Sometimes you can see them at Urvina Bay (Isabela). You can also usually see some at the Charles Darwin Research Station.

Marine Iguana

The endemic Marine Iguana (*Amblyrhynchus cristatus, iguana marina*) is the only sea-faring lizard in the world. Adult marine iguanas are mostly black or dark gray, but some races have a colorful red and green lichen-like covering on their backs, the result of dies in their algal diet. They also have an elongated tail to help them swim; a flat head; a pronounced crest running the length of their backs; and large, webbed feet.

Marine iguanas live on land, but they feed on red and green algae in the cool ocean waters. Smaller iguanas keep to the intertidal zone, but others venture to depths of up to 10 meters and stay submerged for up to ten minutes looking for food. After a swim, they will return to land to bask in the sun or huddle with others for warmth (they are cold-blooded) and perform an unforgettable snort in order to release an excess of salt from their nostrils.

Marine iguanas have the same general reproductive cycle as land iguanas, laying their eggs in the beginning of the year. Their mating behavior, however, is a bit different. Marine iguanas are polygamous, meaning female iguanas accept a number of male partners, often as many as fifteen. Females lay three eggs in their underground nests instead of one, which take up to three months to incubate. Young marine iguanas face the same predatory threats when they hatch, but they have the added challenge of thwarting marine predators. If they survive through the formative period, they are expected to live for 40 years.

Marine iguanas are interesting to watch, not only because they are unusual and entertaining, but because they tell an interesting evolutionary tale. When iguanas originally arrived to the islands, they were strictly land-based creatures; they evolved the ability to swim over time, so that they could make use of unexplored niches. Furthermore, every El Niño year, you can witness the complicated dynamics of natural selection at work upon the marine iguanas: sexual selection favors larger individuals, while climatic conditions work against them, resulting in more medium-sized individuals in subsequent generations. Marine iguanas are found on all of the major islands.

Mammals - Sea Lions

The endemic Galápagos Sea Lion (*Zalophus californianus wollebacki, lobo marino*) is found all throughout the islands and is absolutely fearless of humans. You will definitely have the chance to watch some of the 50,000 inquisitive juvenile sea lions, playful adult sea lions, protective mother sea lions, and competitive male sea lions found in the archipelago from both land (some resting on dinghies and landing points) and sea vantage points. Males, or bulls, can be distinguished from the females, or cows, by their thick necks, bumped foreheads and immense size (full-grown males can weigh up to 250 kg). They jealously guard and protect their territory, a finite area covering land and water space, a harem of approximately 20 to 22 cows, immature sea lions and pups. When bulls lose land battles to other, more aggressive dominant males, they conglomerate in specific island sites, or bachelor pads, to heal and rest until the next challenge.

The mating season varies from island to island, but it generally occurs from June to November. Females give birth to four or five pups over their lifetimes, one every two years. Copulation usually takes place in the water four weeks after a birth, but due to "delayed implantation," the egg is not implanted into the womb for another two months. Gestation takes another nine months, thus finalizing the annual birth cycle. Nine out of ten sea lion pups are females and one-tenth males, and all stay together in "kindergartens," swimming and playing in the shallow water. After five months, the pups can start fishing for themselves, although they still depend on their mothers. After three years, cows have reached sexual maturity and begin to reproduce; and after five years, the slow-blooming males reach their adulthood. Most sea lions live for fourteen or fifteen years.

Sea lions feed mostly on sardines (the cause of their bad breath), for which they may travel ten to 15 kilometers out from the coast over the span of days to hunt. It is in deep water that sea lions encounter and must defend themselves from their only predators, sharks. Sea lions are staples at most islands (even the populated ones). You can see surfing sea lions at Punta Suarez (Española) and North Seymour, and you can see one of the bulls' bachelor pads at South Plaza.

The Galápagos fur seal (*Arctocephalus galapagoensis, lobo de dos pelos*) should technically be called the Galápagos fur sea lion, since it not a true seal. The fur seal is easily distinguished from the sea lion by its smaller size, darker color, shorter snout, and bear-like facial appearance (hence its scientific name, arcto = bear; cephalus = head). It also has a much thicker, denser coat consisting of two distinct layers: on outer coat of long hairs and an inner coat of short, dense fur. Finally, since thick-coated fur seals are less tolerant of the heat than sea lions, they are most often found in shady coves and rock crevices with adjacent deep-water areas. The mating season is from August to November, followed by delayed implantation and fertilization in the next few months and birth the following year. Fur seal cows generally give birth less frequently than sea lions, about once every three years.

Fur seals mainly feed on fish and squid, which they hunt in depths of up to 100 meters during the night hours in order to escape sharks. Unfortunately, fur seals had a more destructive predator, which caused populations to drop to near-extinction in the nineteenth century: humans. The fur seals have made a remarkable comeback since then, and it is predicted that over 25,000 now habituate the archipelago. Although they are fairly abundant, they are not often seen, due to their choice of habitat. Your best bets are the western archipelago (Fernandina and Isabela), Puerto Egas (Santiago) and Rábida.

LAND BIRDS

Few species of land birds inhabit the Galápagos, and three-quarters (22 of 29) of these are endemic. Unlike other Galápagos fauna, most land birds are visually unpleasing, spanning the dull and drab spectrum of the color palette. As if to overcompensate for being color-challenged, these birds have a shining personality, reacting to humans with tame indifference, curiosity or even pestering.

Darwin's finches—the famous little birds that helped to inspire their namesake's evolutionary theories—are known to land on your dinner table (or in your hand, if there are crumbs in it). Mockingbirds, which hop carelessly over any surface, including human feet, are also exemplary of this trusting behavior. The Galápagos Hawk, Short-eared Owl and Galápagos Dove are also surprisingly accessible to visitor viewing and are described here.

YELLOW WARBLER

The Yellow Warbler is frequently spotted in Galápagos, flitting across the trail or snapping up bugs near the water's edge. It is a small, bright yellow bird with black stripes on its wings. The Yellow Warbler is the only small, dazzling yellow-colored bird in the islands: you can't mistake it for anything else. Yellow Warblers are not endemic to Galápagos: in other parts of the world, they prefer the edges of boggy wetlands and fields with trees. They're found all over the western hemisphere, from Alaska to Peru.

GALÁPAGOS

You'd expect to see the tiny warbler feeding on the ground or in a low tree: nevertheless, they have found that there are more insects to be found along the shoreline than in the dry interior of the islands. The Galápagos Yellow Warblers are therefore often seen quickly darting along the shore, nipping up insects. They also occasionally feed on seeds or fruit.

Male Yellow Warblers have distinctive reddish stripes on their breast. Females are a little more drab and have duller stripes, or may lack them altogether. Males also have a reddish "cap" on top of their heads. Their song, which sounds a little like "sweet sweet sweet" is quite pleasant.

DARWIN'S FINCHES

The 13 species of Darwin's Finches (genus *Geospiza, pinzón*) that are found in the Galápagos are perhaps the most famous and sought-after land birds on the islands, given the ecological significance of differences in species' beak morphology and its link to feeding behavior. All of the finches are sparrow-sized with mottled gray, brown, black or greenish feathers and short, rounded wings. Because all 13 species have similar superficial characteristics, it is difficult to impossible (even for naturalist guides) to distinguish them. The only clues they provide are the shape of their beak, the type of food they eat and the type of habitat they occupy.

Although they all originated from a single ancestor, individual species have formed as niche specialists: some eat seeds, some eat leaves, some eat cactus, some eat insects. One species found on Wolf drinks the blood of Nazca or red-footed boobies, a habit that has led to its being dubbed a "vampire finch." Three other finch species—the small, medium and sharp-billed ground finches—have the distinction of eating the ticks and mites off of reptiles. There are even two species—the woodpecker and mangrove finches—that use twigs or spines as primitive tools to extract hidden insect larvae or grubs from holes in trees branches.

The mating season of finches generally begins after the first major rainfall of the rainy season (around February). The male courts the female by building an elaborate dome-shaped nest made of twigs, grass, bark, feathers and other materials, which he locates in his firmly-established and highly protected territory. The male will continually attend to the female at the nest, while she lays and incubates her eggs (two to five, on average), and during the first weeks of the fledglings' lives. Finches are found on all major islands, with each species distributed throughout the archipelago (and within islands) according to its desired habitat.

MOCKINGBIRD

There are four similarly-looking species of endemic mockingbirds in very different home ranges throughout the Galápagos archipelago: the Charles Mockingbird (*Nesomimus trifasciatus, cucuve de Floreana*), found near Floreana on the islands of Champion and Gardner, the Hood Mockingbird (*Nesomimus macdonaldi, cucuve de Española*), found on Española, the Chatham Mockingbird (*Nesomimus melanotis, cucuve de San Cristóbal*) from San Cristóbal, and the Galápagos Mockingbird (*Nesomimus parvulus, cucuve de Galápagos*), occurring on the remaining major islands.

All four species of mockingbird can be recognized as a thrush-sized, long-tailed, gray and brown streaked land bird. The mockingbirds, especially the Hood variety, will also greet you inquisitively with a loud, piercing shrill, loosely translated as "give me any liquid beverage—even your spit will do." Resist the temptation to quench their thirst: years of success employing their bad begging behavior on tourists has caused an increasing reliance on them for water.

The mockingbirds have an extremely interesting social structure, reminiscent of a well-cogged familial machine. During the breeding season, they form cooperative groups comprised of a breeding female, her mate, and the offspring of her previous broods, all of whom participate in the raising of the next brood and maintenance of the territory.

During the rest of the year, large communal territories are formed with as few as nine and as many as forty individuals, each contributing to territory defense. It's a hoot to watch these birds defending their territories: individuals will face off across the imaginary frontier in linear fronts, each enemy pair squawking, flicking their tails and rushing at each other. Mockingbirds are omnivorous, but they occasionally exhibit aggressive, predatory behavior. They will eat just about anything: seeds, insects, baby turtles, young finches and sea lion placenta.

GALÁPAGOS HAWK

The Galápagos Hawk (*Buteo galapagoensis, gavilán de Galápagos*) is an impressive and fearless large, dark brown bird of prey. Adults have a dark banded tail, yellow, hooked bill and strong yellow talons. The female has the same general features but has a larger, more imposing stature. Juveniles are lighter brown and heavily mottled.

Nests—large, disorganized conglomerations of twigs—are usually constructed in trees or on a rocky outcrop. Following an unusual mating system termed "cooperative polyandry," each female will mate with up to four males, which take turns incubating the two or three eggs in the nest and raising the young. Young birds are expelled from the territory after about four months and begin to breed two years later.

A fearsome predator and scavenger with no natural enemies, the Galápagos hawk delights in a smorgasbord of foods, especially baby iguanas, lizards, small birds, dead goats or sea lions and sea lion placenta. It can often be seen flying or perching impatiently near an iguana nesting area during April and May, when baby iguanas begin to emerge from their eggs. The hawk is best viewed at Punta Suarez and Gardner Bay (Española), South Plaza, Santa Fé and Punta Espinosa (Fernandina).

SHORT-EARED OWL

The Short-eared Owl (*Asio flammeus galapagoensis, lechuza de orejas cortas*) is the most commonly seen owl in the Galápagos. It is dark brown in color with light mottled markings, a dark facial disc, yellow eyes and a dark bill. You are most likely to see the diurnal hunter in the early morning or evening, when it is out looking for its next meal of small birds, rats or mice. It makes its nests on open ground, where it lays three to four eggs. This species is found on every major island, except Wolf.

GALÁPAGOS DOVE

The endemic Galápagos Dove (*Zenaida galapagoensis, paloma de Galápagos*) is one of the more attractive land birds, with a chestnut-brown back, reddish-brown head and underparts, bright red legs and a conspicuous pale blue ring around the eye. Active nests are found year-round, but the peak of breeding season usually starts in February. Courtship behavior includes exaggerated flying patterns, a bowing ceremony and the males' release of a deep, quiet cooing call. The female will lay two eggs in nests built under rocks or vacated by mockingbirds. The curved shape of the Galápagos Dove's bill is indicative of its chosen food: seeds picked from the ground, mainly dropped by the opuntia cactus. They will also take caterpillars and insect larvae. The Galápagos dove can be seen in the drier areas of most islands; Darwin and Wolf harbor a larger subspecies of the same bird.

MARINE LIFE

The Galápagos Islands are an amazing place for exploring underwater habitats. Due to the collision of warm and cool ocean currents, there is an astounding diversity and abundance of Galápagos fish species. That does not mean, however, that mastering marine creature identification is impossible. The following pages are an introductory guide to the most common shore animals, cartilaginous fish (sharks and rays), and bony fish that can be seen when snorkeling.

SALLY LIGHTFOOT CRABS

Sally Lightfoot Crabs (*Graspus graspus, cangrejos*) are named for their ability to flitter across rock faces like the famous dancer. Adults have a dramatic red-orange color, with a blue underside. Since red is the first color to disappear underwater, this coloration serves to camouflage the crabs. Juveniles, which are heavily predated, also rely on camouflage: they are black so that they can disappear against the lava background that serves as their habitat.

They are found on lava shores throughout the islands, but common sightings are in Las Bachas (Santa Cruz), Puerto Egas (Santiago) and Sombrero Chino.

SHARKS IN THE GALÁPAGOS

The White-tipped Reef Shark (*Triaendon obesus, tiburón aleta blanca*) is a common—though initially commanding—sight in snorkel spots throughout the archipelago. It is easy to identify by its pointed nose, silvery-gray color, and the white tips on its tail and first dorsal fin. Most white-tipped reef sharks are about the same size as an adult human, 1.5 to two meters in length. They tend to rest around rocky inlays or in caves, often swimming very close to snorklers. Don't worry about these sharks reenacting a scene from Jaws: they feed at night on small fish and are very docile. They are commonly seen snorkeling at North Seymour, Gardner Bay and Turtle Island (Española), and Devil's Crown (Floreana). You can also see them from the beach at Punta Cormorant (Floreana) and Bartolomé.

The Black-tipped Reef Shark (*Carcharhinus limbatus, tiburón alta negra*) is less common than the white-tipped reef shark, but it can still be seen snorkeling. It too is easily recognizable by its pointed nose, silvery-gray color, and the black (instead of white) tips on its fins. It is the same size as the white-tipped reef shark, thus inspiring the same commanding yet graceful presence, but it is more blatantly unassuming, usually swimming away at the sight of humans. These are sometimes seen at Devil's Crown (Floreana). Juveniles are common in Black Turtle Cove (Santa Cruz).

The endemic Galápagos Shark (*Carcharhinus galapagensis, tiburón de Galápagos*) is a stout, silvery-gray to brown shark. Despite its smaller size (up to two meters), it is, arguably, the most threatening of the Galápagos sharks both in appearance and behavior. It is an active carnivore, known to eat other sharks, that swims solitary or in loose groups. It is rarely seen in the typical snorkel spots, but it has been seen at Devil's Crown (Floreana) and at Leon Dormido (San Cristóbal).

The Hammerhead Shark (*Sphyrna lewini, tiburón martillo*) is instantly recognizable by its flattened head, peripheral eyes and nostrils, and large (growing up to four meters long) shark-like physique. The Galápagos are famous for their abundance of these charismatic creatures: divers often see them in large schools of up to thirty or forty individuals. You are less likely to see them while you are snorkeling, but your best chance is at Genovesa. If you are extremely lucky, you may see juveniles in Black Turtle Cove (Santa Cruz) or Post Office Bay (Floreana).

The Whale Shark (*Rhincodon typus, tiburón ballena*) is a massive, but harmless, shark found mostly in the western islands of Darwin and Wolf. Since divers tend to be the only ones to visit these outlying islands, they are the most likely to catch a momentous glimpse or to swim like an impotent little remora next to the gray and yellow-spotted beast. However, ship captains and crew tell tall tales (mostly true) of the world's largest fish swimming past them as they watch in awe from the boat. It has a huge mouth (often lined with cleaner fish) that can swallow vast quantities of their favorite vegetarian plankton diet.

RAYS IN THE GALÁPAGOS ISLANDS

The Manta Ray (*Manta hamiltoni, mantaraya*), with its large lobes, long mouth, thin tail, and massive three-meter wingspan, is an amazingly beautiful, graceful, and unassuming creature. And watching it swim or jump out of the water to remove annoying parasites or remora is a truly unforgettable experience. They feed on plankton near the surface of the water, making visual sightings from the ship or dinghy a fairly common occurrence. They are often seen in open water between the central islands, most often from the cliff at South Plaza or from the beach at Rábida.

Golden Rays (*Rhinoptera steindachneri, raya dorada*) range in size, but they are usually between a half-meter to a meter across the wings. They are aptly named for their golden-colored tops, but they can also be recognized by their blunt heads and long, whip-like tail. They are often seen in the major snorkel sites swimming solitary, but they also swim in large schools in quiet lagoons. The best place to see schools of golden rays is at Black Turtle Cove (Santa Cruz).

Spotted Eagle Rays (*Aetobatus narinari, raya águila*) are also commonly sighted schooling in small lagoons, like Black Turtle Cove (Santa Cruz). They have pointed heads, long tails with a spiny termination, and a wingspan ranging from one to two meters, but their most distinguishing feature is the array of white spots that covers their black tops. They are also occasionally seen snorkeling at Turtle Island (Española) or off Floreana. Stingrays (family Dasyatididae, rayas) are common residents of shallow beach areas and deeper sandy bottoms throughout the Galápagos. They are gray with a flat body and long, narrow tail, which has the nasty stinger at its base. Size and shape of stingrays can vary, from the smaller, angular "diamond stingray" to the larger (up to two meter wingspan), circular "marbled" stingray. You can spot stingrays lurking on the sea floor of some shallower snorkel sites or hiding out in the surf at Punta Cormorant and/or Post Office Bay (Floreana).

SPOTTED EAGLE RAY
The spotted eagle ray (*Aetobatus narinari*) is a large, graceful, beautiful member of the ray family that is common throughout the tropics around the globe. They can reach lengths of up to 2.5 meters (eight feet) across, and counting their long tail, can be found up to 5 meters (16 feet) in length. They can weigh over 230 kilograms (500 pounds). They tend to skim near the bottom of sandy areas, looking for mollusks and crustaceans which make up their diet. In Galápagos, they are relatively uncommon: you'll see ten stingrays for every spotted eagle. They are most often seen by snorkelers in deep-water sites, such as Rábida, Devil's Crown and Turtle Rock. Spotted Eagles are shy, and will generally swim off if approached by snorkelers.

STINGRAYS
Peaceful bottom dwellers, stingrays are quite common throughout Galápagos. They are the rays most commonly seen, as they tend to inhabit shallow, sandy sites popular with snorkelers and divers. They can grow quite large, up to about a six-foot wingspan. When they swim, they sort of glide along, and they appear to be more flying than swimming. They get their name from a small spike they have in their tail, which can whip up and sting an unwary swimmer or wader. They only sting when threatened or stepped upon. If you're wading in a shallow, sandy beach it is best to walk using the "stingray shuffle," scuffing your feet in the sand to frighten them away before you step on one by accident!

FISH IN THE GALÁPAGOS
Galápagos is world-renowned as one of the best places in the world for diving and snorkeling. If you choose to dive snorkel, or take a tour in a glass-bottom boat, chances are very good that you will see a number of beautiful, exotic fish and marine animals.

The most common member of the Angelfish family is the colorful, disc-shaped King Angelfish (*Holocanthus passer*). It is easily identified by its bright yellow tail and white stripe extending the length of its dark body just behind the pectoral fins.

The Flag Cabrilla is a olive/greyish fish commonly seen in most snorkel and dive sites. Damselfish are also very abundant throughout the archipelago. Although all damselfish can be distinguished by their elongated, elegantly flowing dorsal and tail fins, different species in the damselfish family have their own distinguishing characteristics.

The Great Damselfish has a gray body that fades to black near the tail, with breeding males demonstrating a striking silvery-white face. The Yellow-tailed Damselfish (*Stegastes arcifrons*) has a bright yellow tail (obviously) and lips, blue eyes and purple-black body. The white-tail damselfish has a distinctive white stripe at the base of its tail and orange "eyebrows" that make it easy to identify. The Sergeant Major (*Abudefduf troschelii*), a common reef fish throughout the tropics with black and yellow stripes and disc-shaped body, is also a member of this family, commonly spotted at major snorkel sites. Even though all damselfish are attractive (such is the fate of "damsels"), the juveniles are often the most visually pleasing, because they have iridescent blue spots that shimmer as they swim in the water.

Damselfish are usually found solitary or in small groups of up to three. Even though they are often found in the proximity of other fish, they are extremely territorial and will often chase away intruders (even humans) encroaching upon their algae patch. If you're attentive while snorkeling or diving, you may notice something strange about that oddly-shaped rock on the bottom. Look more closely: you may have spotted a stone scorpionfish. By all means, take a closer look: just don't step on it, as the stone scorpionfish has quite the defense mechanism—venomous spines along it's back!

Parrotfish are one of the easiest fish to identify in the Galápagos, because they are large, colorful, scaly, and shallow swimmers. Colors vary depending on species and age, but most parrotfish are orange with silver scales, red and black, or most often blue-green with colorful specks. One species, the Bumphead Parrotfish, has a very distinctive noggin: as the name implies, it has a flat, bulbous forehead.

Besides their bright coloration, all parrotfish have a beak-shaped mouth (hence the family name), which can serve to bite off and grind up large chunks of coral. They are very important for nutrient cycling. Surgeonfish are another guaranteed sighting during a snorkel session in the Galápagos. All surgeonfish are flat and oval-shaped and swim in massive schools. They also have sharp retractable spines at the base of the tail, which can be used to make precise incisions (like a surgeon's scalpel) in their predators. The most abundant species is the Yellow-tailed Surgeonfish, which, besides possessing a yellow tail, has three distinctive horizontal black polka-dots preceding the tail. It is found in just about every snorkel site in the archipelago.

THE FLAG CABRILLA
The Flag Cabrilla (*Epinephelus Labriformis*) is a favorite of divers and snorkelers in Galápagos, as it is very common, prefers shallow water and is not terribly timid. North American divers and snorkelers may think it looks like a bass. It has a greenish/olive to reddish to gray body and is easily identified by its numerous white spots and milky blotches. It also has a distinctive black spot on the upper side of the base of its tail. They prefer rocks and reefs and don't tend to move much: you'll usually see them lurking on ledges and in crevasses as you pass. Approach slowly and you should get a good look.

ZEBRA MORAY EEL
The elusive zebra moray eel (*gymnomuraena zebra*) is smaller and more shy than its moray cousins. It is blackish brown with distinctive white-green to white-blue stripes. It also has a blunter nose than its moray relatives. It prefers rocky walls and areas with boulders and rocks. It is shy and will hide from snorkelers and divers. It eats crabs and mollusks.

WHITE-TAIL DAMSELFISH
The white-tail damselfish (*stegastes leucorus beebei*) is a familiar sight to many Galápagos snorkelers and divers. This fish, much more spectacular when it is a juvenile, is found in most dive and snorkel spots in the islands, where they favor rocky formations in relatively shallow water. They are brownish gray to black. Adults and juveniles are identified by a white stripe at the base of their tail—in some adults, the stripe may disappear. They generally have a bright orange "eyebrow" that makes identifying them easy, and there is often a bright yellow stripe on their pectoral fins. They ignore divers, only retreating into holes and shelter if too closely approached.

KING ANGELFISH
The only member of the Angelfish family to be found in Galápagos, the King Angelfish (*Holacanthus passer*) is a favorite of many snorkelers and divers. This very beautiful fish is common in most snorkeling and diving areas. They prefer rocky areas to sandy bottoms. They are oval-shaped and have a dark blue body with a distinctive white stripe behind the gill. The top and back fins are yellow to orange. They are generally seen alone or in pairs: they occasionally school.

STONE SCORPIONFISH

The stone scorpionfish (*Scorpaena plumieri mystes*) is a master of deception, disguising itself as a rock, clump of vegetation or piece of coral. Loose flaps of skin and scale help it blend into the bottom, where it will wait motionless for prey to swim past. It can also change colors from grey to purple to red in order to better hide. The spines along it's dorsal fin contain a painful poison. However, they are not aggressive and remain motionless if approached. They are fairly common, but often difficult to spot. It's Spanish name is *brujo*, or "warlock."

BRAVO CLINID

This small, colorful bottom dweller is a master of disguise: it can change colors rapidly to disguise itself into its environment. A member of the blenny family, the bravo clinid (*Labrisomus dentriticus*) is endemic to Galápagos, and common throughout the islands. It usually remains motionless when approached by a snorkeler or diver, allowing close inspection. They prefer rocks and crevasses to sandy bottoms.

SERGEANT-MAJOR

A member of the damselfish family, sergeant-majors are commonly seen at most Galápagos snorkeling and diving sites (and around the world, in fact). They are small (up to eight inches) oval-shaped fish, yellow-green with distinctive blue-black stripes. These stripes give it it's name: they resemble the stripes on a sergeant-major's uniform. They are not terribly shy and can usually be easily approached by slow-moving swimmers.

PARROT FISH

A common sight for snorkelers and divers, the parrot fish is very colorful and not terribly shy, which makes it a favorite. Common at most of the dive sites throughout Galápagos, the parrot fish is a large member of the wrasse family. It has a long body, large scales, and a distinctive parrot-like beak with which it crunches coral in order to eat the organisms inside: you can often hear their munching before you see them. Most are bluish-green with hints of yellow and orange.

GEOLOGY

The Galápagos Island region is one of the most volcanically active areas in the world. The first islands were formed between three and five million years ago, when underwater mountains formed by successive volcanic eruptions began to emerge from the sea, and island formation has continued ever since.

Each major island is a large shield volcano, with the exception of Isabela, which was formed by the unification above sea level of six volcanoes. Since 1535, when the islands were discovered, over 50 eruptions have been recorded, the most recent of which was Isabela's Cerro Azul in 1998.

Geologists rely on two widespread geological theories—the theory of plate tectonics and the hotspot theory—to explain island formation and evolution. According to the theory of plate tectonics, a series of mobile pieces of the earth's outer crust, or plates, are continually spreading away from one another, sliding past one another, or colliding with one another.

Near the Galápagos, tectonic activity follows an interesting yet complicated pattern influenced by the convergence of three plates—the Pacific, the Nazca and the Cocos Plates. The island archipelago is located on the northern boundary of the Nazca Plate near its junction with the Cocos Plate, but it is not at rest there. Sea-floor spreading along the Galápagos Rift causes the islands to move south and east at the rate of 7 cm per year. This may not seem that fast, but in a million years (a geologic heartbeat), that amounts to 70 km (43.5 miles). The hotspot theory says that, in certain areas around the earth, there are stationary areas in the mantle that occasionally get superheated. When the heat from these hot spots increases enough to melt the earth's crust, it will produce a volcanic eruption with enough magnitude to project molten lava toward, and eventually above, the ocean's surface.

GALÁPAGOS

As tectonic plates move across the fixed hot spot, a trail of volcanoes follows, each aging and eroding with time. Since the Galápagos are moving southeast over the hot spot, geologists speculate that the oldest islands must be San Cristóbal and Española, which are found in the southeast archipelago. Following the same logic, the newest islands must be the north-western islands; according to form, the western islands of Fernandina and Isabela, which are situated directly over the hot spot, are still in the process of formation.

Most of the volcanic rocks and magma forming the eruptions in the Galápagos are basaltic, which have low levels of silicon and oxygen and flow more easily. Since eruptions thus take the form of lava flows instead of explosions, the volcanoes that develop tend to have smooth, shield-shaped outlines with rounded tops instead of the more well-recognized cone-shape.

As lava flows, its surface layer comes into contact with the air, cools, and slows down. The result is the formation of a crust with a distinctive surface type: pahoehoe (braided), aa (jagged, ow! ow!), or schrict (ropy). These lava formations are commonly seen at Sullivan Bay on the eastern side of Santiago.

Photo by Dr.Crit Minster

VISITOR SITES

Tourists in the Galápagos will be amazed by the number and variation of visitor sites throughout the archipelago. There are over fifty accessible visitor sites in Galápagos National Park territory, each offering its own unique history, landscape, vegetative characteristics and faunal features. And when taken in tandem, visitors can begin to understand the complex evolutionary process that have shaped island biogeography. Most cruise tours visit two island sites and one or two additional snorkel sites per day.

NORTHERN VISITOR SITES

Visiting the northern islands of Genovesa, Marchena and Pinta can be a special experience for tourists, because it implies earning a rite of passage across the equatorial line. Unfortunately, Marchena and Pinta are off-limits to tourists, but Genovesa is most certainly a Galápagos highlight. It is one of only two islands where you can see groups of red-footed boobies, and the surrounding bay is often a haven for hammerhead sharks, which are occasionally visible while snorkeling.

Although Santiago, Bartolome (and nearby dive-site Cousin's Rock), Sombrero Chino and Rabida are closer to the central island of Santa Cruz than the three northern outliers, we consider them "northern islands" because they are located outside the central island conglomeration. These islands are geologically interesting and offer some of the best photographic opportunities in the Galápagos Islands.

GENOVESA

Also known as tower, Genovesa is the island in the northeastern extreme of the archipelago, north of the equator. Travel to Genovesa is not always included in the eight-day cruise itinerary because of the extra gas needed to visit it. However, a number of the larger, more expensive yachts do visit here, so if you are interested in seabirds and exciting snorkeling opportunities, you may want to prioritize this island on your itinerary when selecting cruises. Genovesa covers 14 km squared and is fairly flat and round, with a large, almost landlocked cove on the south side called Darwin Bay. During the dingy ride from your boat to the first visitor site, Prince Philip's Steps, you will have a good view of red-billed tropicbirds, great frigatebirds, swallow-tailed gulls, Nazca boobies, and red-footed boobies flying, fishing and potentially nesting in cracks in the seaward side of the cliff.

PRINCE PHILLIP'S STEPS

A dry landing leads you to the base of Prince Philip's Steps, a steep, rocky path up the 25-meter cliff face. At the top of the cliffs, the 1-km-long trail leads inland through palo santo vegetation, where the red-footed boobies may be nesting, colonies of seabirds, and an expanse of lava where short-eared owls, Galápagos swallows, Galápagos doves and storm petrels can often be seen. This is an amazing site for bird enthusiasts. But be sure to watch your head for the inevitable guano shower!

DARWIN BAY

The second visitor site, Darwin Bay, is a white-sand beach accessed by a wet landing. Here a .75 km trail passes through mangrove patches frequented by land birds as well as colonies of Nazca boobies, red-footed boobies and swallow-tailed gulls. Further along the trail, beautiful tide pools house the occasional playful sea lion and cliffs offer an amazing view of the island and the sea.

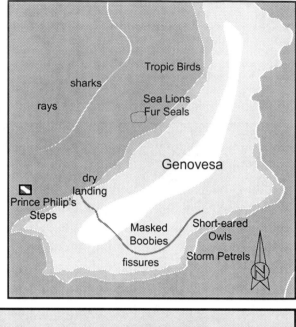

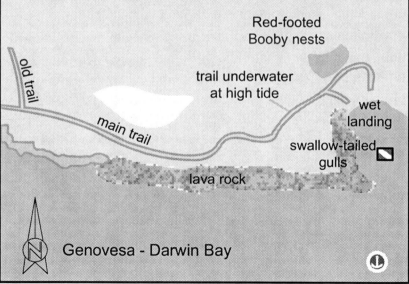

SNORKELING

Because of the steep underwater terrain of Genovesa, snorkeling conditions can vary. If you like to dive and can hold your breath for extended periods of time, you may see interesting bottom-dwellers, tropical fish found only in the northern archipelago, or even a hammerhead shark. However, if you are uncomfortable in the water, you may be disappointed by the marine life visible from the surface.

MARCHENA

Also known as Bindloe, Marchena is a large (130 km-squared) active shield volcano located due west of Genovesa. Although it is the seventh-largest island, it has a fairly desolate terrain and absolutely no visitor sites. There are some good scuba sites nearby, so you may get to see the island up close if you are on a dive tour.

PINTA

Also known as Abington, Pinta is an elongated shield located northwest of Marchena that used to serve as Lonesome George's abode. Visitation to the island is limited to scientists and researchers, who must attain a permit before landing there.

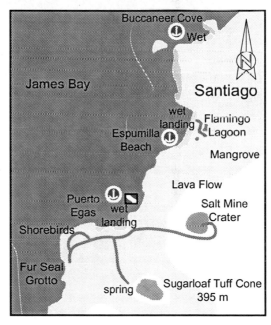

SANTIAGO

Also known as San Salvador or James, Santiago is the fourth largest island at 585 km-squared. This island is especially interesting for people interested in geology, volcanology or succession. Since it provides zero shade and the black rocks can produce an uncomfortable amount of heat, try to visit this island early in the morning or close to dusk.

PUERTO EGAS

The most popular visitor site is Puerto Egas, on the west side of Santiago, where a wet landing places you on a flat, black sandy beach from which you can snorkel or play a game of soccer.

Further along the trail, lava formations eroded to form pools, caves and inlets provide the home to coastal seabirds and a variety of interesting inter-tidal organisms. This is an excellent place to see colonies of Sally Lightfoot crabs scuttling about and marine iguanas munching on algae. Don't be surprised if you find a sea lion or fur sea lion nestled in one of the inlets or playing along the coast.

DARWIN'S TOILET

Near the end of the coastal trail is Darwin's toilet, a rock formation that causes a vertical chute of water to rise when the waves collide with the rock face. You may also see Galápagos swallows, herons and the occasional lava lizard hiding under the rocks. On the east coast of Santiago, across the bay from Bartolomé, is Sullivan Bay. Here, a century-old volcanic eruption has left the island landscape barren. You can see the path of lava flow as well as the various igneous rock structures formed from varying rates of flow, temperature of formation, and pressure. Here you can see examples of three lava types—pahoehoe (braided), aa (jagged and painful) and schrict (ropy). You can also find *hornitos*, little ovens, formed when bubbles escape from hot lava to form mini-volcanoes. Witness the regeneration of the island in the form of pioneer plants—Brachycereus cactus and Mollugo carpetweed—and colonizers—grasshoppers, lizards and snakes.

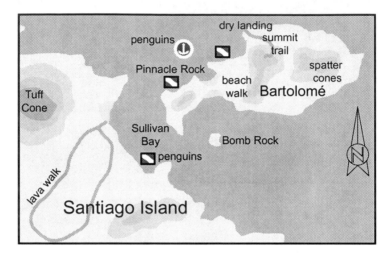

BARTOLOMÉ

Bartolomé, a small islet (1.2 km-squared) just off Sullivan Bay, is the most recognizable island given its distinctive Pinnacle Rock, a towering rock face that has been eroded both naturally and with the help of sure-shots to a point. You may recognize it from the ample coverage it received in the film, Master and Commander.

Visitors can disembark opposite Pinnacle Rock (dry landing) to climb to the 114-meter summit of the island and witness the spectacular views off all neighboring islands. Try to arrive at the top as close to dusk as possible and stay until 6 p.m. when you must leave the island. A staircase and wooden boardwalk has been constructed to mitigate erosion on the slopes. Erosion has been especially grave due to the high frequency of visitation on this island. You can also see pioneer plants like the candelabra cactus and a truly unique lava landscape.

The other visitor site on Bartolomé is a series of small, white, sandy beaches at the narrow center of the barbell-shaped island. From here, you can snorkel around Pinnacle Rock, searching for Galápagos penguins, marine turtles, white-tipped reef sharks and a variety of tropical fish. You can also walk along a sandy trail to the other side of the island, where there is an identical white-sand beach. From the surf, you can often see white-tipped reef sharks hungrily awaiting baby green sea turtles that have been hatched on-land.

SOMBRERO CHINO

The appearance of this island is pretty well-described by its name, *Sombrero Chino*, or Chinese Hat. It is a very small island (less than 1 km-squared) off the southeastern tip of Santiago. It is a fairly recent volcanic cone with a few small but intact lava tunnels. The ambience created by the volcanic cone background, crashing waves along the rocky coast and surrounding islets makes Sombrero Chino an exceedingly pleasant stop. The 400-meter trail starts on a small, white-sand beach, where you can often see American oystercatchers and sea lions. From the beach you can swim in tranquil blue waters along the cove, playing with sea lions and spotting tropical fish. The trail continues along the cove, passing marine iguanas, Sally Lightfoot crabs and lava lizards. If you visit during the cold season (May-June and November-December), the island may have some small tide pools lined with green algae, which attract more marine iguanas.

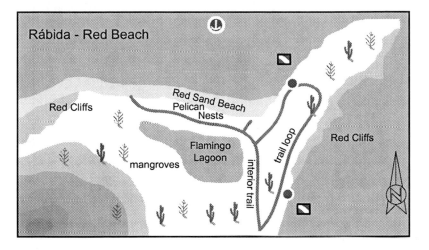

RÁBIDA

Also known as Jervis, Rábida is a small island (5 km-squared) south of Santiago whose colorful splendor makes it a photographer's dream. Visitors will be struck by the sharp contrasts between the turquoise waters, maroon sandy beach, beige rock substrate and lush green highlands. There is a wet landing onto the long, red beach where sea lions lounge, pelicans nest and the occasional manta ray jumps in the distance. A short walk away from the beach takes you to a brackish lagoon, where you can sometimes see flamingoes despite the fact that sea lion fecal contamination of the lagoon has prevented the growth of crustaceans, the flamingos' food source. A .75 km circular trail begins at the lagoon, winding through cactus (look for Mickey Mouse) and palo santo stands, which are home to a few land iguanas. The walk offers amazing views of the sea as well as the island's 367 m volcanic peak.

You can also snorkel from the beach or take a dingy ride along the cove to look for green sea turtles, marine iguanas and fur sea lions. The deep-water snorkeling off of Rabida's walls is fantastic.

CENTRAL ISLAND VISITORS SITES

The central islands of Santa Cruz and Baltra serve as the hub of tourist traffic, since the main town of Puerto Ayora and the airport are located here. The majority of organized tours and independent travelers begin and end their adventures here. The surrounding islands—Daphne Major and Minor, North Seymour, South Plaza (and the nearby dive-site of Gordon Rocks), and Santa Fe—are thus the most visited by tourists due to their close proximity to Puerto Ayora. But they also offer some of the best opportunities for seeing seabirds and large marine creatures, like hammerhead sharks, in abundance.

GALÁPAGOS

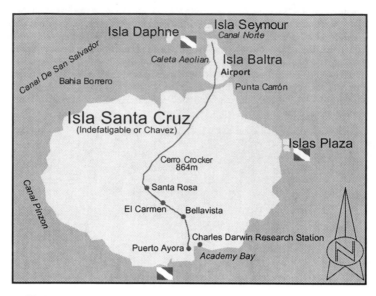

SANTA CRUZ

Santa Cruz is the most tourist-friendly island with close proximity to the main airport at Baltra and the largest resident population. It is also the second-largest island in the Galápagos Islands. In addition to its easy access and tourist infrastructure, Santa Cruz offers visitors the opportunity to explore lava tunnels and sinkholes, creep next to a giant land tortoise in its natural environment, swim at the beach or in a rocky crag, learn about scientific methodologies being utilized on the islands to confront the conservation threat of introduced species or dance the night away in Puerto Ayora.

VISITOR SITES AROUND SANTA CRUZ

There are several highland sites on Santa Cruz, which can be reached in tour vehicle or private transportation, by bicycle or on foot from the trans-island road. From the village of Bellavista, 7 km north of Puerto Ayora, you can either venture north into the national-park highlands, east, eventually hitting the beach, or west, toward the Baltra airport.

NORTH TRAIL-MEDIA LUNA

The north route is a 5 km trail to a crescent-shaped hill called Media Luna, which serves as the base point for access to two other hills, Cerro Crocker, the highest point on Santa Cruz, and El Puntudo. You can either hike, bike, or ride horseback the 3 km from Media Luna to the other two hills, taking in the typical highland flora—Scalesia, Miconia and fern-sedge zones—and fauna—vermilion flycatchers, Galápagos rails, finches and dark-rumped petrels. Since this area is national park land, you must go with a guide either with a formal tour or with a private group, both of which can be arranged in Puerto Ayora.

GARRAPATERO BEACH

Going east from Bellavista along a hilly yet scenic road through the village of Cascajo brings you to a coastal trail that leads to Garrapatero, a gorgeous white-sand beach. Some say this is the most romantic spot in the Galápagos, but besides serving as a mating site (mostly for humans), the beach is great for running, swimming, snorkeling, kayaking or just watching the "wild" life. It is about a two-hour bike ride (up and down) to the coast and a 15-minute walk to the beach.

WEST TRAIL

The other highland attractions can be accessed from the road going west out of Bellavista. First, about 2 km up the road, you will encounter the *Tunel del Mirador*, a lava tube extending more than one kilometer underground. You can explore the tunnels on your own or with a tour organized in Puerto Ayora. The admission fee is about $2, which includes information about the formation of the lava tubes, guides and flashlights (although the tunnel also has some lighting, it is a good idea to supplement what is provided with your own torch or head lamp).

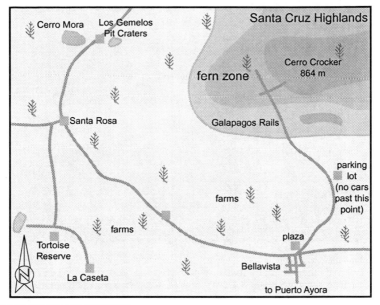

EL CHATO TORTOISE RESERVE

Further along the road near the town of Santa Rosa is El Chato Tortoise Reserve, where you can follow a 1.6 km trail through lagoons to observe giant tortoises in their natural habitat, vermilion flycatchers, yellow warblers, Galápagos rails, short-eared owls and white-cheeked pintails. You can continue on foot or horseback through private farmland to the boundary of the national park area, where you can turn left to go to La Caseta (2 km) or right to go to Cerro Chato (3 km). You can organize guided day-tours in Puerto Ayora for about $20-30. Many cruise tours will also make a stop here, or at the adjacent private ranch owned by the Devine family, to see the tortoises. The entrance fee to the private ranch is about $2, which allows you to wander around at will (in boots provided by the owners) or partake in a soda, beer or hot beverage at the cafe.

LOS GEMELOS

The final attraction, located just off the main road 2 km north of Santa Rosa, is Los Gemelos. These are twin sinkholes—not volcanic craters—surrounded by Scalesia forest, where you can search for vermilion flycatchers, short-eared owls and finches.The remaining visitor sites on Santa Cruz are located on the north coast and are reached by boat and with guides.

BACHAS BEACH

Bachas Beach is often the first destination on a cruise tour, since it is close to the embarkation area and a relaxing introduction to Galápagos travel. Here you can walk along the white-sand beach (wet landing), looking at Sally Lightfoot crabs, remnants of pencil-spined sea urchins, mounds where green sea turtles lay their eggs and mangroves. There is also a small lagoon, where you can often see flamingos and the remains of abandoned barges (from which the area receives its name).

Black Turtle Cove

Black Turtle Cove, or *Caleta Tortuga Negra*, is a shallow inlet surrounded by mangrove stands that provides protection for juvenile marine creatures. From a panga or a kayak (there is no landing site), you can see black- and white-tipped reef sharks, sea turtles, golden cowrays, spotted eagle rays, and on the rare occasion, juvenile hammerhead sharks. Seabirds, like pelicans and blue-footed boobies, also come here to feed.

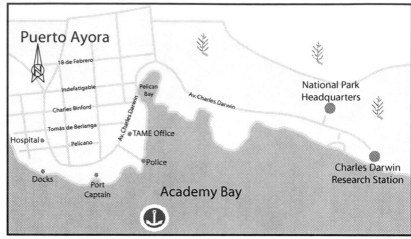

Puerto Ayora

Santa Cruz's main town is Puerto Ayora, which is located on the island's southeast side. The majority of land tours, scuba diving tours and adventure tours originate and/or are based here. Visitors intending to arrange cruise tours locally will stay here waiting for availability on boats to open up. And virtually every cruise tour makes a day stop here—usually near the halfway point of an eight-day trip or at the extremes of the four or five-day trip—so that visitors can visit the Charles Darwin Research Station and highlands and stock up on medicine, film, batteries and snacks if supplies were beginning to run low. Since Puerto Ayora caters to tourist activities, visitors can find virtually any item unintentionally left behind. There is a wealth of hotels, restaurants, bars, stores, tour agencies, dive shops, internet cafés and phone centers. There is also a post office, a TAME office, a basic public hospital and a hyperbaric chamber.

Transportation Around Puerto Ayora

Transportation around Puerto Ayora is generally satisfied by your own two feet. Many of the local residents have bicycles for getting around, but unless you are planning to visit Puerto Ayora's surrounding residential neighborhoods, you should not require one. Bicycling is a fun way to get to know the town, though, if you are stuck for things to do or want to pretend you are a local. Bicycles are also a good way to travel to visitor sites on Santa Cruz within a two- or three-hour radius. Beware: bike rides in the highlands can be challenging. Rentals start at $10 per day. Tours with a guide and/or support vehicle are also available. Transportation within the bay—either to the Playa de Los Alemanes and Las Grietas or to the harbor—is serviced with water-taxis (50-cents one way).

If you organize a day-trip with an agency either as part of a packaged tour or separately, that agency will coordinate all transportation logistics for you: all you have to do is show up at an agreed-upon location in town. If you want to visit the non-National Park sites on your own, you will have to arrange your own transportation. You can contract a taxi to take you anywhere on Santa Cruz (the price of about $10/hour is negotiable).

This can often result in an inexpensive, interesting and personalized experience, since the taxi drivers will undoubtedly serve as your tour guide for the day and give you a resident's perspective. City buses (CITTEG) leave in the morning for Baltra, to make a connection with the flights. Bus tickets and schedule information is available at the office near the "Y". There are usually six buses per day. Local pick-ups and trucks run regularly to Bellavista ($.25) and Santa Rosa ($1), leaving from Avenida Baltra and Calle Española (according to the tourism office map), two blocks from the city market. The Parada is marked, in front of the building with the green awning.

TRANSPORTATION TO PUERTO AYORA

After you de-plane in Baltra, you will either meet the naturalist guide leading your pre-arranged tour or you will head off individually to Puerto Ayora. If you have an organized cruise tour, you will go with your guide and boat-mates on a 5-minute TAME or Aerogal bus-ride to the *muelle*, or dock, where your boat is anchored. If you have arranged a day-tour from Puerto Ayora, you will take a similar bus-ride to the canal, where you will meet a ferry, take a five-minute trip to Santa Cruz and board a tour bus.

If you are on your own and heading to Puerto Ayora, follow the day-tour groups: you can ride the same TAME or Aerogal bus to the canal (for free) and take the same ferry to Santa Cruz ($.50 one-way). Once you get across the channel to Santa Cruz, you can either catch a taxi (about $15 per truck, so try to share) or public bus ($1.80) to take you the final leg to Puerto Ayora. Ideally, the ferries and buses are scheduled to coincide with flights landing and taking off, so you should not have to wait long. The taxi or bus will drop you off in any of the most frequented central spots—like the main pier or boardwalk—or the hotel you specify to the driver.

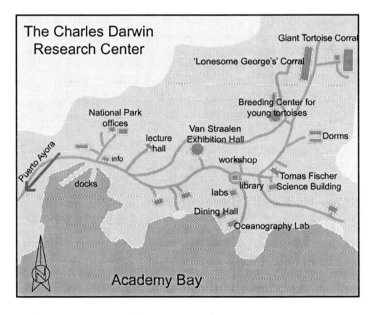

THINGS TO SEE & DO
THE CHARLES DARWIN RESEARCH STATION

Most tours visit the Charles Darwin Research Station. In 1959, the same year the National Park was established, the Charles Darwin Foundation—an international non-governmental organization—was formed. Its basic objectives were to promote scientific studies and environmental education in partnership with the Galápagos National Park, through the management of an on-site investigative facility, the Charles Darwin Research Station (CDRS). Since

Have a great travel story? Tell it at www.vivatravelguides.com

its foundation, the Charles Darwin Foundation and its Research Station have gathered baseline scientific data for a variety of conservation initiatives.

An important nexus of these conservation efforts has been the mitigation of the harmful effects of introduced species and the regeneration of native populations, a process that visitors to the CDRS can watch with their own eyes. Following the interpretive trails along the wooden boardwalk, you will meet Lonesome George, who was thought to be the last of a subspecies of giant Galápagos tortoise to survive introduced predators. However, there may be hope for George, recently another male of his species was found. At the station you will also see the solution to the turtle population problem: a tortoise captive breeding center that has been successful in restoring healthy populations to the wild.

Other attractions at the CDRS include close-up views of several of the 11 subspecies of tortoise, land iguanas, Darwin's finches, paths through coastal and arid-zone vegetation, including salt bush, mangroves, prickly pear, and other cactus, an elaborate presentation and video of the station's conservation efforts in the Van Straelen Exhibition Center, access to a white-sand beach, and the customary souvenir kiosk, whose profits go to support the station (since it is 100% privately funded, receiving zero support from the Ecuadorian government).

PUERTO AYORA SHOPPING

Shopping in Puerto Ayora includes the typical t-shirts and souvenirs-covering a wide range of books and references-along with books, postcards, and some finer arts and crafts. A percentage of the proceeds generated from the Charles Darwin Research Station's souvenir stand goes to support conservation projects. Avoid buying any craft items made from derivatives of island fauna, especially black coral or tortoise shell; it is prohibited by the Galápagos National Park.

OPUNTIA SHOP

The Opuntia Shop is cute souvenir shop/bar nestled in a lovely little courtyard decorated in intricate mosaics. After purchasing a t-shirt or postcard, you can sit at one of the outdoor tables, have an ice cream, soda or beer and relax amid the refreshing surroundings. Avenida Charles Darwin.

GALÁPAGOS GALLERY

A small gallery with creative artistic pieces, ranging from wooden crafts and tagua, or vegetable ivory figurines, to paintings and clothes. Visa and MasterCard accepted. Avenida Charles Darwin.

GALERIA JOHANNA

A typical souvenir shop with the novelty of being located in a red, wooden boat. It is air-conditioned and accepts Visa. Avenida Charles Darwin near the cemetery.

GALERIA AYMARA

A small gallery selling arts and crafts from the Galápagos and the mainland. Pieces range from intricate weavings, creatively patterned ceramics, tagua, or vegetable ivory figurines, and jewelry. Visa and MasterCard accepted. Avenida Charles Darwin.

DIVE SHOPS IN PUERTO AYORA

SCUBA IGUANA ($100-120 PER DAY DEPENDING ON DIVE SITES)

Scuba Iguana is the most efficient, detail-oriented and professional dive operation in Puerto Ayora. Gear and equipment is available in all sizes, well-maintained, and replaced annually, so you will never feel uncomfortable due to ill-fitting gear or malfunctioning equipment. Pre- and post-dive periods are restful and relaxing on Scuba Iguanas spacious and cushy boat, but don't expect too much down-time, since the boats twin engines get you to your dive location in record time.

Safety is also a priority: all new divers must complete a check dive and receive an extensive safety briefing. In addition to employing a smooth operating style, the Scuba Iguana staff is friendly, accommodating, and professional. English-speaking guides—which are assigned to small groups with a maximum of four divers—know the dive sites like the back of their hands and have a knack for finding what you are looking for. Dive center staff is also bilingual and extremely helpful, offering tourist information beyond the scuba-diving scope. Full certification courses, daily dive trips, and pick-up service can be arranged. Regardless of your scuba-diving expectations in Galápagos, you are bound to be satisfied with Scuba Iguana. Avenida Charles Darwin across from the cemetery, Tel: 593-05-252-6497, 7 days/week: 7 a.m.-6 p.m., price includes 2 immersions, full equipment rental, lunch, snack, hot shower and transportation to dive sites.

GALÁPAGOS SUB-AQUA ($100-120 PER DAY DEPENDING ON DIVE SITES)
Galápagos Sub-Aqua is a full-service dive center in Puerto Ayora. PADI-certification courses, from open-water to divemaster, are provided for a reasonable cost. Already certified divers can arrange daily immersions individually or as a tour package. Most guides and instructors are English-speaking, professional, and knowledgeable. The dive center staff may not be the friendliest, but it also changes constantly depending on volunteers. Equipment is well-maintained and in good condition. Open Monday - Sunday 7 a.m. - 6 p.m. Price includes 2 immersions, full equipment rental, lunch, snack and transportation to dive sites. Avenida Charles Darwin across from the fishing port, Tel: 593-05-252-6350.

NAUTI DIVING ($100-120 PER DAY DEPENDING ON DIVE SITES)
Nauti diving offers certification courses, daily dive trips and dive tours to regular dive sites as well as to the outlying islands of Darwin and Wolf. Although the mechanics of the dive operation are less than perfect (gear is older and limited in sizes; the dive boat is small and often a bit cramped; the vegetarian lunch is barely digestible), Nauti diving has the competition beat in one important respect: the friendly and personalized service offered by their staff. Open Monday - Sunday 7 a.m. - 6 p.m. Price includes 2 immersions, full equipment rental, lunch, snack and transportation to dive sites. Av. Charles Darwin y Isla Floreana, Tel: 593-5-252-7004, E-mail: info@nautidiving.com, URL: www.nautidiving.com.

LODGING
Puerto Ayora offers an abundance of hotel choices for all tastes and budgets. Budget hotels are fairly clean, private and comfortable and put a much smaller dent in your pocketbook than the luxurious first class hotels.

Prices are set by the *Camara de Turismo* (Chamber of Tourism), but they may still fluctuate between the high and low tourist seasons. Almost all hotels can be found on or near Avenida Charles Darwin, so search the main drag until you find what you are looking for.

BUDGET
PENSION GLORIA ($5-7/PERSON)
Pension Gloria is the option for the backpacker who has overstayed his welcome and over-spent his budget. It is the least expensive—and least frilly—place to stay in the Galápagos, at $7 per person per day or $5 per person for five or more days. There are a few (dark) rooms opening out to (an even darker) courtyard, each with fans and their own flair (the walls have painted Galápagos scenes). Bathrooms are shared and kitchen facilities can be made available upon request. Avenida Charles Darwin near Seymour.

HOTEL SANTA CRUZ ($7/PERSON)
The Hotel Santa Cruz is a haven for backpackers and national tourists. Even though it is a bit far from the boardwalk (in Puerto Ayora standards) and accommodations are basic, the Hotel Santa Cruz is the cheapest and most family-oriented in town. It is owned and operated by Cristobal and Angela Erazo, a kind, laid-back elderly couple, who can share with you some interesting historical anecdotes of the Islands. There are eight rooms—two singles, four doubles, one triple and one quadruple—with private bathrooms, tepid-water showers and portable fans. It is a safe and relatively comfortable option for travelers on a fixed budget. Avenida Baltra and Indefatigable. Tel: 593-5-252-6573.

GALÁPAGOS

HOTEL LIRIO DEL MAR ($10-15/PERSON)

The Hotel Lirio del Mar is a decent option for budget travelers. It is a three-story hotel with conspicuous orange walls and a second-floor terrace overlooking Academy Bay. Although its exterior is not lacking for character, the rooms are fairly basic and ordinary. Twenty-four single, double, triple and quadruple rooms have private hot bath and fans. There is also a small, dark lounge area near reception that has sofas and a television. Its no-frills eccentricity is forgettable but endearing, an overall comfortable choice for an economical price. Islas Plaza between Tomas de Berlanga and Avenida Charles Darwin, Tel: 593-05-252-6212.

MID-RANGE

HOTEL NEW ELIZABETH ($12-25 + TAX)

The Hotel Elizabeth is a good budget choice for couples or individual travelers. Even though it is centrally located just off of the main drag of Avenida Charles Darwin, the 22 rooms are private, quiet and clean, and well-equipped with private bathroom, hot water, fans and televisions upon request. The female owner Vilma Lucio is extremely friendly and accommodating, and will most likely respond to your needs after a short conversation in the airy (paved and a bit unattractive) outdoor courtyard. The hotel also has a storage area and laundry service.

HOTEL SALINAS (ROOMS: $11.20-44.80 + TAX)

Hotel Salinas is one of the more spacious and professional budget hotels in Puerto Ayora. It has 22 plain, yet comfortable, rooms with private baths, which are distributed on three floors. As you climb the courtyard staircase, you encounter more frills and perks. First floor singles and doubles have tepid water and fans; second floor doubles, triples, and quadruples have hot water and fan; and third floor suites, which may or may not still be under construction, have hot water, air-conditioning, and cable. The hotel also offers 24-hour coffee, laundry and tour information services. Even though the Hotel Salinas lacks the kitschy character that other budget accommodations in Puerto Ayora provide, rooms are clean, location is central, and staff is friendly and helpful. The small central garden also provides a refreshing area for sipping cold drinks or chatting with new friends. Islas Plaza between Avenida Charles Darwin and Tomas de Berlanga, Tel: 593-05-252-6107.

HOTEL ESTRELLA DEL MAR (ROOMS: $20-76)

The Hotel Estrella del Mar is the only budget hotel that can offer ocean views. Four of the hotel's 12 rooms face Academy Bay and receive fresh breezes off the water through their screened-in windows. All other rooms are cute, clean and spacious, and have private hot showers and fan. A few select rooms have air-conditioning and television at the same prices, so request these rooms if you come between February and April and need solace from the unbearable heat. It is a friendly place near the water with a comfortable eating area (breakfast is available for a small price), self-service coffee bar, and lounge. The only downfall is the unfortunate recurrent conglomeration of moths in the main hallway. 12 de Febrero just off Academy Bay, Tel: 593-05-252-6427.

HOTEL SOL Y MAR (ROOMS: $55-75)

The Hotel Sol y Mar is filled with delightful characters, from the friendly receptionist (and owner's mother) Shirley Fuentes to the lava heron, sea lion and marine iguanas that stay as permanent hotel guests. The hotel has eight rooms, six on the waterfront and two on the other side of Avenida Charles Darwin. Each room is spacious, immaculate and secure, and comes with hot private bath and fan. A small deck with picnic tables serves as a great resting or meeting area, with views of the nearby not-so-wildlife and adjacent Academy Bay. The hotel is family-owned and operated, so you are guaranteed personalized, caring, and detail-oriented service. Avenida Charles Darwin between Tomas de Berlanga and Charles Dinford (next to the Banco del Pacifico), Tel: 593-05-252-6281, Fax: 593-05-252-7015.

GRAND HOTEL LOBO DEL MAR (ROOMS: $20.74-70 + TAX)

The Grand Hotel Lobo del Mar may be "grand" in terms of size, due to its recent four-story addition, but it is nowhere near grand in terms of service, despite the variety of activities it coordinates. The hotel has a day-boat, the Galápagos Shark, and a cruise-boat, the Lobo del Mar III, and it also has partnerships with a variety of day-tour operators. This means that you may wind up having to stay in the already paid-for Lobo del Mar, and it is a toss-up whether you will be placed in the swanky, newer, more expensive section of the hotel or the lifeless, older, more economical section. If you are lucky, you will have one of the newer rooms, complete with lush comforts, television, and air-conditioning. Less-fortunate tourists will get a room in the older, darker section, which comes with a fan and private hot bath. Older rooms with fan, including breakfast. 12 de Febrero just off Avenida Charles Darwin toward the bay, Tel: 593-05-252-6188, URL: www.lobodelmar.com.ec.

HOTEL PALMERAS (ROOMS: $28-70)
The Hotel Palmeras is your typical cookie-cutter hotel, with a touch of added elegance. It has a capacity for 70 guests in 32 single, double, triple and quadruple rooms. Rooms on the first floor have fan and private hot water facilities. Second-floor rooms have air-conditioning, private hot bath and television. A bright top-floor restaurant, disco, swimming pool and game room add entertainment options for its varied clientele. There are also laundry, telephone, fax, and internet services available. The Hotel Palmeras works with SERVITUR and other local tour operators to organize combination tours that utilize their own boat, the Verito. Since the hotel caters to large groups and tours, they have mastered the art of providing efficient, friendly, and personalized service. Tomas de Berlanga and Islas Plaza, Tel: 593-05-252-6139, Fax: 593-05-252-6373, E-mail: hotelpalmeras@hotmail.com.

LUXURY
CASA DEL LAGO (ROOMS: $60-100)
The Casa del Lago is part of an effort by owner Elena Albarado to offer tourists alternatives that emphasize social and cultural responsibility. Suites are rented on a daily, weekly or even monthly basis. Both housing units have fully-stocked kitchen units and stylish architectural design and furnishings. Recycled glass fragments in window frames play with incoming light; hand-painted tiles add flair to showers and staircases; and wild fabrics give the walls, ceilings and beds a spicy character. The residence is adjacent to the Casa del Lago Cafe Cultural and looks out on the spectacular Laguna Las Ninfas. The owner can also arrange custom-designed tours for student groups and other parties interested in educational tourism. Tours visit local hot-spots, farms, and residences and generate proceeds that directly benefit Santa Cruz residents. Tel: 593-098-51-40-15/593-09-971-4647, E-mail: Galápagoscultural@hotmail.com, URL: www.Galápagoscultural.com.

HOTEL SILBERSTEIN (ROOMS: $84-126)
The Hotel Silberstein, formerly known as the Hotel Angermeyer, is a modern, intimate and beautifully-landscaped hotel. It has 22 clean, romantic rooms, each containing private hot bath, ceiling fan and air-conditioning and a view toward the lush courtyard/swimming pool area. There are 11 matrimonial double rooms, eight double rooms with twin beds and three triple rooms. Comfort, style and attention to detail (not to mention price) are at a maximum at the Hotel Silberstein. A sandy space near the pool can serve as a barbeque-pit or playplace for youngsters. The garden surrounding the open-air bar provides a diverse, eye-catching landscape (as well as providing interesting data for plant and bird surveys conducted by the Charles Darwin Research). And the restaurant and its island-famous gourmet chef serve spectacular and unique dishes to please. The hotel partners with the Galextur to offer four to eight-day tours with overnight accommodations in Puerto Ayora. It can also arrange cruise tours on the sailboat Sulidae. Avenida Charles Darwin and Seymour, Tel: 593-05-252-6277, E-mail: blectour@iuo.satnet.net.

RED MANGROVE ADVENTURE INN (ROOMS: $88-285 + TAX)
The Red Mangrove Adventure Inn is an intimate, relaxing, and unique ecological paradise. Nine spacious, creatively-decorated rooms and suites—each carrying a color-theme—offer you the finest of accommodations in a private bungalow nestled among red mangrove trees. Each room is clean, comfortable and equipped with private hot bath, ceiling fan. There is also a small pool, a meeting area with plush tables and chairs, a common room with television and plenty of hammocks for lounging. The inn has its own boutique, which sells artistic goods

GALÁPAGOS

and organic coffee and an amazing sushi restaurant/bar. The Red Mangrove Adventure Inn is pricey, but it will guarantee a truly individual and unforgettable experience. The inn also coordinates a variety of tours, including camping, sea kayaking, fishing, mountain biking and horseback riding. As such, it offers excellent, custom-tailored alternatives to pre-arranged tours. Avenida Charles Darwin near the cemetery, Tel: 593-05-252-7011, Fax: 593-05-252-6564, E-mail: recepcion@redmangrove.com, URL: www.redmangrove.com.

HOTEL ROYAL PALM (ROOMS: $345-825)
The Hotel Royal Palm is tucked up in the jungle-like brush on Santa Cruz island in the Galápagos. It's a secluded hideaway for luxury travelers, providing high class service in accordance with the awe-inspiring environment of the islands. Hotel Royal Palm consists of ten exclusive villas, four veranda studios and three suites, all individually decorated. The hotel offers indoor and outdoor Jacuzzis, DVD and CD players, a wellness club with spa, internet access, and a wonderful art gallery that showcases works of leading Ecuadorian, Galapageno and international artists. One of the biggest draws of this hotel is its truly outstanding international gourmet cuisine. Via Baltra, Tel: 593-05-252-7408, E-mail: info@royalpalmGalápagos.com, URL: www.royalpalmGalápagos.com.

PUERTO AYORA RESTAURANTS
Along the main drag, Avenida Charles Darwin, there are a variety of open-air cafés, restaurants, and bars (or sites serving as all three). Seafood and Italian cuisine seem to dominate the food scene, but you can also find sandwiches, salads, amazing coffee and juices, and homemade ice cream. Even if you don't want to dine, stop in any street-side establishments, order a refreshing beverage and watch the mesmerizing mix of people walk by. Another hot-spot for good eats is the *Calle de los Kioskos*, a line of outdoor stalls specializing in inexpensive, mouth-watering local dishes.

ASIAN
RED SUSHI (ENTREES: $3-13)
Red Sushi, in the Red Mangrove Adventure Inn, is a bar/restaurant specializing in Japanese delights. The sashimi and maki rolls are perfectly delectable, and popping them in your mouth in the colorful, waterfront establishment makes the dining experience truly enjoyable. There is also a selection of Japanese soups and main dishes, as well as a full menu of exotic drinks (not country-specific) served at the bar. Charles Darwin near the cemetery.

ECUADORIAN/SEAFOOD
KIOSKOS (ENTREES: $3-8)
Eat at the kioskos, a series of outdoor food stands, and you will get the tastiest, most reasonably-priced, and fastest fresh food in town. Most locals eat here, so don't be surprised if you have to fight for a seat during the dinner hour. Almost all of the stalls have the same menu: beef, chicken, fish, and/or shrimp prepared according to your tastes or *encocado*, covered in a delicious coconut sauce. Most dishes come with rice, beans and salad and cost around $5. Some stalls will also serve lobster, an especially tasty treat, for a pretty price. Calle de los Kioskos, an extension of Charles Dinford between Islas Plaza and Avenida Baltra.

ANGERMEYER POINT (ENTREES: $10-12)
Puerto Ayora's finest restaurant was founded by the Angermeyers, one of the earliest colonist families of the town. Set in the cabin of Karl, it is decorated with photos and memorabilia of those early days of island life. On the deck facing the bay, you can enjoy an evening meal of fish or Galapagan beef, as succulent as that of Argentina. Meat portions are generous; the sides are delicious but disappointingly small. This is an unforgettable dining experience that is well worth the expense. Open evenings.

RESTAURANTE EL DESCANSO DEL "GUIA" (ENTREES: $5-8)
The eclectic Restaurante El Descanso del "Guia" is a local staple, its friendly and unassuming owner Irlanda Banguera has served typical Ecuadorian dishes there for over ten years. It is

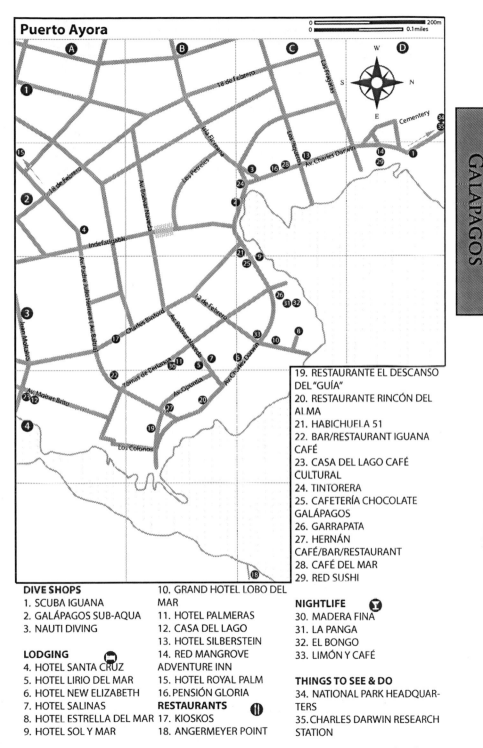

Puerto Ayora

DIVE SHOPS
1. SCUBA IGUANA
2. GALÁPAGOS SUB-AQUA
3. NAUTI DIVING

LODGING
4. HOTEL SANTA CRUZ
5. HOTEL LIRIO DEL MAR
6. HOTEL NEW ELIZABETH
7. HOTEL SALINAS
8. HOTEL ESTRELLA DEL MAR
9. HOTEL SOL Y MAR
10. GRAND HOTEL LOBO DEL MAR
11. HOTEL PALMERAS
12. CASA DEL LAGO
13. HOTEL SILBERSTEIN
14. RED MANGROVE ADVENTURE INN
15. HOTEL ROYAL PALM
16. PENSIÓN GLORIA

RESTAURANTS
17. KIOSKOS
18. ANGERMEYER POINT
19. RESTAURANTE EL DESCANSO DEL "GUÍA"
20. RESTAURANTE RINCÓN DEL ALMA
21. HABICHUELA 51
22. BAR/RESTAURANT IGUANA CAFÉ
23. CASA DEL LAGO CAFÉ CULTURAL
24. TINTORERA
25. CAFETERÍA CHOCOLATE GALÁPAGOS
26. GARRAPATA
27. HERNÁN CAFÉ/BAR/RESTAURANT
28. CAFÉ DEL MAR
29. RED SUSHI

NIGHTLIFE
30. MADERA FINA
31. LA PANGA
32. EL BONGO
33. LIMÓN Y CAFÉ

THINGS TO SEE & DO
34. NATIONAL PARK HEADQUARTERS
35. CHARLES DARWIN RESEARCH STATION

Have a great travel story? Tell it at www.vivatravelguides.com

popular for breakfasts, especially fruit salads and *secos de carne y pollo* (chicken and beef stew) to-go. There is also an inexpensive yet hearty fixed lunch menu, which often includes Irlanda's famous meatballs. The sparse decorations and assorted furnishings make the interior a bit drab, but the surrounding greenery, cool breeze from the ocean and friendly service add refreshment and life to the establishment. Avenida Charles Darwin, next to the bus station.

RESTAURANTE RINCÓN DEL ALMA (ENTREES: $6-10)

The Rincon del Alma has all of the typical Galápagos food choices—seafood, meats and some Italian choices—in a central location across from the park. The Rincon del Alma has a local, familial feel and is popular among breakfast crowds. Food is tasty and served in man-sized portions, so you may want to share a few dishes among friends. The fish, lobster, octopus and shrimp ceviches are satisfying (said to cure your *chuchaqui*, or hangover) and served with a bottomless supply of homemade banana chips. You can order the ceviche at any hour, sit along the main drag of Avenida Charles Darwin, and watch the hustle and bustle of Puerto Ayora. Avenida Charles Darwin between Avenida Baltra and Islas Plaza, Tel: 593-05-252-6196.

NOTE: For super cheap treats (and an adventure) head to the Mercado Municipal on Avenida Baltra (i.e. Padre Julio Herrera) and Calle Isla Duncan. Another good option is the feria libre (country market), which occurs once a week on Saturday mornings, at the Perimetral on Calle Isla Duncan, six blocks north of the city market.

CAFÉ/BARS

BAR/RESTAURANT IGUANA CAFE (ENTREES: $3-6)

An enormous bamboo bar, tree-trunk tables, and bright sarong wall treatments give the Bar/Restaurant Iguana Cafe an eclectic, bohemian, and ultimately welcoming feeling to tourists and locals alike. Amazing mixed juices, spaghetti and lasagna, and seafood specialties make it worth their while gastronomically. Avenida Baltra between Tomas de Berlanga and the Calle de los Kioskos, Breakfasts and sandwiches: $2-4; Main dishes: $3-6.

HABICHUELA 51 (ENTREES: $2-5)

Habichuela 51 is well-frequented for its prime location and laid-back, open-air atmosphere and not for its outstanding food. Sandwiches, hamburgers and other bar food is served, but most people sit at one of the few patio tables, order a beer and watch the people on Avenida Charles Darwin stroll by. The selling point for Habichuela 51, besides its excellent vantage point, is the bottomless bowl of popcorn that comes complimentary with your beer order. Avenida Charles Darwin and Charles Binford.

INTERNATIONAL/VEGETARIAN

CASA DEL LAGO CAFÉ CULTURAL (MEALS FROM $4)

The Casa del Lago Cafe Cultural was opened in 2004 by former guide and Imbabura resident Elena Albarado to provide a space for local artists, performers, movie screenings, festivals, special events and other cultural activities. The cafe serves organic coffee grown on the islands and fantastic coffee drinks, perfectly complemented by *helados de paila*, homemade ice cream. It also serves tasty and inexpensive breakfasts and vegetarian dishes, including healthy soups, salads, middle-eastern food and bagels, those *panes raros* (strange breads) that U.S. tourists constantly crave. Internet, musical instruments and board games are available for short-term use, and paintings and wooden crafts created by local elderly residents are for sale. Come and enjoy participating in a socially responsible, delicious and eye-catching (picture windows face the Laguna Las Ninfas) production. Moises Brito and Juan Montalvo, near Laguna Las Ninfas, Tel: 593-09-851-4015/971-4647, E-mail: Galápagoscultural@hotmail.com, URL: www.Galápagoscultural.com.

TINTORERA (DISHES: $2-5)

Owners Linda Kerrison and Emma Ridley have given Tintorera a fresh, eco-friendly spin. Produce is organic and locally-grown; cheeses are made locally; jams are produced by the Orgnization of Artisan Women in Isabela; and re-usable glass soda bottles—not plastic throwaways—are used. Ice cream, cakes and bread products are homemade and delectably moutwatering. Breakfast is the best meal here, not only because you can partake in any of the items baked fresh, but also because you get a bottomless cup of tea or organic Galápagos coffee. Lunches, however, are not far behind: sandwiches on homemade bread, bagel sandwiches, veggie burgers, salads, soups and middle-eastern food provide delicious vegetarian options. Avenida Charles Darwin and Isla Floreana.

CAFETERIA CHOCOLATE GALÁPAGOS (DISHES: $3-8)
The Cafeteria Chocolate Galápagos is a friendly, spacious and comfortable space for gluttonous, voyeuristic, or group-oriented travelers. A few covered four-person tables on the café's patio provide the perfect space for drinking hot chocolate, watching traffic stroll along the main drag, or playing cards well into the night. Soup, salad, Italian dishes and sandwiches made with homemade bread provide a sumptious start before digging in to the real draw: chocolate in all of its delicious forms. Avenida Charles Darwin between Charles Binford and Tomas de Berlanga.

GARRAPATA (ENTREES: $7-10)
Garrapata is often considered (by tourists) to be the best restaurant in town. It serves fresh seafood and creative meat dishes, as well as nine different pastas. The restaurant also counts on a friendly waitstaff, ample bar and candle-lit outdoor seating. If the food alone does not sell you, a stroll past the romantic atmosphere and full tables will convince you to stop in and eat before hitting the bars next door. Avenida Charles Darwin between 12 de Febrero and Tomas de Berlanga, Tel: 593-05-252-6264.

HERNAN CAFÉ/BAR/RESTAURANT (ENTREES: $6-18)
Hernan Cafe/Bar/Restaurant generalizes in a wide variety of food options, as its name suggests. Its most popular menu items are pizza and spaghetti, but it also offers soup, sandwiches, salads, fish, chicken and beef dishes. Its specialties are fish and steak, prepared in delectable combinations of herbs and spices. The establishment also has a small bar and ice-cream machine, which frequently produce crowds or long lines, especially if there is a soccer game on television or recess from school. The central location, relaxed open-air atmosphere, and plethora of options available at owner Hernan Herrera's familial eatery make it a popular choice among tourists and locals alike. Avenida Baltra and Avenida Charles Darwin, Tel: 593-05-252-6573.

V!VA Member Review-Hernan Café/Bar/Restaurant
Great location across from the waterfront area near the main dock. Service was quick and friendly. Prices were reasonable (under $10 per person w/ drinks included). 50 cent ice cream cones were a treat! 2 Feb 2006. New York.

CAFÉ DEL MAR
The aroma of grilled meats and the sizzle of the fire greet you as you walk into this brightly lit cavernous space with bamboo walls and large, wood slab tables. On one wall, videos about the Galápagos are being shown. The shish kabobs—beef, seafood or mixed—are the best bargain at $5. They come with generous portions of steamed potatoes lightly drizzled with a cheese sauce and a salad. Café del Mar has a full bar. The wines are a bit overpriced. Open evenings after 6:30 p.m. Av. Charles Darwin, across from the WWF (World Wildlife Fund) offices.

NIGHTLIFE
The selection of bars and discos in Puerto Ayora is pretty slim. But the lack of options means that the nighttime hotspots are pretty heavily-trafficked by both locals and tourists and open until the wee hours.

LIMÓN Y CAFÉ (BEER: $1-2, COCKTAILS: $2-4)
A laid-back local hangout, Limón y Café is the most common nighttime meeting place on the island. You can sit at the bar or at any of the wooden tables, sipping ice-cold beers, playing cards or chatting with new friends. It also has a pool table and plays (badly) subtitled movies on the bar television. Limón y Café is always open and crowded. Regardless of when you come, you are

bound to see a friendly face. It is Puerto Ayora's own Cheers: the place where everybody knows your name. Open 7 p.m.-2 a.m. daily. Avenida Charles Darwin and 12 de Febrero.

MADERA FINA (BEER: $1-2 COCKTAILS: $2-5)
Madera Fina is, as its name "Fine Wood" suggests, the most shi-shi disco in Puerto Ayora. It is populated by an older crowd and guests of the adjacent Hotel Palmeras. It is a good option for couples looking for a nice, relaxed and roomy place to dance. Open 8:30 p.m.-3 a.m. on weekends.Tomas de Berlanga between Avenida Baltra and Islas Plaza, adjacent to the Hotel Palmeras.

LA PANGA (BEER: $1-2 COCKTAILS: $2-5)
La Panga is the most popular-and only-main drag disco in town, which means it is always hopping on the weekends until the closing hour. It has a full bar, serving drinks with a local flavor. A small dance floor with video screen is usually crowded with salsa partners and foreigners shaking their booties to the strange but lively mix of latin, electronic and pop music. It also has some plush lounge booths and a pool table for the more tuckered out. Open until 3 a.m. on weekends. Avenida Charles Darwin between 12 de Febrero and Tomas de Berlanga.

EL BONGO (BEER: $1-3.COCKTAILS: $2-5)
El Bongo is an internet cafe/bar with a pretty loyal local following. It has a few tables outside where you can sip your drink, enjoy the night air and look at the stars. Inside there is a pool table, some booths and a fairly extensive bar. Modern decor, spaciousness and beer on tap give El Bongo the perfect mix of sterility and character. It is a comfortable place to start the night out with a few drinks or to stay into the late night hanging out with friends. Open until 2 a.m. every night. Avenida Charles Darwin between 12 de Febrero and Tomas de Berlanga, above La Panga.

AROUND PUERTO AYORA

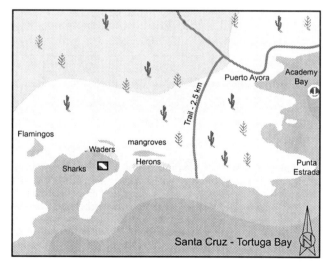

Santa Cruz - Tortuga Bay

TORTUGA BAY, LAGUNA LAS NINFAS
One popular Puerto Ayora visitor site is Tortuga Bay, located at the end of a paved 3 km trail southwest of town. Once you arrive at Tortuga Bay (a guide is not needed), you will encounter a long, white-sand beach and some pretty powerful waves offshore. If you came to surf, stay and try your luck, but if you came to swim or relax on the beach, keep walking until the end of the beach, where there is a spit of secluded beachland (hopefully not filled with visitors) and a protected swimming area. Do not stay at the first beach; not only have numerous children and adults drowned in the hard-to-read waters, but the second beach area is much nicer. There you can rest alongside mangroves, dodge mockingbirds, watch pelicans, follow marine

iguanas or snorkel with sharks. Make sure you bring food, water and sunscreen, because there are no facilities and very little shade. Also on the southwest side of town is the Laguna Las Ninfas. This is a beautiful, refreshing place to swim (if you come when the little kids who usually frequent the swimming area are at school) or look for wildlife.

La Playa de los Alemanes, Las Grietas

La Playa de los Alemanes, another beautiful white-sand beach, and Las Grietas, a series of rock crevices filled with water, are close to town. Take a 50 cent water-taxi across the bay to the second dock, where you will encounter the head of the walking trail. Following the trail for about five minutes, you will arrive at La Playa de los Alemanes, where you can relax, swim and enjoy the mangrove (and Finch Bay Hotel) surroundings. Make sure you get to the beach during low tide, because it can disappear at high tide. Past the beach, the trail becomes rocky and potentially treacherous for balance-deficient or barefoot visitors. The trail continues for about 20 minutes past a small salt mine, arid-zone vegetation and the occasional bird to the top of the first of two approximately 12-meter deep crevices known as Las Grietas. If you are daring, you can jump from there into the cool water below, or you can follow the wooden staircase down to the water. There you can swim, play with the fish that have made their home among the submerged rocks or jump from the various rocky platforms. Make an effort to arrive at mid-day, when the sun shines directly overhead and illuminates the crevice.

Baltra

Most visitors to the Galápagos archipelago arrive by way of the airport on Baltra, which originally served as a US Navy base. There are no visitor sites or accommodations on Baltra (and the land iguana species that used to live on Baltra has been eliminated), and the only facilities available on Baltra relate to air traffic and transportation. From the airport you can catch a bus to the canal, where you can catch an 80 cent ferry to Santa Cruz, and to the port, where visitors with pre-arranged tours meet their boat.

North Seymour

Since the 1.9 km-squared uplifted island of North Seymour is located just north of Baltra, it is a popular first excursion or finale of a cruise tour and a good day trip from Puerto Ayora. A dry landing leads to a circular trail (about 2.5 km long) through some of the most active sea bird breeding colonies in the archipelago. Following the trail along the beach, you should see blue-footed boobies and pelicans fishing, swallow-tail gulls and frigatebirds flying, and marine iguanas resting on the rocky shore. If you take a rest on the rocks and patiently look out at the sea, you will probably see a sea lion or two surfing the waves. Further along the trail, you will see hordes of male frigatebirds nesting—attracting females with their inflated red sack—and the occasional land iguana.

Regardless of the time of year you visit, you are likely

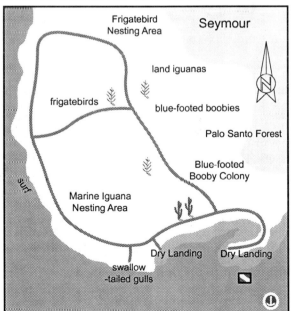

to observe some kind of courtship, mating, nesting, or chick nesting on North Seymour. And since both boobies and frigatebirds often make their nests close to the trail, you may get a very good close-up shot. The snorkeling and diving at North Seymour is also excellent. From the surface, you are bound to see white-tipped reef sharks, triggerfish, surgeonfish and other colorful fish. If you are diving in the canal, you are likely see a host of Galápagos garden eels, moray eels and the occasional diamond, golden, or manta ray. At Punta, hunt for white-tipped reef sharks and moray eels in caves and crevices.

SOUTH PLAZA

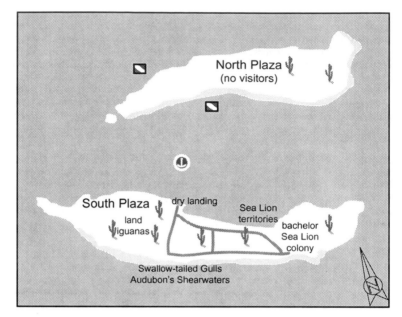

South Plaza is a small island off the east coast of Santa Cruz that was formed by uplift due to faulting. The small size of the island combined with interesting geological, floral, and faunal characteristics makes it a definitive highlight for cruise travelers or for day-trippers from Puerto Ayora. There is a dry landing onto a shore covered with white rocks, polished to a brilliant sheen by the oily sea lions as they travel up and down the shore. A 1 km trail circuit leads you first through an opuntia cactus forest frequented by richly yellow land iguanas, yellow warblers and finches. There is also one land-marine iguana hybrid that has been hanging out at the beginning of the trail since 2003, but it is only rarely seen. The trail continues along a 25 meter high cliff, which provides excellent landscape vistas of the neighboring Santa Cruz as well as sights of numerous seabirds, such as red-billed tropicbirds, Audubon shearwaters, swallow-tailed gulls, pelicans and frigatebirds. You may also see a conspicuous line of mullets swimming offshore and, if you are lucky, a shark or two lurking in the rocks below or a manta ray jumping in the distance. Further east along the trail, you will encounter a sea lion bachelor colony, where males defeated in the battle for territory feat the difficult climb up the rocky crag to congregate, enjoying a bit of camaraderie before returning to challenge for territory. The final part of the trail passes through a distinct sea lion territory, where you may see newborn pups (if arriving in October-December) or playful juveniles (February-April).

DAPHNE MAJOR AND MINOR
These two small islands about 10 km west of Baltra provide the first macro view of the archipelago after landing in the airport. If you have the opportunity to visit Daphne Major, the island home where Rosemary and Peter Grant conducted their study on Darwin finches

that inspired the novel, The Beak of the Finch, consider yourself among select company: the island is only accessible to one scientific group per month in order to reduce erosion.

It is clear from the beginning of the visit—a landing which requires stepping from the moving dinghy onto a vertical cliff face and scrambling up the rocks to the head of the steep, rocky trail—that a trip to Daphne is a special experience. The short trail leads up the side of the volcanic island to a 120-meter high summit, passing Nazca boobies, swallow-tailed gulls and finches along the way. At the top of the cone are two small craters, where hundreds of blue-footed boobies and frigatebirds settle to find their mates (a veritable bird motel!).

Daphne Minor is fairly eroded and not accessible to tourists—although the surrounding waters are very popular dive site. The underwater geology of Daphne is very interesting, with recesses and steep cliffs, and a high possibility of seeing sharks—white-tipped, Galápagos, and occasionally hammerheads—along with sea turtles and rays.

SANTA FE

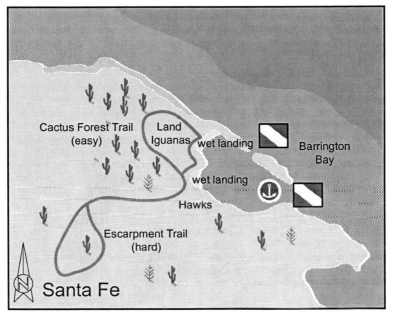

Santa Fe, located about 20 km southeast of Santa Cruz, is a popular destination for day trips and cruise itineraries. A wet landing on a white-sand beach—home to a colony of sea lions—provides visitors with the opportunity to follow two different trails. The first trail, a 300-meter circuit, takes you to one of the tallest stands of opuntia cactus in the archipelago, some reaching heights of over 10 meters. The other trail, a 1.5 km hike through palo santo forest, may expose you to a variety of land birds, the Galápagos hawk and the elusive species of land iguana endemic to Santa Fe.

SOUTHERN ISLAND VISITOR SITES

The three southern islands of San Cristóbal, Española and Floreana provide some of the most exciting, unique and unforgettable visitor sites in the Galápagos. San Cristóbal and its main port town, Puerto Baquerizo Moreno (it is also the capital of Galápagos), have the best surfing spots in the archipelago. There is good diving and snorkeling nearby, as well as some good beaches.

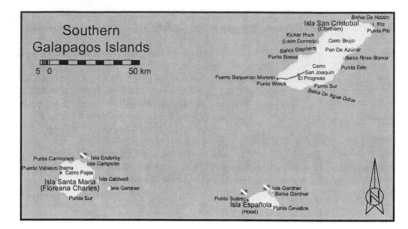

Española is famous as the only place in the world where the waved albatross nests. You can see their awkward waddling take-off during the months of the year when they are there. Finally, the island of Floreana boasts one of the best snorkel spots in the islands, Devil's Crown.

SAN CRISTÓBAL

San Cristóbal is the fifth-largest island (558 km-squared) and lies on the southeast extreme of the archipelago. Rapid development of tourist and educational facilities, as well as the existence of an airport, has caused island visitation to grow in recent years. San Cristóbal boasts the only freshwater lagoon in the archipelago, beautiful beaches, amazing snorkeling and scuba-diving opportunities, and some of the best surfing spots in the archipelago. The island also provides an interesting socio-environmental element missing from other islands: visitors interested in the human component of the Galápagos Islands can see colonial architecture, visit organic coffee plantations and other agricultural centers and even dabble in local politics in the provincial capital, Puerto Baquerizo Moreno. Tourists can either arrive by air from Baltra or by private boat from Puerto Ayora.

LEÓN DORMIDO/KICKER ROCK

León Dormido ("sleeping lion") is a medium-sized distinctive island off the coast of San Cristóbal Island. It is also known as "Kicker Rock" in English due to the fact that it vaguely resembles a foot. The small island is host to numerous sea birds such as boobies. It is also one of the best Galápagos Islands dive spots.

PUERTO BAQUERIZO MORENO

The capital and administrative center of the Galápagos, Puerto Baquerizo Moreno, has the second-largest population (5,600 inhabitants) in the archipelago, after Puerto Ayora.

Although the tourist infrastructure is less advanced here than in Puerto Ayora, visitors to Puerto Baquerizo Moreno are not without options. Hotels, stores, restaurants and travel agencies line the boardwalk, and internet cafes, telephone centers and banks are common. There is also a small post office, police station and hospital. The Galápagos campus of the San Francisco University is also in Puerto Baquerizo Moreno, so university staff and students reside here.

Day-trips to various on-land, offshore and marine sites are available and can be arranged through travel agencies and dive centers located in town. Private vehicles (taxis) provide fairly inexpensive and reliable transportation and are often a good alternative to arranged tours when visiting highland sites. There are also infrequent public buses that run from Puerto Baquerizo Moreno to the village of El Progreso (8 km to the east).

Some boats begin their tours here, and periodic closings of the Baltra airport for cleaning or maintenance can cause tourist activity to shift to San Cristóbal. As a result, visitor services and facilities are constantly improving in Puerto Baquerizo Moreno to provide alternatives for tourists and to meet tourist demand.

THINGS TO SEE & DO

THE GALÁPAGOS NATIONAL PARK INTERPRETATION CENTER

Inaugurated in 1998, the Galápagos National Park Interpretation Center, located on the northeast side of Puerto Baquerizo Moreno, has a series of interactive exhibits providing information about the history and biodiversity of the Galápagos Islands. The self-guided walking tour lasts about one hour, is offered in English and in Spanish, and is appropriate for all ages.

NEARBY BEACHES

Walking trails from the interpretation center lead to Las Tijeretas and Playa Cabo de Horno. Las Tijeretas (sometimes referred to as Frigatebird Hill), a 1.5 km hike from the Interpretation Center, provides a spectacular view of the bay below and the town behind, as well as snorkeling and swimming opportunities and possible glimpses of the two species of frigatebird. Playa Cabo de Horno is a white-sand beach at the northern end of town that offers swimming and snorkeling opportunities, sports facilities and beautiful views.

In addition to Cabo del Horno, Puerto Baquerizo Moreno also has some excellent public beaches. Playa Man is a beautiful white-sand beach with volleyball courts, a view of the bay (and the boats and sea lions maneuvering through it) and swimming and snorkeling opportunities. Since the beach is located across from the San Francisco University, you are likely to find college students "studying" there if school is in session. Playa de Oro, at the end of the boardwalk, is a small white-sand beach perfect for lounging, swimming or playing sports. The town also boasts two excellent surfing spots. The first, Carola Point, is located at the north extreme of town, while the second, El Cañon, is west of town near the airport. Another popular attraction is La Lobería. Accessed via a long trail beginning at the west-end of town, visitors to La Lobería can watch the antics of a playful sea lion colony and enjoy the nice landscape views.

MORE SAN CRISTÓBAL VISITOR SITES

Located in the highlands of San Cristóbal at an altitude of 700 meters, El Junco Lagoon is the only freshwater lake in the Galápagos. As you rise from Puerto Baquerizo Moreno to El Junco, you can see marked differences in climatic composition and, as a result, vegetative zones. The highland vegetation comprising of Miconia bushes and endemic tree ferns surrounds the lake, contributing to a lush landscape. Here you can also observe white-cheeked pintails and common gallinules. Another common visitor site on the west side of San Cristóbal is *Cerro Brujo* (Wizard Hill), a white-sand beach (accessible by wet landing) that is the home to Sally Lightfoot

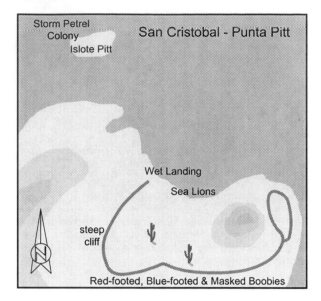

Storm Petrel Colony

Islote Pitt

San Cristobal - Punta Pitt

Wet Landing

Sea Lions

steep cliff

Red-footed, Blue-footed & Masked Boobies

crabs, marine iguanas and sea lions. If you visit during the wet season, tide pools formed by filled crevices in rocks aligning the shore harbor interesting inter-tidal creatures (even the occasional octopus).

You can swim or snorkel from shore, hike or run along the beach trail, or enjoy the majestic offshore view of the geological formation, Leon Dormido, also known as Kicker Rock. This rock structure (resembling a sleeping lion, hence the name) protrudes out of the sea and rivals Bartolomé's Pinnacle Rock. Small vessels can pass through a channel formed between the rocks, allowing visitors to see the wealth of barnacles attached to the rock surface. Divers and snorkelers can enjoy the colorful coral formations and tropical fish, search for macro-sized creatures in the eroded underwater crevices or stalk Galápagos sharks swimming along the shelf. Punta Pitt, located at the northwest tip of San Cristóbal, is one of two places in the archipelago (Genovesa being the other) where you can see a colony of red-footed boobies and it is the only site where you may see all three Galápagos booby species nesting. You can also see Galápagos hawks, sea lions and interesting volcanic tuff formations here.

DIVING AROUND SAN CRISTÓBAL
There are a few good dive shops in the small town of Puerto Baquerizo Moreno, on San Cristóbal Island. Popular dives from San Cristóbal include Isla Lobos, where you can Scuba and snorkel in a colony of sea lions, Kicker Rock, where you have a fair chance of seeing a hammerhead shark and Punta Pitt. San Cristóbal is also within range of Española Island, which also has some dive sites.

ISLA LOBOS
Isla Lobos is the closest dive site to Puerto Baquerizo Moreno, only about a half hour away by boat. The popular dive/snorkeling site is formed by San Cristóbal island on one side and long, narrow Lobos Island on the other. The result is a shallow, protected bay of sorts which is somewhat cloudy, but very popular among novice divers and snorkelers, as the water is warm, there is a lot to see, it's not very deep (about 25-30 feet maximum, most of it is shallower), there are no currents or big waves and you're almost guaranteed to see sea lions frolicking nearby. If you go late morning or early afternoon, there is also a good chance you'll see marine iguanas eating seaweed underwater. Most dive shops in Puerto Baquerizo Moreno will offer Isla Lobos as part of a two-dive day trip with Kicker Rock.

RESTAURANTS
LA PLAYA
One of the best restaurants in Galápagos, La Playa is located in Puerto Baquerizo Moreno, San Cristóbal. A casual, laid-back place with an ocean view, nothing about the restaurant's plain exterior will cause you to suspect how good the food is. Specializing in seafood, La Playa is a local favorite and often fills up on weekends. There is a full menu, with non-seafood options for those who wish. The service is a bit surly, and the prices are quite steep by Puerto Baquerizo Moreno standards, but you'll forget all about that when the food comes. If you're very hungry, try a plate of *chicharron de pescado*-little fried bits of fish served with a dipping sauce—as an appetizer. Av. Armada Nacional, Tel: 593-05-252-0044.

MICONIA
With excellent food and service, this restaurant caters to the tourists who do not have the stomach for, or interest in eating traditional Ecuadorian-style meals (which is usually fish and rice). Instead Miconia offers Italian (pastas and pizza) or American (sandwiches, burgers, salads) and there is one Chinese dish (chicken and vegetables with rice). It also has a variety of seafood platters. The quality of the food is good, and the portion sizes are perfect, so this restaurant definitely gives you your money's worth. In addition they have menus both in Spanish and English. The views from the second floor of the restaurant are amazing: it overlooks the bay area (best at sunset). The restaurant serves breakfast, lunch and dinner and offers delivery service. The owner, Katy, is a wonderful, energetic local woman who also teaches aerobic classes in the gym which is located behind the restaurant (adjacent to the newly opened Miconia Cabanas). From the pier, turn Left.

ESPAÑOLA
Española, also known as Hood, is the southernmost island in the archipelago, located about 90 km southeast of Santa Cruz. Punta Suarez, a visitor site on the western side of the island, is consistently touted as a favorite among visitors due to its abundance of birds. Visitors have a dry landing—often having to sidestep marine iguanas and sea lions resting on the jetty and on the adjacent rocks—that passes into a small, white-sand beach. Here you will find one of the distinct sea lion colonies that inhabit the beaches riddled along the coast of the island.

From this beach, a long and rocky, tremendously action-packed 2 km trail circuit begins.

Continuing along the coastal trail, you pass colonies of blue-footed boobies and Nazca boobies nesting on the cliffs, most likely spot a finch or two, and probably locate a few seabirds—the red-billed tropicbird or swallow-tailed gull—flying offshore. You immediately learn to avoid the lava lizards darting under your feet and Hood mockingbirds begging for water. Next, you walk down the rocky steps to the beach where waves crash up on the rocks in a breathtaking display and where hordes of marine iguanas monitor the eggs they have laid between the months of January and March. If you arrive when the eggs begin to hatch, chances are you will see a Galápagos hawk hovering around this area, waiting to prey upon the new hatchlings. Just beyond lies a flat section of the

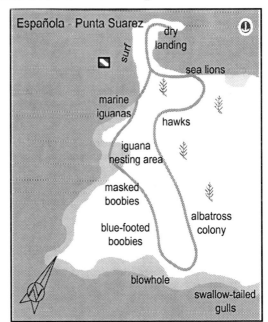

Española - Punta Suarez
surf
dry landing
sea lions
marine iguanas
hawks
iguana nesting area
masked boobies
blue-footed boobies
albatross colony
blowhole
swallow-tailed gulls

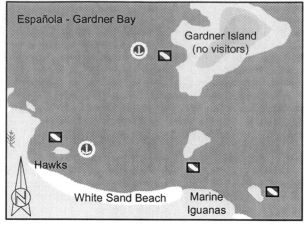

Española - Gardner Bay

Gardner Island (no visitors)

Hawks

White Sand Beach   Marine Iguanas

trail, an "airport" where, from late March until late December, waved albatrosses can take flight, land, await the return of their mates from the mainland, or proceed with their elaborate courting rituals.

Further along the trail is a blowhole, a slit in the rocky coastline through which waves force water to spout about 20 meters in the air. Here you can sit on the cliff and watch the spectacle, relax and reapply sunscreen (you have probably already been walking for an hour!), and watch seabirds flying overhead. The rocky trail back to the beach cuts inland through the dry vegetation of the island, where an albatross or a land iguana may be hiding. Gardner Bay is a beautiful, white-sand beach at the east end of Española, where you can nap next to sea lions, play in the sand, or snorkel at an island just offshore. Wet landings here can get very wet (especially when the tide is rolling out), so be careful with your belongings. If you walk down the beach to the rocky limits, you can probably see some marine iguanas. Late in the year (October-December) you may also see green sea turtles mating. Near Gardner Bay is an excellent snorkeling spot, Turtle Island.

FLOREANA
Also known as Santa María or Charles, Floreana is the sixth-largest island (173 km-squared) and has the fourth-largest population. There are three visitor sites on the north coast of Floreana.

POST OFFICE BAY
The first, Post Office Bay, is a short, white-sand beach (requiring a wet landing) with a make-shift barrel adorned with a rustic, yet international decor. Although originally utilized by whaling ship captains, post office bay now counts on other tourists to provide mail service: if you encounter a postcard addressed to someone in your home town (or home country), you are required to personally deliver it. The system works, because the number of postcards kept in the barrel at Post Office Bay remains low. Also nearby are the remains of a canning factory, a lava tunnel with a small, brackish (and chilly) pool for swimming in the dark and a soccer field. You can also swim or snorkel from the beach. Be careful of the stingrays hiding in the surf!

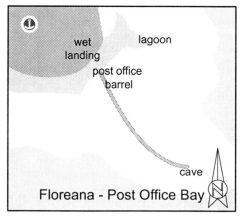

wet landing   lagoon

post office barrel

cave

Floreana - Post Office Bay

PUNTA CORMORANT

The second visitor site is Punta Cormorant. After a short dingy ride along a cliff with nesting seabirds, visitors disembark (wet landing) onto a brown-sand beach, which is tinted green due to its composition of olivine crystals and inhabited by sea lions and crabs. A short distance up the beach is the first trail, which leads to a promenade overlooking a flamingo lagoon.

Dozens of flamingoes make their home here, building their nests toward the end of the year (October-December). They make intricate patterns in the mud as they kick up their food, and occasionally exhibit their flamenco-style mating dance. If you are lucky, you will be able to witness this from June-October. This is also a good place to see other wading birds, such as white-checked pintail ducks, black-necked silts, American oystercatchers, whillets, and whimbrels. Another 400-meter trail follows the perimeter of the lagoon through the island's distinctive mangrove and palo santo stands to a white-sand beach where turtles often lay their eggs. From the beach, you have an excellent view of two small islands in the distance, Enderby and Champion, which are excellent snorkeling and dive spots. You may also be able to spot sea turtles and stingrays in the surf.

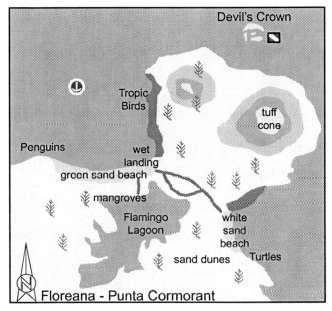

DEVIL'S CROWN

The third visitor site, Devil's Crown, is the remains of a half-submerged volcanic cone a few hundred meters from Punta Cormorant and the best snorkeling site in the Galápagos Islands. Snorkelers enter the water on the outside of the rocky crater, where white-tipped reef sharks, sea lions, sea turtles, rays, and large schools of tropical reef fish are commonly seen in the deep water. You continue to swim around the volcanic semi-circle (or through an underwater opening in the rocks) to the shallow crater center, where white-tipped reef sharks hide in cave openings; moray eels poke their heads out of rock and coral formations; and colorful reef fish abound.

PUERTO VELASCO IBARRA

The port town of Puerto Velasco Ibarra, the only settlement on the island with inhabitants, provides limited tourist attractions. There are a few hotels, stores and restaurants along with a soccer field. Infrequent public transportation and private vehicles offer access to the highlands. The family of Margaret Wittmer, one of the early (and scandal-ridden—read "A Galá-pagos Affair" to get the full history) inhabitants of Floreana, has a farm with intact relics and giant tortoises, which passengers on either of their boats (Tip Top II and III) may get to visit.

WESTERN ISLAND VISITOR SITES

The western islands of Isabela and Fernandina are the least frequented by tourists due to their distance from the main islands. However, if you are lucky to visit these outliers, you will have the rare opportunity to witness volcanology in action, to see the unusual flightless cor-morant and to cross pods of whales and dolphins. The northwestern islands of Wolf are even more remote, so scuba-diving tours here offer an extra-special occasion to experience some of the most abundant and diverse marine life in the world. You also have the best possibility of encountering the big draws, like whales, hammerhead sharks and whale sharks.

ISABELA

At 4588 km-squared, Isabela is the largest island in the archipelago and often touted by locals as the gem of the Galápagos. It is relatively young island given its proximity to the geological hot spot and consists of a chain of five active volcanoes: Volcán Wolf, the highest point in Galápagos at around 1700 m; Cerro Azul, whose last eruption was registered in 1998; Sierra Negra; Volcán Alcedo; and Volcán Darwin. Unfortunately, since many of the visitor sites are on the west side of the island and require a long passage (and fuel use) from Santa Cruz, few pre-arranged tours—limited to the larger, more expensive cruises visit Isabela. Although not a common visitor site for cruising, Isabela has recently gained popularity among visitors (and locals) as a side trip due to the island's spectacular landscape and biodiversity. The variety and abundance of avifauna in the various ecological niches of Isabela is especially notable. In the volcanic highlands, visitors can get close views of Galápagos hawks, flycatchers and finches. In the island's wetlands, visitors can see flamingos, great blue herons and sandpip-ers. And along the coast, visitors can spot penguins, cormorants, frigatebirds and blue-footed boobies. Urbina Bay is a good place to see land iguanas, and you can also snorkel there.

Isabela can be accessed directly from Santa Cruz, by boat from Puerto Ayora. It takes about eight hours to get to Isabela via Floreana and about four hours to return. It is also possible to reach the island by plane from Baltra (30 minutes). Puerto Villamil, Isabela's main town is a much mellower version of Puerto Ayora and the second-most popular port to hang out in a hammock and watch the boobies fly by. True to island attitude, expect only the most basic tourist accommodations, restaurants and bars.

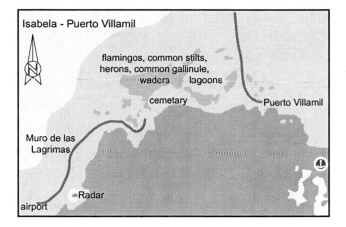

ISABELA HOTELS

Isabela offers fewer hotels than Santa Cruz, but still manages to offer a range of budget options. You can rent a cozy cabin, stay in a youth hostel, or splurge and spend a few nights at La Casa de Marita.

PUERTO VILLAMIL

Puerto Villamil is a small port town on the southeast side of Isabela. It has about 2,000 inhabitants, most of whom make their living from fishing. As such, it maintains the quaint, community atmosphere of a fishing-town—main streets are unpaved—despite the fact that tourism is rising as an important economic activity. The white-sand beach extends the length of the town, providing visitors with excellent swimming, snorkeling, surfing and sporting possibilities. Although the town only consists of a few main streets, it does have a telephone center, a bank, a post office, a police station and a small hospital. There is little selection when it comes to accommodations and food, but the quality and friendliness of service will not leave you disappointed. There are also some amazing camping spots. The town's beach is a spectacular two-mile stretch of silky bone-colored sand sprouting swaying palms in just the right spots. A five-minute walk from town, you will find a tucked-away lagoon sprouting flamingos. Hikers will appreciate the numerous trails heading inland and up the sides of the Island's volcanoes.

AROUND PUERTO VILLAMIL

West of the town center, there is a scenic trail leading north off of the main road to two visitor sites. A short distance after the start of the trail, you will encounter La Poza de los Flamingos, a small lagoon where you can spot flamingos and other migrant birds. Continuing north along the trail, you will find the Centro de Crianza de Tortuga Terrestre, a land tortoise breeding facility open to the public. Shortly beyond the breeding facility, the trail merges with the main road and continues north toward Volcán Sierra Negra, an active volcano (1490m) 27 km from Puerto Villamil, where visitors can camp, horseback ride, hike or simply enjoy nature. You can walk around the caldera, which is roughly 10 km in diameter, passing fumaroles and interesting lava formations, Galápagos hawks, short-eared owls, finches and flycatchers.

ORGANIZING TOURS

Trips to the volcano with naturalist guides can be organized by tour agencies in Puerto Villamil, but if you decide to go it alone, you can hire private transportation from the town center to take you to Santo Tomás, a small settlement at the flanks of the volcano. From there, it is 9 km to the top of the volcano, which you can hike or complete on horseback. Horses can be rented in the town. Be sure to bring plenty of food, water and a compass—it's easy to get lost.

OTHER ACTIVITIES AROUND PUERTO VILLAMIL

Off the southeastern end of Puerto Villamil is the island of Las Tintoreras, which has nice views, hiking possibilities and wildlife watching. If you follow the coastline on the other end of town, you will eventually arrive at *El Muro de las Lágrimas*, The Wall of Tears, an instrument of torture used to punish the prisoners of a penal colony established on Isabela from 1945-1959. Although the site sounds grim, it provides an interesting bit of the island's history and the long trail along the coast provides excellent scenic views and wildlife watching opportunities.

MORE ISABELA VISITOR SITES

With the exception of Puerto Villamil and the surrounding areas, all of Isabela's visitor sites are on the western side of the island.

TARGUS COVE

Tagus Cove, just west of Volcán Darwin, was once a favorite anchor-spot for early whaling and pirate ships, the names which are still etched into the cliffs around the cove. In a dinghy ride along the cliffs, you can see this historical graffiti, as well as the Galápagos penguin, the flightless cormorant and other seabirds. A dry landing drops you at the head of a 2 km trail, which leads up the lower slopes of the volcano to a high-point, where you can see an impressive crater lake, the paths of lava travel and a variety of interesting volcanic formations.

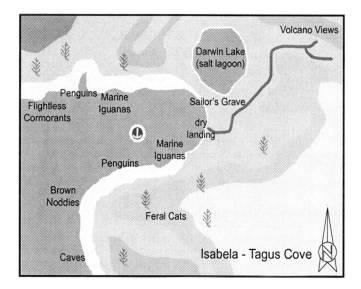

URBINA BAY

Urbina Bay, south of Tagus Cove in the center of the western coast of Isabela, is a flat area formed by uplift from the sea characterized by a unique terrestrial coral reef. A 1-km trail beginning at the beach (wet landing) leads you to the corals and a decent view of Volcán Alcedo. On land, you can see flightless cormorants, pelicans and marine iguanas. In the bay, you may see rays or sea turtles swimming near the surface. Following the western coast of Isabela south from Urbina Bay until the shoreline bends sharply toward the lower arm of the island, there is a visitor site known for its marine life called Elizabeth Bay. There are no landing sites, but you can take a dingy ride to the Mariela Islands at the entrance of the bay to see penguins or to a narrow passage in the sea lined with mangroves that leads into an enclosed cave at the opposite end of the bay. As you ride in the panga, look along the coast for seabirds and in the water for sea turtles and rays.

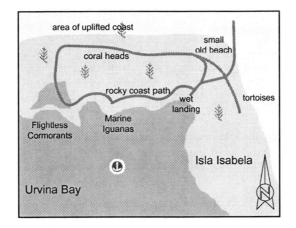

RESPONSIBLE TOURISM ON THE ISLANDS

The following is a list of pretty common sense tips to ensuring that the Galápagos will remain as beautiful for future generations as they are for you:

Do NOT bring any items that could introduce invasive (non-native) species to the islands. There is a costly and effective program to eliminate them, as they can damage the environment, and endanger endemic species. SICGAL (Galápagos customs) has a list of permitted, restricted and banned items.

Do NOT purchase souvenirs made from native plants or animals.

Do NOT remove plant, animal or other natural objects from the islands.

Do NOT venture off the trail or away from the tour group. This is not only to protect the land and local wildlife, but also because the environment is quite harsh and even experienced persons (locals, military and scientists) have disappeared and been presumed dead.

Do NOT visit unofficial or unapproved park areas.

Do NOT throw anything into the water, from land or boat.

Do NOT touch, feed or startle the animals.

DO visit the Park with only licensed National Park Guides.

DO choose a tour operator with a Responsible Tourism Policy (IGTOA is a good source for company information, visit their website: www.igtoa.org. You can also look for companies using the SmartVoyager logo, an indication that they have gone the extra mile to earn sustainable tourism certification. For more details check out the Rainforest Alliance website: www.rainforest-alliance.org).

DO participate in the recycling and compost program in Puerto Ayora, recycling bins are everywhere.

DO carry out highly toxic articles like batteries, where they can be disposed of properly.

Have a great travel story? Tell it at www.vivatravelguides.com

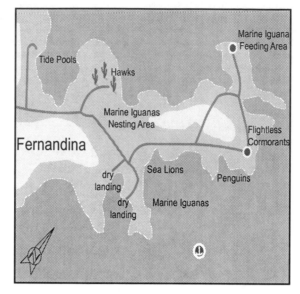

FERNANDINA

Fernandina, the westernmost—and youngest—of the main islands, is situated directly above a geologic hot spot and as such, has the highest volcanic activity of any of the islands. Many eruptions have been recorded since 1813, the most recent of which occurred in 1995. There is one visitor site, Punta Espinosa, where flightless cormorants, pelicans, penguins, sea lions, and an abundance of marine iguanas reside. There are two short trails (.25 km and .75 km long and accessible by dry landing) that lead to recently formed lava fields, where you can see pahoehoe and aa lava formations and pioneer plants.

The marine ecosystem around Fernandina, where the cold Cromwell current has its greatest impact on water temperature and nutrient upwelling, hosts organisms not found in other sectors of the archipelago. In fact, since Bryde's whales, pilot whales, and bottlenose dolphins feed here, so keep your eyes open when you are cruising! This area has been declared a Whale Sanctuary. Unfortunately, since Fernandina, like Isabela, is far to the west, only the larger, more expensive boats include it in their itinerary.

PUNTA ESPINOSA

Fernandina's most popular visitor site, Punta Espinosa is a great place to see some Galápagos wildlife that you don't often see. Most noteworthy is the endemic flightless cormorant, which is only found in western islands. After a dry-ish landing on a rocky shore, visitors will have the opportunity to peek into some tidal pools, which often are home to interesting marine life. You may even spot a ray or sea turtle in the lagoon.

After the landing, you'll head to the main trail, passing a large colony of marine iguanas as you do. Stop for some photos, and then head along the trail to see the cormorants. If you're lucky, you'll be able to get a good look at them as they swim and explore. The other end of the trail leads to some interesting lava formations, an abandoned ship's engine and some more lagoons.

Along the rocky shore near Punta Espinosa, visitors will occasionally see the rare Galápagos penguin. If you're lucky, your cruise ship will send pangas or zodiacs along the shore, where your keen-eyed naturalist guide will help you spot the penguins: they're difficult to see against the black lava background.

DARWIN AND WOLF

Darwin (Culpepper) and Wolf (Wenman) are two tiny, outlying islands in the northwest archipelago that harbor an incredibly diverse and abundant marine life. As such, the islands are only visited on live-aboard scuba diving tours. Certain species of Tropical Indo-Pacific fish and coral can only be found here, but the main attraction for divers is the high possibility of seeing big stuff, and lots of it, like whales, hammerhead sharks and whale sharks.

RECOMMENDED READING LIST

Constant, Pierre. Marine Life of the Galápagos: A Diver's guide to the Fishes, Whales, Dolphins, and Marine Invertebrates. 2003, Twin Age Limited: Hong Kong.

Constant, Pierre. The Galápagos Islands. 2000, Odyssey: New York.

Constant, Pierre. Marine Life of the Galápagos. 1992, Twin Age Limited: Hong Kong.

Epler, Bruce, Alan White, and Charles Gilbert. Galápagos Guide. 1986, United States Peace Corps: Quito.

Fitter, Julian, Daniel Fitter, and David Hosking. Safari Guides: Wildlife of the Galápagos. 2000, Harper Collins: London.

Harris, Michael. A Field Guide to the Birds of Galápagos. 1988, Collins: London.

Hickman, Jr., Cleveland P. A Field Guide to Sea Stars and other Echinoderms of Galápagos. 1998, Sugar Spring Press: Lexington.

Hickman, Jr., Cleveland P. and Todd L. Zimmerman. A Field Guide to Crustaceans of Galápagos. 2000, Sugar Spring Press: Lexington.

Hickman, Jr., Cleveland P and Yves Finet. A Field Guide to Marine Molluscs of Galápagos. 1999, Sugar Spring Press: Lexington.

Horwell, David and Pete Oxford. Galápagos Wildlife: A Visitor's Guide. 2002, Bradt Publications: UK.

Humann, Paul and Ned Deloach. Reef Fish Identification: Galápagos. 2003, New World Publications: Jacksonville.

Jackson, Michael. Galápagos: A Natural History Guide. 1989, University of Calgary Press: Calgary.

Lawesson, J.E., et al. Botanical Research and Management in Galápagos. 1992, Missouri Botanical Garden: St. Louis.

Schofield, Eileen K. Field Guide and Travel Journal: Plants of the Galápagos Islands. 1984, Universe Books: New York.

Stephenson, Marylee. The Galápagos Islands: The Essential Handbook for Exploring, Enjoying, and Understanding Darwin's Enchanted Islands. 1989, The Mountaineers: Seattle.

Treherne, John. The Galápagos Affair. 1983, Penguin Books: London.

White, Alan and Bruce Elper. Galápagos Guide. 1972.

Wittmer, Margret. Floreana. 1989, Anthony Nelson Ltd: Oswestry.

Have a great travel story? Tell it at www.vivatravelguides.com

Northern Andes

The Northern Andes in Ecuador span the area north of Quito to the Colombian border. This part of the country is beautiful with a wide range of ecosystems, from cloud forests to deserts, and everything in between. The rolling countryside around the famous markets in Otavalo is scattered with *haciendas*, many of which have opened their doors to tourism. This is an area where few foreign tourists have ventured until relatively recently. There are opportunities to explore local *campesino* tracks, trek in unspoilt *páramo*, explore rural villages where the pace of life remains unchanged, have a go at *pelota del mano* (a traditional handball game), soak in the new Arco Iris hot springs, and explore the ancient *Caranqui* culture.

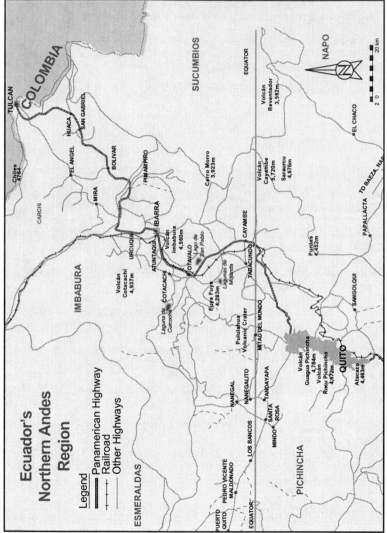

Ibarra

Ibarra, Imbabura's provincial capital, is also known as the "White City" due to its colonial whitewashed buildings (though some visitors find it a bit more lackluster than it sounds). Cobblestone streets, red-tiled roofs and horse-drawn carts add to the historic ambiance. In the past, busloads of travelers came to Ibarra to hop aboard the train, which rolled its way down from the Andes to the coastal town of San Lorenzo 193 miles away. Unfortunately, the rails are currently under construction, and only a truncated version (the *autoferro*) runs as far as Primer Paso 45 kilometers away. Even without rail trail, however, Ibarra is a peaceful, pleasant place to spend a day or two. Take a stroll to the Basílica de La Merced, with its lofty red-and-gold altarpiece, then head to the old infantry barracks near Parque La Merced and snack on *nogadas* and *arrope de mora*, some of Ibarra's sweeter specialities. After your sweet-tooth fix, make your way to Plaza de la Ibarreñidad and stop by the Museo Banco Central, where you can brush up on your Ecuadorian archaeology and Northern Highlands history, while browsing an array of pre-Inca and Inca artifacts.

If history isn't your thing, check out the Mercado Amazonas on Avenida Pérez Guerrero, or the crafts market on Plaza Atahualpa. And no trip to the White City would be complete without sampling its most famous speciality: *helados de paila*. This sweet, fluffy, sorbet-like treat is whipped up in oversized copper pans, known as *pailas*, and sold at a number of *heladerías* in town. For day tripping outside the city, head to the peaceful shores of Laguna Yahuarcocha, or the woodcarving capital of San Antonio de Ibarra. Ibarra is also en route to Esmeraldas, if you crave a quick dip in the ocean.

LODGING

IMBABURA ($5/PERSON)
Those on a budget or interested in spending the night in a converted colonial building should make their way to Imbabura. The hotel is complete with an interior courtyard, soaring ceilings and a distinct monastery-like feel. Rooms are simple, but spotless, and some boast excellent views of the stunning scenery spread across Ibarra's horizon. Oviedo 9-33 and Chica Narváez, Tel: 593-6-950-155 / 593-6-295-1155.

HOSTAL EL EJECTIVO (ROOMS: $6-22)
For 28 years, this hostal has been operated by the Chacon family of Ibarra. The cleanliness, 24-hour hot water, comfortable beds and hospitable staff have kept it a leader in Ibarra's hostal community. It has 16 rooms l with private baths, comfy beds, cable TV and telephone. Some rooms even have a balcony that overlook the city. . Bolivar 969, Tel: 593-6-295-6575, Fax: 593-6-295-6511, E-mail: mchaconf@yahoo.com.

HOTEL MONTECARLO (ROOMS: $16-50)
Centrally located near downtown Ibarra, Hotel Montecarlo is a larger hotel with 33 rooms and 2 suites, all of which have private bathrooms, hot water, cable TV and a telephone. While not a luxury retreat, it is a solid budget to mid-range option. Enjoy the jacuzzi, Turkish Spa, or sauna, or make a splash in the pool. The onsite restaurant serves up decent national and international cuisine. Jaime Rivadeneira 5-55 and Oviedo, Tel: 593-6-295-8266, E-mail: montecarlohotel@gmail.com.

IMPERIO DEL SOL (ROOMS: $25-40)
The largest hotel complex at Laguna Yaguarcocha is located on the northeast side of Ibarra away from the city and in a valley. Clean and comfortable, the rooms all have private bathrooms with hot water, cable TV and telephones. The hotel offers volleyball, tennis and squash courts. An amazing outdoor patio is often the centerpiece for local weddings and conferences. Although breakfast is not included, for $2.50 an "Americano" breakfast—eggs, bread, juice or coffee—is available at the Imperio del Sol Restaurante. Snag yourself a table near the windows for a spectacular view of the lake and mountains. 1557 Ibarra Yahuarcocha.

> *V!VA Member Review-Imperio del Sol*
> *Our family enjoyed the entire visit. The hotel and restaurant are superb. The quality of the food and atmosphere is top notch and we highly recommend it. It is a perfect place for well needed rest and relaxation. 25 June 2007. Florida, USA.*

Find more reviews from travelers at www.vivatravelguides.com

HOSTERÍA PANTAVÍ (ROOMS: $30-75)

Hostería Pantaví was constructed on the ruins of the old San Clemente hacienda. It has twelve lovely rooms and offers a beautiful, peaceful setting and excellent food. Pantaví is conveniently located near the Cotacachi-Cayapas Reserve, the Arco Iris and Chachimbiro hot springs, El Ángel Ecological Reserve, a number of archaeological sites from the ancient Caranqui people, and is not far from the Chota valley, of interest due to its Afro-Ecuadorean heritage. The hostería itself has a swimming pool and conference facilities, as well as areas for tennis, volleyball, and basketball. There are 12 rooms, which vary in capacity and bed size. English, French, German, Dutch and Italian are spoken. Private transport from Quito to the Hosteria Pantaví can be arranged. Km. 6 en la via Salinas, Tel: 593-2-2347-476, URL: www.infohosteriapantavi.com.ec.

HOTEL AJAVI (ROOMS: $35-70)

One of Ibarra's nicest hotels with many luxury features—you would pay double for this in a bigger city like Quito. Among the extras are: a huge outdoor pool, gym and spa facilities, playing fields, a casino and game room. The hotel has a Quito office at Santa María 482 and Amazonas, 5th floor. Mariano Acosta 1635, Tel: 593-6-295-5555, E-mail: h-ajavi@imbanet.net.

HACIENDA CHORLAVI (ROOMS: $40-70)

If you're one for rustic, but comfortable and charming accommodation, then Hacienda Chorlavi is the place to unpack. A converted colonial hacienda, complete with whitewashed buildings and a monastery-converted cocktail bar, this lovely place is bursting with character. Rooms are appointed with period furnishing, big beds and private bathrooms. Even if you don't plan on spending the night, stop by and dine in the locally famous restaurant, a popular spot for Ecuadorian families. On weekends you can indulge in local fare while enjoying live music. Panamericana Sur Km 4.5, Tel: 593-6-293-2222 / 593-6-293-2223, E-mail: reservaciones@haciendachorlavi.com, URL: www.haciendachorlavi.com.

RANCHO DE CAROLINA

Set back on a small dirt road away from the nearby Pan American highway. Swim in the pool, enjoy a hydro massage, play tennis, hit the horse trails, shoot some billiards or just lay in the open green fields with a blanket and read a book. Eighteen rooms all with private baths, televisions, telephones and hot water are available. Panamericana Sur Km 4, Tel: 593-6-293-3113, E-mail: ranchodecarolina@yahoo.com.

POLYLEPIS LODGE

A unique eco-lodge tucked away on the El Ángel reserve protecting 30 acres of rare polylepis forest that dates back between two and four million years. Fourteen huts and cottages housing 2-12 guests have private bathrooms, fireplaces, and some have private jacuzzis. A restaurant, bar and game room make for perfect places to unwind at the end of an outdoorsy day. Tel: 593-6-295-4009 Cell: 593-9-403-1467, E-mail: info@polylepislodge.com, URL: reservas@polylepislodge.com.

RESTAURANTS

LA ESQUINA (SNACKS: $.50-2)

One of the more modern cafés/heladerías in Ibarra, La Esquina offers a short menu of Ecuadorian specialties including *humitas*, *quimbolitos* and *empanadas*. It also offers a simple breakfast menu, sandwiches, yogurt, desserts, water, sodas and of course, a range of traditional Ibarra ice cream (fluffy ice cream with a consistency similar to sherbet). On the corner of Olmedo and Flores.

EL ENCUENTRO (DRINKS: $1-3)

From the street this place may seem deserted, but make the short jaunt inwards—down the narrow pathway, past the pleasant garden area—and you'll find a laid-back but lively bar buzzing with locals chatting and tossing back a few drinks. Full of character, the bar and seating area features an eclectic collection of cowboy-styled art and artifacts, interspersed with the odd antique sewing machine. The low-lit, smoky atmosphere, coupled with 1930s décor and bucolic furnishings, gives the impression that a swaggering, bad-mouthing gaucho might swing through the doors at any moment. Despite a rather rough-around-the-edges, down-home feel, this place appeals as the local romantic rendezvous for couples, who come to share a few drinks on the garden terrace. Olmedo 9-59.

CAFÉ PUSHKIN (BREAKFAST: $2-3)
This small but friendly café is a great place to enjoy an early morning breakfast or mid-afternoon snack. In the mornings, Ibarran locals filter in to grab a bite to eat before starting the day, and the small café quickly comes to life with conversation. Although there is no official menu (unless you count what they've written on the window) set dishes include traditional fare, such as sandwiches, *quimbolitos* and *café con humitas*. Olmedo 7-75.

CAFÉ ARTE (ENTREES: $1.50-5)
An art-infused café, Café Arte lives up to its name with a dash of funk and good food to boot. A variety of artwork by local arstists—from modern paintings to photo exhibits—cover the walls, mosaic tiles line the floor, dark and rustic wooden tables fill the dining room, and candlelight makes for a cool, retro, relaxing café. Some evenings live music by a local folk or rock band echo throughout. While not as cheap as other eating or drinking establishments in town, you are really paying for an eclectic atmosphere and experience that you won't find anywhere else in Ibarra. An assortment of dishes decorate the menu, from lavish salads to a western-style gourmet roast chicken dish. On the high-end, you can indulge in Filet Mignon for $5, or try a plate of tacos or a burrito for around $3. Salinas 5-43.

RESTAURANT EL CHAGRA (ENTREES: $2.50-3)
True Ecuadorian cuisine is the specialty here. Soups range from 50 cents to 70 cents a bowl. A daily selection of *Platos Fuertes* (main plates), including a trout or meat dish, will run you about $3.20. If you are looking for a less expensive meal, try one of the mixed rice dishes for $2.80. Breakfasts too. Olmedo 748 and Flores.

DONDE... EL ARGENTINO CARNES AND PARRILLADAS (ENTREES: $4-12)
Tucked away in the corner of a quiet plaza far from tour buses and boisterous backpackers. Despite its ostensibly simple appearance, the restaurant serves up outstanding Argentincan-style dishes overflowing with food and literally dripping with flavor. Meat—grilled and served with heaps of spicy sauces and mouth-watering sides—is the specialty here, and you're almost guaranteed to leave with a full belly. This is a well-kept Ibarra secret... shhh... don't tell anyone we told you! Monday - Saturday, 12 p.m. - 9:30 p.m., Sunday, 12 p.m. - 3:30 p.m. Sucre and Pedro Moncayo, Plazoleta Francisco Calderón Local 4, Tel: 593-9-938-4857.

BAR BUD
Although housed in a tiny space in Plaza Ibarrenidad, this American/European style bar occupies two floors, offers a full bar serving up a variety of cocktails, from Peruvian Pisco Sours to traditional Cuba Libres, to a selection of beers. Not the cheapest bar in town—cocktails run $2 to $3 a pop—but a good watering hole to grab a late afternoon beer. As the night grows old, the place gets hopping and the party typically spills out into the plaza. Popular with college-aged Ecuadorians. Wednesday - Saturday, 4 p.m. - 12 a.m., Sunday, 10 a.m. - 4 p.m. Plaza Ibarrenidad.

AROUND IBARRA
LAGUNA YAHUARCOCHA
A pleasant side-trip from Ibarra if you're looking to escape the city. Sitting on the outskirts of the city amidst mist-enshrouded rolling green hills, this peaceful glass-top lake was the site of a bloody massacre of the indigenous *Cara* people by Huayna Capac and his Inca army. The 1495 grudge-match marked the climax of a seventeen-year military campaign. In Quichua, the lake's name translates to "lake of blood," so chosen to recall the twenty-fifty thousand bleeding bodies that turned the lake waters crimson. Today crystal-clear water and the oc-

casional call of resident herons greet visitors, who come to relax in the peaceful, almost-picture-perfect setting (someone got the bright idea to construct a massive race track around the lake; competitions are held in September when Ibarra erupts in fiestas). Getting to the lake is easy: head to Oviedo at the corner of Sánchez and Cifuentes and hop on a bus (every 15 min, 25 cents), or walk, following the path that heads east from Oviedo, over the bridge and along the Panamericana.

SALINAS VALLEY

Just 30 kilometers from Ibarra, Salinas gets its name from the high concentration of mineral salts in its soils. Up until fairly recently, people were still extracting mineral salt by traditional methods. You can visit one of the salt mines and see for yourself how this was done. Ask in the village for more information. Although the valley is now mostly dedicated to the cultivation of sugar cane, it once was a meeting point and market area for indigenous groups from all different directions. In Northern Ecuador, this valley holds the easiest passage from the coast, across the two Andes ranges and down to the Amazon. Therefore, it has been a location of strategic importance throughout history.

OTAVALO

Set in a valley in the northern Andes, Otavalo is right at the top of any Ecuador traveler's must-see list, famous throughout South America for its weekly Otavalo market where one can find an overwhelming variety of Andean crafts and is reportedly the biggest of its kind in Latin America. Every Saturday from about 8 a.m., local craftsmen pour into the town and unfold their wares in the *Plaza de Ponchos* and surrounding streets, the whole area exploding into a hodgepodge of colorful rugs, clothes, paintings and other crafts. There is also an animal market early on Saturday mornings which is worth a visit.

During the week, Otavalo is a sleepy little town, which can be hard to believe if you've seen it during Saturday's mid-market frenzy. Architecturally, it is mainly modern (if you count 1960s and 70s vintage cinderblock as modern), although there are a few Colonial buildings left, mainly at the southern end of town around the *Plaza Bolívar*. There are also a couple of museums that are worth a peek, including the *Instituto Otavaleño do Antropología*. But apart from a small daily craft market in the Plaza de Ponchos, there's not much going in the town, and Otavalo hotels and restaurants are often empty, particularly in low season. Nightlife is virtually nonexistent during the week, although there are a few good live music venues, usually traditional Peñas that play Andean music and are open on Friday and Saturday nights.

However despite its quietness —or perhaps because of it—many travellers opt for an extended stay here, often to study Spanish for a few weeks, or to explore the area surrounding Otavalo spotted with waterfalls and ancient Inca trails that weave in and out of the mountains.

THINGS TO SEE & DO

OTAVALO'S MARKETS

The Otavaleños have been long renowned for their weaving skills, and over the last couple of decades have become one of the most successful indigenous groups on the continent, thanks to the growing popularity of their weekly craft market. Although most still live up in the hills around the town and wear traditional clothing, this doesn't mean they are poor—it is not unusual to see families of six or seven loading rugs into their brand new LandCruisers at the end of the day, or women carrying baskets of grain up the hill while talking on cell phones.

The main market takes place on Saturday, with stalls in the *Plaza de Ponchos* and surrounding streets. Although it is possible to visit the market in a day from Quito (it's only two hours or so by bus), many tourists arrive on Friday night. Doing this will not only give you a chance to enjoy virtually-empty craft market before the day-trippers arrive (and prices rise), but you will also be able to visit the weekly animal market on Saturday morning.

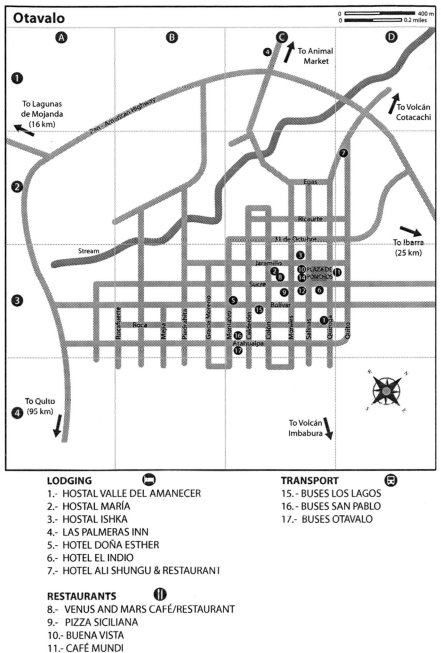

Otavalo

0 — 400 m
0 — 0.2 miles

To Animal Market

To Lagunas de Mojanda (16 km)

Pan - American Highway

To Volcán Cotacachi

Egas

Ricaurte

31 de Octubre

To Ibarra (25 km)

Stream

Jaramillo

PLAZA DE PONCHOS

Sucre

Bolívar

Rocafuerte
Roca
Mejía
Piedrahita
Gracia Moreno
Montalvo
Calderón
Colón
Morales
Salinas
Quiroga
Quito

Atahualpa

To Quito (95 km)

To Volcán Imbabura

NORTHERN ANDES

LODGING

1.- HOSTAL VALLE DEL AMANECER
2.- HOSTAL MARÍA
3.- HOSTAL ISHKA
4.- LAS PALMERAS INN
5.- HOTEL DOÑA ESTHER
6.- HOTEL EL INDIO
7.- HOTEL ALI SHUNGU & RESTAURANT

RESTAURANTS

8.- VENUS AND MARS CAFÉ/RESTAURANT
9.- PIZZA SICILIANA
10.- BUENA VISTA
11.- CAFÉ MUNDI
12.- TABASCO'S
13.- ÁRBOL DE MONTALVO
14.- SHANANDOA PIE SHOP

TRANSPORT

15.- BUSES LOS LAGOS
16.- BUSES SAN PABLO
17.- BUSES OTAVALO

Although haggling may feel uncomfortable at first, remember that it is commonplace here, and locals do it all the time. It is difficult to know what items should cost, but you can generally expect to pay half to two-thirds of the original asking price. Offer half and settle at just above.

The animal market also takes place on Saturday, and goes on from sunrise until around 9:30 a.m. in a grassy square on the outskirts of town—just follow the stream of locals, squealing piglets and braying donkeys. It's a fascinating and noisy spectacle, and definitely worth the early start. It can be fun to stroll through the fruit and vegetable market as well—it's a few blocks south of the Plaza de Ponchos and provides a nice taste of local flavor as well as an escape from the crowded chaos of the craft market. The market starts at about 8 a.m. and goes on all day.

LODGING

As you might expect from such a tourist hotspot, Otavalo has quite a choice of hotels and hostels catering to every type of traveller. The town itself features a lot of budget and midrange accommodation from around $5 per night for a dorm bed, up to around $30 for a private room with TV, heating, etc. Some of the nicest places to stay are a few miles outside town up in the hills. These tend to be a bit more expensive (you can pay up to $280 for pure spa luxury), but there are a couple of options to suit the backpacker pocket, too. They offer great views, direct access to walking routes in the countryside and can be great places to chill out for a few days.

BUDGET

HOSTAL VALLE DEL AMANECER ($7-10/PERSON)

A gem of a hostel, this is a chilled out little place with lots of reasons that make it a choice spot, including friendly owners, a helpful travel desk, a café/restaurant that is open all day and a central patio with a huge avocado tree, lots of plants and hammocks. The rooms are small and very basic, and it can get quite noisy if there are a lot of people staying, which there invariably are on weekends. A few of the rooms have private bathrooms but most are shared. It's convenient both to the bus terminal and to Poncho Plaza. You can rent a mountain bike from here for $7 per day, or $5 for half a day, and the owners will also arrange day trips and activities. Corner of Quiroga and Roca, Tel: 593-6-292-0990.

HOSTAL MARÍA ($5/PERSON)

The bright green Hostal María is an unremarkable but friendly enough place, close to Poncho Plaza. The medium-sized white rooms lack character but they're clean and all have private bathrooms. The price is $5 per person, whether you want a single, double or triple, which makes it a good deal for single travellers. However, there's no common area or café so when you're in the hotel you're pretty much restricted to your room. Breakfast is available at the deli-style Café Rio Intag underneath the hotel—you can choose from a few set menus, including American and Ecuadorian, which cost from $1.25 to $2.50. Modesto Jaramillo and Colon, Tel: 593-6-292-0672.

HOSTAL ISHKA ($3-5/PERSON)

Shabby and in need of a paint job, but if you don't mind roughing it a bit, you'll be fine. It's a good place to meet other travellers, too. There isn't a café or restaurant, but you can get breakfast next door at La Cascada from 8a.m. on. The usual fare—coffee, juice, bread and eggs—goes for around $1.50. Modesto Jaramillo 569 and Morales, Tel: 593-6-292-0684.

RUNA TUPARI ($15/DAY WITH THREE MEALS)

A community operation run by UNORCAC—an organization representing the rural indigenous people of Cotacachi—located in the rural region near the Cotacachi-Cayapas ecological reserve. Lodges house up to three people and are located in four different local communities sprawling the base of the Cotacachi Volcano. Rooms are cozy and warm, most having a bedroom with a fireplace, a bathroom with hot shower, and stunning views of surrounding foothills. Family hosts provide traditional meals prepared using fresh veggies from nearby crops. A wide range of 1-4 day tours and treks with native guides that include a mix of cultural, natural and adventure experiences are available. Plaza de los Ponchos, Sucre and Quiroga, Tel: 593-6-292-5985, Cell: 593-9-728-6756, E-mail: nativetravel@runatupari.com, URL: www.runatupari.com.

MID-RANGE

LAS PALMERAS INN (ROOMS: $15-30)

A small lodge just a few minutes outside of Otavalo with spectacular views of Imbabura and Cotocachi Volcanoes, set in a gorgeously landscaped graden. Most of the inn's rooms are in cozy cabins apart from the main house. There are larger, more luxuriously rooms available as well as a few beds available in a hostel-style shared room for budget travelers. 3 km west of Otavalo, past Animal Market, Tel: 593-6-292-2607.

HOTEL DOÑA ESTHER (ROOMS: $22-42)

Set back from the street in an unassuming colonial building, this hotel has a friendly, homey feel. Arranged around a small leafy courtyard are three floors of moderately-sized rooms, all of which are tastefully decorated with simple wooden furniture, local art and craftwork. The suite on the top floor has a kitchenette, sitting area and double bedroom, all with stunning views over the rooftops and mountains beyond—a deal at $39. On the ground floor there's a small sitting room with a good book exchange. The restaurant is justly famous for its delicious thin crust pizzas, served between 6 p.m. and 9 p.m. every day. The Mediterranean-style restaurant is open from midday on weekends until 10 p.m. Juan Montalvo 4-44 and Bolivar, Tel: 593-6-292-0739 / 593-6-292-5381, E-mail: info@otavalohotel.com, hostalesther@yahoo.com, URL: www.otavalohotel.com.

HOTEL EL INDIO (ROOMS: $10-30)

The Hotel El Indio's concrete and glass façade and tired neon signs do little to tempt tourists. But those who do make it through the front door will be rewarded with a warm welcome from the smiley Otavaleño owners and good value accommodation in spotlessly clean rooms, all with private bathrooms. The decoration is a curious mix of 70s kitsch—thick black leather armchairs and bright strip lighting—and Otavaleño, with large brightly colored murals and wall-hangings scattered about white walls. It's in a good location, bang in the centre of town within spitting distance of Poncho Plaza. The best room is 403, which boasts a balcony with views over the street and plaza, however things get going early in Otavalo so if you're counting on a lie-in, go for a room at the back of the building instead. Don't confuse this place with the more expensive Hotel El Indio Inn, which is run by the same family. Sucre 12-14 and Salinas, Tel: 593-6-292-0060.

HOTEL ALI SHUNGU (ROOMS: $55-200)

The Hotel Ali Shungu is a beautiful accommodation option in Otavalo. Margaret and Frank, the American owners, have done a fabulous job in deocrating the hotel with wonderful handicrafts from Ecuador, Peru and Bolivia. In fact, they have one of the nicest gift shops in town, filled with quality wares versus the "same-old, same-old" found in the Otavalo market. On Friday nights, there is live Andean music in the dining room for both hotel guests and the public to enjoy while trying out some of the delicious and imaginative fare. Ask for one of the rooms on the right side (on Calle Quito). No traffic noise there! Also, the hotel runs a foundation to aid the local, less fortunate families. If you're keen for something a bit further outside the city (and a good bit quieter), but don't want to sacrifice the comfort and first-class service, head to the owner's newest establishment: Ali Shungu Mountain Top Lodge. Calle Quito and Miguel Egas, Tel: 593-6-292-0750, URL: www.alishungu.com.

RESTAURANTS

Considering the amount of traffic that Otavalo gets, the choice of restaurants in the town is fairly limited. There are a few places geared at tourists around the Plaza de Ponchos, plus the usual rice-with-everything Ecuadorian places on every other corner. For really good, international food in town try some of the upper-end hotels. Most of the hotels and hostels outside town serve up delicious, healthy food as well, often using vegetables grown in their own gardens.

Find more reviews from travelers at www.vivatravelguides.com

VENUS AND MARS CAFÉ (ENTREES: $1-2)

This tiny little place opened in summer 2004, and is surely one of the only places in town where you can still get a sandwich and a coffee for under a dollar. It's a great place to sit and watch the world go by, and the welcoming owners won't hassle you if you do. Sucre, between Morales and Colon.

PIZZA SICILIANA (ENTREES: $2-7)

Pizza Siciliana's warm atmosphere, famous pizzas and wood-burning stove have been enticing both foreigners and locals for years. Pizzas are expensive, averaging around $7 for a small (medium and large are also available). Other dishes, however, such as salads, hamburgers and sandwiches are more reasonable at $2-3. Every Friday and Saturday night a live Andean band provides the soundtrack to your meal. Morales 5-10 and Sucre, Tel: 593-6-292-5999.

BUENA VISTA (ENTREES: $4-5)

On the second floor of a building on the edge of the Plaza de Ponchos, Buena Vista certainly lives up to its name (Good View), especially if you're lucky enough to get one of the two tables on the balcony. It's a great spot for breakfast on a Saturday morning when you can watch the empty plaza turn into a sea of rugs, ceramics, jewelry and other handicrafts as the market takes shape. There's a small book exchange, and they play movies in Spanish and English daily. The menu features a lot of pastas and meat dishes, and the salads are good too. Try the hot fruit juice with cane-sugar alcohol, a local specialty. Salinas between Sucre and Modesto Jaramillo (Plaza de Ponchos), Tel: 593-6-292-5166.

CAFÉ MUNDI (ENTREES: $3-4)

Run by a charming local couple and their children, Café Mundi is an Otavalo institution. It's a small place with a few dining tables and one long, low coffee table surrounded by surprisingly comfortable leather benches, and the windows are plastered with testimonials from former customers. The food ranges from just passable to excellent—the Ecuadorian main dishes (*platos fuertes*) tend to be the best. It's right on the Plaza de Ponchos, so you can duck in for a quick coffee or a bite to eat when you need a break from the bustle of the market. Open daily: 8 a.m. - 10:30 p.m., but closes earlier if it's quiet. Quiroga, between Sucre and Modesto Jaramillo, Tel: 593-6-292-1729.

TABASCO'S (ENTREES: $5-7)

A great spot for breakfast or lunch, Tabasco's is on the second floor of a building on the Plaza de Ponchos, and boasts a terrace with tables overlooking the square. The food is the usual Mexican fare, and it's good (though nothing special), and prices are a fair bit higher than average. You pay for the smiley service and the superb people-watching. Salinas 617 and Sucre esquina (second floor), Tel: 593-6-292-2475, E-mail: tabascosmexicanfood777@hotmail.com.

ÁRBOL DE MONTALVO

The Árbol de Montalvo restaurant is located in the back of the Hostal Doña Esther. It has a cosy bistro-like atmosphere, especially for the big wood-burning oven in the middle of the restaurant. The restaurant serves Mediterranean food. Besides the variety of plates, it specializes in pizzas, which are made in the wood-burning oven, right before your eyes. The typical national dishes also found their place onto the menu. Juan Montalvo 444 and Bolivar, Tel: 593-6-292-0739, Fax: 593-6-292-0739, E-mail: info@otavalohotel.com, URL: www.otavalohotel.com.

SHANANDOA PIE SHOP (ENTREES: $1.50-2)

Maybe the spelling is off, but the pies aren't... they're orgasmic! The owner, Aide Garzon, has been in the same location for 25 years, making all of the pies herself. She bought a book on pie receipes and fooled around with the different receipes for a month before she found the perfect one. Now she has 10 different flavors, all made from fresh fruits and other ingredients. She also makes wonderfully huge, over-stuffed sandwiches and salads, along with milkshakes and fresh fruit juices. Calle Salinas on the Plaza de Ponchos.

Ali Shungu Restaurant (entrees: $5-10)

The Ali Shungu Restaurant has delighted travelers in its internationally renowned natural foods restaurant for 14 years. Breakfast, lunch, dinner, snacks and cocktails are served in a beautiful Andean folklore-decorated dining room, next to the fireplace or on the garden patio under the volcano. You'll find many healthy and delicious international selections on the menu; gourmet organic vegetarian fare and only the choicest of meats, all prepared with loving care and the very best quality ingredients. Ali Shungu restaurant uses no chemicals, MSG or aluminum cookware. Calle Quito and Miguel Egas, Tel: 593-6-292-0750, E-mail: hotel@alishungu.com, URL: www.alishungu.com.

Around Otavalo

Although many tourists come to Otavalo just for the market, there's plenty more to do in the highlands around the town. Spread out in a valley of the northern Andes, Otavalo is surrounded by extinct volcanoes, rugged Andean peaks and fertile highlands scattered with villages, plus an abundance of lakes and waterfalls. It's easy to get around—the combination of ancient Inca trails and cobbled roads and tracks make the possibilities for walking and cycling almost unlimited.

There are a couple of tour agencies in town that can arrange trips from Otavalo—the most popular ones are visits to local villages where you can visit indian homes, see carpets being woven the traditional way and learn about weaving processes. Hiking, cycling and horseback riding trips are also available.

For hikes, the area around Lagunas de Mojanda is an excellent spot—beautiful, yet not at all crowded. Set in high páramo land 17 km south of Otavalo, there are numerous trails around the lakes, and you can walk for just a couple of hours, or up to a whole day. There are two hotels along the road that provide easy access to the area, and both can recommend good routes.

The huge Laguna de San Pablo a few miles southeast of the town is another good choice, with several places to stay on the water's edge. There's a paved road encircling the lake, and you can walk around it in a day—the views are spectacular.

Another good excursion is to Laguna de Cuicocha, a volcanic crater lake which is a haven for wildlife. There is nowhere to stay around here, but there is a restaurant, and you can take a boat trip onto the lake for an hour or so. There's a trail around the lake but it's very eroded in places and can be difficult to follow. On a clear day views are stunning.

A popular walking or cycling trip from Otavalo is to the Cascada de Peguche (waterfall). Follow the railway tracks north to the town of Peguche (about 3 km), where you may be lucky enough to see weavers at work. It's a further 2 km along a trail southwest to the waterfall. It can be fairly busy with locals during the weekend but quieter during the week.

Cotocachi-Cayapas Ecological Reserve

The Ecological Cotocachi-Cayapas reserve preserves 204,420 hectares of the Western Andes ranging in elevation from the summit of Cotocachi (4,939 meters) to coastal rainforest (300 meters). Access to the reserve is difficult since most of the area is covered by thick cloudforest and mountain and rainforest vegetation, with the exception of the eastern edge, which is páramo. Most people choose to visit the edge of the reserve from Otovalo or Ibarra but it is also possible to access by traveling up the Cayapas River from the coastal Afro-ecuadorian community of Borbon.

The Piñan area is located at the eastern end of the Cotocachi-Cayapas reserve and provides the visitor with high, unspoilt páramo and incredible views from the summit, which many consider the best in Ecuador. The trek takes 3-4 days and begins from the small village of Iruguincho, northwest of Ibarra. The hike climbs high into unspoilt páramo, and gives a wonderful insight into traditional farming practices in the area, which have remained largely unchanged for centuries.

NORTHERN ANDES

Herds of wild horses, an abundance of small lakes, spectacular páramo vegetation and a wonderful variety of wild flowers dot the landscape. Due to the unspoilt nature of the area, it is one of the best places in Ecuador to see condors and white-tailed deer. For those interested in birds, there are also caracaras, finches, flycatchers and a large variety of hummingbirds. From the summit of Yanaurco the views are breathtaking—on a clear day you can see the whole of the Ibarra/San Pablo valley with more than 40 lakes scattered across the páramo. Campus Trekking Agency based in Quito is the main operators in Ecuador offering the guided Piñan Trek. Contact: Campus Trekking, Tel: 593-2-234-0601, URL: www.campustrekking.com.

IRUGUINCHO

Iruguincho is a small, poor, rural village close to the Cotocachi-Cayapas Reserve, where people subside on basic agriculture. The community has recently become involved in community tourism and can provide visitors with local guides and horses.

From here you can arrange a day hike to Churo, one of the best preserved pre-Columbian temples to be found in the area (3 hours). It is thought that the form of the temple corresponds to the shape of a shell and that the temple was used to worship the volcano, Cayambe.

The community also offers shorter walks to the cloudforest, a beautiful local waterfall and the Timbuyacu hot springs (owned by the community, very basic but a completely different experience!). Ask for Galo Vargas in the village, who can arrange horses for longer trips and act as a guide for the C-C Reserve (Spanish only).

There is currently no accommodation available in Iruguincho, but the community is planning to offer stays in their homes in the near future. In the meantime, you can camp near the village or stay in Tumbabiro.

CAHUASQUI

Cahuasqui is a beautiful remote village. People depend on agriculture for subsistence and use methods that have remain unchanged over the centuries. There are about 20 burial and ceremonial mounds scattered all around the Cahuasqui plateau. This was a strategic stronghold of the Caranqui culture 1500-500 B.C., and agricultural terraces from this culture can still be seen here.

In days past, cotton and maize were grown on the terraces and today they continue to be used by the local people for the cultivation of maize and other vegetable food crops. Cahuasqui also has a huge ceremonial pyramid, which has been partially destroyed by bulldozers in order the use the ground for agriculture, but it is nevertheless worth a visit if you are in the area.

In the smaller park in Cahuasqui there is evidence of the only Caranqui calendar which exists in Ecuador. It is carved on a huge stone, and in order to protect this archaeological piece, the local people mounted the stone in cement such that half only the main façade can be appreciated.

There is also a small private archaeological museum in the main plaza (park) close to the church. Ask for Pablo Montalvo, a young enthusiast (collector of archaeological pieces) who will be happy to show you his museum for free—but might expect a small tip. He only speaks Spanish, but can also act as a guide for *tolas* (mounds) and pyramids in the areas.

TUMBABIRO

Tumbabiro is a small rural village approximately 40 minutes northwest of Ibarra. Most of the people who live in this area still cultivate crops using largely traditional methods. Many of the buildings in and around the main square are ancient and constructed using adobe mud bricks and local timbers. There are also a number of very old adobe walls surrounding nearby fields.

Find more reviews from travelers at www.vivatravelguides.com

The main square provides a relaxing setting to admire local men playing a traditional ball game, *Pelota en Mano*, on the weekends. You can also catch buses to Urcuqui and Cahuasqui and Ibarra from here.

About 4 kilometers north of Tumbabiro, close to Ajumbuela village there is a double-ramped, complete Caranqui pyramid. Although covered with vegetation, this pyramid is in excellent condition and many pottery fragments dating from 1500-500 B.C. have been found there. More information in English, German and Spanish is available at Hosteria Pantavi, and guides can be recommended and arranged from there.

Another loding option is Tio Lauro, located near the town of Tumbabiro, about 40 minutes north of Ibarra, roughly three hours from Quito. It offers basic accommodation with shared bathroom with shower for $8 per person per night including breakfast. The hostel is clean and friendly. No English is spoken.

VERDE MILENIO FOUNDATION
The Verde Milenio Foundation is a non-profit organization dedicated to protecting the environment and preserving the cultural heritage of the native communities who live in the endangered areas of Ecuador.

Verde Milenio's principal area of operation is currently El Chocó, on the north coast of Ecuador in the Cotocachi-Cayapas Ecological Reserve. It manages a number of projects including supporting the development of community eco-tourism. San Miguel and Playa de Oro are two tourist destinations that offer their guests a truly unique experience.

Verde Milenio has been designed to offer the visitor the best comfort in the heart of the tropical Choco rainforest; one of the most spectacular coastal humid forests, and known worldwide as a bio-diverse hotspot. These destinations therefore offer an ecological and cultural experience without comparison in a pleasant and calm atmosphere.

Verde Milenio works in collaboration with the local Chachi and Afro-Ecuadorian communities to support the development of these ecotourism projects. The projects provide communities with an ecologically and culturally sound alternative for sustainable development. In addition to ecotourism projects, Verde Milenio also manages education, health, conservation, small business development and volunteering projects. Obs. Miguel and Solier #122 and Selva Alegre, Tel: 593-2-290-6192, Cell: 593-9-984-2256, E-mail: info@verdemilenio.org, URL: www.verdemilenio.org.

CHOTA VALLEY
Situated 34 kilometers to the north of Imbabura Province, the Chota Valley is home to much of the Afro-Ecuadorian community. These people were originally brought to Ecuador as slaves and many now work in sugarcane production and agriculture. The community, however, maintains a unique culture expressed through music and dance. The "bomba" is a typical dance—a mixture of African and highland Indian components (an indigenous-hispanic-african hybrid), a dance in which women shake and move their hips whilst carrying a bottle on their heads. Women wear wide colourful skirts and men dress all in white. The music is rhythmic and based around the *bomba*—a drum played with both hands.

The community welcomes tourists, and provides basic, clean accommodation for $8 per night including breakfast. Various craft products are sold, including wonderful clay masks, candelabras and other objects. The also community has a volunteer program, and can arrange dance classes and a range of other activities. For more information, contact Mirium Ghysselinckx, Tel: 593-9-449-4029, E-mail: miri2002es@hotmail.com.

TOURS AROUND OTAVALO
OTAVALO KICHWA TOURS
Quiroga 4-05 and Sucre St, close to Poncho Plaza, Tel: 593-6-292-4674, Fax: 593-6-292-4674, E-mail: ethnostek@yahoo.com, URL: www.otavalotours.org.

LODGING
The highlands outside Otavalo are home to numerous hotels and hostels, often in converted haciendas. They range in price from a couple of dollars a night up to nearly $300, depending on how many home comforts you want. All offer beautiful views, direct access to walking routes in the countryside and can be great places to escape the bustle of the town.

CASA LUNA COTACACHI (ROOMS: $15-30)
Casa Luna Cotacachi is a charming B&B with a warm atmosphere, located in a small indigeous community at walking distance from the centre of the lovely town of Cotacachi, close to Otavalo. It is a great place to relax, surrounded by a lovely garden, with great views of the nearby volcanoes. Tours can be arranged to Otavalo and other surrounding areas, as well as Ibarra, El Valle del Chota and the Cloud Forest of Intag. Or ride for free on a mountain bike and discover hidden, but authentic places. Via Pilchibuela / El Sagrario / Cotacachi, Tel: 593-6-291-4000, URL: www.casaluna-cotacachi.com.

HACIENDA GUACHALÁ (ROOMS: $30-60)
Originally built in 1580, Guachalá is one of the oldest haciendas in Ecuador. In its heyday (around 1700), Guachala was the administrative center for about 12,000 hectares of land and employed 500 workers, mostly in textiles which were shipped to Spain. Converted to a hotel in 1993, it offers one of the more affordable options for those who wish to have a true hacienda experience. It is located between Quito and Otavalo, about an hour from Quito and a half hour from Otavalo. The complex itself has wide hallways, attractive gardens, ample rooms, a swimming pool and a chapel. Many animals are kept there, including llamas, horses, mules, geese, etc., and a number of activities are available, including: horseback riding, fishing, areas for basketball, soccer, and volleyball. There is a bar area and even satellite TV and internet. Tel: 593-2-236-3042 / 593-2-236-2426, E-mail: info@guachala.com, URL: www.guachala.com.

LA CASA SOL - OTAVALO (ROOMS: $30-70)
La Casa Sol is more than a hotel, it is a home integrated into the daily life of the indigenous communities of the sector. The lodge is located inside the "Cascada de Peguche" (Waterfall of Peguche) protected forest. The Kichwa de Peguche community is a privileged and energetic place, where guests enjoy evenings and sceneries that leave them breathless. 3 Km north of Otavalo, Tel: 593-2-223-0798, Fax: 593-2-223-383, E-mail: info@lacasaandina.com, URL: www.lacasaandina.com.

> V!VA Member Review- La Casa Sol - Otavalo
>
> La Casa Sol Otavalo is the most beautiful hotel I've ever visited, and for such a great price! The staff is most amiable and helpful, and the connection with La Casa Sol in Quito makes the trip a breeze. 25 June 2007. USA

HOSTERÍA PANTAVÍ (ROOMS: $30-75)
Hostería Pantaví was constructed on the ruins of the old San Clemente hacienda. It has twelve lovely rooms and offers a beautiful, peaceful setting and excellent food. There is also a variety of wonderful ethnic art on the walls in the main house, painted by the owner, Camilo Andrade. Pantaví is conveniently located near the Cotacachi-Cayapas Reserve, the Arco Iris and Chachimbiro hot springs, El Angel Ecological Reserve, a number of archaeological sites

from the ancient Caranqui people, and is not far from the Chota valley. The hostería itself has a swimming pool and conference facilities, as well as areas for tennis, volleyball, and basketball. There are 12 rooms, which vary in capacity and bed size. English, French, German, Dutch, and Italian are spoken. Private transport from Quito to the Hosteria Pantaví can be arranged. Located near the town of Tumbabiro, about 35 minutes north of Ibarra, or roughly three hours from Quito. Tel: 593-2-234-0601, URL: www.hosteriapantavi.com.

HACIENDO SAN FRANCISCO (ROOMS: $36-71)
For the traveler looking for the hacienda experience at a more reasonable price. Located in Imbabura province in the Salinas Valley, Hacienda San Francisco has been in the same family since 1640. It is convenient to many places of interest, including Otavalo, Chota, and the Cotacachi-Cayapas reserve. Also nearby are the Chachimbiro thermal springs, but guests needn't bother. San Francisco has its own, natural hot spring and thermal bath! Beautiful airy rooms and hiking, swimming pool, tennis court and horseback riding. Tel: 593-6-293-4161.

HACIENDA CUSIN (ROOMS: $75-220)
One of the most elegant and prestigious haciendas in the northern highlands, Hacienda Cusin is a beautiful and peaceful complex of buildings, gardens and patios. Some of the buildings date back to the colonial era, when the owners of Cusin oversaw more than 100,000 acres in the nearby valleys. Today, it is a favorite for visitors and also hosts numerous weddings and special events. It is only about 30 minutes from Otavalo, and tends to fill up on weekends with tourists headed to the market. Cusin offers horseback riding, mountain biking, a game room and sports courts, and can also arrange tours or even Spanish classes. Breakfast is included. Their special "umbrella rate" of $100/person per day is worth checking out: it includes all meals, horseback rides, mountain bikes, use of the internet, and room upgrades when available. Reservations made via the internet get a 10% discount. Tel: 593-6-291-8013, E-mail: hacienda@cusin.com.ec, URL: www.haciendacusin.com.

HACIENDA PINSAQUI (ROOMS: $78-130)

Located exactly between the market towns of Otavalo, Cotacachi (known for leather goods) and San Antonio de Ibarra (known for wood carvings), Pinsaqui is one of the most historic haciendas—Simón Bolívar used to visit here when he would travel between Ecuador and Colombia (the 'Simón Bolívar Room' is the most elegant suite in the hotel), and "The treaty of Pinsaqui" was even signed in one of the haciendas' grand salons, ending a war between Ecuador and Colombia in the nineteenth century. Recently converted, Pinsaqui still feels more like a home than a hotel. The staff is friendly, helpful and courteous. The complex is a maze of well-kept, beautiful gardens, patios, airy hallways, unique guest rooms (all of which have private bath and either a wood stove or a fireplace) and fountains. Pinsaqui can arrange for horseback rides along the trails in back of the hacienda. It also boasts large rooms which can serve as conference facilities, and can host special events such as weddings. Tel: 593-6-294-6116, E-mail: info@haciendapinsaqui.com, URL:www.haciendapinsaqui.com.

HACIENDA PRIMAVERA ($83/PERSON)

Hacienda Primavera is a gorgeous hacienda located in the El Choclo rainforest reserve. Owned by the same family for over 90 years, the hotel is located three hours northwest of Quito. The hacienda is a working ranch with horses, pigs, goats, cattle, llamas and donkeys, and is surrounded by a lush forest with prolific bird life. There are eight suites with exquisite views of the rainforest, all with private bathrooms and balconies. Because the hacienda is also an eco-lodge, the proprietors make every effort to keep their hotel eco-friendly through organic recycling and other earth-conscious efforts. Hacienda Primavera offers gourmet meals daily, as well as such varied activities as horseback riding, whitewater rafting, Autoferro train rides, hiking, and the opportunity to participate in the day-to-day running of the hacienda. Tel: 593-2-282-7129, URL: www.haciendaprimavera.com.

HACIENDA ZULETA ($170-205/PERSON)

Like the haciendas of old, Zuleta is a working, 4,000 acre farm with a stable of over 90 horses just outside of Otavalo. There is an embroidery workshop and a working dairy farm on the premises. Built in 1691, the hacienda has wide halls, spacious rooms, beautiful gardens, and fine dining. Unlike most of the other converted haciendas in the region, Zuleta still considers tourism and guests as a secondary source of income; it is still primarily a large farm. There are only nine guest rooms, reservations are required, and there is a two-night minimum stay. The restaurant features fine organic food, most of which is produced at the hacienda. Zuleta offers the usual hacienda activities, such as horseback riding, mountain biking, trekking, and tours of the nearby pre-Columbian Caranqui pyramids. They pride themselves on their horses, however, and offer classes and week-long riding programs. The hacienda is about two hours from Quito—contact a representative in advance if you want them to pick you up at the Quito airport. E-Mail: hacienda@zuleta.com, URL: www.zuleta.com.

LA MIRAGE (ROOMS: FROM $250)

Ecuador's most elegant and upscale resort is located at the end of a nondescript dirt road leaving the northern town of Cotacachi, known for its leather goods. La Mirage was once an elegant colonial hacienda, but since its purchase and renovation by the prestigious French hotel Chain Relais and Chateaux, it has become Ecuador's most exclusive spa and retreat. Twenty-three suites, each of which features a fireplace, are adorned with original paintings, elegant four-poster beds and tasteful decorations. Terrycloth robes are spread out on the bed for your use while at the hotel, sprinkled with rose petals. The bathrooms are sparkling clean and roomy. All rooms also have cable TV. The spa is one of the main attractions. The treatments are expertly done: you can choose from options from a simple massage or reflexology (basically a foot massage) to decadent choices such as "Cleopatra's bath," a two-hour treatment which includes massage, rose-petal bath and more in the "Cleopatra Room," tastefully decorated and painted in an Egyptian style (the real Cleopatra probably never had it this good). Remote, yes. Expensive, yes. But if you're the sort of person who only has time for the best, it's tough to beat this place in terms of elegance. Tel: 593-6-291-5237 / 593-6-291-5561, Fax: 593-6-291-5065, E-mail: mirage1@mirage.com.ec, URL: www.mirage.com.ec.

NORTHERN ANDES

LAGUNAS DE MOJANDA

One of the most popular spots for hiking is the area around Lagunas de Mojanda. Seventeen kilometres from Otavalo, the lakes are set in high páramo grassland at around 3,500 m. A taxi up to the lake from the town costs about $12-14. Expect to pay another $6-7 per hour if you want the taxi to wait. If you come hiking up here, make sure you take some warm clothes and a windproof jacket—the altitude and the exposure make it much colder than sheltered Otavalo. The road between the lake and the town is itself a nice walk, cobbled the whole way and affords great views over the valleys, passing through little villages. There's no transport up there, so if you walk up, you should order a taxi to pick you up at the top (the walk takes five to seven hours with breaks), or be prepared to walk back as well. Some people get a taxi to the top and walk back down. If you do this hike, go in a group as some parts are isolated and there have been reports of robberies on the route. The lower six or seven kilometres are generally considered to be safer.

There are two main places to stay along this road. On the right hand side, 3 km from town is the top-end hotel Casa Mojanda. About 1 km further along on the left is La Luna, which is more geared toward backpackers. Both have great views down into the valley.

Once you reach the lake, there are numerous possibilities for hiking. A good trek (well, half hike, half scramble) is from the lakeside, close to where the road stops, up to the top of Fuya Fuya, an extinct volcano—it's the highest point around the lake at 4260 meters, and the views from the top are stunning on a clear day. Another shorter walk, is to the top of the first hill on the left as you face the lake from the parking area. You'll see the trail leading steeply upwards from the lakeside. It's a steep, 20 to 30-minute climb to the highest point, from here you can make your way along the ridge. Take one of the paths down the hill to the lakeside, from where you can walk back to the parking area. Although there is a trail around the lake, it's almost impossible to hike it in a single day unless you run! Most people simply walk along the trail for a couple of hours then backtrack. There are also several circular routes that start off on the lakeside trail then bend into the mountains—these can take anywhere from a couple of hours to a full day. Both hotels mentioned above can suggest good walking routes and can sometimes arrange tours.

LA LUNA (CAMPING: $3, DORM: $4.50, ROOMS: $8-12 + TAX)

Set in the hills a couple of miles south of Otavalo, La Luna is an excellent choice for backpackers who want to chill out for a few days. It's a charming place with great views of the valley. The hammocks on the terrace make fine viewpoints and there's a cozy restaurant with basic but wholesome food and a wood-burning fire for colder evenings. They sometimes have live Andean music on Saturday nights. In the lounge there are plenty of games to keep you occupied, as well as a DVD player and a selection of DVDs in English. There are several good walks in the area, and the helpful English/Ecuadorian owners can provide you with a map and suggest some good routes. They can also arrange transport to the Lagunas de Mojanda, as well as horseback riding and mountain biking trips. Kilometro 4 1/2 via Mojanda, Tel: 593-9-973-7415 / 593-9-829-4913, E-mail: lalunaecuador@yahoo.co.uk.

CASA MOJANDA ($45-90/PERSON, DISCOUNTS FOR CHILDREN)

Casa Mojanda is a comfortable retreat just over 3 km outside Otavalo on the road to Lagunas de Mojanda. All the rooms have en-suite and are tastefully decorated, located in rammed earth cottages overlooking the valley and mountains. The food consists of mainly Ecuadorian recipes made with organic ingredients from the garden and is delicious and wholesome. There is a sociable atmosphere at mealtimes and the hosts, a US/Ecuadorian couple, often eat with the guests. They are also very knowledgeable about the local area and can provide information about local walks and tours. Ask them about their community-based projects, which include building a kindergarten and health center. There is a hot tub, home cinema with plenty of videos, a ping-pong table and a great library with hundreds of books to chose from, mainly in English and Spanish. Kilometro 3 1/2 via Mojanda Tel: 593-9-973-1737, E-mail: info@casamojanda.com, URL: www.casamojanda.com.

LAGO SAN PABLO

The Lago San Pablo a few miles southeast of Otavalo is another good destination in the northern Andes. It is a large lake with several places to stay on the water's edge. There's a paved road encircling the lake, and you can walk around it in a day. The views are beautiful. Water activities can be arranged and include sailing, canoeing and waterskiing.

LODGING

HOSTERÍA PUERTO LAGO (ROOMS: $60-90)

On the shore of San Pablo Lake, about 15 minutes south of Otavalo. It is an attractive complex of well-manicured lawns, spacious rooms, and features one of the most elegant restaurants in the area. There are 27 rooms in the complex, the best of which have a magnificent view of the lake and Imbabura volcano on the other side. The rooms are cozy, neat and comfortable, and have fireplaces and cable TV. Puerto Lago also owns a motorboat, making tours of the lake, fishing, and water skiing possible. The restaurant is probably the best part of Puerto Lago. Constructed right on the shore, there are spectacular views and the food is outstanding. There are also conference facilities, and Puerto Lago can host special events. Tel: 593-6-292-0920, E-mail: puertolago@andinanet.net.

FUYA FUYA

Fuya Fuya is located 20 km south of Otavalo. It's a straightforward climb that provides spectacular views of the Lagunas de Mojanda, three pristine lakes located at the base of the mountain, and wide expanses of páramo grasslands.

GETTING TO FUYA FUYA FROM QUITO

From Quito, take the Pan American Highway north toward Otavalo. After you reach Lago San Pablo, you will pass a Repsol gas station on the right. Just past the gas station, turn left at the sign for Mojanda and follow the cobblestone road to the left for about 15 minutes until you come to the lakes. Fuya Fuya is easily visible from here. If you don't have your own transportation, take a bus to Otavalo and hire a taxi up to Lagunas de Mojanda.

HIKING FUYA FUYA

You can follow any of the various footpaths up to the pass or to the peak at 4263 meters (13,986 feet). It takes only two to three hours to summit from the lakes, and the total elevation gain is approximately 550 meters, making Fuya Fuya a good, quick mountain for climbers hoping to acclimatize for some of Ecuador's higher peaks. It's a good idea to take a topographic map of the region if you decide to hike in the areas beyond the lakes or trek to other mountains, such as Imbabura, in the area.

Photo by Caroline Bennett

NORTHERN ANDES

CENTRAL ANDES

To the south of Quito, the Central Highlands area is reached by the Avenue of the Volcanoes, characterized by striking volcanic peaks and rugged Andean scenery. Some of Ecuador's most visited sites lie in this area, including the Cotopaxi National Park, the lively little holiday town of Baños, the hot springs at Papallacta, the Laguna de Quilotoa (the huge crater lake on the route of the popular "Quilotoa Loop") and, of course, Ecuador's highest peak, Chimborazo.

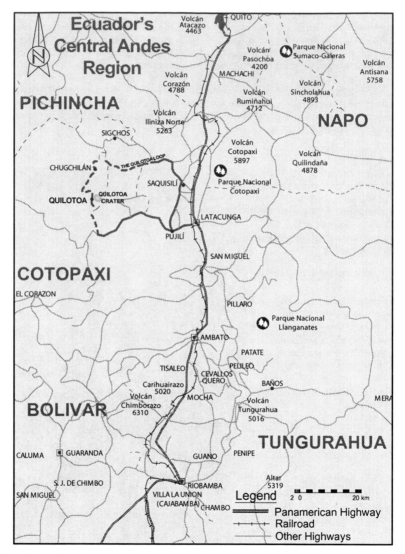

LATACUNGA

A medium-sized town about an hour south of Quito, Latacunga appeals to the traveler interested in a more native or genuine Ecuadorian experience. Latacunga is a tranquil, non-touristy town with a decent tourist infrastructure. Latacunga was destroyed by earthquakes and eruptions of Cotopaxi on three occasions: in 1742, 1768 and 1877. The capital of Cotopaxi province, it is convenient to the Cotopaxi National Park as well as the Quilotoa-Zumbahua loop, Saquisilí and Pujilí. In spite of the repeated destruction, it is a historical town, boasting a well-preserved colonial downtown that is worth a visit even for the traveler who is merely passing through. Once a somewhat grungy city, Latacunga has done a great deal in recent years to beautify itself, improving gardens in the town squares and adding ornate metalwork to the bridges that connect it to the highway.

There are a variety of hotels and restaurants in Latacunga, catering to every budget level. Try one of the city's most famous dishes: *chugchucaras*, a plate of pork with boiled corn, fried plantains and popcorn.

THINGS TO DO
The city hosts a most impressive Saturday market. Unlike Otavalo, the main participants in the Latacunga market are not foreigners but locals who do their weekly shopping and socializing. Even on other days of the week, the market is often bustling and worth a visit.

Two museums are of interest: La Casa de los Marqueses de Miraflores (Sanchez de Orellana and Abel Echeverria) is a restored colonial mansion with traditional furniture and colonial art, and La Casa de la Cultura (Antonia Vela and Padre Salcedo) has an interesting collection of pre-conquest artifacts as well as an art gallery with rotating exhibitions.

The town festival, *La Fiesta de la Mama Negra*, is held both on the last weekend in September and in early November, featuring parades, fireworks and dancing.

It is easy to get to Latacunga from the Quito terminal—buses run every 10 or 15 minutes and cost between $1.50 and $2. Be warned, however: buses to Latacunga will often drive all over Quito after departing from the terminal, hoping to fill with passengers. This means that the one-hour trip may well take up to two hours. If you're trying to catch the bus from Latacunga to the Quilotoa loop (with daily departures at 11:30 a.m. and noon), be sure to arrive early enough to have time to spare.

QUILOTOA LOOP
With some of the most breathtaking scenery in Ecuador, the region that has come to be known as the Quilotoa Loop is perfect for travelers seeking a taste of indigenous farm life and spectacular mountain landscapes a bit off the usual tourist path.

Starting in Latacunga, 200 kilometers of mostly unpaved road winds through patchwork hills and along riverbeds, connecting tiny mountain villages to the west, then circling back to Latacunga. Though riding the entire loop in one fell swoop would take about eight hours by bus, the real thrill of the expedition is in hiking and bumping along the dusty road from village to village, staying the night and hanging out with the locals.

QUILOTOA LOOP HIGHLIGHTS
The magnificent Quilotoa Volcanic Crater Lake is one of the most striking sites in Ecuador and one of the most beautiful craters in Latin America, with lustrous emerald waters and excellent hiking paths.

The indigenous market at Sasquisilí. You won't find many souvenirs, but many consider this the best market in Ecuador, and it's certainly one of the most authentic. Filled with locals bartering for everything from pigs' ears to fresh produce, Thursdays in Saquisilí transform into a colorful spectacle for the senses.

The tiny town of Chugchilán landed on the map because of a few fantastic hostels, and its popularity as a base for exploring the area continues to rise. With some of the region's most incredible vistas, an array of hiking and horseback riding trails into canyons and cloud forests, and exceptionally warm and hospitable people, it's no wonder that business in this tiny mountain town has flourished.

CENTRAL ANDES

The artisan village of Tigua is probably best known for the unique style of colorful paintings made locally and sold all over the country. In addition to visits to local art galleries and workshops, there are many hikes in the area and an excellent working-farm posada.

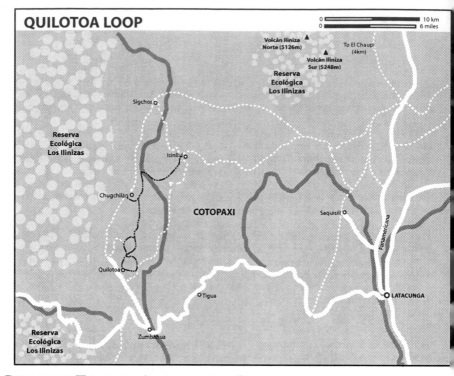

GETTING TO AND AWAY FROM QUILOTOA

Buses departing Latacunga headed for Chugchilán clockwise around the loop pass through Quilotoa between 2 - 2:30 p.m. ($2, two hours to Chugchilán). Moving counter-clockwise, buses coming from Chugchilán on the way to Latacunga pass through Quilotoa around 6 a.m. on Monday-Friday, an hour earlier on Saturday, and with more frequency on Sunday. As schedules change often, ask around—there may be additional buses passing through during busier times of year.

THINGS TO DO & SEE

HIKING IN THE QUILOTOA REGION

From traversing deep rugged canyons, volcanic crater lakes and climbing around in cloud forests, to gentle walks through rolling patchwork hills and to high-mountain cheese factories, the Quilotoa region presents some of the best hiking in Ecuador. If you have a few days, walk the whole loop from village to village, hopping on the bus or a local milk truck when you've had enough. Alternatively, base yourself in Chugchilán, Tigua or Quilotoa and indulge in several fantastic day hikes.

HIKING IN THE QUILOTOA REGION

The walk from the Quilotoa crater to Chugchilán is undoubtedly one of the best short hikes in Ecuador. The trek takes four to five hours, depending on how long you stop to let your jaw drop at the alternating views between glistening green volcanic crater lake and endless green pastures backed by distant jagged mountains.

Isinliví to Chugchilán, passing through the small village of Guantualo. A good five hours with plenty of stops to admire the landscape. Hit the Monday market in Guantualo if you can.
Hike from Tigua to Quilotoa. Another four hours of breathtaking views and gentle trekking, rewarded with the glimmering waters of the Quilotoa Crater Lake at the end.

The list of possibilities go on! Read about things to do in specific towns, and ask around to determine which trails are currently best while you're in the region. Any of these trips can be made in reverse. Always pay attention to the notoriously rapidly changing weather, and be sure to leave ample time to complete hikes well before afternoon rains and dark.

Photo by Caroline Bennett

BIKING IN THE QUILOTOA REGION
The Quilotoa Loop presents some awesome trips for bicyclists, with gentle inclines and awe-inspiring views around nearly every corner. Most people begin the journey in Latacunga, though you can also enter the region from Lasso or Zumbahua. Biking any good part of the loop takes a comfortable three to five days, depending on your speed and length of overnight stays. While the route is easy going in most places, watch out for cobbled stones and steeper hills around the Sigchos area.

A few popular routes that diverge from the typical towns on the loop are:

In the North: Latacunga-Guingopana-Guangaje-Guantualo-Isinliví-Sigchos. From Sigchos, you can take a bus back to Latacunga.

To the South: Zumbahua-Angamarca-Shuyo-Moraspungo-Quevado or Salinas.

GETTING AROUND THE QUILOTOA LOOP
Though transport can be a bit tricky, getting around the loop via public transport is doable with a little patience, planning and some very early morning rises. The destinations more than make up for the arduous journeys, and the scenery is stunning by golden dawn light. Many choose to travel the loop in a circle, walking, busing, horsing, or biking from village to village in either direction, and staying in a different place each night. Another option is to base yourself

CENTRAL ANDES

in either Chugchilán or Tigua, where accommodation options are considerably more pleasant and buses can take you back to Latacunga when you've finished exploring the area.

Buses from Latacunga leave for Chugchilán via Sigchos (stopping in Saquisilí around noon, then in Sigchos for about 15 minutes around 2 p.m.) on the northern route at 11:30 a.m. daily, and for Chugchilán via Zumbahua (passing through at about 1:30 p.m.) on the southern end at 12:00 p.m. Either journey takes about four hours.

Buses returning from Chugchilán to Latacunga leave early and pass through towns on their respective routes along the way. In general, buses headed to Latacunga via Sigchos leave around 3 a.m. every day, with several additional times later in the week. Buses taking the southern route from Chugchilán leave daily at 4 a.m., with several additional departures later in the week and on market day.

General bus transportation from Chugchilán is as follows; see specific town information for further information on getting to and away from other towns along the loop.

Monday:
Chugchílan to Latacunga via Sigchos 3 a.m.
Chugchílan to Latacunga via Zumbahua 4 a.m.

Tuesday:
Chugchílan to Latacunga via Sigchos 3 a.m.
Chugchílan to Latacunga via Zumbahua 4 a.m.

Wednesday:
Chugchílan to Latacunga via Sigchos 3 a.m.
Chugchílan to Latacunga via Zumbahua 4 a.m.
Chugchílan to Zumbahua / La Mana 5 a.m.

Thursday:
Chugchílan to Latacunga via Sigchos 3 a.m.
Chugchílan to Latacunga via Zumbahua 4 a.m.

Friday:
Chugchílan to Latacunga via Sigchos 3 a.m.
Chugchílan to Latacunga via Zumbahua 4 a.m.
Chugchílan to Zumbahua / La Mana 6 a.m.

Saturday:
Chugchílan to Latacunga via Sigchos 3 a.m.
Chugchílan to Latacunga via Zumbahua 3 a.m.
Chugchílan to Zumbahua / La Mana 4 a.m.

Sunday:
Chugchílan to Latacunga via Sigchos 4 a.m., 4:30 a.m., 5:30 a.m., 12 p.m.
Chugchílan to Latacunga via Zumbahua 6 a.m., 9 a.m., 10 a.m., 2 p.m.

*During the school year (Sept-June) there is a daily bus from Chugchilán to Sigchos departing at 5:30 am (you can change in Sigchos for the 7 a.m. bus to Latacunga); note that the bus doesn't run when there are no classes, so ask around.

*Buses leave from Zumbahua headed to Latacunga every 30 minutes during the day.

*Buses leave from Sigchos headed to Latacunga and Quito in the afternoon. Monday through Saturday there is also a milk truck that makes the journey from Chugchilán to Sigchos. From there you can then take an afternoon bus to Latacunga. The truck usually passes through town around 9 a.m., though this can vary so ask the locals to be sure.

If you get stuck or aren't eager to brave the early mornings, you can hire a private pickup from any of the towns with hostels. Private transport from Chugchilán to Quilotoa is $25 for up to five people; $30 to Zumbahua or Sigchos for up to five; and $60 all the way back to Latacunga.

SAQUISILÍ
A small town in Cotopaxi province, Saquisilí is gaining fame for its bustling local Thursday market. Only two hours south of Quito by bus and a few kilometers off the Quito-Ambato stretch of the Pan American highway, the market's accessibility and authenticity are making it a more and more popular stop with tourists.

Each Thursday, the town is transformed by a lively, sprawling display of goods brought in by locals from surrounding villages in all directions. Unlike the Otavalo market that is primarily a show for tourists, the Saquisilí market is truly a local event that has existed since Pre-Columbian times. Men and women from surrounding small villages swarm in in herds at the crack of dawn, toting every item imaginable from household necessities to baskets full of squawking chicks. The market takes up eight main plazas and offers everything from reed mats to herbal remedies, meat products to the squealing livestock itself. To explore the latter, walk for about 10 minutes past the market's main plaza along the dirt road that leads out of town. Come early, as the animal market excitement begins to subside by about 9 a.m. As if there weren't enough to tickle the senses into overload in the main squares, every adjoining street connecting the courts see vendors selling more randomness, from painted key rings to hot cell phones and electronics.

Like many local highland markets, the market at Saquisilí is not only for commerce: it is also a very important social and cultural affair. Indigenous men and women can be seen donning traditional dress and felt fedora hats, bartering with their neighbors and mingling over lunch.

For the traveler, much of the market is of little commercial interest. Though there is a growing artisan section with colorful local crafts and tourist items at cheaper prices than can be found in Quito and Otavalo, the essence of the market is in its fruits and vegetables plaza, the lively animal market and the smells that come from the array of edibles sizzling on every corner. Though you're not likely to be in the market searching for a dish rack or a new alpaca, Saquisilí provides a genuine look at native life and culture, and photographic opportunities abound.

There's no shortage of traditional food to sample—some options are quite tasty, while others can be a bit nauseating to the unaccustomed stomach. Locals will tell you that you haven't been to Saquisilí if you didn't try *tortillas de maíz*—a sizzling hot corn pancake oozing with cheese and smothered in sauce. If you haven't yet given *cuy* (guinea pig) a taste, Saquisilí is a famed place to do so. Prices are cheap—about $4 for a half—and you can choose your own skewer from the charred faces on offer.

Saquisilí is only a few miles off the highway, so it is easy to combine with a trip to the Cotopaxi area or on a travel day between Quito and Baños or Riobamba. It is also easily accessible by bus from Latacunga and other points in the south.

GETTING TO AND AWAY
Though with little posted information the trip may seem daunting, getting to and away from Saquisilí is really quite easy. Buses passing the Pan American highway heading north or south will let you off a few kilometers outside of town, where a bus comes and goes and pickup trucks are always waiting on market days. There are frequent bus services between Latacunga and Saquisilí ($0.40, 25 minutes) and Quito and Saquisilí ($2.50, 2 1/2 hours). In the Quito

CENTRAL ANDES

bus terminal or just outside, you can get any bus headed south and ask the driver to leave you at the junction for Saquisilí. From here, jump on the bus if it happens to be there when you arrive, otherwise ask a truck driver to take you to town for about 50 cents. You'll know when you've reached the town center; from here, the market is a short walk away.

Buses heading back to Quito and elsewhere leave from the corner of the food market. Follow Mariscal Sucre down to the square, where buses leave as they fill (about every 15-30 minutes early in the afternoon, tapering off throughout the day). The last bus to Quito leaves around 4 p.m. Alternatively, some Quito hotels (Hilton Colón and Hotel Quito) offer half-day tours to the Saquisilí market on Thursdays. Several Latacunga agencies offer Saquisilí in their tours as well.

LODGING

Though many travelers prefer to stay in nearby Latacunga and take a crack-of-dawn bus to the Thursday market, Saquisilí does offer basic accommodation and a number of hole-in-the-wall restaurants.

SALON PICHINCHA ($4/PERSON)

A quiet option with simple rooms, a restaurant and friendly owners. Beds are $4 per person with shared bath and hot water. Walk down past the park on Bolivar, one-and-a-half blocks past the clothing market, continuing on the left to a signed doorway and enter through the restaurant. Rooms tend to fill up fast on Wednesday nights before market days.

PENSIÓN CHABELA

A tiny overhead sign claims that this place has rooms, though several attempts at trying to find someone to show one proved fruitless. Look for a tucked-away hallway, leading to a colorful stained-glass door next to Abarrotes Normita *tienda* and the dentist office on the plaza. Mariscal Sucre and Bolivar, Tel: 593-3-372-1114.

SAN CARLOS (ROOMS: $8-12)

Probably your best bet, if you can handle the cheesy décor and a little Jesus paraphernalia. San Carlos is a one-stop shop with an in-house hotel, bar and cafeteria overlooking the central plaza. The area can be a bit noisy with the frequent squawking of a clown that broadcasts sales throughout the afternoon in the store below. Rooms are simple and dark, but will do the trick for one night and an early market morning rise. The restaurant is decent for the area, serving up secos de pollo/carne and simple fare. You can't miss the building—a broken, hanging neon marks the spot off Bolívar and Sucre at the corner of the park. Bolivar and Sucre, Tel: 593-3-720-1981, 593-3-272-1057.

HOTEL CUELLO DE LUNA (ROOMS: $15-75)

A fancier alternative to sleeping in Saquisilí while still staying nearby, Cuello de Luna sits just out of town between Cotopaxi National Park and the market town. From spotless dorms to luxurious private rooms with bath and fireplace, this hotel is nestled in the scenic Andean peaks. The hotel offers tours and will also provide transport to the park, Saquisilí and other towns, including Quito, Baños and Chimborazo, for a price. El Chasquí, Panamericana Sur Km 65, just in front of the entrance to Parque Nacional Cotopaxi, Tel: 593-9-970-0330 / 593-2-290-5939, URL: www.cuellodeluna.com.

RESTAURANTS

The best bet for eats is in the market or in the simple but adequate restaurants on the park square. You can also check out the adjoining streets just off it in all directions. Though a few are worth mentioning, they're all pretty similar in price and selection. Scope out a place that seems popular with the locals at the moment.

SURTIPAN

The best bakery in town, with a wide variety of cakes and colorful pastries. On the corner of Mariscal Sucre and 24 de Mayo.

POLLOS A LA BRASA
A tasty spot off the food market square, if you don't have the stomach for what's on offer in the market itself. Healthy portions of roasted chicken and cheap almuerzos, just across from the Medico Familiar sign (though hopefully you won't need the neighbor's services!). Just off the food market square.

CEVICHERIA PATY
A seemingly popular spot next to San Carlos on the plaza, directly across the square from the church. Almuerzos, ceviches, crab, meriendas, encebollados and typical plates for cheap. In a hurry? Grab a cuy or roasted pig part to go from the lady grilling just outside on the sidewalk. Next to San Carlos on the plaza.

RESTAURANT ELISABETH
Red and white checkerboard cloths mark the tables that line this hole-in-the-wall spot off the plaza. Small, simple and good typical plates and $1.25 set menu almuerzos. Calle Bolivar on the park.

PUJILÍ
A small market town located only a few miles away from Latacunga and the Quito-Ambato highway, Pujilí has a rich culture and history. Most of the inhabitants of Pujilí are indigenous, and the best time to see native customs and clothing are the market days: Wednesdays and Sundays. Unlike Otavalo, which is mainly for tourists, the market in Pujilí is still a local affair. Men and women from surrounding villages will pack up their llamas and *burros* early in the morning in order to come to the market and sell their extra produce for whatever money they can make. Professional vendors also come, bringing their wares, which are generally basic essentials like rope, knives, dishes, batteries, clocks, etc.

Like the market in Saquisilí, it is more than simply a time to shop: it is also an important social activity, and locals will dress nicely and spend a good amount of time socializing. Tourists are discovering Pujilí (as well as Zumbahua and Saquisilí, the other market towns in the area), so there will be some stalls dedicated to Otavalo-style weavings or other popular tourist goods. Pujilí itself is known for clay pottery and ceramics, which are also sold at the market. Of particular interest in Pujilí is the Corpus Christi festival in June, which features the El Danzante parades. It is a fascinating mix of Catholic and ancient native religious practices. Pujilí's location makes it an ideal place to combine with other daytrips to the Cotopaxi area or on a travel day between Quito and Baños or Riobamba. It is especially convenient if you have your own transportation. If you don't, it is still possible to visit by bus from Latacunga.

For a small town, it has an interesting history: the citizens of Pujilí fought bravely in the war of independence. One of Ecuador's presidents, General Guillermo Rodríguez Lara, was a native of Pujilí. The town was devastated by an earthquake in 1996, but has since been reconstructed.

QUILOTOA
Just off the loop road about 14 kilometers north of Zumbahua lies the wee village of Quilotoa and the mysterious emerald waters of its illustrious volcanic crater lake. Jagged rocky cliffs drop 400 meters down from a fully encircling rim trail to meet the massive reflective pool below. The bizarre opaque-green of the lake, paired with the distant snowcapped peaks of Iliniza Sur and Cotopaxi, set a truly awe-inspiring scene.

In 30 minutes, you can climb down to the shores on a cut path just below the parking area—the steep return trip takes at least double that (or for a few bucks you can hop on a donkey and save weary legs). Kayaks are available for rent at the end of the trail, though the lake has no outlet and you mustn't swim or drink from the stagnant alkaline waters. Relatively fit hikers can make the four to five-hour trek around the entire circumference of the crater, or walk a third of the way around it and on to Chugchilán.

One stretch of dirt road and the scattering of houses and tiny businesses make up the small village of Quilotoa, which lies just before the crater lake and seems to only exist in response to tourism. There are several extremely basic hostels that also serve as restaurants and shops, and not much else.

Quilotoa is a good place to find local indigenous art, especially paintings of the famous Tigua style. There are a few shops where artists sell their work that are mostly part of hostels or houses in town. If the doors are locked, ask around and someone will likely come let you in. Be aware that nights can be pretty chilly in the Andes, and some simple accommodations may not be adequately equipped to keep you warm.

LODGING

HOSTAL CHOSITA ($6/PERSON INCLUDING MEALS)
A tiny shop on the right as you walk from the main road toward the crater. Eight small and extremely basic rooms run at $6 per person including meals. Halfway through the village on the right.

PACHA MAMA ($8/PERSON INCLUDING MEALS)
A very basic but friendly option run by a local family, Pacha Mama is the last stop on the left as you approach the crater. Four upstairs rooms are surprisingly warm for the area as heat is carried up and radiated through a large metal pipe. There is also a small shop where you can buy water and snacks if you're just passing through before a hike. Cells: 593-8-554-9953/ 593-9-212-5962.

PRINCESA TOA ($8/PERSON INCLUDING MEALS)
The second to last place on the left as you walk from town to the crater, Princesa Toa is organized by the Fundacion Ecuatoriana del Habitat and is community-run. Though accommodations are basic, the indigenous locals who work there are friendly and proud. One large dorm has 6 beds of various sizes; across the hall there are two doubles. Prices include breakfast and dinner in a pleasant open dining room upstairs, which is also a good place to grab a cup of coffee and take a last look at the map before heading off on the trail if you're just passing through. Across from the crater overlook.

HOSTAL CABAÑAS QUILOTOA (ROOMS: $8-12)
A bigger place, though still family-run and by a super-nice bunch at that. Beds in a large dorm are $8 per person, while several smaller rooms go for $10-12 with shared/private bath. Both prices include a typical local dinner and breakfast, with *cuy* (roasted guinea pig) on special nights. A large room downstairs serves as the common room and restaurant to both guests and the family, and also houses a small shop selling local indigenous landscape paintings by the artist owner. On the right at the village entrance, Cell: 593-9-212-5962.

QUILOTOA CRATER LAKE LODGE (ROOMS: $35-45)
A diamond in the rough of the concrete village, the Crater Lake Lodge is certainly unique among area accommodations, though you'll pay for the difference. The hacienda-style lodge was built with respect for the environment and lush surrounding area in mind, and offers clean and comfortable double and triple rooms. Travelers on a budget can seek refuge in the camping area, though remember that nights can be quite chilly in the Andes. A well-decorated restaurant with panoramic views and a massive stone fireplace is home to hearty local and international cuisine. Note the several dogs, cats, turkeys, guinea pigs, rabbits, roosters, hens, pheasants, peacocks and llamas on the grounds. At the entrance to Quilotoa village, Tel: 593-2-223-8665 / 2527 835, E-mail: info@quilotoalodge.com, URL: www.quilotoalodge.com.

TIGUA
Climbing up from Pujilí, the scenery begins to change as hillsides ascend and the jagged peaks of Cotopaxi and the Ilinizas jut through the clouds. Just before reaching the larger town of Zumbahua lies the village of Tigua, a wee community that has become world-famous for a special style of painting by the same name. Here you can buy colorful pieces depicting

Andean life directly from the artists at the Galería de los Pinturas de Tigua, run by the association of indigenous painters of Tigua. Be on the lookout for paintings by the Toaquiza family, who originally conceptualized the Tigua style.

There's not much of town center, more a scattering of several clusters of houses and the occasional shop, but it is close to Quilotoa and Zumbahua. There are pretty walks in the area, and two excellent lodging options make Tigua an appealing place to base yourself in while exploring the region.

Mount Amina hovers over the eastern side of the village near La Posada de Tigua, which according to local Quichua legend, is the formation of a giant who came from the coast to rest in Tigua and has been sleeping there ever since. Every summer locals gather on the mountain in ceremony.

THINGS TO SEE & DO
Most of the activities in Tigua are outdoors: local guides can take you on breathtaking hikes with views of the mountains, let you in to visit a local home, or take you to see the workshop of one of the local painters. There is also a co-operatively owned art gallery right next door to Semana Huasi. Besides that, there is the traditional market in the town of Zumbahua (worth a visit, plan on about 45 minutes to an hour—see Zumbahua for more details) and the volcanic crater at Quilotoa (if you have your own transportation for these trips, you'll save yourself a lot of hassle!).

GALERÍA DE LOS PINTURAS DE TIGUA
Home of an impressive collection of art by local indigenous painters, run by friendly Alfredo, president of the Association of Indigenous Painters of Tigua, and an artist himself. Located at Kilometer 53 on the loop and arguably the best place to purchase authentic Tigua art. If the door's locked, give Alfredo a call (Cell: 593-9-934-3969) and he'll come open the shop for you. Kilometer 53 on the loop, next to Semana Huasi, Tel: 593-3-281-4868, Cell: 593-9-934-3969, E-mail: www.atoaquizauotmail.com.

LODGING
HOSTERÍA SEMANA HUASI ($15/PERSON WITH BREAKFAST AND DINNER)
Hostería Semana Huasi is a cozy, community-run hostel, overlooking the valley as you come into town. There are two comfy dorm rooms and a few private doubles, all sharing eco-friendly bathrooms. A restaurant upstairs serves dinner and breakfast (included in the price) and has lovely vistas of the valley below. Next door to the Galería de los Pinturas de Tigua as you come around the bend, you can't miss the rust-colored roof. Tel: 593-3-381-4868, E-mail: huasi@yahoo.com.

LA POSADA DE TIGUA ($22-29/PERSON INCLUDING MEALS)
An old sprawling hacienda that is a working farm-turned-guesthouse with an authentic feel and the warmest of hosts, the posada is truly a destination in itself. While this place may sound a bit pricey for the region, you pay for what you get here, and it's worth it. Seven cozy rooms of varying décor and layout make up the first floor of a large farmhouse, convening in a snug living room with a woodstove and old west feel. Running the business is truly a family affair, with Margarita, Marco, and their children eager to show you the ropes at the farm and ensure that your stay is memorable. The farm works to fuel the posada, providing fresh veggies, milk, yogurt and meat that the family continually transform into some tasty meals that would give your grandma a run for her money. Be sure to try the yogurt made on-site, mixed with *manjar de leche*—an incredible caramel treat! Hosts are more than happy to show you the farm, send you off on horses, or even take a stab at milking the cows or riding a llama. Three km from Tigua "town," 800 m down a dusty dirt road from the main road, Tel: 593-3-281-3682, Cell: 593-9-161-2391, E-mail: laposadadetigua@latinmail.com.

ZUMBAHUA

Winding along the loop about halfway between tiny Tigua and the Quilotoa crater, lies the sleepy town of Zumbahua. Sitting low and surrounded by mountain peaks and quilted hills more barren than other parts of the region, the town seems as if it has sprung up out of nowhere. Though you may be the only tourists around on any given weekday, the area is pleasant and has great hiking and stunning views.

On Saturdays, the place springs to life, as locals from surrounding villages stream in with goods and creatures to sell at one of the most colorful and authentic markets in the area. The real highlight is watching the town transform early in the morning, as traditionally dressed families come parading in by the bus and llamaful. Though you probably won't find much of interest to buy, it's a lively scene and a photographer's delight.

GETTING TO AND AWAY

There is a frequent bus service from Zumbahua to Latacunga and vice versa. Buses leave from Avenida 5 de Junio in Latacunga ($2, 2.5 hours), some of which continue on to Quilotoa and Chugchilán. Transportes Ilinizas also has a frequent service to Saquisilí ($0.50, 35 minutes), Chugchilán and Sigchos. If you find yourself in a bind, trucks can be hired from Zumbahua to Quilotoa (about $15) and Chugchilán ($35).

LODGING

Though travelers do make their way through here in transit and for market days, you may well be the only foreigners in town on any given overnight. Beware that it can be quite chilly at night in the Andes—be sure there are plenty of blankets available when choosing a room.

HOSTAL CONDOR MATZI ($5/PERSON)

This market-side hostel used to be about the only show in town and has gotten more guidebook coverage than the others, but isn't your only bet these days. The building is a bit tired and sits to the left of the church on the main square facing the mountains. Simple and cheap, it'll do for a night. Call ahead, or ask around at the corner store if you arrive and no one is there to let you in. For a buck, the hostel will also watch your bags for the day even if you aren't staying there so you won't have to lug them around the market. Sits to the left of the church on the main square facing the mountains, Tel: 593-3-281-4611.

HOSTAL RICHARD ($5/PERSON)

On the corner of the square where the Pan American meets Calle Angel Maria Umajinga, Hostal Richard is a small but friendly, family-run place above a small store. Two large dorm rooms, a double and a triple share bathrooms and a kitchen. Pan American and Calle Angel Maria Umajinga, Tel: 593-3-524-6282.

HOTEL QUILOTOA ($5-7/PERSON)

A lesser known place across the square from Condor Matzi, but perhaps the best option in Zumbahua. Simple rooms on the second floor share a terrace that looks out over the market square below. The first floor is home to a restaurant with good roasted chicken and $1.50 lunches with friendly service. $5 per person, $7 with private bath and hot water. Across the square from Condor, Cell: 593-8-684-0616.

CHUGCHILÁN

Sitting high to the west between Sigchos and Quilotoa, tiny Chugchilán and its friendly inhabitants are a real Andean gem. With stunning scenery, hikes into plummeting canyons, primary cloud forests, cheese factories and some of the homiest accommodations in Ecuador, Chugchilán should not be missed.

Chugchilán landed on the map because of a few fantastic hostels, and its popularity as a base for exploring the area continues to rise. Built into the mountainsides and overlooking the impressive Río Toachi canyon, the village is one of those places where people come passing through and end up staying for days. There are three excellent lodges at the end of town, each with its own warm touches and all offering hearty home-cooked meals, horseback riding trips, local transportation and hiking information.

The "town" itself consists of a small basketball court in front of a church facing a few simple houses that also serve as local businesses, vending ice cream or sewing up saddles. A street stall or two dish out simple meat and rice plates in the evenings, catering to locals and also serving as the town hangout. Don't be fooled by the sign "Pension Popular Diocesana" next to the church—the old building is not a hostel! Hostels and most things of interest to tourists can be found heading down the hill just outside of town.

Getting To and Away
Buses from Latacunga leave for Chugchilán via Sigchos (stopping in Saquisilí around noon, then in Sigchos for about 15 minutes around 2 p.m.) on the northern route at 11:30 a.m. daily, and for Chugchilán via Zumbahua (passing through at about 1:30 p.m.) on the southern end at 12:00 p.m. Either journey takes about four hours. Buses returning from Chugchilán to Latacunga leave early and pass through towns on their respective routes along the way. In general, buses headed to Latacunga via Sigchos leave around 3 a.m. everyday, with several additional times later in the week. Buses taking the southern route from Chugchilán leave daily at 4 a.m., with several additional departures later in the week and on market day.

Things to see & do
Artesanias Grupo de Mujeres Chugchilán
The organization runs a small shop filled with lovely hand knit goods made by local women and benefiting the community. To the right of church, if you're facing it from the road, ask around if the door's locked and someone will come open up for you.

Hiking
There are a number of fantastic hikes in the area, ask around to determine which trails are currently best at the time of your stay.

The walk from the Quilotoa crater to Chugchilán is undoubtedly one of the best short hikes in Ecuador. The trek takes four to five hours depending on how long you stop to let your jaw drop at the alternating views between glistening green volcanic crater lake and endless green pastures, backed by distant jagged mountains.

Hike from Chugchilán to Isinliví, passing through the small village of Guantualo. This takes a good five hours with plenty of stops to admire the landscape. Hit the Monday market in Guantualo if you can.

Either of these trips can be made in reverse. Always pay attention to the notoriously quickly changing weather, and be sure to leave ample time to complete hikes well before afternoon rains and dark.

Any of the area's accommodations will happily arrange guides for a number of incredible scenic hikes, and prices for such services are relatively established at $10-15 per four to six-hour trek. Alternatively, you can give a local guide a call yourself—ask around, or try: Bernacho, Cell: 593-8-810-2369 or Miguel, Cell: 593-8-811-1010.

Hiking from Quilotoa to Chugchilán
This 7.5-mile trek is one of the most astonishingly beautiful day hikes in Ecuador. The hike takes approximately five hours, and walks past Quilotoa's volcanic crater lake, down into the valley through the town of Guayama, and finally up the canyon into Chugchilán. While the hike is not extremely challenging, pay close attention to the route and as always, the weather. The route begins in the tiny town of Quilotoa. Signs are used to demarcate the hike, but they have since been removed or blown over.

Get your writing published in our books, go to www.vivatravelguides.com

From El Mirador—the lookout over the crater (across from Pacha Mama)—look left across the lake where three sandy patches will be visible along the ridge. Your aim in this first section is to make it to the third sandy spot—the lowest along the ridgeline—where you will descend from the ridge into the valley. From El Mirador, walk to your left along the ridge on the well-defined path. At the beginning of the path, a sign with helpful hints also has a map painted on the back of it. The path will wind along the top of the ridgeline, giving the hiker breathtaking views that swap between the emerald lake and patchwork valley. While you will walk through more than three sandy patches, be sure you have reached the lowest sandy spot before turning down into the valley. This correct sandy patch has a rock cairn in the middle of it, with an empty signpost sticking out.

From the sandy spot you will be able to see your next objective, the small town of Guayama. Take the path that descends straight down the hill, past a small house. Once you reach the bottom of the hill, a road will take you through the middle of the town. This tiny village has few amenities, though there is a basic shop with drinks and a new small hostel (Hostal El Chucurito, $5 per person) in a house at the far end of town by a cemetery.

At this end of town, the road will curve left past the cemetery. You will find the continuation of the path to Chugchilán at the third right. In the final section of the hike, the path will wind through beautiful pastures and then steeply down into the river basin, before climbing up into the town of Chugchilán.

The path obscures a bit in one spot, where three options present themselves in a small, grassy clearing. Take the middle route that looks like a tunnel, which leads down into the canyon on a narrow path with tall steep rock walls. Once at the bottom, just keep following the well-trodden trail past local dwellings and up and into Chugchilán.

The hike in this direction is mostly downhill, however the final section is steep and challenging. It also can be difficult to find your way on this hike, especially if it is cloudy. Only undertake this adventure if you are confident in your sense of direction! Make sure that you have enough time to complete the hike before the afternoon weather moves in; never leave from Quilotoa after 1:30 p.m. If you have any doubts, hire a local guide for $10-15 in either Quilotoa or Chugchilán, or ask locals along the way. Andino people are friendly and will point you in the right direction!

HORSEBACK RIDING
The area around Chugchilán is fascinatingly diverse in landscape, and great for exploring by horse. The relatively small region is home to the Paramo highlands, vast expanses of Andean farmland, the lowland riverbed of the Río Toachi, and both primary and secondary cloud forests. Within just a few hours, you can experience several dramatically different terrains and climate zones, visit a highland cheese factory and stick your toes into one of several nearby waterfalls.

Any of the hostels can arrange horses and a local guide for four to six-hour expeditions, costing around $10-15 per person. Horses are generally in pretty good shape though seem a little tired; be sure you have a happy trotter before heading for the hills.

LODGING
There are three superb lodging options in Chugchilán that are destinations in themselves and cater to every budget and type of traveler. The Hostal Cloud Forest has the best value and is popular with backpackers, while the award-winning Black Sheep Inn has won over the eco-tourism crowd. Mama Hilda's has found a special place somewhere in the middle. All offer scrumptious home-cooked meals included in their prices and can arrange horseback riding tours, hiking guides and information, and private transportation.

Central Andes

252

LODGING
HOSTAL
Hostal
© map
is

HOSTAL CLOUD FOREST ($8/PERSON WITH BREAKFAST AND

The cheapest of the three options, but comparable in quality, Cloud
great value choice for backpackers. Rooms are a bit small, but open
outdoor common area with thatched-grass covered picnic tables a
about. The large dining and lounge area, reminiscent of a ski lodge,
post-hike with its cozy woodstove and festive corner bar, serving up ev
no to piña coladas to whiskey. There's also a book exchange and interne
desperate. At $8 per person, with breakfast, a hearty dinner and shared
private bath), the place is a real area bargain. Just down the hill, on the
as you head out of town, Tel: 593-3-281-4808, E-mail: Jose_cloudfores

HOSTAL MAMA HILDA (ROOMS: $17-20)

A lovely complex of clean and cozy rooms with spectacular views and the warmest of hosts,
you're sure to be taken care of and then some at Mama Hilda's. Running the place is a full-
out family affair with hearty group meals in a homey dining room (veggie friendly too!), and
Mama herself seemingly everywhere at once ensuring that everything is up to par. Comfy
brick-walled rooms, some with woodstoves and private bath, all share decks with colorful
hammocks looking out over Mama's flower garden and green patchwork hills beyond. Lounge
on the balcony during the magical dusk hour when a hanging mist drapes over the mountains
and you can hear the distant hum of kids playing futból in the town center. Families and
larger groups can stay in "El Refuge"—the newest of buildings—which houses spacious rooms
with lofts that sleep up to six. Other rooms share bathrooms that are spotless and plentiful.
Friendly owners will happily arrange horseback tours, hikes and private transport. On the left
as you start walking down the hill from the center of town, Tel: 593-3-281-4814, Quito: 593-
2-258-2957, E-mail: info@hostalmamahilda.org, URL: www.hostalmamahilda.org/.

> *V!VA Member Review-Hostal Mama Hilda*
> *Hostal Mama Hilda is a wonderful place to stay on the Quilotoa loop. My wife and I*
> *were originally only going to stay for 1 night, but ended up staying for three. The family*
> *that runs the hostal is so welcoming and friendly and the standard of accommodation*
> *and food is excellent. 13 June 2007. England.*

THE BLACK SHEEP INN ECOLODGE (ROOMS: $25-70)

This friendly, remote mountain lodge set in the Andean highlands of Ecuador caters to international travelers interested in hiking, biking, horseback riding and getting involved with the
community. The lodge makes a strong effort to promote environmental awareness in the local
community and with guests. Vegetarian meals, permaculture practices and shared compost
bathrooms all work toward that goal. From the inn, hike to the spectacular Quilotoa Volcanic
Crater with its turquoise waters, passing a handful of farms and local families going about
their daily business on the way. Bike the mostly downhill ride to the Sunday market at Sigchos.
Rent horses for a morning ride to the local cheese factory or visit the cloud forest with waterfalls, plants and wildlife to see. Or, if you are more interested in staying close to home, relax
in the cozy main lodge; listen to music, partake in the book exchange, relax or go for a ride
on the zip-line. The lodge staff are helpful and will happily help you plan your day's activities,
arranging transportation and guides. There is hot water 24-hour, which you will be grateful
for in this chilly mountain climate. Tel: 593-3-281-4587, E-mail: info@blacksheepinn.com,
URL: www.blacksheepinn.com.

ISINLIVÍ

A tiny village just off the Quilotoa Loop southeast of Sigchos. This town is only really on the
map due to the fantastic Hostal Llullu Llama. There's not much else here —a small woodshop
and a handicraft store that are worth a stop—but the area is stunning and makes for a good
hiking destination or base.

CENTRAL ANDES

Get your writing published in our books, go to www.vivatravelguides.com

LULLU LLAMA ($6-9/PERSON + TAX)

lullu Llama was once a traditional farmhouse, but was recently converted into a ro-
tic mountain hostal high up in the Ecuadorian Andes. Due to its location, the hostal
a prime spot from which to start hikes and treks; pick up free hiking maps, or organize
a multi-day tour. You can also head out to nearby indigenous markets and communities,
check out hidden valley trails, or just enjoy the local flora and fauna—including orchids and
hummingbirds. The hostal prepares hearty three-course meals, including a healthy breakfast to start the day. The hot showers and woodstove are the perfect way to warm up and
get rid of that Andean chill. Isinliví, Tel: 593-3-281-4790, E-mail: info@llullullama.com,
URL: www.llullullama.com.

SIGCHOS

Aside from bus transfers and a small Sunday market, there's really not much to see in the
small dusty town of Sigchos. People are friendly and there is very basic accommodation if you
find yourself here for a night, though with Isinliví and Chugchilán's fantastic lodging options
both less than 25 kilometers away, it's hard not to simply pass through Sigchos en-route.

Winding along the road from Latacunga, a church, school and a few houses dot the road for
about 3 km before opening into the main town. A drab, concrete plaza marks the center of
town, which is also where buses arrive and depart. Businesses are mostly industrial, vending home goods, building supplies, mechanic and legal services, and the like to surrounding villages. Small, colorful buildings pop out to face lush, green hills that are marking of
the region, providing for more miles of gorgeous hiking and luring travelers away from the
otherwise lackluster town.

GETTING TO AND AWAY

There is relatively frequent bus service to and from Latacunga ($1.50, 3.5 hours), and a daily
bus that passes through Sigchos on the route between Latacunga and Chugchilán. The more
sure-fire daily buses to Latacunga depart at 7 a.m. and 2:30 p.m. from beside the church, with
more frequent buses on Wednesday, Saturday and Sunday. All buses make a stop in Saquisilí
on their way to and from Latacunga. Heading farther west you can catch the daily milk truck
($1, about an hour) to Chugchilán, which leaves Sigchos around 7:30 a.m.

LODGING

RESIDENCIAL TOURISMO ($5/PERSON)

A large colorful sign hangs above the corner store near the center of town marking Residencial Tourismo. This is about the only show in town, and probably your best bet for sleeping
and eating if you decide to stay overnight in Sigchos. The large building caters to groups passing through and can house 30 to 40 guests in simple but clean rooms, some with private bath.
Meals available and the owner and shop runner Yolanda will take care of you with a smile.
Calle Carlos Hugo Páez, Cell: 593-8-875-2984.

HOSTAL TUNGURAHUA ($5/PERSON)

$5 per person for the basic of basics in a three-story house. Let them know in advance if
you'd like to eat meals during your stay, and they'll arrange preparation. Off the main square,
ask around town.

RESTAURANTS

A few basic, but good restaurants don't have names. They can be found scattered around 24
De Mayo Plaza, a few blocks from where the bus drops you off. Both Residencial Tourismo
and Hostal Tungurahua will prepare meals if you ask in advance.

SINCHOLAGUA VOLCANO

Sincholagua is an inactive volcano located 45 km (28 miles) southeast of Quito and about 15 km (9 miles) northeast of Cotopaxi Volcano. It's less frequently climbed than any of the other mountains listed for the simple reason that it's difficult to access. Nevertheless, those who make the effort to get to Sincholagua will be well rewarded with a beautiful hike and spectacular views of Cotopaxi, Rumiñahui and the backside of Pasochoa.

GETTING TO SINCHOLAGUA FROM QUITO

Drive one hour south on the Pan American highway to the town of Machachi. Go to the main plaza in Machachi and then turn right just after you pass the plaza's northeast corner. This road will take you through town to a cobblestone road that continues on into the countryside. About five minutes outside of town, the road dips down into a river valley and then winds up for approximately one hour through a number of small villages and past the Guitig factory on the left. Stay on the main road; there a number of secondary roads that can be hard to distinguish from the principal one. You will eventually come to a "T." Go right for about another 10 minutes until you reach the north entrance to Cotopaxi National Park.

Even though Sincholagua resides outside of the National Park's boundaries, rangers will likely charge you a fee of either $2 or $10 (depending on whether you are a resident or foreign visitor) per person to drive through the Park.

Immediately after the ranger station, take a left on the dirt road and follow it east and south for 10 to 15 minutes. When you start driving downhill, to your right you will see a collection of small white buildings at the bottom of a gulley. Take the switchback left and then right to get down to these buildings. There is a gate but it is generally not locked. Continue on about 500 meters past the building to a well constructed concrete bridge spanning the Río Pita. If the gate is open, drive across the bridge and park along side the dirt road. If it's closed, park in the grassy area adjacent to the bridge and continue on foot.

HIKING SINCHOLAGUA

Once you have crossed the bridge, follow the vehicle tracks northeast up the ridge through a series of pine groves and meadows. After about 1.5 hours of steady walking, you will find a concrete survey marker from where you should be able to see a clear approach along a rocky ridge to the mountain. Make your way across this ridge and then traverse the right side until you reach the barren base of the mountain. From here, traverse left and up the northwest face.

You will drop down into a basin and then climb up to a saddle below the summit. The final ascent and the summit itself are exposed and require good scrambling skills. For rock enthusiasts, a great nearby climb is Pico Hoeneisen, which is the prominent peak below Sincholagua. Hoeneisen should only be done by experienced climbers with technical gear.

ILINIZA VOLCANOES

The twin peaks of Iliniza Norte (elevation: 5,126 m, 16,817 ft) and Sur (elevation: 5,248 m, 17,220 ft) rise up in sharp contrast to the páramo 55 km (34 miles) south of Quito. Today, the two mountains are connected by a one-kilometer long saddle, but in prehistoric times, they comprised one solid volcano.

Though similar in height, they vary greatly in technical difficulty. Norte requires no technical skills or equipment (unless there has been considerable snowfall, in which case you may want rope and even crampons). On the other hand, Iliniza Sur is one of Ecuador's more technical climbs and should only be attempted by experienced climbers.

GETTING TO THE ILINIZAS FROM QUITO

To reach the Ilinizas, drive south on the Pan American highway and turn right (west) eight kilometers after Machachi onto a cobblestone and dirt road that leads to the community of El Chaupi. Go seven kilometers on this road until you reach El Chaupi's main plaza. Go right out of the plaza on a road to the right of the church. Travel three kilometers up this road and make a left turn. Continue on until you reach a series of switchbacks that take you up a hill to a parking area marked by a shrine to the Virgin Mary.

From the parking area, follow a dirt road that leads to a well trodden trail. Follow the trail as it winds upwards to a steep ridge, and then climb the ridge until you reach a simple refuge made of cement blocks. On a clear day, you will see Iliniza Norte to the northwest and Iliniza Sur to the southwest.

HIKING ILINIZA NORTE
To climb Norte, walk approximately 45 minutes up the left side of the southeast ridge. You will be on a slope of sandy scree and loose rock until you reach a ridge of solid rock. Follow this ridge of solid rock to a false summit at 5,060 meters, and then traverse right across a number of sandy ledges, including one called the *Paso de Muerte*, or "death pass." These can be intimidating to inexperienced climbers, especially when they are covered with snow. Continue on until you reach a gully. Ten minutes more of scrambling up loose rock will lead you to the true summit marked by an iron cross. The danger of falling rock during the last part of the climb should not be understated; wearing a helmet is always a good idea. It takes between two and three hours to reach the summit from the refuge, and the total climbing time to the summit and back to the shrine is approximately eight hours.

COTOPAXI NATIONAL PARK
An hour and a half south of Quito, along the Avenue of the Volcanoes, lays the dominant image on the Ecuadorian national psyche: the perfectly conical Cotopaxi volcano (5,897 m, 19,350 ft), claiming to be the world's highest active volcano. Even novice climbers can summit the glacier-topped peak with the help of a good guide, glacier climbing equipment and a hardy jacket. The views from the top on a clear day are incredible. Even so, it's a physically demanding climb, (if not technically demanding, depending on snowfall and current glacier conditions) so proper acclimatization, good fitness and training is essential. A week in Quito or any other Andean town with ample walking and summiting of a lesser peak or two should be sufficient.

Photo by Jason Halberstadt

GETTING TO AND AWAY
The main entrance to Cotopaxi National Park is located just a few kilometers before the town of Lasso. Drive south from Quito for approximately two hours on the Pan American highway until you see a large sign for "Parque Nacional Cotopaxi." Turn left (east) at the sign, immediately cross a set of railroad tracks, and follow a dirt road east for 15 km until you get to the Park's main entrance. Unlike the north entrance accessed via Machachi, the road to this one is relatively well-marked. There is an entrance fee of $2 for Ecuadorians and permanent residents, and $10 for foreign visitors. If you don't have your own car, buses run regularly along the Pan American highway from Quito. Ask to be let off at the entrance and walk or hitchhike to the entrance.

Many travelers get a kick out of taking the train from Quito. This unforgettable experience costs around $5 one-way. Ecuadorians have the curious habit of riding on the roof of trains and a small rail is set up around the edge of the bus-looking train to keep passengers from flying off. The train runs Saturdays and Sundays leaving Quito at 8 a.m. and leaving Cotopaxi at 2 p.m. The trip takes a little over three hours and takes you inside Cotopaxi National Park. See www.codeso.com/TurismoEcuador/TurismoTren01E.html for more information.

Hiking to Cotopaxi's Refuge

From the entrance, follow the road for about 20 km to a parking area below the refuge. The Park Service has placed signs at most of the key intersections and, unless it's foggy, for most of the drive up, you will see Cotopaxi and the road leading up to it on your right. There is a steep, one-hour climb from the parking area, situated at 4,500 m, to the refuge (4,800 m). If you intend to climb to the peak, it's wise to settle into the refuge by mid-afternoon as you will have to leave the comfort of your sleeping bag between midnight and 2 a.m.

Summiting Cotopaxi

Though the route has changed over the years due to recession and shifting of the glacier brought about by global climate change, it generally takes you up the right (east) side of the volcano's north face to the huge rock wall called Yanasacha, and then it cuts back left (west), traversing a steep slope to the summit. The ascent along this route, which is usually well-marked by footprints and wands, takes between five and seven hours, and the descent approximately half that time. If there is any doubt about your pace and climbing time, start earlier rather than later, as the snow becomes sticky and difficult to travel on soon after sunrise.

Though not very technical by mountaineering standards, Cotopaxi is not without its dangers. Along the lower section of the mountain you will encounter a number of large crevasses spanned by ice bridges and, just after Yanasacha, you must climb a short but steep, nearly vertical, wall of ice and snow in order to access the final stretch of glacier leading up to the crater. If you are lucky enough to have a clear day when the sun comes out, Cotopaxi provides dreamy views of the mountainous Andean landscape for hundreds of kilometers in every direction.

Camping

For travelers more interested in views of the volcano without actually climbing, there are campgrounds near the train station. For $10 per person ($5 for Ecuadorians), you can have multiday access to rustic cabins about 400 meters from the entrance. For $5 per person ($3 for Ecuadorians), you can camp out with your own tent along any of the trails around the campground.

Mountain Biking

Mountain biking in Cotopaxi is a spectacular once-in-a-lifetime experience. Descend from the refuge parking lot cutting through the thin air at bone-chilling speed. Most of the park is very flat due to historical eruptions that caused the glacier to melt and form literally flat lake beds around the volcano. This is all good news, since riding uphill at this altitude, you're likely to bust a lung—or two.

Other Hikes around Cotopaxi

From the campground, you may access a trail that goes to the peak of Ruminiñahui Volcano (4712 m), a six to eight-hour round-trip spectacular walk. In reality, walking most any path through the paramo from either the campgrounds or Lago Limpiopungo towards the ridge to the right of the Southern-most peak of Rumiñahui will lead you to the peak (the furthest to the left, the South). There are popular treks that go around the volcano and another, called Trek of the Condor, which starts near Papallacta, passes near Volcan Antisana and finishes at Cotopaxi.

Horseback Riding

There is also available horseback riding for $1 per loop from the entrance to the campsite and back. Along with great hiking trails, you can spot domesticated llamas, wild horses, raptors, andean gulls, deer and other wildlife.

Lodging

Hostería Papagayo ($5-9/person)

Hostería Papagayo is an attractive hotel, 45 minutes south of Quito, with a variety of rooms of differing capacities, with and without private bath. Guests can use the camping area for a mere $3 per person. For such an affordable place, it has a wide variety of services, including laundry, restaurant, book exchange, internet access and even a petting zoo. Papagayo encourages backpackers and budget travelers: there are detailed instructions on their website for those who wish to arrive by bus from the terminal in Quito. Horseback rides, mountain biking and tours to the nearby hot springs or the volcanic crater at Quilotoa are available. It is also possible to visit the Santa Martha Animal Rescue Center. For those interested in volunteer work, Papagayo sometimes accepts volunteers to work at the hostel itself and with a program they have in local schools. Tel: 593-2-231-0002, E-mail: info@hostería-papagayo.com, URL: www.hosteria-papagayo.com.

TAMBOPAXI ($37/PERSON WITH MEALS)

Set just inside the bleak, beautiful wilderness that is the Cotopaxi National Park, Tambopaxi advertises itself as an acclimatization center: "the best place to stay and climb Cotopaxi." At an 3,750 m elevation, this is probably a reasonable claim. Tambopaxi offers hostel accommodation. There are two dormitory huts, one with 27 beds spread across four rooms and the other with eight beds in three rooms. While the buildings are the only ones visible for miles within the national park, the careful use of construction materials and close attention to aesthetic detail mean that the environment is not detrimentally impacted by the presence of the buildings. It is also possible to camp at Tambopaxi. Campers enjoy the same facilities as those staying in the huts. For those who do not wish to spend an overnight in the national park, Tambopaxi also has a restaurant which offers delicious, hearty set meals with a stunning view of Cotopaxi itself on a clear day. Parque Nacional Cotopaxi, Tel: 593-2-222-0242, E-mail: tambopaxi@tambopaxi.com, URL: www.tambopaxi.com.

HACIENDA HATO VERDE

Hato Verde Country House is about 150 years old and still serves as home of the owner and his family. In keeping with the original style of the old house, there are six luxurious rooms, each one with private bathroom and fireplace. You can appreciate the impeccable masonry work on the walls, developing the colonial/rustic style of the region. This generates a warm and inviting atmosphere with all the comforts and necessities of a boutique hotel. Panamericana Sur Km. 55, Tel: 593-3-271-9348, Fax: 593-3-271-9902, E-mail: haciendahatoverde@hotmail.com, URL: www.haciendahatoverde.com.

HACIENDA EL PORVENIR (ROOMS $40-100)

Hacienda El Porvenir, is located one and a half hours from Quito, on the slopes of Rumiñahui Volcano, and is a mere four kilometers from the northern entrance of Cotopaxi National Park. A beautiful traditional Andean hacienda that provides comfortable rooms, built using materials such as brick, straw, wood and adobe. San Ignacio N27-127, Tel: 593-2-3237372, Fax: 593-2-223-1806, E-mail: info@tierradelvolcan.com, URL: www.tierradelvolcan.com.

VOLCANO LAND ($40-100/PERSON)

In Cotopaxi province is Volcano Land, a small hacienda specializing in adventure travel. It is about an hour and forty minutes from Quito. Visitors leave the highway near Machachi and continue up the road for another half hour. The hostería complex boasts a social area/mess hall, a store where you can purchase necessities and souvenirs and a working farm, where hotel guests are encouraged to help out with daily activities such as milking. The rooms are small, but cozy and neat. Volcano Land caters to tourists with a bit more cash than the typical backpacker. Specialists in adventure travel, Volcano Land offers horseback riding, birdwatching, trekking, camping and other outdoor activities. Volcano Land has adventures and activities for all: from simple walks and hikes to far more difficult challenges. It is even possible to arrange to climb Cotopaxi. Quito Address: San Ignacio 1015 and Gonzáles Suarez, Tel: 593-2-223-1806, E-Mail: info@volcanoland.com, URL: www.volcanoland.com.

HOSTERÍA SAN MATEO (ROOMS: $55-70)

A small, attractive inn located very close to Cotopaxi park, San Mateo is a good option for travelers in the medium price range. Formerly the country home of a high-ranking government official, the building was built in the 1970s and recently converted. There are only seven rooms, so space is limited. San Mateo is a family-friendly hotel, with a playground for children and some bunnies, geese, and other farm animals. The restaurant offers a variety of food, including the house special, a grilled steak served on a hot volcanic stone. Breakfast is superb. Tel: 593-3-271-9015, International: 593-3-2719-015, US Toll Free: 1-877-641-2117, E-mail: info@hosteriasanmateo.com, URL: www.hosteriasanmateo.com.

HOSTERÍA LA CIENEGA (ROOMS: $56-98)

This 400+ year-old hacienda near the base of the famous Cotopaxi Volcano is spacious and caters to the international traveler seeking extra luxury. The walls are made with volcanic rock and have withstood countless tremors from its active volcanic neighbor. There are 32 rooms which are a mixture of double rooms, junior suites and luxury suites. All have private bathrooms, hot water, telephones and heaters. The hacienda's restaurant serves international cuisine. Other facilities include a chapel—mainly used for weddings—two seminar rooms, a bar, sports facilities and gardens. Among the activities available at La Ciénega are: sport fishing, hikes and horseback riding. Quito office: Cordero 1442 and Av. Amazonas, Edif. Fuente Azul, Tel: 593-2-254-1337, Fax: 593-2-222-8820.

HACIENDA LEITO (ROOMS: $85-160)

Whether you're an adventurer in search of a relaxing break or a couple looking for a romantic getaway, Hacienda Leito can cater to your needs. This spectacular hacienda is located just three hours south of Quito and conveniently close to Ecuador's rainforest, as well as the hulking Tungurahua Volcano. It offers a spectacular setting coupled with a warm, family atmosphere. Bright spacious rooms appointed with tasteful antique furniture boast soft, comfy beds that promise a restful sleep. (Did we mention that all rooms have a fireplace?) Kick back and relax in the charming social spaces, or request a tailor-made tour: the hacienda can arrange hiking, horseback riding, river rafting, biking and cultural expeditions. From nature lovers and active travlers to families and photographers, this place has something for everyone. Kilometer 8 on the way to Leito, Tel: 593-3-285-9329 / 593-3-285-9331, E-mail: llanganates@andinanet.net, URL:www.haciendaleito.com.

SAN AGUSTÍN DE CALLO (ROOMS STARTING AT: $195)

San Agustín de Callo is one of the most intriguing haciendas available in Ecuador. Originally the site of a pre-Columbian Inca residence, it is one of few important Inca archaeological sites in Ecuador. Originally built around 1440, it is specifically mentioned in the chronicles of Pedro Cieza de León, a Spanish conquistador who wrote a narrative describing his travels in the mid-sixteenth century. The Spanish built on the site, which was given to the Augustinian religious order in 1590 before becoming private property. It has been in the Plaza family (which boasts two Ecuadorian presidents) since 1921. The University of Texas has an ongoing archaeological project at the hacienda. Like most haciendas, it has spacious rooms, beautiful gardens, full dining, and good service. The rooms and suites are particularly elegant, and boast names like Inca Tambo Suite and Bonpland Room. Some of the rooms even feature original Inca stonework walls. Highway 5 km from the entrance to Cotopaxi National Park, Tel: 593-2-290-6157, E-Mail: info@incahacienda.com, URL: www.incahacienda.com

AMBATO

Ambato, which is located about an hour and a half south of Quito, tends to be more of a bus stopover than a tourist destination. Rightfully so, there is little for tourists to see or do in Ambato. If you do happen to need to spend some time in the city, there is a selection of hotels, restaurants and a museum or two to keep you occupied. However, you are really better off taking the 80 cent bus to Baños, which is a much livelier town, and spending the night there. Carnival is the exception to this rule. Ambato holds a huge festival, called "Fiesta de las flores y las frutas." It is usually held during the last two weeks of February. During the festival, there are colorful parades and other festivities such as bullfights. If you choose to come to Ambato during this celebration, be sure to book early, because accommodations tend to fill up quickly.

GETTING TO AND AWAY

The bus station in Ambato is located about 2 km north of the Centro on Ave. Columbia and Paraguay. The phone number is 593-3-282-1841. It is one of the more major bus hubs in Ecuador, and there are daily buses to Guayaquil, Quito, Baños, Cuenca, Latacunga, Santo Domingo, Riobamba, Guaranda, Tena, Macas, Puyo, Loja, Machala and Esmeraldas. To get to the Centro from the bus station, walk up the hill from the bus stop and take a right at the first major road. Cross the railroad track, and follow the signs to the Centro.

LODGING

Although there are plenty of accommodation options in Ambato, most are overpriced and dingy. Many places seem to have been decorated at the height of the 70s. By your Grandma. However, if you can look past the décor, they are fairly comfortable for a night or two stay. Most of the hotels are located in El Centro, so if you get to town without a reservation, cruise down and find a place. They are rarely booked, with the exception of Carnival, when a reservation is necessary for any hotel in town.

GRAN HOTEL (ROOMS: $15-20)

A fine option, although it is priced a little on the high side for what you get. The rooms are clean and spacious, a bit oddly decorated, but perfectly acceptable. Ample amenities are provided; there are televisions, phones and bathrooms in all the rooms. Also, breakfast is included in the price of a room. Rocafuerte 11-33, Tel: 593-3-282-5915.

HOTEL SEÑORIAL (ROOMS: $24-29)

Hotel Señorial may have odd decor, seemingly right out of a bad 80s film, but once you look past the pastel colors, you can see it is a perfectly nice place to stay. The rooms are well-kept, quiet and large. The large windows provide a good amount of light, giving the rooms a brighter feel. All their rooms have cable television, which is a must while staying in Ambato, as there is unfortunately, little to do at night. Cevallos and Quito, Tel: 593-3-282-5124 / 282-6249.

HOTEL AMBATO (ROOMS: $40-60)

Hotel Ambato is the fanciest place in town, with a price to match. If you happen to be in town, and have a decent sized budget, this is probably your best choice of a place to stay. The rooms are large and modern, all with private bathrooms. There are suites available. The hotel conveniently located in El Centro near to restaurants and shops. There is a café, restaurant and casino located on site. Guayaquil and Rocafuerte, Tel: 593-3-242-1791, URL: www.hotelambato.com.

RESTAURANTS

El Centro is the place with the greatest concentration of restaurants in Ambato, particularly chicken restaraunts. Everywhere you look you will see a different restaurant roasting up chickens. You can also find cuy, pizza and even shawarmas in Ambato. If you are only in town for a while, wander downtown for a gelato. There are a few shops that sell it, and they are cheap, at about 50 cents for a cone. If you happen to be in Ambato overnight, there are a couple of bars that have a bit of a nightlife that you could check out. El Coyote is a discoteca that is located on Bolívar and Guayaquil. Cerveceria Bufalo, located on Olmedo and Mera, is another option for either drinking or dancing.

OASIS CAFÉ AND HELADOS DE PAILA (SNACKS: $1-3)

This lovely café, hidden by being a little off the strip, specializes in gelato. It is sharply decorated, with simple modern fixtures, and is probably the hippest place in town. Their gelatos come in a variety of yummy flavors, and a simple cone only costs 50 cents. You can't beat a bargain like that! This café is a lovely place to spend a few hours relaxing with desert and a coffee catching up on some reading. Mariano Egüez Antonio and Jose de Sucre.

CUBANO'S PIZZA (ENTREES: $1.50-2)

Cubano's is a chain pizza company in the city of Ambato, with a couple of locations around the area. The pizza is nothing to write home about, but it is cheap, so those on a budget may want to stop by for a snack. The restaurant does not hold a large amount of ambiance, but it is clean and simple. Personal size pizzas only cost between $1.50 and $2 and come in the usual variety of flavors. Calle Quito and Pedro Fermin Cevallos.

NOCHES DE ARABIA
Noches de Arabia is a small restaurant without a whole lot of ambiance. Despite the plastic tables, this is a good place to stop, get a snack and have a few beers in the afternoon or evening. The specialty is shawarma, but other Middle Eastern cuisine is offered as well. Everything is well-priced, making it perfect for the traveler on a budget. 18-31 Pedro Fermin Cevallos.

GRAN ÁLAMO (ENTREES: $4-6)
This cozy restaurant feels straight out of the Wild West with its all wooden walls and large wooden booths. Even the décor has a definite old-time American feel. However, one look at the menu and you will be reminded that you are indeed still in Ecuador. The restaurant serves up mostly Ecuadorian cuisine, your normal rice and meat sort of entrees. However, the food is tasty and portion sizes are good. The restaurant has also has a full bar, making it a good choice for an evening cocktail or two. Entrees run between four and six dollars, and credit cards are accepted. 17-19 Pedro Fernub Cevakkis, Tel: 593-3-282-4704.

BAÑOS
Baños is one of the most popular tourist destinations in the Ecuadorian Sierra. Its full name, Baños de Agua Santa (literally, "baths of the holy waters") reflects the natural hot springs running off neighboring Volcán Tungurahua (5,023 m, 16,480 ft). The town is surrounded by a curtain of bright green mountains, rich in waterfalls, flora and fauna. There are natural hot springs under the waterfall splashing into town which, unlike the clear hot springs in Papallacta, are a chocolate brown color and almost always packed to capacity. The town is full of hostels, restaurants and cafés.

With plenty of hiking, bike paths, spas and tours, it is not hard to find something to do. Activities include tours outside of town. Tourism in Baños hit a pretty serious bump when, in 1999, the Tungurahua volcano burst to life and the city was evacuated. For almost two years, tourism was brought to an almost complete stand-still as residents and travelers alike held their breath and waited for the inevitable explosion. It never came, and life slowly trickled back to this small mountain town.

There is, however, a threat of volcanic activity. Heightened activity was reported in May 2006, followed shortly afterwards in July and August 2006 with eruptions that required evacuation of the surrounding villages, although the residents of Baños were reluctant to leave. Though the volcano has since been emitting ominous gurgles and ashy plumes of smoke, activity has been limited to taunting the town and its visitors with such displays.

Check for news on volcanic activity before visiting Baños. The Smithsonian keeps a running watch on activity worldwide on their website: www.volcano.si.edu. As much of Ecuador lives under the threat of volcanic eruption, you may be surprised at the relaxed attitude locals have toward their fiery neighbor.

THINGS TO SEE & DO
With striking natural beauty and an adventuresome crowd, there's no shortage of things to do in Baños.

Tours to view the naturally illuminated Tungurahua Volcano, which should only be taken on very clear nights, depart every night at 9 p.m. and return at 11 p.m. If there are any clouds, you won't be able to see the volcano at all. There are two basic tours to choose from: a chiva tour and a van tour. The Chiva Tour is generally $1 cheaper, at $3, and while it doesn't offer the highest lookout, it does include music, a campfire and hot chocolate or coffee. The van

CENTRAL ANDES

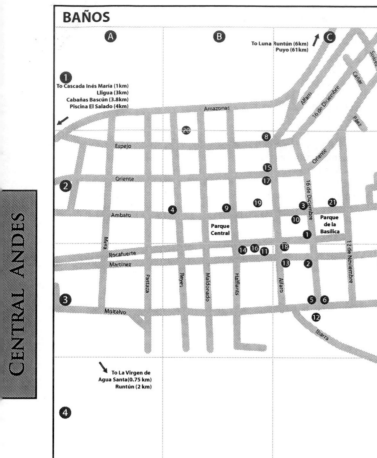

BAÑOS

LODGING 🛏

1. HOSTAL RESIDENCIAL LUCY
2. HOSPEDAJE SANTA CRUZ
3. ROSS HOTEL
4. HOTEL EL BELÉN
5. LA PETITE AUBERGE
6. GALA HOTEL
7. LA POSADA DEL ARTE
8. HOSTAL DONDE IVÁN

RESTAURANTS 🍴

9. BLAH BLAH CAFÉ
10. LA ABUELA CAFÉ
11. CASA HOOD
12. PANCHO VILLA
13. SWISS BISTRO
14. RINCÓN DE SUIZA
15. TALMANA'S

16. SUPERMERCADO SANTA MARÍA NEW

NIGHTLIFE 🍸

17. LEPRECHAUN BAR

TRANSPORT 🚌

18. BUS STOP FOR AGOYÁN
19. BUS STOP FOR PISCINA EL SALADO
20. BUS TERMINAL

THINGS TO SEE & DO

21. BASÍLICA DE NUESTRA SEÑORA DE AGUA SANTA
22. PISCINA DE LA VIRGEN

tour, at \$4, gives you a better chance to see the volcano. However, if there offers no alternative to staring at the cloudy horizon while standing on t Bring a jacket, it is cool at night.

Tour agencies fill pretty much every block in Baños offering every varie from bungee jumping off bridges to rafting and everything in-between Basin are also popular.

RAFTING IN BAÑOS

Baños has programs for rafting for beginners through to experts—the river Pastaza is an exciting river with decent rapids. The company Team Adventure provides good rafting trips. Rafting for a half day runs at about \$35 per person. Oriente and Thomas Halflans, Tel: 593-3-274-2195, E-mail: teamfulladventure@yahoo.com, URL: www.teamecuador.com.

BUNGEE JUMP/FALL

This is not quite as scary as a bungee jump, but just hairy enough to get your heart beating and your legs wobbly. Carlos will strap you in and give you the choice of whether you want to jump off the bridge facing forwards or fall backwards. Falling backwards is not nearly as scary as going forward. You are harnessed to a rope, so you swing under the bridge instead of bouncing back up. It's not as jarring as bungee jumping. A jump will cost you \$10 or so. Approximately 5 km outside of Baños on the road to Puyo. Ask any shop offering tours in Baños.

BIKE RIDE TO PUYO

For the more athletic traveler, there is the option to rent bicycles and ride 60 km from Baños to Puyo in a single day. Allegedly, the bike ride is mostly downhill, but it seems to be equal parts uphill and downhill. The good news is you can catch a bus heading to Baños at any point on the ride and head back into town if you can't make it all the way.

The ride is wonderful—in the first 20 km or so, there are many different waterfalls of all shapes and sizes that culminate in the powerful El Pailón del Diablo waterfall, at about 17 km into the ride. The ride is beautiful along the river and you can stop to bridge jump with locals. Further on, you can stop to ride the cable car across the valley to see another waterfall or wander through the lush greenery and flowers.

A few things to know before you do the ride: you will be sharing the highway with speedy, if not suicidal, truck and bus drivers. At some points, you will have to go through pitch-black tunnels with the traffic. It can be very frightening. There is always the risk of your bike breaking down or being faulty in some way and it may rain, leaving you in between towns and nowhere to take cover. You can always catch a bus and head back to Baños. The ride can take anywhere from five to eight hours, depending how long you dilly-dally at each waterfall. To rent a bike costs approximately \$5.

EL REFUGIO SPA

For a one-of-a-kind spa experience that won't break the bank, an afternoon at El Refugio is a must. The Bohemian-friendly spa compound is nestled deep in the tranquil valley under the Tungurahua volcano and overlooking the Río Pastaza, about 2 kilometers outside of Baños just off the road to Puyo. Choose from a full menu of á la carte treatments, including: mud baths, massage and ear candling, or treat yourself to the whole package for \$45. Treatments start with a visit to a lookout point facing a mountainside, where all are encouraged to let it all go with a scream into the ethers of the valley. For a memorably invigorating experience, try the *baños de cajón*—for \$5, you'll be seated in an enclosed sauna box with only your head poking out of the top while hot vapors deep cleanse your pores. Every 15 minutes, you'll be doused with icy-cool water before returning to the warmth of the box—amazingly refreshing, and letting out a few yelps as the water meets your face is all part of the fun. Couple a cleansing with a soothing hot-stone message for a relaxing full body experience. Camino Real and Barrio San Vicente, Tel: 593-3-2740-482, Cell: 593-9-7850-607, E-mail: info@spaecuador.info.

> **!VA Member Review-El Refugio Spa**
> A really unique and invigorating "spa" experience. A wonderful way to spend an afternoon soothing tired biking legs or aching rafting muscles, without shelling out a bunch of cash. Try the baños de cajon! 22 March 2007. Maine, USA.

LODGING

Hotels in Baños are, in general, exceptionally affordable and abundant, except during Ecuadorian holidays when nationals flock to the area to enjoy the exceptional climate and numerous activities. During the holiday seasons, advanced reservations are a must, but the rest of the year, one normally has their pick of where to stay. There are hotels in Baños for every price range, but value is good. You get what you pay for, so don't hesitate to look around before deciding where to stay.

HOSTAL RESIDENCIAL 'LUCY' ($3-10/PERSON)

A family-run hotel with some of the cheapest rates in Baños, Hostal Residencial Lucy has dark, dank rooms with saggy mattresses and tiny bathrooms. On the plus side, it is well-located, right between the two plazas and half a block from the supermarket. There is also cable TV in every room. There is no checkout time; you can leave whenever you want. Prices double during Carnival (end of February) and Semana Santa (the week leading up to Easter). Rocafuerte 240 and 16 de Diciembre, Tel: 593-3-274-0466.

HOSPEDAJE SANTA CRUZ ($5.50-7.50/PERSON)

Hospedaje Santa Cruz has two locations in Baños, both on 16 de Diciembre just south of Martinez and across from Le Petit Auberge. Both are pretty much the same, although the southern branch is $1 cheaper (maybe because it's a few steps farther than the center of town). With a community lounge, fireplace, garden and self-service drinks and cocktails, the atmosphere is relaxed and cozy. The paint jobs in some rooms are fairly eccentric uses of spray paint, but are full of personality. A continental breakfast is served in the morning for $2. Additionally, there are hammocks to lounge in, a kitchen area and a garden with tables to sunbathe. 16 de Diciembre and Luis A. Martínez, Tel: 593-3-274-0648, E-mail: santacruzhostal@yahoo.com.

HOTEL EL BELEN ($6-15/PERSON)

Hotel El Belen, about two blocks from the bus station on Reyes, is a cozy, comfortable hotel with cable TV in every room, a small hot tub and steam bath. An on-site cafeteria offers breakfasts. Prices raise during Carnival at the end of February and during Semana Santa, the week leading up to Easter from $6 per person to $15. Oscar Efren Reyes and Ambato, Tel: 593-3-274-1024, E-mail: info@hotel-elbelen.com, URL: www.hotel-elbelen.com.

ROSS HOTEL (ROOMS: $10)

A four-story building on the main plaza, Ross Hotel was officially opened December 2004. Inspired by big-chain American hotels, the owner has added some interesting features you won't find in any other hotel in Baños, like a breakfast buffet (included), cable TV and DVD players in every room (and a free DVD rental in the reception). Ask for a room with a view of the plaza and the waterfall in the distance. Room service from the sandwich shop downstairs is available 24 hours. 16 de Diciembre and Ambato, Tel: 593-3-274-1709.

HOSTAL DONDE IVAN (ROOMS: $12)

The highlight of this place is its third floor restaurant, with a spectacular panoramic view of the countryside. A terrace garden, located on the fourth and fifth floor, is also a great place to sit and relax with a good book or friends. The hostal has single, double and triple rooms (all with hot water) and a restaurant, where you can eat your fill of traditional Ecuadorian fare. Laundry service and luggage store are available, as well as bicycle, horseback riding or rafting excursions. Eloy Alfaro 10-22 and Espejo, Cell: 593-9-972-2445, E-mail: dondeivanres@yahoo.com.

La Petite Auberge (Rooms: $9-14)

La Petite Auberge is a pleasant, peaceful hotel tucked in a garden with views of the mountains towering over Baños. Relax in the garden, chat with other travelers by the fireplace in the lounge or exchange books in English, French, Dutch, German and Hebrew (the deal is give two books, get one). The per person price includes a continental breakfast in Le Petit Restaurant of french bread, homemade marmalade, juice and coffee. All credit cards are accepted with a $20 minimum and a 10% surcharge. Prices bump up about $3 if you are traveling alone. Calle 16 de Diciembre 240 and Montalvo, Tel: 593-3-274-0936, E-mail: lepetitbanos@yahoo.com.

Gala Hotel (Rooms: $10-15)

Gala Hotel was opened in November 2004 on a quiet street to the southeast of the center of Baños. With a sterile, modern feel, the hotel makes up for what it lacks in character in comfort and cleanliness. The rooms are spacious and all have TVs with cable. Ask for one of the two rooms with a balcony and view of the mountains and waterfall. The highlight is Pancho Villa, a delicious Mexican restaurant, on the ground floor of the hotel. The per person rate of $10 jumps up to $15 during Carnival and Semana Santa (the week before Easter). Av. 16 de Diciembre and Juan Montalvo, Tel: 593-3-274-2870.

La Posada del Arte (Rooms: $16-48)

For art aficionados and discriminating travelers, La Posada del Arte is certainly a Baños gem. In addition to comfy beds and plenty of hot water, the hostel has a cozy sala where you can relax, listen to music or read in front of an inviting fireplace. The hostel is also a showcase for Ecuadorian paintings, including work by artists like Whitman, Soriano, Rueda, Endara and Sanchez. When your tummy starts to rumble, head to the hostel's restaurant, which features traditional Ecuadorian dishes, and international plates like curries and pasta. Vegetarian options are also available. If you're in the mood to learn more about the city, the friendly staff can arrange a tour. The owner is particularly knowledgeable about treks and trails through the area, and even has a notebook full of helpful maps he's made himself. Calle Velasco Ibarra and Av. Montalvo, Tel: 593-3-327-4083, E-mail: artehostal@yahoo.com, URL: www.posadadelarte.com.

Luna Runtun (Rooms: $70-245)

A gorgeous luxury spa set in the mountains above Baños with views of the Tungurahua volcano, Luna Runtun is 6 km off the main road from Baños to Puyo. To get there from Baños, get a taxi, rent a car or make arrangements through a tour company. You can stay in Baños and go to the spa as a day trip, or stay at the spa as long as you like. Services offered at the spa include body treatments like volcanic ash and salt exfoliation, honey exfoliation, or rose bath from $15-25; massages from $14-36; facials for $15; hair care; manicures and pedicures for $10; and waxing for $5-15. For overnight guests, rooms range in price from $70-245 per room which includes a welcome cocktail, dinner, breakfast and full use of the sauna. Caserío Runtun Km 6, P.O. Box 18-02-1944, Tel: 593-3-274-0882, Fax: 593-3-274-0376, E-mail: carmen@lunaruntun.com, URL: www.lunaruntun.com.

Restaurants

Talmana's

Serving up scrumptious soups, salads and sandwiches, including vegetarian options, Talmana's is a good place for cheaper meals that don't skimp on service. The chilled out music and friendly atmosphere is an added bonus. Calle Oriente and Eloy Alfaro, Cell: 593-9-410-2600, E-mail: talmana@gmail.com.

Rincón de Suiza (Snacks: $1-3)

Rincón de Suiza has excellent coffee, homemade cakes, Swiss specialties, fruit juices and smoothies, cocktails, wines and liquors, fine tobaccos, billard/pool tables, table games, sofa corner, newspapers, magazines, book exchange and a pleasant and cozy atmosphere. Luis A. Martinez, Tel: 593-3-274-2807, E-mail: cafeteria@rincondesuiza.com, URL: www.rincondesuiza.com.

BLAH BLAH CAFÉ (ENTREES: $2-5)
Blah Blah Café has graced Baños for more than 10 years. With magazines and books in English and Spanish, incense and music, the café has an incredibly relaxed and comfortable environment. The cappuccino is excellent and there are several snack-like food options (sandwiches, breakfasts, salads, etc.) including a good selection for vegetarians. T. Halflants and Ambato, Tel: 593-9-924-3723.

CASA HOOD (ENTREES: $3-6)
With a long history in Baños, Casa Hood is one of the best spots for delicious international cuisine, coffee, drinks, desserts, books or just a relaxing time. The book exchange, while not the biggest in Ecuador, maintains a high level of quality by only allowing exchanges for books of similar caliber. Movies are shown almost every night at 8 p.m. Luis A. Martinez (behind the supermarket), Cell: 593-9-462-0269.

> *V!VA Member Review-Casa Hood*
> *A great place to chill out. Drink some of their great teas, their food is very tasty and spicy, just great. 27 June 2007. Germany.*

PANCHO VILLA
Pancho Villa is located in the southeast corner of the city. The decor is an eclectic mix of posters of Ecuador, Mexico and everything in between. Outdoor seating is available. Montalvo and 16 de Diciembre, Tel: 593-3-274-2870.

LA ABUELA CAFÉ
La Abuela Café is a small café that has a great selection of breakfasts from $1.90 to $2.90. For lunch and dinner, there are simple dishes like salad, sandwiches and pizza, but not much selection for vegetarians. Try the pancakes. Eloy Alfaro between Ambato and Oriente, Cell: 593-9-965-4365.

SWISS BISTRO (ENTREES: $5-6)
Specializing in culinary creations from Switzerland and other parts of Europe, this restaurant features an extensive menu that is sure to please even the most difficult of palates. Some might say that the meat or cheese fondues are a highlight, but you would have to first try the Beef Stroganov, Chicken Cordon Bleu, or fresh Steamed Trout, to be sure. Of course, you would probably also have to sample one of their delicious soups or salads as well. What is certain, however, is that no meal is complete without one of the Swiss Bistro's desserts, which are sure to tickle the sweet tooth. Choose from a variety of treats, including special Swiss ice cream and banana flambé. The restaurant also features a variety of Argentinian and Chilean wines, beers, juices and gourmet coffees (and of course hot chocolate!). Calle Martinez and Alfaro, Cell: 593-9-400-4019.

NIGHTLIFE
LEPRECHAUN BAR (DRINKS: $1-3)
A small, but fun bar in the heart of Baños. There is no cover and a welcome flaming shot if you get in early. Leprechaun Bar has a bumping dance floor on the weekends featuring salsa, merengue, hip hop, rock and more. Eloy Alfaro and Oriente.

AROUND BAÑOS
RÍO VERDE

Río Verde is about 17 km south of Baños. An area rich in waterfalls and lush vegetation, most travelers see this area on a day trip from Baños by bike, tour bus, chiva, scooter or motorbike. The biggest waterfall in the area, El Pailón del Diablo is the stopping point to the south for most tours from Baños and features a less than 1 km path leading through the forest and to the waterfall as well as some restaurants and lodges set deep in the woods.

EL PAILÓN DEL DIABLO

A beautiful waterfall about 1 km off the main road from Baños to Puyo, El Pailón del Diablo (the Devil's Cauldron) is well worth the day trip from Baños. Don't miss the cable car (or, more appropriately, cable basket) to see the Manta de Novia waterfall (Bride's Veil Waterfall) on the way. The walk down to El Pailón del Diablo costs $1 roundtrip and is well-worth the views directly over the waterfall. Park at the Restaurante las Hortensias just after a small bridge and head downhill on a small footpath which weaves through beautiful cloud forest for less than 1 km until you reach a suspended bridge. You can view the waterfall from the bridge, or, for 50 cents, pass through El Otro Lado restaurant and walk on their private path until you are almost close enough to touch the waterfall. There is great birdwatching and you will see a variety of butterflies and orchids along the way. El Otro Lado and El Pailón Restaurant have small cafés and a few rooms which are between $10-15 per person per night.

Large flatbed trucks often park in front of the Hotensias restaurant offering rides back to Baños (around $1.50 per person). The bus is much cheaper, but you will save the trek to the main road. Río Verde, 17 km de Baños to Puyo.

EL PAILÓN RESTAURANT

The owners of this small restaurant have taken the initiative to carve out paths through the cloud forest leading to the waterfall Pailón del Diablo. For 50 cents, you can take a walk through the forest lined with orchids until you are almost close enough to reach out your hand and touch the waterfall. The restaurant itself doesn't have a view of the waterfall, but has open-air seating looking out at the lush forest hills. Rio Verde 17 Km Via Banos, Tel: 593-3-288-4204.

RESTAURANTE LAS HORTENSIAS

Right off the main road from Baños to Puyo and the entrance to the path down to Pailón del Diablo, Restaurante Las Hortensias offers typical Ecuadorian cuisine like trout, grilled chicken and *churrascos* (beef with a fried egg on top). This restaurant is a perfect place to park your bike or scooter and catch your breath before heading down to see the waterfall.

EL OTRO LADO (ROOMS: $35)

This open-air restaurant has great views of the waterfall and is a perfect place to build up energy for the hike back up to the road. The cabañas sleep four. El Otro Lado restaurant has appetizers, salads, Mexican dishes and some vegetarian dishes all for under $4. One kilometer off the main road from Baños to Puyo, on the path to the Pailón del Diablo waterfall, just across the suspended bridge, Tel: 593-3-228-4193, Cell: 593-9-261-4798, E-mail: pmalopozo@hotmail.com.

HACIENDA MANTELES (ROOMS: $45-50)

An elegant, full service hostería located about a half-hour from Baños. First constructed in 1580, Hacienda Manteles is one of the oldest in Ecuador. It is relatively small, with only ten rooms, each with private bath and hot water. Because of its location, Manteles is home to several species of hummingbirds and orchids. There is an on-site restaurant, specializing in traditional cuisine. The hacienda owns 250 acres of rainforest, and part of the profits go to preservation. The hacienda also offers activities such as horseback riding, bird watching and "agriculture day," in which guests are encouraged to participate in the planting and care of local crops. Breakfast is included, along with a welcome cocktail and coffee. Cell: 593-9-871-5632, E-mail: info@haciendamanteles.com, URL:www.haciendamanteles.com.

CENTRAL ANDES

CHIMBORAZO

At 6,310 meters (20,702 ft), Chimborazo is the highest mountain in Ecuador and—thanks to the equatorial bulge—its peak enjoys the distinction of being the furthest point from the center of the Earth. Chimborazo is actually an extinct volcano that is believed to have last erupted some 10,000 years ago. The volcano's massive glacier persists but it has dwindled in recent years due to global climate change and ongoing eruptions of near Tungurahua, which spews black ash onto the Chimborazo's eastern slopes. This causes it to conduct more of the sun's heat and thus melt at a greater than normal rate. Despite the snowcap's decline, Chimborazo's white crown is still among the most beautiful sights in Ecuador.

GETTING THERE FROM QUITO

Chimborazo is located approximately 150 kilometers southwest of Quito. The best way to reach the mountain is via a dirt road that branches off southeast from the Ambato-Guaranda road.

Take the Pan American highway south to Ambato and then head southwest towards Guaranda. About 56 kilometers from Ambato, you will arrive at a dirt road that leads to the Whymper refuge, named after Edward Whymper, the British climber who made the first ascent of Chimborazo in 1880. This juncture is sometimes referred to as *el cruce del Arenal* and is marked by a deserted block house. The road winds 12 kilometers across the windblown countryside to a parking area and lower refuge below the Whymper refuge.

If you do not have a vehicle, you can take a bus to "El Cruce del Arenal" and walk to the lower refuge via the main dirt road or cross country. If you decide to take the cross-country route, walk southeast on the dirt road for about four kilometers until you come to a sharp bend where you must turn left and climb due east for approximately four more kilometers until you see the lower refuge and parking area. This takes approximately four hours. You can also hire transportation from Ambato or Riobamba. Riobamba is more pleasant than Ambato and offers a better selection of accommodation and restaurants. The trip to the parking area directly from Quito takes between three and four hours in a four-wheel drive vehicle. Hiking to the Whymper refuge is straightforward and takes about 45 minutes from the parking area.

SUMMITING CHIMBORAZO

Though Chimborazo is not Ecuador's most technically difficult climb, it requires previous glacier experience, knowledge of the complete array of climbing gear, stamina and adequate acclimatization. Climbers should make ascents of other nearby peaks, such as Iliniza Norte and Cotopaxi, and consider spending a couple of nights at the Whymper refuge to properly acclimatize.

Chimborazo has five summits: Whymper Peak (6,310 m), Veintimilla Summit (6,267 m), North Summit (6,200 m), Central Summit (6,000 m) and Eastern Summit (5,500 m). Most people that make the effort to climb Chimborazo choose to try for its highest point, Whymper Peak. There are several routes to Whymper Peak, and they vary slightly year-to-year because of the ever-changing glacier.

Climbers usually depart from Whymper refuge at midnight to make the eight to 10-hour slog to the summit. Generally, the route takes you to the left of Thielman Glacier to El Corredor which begins just below some large rock outcroppings. Traverse right of these outcroppings, and then climb left up a steep snowfield until you reach another large rock outcropping called El Castillo. From here, ascend northwest toward the Veintimilla summit. The final leg of the climb changes frequently due to a shifting, large crevasse, so it is strongly advised to go with a local guide who knows the current route. The descent takes between two and four hours.

LODGING

CHIMBORAZO HILL STAR (ROOMS: $40)

The Historical "Tambo de Totorillas" (roadside inn) was once located in this place, along the old "Royal Road" between Guayaquil and Quito. The owners have rebuilt the inn, combining its traditional architecture with modern comfort and services. The shelter is at the center of the base camp a place where guests can rest, eat and acclimatize comfortably. Professional mountain guides can be provided to climb to the summits of the Chimborazo and Carihuayrazo, along with naturalist guides for high mountain and wasteland excursions in the mountains areas and in the páramo. Next to the mountain refuge "Chimborazo Hill Star," a few meters from the creek, there are two cabins named "Condor" and "Curiquingue" after the two Andean birds. All construction was made by using materials from the region and preserving the native architecture from the wasteland. Each cabin has four double bedrooms, two full bathrooms—one per floor—and a small family room with a wonderful view. Urb. "Las Abras" Km.3 vía a Guano, Riobamba, Tel: 593-3-296-4915 / 593-3-294-0818, E-mail: marcocruz@andinanet.net, URL: www.expediciones-andinas.com.

> V!VA Member Review-Chimborazo Hill Star
> The refugio surroundings really do look like the pictures in the write-up. It is bitterly cold, and the altitude is high, making everything more difficult, but the scenery and sense of isolation is absolutely amazing. When we woke up in the morning, there were llamas grazing in the immediate areas surrounding the buildings. 1 June 2006. England.

RIOBAMBA
Broad streets and aging, but still-charming colonial buildings characterize this buzzing town situated in the heart of the central Andes. The capital of Chimborazo Province, Riobamba is a commercial hub and cultural center for both nearby indigenous communities and the city's more European-styled constituents. It was originally located 20 kilometers south—until an earthquake leveled it in 1797. Today's Riobamba features several attractive cathedrals, plazas and parks, including the noteworthy Parque Maldonado, Parque Sucre, Parque Guayaquil and Santa Bárbara Cathedral. On clear days, the city boasts unparalleled views of five of the region's volcanic peaks: Chimborazo, Altar, Tungurahua, Carihuairazo and Sangay. (Find a hotel with a rooftop terrace and spend the morning savoring the stunning view). Saturday is market day, when indigenous people from all over come to sell their wares.

While the market in Plaza de la Concepción (Orozco and Colón, south of the Convento de la Concepción) is geared towards tourists, the San Alfonso (Argentinos and 5 de Junio) and La Condamine (Carabobo and Colombia) markets are also worthwhile stops, especially if you're looking for fresh fruit or traditional textiles. Despite its agreeable, laidback-but-busy atmosphere, Riobamba is probably more known as a gateway to nearby sites than as a destination in itself. You can go off-the-rails with the famous *Nariz del Diablo* (Devil's Nose) train ride, venture into the wilds of nearby Chimborazo, or trail-blaze through the northern stretch of Parque Nacional Sangay.

GETTING TO AND AWAY
The bus station is located about 2 km north of El Centro in Riobamba on León Borja. It is feasible to walk from the station to the city's center, but if it is late at night or you have a lot of luggage, it is probably best to just take a taxi. There are regular buses from the terminal to Quito (4.5 hours), Guayaquil (5 hours), Cuenca (7 hours), Guaranda (2.5 hours) and Santo Domingo (5.5 hours). As usual with Ecuador, the fares will run you about a dollar per hour.

THINGS TO SEE & DO
NARIZ DEL DIABLO
El Nariz del Diablo, or The Devil's Nose, is the highlight of a fantastic rail trip that meanders through the rich tapestry of cultivated fields and páramo spread across the southern half of Ecuador's 400-kilometer long Central Valley, aptly christened "The Avenue of the Volcanoes" in 1802 by the German explorer Alexander Von Humboldt. The journey begins in Riobamba. The train travels south from Chimborazo through a number of small villages and large ex-

CENTRAL ANDES

panses of open country before arriving at the small town of Alausí, where it begins a hair-raising descent. Most travelers sit on top of the railcars to take advantage of the spectacular vistas provided by the engineers' ingenious solution of carving a series of tight zigzags into the side of the mountain, which allow the train to climb a gradient of 1-in-18 from 1800 to 2600 meters, by going forwards then backwards up the tracks. A hundred years after it was constructed, the steep grade of the Devil's Nose stretch of track precludes its use as a freight or efficient passenger line, but affords the perfect means for present-day explorers who want to discover the rugged and breathtaking Ecuadorian countryside. The train runs on Wednesday, Friday and Sunday and the cost is $11.20. You can buy tickets on the train, but it is suggested to buy them a day earlier, a task for which you may need your passport. It is recommended to be at the station at 6 a.m. although the train departs at 7 a.m. The return train from Alausí to Riobamba is scheduled to leave Alausí at 12.30 p.m. but invariably departs later. Estación de Riobamba, Av. 10 de Agosto and Carabobo, Tel: 593-3-296-1909.

Viva Travel Guides Update: Due to safety concerns, as of April 2007 and until the time of writing, passengers are not allowed to ride on the roof of the train.

LODGING

The majority of tourists who visit Riobamba do so to take the train to Alausí and ride through the famed Devil's Nose. For this reason, the majority of places to stay are concentrated around the train station. If you are on a budget, and will only be in town for a short while, there are a number of cheap hostels. They may not have as many amenities as a fancy hotel, but for one night they tend to do the trick. If you are planning on staying in town for a few days, have a larger budget and are looking for a quiet holiday, it is worth staying at one of the hotels that are located outside of the city of Riobamba. They tend to be fancier, and the scenery is unforgettable.

HOTEL TREN DORADO ($8/PERSON)

Clean bathrooms, spacious comfortable rooms, friendly service and an excellent location makes Hotel Tren Dorado a great place to lay your backpack for a few days while you explore the south-central city of Riobamba. Hotel Tren Dorado is a great value, offering a few room sizes, but regardless of which accomodation you choose, the cost is $8 per person. Painted bright green and pink on the outside, Tren Dorado is hard to miss. Not only convenient to the train station, Tren Dorado is also one of the only places in town that serves up breakfast early enough so that those who have tickets for the train ride can eat breakfast before the 7 a.m. departure. Starting at 5:30 a.m. on Sundays and Wednesdays (the ONLY two days that the train runs), there is a deleicious continental breakfast buffet of bread, fruit, granola, yogurt, coffee, juice and tea. Carabobo 22-35, Tel: 593-3-296-4890, Fax: 593-3-296-4890, E-mail: htrendorado@hotmail.com.

HOSTAL MONTECARLO (ROOMS: $12)

Located only a few blocks from the train station, this is a very convenient and good place to stay. Rooms are comfortable—not the most elegant, but they do the trick. There is also a café on site, which is one of the only two in the city that serve a special early bird breakfast on the days the train runs. The price includes continental breakfast. 25-41 10 de Agosto, Tel: 593-03-295-3204/3-2961-577, Fax: 593-3-296-0557, E-mail: montecarloriobamba@andinanet.net.

HOTEL ZEUS INTERNACIONAL (ROOMS: $24-80)

One of the nicer hotels in Riobamba, but it does have a price tag to match. If you don't mind spending more for a bit more of luxury, then the Hotel Zeus is probably where you will want to stay. However, do know that luxury does not mean 5-star hotel. It may be nicer than other places to stay, but it is nothing amazing. Prices range from $24-80 dollars, depending on your room choice. Suites are available. There is also a restaurant and bar located in the hotel. Ave. Daniel León Borja 41-29, Tel: 593-3-968-036/593-3-968-037/593-3-968-038, E-mail: info@hotelzeus.com.ec.

EL TROJE (ROOMS: $40-60)

Located in the pleasant countryside just 5 minutes from Riobamba, El Troje is a traveler's dream. Rustic meets modern in this lovely hostería, which boasts 48 stylish rooms (fully equipped with TV and phone) and spectacular views of Ecuador's highest peak, Chimborazo. Relax and unwind in the warm and cozy setting, where you can spend the day pampering yourself in the turkish sauna or breaking a sweat on the basketball and volleyball courts. The more adventurous can organize a tour; mountain biking, hiking, trekking and horseback riding expeditions are perfect for exploring the surrounding countryside. After a hard day of trail blazing or lounging by the pool, head to El Troje's charming restaurant, La Arquería. Top-notch local and international cuisine paired with first-class service ensures a memorable dining experience.Kilometer 4.5 via Riobamba-Chambo, Tel: 593-3-296-4572/593-3-296-0826, Fax: 593-3-296-5338, E-mail: sales@eltroje.com, URL: www.eltroje.com.

HOSTERÍA LA ANDALUZA (ROOMS: $40-80)

This charming hotel is located about ten minutes away from Riobamba, and is the perfect place to stay if you want a quiet countryside experience. Located near Chimborazo, you can enjoy its splendor from your hotel room. The hostería offers suites and junior suites as well as regular rooms. All rooms feature a private bathroom, heating system and TV. There is a gym, sauna, steam bath, a bar and restaurant on-site. Panamericana Norte, Tel: 593-3-294-9470.

RESTAURANTS

There is no shortage of places to eat in Riobamba, however most of the restaurants are mom and pop run holes in the walls. Their food usually is not bad, and is cheap, but sanitary conditions often seem questionable. If you are looking for a little nicer place to eat, a walk up the main street in town, 10 de Agosto, will lead you to most of your more upscale (and clean) options. On train days, both the Hotel Tren Dorado and the Hostal Montecarlo offer early bird breakfasts, starting at 5:30am. If you don't have a train to catch early in the morning, or want to party anyways, there are a good selection of discotecas in town.

CAFÉ ORFEO (SNACKS: $2-4)

This Café turns into more of a bar during the night. It is a great place to go if you want a more relaxing night out, instead of a drunken night at the discoteca. They tend to have live music often, especially on the weekends. It is located just one block off of 10 de Agosto, and is very near to the Centro of Riobamba. Primera Constituyente and García Moreno, Cell: 593-9-359-5258.

HOLLYWOOD COFFEE (SNACKS: $2-5)

Perhaps the most random coffee shop in Ecuador, Hollywood Coffee seems to be trying to be a Planet Hollywood meets Starbucks. Outside of the coffee shop, "handprints" of famous people line the sidewalk. Inside it is decorated with various posters of quintessential celebrities such as Marilyn Monroe. The coffee is not great, but at least it is not Nescafé. 10 de Octubre.

ZUCKER CAFÉ (ENTREES: $1.50-4.50)

This restaurant has a definite hipness, with its sleek modern furniture and orange mood lighting. It's the sort of place you would imagine the cool kids come on the weekends to sip fancy drinks and smoke cigarettes. If that is not your scene, a trip during the week will bring you tasty lunch fare, such as sandwiches and crepes. They also have an extensive dessert menu, if you just want to stop in for an afternoon snack. 27-46 10 de Agosto.

D'BAGGIO (ENTREES: $2.60-5)

Anyone who has spent a reasonable amount of time in Ecuador probable knows that generally the pizza is nothing to write home about. D'Baggios is the exception to this rule. A small restaurant, its attempt to look like a quaint Italian eatery may not be spot on, but is endearing. The pizzas are completely homemade in an area in the front of the restaurant. As you sit and wait for your meal, you can watch the chef flipping the dough in the air and whipping pizzas in and out of the wood oven. The delicious pizzas are all made with fresh ingredients. The restaurant also has a selection of pastas. Miguel A León and 10 de Agosto.

PIZZERIA SAN VALENTIN (ENTREES: $3-5)

Pizzeria San Valentin is a downhome, pizza joint that has shadows of an old-school American pizza place, with tasty pizzas, chilled beers and a jukebox. While its trademark is pizza, San Valentin also serves up Mexican food, and while it's not the spicy food that you'd get if you were in Mexico, it's some of the better Mexican food you'll find in Ecuador. A favorite spot for locals to throw back a few beers and chill out, the restaurant also sees its fair share of gringos, as it is on Avenida Leon Borja, the main drag in town. Although a good, comfortable and casual restaurant for just about anyone, families going for dinner should get there early as the place fills up by about 9 p.m., and the music grows louder with each hour. Avenida Leon Borja.

SALINAS

A windy bus ride on dirt roads through the Ecuadorian countryside will bring you to the small town of Salinas. Not to be confused with the beach destination, its official name is Salinas de Bolívar. If you are looking for peaceful relaxing country life in Ecuador, Salinas is the perfect place to see it. The town is famous for its cheese, chocolates, salamis and sweaters. Everything is made in fair-trade factories, which can be visited Monday through Saturday. If you can't make it to the factory, no worries, everything can be bought in a store right off of the main square called Tienda El Salinerito for the same price. One taste of the chocolates and cheeses, and you will be wondering if it would be acceptable to fill up an entire suitcase to bring home. That is, if you don't accidentally eat them all before you even leave Ecuador.

There are few options of places to stay or eat in Salinas, however what is there is acceptably quaint. Nothing is five-star, but you can find clean and cozy accommodations. The restaurants in town all serve typical Ecuadorian cuisine, with daily almuerzo specials.

LODGING

EL REFUGIO

Probably your best option if you are planning to spend a night or two in Salinas. It is located a short, two-block walk from the main plaza. Hot showers are available. Also there is a small restaurant on-site. Be sure to call ahead if you are planning a visit; often, if there are no planned guests, the owners are nowhere to be found. Tel: 593-3-239-0022/3-239-0024.

RESTAURANTS

SCROP

Right at the corner of the main square, this is one of the nicer restaurants in town. It may be small, but it tends to be packed, particularly on the weekends. There is a TV in the corner with cable, which locals seems to enjoy sitting in front of for hours at a time. The food served is your classic Ecuadorian rice and meat, satisfying and well-priced. At night the place is transformed into a bar. The tables are pushed to the side so people can dance to the loud music. If you are spending the night, it is a great place to meet some locals and have a good time.

GUARANDA

Guaranda is best known for its massive Carnival celebration. Carnival, which traditionally falls at the end of February, is the week or so before the beginning of Lent. In Guaranda, there are parades, parties and water-throwing on the streets for about five days before Ash Wednesday. If you want to party during Carnival, Guaranda is the place to go. During the rest of the year, Guaranda is a pretty sleepy town that sees very few tourists. It is a good place to go if you want to see a more authentic view of what a typical life in Ecuador consists of. Be aware though, that you will be an outsider in town—Guaranda sees few travelers throughout the year. Also, if you want to go visit the country village of Salinas, you can catch buses headed that way in Guaranda.

GETTING TO AND AWAY

The bus station in Guaranda is located a little way from the main square. It is walkable, but with your gear, it is probably best to get a cab. There are frequent buses to major cities, such as Guayaquil, Quito, Riobamba and Ambato. There is also daily bus service to the nearby village of Salinas. Times, and number of daily buses vary, so best to check ahead of time to ensure there will be a bus to where you need to go.

LODGING

Accommodation options in Guaranda are a bit sparse, understandably so since it is not a place that draws a huge amount of tourists. There are a few good options to stay in the town, however. Nothing fancy, but definitely acceptable. They are all priced very reasonably; a private room with a bathroom should run you around ten to fifteen dollars. Beware that if you plan to visit the area during Carnival and do not book ahead, you could end up in being a less then savory hotel.

HOSTAL DE LAS FLORES (ROOMS: $8-10)

The Hostal de las Flores offers travelers a friendly comfortable stay in Guaranda. It is housed in a renovated old building, which includes a quaint courtyard in its interior. The rooms are simple, but adequate. All rooms include a television and telephone. It is located near the main square in town, making it easy to get to restaurants in the area, but is far enough away that it tends to be quiet. Pichincha 4-02, Tel: 593-3-298-0644.

HOTEL BOLÍVAR (ROOMS: $8-16)

Hotel Bolívar is another good option for those staying in Guaranda. Rooms are clean and quiet and well priced, between 8 and 16 dollars per night. Plus there is a restaurant and café attached, which sets it apart from other accommodations in the area. It is handy spot to relax with an afternoon coffee or catch a breakfast before a day of exploring the area. Sucre 704 and Rocafuerte, Tel: 593-3-298-0547.

RESTAURANTS

In general, Guaranda has the general small town Ecuador fare, lots of small restaurants serving meat and rice. They are usually a good value, just make sure you are comfortable with the cleanliness of the restaurant—it is often a good indicator of how safe the food is to eat. Also, if you are itching to try cuy, Guaranda has a handful of decent restaurants that sell it for a lower price then you might find in bigger cities such as Quito.

LOS 7 SANTOS

Los 7 Santos is probably the place with the most ambiance in town. It feels like the sort of coffee shop you might find in a hip neighborhood in New York, not Guaranda. They offer coffee, snacks and light meals. Los 7 Santos is a great place to relax and plan out your day, with a good breakfast. The coffee is not the best ever, but that tends to be typical in Ecuador. Convección near 10 de Agosto.

QUESERAS DE BOLÍVAR

If you are unable to get over to Salinas during you stay in the area, definitely plan to visit this shop in Guaranda. It sells a wide selection of the cheeses, chocolates and other goods that are made in the Salinas area. The chocolates are smooth and milky and make a great gift for friends back home. That is, if they don't mysteriously disappear before you get home. They are hard to resist once you have a stash in your backpack. Av Gral Enriquez, Tel: 593-3-298-2205.

ALAUSÍ

Most tourists that end up in Alausí do so to take the famed Devil's Nose train ride. Besides the train ride, there is little to see in this sleepy countryside village. If you arrive on days when the train is not running, you will likely be the only visitor in town—a good opportunity to see typical small town life and chat up a few locals. There is a large statue of St. Peter in town, which is worth hiking up to. Also, there is a hill near the statue which gives a wonderful view of the town. There are a few restaurants in town, which all serve typical Ecuadorian food. There are also a couple of bars that are usually absolutely packed with local men enjoying a fútbol game. The bus and train station in town are located right on the main strip, near all the restaurants, hotels, stores and banks in Alausí.

Restaurants

Trigo Pan
If you are in the mood for a little snack, perhaps something to bring along with you on the train, Trigo Pan is the place to go. This panaderia, or bakery, offers a variety of baked goods, including empanadas, rolls and cakes. They also take orders for specialized baked goods, such as birthday cakes. Probably nothing the average backpacker is ever going to need, but you never know. 5 de Junio and Estaban Orozco, Tel: 593-3-293-1341 / 593-3-293-1398.

Llovy Burger
Conveniently located near the train station, Llovy Burger is the one place in town offering American food. If you can just not stand another dinner of rice and chicken, stop in for a hamburger, hot dog and fries. The food is not amazing, but acceptable—about the grade of any American fast food restaurant out there. The prices are very reasonable, ranging from one to five dollars, depending on what and how much you want. 5 de Junio near the train station.

Cafetería La Higuera
Cafetería La Higuera offers more or less typical Ecuadorian fare. However, its quality seems to be a bit better than most. The portions are large and the food flavorful. It is in particular a good place to catch breakfast before a ride on the train. They have many breakfast special options; the most popular includes eggs, bread, juice and coffee for around 2 bucks. 5 de Junio, near the train station, Tel: 593-3-293-1582, Cell: 593-9-145-7284.

Photo by Caroline Bennett

SOUTHERN ANDES

Leaving the rugged, rumbling volcanoes of the Northern Andes, and heading south along the Panamericana, one enters the softer and slightly more isolated scenery that runs across the impressive Southern Andes. No longer bearing the scars of a violent volcanic past, the region erupts into long, lonely stretches of untamed, uninhabited, historically and culturally rich landscapes. Lower elevations give way to warmer, drier climates, which in tandem with the stunning countryside, make the Southern Andes supreme walking and trekking territory.

The seat of southern culture, and the South's only large urban center, Cuenca is a remarkable city graced with spectacular colonial architecture and a wealth of local artesanía. Just a short shot from Cuenca is Ingapirca, Ecuador's only major Inca ruins.Draped in dramatic scenery and festooned in history and culture, the Southern Andes are amply armed to entertain intrepid trekkers and cultural explorers alike.

Help other travelers. Publish your favorite places at www.vivatravelguides.com

SOUTHERN ANDES

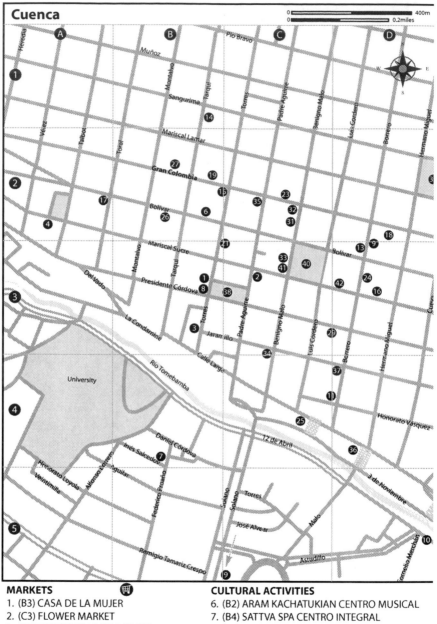

Cuenca

MARKETS 🏪

1. (B3) CASA DE LA MUJER
2. (C3) FLOWER MARKET
3. (B3) MERCADO 10 DE AGOSTO

MUSEUMS 🏛

4. (A2) POPULAR ARTS MUSEUM
5. (E5) PUMAPUNGO MUSEUM

CULTURAL ACTIVITIES

6. (B2) ARAM KACHATUKIAN CENTRO MUSICAL
7. (B4) SATTVA SPA CENTRO INTEGRAL
8. (B3) MAMA KINUA CENTRO CULTURAL
9. (C5) EL SURTIDO ALMACÉN DE MUSICA
10. (D5) MIRADOR TURI 🚌

LODGING

11. (C4) HOSTAL SANTA FE
12. (E4) VERDE LIMÓN HOSTAL

13. (D3) HOSTAL LA ORQUÍDEA
14. (B1) HOSTAL MACONDO
15. (B2) HOSTAL CHORDELEG
16. (D3) HOTEL EL CONQUISTADOR
17. (A2) HOSTAL POSADA DEL ÁNGEL
18. (D2) HOTEL PRESIDENTE
19. (B2) SAN ANDRÉS HOTEL
20. (E2) HOSTERÍA HUERTOS DE UZHUPUD
21. (C3) HOTEL INCA REAL
22. (E5) HOTEL ORO VERDE
23. (C2) HOTEL CARVALLO
24. (D3) HOTEL SANTA LUCÍA
25. (C4) HOTEL CRESPO
26. (B2) MANSIÓN ALCAZAR

RESTAURANTS
27. (B2) VILLA ROSA
28. (E3) GOOD AFFINITY RESTAURANT AND TEA HOUSE
29. (C3) EL JARDÍN RESTAURANT
30. (E5) EL MAÍZ RESTAURANTE
31. (C2) HELADERÍA HOLANDA
32. (C2) CAFÉ EUCALYPTUS
33. (C3) RAYMIPAMBA CAFÉ RESTAURANT
34. (C3) CAFÉ AUSTRIA
35. (C2) EL PEDREGAL AZTECA
36. (D4) WUNDERBAR CAFÉ
37. (D4) CACAO Y CANELA CAFÉ BAR

THINGS TO SEE & DO
38. (C3) PLAZA SAN FRANCISCO
39. (D2) PLAZA ROTARY
40. (C3) CENTRAL PARK (Parque Calderón)
41. (C3) CATEDRAL DE LA INMACULADA CONCEPCIÓN (New Cathedral)
42. (D3) EL SAGRARIO (Old Cathedral)

TRANSPORT
43. (E2) BUS TERMINAL
44. (E2) AIRPORT

SOUTHERN ANDES

CUENCA

If you measure a city on size or population alone, Cuenca ranks third in Ecuador. If you consider charm, beauty and the opinion of all Ecuadorians, however, Cuenca leaps into first place. It is a lost colonial jewel: a neat, orderly city set in the picturesque rolling hills of southern Ecuador. Like Quito, Cuenca has a centuries-old colonial center full of stunning architecture, venerable churches and well-kept parks. Unlike Quito, however, the colo-

Photo by Dr. Crit Minster

nial center is still the heart of the city: a place to be enjoyed by all cuencanos, day or night. As you wander around the center, notice the finely carved wooden doors—they're quite striking. The best hotels and restaurants are to be found there, as well as ice cream parlors, cafés, shops and more. Cuencanos are immensely proud of the fact that their colonial downtown was named a UNESCO World Heritage Cultural site in 1999.

HISTORY

Cuenca is an ancient city, older than even the Spanish occupation. Before it was Cuenca, it was Guapondelig, a Cañari settlement. When the Incas came, they conquered the Cañari and changed its name to Tumipamba. The Spanish continued the tradition, building on the city of the vanquished Inca: then named it "Santa Ana de los Cuatro Ríos de Cuenca," or "Saint Anne of the Four Rivers of Cuenca." Four rivers do indeed flow through and around Cuenca, the most visible being the Río Tomebamba, which is overlooked by the southern edge of the old city.

THINGS TO SEE & DO

Cuenca has a lot to offer the visitor. Apart from the obvious architecture and colonial churches, Cuenca is close to the breathtaking El Cajas national park and reserve as well as Ecuador's most significant Inca ruins, Ingapirca. Cuenca is surrounded by quaint villages, each of which is worth a visit: Gualaceo is a small town with colonial roots and a pleasant river park. Chordeleg is known for the numerous silver shops that line the main street and park. Sigsig is a bit far off, but a good place to see Panama hats being made in the traditional way. Bulcay is the last place to see the dying art of ikat weaving: there are less than 30 weavers who still practice it today. Girón boasts colonial architecture and the nearby waterfall of El Chorro. Jima is known for hiking.

TOURS

EXPEDICIONES APULLACTA

A very professional travel agency which specializes in domestic travel. Extremely reliable for domestic flights, Cuenca-based day travel and visits to indigenous community tourism projects. Has English-speaking staff who are very comfortable working with travelers. Corner of General Torres and Gran Colombia

SHOPPING

You a shopper? Great news! Cuenca is known for handicrafts. The most famous Cuenca handicraft is the Panama hat, which is, of course, made in Ecuador and not Panama. The hats are handwoven out of a special sort of straw—*paja turquilla*—that is native to the region. Many families and individuals weave Panama hats as a full-time job or as a way to make extra money. A simple Panama hat can be woven in about two days and might fetch five to ten dollars for the weaver, whereas a finely woven one can take weeks and can cost up to $500. Your best bet to see Panama hats being woven is in the town of Sigsig or at the Homero Ortega factory.

Cuenca is also known for pottery and ceramics. Check out the Vega gallery near the Turi overlook, or browse the shops near the center of town. If you're more a fan of textiles, arrange a tour to the town of Bulcay, where you can see the last of the ikat weavers. Silver is also worked in Chordeleg: you can't miss all the jewelry stores.

Cuenca Activities

Cuenca is one of Ecuador's most elegant and beautiful cities: it is considered a UNESCO World Heritage Cultural site, a fact of which the locals are immeasurably proud. The easiest and most obvious activity is to simply stroll around the historic downtown, marveling at the architecture in and around the well-kept main park. The central park is dominated by a monument to Abdón Calderón, a young cuencano who fought valiantly at the battle of Pichincha in 1822. Cuenca's most famous cathedral is La Inmaculada, a massive stone-and-brick structure on the eastern side of the central square. It is instantly recognizable by the blue domes that dominate Cuenca's skyline.

If La Inmaculada isn't enough for you, be reassured: there are supposedly 52 churches in Cuenca, one for every Sunday of the year. It is impossible to wander far in any direction in Cuenca without running into a colonial church.

If you've seen enough churches and want a taste—or, rather, a whiff—of local culture, head over to the 10 de Agosto market. This market, once considered by cuencanos to be shabby and dangerous, has had a complete makeover. It is a sprawling two-level complex, with a working escalator and signs on the ceiling telling visitors where to find meat, fruit, vegetables, etc. The stalls are orderly and neat: South American market-going veterans may be stunned at the very orderliness of the place. There isn't much to buy for tourists, but bring your camera: the fruit "aisle" is particularly photo-worthy.

Another place frequented by locals but worth a stop for visitors is the Plaza Rotary. It's an open-air market featuring assorted "stuff"—there's really no better word for it. Need a basket made of old car tires? Plaza Rotary. How about a neon-colored SpongeBob piggy bank? You bet. In the market for a handmade wicker fire-fanner? You've come to the right place.

If you have all the SpongeBob piggybanks you need and want to do some real shopping, Cuenca is your place. There are several antique stores near the Las Conceptas church: buyer beware, especially when purchasing "pre-Columbian" pottery, colonial paintings and carved wooden statues: some are certainly forgeries or replicas. Most stores will tell you when something is a reproduction, but not all: look closely at any "antique" you wish to purchase. If you want to purchase some of Cuenca's famous pottery, head to the Eduardo Vega Gallery, just down the hill from the Turi overlook.

If you're on a tour, they'll probably take you to the Homero Ortega Panama hat factory (Ramírez Dávalos 3-86). There are several factories (and individuals) in and around Cuenca who make Panama hats. The Homero Ortega factory is the only one which is open to the public.

No trip to Cuenca is complete without a trip to the Turi overlook. It sits on a modest hill to the south of the city: on a clear day, the view is spectacular. There is a small church there and some coin-operated binoculars.

If you're staying awhile, Cuenca has some reputable Spanish schools that can set you up in a homestay if you like. There are also several museums of note, including the Pumapungo museum complex which has very good exhibits for those interested in the complete history

SOUTHERN ANDES

of the region and city. The Popular Arts Museum is a good place to see modern art that has been influenced by traditional techniques and styles. Don't forget to visit the San Joaquín neighborhood, where you can get some great barbecued meat.

There is as much to do outside of Cuenca as inside the city. The two biggest attractions are El Cajas national park and the ancient Inca ruins at Ingapirca. Many tours will take you to the towns of Gualaceo and Chordeleg. Gualaceo is a small, pleasant town with a nice park by the river, and Chordeleg is known for the dozens of silver shops that line the streets and main square. Occasionally, the tours will continue to the town of Sigsig, which is known for Panama hats. Many tours will stop for lunch at the beautiful Hosteria Uzhupud.

The town of Girón is also popular with visitors for its attractive old colonial homes and the nearby el Chorro waterfall. The nearby town of Jima is developing a fledgling tourism industry: it offers good hikes.

SPANISH SCHOOLS

While not offering Quito's variety of options and competition, Cuenca has a good selection of Spanish schools. Studying here as opposed to Quito is appealing to many travelers due to Cuenca's smaller size, and relative safety. You will also have greater opportunities to interact with locals as you practice conjugations, due in part to the much smaller tourist crowd. Cuenca is one of Ecuador's most expensive cities, but its quaint, colonial atmosphere will continue to attract Spanish students for years to come.

PARKS

CUENCA'S CENTRAL PARK AND FLOWER MARKET

Cuenca's beautifully tended Central Park, Parque Calderón, is an attractive, expansive area of flowers and trees. It is also a monument to Abdón Calderón, a native cuencano who fought in the battle of Pichincha, a pivotal confrontation in Ecuador's struggle for independence. According to local legend, a critically injured Calderón crawled to the summit of Pichincha Volcano, where he planted the Ecuadorian flag in defiance of the Spanish. This legend is probably embellished somewhat, but it is true, according to historical documents, that he received four wounds in the battle yet continued to fight. He died in Quito five days later, and to this day, Ecuadorian soldiers who show tremendous courage are awarded the Abdón Calderón medal.

The park is flanked on two sides by churches: to the east is the colonial El Sagrario church, which is today more of a museum than a church. On the west is the massive La Inmaculada Church, which features the blue domes for which Cuenca is famous. Next to La Inmaculada is a restaurant and an ice cream shop.

A half block away to the west, sort of to the side of the Inmaculada Church, you'll find the Cuenca flower market, where women sell locally grown flowers from about a dozen stands. The entrance to La Carmen de la Asunción convent is there as well: the nuns sell religious items through a special window. The market is picturesque, but the sellers are a bit short with tourists who snap photos but don't buy anything.

CHURCHES AND CATHEDRALS

Instantly recognizable by the blue domes that dominate Cuenca's skyline, La Inmaculada is Cuenca's most famous cathedral, but it's practically impossible to wander far in any direction in Cuenca without running into a colonial church. One notable one is the old cathedral, (El Sagrario), which sits across the park from La Inmaculada. Today, El Sagrario is more museum than church: if you wander inside, you'll see no pews or altars, but many interesting artifacts. There is even a glass window in the floor through which you can see a small section of the catacombs below: it looks sort of like a shallow well with several neatly arranged skulls. If you still need a church fix, head over to Todos Los Santos Church, the oldest in Cuenca. You can see the statue of Santa Ana, patroness of the city. It's at the corner of Calle Larga and Bajada de Todos Los Santos.

MARKETS
MERCADO 10 DE AGOSTO

Once considered to be one of the more dangerous markets in town, in the last few years the 10 de Agosto Market has had a tremendous face lift. Redesigned and cleaned up, it now proudly flaunts its new image; it also has the privilege of being the only market in Cuenca with an escalator. For a taste of real Cuencan life, come to the market and meander down the aisles of women selling fresh fruit and medicinal herbs. Or sample one of the mouth watering smoothies, which come in any number of flavors here. For a cheap and hearty lunch, head to the second floor. If you have any specific ailments, the far right hand section on the second floor is filled medicinal plants to make teas, and the women selling them will be happy to let you know what plant will best assuage your respective ailment. On Calle Larga between Tarqui and General Torres.

V!VA Member Review–Mercado 10 de Agosto
The locals in Cuenca don't have much in the way of supermarkets, so they go to the 10 Agosto market for their food and stuff. The market is fascinating if you're intertested in the day-to-day lives of the locals. Not much to buy if you're a visitor, but a neat place to check out and take some photos. 10 April 2007. New York, USA.

PLAZA ROTARY

Plaza Rotary is located about four blocks away from the central square. It is the best place in Cuenca for shopping for artesanía (local handmade goods). Market day is Thursday, but you can find some stalls and sellers there any day. This market is mostly known for ceramics, wooden utensils and household items and finely-made baskets. Located about seven or eight blocks to the northeast of the central square in Cuenca, Plaza Rotary hosts an outdoor market of random, non-touristy handicrafts made by and for locals. Hand-tied rope, baskets made of old car tires, brass bells, garish piggybanks and more are for sale here. The spot is well worth a visit, but don't plan on buying much of anything: there just isn't much of interest for travelers. Plaza Rotary is located on Vargas Machuca and Gaspar Sangurima. You can walk there from the central square, but it will take you about 20 minutes. A cab can get you there much quicker and won't cost more than a dollar or two.

PLAZA SAN FRANCISCO

If you still want to shop, head over to the Plaza San Francisco, about a block away from the flower market to the west. You'll find a lot of low-quality stuff for locals (like shoes) but also some vendors from Otavalo selling the usual blankets, scarves, etc. Some of the stores around the square sell clothes for religious icons, such as gold-embroidered capes. On the western side of the plaza, you'll find La Casa de la Mujer/Cemuart, a tidy collection of stands selling jewelry, panama hats and other handicrafts.

CASA DE LA MUJER

Casa de la Mujer is a building in the center of Cuenca filled with stalls selling every type of craft typical to Ecuador, and especially the Azuay province. Products include knit sweaters from Otavalo, traditional Andean musical instruments, Panama hats, jewelry, ceramics and weavings. More orderly than the San Francisco market just outside, you can peruse the stalls at your own pace with no one pressuring you to buy anything. There are two stories of stalls and public bathrooms ($0.10) on the second floor. You can also get a cheap lunch here for $1. Located on General Torres Across the street from the Plaza San Francisco Market.

MUSEUMS
POPULAR ARTS MUSEUM

El Museo de las Artes Populares, or Popular Arts Museum, is a small but interesting museum dedicated to the popular art of the Americas. It contains old pieces of ethnographic significance as well as local art from many Central and South American cultures. Well worth a visit if you're interested in this sort of thing. Open Monday-Friday 8 a.m.-6 p.m., closed weekends. Hermano Miguel 323 and Calle Larga.

Help other travelers. Publish your favorite places at www.vivatravelguides.com

PUMAPUNGO MUSEUM

The Pumapungo Museum, also known as the Central Bank Museum, is actually a complex of several other smaller museums, each dedicated to a different aspect of Cuenca life or history. The museum itself is at the site of Tombebamba, an ancient Inca city which is being excavated. The Ethnographic museum is based on the theory that a great deal can be learned about a culture through their everyday objects. They have informational displays about Ecuador's various cultures: most of the major cultures in Ecuador are represented. The Archaeological museum contains many pieces and relics unearthed nearby, mostly from the Inca and Cañari cultures. There are also exhibits and it is possible to visit the excavation site. Also on the premises is a museum of religious art and a numismatic museum (which has displays of coins and currency). Open Monday-Saturday, 9 a.m.-6 p.m., closed Sundays. Larga and Huayna Capac, Tel: 593-7-281-1706.

CULTURAL ACTIVITIES

ARAM KACHATUKIAN CENTRO MUSICAL

Aram Kachatukian is an excellent place to pick up an instrument or two, especially if you are curious about traditional Andean music. The center does offer classes in classical music and instruments, but its specialty is instruction in the traditional rhythms you hear all over Ecuador. If you'd like to learn how to pick out a San Juanito on a charango or a Huayno on a zampoña, or even a Capishca on the Kena, this is the place to go. Other instruments offered are electric bass, guitar, piano and violin. For $25 a month, you receive two 45-minute classes a week. There is a one-time $10 registration fee. Bolivar 11-28 and Tarqui, Cell: 09-878-7870.

SATTVA SPA CENTRO INTEGRAL

Walking into Sattva feels like a spa treatment in itself. The calming but simple décor of this center creates the perfect environment for the wealth of classes offered here, many of which cannot be found anywhere else in Cuenca. Classes include Yoga (including pre-natal), Capoeira, Tai-Chi, Flexibility and Body Consciousness, Chi-Kung, Meditation and Relaxation, Modern Dance, Hip-Hop and Ninjitsu. On nice days, some of the classes are held in parks around the city, so call ahead if you'd like to observe a class. Each class has a different price, but the range is between $20 and $30 per month. Calle Ines Salcedo 1-52 and Federico Proaño (behind the Clinica Santa Ines and the Universidad Estatal de Cuenca), Tel: 593-7-288-3131, Cell:09-927-7966.

MAMA KINUA CENTRO CULTURAL

Mama Kinua can be a quick stop if you are in the center of the city and feel like you need a break from the typical tourist magnets. The center acts as a place for gathering and disseminating cultural information. There is a small library of indigenous texts, a café where breakfast and lunch is served, and postings of various cultural events going on in the vicinity. Mama Kinua has connections to La Casa de la Mujer, next door, as well as to Fundación de Salud Jambi Runa, a rural health organization, to Turismo Rural Kushi Waira, and to Queseria Ñucanchik Kawsay, a cooperative of cheese producers. If you are interested in volunteering in any of these areas or in exploring community based tourism in rural areas, Mama Kinua can assist you. Open Monday-Friday, 9 a.m.-5 p.m., closed weekends. General Torres 7-45 and Presidente Cordova (next to Casa de la Mujer on the Plaza de San Francisco), Cell: 09-821-2659.

EL SURTIDO ALMACEN DE MUSICA

If the music you have heard in Ecuador has piqued your interest, El Surtido offers the largest selection of *Musica Nacional* and *Musica Folklorica* for sale. The friendly, knowledgeable staff can help guide you in your selection. Also for sale are musical instruments and accessories, DVDs, music instruction booklets and sheet music. Connected to the store is a delicious and healthy juice bar selling fresh orange, apple and carrot juice, among others. Borrero 8-68 and Bolivar, Tel: 593-7-283-1409/593-7-284-1949.

MIRADOR TURI

Turi, or "brother" in Kichwa, serves as a quick escape away from the center of the city. Most enjoyable at sunset, Turi sits atop a steep hill, providing gorgeous views of the city lights below and the mountains that surround it. You can usually count on a backdrop of pink and purple sky, cuddling couples and traditional music blaring from the church loudspeakers at dusk. The actual lookout point is just in front of the church, the side of which is covered in interesting murals that depict daily indigenous life. On Sundays, Turi is filled with churchgoers and provides an interesting perspective of what town life is really about. Turi is located to the South of Cuenca. From the center of the city a cab ride should not cost more than $3, by bus ($0.25), take any that say "Turi" from the intersection of Fray Vicente Solano and 12 de Abril.

LODGING

The hotels in Cuenca are a great value for any budget level. The best hotels are the converted colonial homes in the center of town, such as the Santa Lucía, Mansión Alcázar or Hotel Crespo, but there is the elegant Oro Verde outside of town for those well-heeled guests who don't want to be in the center of town. There are also any number of mid-range hotels and budget options.

BUDGET
HOSTAL SANTA FE (DORMS: $5, ROOMS: $8)

Private room with bathroom ($8/person). Dorm-style room ($5/person). Borrero 5-57 between Jaramillo and Vasquez about three blocks SE of the central square of Cuenca. Tel: 593-7-282-2025, E-mail: hostalsantafe2005@yahoo.com.

VERDE LIMON HOSTAL (ROOMS: $8-12)

Located near the center of the city, close to the major museums, churches and artesian shops, this simple hostal has 13 clean, well-maintained rooms, in addition to a welcoming living room appointed with TV and DVD, a shared kitchen and a restaurant. Internet is available, as well as tourist information. Juan Jaramillo 4-89 and Mariano Cueva, Tel: 593-7-282-0300, Fax: 593-7-283-1509, E-mail: cuenca@verdelimonhostal.com, URL: www.verdelimonhostal.com.

HOSTAL LA ORQUÍDEA (ROOMS: $16-25)

Hostal La Orquídea is a converted colonial home in downtown Cuenca. Its rates are lower than many of its competitors, so the small place tends to fill up fast: call ahead or arrive early. The hostal is quite pleasant and known for good service. Borrero 9-31 and Bolivar, Tel:07-282-4511.

HOSTAL MACONDO (ROOMS. $16-25)

This is a very nice budget hostal and will serve sleepy backpackers well: rooms are priced under $30 for two people. While it's not your most luxurious place, rooms are clean and comfortable and there is a continental breakfast and kitchen access. Tarqui 11-64, Tel: 593-07-284-0697, Fax:833-593, E-mail: info@hostalmacondo.com, URL: www.hostalmacondo.com.

MID-RANGE
HOSTAL CHORDELEG (ROOMS: $20-40)

An excellent choice for those in the lower mid-range budget zone, Hostal Chordeleg is a converted colonial home in the center of Cuenca. The courtyard, with its neat garden and wooden upper floors, is beautiful. The rooms are well-maintained and come equipped with TV and clean bathrooms. Gran Colombia 11-15 and General Torres, Tel: 593-7-282-2536, Fax: 593-7-282-4611, E-mail: hostalfm@etapa.online.net.ec, URL:www.ecuaventura.com/azuay/wdis_ac_hhosta_chordeleg.html.

HOTEL EL CONQUISTADOR (ANEXO) (ROOMS: $30-41)

An elegant hotel in central Cuenca, Hotel El Conquistador is modern and neat. It lacks the character of converted colonial homes, but it costs less. This is a good choice for mid-range tourists who want to keep costs down without sacrificing comfort. Note: this is the *Anexo*—or Annex—to the Hotel El Conquistador, which is also in Cuenca but has a different location and rates. Sucre 6-80, Tel: 593-7-284-0215, E- mail: anexo@hconquistador.com.ec, URL: www.hotelconquistador.com.ec.

HOSTAL POSADA DEL ANGEL (ROOMS: $25-50)

One of the best mid-range options in Cuenca, the elegant Posada del Angel is located not too far west from the center of town (about a five or six block walk). It is a friendly, well-kept, laid back place that tries to maintain a family atmosphere. The hotel is spacious and airy, with comfy rooms. Bolivar 14-11 and Estevez de Toral, Tel:593-7-284-0695, Fax: 593-7-282-1360, E-mail: reservas@hostalposadadelangel.com, URL: www.hostalposadadelangel.com.

HOTEL PRESIDENTE (ROOMS: $28-50)

Hotel Presidente is a modern, clean hotel not far from the city center. Breakfast is included. G.Colombia 6-59 and Hno. Miguel, Tel: 593-7-283-1066, Fax: 593-7-283-1341, E-mail: hotelpresidente@yahoo.com.

SAN ANDRÉS HOTEL (ROOMS: $25-45)

Considering the quality of accommodation and prices, this is quite possibly the best value (without feeling budget) place in town. Spacious rooms feature oversized beds, elegant comforters and classic dark-wood furniture. The caféteria and bar is as good a place as any in Cuenca to enjoy a drink (or two) and sample the local fare, served with the same first-class attention and care that accompanies guests in the hotel. Gran Colombia 11-66, Tel:593-7-284-1497/593-7-285-0039, E-mail:info@hotelsanandres.net, URL: www.hotelsanandres.net.

HOSTERÍA UZHUPUD (ROOMS: $50-55, SUITES FROM $82)

Located about 45 minutes outside of Cuenca, Hostería Huertos de Uzhupud is a good option for those who want to be near Cuenca, but still have more of a countryside experience. The hostería has hiking trails, horses for riding, tennis courts, a pool and sauna in addition to soccer field, volleyball court and children's games. On weekends and holidays, Uzhupud is popular with Ecuadorians who go to relax: you can pay day rates to use the pool and sauna area. Many tours to nearby Gualaceo and Chordeleg will stop for lunch at Uzhupud. Km 32 Via Paute Valley, Tel:593-7-225-0339/593-7-225-0329/593-7-225-0374, Fax:593-7-225-0373, E-mail: uzhupud1@cue.satnet.net, URL: www.uzhupud.com.

HOTEL INCA REAL (ROOMS: $36-75)

Located in the heart of colonial Cuenca, Hotel Inca Real straddles the line between budget and mid-range hotels in terms of costs. A converted home, the hotel and courtyards are quite nice and attractive, but the rooms are very small, almost to the point of being uncomfortable. There is no restaurant on the premises. General Torres 8-40, Tel: 593-7-282-3636, E-mail: incareal@cue.satnet.net.

LUXURY

HOTEL ORO VERDE (ROOMS: $95-160)

Hotel Oro Verde ("Green Gold" in Spanish, referring to bananas) is Cuenca's most luxurious hotel. It is a destination in itself, offering such amenities as a swimming pool, exercise room, fine dining, tennis and horseback riding. The Oro Verde has 79 rooms, meaning there is usually plenty of space. This hotel is one of several luxurious Oro Verde hotels in Ecuador, and like the others, it features large, well-designed rooms, gorgeous gardens and elegant restaurants. Oro Verde Cuenca is located outside of town, too far to walk, but taxis are inexpensive and the hotel staff are happy to arrange one for guests. Av. Ordóñez Lazo, Tel: 593-7-283-1200, Fax: 593-7-283-2849, E-mail: ov_cue@oroverdehotels.com, URL: www.oroverdehotels.com.

HOTEL CARVALLO (ROOMS: $76-147)

Located in the beautiful Centro Histórico, this recently converted colonial home integrates classic charm with all the comforts of an elegant modern establishment. Warmth and refinement greet visitors at every corner, from the tastefully appointed furnishings to the stylish décor. Rooms are spacious and airy, and feature large beds with fluffy comforters and plenty of throw pillows. Be sure to sample the local fare at Carvallo's classy restaurant; meals are sure to satisfy even the most difficult palates. Gran Colobia 9-52 between Padre Aguirre and Benigno Malo, Tel: 593-7-832-063.

HOTEL SANTA LUCÍA (ROOMS: $65-100)

Hotel Santa Lucía is a beautiful converted home in central Cuenca (the home once belonged to Don Manuel Vega Davila, first governor of Azuay province). The hotel is owned by the Veintimilla family, who also own other successful hotels and restaurants. They know what they're doing and it shows: the hotel won a Cuenca award in 2002 for best building restoration. The restaurant is very good—the food style is Italian-Ecuadorian. Breakfast is included. The restaurant doubles as a café of sorts for breakfast and lunch and an elegant restaurant for dinner. The website is in English, Spanish and German, and is good for info and making reservations. Antonio Borrero 8-44 and Sucre, Tel: 593-7-282-8000, Fax: 593-7-284-2443, E-mail: info@santaluciahotel.com, URL: www.santaluciahotel.com.

HOTEL CRESPO (ROOMS: $60-80)

One of the most popular hotels in Cuenca, Hotel Crespo is a converted family estate, dating back over one hundred years, and located not far from the center of town. It is a gorgeous place, set right on the banks of the Tomebamba River. The hotel has 48 elegant, airy rooms, each of which has Cable TV, phone and mini bar. Many of the rooms have been renovated recently, but this has in no way decreased their charm. There is also a bar and first-class restaurant featuring French cuisine. Breakfast is included. The hotel will pick you up for free at the airport if you have reservations. Larga 793 and Cordero, Tel: 593-7-284-2571, Fax: 593-7-283-9473, E-mail: info@hotelcrespo.com, URL: www.hotel-crespo.com.

MANSIÓN ALCÁZAR (ROOMS: $64-185)

In 2000-2001, the owners of this fine colonial mansion in central Cuenca renovated it into a modern, elegant hotel. The setting is quite pleasant and the rooms are large and comfortable (if a bit formal). The hotel features an excellent restaurant and attractive courtyard where guests can relax. Calle Bolívar 12-55 and Tarqui, Tel: 593-7-282-3918, Fax: 593-7-282-3554, E-mail: info@mansionalcazar.com, URL: www.mansionalcazar.com.

RESTAURANTS

Cuenca is a great place to eat. The restaurants in the city center are diverse and appeal to every taste and budget. The best restaurants are often associated with hotels, like the Santa Lucía or the Hotel Crespo, but they're still quite reasonably priced, with main dishes going for an average of about $8.50 or so. Not bad for a steak in one of Cuenca's finest restaurants! As in all of Ecuador, portions are generally huge.

There are also any number of smaller cafés and ice cream joints for a lighter meal. One very popular hangout is the Angelus café, also known as "tutto fredo," on the main square to the right of the massive Inmaculada Cathedral. Regional food in Cuenca is similar to that of northern Ecuador: a lot of pork, corn, potatoes and rice. Cuenca is also a good place to sample *cuy* (guinea pig!), and if you look as you drive around town, you'll see women cooking cuyes on sticks over open grills. The San Joaquín neighborhood is known for having very good barbecued meat.

If you're feeling very adventurous, head to the market for a meal. There, you'll see dozens of roasted pigs all lined up: for a couple of bucks, you'll get a steaming plate of pork with tasty yellow mashed potatoes known as *llapingachos*. If you wander up and down the market, one of the ladies may offer you a piece of crunchy pork skin, considered the tastiest part by the locals. She's hoping to make a sale: the prices of a plate of pork are all about the same, so the vendors try to out-do each other with flavor. Go ahead and try, if you've got a strong stomach. Don't forget that in Cuenca as in all of Ecuador, 10% service and 12% taxes will be added to the cost of your meal.

HELADERIA HOLANDA (SINGLE SCOOP: $.70)

This is unanimously considered the best place to get ice cream in town. In its central location you can't miss sampling the dozens of flavors, including many only found in Ecuador. Grab a fresh scoop and sit on the pine benches while admiring scenes of Dutch countryside on the walls. Or you can opt to sample the delicious yogurts, cakes, and sandwiches. Benigno Malo 9-51, Tel: 593-7-283-1449.

Help other travelers. Publish your favorite places at www.vivatravelguides.com

CAFÉ EUCALYPTUS (FOOD AND DRINKS: $1.50-5)

A staple for many foreigners living in Cuenca, as well as a local crowd, this restaurant offers comfort food you can't easily find elsewhere: from Pad Thai to Jamaican jerk chicken to typical Ecuadorian food, as well as a long drink list. Located in a renovated colonial house and owned by an American woman, the restaurant fills two floors, with a full bar on the lower level and a dance floor in the covered patio. The back wall is filled with caricatures of all of the regulars that frequent the café. At night the place fills up and there is often live salsa music, so be sure to bring your dancing shoes. Sometimes when there is live music there is a cover of $3 after 9 p.m. Monday - Thursday, 11 a.m. - 12 a.m. Friday, 11 a.m. - 1 a.m., Saturday, 5 p.m. - 12 a.m., Sunday 8:30 a.m. - 9 p.m. Gran Colombia and Benigno Malo, Tel: 593-7-284-9157.

EL MAÍZ RESTAURANTE (ENTREES: $3-5)

One of the most tranquil restaurants in town, El Maíz is located in an old colonial building with a beautiful courtyard, a wonderful place to soak up the peaceful atmosphere of Cuenca. With sunny rooms and outdoor seating, this restaurant specializes in typical Ecuadorian dishes and fresh juices, as well as more experimental, but just as delicious, fusion meals. Away from the bustle of the center of the city, the restaurant is a close walk from the Museo del Banco Central. Calle Larga 1-279 and Calle de los Molinos, Tel: 593-7-284-0224, E-mail: elmaiz@etapaonline.net.ec.

RAYMIPAMBA CAFÉ RESTAURANT (ENTREES: $3-5)

Perhaps the most famous restaurant in Cuenca, it is hard not to stop in, if just for a coffee or dessert. With terraced seating and windows facing out onto Parque Calderon, this café is perfect for a break during a busy day. The menu offers anything from crepes and fresh juices to pastas, *humitas, tamales, chaulafan* and ceviche. Make sure to steal a peek at the walls adorned with old photos of Cuenca. This is just as much a magnet for locals as it is for foreigners. Benigno Malo 8-59, Tel: 593-7-283-4159, Monday-Friday, 8:30 a.m.-11 p.m. Saturday -Sunday, 8:30 a.m-9:00 p.m.

CAFÉ AUSTRIA (ENTREES: $5)

This charming café is perfect for a pick-me-up snack and coffee in the afternoon, or for a delicious meal for dinner. Run by the same owner as the Wunderbar, this locale is smaller and more reminiscent of a European café, filled with wooden tables and chairs. At night the café fills up, accommodating both young and middle-aged, local and foreign. Most weekends there is live music or events such as poetry readings. Benigno Malo. Tel: 593-7-284-0899.

EL PEDREGAL AZTECA (ENTREES: $4-8)

El Pedregal Azteca is a Mexican restaurant, very popular in Cuenca, particularly on Thursday, Friday, and Saturday nights when there are live Mariachi musicians playing. Gran Colombia 10-29.

WUNDERBAR CAFÉ (ENTREES: $5)

This funky German-owned café is a crowd pleaser. Divided into different segments, once seated you can choose anything from a good *canelazo*, international fare, or a game of Jenga or foosball. During the day it is a pleasant place to have lunch (when the weather is good try eating in the garden), while at night the bar comes alive accompanied by occasional live music Thursday to Saturday. Hermano Miguel 3-43 and Calle Larga (Escalinata), Tel:593-7-283-1274, E-mail: wunder@etapaonline.net.ec.

CACAO AND CANELA CAFÉ BAR (DRINKS: $1-3.50)

A delightful café serving, as the name suggests, all things chocolate and cinnamon. The menu consists of a long list of every kind of hot chocolate imaginable. The *cacao* used to make the chocolate is grown in Ecuador (this cacao is so good that at one time the Swiss wanted to import it). Beer, mixed drinks, sandwiches and salads are also offered. During the daytime, it serves as a quiet place to read a book or chat with a friend and at night the café fills up and noise volume rises. Seating is limited as the space is quite small, but you can take advantage of the loft space and the owners always find a way to squeeze you in. On most weekends there is live music. Open for lunch and dinner. Presidente Antonio Borrero (5-97), Tel: 593-7-282-0945.

GOOD AFFINITY RESTAURANT AND TEA HOUSE (LUNCHES: $2)

This vegetarian restaurant is a peaceful retreat from the noisy streets. Owned by a Taiwanese couple, the restaurant is filled with calming music and has outdoor seating surrounded by bamboo and bonsai trees. The basic lunch comes with soup, juice and a plate of rice accompanied by some sort of vegetables and tofu. They also serve soymilk and sell bags of soy products. The restaurant is located on Gran Colombia 1-89 and Capulies, across the street from the Universidad del Pacifico. Due to construction nearby, the bus routes are constantly changing, but you can take any bus that goes to the Coliseo and walk three blocks from their towards the gas station on Gran Colombia. Gran Colombia 1-89, Tel: 593-7-283-2469.

SAN JOAQUÍN - FOR "CARNE ASADA"

San Joaquín is a neighborhood in Cuenca that has emerged as the place to eat *carne asada* (grilled meat). Lining the dirt roads are family-owned restaurants that serve the large Cuencano families that come to devour savory lunches. This is one place in the city where you will be virtually the only foreigner. Many of the restaurants have playgrounds for children, can accommodate large groups, and have both indoor and outdoor seating. San Joaquín is not ideal for vegetarians. Specializing in all types of grilled meat (pork, beef, chicken, and cuy), most plates come with *mote*, potatoes, and *humitas/tamales*. The most well-known restaurants are Las Palmeras, Las Cabañas de San Joaquin and El Tequila.

You can get to San Joaquín by taxi (shouldn't cost more than $3), which takes about 15 minutes from the center, or take bus #19 ($0.25) from the corner of Presidente Cordova and Juan Montalvo or from the Feria Libre market.

VILLA ROSA

The Villa Rosa is one of Cuenca's most elegant restaurants, and one of the best that is not affiliated with a hotel. It is located in a converted colonial home. It isn't too far from the center of town: it's about five blocks away from the central park to the northwest and you may want to consider taking a taxi if you're located south or east of the central square. The food is excellent, specializing in Ecuadorian and international cuisine. You may want to make reservations, especially on weekends. Dress is relatively casual: no tie and jacket is required, but you'll feel out of place in a t-shirt or tennis shoes. Gran Colombia 12-22, Tel:593-7-283-7944.

EL JARDÍN RESTAURANT

One of Cuenca's best and most elegant restaurants, El Jardín is a good place to splurge on a fine meal if your budget is not too tight. The service is exceptional. Presidente Córdova 7-23, Tel: 593-7-283-1120.

NIGHTLIFE

If Cuenca is lacking in anything, it's nightlife—it's just not a party town. Still, there are places where you can go out and have a good time: check out Wunderbar or some of the other bars and cafés by the river.

AROUND CUENCA

There is as much to do outside of Cuenca as inside in the city. Apart from the obvious architecture and colonial churches, Cuenca is close to the breathtaking El Cajas National Park and reserve, as well as Ecuador's most significant Inca ruins, Ingapirca. The city is also surrounded by quaint villages, each of which is worth a visit: Gualaceo is a small town with colonial roots and a pleasant river park. Chordeleg is known for the numerous silver shops lining the main street and park. Sigsig is a bit far off, but a good place to see Panama hats being made in the traditional way. Bulcay is the last place to see the dying art of ikat weaving: there are less than 30 weavers who still practice it today. Girón boasts colonial architecture and the nearby waterfall of El Chorro. The nearby town of Jima is developing a fledgling tourism industry: it offers good hikes. Many tours will stop for lunch at the beautiful Hosteria Uzhupud.

INGAPIRCA

Ingapirca is a ruined Inca city, and probably the most important set of Inca ruins in Ecuador. That being said, the ruins at Ingapirca are not very impressive, especially when compared to Macchu Picchu or other pre-Columbian ruin complexes in Peru. Ingapirca was once an important Inca military and religious center, but over the centuries, the site was cannibalized by the Spanish who used the finely chiseled stones to build their own homes and churches. Before the arrival of the Incas, the site had been an important Cañari observatory. Today, the best-preserved structure is an oval-shaped platform known as the Temple of the Sun. Efforts are underway to restore the site.

Although those who have seen the impressive ruin complexes in Peru (or Mexico and Guatemala, for that matter) may be disappointed by Ingapirca, it is still worth the trip, particularly if you are a ruins buff or if you won't get the chance to go to Peru.

GETTING TO INGAPIRCA

Ingapirca is located in the middle of nowhere, about 90 km away from Cuenca. Guided tours to the site can be arranged in Cuenca, or if you get there by yourself (wheel and deal with the taxis in Cuenca, make sure they stick around to take you back) there are guides hoping for clients at the entrance to the ruins. Alternatively, there are two daily buses from Cuenca to Ingapirca, leaving at 9 a.m. and 1 p.m. from the terminal and returning at 1 p.m. and 4 p.m. Plan on spending about two hours visiting the ruins. The ruins are open daily from 8 a.m.-5 p.m. and entrance costs $5.

LODGING

POSADA INGAPIRCA/INGAPIRCA INNS (ROOMS: $37-49)

The hotel is a surprisingly attractive converted 200-year-old hacienda: it features 20 rooms, elegant social areas and well-kept gardens. There is more to do than just see the ruins: the Posada can arrange hikes along the Inca trail that passes through the area, and there is a billiard room on the premises. An appealing option for someone who wants to see the ruins and who also would like to escape the cities for the quiet, elegant night away. Prices are quite reasonable for a converted hacienda. The Posada is managed by the Grupo Santa Ana, which also manages the Victoria hotel and El Jardin restaurant in Cuenca: information is available at the hotel. Calle Larga 6-93 and Borrega, Tel: 593-7-282-7401, Fax: 593-7-283-2340, E-mail: santaana@etapaonline.net.ec.

EL CAJAS NATIONAL PARK

El Cajas National Park and Reserve is a starkly beautiful wilderness of valleys, lakes, highland vistas and rock formations. It consists of 29,000 hectares of páramo (a páramo is a grassy highland generally unfit for cultivation, the closest translation is probably "badlands") known for hiking and trout fishing. To visit the park, you will first stop at the information building located at next to Totoras Lake. There, you will pay your entry fee ($10) and you'll be given a map of the park. There are several trails of interest, most of which are meduim in terms of difficulty level. Note that fog and rain are common in El Cajas National Park, so pack accordingly. There are several tour operators in Cuenca who offer guided day tours to El Cajas National Park and Reserve. 45 minutes by car or bus from Cuenca along the highway that leads to Guayaquil and the coast. Informational center open from 7 a.m.-5 p.m.

BAÑOS

A few kilometers west of the city of Cuenca is the small town of Baños, not to be confused with the larger tourist town of the same name near Ambato. Baños-Cuenca is a pleasant, peaceful little village named for the hot thermal waters there. The water is channeled into four different commercial complexes, the best of which is the Balneario Durán (open daily 7:30 a.m. - 8 p.m., closes earlier Wednesday and Sunday). Once you're done at the thermal baths (costing between 50 cents and $3), you can explore the small town, the highlight of which is probably the church, from which there is a good view of the valley.

LODGING
HOSTERÍA DURÁN (ROOMS: $36-78)
About five minutes from Cuenca, Hostería Durán is a suprisingly large hotel and visitor complex with hot springs, restaurant, conference facilities, game room, waterslides and more. It is far and away the best place to stay in the tiny town of Baños and stacks up well against hotels in Cuenca, too. They can take reservations through their web site, which is somewhat difficult to use. Av. Ricardo Durán, Tel: 593-0-789-2485, E-mail: bduran@az.pro.ec, URL: www.hosteriaduran.com.

BULCAY
About a half hour outside of Cuenca, the tiny town of Bulcay is home to the last remaining weavers of the ikat tradition. The women weavers use traditional hand looms (often handed down from generation to generation) to produce strikingly colored shawls and sweaters (as well as purses, shoulder bags, etc.). They commonly use cotton, wool and alpaca for their creations, which they sell from their homes or to agents who then sell them in markets or shops in Quito. Sadly, the ikat (pronounced "ee-cot") tradition is dying out. There are only about 30 weavers still producing the textiles today. Bulcay itself is a pleasant little town, but there is little to see or do besides visiting the homes of the weavers, which is generally only possible if you're on a tour from Cuenca. Bulcay is on the way to Gualaceo, and tours may stop there if you ask them. The modest Pachaíma hotel in town is the only one, but Bulcay is only a few minutes from the Hostería Uzhupud and Gualaceo.

CHORDELEG
Chordeleg is a small town outside of Cuenca, often combined with Gualaceo for day trips. It is known for the many jewelry stores that line the streets and main square: there must be at least 20 of them. The jewelry—particularly the silver—is made locally and there is an impressive selection of pendants, bracelets, earrings, etc. Other than shop, there isn't much to see and do in Chordeleg. Most of the tours take visitors to have lunch at the nearby Uzhupud hosteria. Buses leave Cuenca regularly for Gualaceo (from the corner of Espana and Benalcazar), where it is easy to catch a second bus to Chordeleg.

JIMA
Jima is a small charming town an hour and a half southeast of Cuenca. Seated at the foot of a steep green mountain ridge, this is the place to go if you are tired of tourist traps. With the help of a Peace Corps volunteer and the Fundacion Turistica Jima, the town has developed its own community-based tourism, so you know that the money you spend here will go directly back to the community members, not to a big company. From Jima, there are a number of trails and hikes of varying lengths and difficulty. Many of these go to the peaks of the mountains surrounding the town, where you will be rewarded with beautiful views. To cool off after a hike, try taking a dip in the clean Rio Moya.

HIKES AROUND JIMA
Jima serves as a good base for longer hikes in the area. An hour from the town is the primary cloud forest, Bosque de Tambillo, which has hundreds of different animal species and more than 200 types of orchids. There is also a three-to four-day hike that takes you from the Sierra to the Oriente. The hike begins 22 km to the east of Jima in the Cordillera Moriré and drops 1,800 meters by the time you reach the Oriente. It is also possible to rent horses and camping gear in Jima.

LODGING
There are two options for places to spend the night. One is the Hostal Chacapamba (593-7-241-8035 or 593-7-247–8046), a new two story house with balcony. The other option is to spend the night in a building owned by the local high school (593-7-241-8398): rooms with shared bathroom cost $4.50. All of the proceeds go towards improving the schools in town. You can also make reservations for rooms at the information center (593-7-241-8270).

Tourist Information

For reservations and information about hikes, place to stay, and other activities, contact the information center at 593-7-241-8270. Cultural activities such as traditional dances and music can be arranged for large groups. Email: jimaecuador@yahoo.com URL: www.projectsforpeace.org/jima.

Gualaceo

An attractive little village on the river of the same name, Gualaceo is known as "The Garden of Azuay" (Azuay being the name of the province). It is located about an hour away from Cuenca, in the heart of a fertile agricultural region known for fruit. The best time for visitors is Sunday, market day. Gualaceo's market is small but picturesque, and shoppers can find handmade baskets and other articles. Buses to Gualaceo leave every half-hour or so from Cuenca. Also, travel agencies in Cuenca offer tours that normally include the towns of Gualaceo, Chordeleg and (sometimes) Sigsig.

Sigsig

Sigsig is a small agricultural town one and a half hours southeast of Cuenca that sits in a valley surrounded by steep mountains. It is best known for being the source of many of the Panama hats sold within and outside of Ecuador. A quick walk around town will give a glimpse of the many stages of toquilla hat production. Arriving from Cuenca, you will be let off in the first of two of the town's parks. This park is filled with soccer fields and basketball courts and is dominated by two enormous and eerie welded statues of angels on stilts. To get a glimpse of the scenery and to orient yourself, walk up the flight of stairs toward the basketball court on the hill, where you will be able to take advantage of the height and enjoy the vistas.

The town is very straightforward, and by walking around for about an hour or so, you can cover just about all of the streets. The streets are laid out in a grid formation, with the uphill side of town being north, and the downhill side, towards the market, being south. The houses are old colonial buildings with flowers dripping off balconies. There are not many formal activities to entertain you with in Sigsig, but walking around the town and peeking into doors where women are weaving hats can be quite interesting. Toward the east of town there is another park with a statue dedicated to Cacique Duma, the chief of the Cañari Confederation from Sigsig who defeated the Incan conquistadors from Cuzco.

Around Sigsig

If you get tired of walking around town, head towards the South of town where a five to ten minute walk will lead you to the "playa," or bank of the river. Along the way you can stop at the Asociación de Toquilleras Maria Auxiliadora and take a look at the Panama hat production. If you are interested in buying, this is probably the best place to look. The "playa" is a refreshing stop, surrounded by eucalyptus trees and steep green mountains, and a perfect place to picnic. Swimming and fishing are allowed, but some spots can get deep, so be careful. Those interested in exploring the surrounding areas should visit the Zhavalula and Chobshi caves, once used by the Incas. These can be reached in about five to ten minutes by pick-up truck, which you can hire (about $3) either at the southeast corner of the park when you first arrive in town, or at the market. If you would like to walk there, follow the road to the "playa" then stay straight and follow signs to the caves.

Lodging

There are not many hotels in Sigsig but if you do plan on spending the night you can stay at Residencial Lupita (593-7-226-6257). Directions: Sigsig is 18 km past Chordeleg. Take a bus from the Terminal in Cuenca for $1.25.

Restaurants

For a good and cheap bite to eat, try Chunucari Bar Restaurant, located on Calle Davila between Sucre and Bolivar. Open for breakfast, lunch and dinner, this restaurant serves a delicious meal in the courtyard of a rustic colonial house. Lunch includes a large bowl of soup, a rice plate with vegetables and fish or meat, juice and dessert for $1.50. There is also a small gift shop attached to the restaurant.

GIRÓN

Girón is a small sleepy town tucked into the mountains 45 km southeast of Cuenca. Just an hour drive to the town, the climate is significantly milder than its larger neighbor. Most of the old colonial houses that line the street have not been remodeled in years, but this antiquity is what gives the town much of its charm. There is a quaint central plaza with a somewhat out-of-place modern church. If you have time, it is worth walking around town and on the outskirts, where the paved roads quickly turn to dirt and you are soon walking in farmland. Girón has a huge emigration rate to the US; don't be surprised if some of the townsfolk speak surprisingly good English.

One of the main draws to the vicinity of Girón is El Chorro, the waterfall that flows down the cliffs outside of town. The walk to the waterfall makes for a nice day hike, including beautiful views of the valley below and trails in dense forest. There are two options to reach the waterfalls: one is by walking up a 5 km dirt road, which takes about two hours (ask for directions in town); the other is a bit hardier, along an uphill trail through the woods. This second hike gets you to a higher waterfall, much more isolated, but well-worth the sweat. From Cuenca, buses to Girón ($1) leave from the terminal at the Feria Libre market every hour. You can also take any bus that heads towards Machala or Santa Isabel and ask the driver to let you off at Girón. The ride takes 45 minutes to an hour.

SOUTH TO LOJA

Riddled with potholes and assaulted by the occasional landslide, the road from Cuenca to Loja boasts its fare share of obstacles. But dodge the ditches and sail past the landslides and you'll be stunned by the scenery unfolding before your eyes. On a clear day, as the road climbs in altitude, a remarkable panorama of mountain ranges and verdant valleys stretches out below. Only occasionally does a traditional pueblo pop up among the otherwise uninhabited landscape. These sleepy little towns, such as Saraguro, offer a rare glimpse of life in rural Ecuador, as untouched by tourism as the land is by people. Meandering past the quiet backcountry communities and cutting across the barren but beautiful landscape, the road continues its serpentine route south towards Peru, astounding the onlooker with more breathtaking views around each twist and turn. This is a drive not to be missed.

SARAGURO

The modest agricultural town of Saraguro is a must-stop on route to Loja, made famous for its vibrant local culture and beautiful weaving and jewelry. To really get a feel for Saraguro it is worth hiring a guide to take you not only through the city, but to the surrounding towns, which hold just as much cultural importance and interest. A great place to start any visit to Saraguro is at Fundación Kawsay, whose goal is community eco-tourism and revitalization of the indigenous culture and ethnicity of Saraguro. Through this agency you can tour weavers' workshops and medicinal plant projects, as well as hike to sacred waterfalls where traditional ritual cleansings are still performed. The profits of this organization go directly to the different communities visited, so you know exactly where your money is going. And if you have a hankering to pick up some Quichua, this is the place to do it, as most people in the area, especially in the surrounding towns, speak this native language. At 64 km north of Loja, there are not very many places to stay the night in Saraguro.

Fundacion Kawsay, located just outside of town, has the most comfortable hostel, accompanied by beautiful views. Hotels Samana Wasi, Sara Allpa, and Saraguro, are all budget and adequate options. The best place to eat is Mama Cuchara, serving typical meals on the main plaza and run by the indigenous federation. A trip to Saraguro is truly eye-opening and refreshing: tourists rarely frequent this region bound by stunning landscapes and home to a captivating culture. For more information go to www.kawsay.org, or call 593-7-220-0331.

SOUTHERN ANDES

LOJA

Founded in 1548 by Alonso de Mercadillo, Loja is somewhat of a political and cultural island, surrounded by mountains and stranded at the far southern end of Ecuador. Besides being the provincial capital, Loja warrants recognition as the first city in Ecuador to generate electricity (1897). Today, it is an intellectually and architecturally unique city, boasting two universities set among a peculiar mix of urban concrete and colonial structures.

Approximately 500 meters lower than most southern cities, Loja enjoys noticeably warmer weather—an appropriate complement to its congenial cultural climate and exuberant atmosphere. There is a lot to see and do in Loja. Situated around the sprawling palm-tree studded central park are a number of interesting buildings, including the Cathedral, Casa de Justicia, which houses the Museo del Banco Central, and the modern municipio, with its pleasant courtyard and vibrant murals, which play out various indigenous scenes. Beyond the park, further south along Bolívar from the Iglesia Santo Domingo, is the Plaza de la Independencia, where the citizens of Loja gathered on November 18, 1820 to denounce the Spanish Crown and assert their independence. Perhaps the most attractive section of the city, the square is enlivened by the brightly painted facades of colonial-style buildings, and neatly framed by resplendent hills rising in the distance.

Between the historic center of the city and the northern areas, you'll find the Entrada a la Cuidad, a towering structure designed to look like a medieval castle gatehouse. The building houses an art museum and snack bar and is worth a quick visit. Beyond the city center and its magnificent squares are the Parque de Recreación Jipiro, Parque La Argelia and Jardín Botánico Reynaldo Espinosa, all perfect for day-strolls. For stunning panoramic views of the city, head up to the statue of the Virgen de Fátima, sitting in the hills east of the city. Located just beyond Loja, Parque Nacional Podocarpus offers more sweeping views and stunning landscapes to explore.

Most visitors to Loja are delighted to discover that the city is still quite inexpensive: you can stay and eat for less money than you can in most of the rest of Ecuador. As for lodging in Loja, visitors have several options: you'll find dirt-cheap hostels, elegant, classy hotels and everything in between. Restaurants in Loja tend towards the regional: most of the food you'll find is heavy southern Ecuadorian fare, heavy on the soups and pork, but there are a few places that feature international cuisine.

GETTING TO LOJA

Loja is in a remote part of southern Ecuador and the best way to get there, by far, is to fly. There are a few daily flights to and from Quito, which take about 45 minutes and cost roughly $140 (roundtrip). The airport in Loja is located about 40 minutes away from the city: cab fare from the airport to the city will cost you about $10-15, or you can take the cab to the nearby little town of Catamayo, where you can catch a bus to Loja. They leave regularly, especially when a flight has just come in. If you have heavy bags, it may not be worth it to lug them to Catamayo: you may want to just suck it up and go for the direct taxi. Note that Loja's airport has a very small runway and is precariously carved out of the rolling hills in the area. The airport closes regularly for bad weather: they'll postpone flights in or out indefinitely until they're sure that conditions are safe. In other words, don't plan your time very tightly coming into or out of the city, or you may be in for a nerve-wracking day of waiting out a rainstorm.

By bus: Getting to Loja by bus is a long trip. From Quito, it's a grueling 15 hour trip. Panamericana (Colon and Reina Victoria in the Mariscal, phone 593-2-250-1585) makes the trip, as do some companies at the Terminal Terrestre in Quito. A bus ticket from Quito to Loja costs about $15-20 depending on operator, quality of bus, if it goes directly, etc. From Guayaquil, the bus trip is 9-10 hours and costs about $10. Buses tend to leave at night and arrive in the morning. From Cuenca, buses tend to go more or less hourly all day. It's a five-hour trip that costs roughly $7. You can also get from Piura, Peru, on the border, to Loja. It's an eight-hour trip, costing about $8. Buses leave early in the morning and late at night. Buses leave every half hour or so from Loja to Catamayo, where you'll find the La Toma airport (45 minutes).

Tourist information
Municipal Building

On the corner of the Parque Principal in Loja is the Municipal Building, a good reference point that offers a wealth of information. There is a public library, which includes a braille library, as well as an turism office, which can help you plan your stay in Loja and the surrounding areas. Next to the office is a beautiful mural of traditional musical life in Loja, painted by Oswaldo Mora, that is definitely worth visiting. On the corner of the Parque Principal on Eguiguren and Bolivar.

Things to See & Do

Most visitors to the city of Loja are just passing through on their way to peaceful Vilcabamba, which is a pity: Loja is a charming city in its own right, with lots to see and do. The hotels in Loja are affordable and pleasant, and the restaurants in Loja are quite good. If you're passing through, you should consider spending a day or two checking out what Loja has to offer.

The most recognizable landmark in the city is certainly the Entrada a la Ciudad, a towering structure designed like a medieval gatehouse, complete with towers, crenellated walls and a portcullis. It houses an art museum and is a good place to explore, especially for kids.

Jipiro Park is located to the north of the city. It is a city park hugely popular with Lojano families, especially on weekends. It's low-cost entertainment at its friendly best: check out an ultra-cheesy planetarium show for twenty-five cents, rent a paddleboat for a dollar or watch the locals play soccer for free. The park is full of small replicas of famous buildings: St. Basil's Cathedral has slides for kids, an Arabic mosque hosts the planetarium, and the bathrooms are in the Polynesian Tiki House.

There are several other parks surrounding the city, including Parque Universitario la Arquelia and the Reinaldo Espinoza Botanical Garden. Loja's historic downtown, while not as nice as Cuenca's, is still worth a visit. There are several cathedrals and city squares and a number of interesting museums, including the Music Museum and the Central Bank Museum.

Entrada a la Ciudad

Also known as Puerta de la Cuidad or Portal de la Cuidad, the Entrada a la Cuidad de Loja is without a doubt Loja's most recognizable landmark. Built to look like a medieval gatehouse, complete with (fake) portcullis, the Entrada a la ciudad straddles Sucre Street as it leaves downtown to the north. The Entrada crosses a very small river (it seems like overkill, in fact: you could probably jump over the "river") and there is a small park-like area on either side. There is even a very small parking lot for those who wish to see the building.

Inside the castle-like structure, you'll find a free art museum, open daily, a snack bar, and a wandering maze of stairways, balconies and towers. There is a small information desk. The gatehouse is well-kept, attractive and more than a little fun: you'll want to stop and see it, and you'll only need about 20 minutes. Across the street to the south are two dazzling murals dedicated to Simón Bolívar and José Antonio de Sucre, heroes of Ecuadorian independence. Where 18 Noviembre, Sucre and Nueva Loja streets converge.

Musuems
Museo de la Música (Museum of Music)

This small museum set around a sunny courtyard is dedicated to the musicians and composers of Loja. The displays include many of their original instruments and sheet music. The museum also has occasional musical performances and a nice café that serves fresh juices, coffee, and typical Lojano snacks, such as tamales. Open Monday - Friday, 9 a.m.-1 p.m., 3 p.m.-7 p.m. Bernardo Valdivieso 09-42 and Rocafuerte, Tel: 593-7-256-1342.

SOUTHERN ANDES

MUSEO DEL BANCO CENTRAL

This museum contains an extensive collection of archaeological pieces, including 10,000 year old weapons and tools from the region around Loja, and other objects pertaining to the most well known cultures of Ecuador, such as Valdivia, Machalilla and Chorrera. There is also an ethnographic section that focuses on the region of Loja and Saraguro, as well as a fine arts section with religious art as well as contemporary pieces. In the mornings, there are occasional free guides in the museum—local tourism students doing internships. Although they do not charge, it is appropriate to give them a small tip if they are informative and helpful. 10 de Agosto 13-30 between Bolivar and Bernardo Valdiviezo, Hours: 9 a.m.-1 p.m., 2 p.m.- 5 p.m.

PARKS

PARQUE JIPIRO

One of the best known parks of Loja, Jipiro lies to the North of the city and spans 10 hectares. It is well-kept, clean and a great place to take a stroll. There is a lake, sports fields, a "cyber train" with internet service, a zoo, and pools, as well as many replicas of the world's great buildings. It is possible to camp here and on the weekends it fills up with Lojano families who come for the many activities and events. One of the buildings houses a planetarium: shows cost 25 cents and are well worth it, if just for humor value. The planetarium screen is the size of a large beach umbrella and the show basically consists of a guy with a slide projector showing dim photos from a science textbook on one section of the ceiling while the voice-over talks about planets, comets and constellations. It lasts about 15 minutes and shows continually, whenever the seats fill up, which usually doesn't take long, especially on weekends. Masochists will enjoy an interesting ride: for a quarter, a guy will strap you into a gyroscope-looking thing and give you a hearty spin. The paddleboats are also fun for a couple of bucks. In the North of the city, a few blocks East of the bus terminal. Five minutes from city center by bus marked "Jipiro" from Universitaria, Tel: 593-7-258-3357 (ext 251).

PARQUE UNIVERSITARIO LA ARQUELIA

La Arquelia is a beautiful 90 hectare park on the edge of the city. There are 7 km of excellent hiking trails that go through forest, streams and the páramo. There is a small museum and information center, and at the entrance to the trails, there is a map that shows the various hikes. Also part of the park, with an entrance across the street, is the impressive botanical garden, including many species of plants native to Ecuador, such as cinchona trees, various medicinal plants and an orchid garden. La Arquelia is on the road from Loja to Vilcabamba. Take any bus heading toward Vilcabamba and get off at the gate (12 minutes, 50 cents). Or take an Argelia-Pitas bus (10 minutes, 20 cents) that drops you off at the campus. From there it is a ten-minute walk. Open 8 a.m.-12 p.m., 2 p.m.-5:30 p.m.

LODGING

Loja has a variety of hotel options for visitors, from $5/night hostels (Londres Hotel) to business-class (Quo Vadis) to comfortable, elegant hotels (Casa Lojana). You'll also find everything in-between.

If you're looking to sleep cheap, head to the old town. West of the central square, you'll find an array of budget hostals in varying states of upkeep and cleanliness. The best of them are Hostal Las Orquideas and Londres Hotel, but there are many more. The old town is a bit noisier than other areas of Loja, but if you're on a budget, you're pretty much stuck there. Loja is still an inexpensive town, and there are several good hotel deals in the mid-range category. Quo Vadis is new, and its rates are still low for the time being. The Hostal Aguilera Internacional is a good choice and has rates which compete with some of the pricier downtown locales.

The best hotel in town is probably Casa Lojana, set in a converted home outside of town. In the Centro Histórico, the seen-better-days Hotel Libertador is a good option for families with kids, as it has a pool, restaurant, sauna, etc. and it's also very centrally located. One thing to always bear in mind when selecting lodging in Loja is that prices are relatively low there: unless you're on the tightest of budgets, you may want to spend a little more. For the cost of a lower mid-range hotel in Quito, you can stay at a nice mid-range or business-class hotel in Loja.

HOTEL LONDRÉS (ROOMS: $5)

The Hotel Londres is located in an old, unassuming building that was obviously cut in half at some point in the past. Tall and narrow, the hostel has 12 rooms with a varying number of beds in each: the rock-bottom price of $5 will get you one. Bathrooms are spread out and shared: none of the rooms has private bath. There is a small community kitchen in back. The old wooden floors are charming though, and there is even a little nook where guests can hang out. There isn't real hot water, but heating devices on the showers (think a cross between a shower head and a toaster) should provide at least lukewarm water. Sucre 07-57 and 10 de Agosto, Tel: 593-7-256-1936.

HOSTAL LAS ORQUÍDEAS (ROOMS: $10-24)

Probably the best all-around low-budget lodging option in downtown Loja, Las Orquídeas is a small, but clean and friendly, hostal just around the corner from the central park. It's also about the most economical place to stay in Loja that still features private bathrooms. The interior is not nearly as gloomy as most of the other downtown hotels, and efforts have been made to liven it up with plants, wall art, etc. There is no restaurant on the premises but there are several nearby. Bolivar 08-59 entre 10 Agosto and Rocafuerte, Tel: 593-7-256-2162/593-7-258-7008, E-mail: hlorquideas@easynet.ec.

SARAGURO RIKUY

Simple rooms run by Saraguro Rikuy, a non-profit community organization supporting community organization and development through education about the tradition, environment, and sustainable development. Doubles to dorm rooms house up to 33, many have private baths with hot water. Decent on-site bar and restaurant. Calle 18 de Noviembre and Avenida Loja, Tel: 593-7-220-0331, E-mail: info@kawsay.org, URL: www.kawsay.org.

COPALINGA (ROOMS: $14-34)

Located 3 km from Podocarpus Nacional Park, Copalinga is a mecca for birders and nature lovers, surrounded by a complex network of trails with bird viewing spots. Six cozy cabins house up to 12 and four smaller doubles each have private bath, hot showers, and a balcony. There are also more budget "rustic" cabins with bunks and a shared bath. The owners will make you meals in an on-site restaurant and bar, but make reservations ahead of time if you plan to eat. Halfway between Zamora and Copalinga (3 km) on the road to the Podocarpus National Park, Tel:593-9-347-7013, E-mail: info@copalinga.com, URL:www.copalinga.com.

HOTEL ACAPULCO (ROOMS: $16-36)

Rooms are slightly brighter than the murky passageways and stairwells, but the bathrooms smell funky enough to make you wonder if cleanliness is really a priority. The service, while not exactly friendly, is at least efficient and polite. It does have Cable TV, which is a bonus and as hotels in the area go, there are worse values. The best that can be said about the Acapulco is that it is well-located, being only a couple of blocks from most of the attractions in downtown Loja (such as they are). You're better off heading a couple of doors down to the Londres Hotel, or better yet, a couple of blocks over to the Hostal Las Orquídeas. Sucre 07-61 and 10 de Agosto, Tel: 593-7-257-0651/593-7-257-9652/593-7-257-0199, E-mail: hacapulco@easynet.net.ec.

HOSTAL AGUILERA INTERNACIONAL (ROOMS: $22-47)

Located directly across the street from the impossible-to-miss Entrada de la Ciudad, the Hostal Aguilera Internacional is an airy, bright hotel with small but clean rooms, ample parking, and an array of services that include a social room (for wedding receptions, etc.), a playground, a conference room and a restaurant. There is even a sauna, steam room and gym. The hotel is a significant step up from similarly priced downtown hotels such as the Acapulco and the Central Park Hostal. It is still possible to walk to downtown areas of interest and proximity to Puerta de Loja is a bonus. Sucre 01-08 and Av. Emiliano Ortega, Tel: 593-7-258-4660/593-257-2892,/593-7-257-2461/593-7-257-2894.

QUO VADIS (ROOMS: $29-65)

One of the newest hotels in Loja (completed in early 2007), the Quo Vadis is a modern, reasonably priced hotel well located within walking distance of Jipiro Park. The Quo Vadis features a restaurant but no pool or gym, and oddly does not have an elevator (if you don't like stairs, stay elsewhere or request a room on the first floor). The rooms are very nice, comfortable, and clean, and the hotel is very tastefully decorated. As an added bonus, the Quo Vadis is one of very few places in Loja to get a decent expresso or cappuccino: an important consideration for you java-heads out there. Rates are currently low, as the hotel is still making a name for itself, but may go up at some point in the future—be sure to double-check before booking. On Sundays, the restaurant at the Quo Vadis has a lunch buffet popular with locals and guests alike. Isidro Ayora and 8 de Diciembre, E-mail: quovadishotel@gmail.com, URL: www.quovadishotel.com.ec.

HOTEL LIBERTADOR (ROOMS: $45-69)

The Hotel Libertador is the best of the hotels located in Loja's historic district. The interior is dimly lit and gloomy, but the rooms are nice, the service is very good, and there are a variety of extras that other hotels in the area do not have, such as a swimming pool, sauna, steam room and restaurant. It also offers free internet for guests, Cable TV and parking, which is a bonus in the chaotic Loja city center. Colon 14-30 and Bolivar, Tel: 593-7-256-0779/ 593-7-257-8278, URL: www.hotellibertador.com.ec.

CASA LOJANA (ROOMS: $61-110)

Casa Lojana is one of Loja's best high-budget options. The building that houses the hotel was once an elegant home, which has since been converted. There are gardens, balconies, a fine restaurant and luxurious, well-decorated rooms. The hotel is efficiently run by the University of Loja, who use it as a learning tool for their students in hotel industry courses. The hotel is located outside of town on a hilly street: a taxi ride from just about anywhere in Loja should cost about $1. The rates are quite high for inexpensive Loja, but they're relative. A night at a place like Casa Lojana would be much more expensive in Quito or other parts of the world. Paris 00-08 and Zoilo Rodríguez, Tel: 593-7-258-5984/593-7-258-5984, E-mail:casalojanahotel@utpl.edu.ec, URL: www.casalojanahotel.com.ec.

RESTAURANTS

CAFÉ REAL (BREAKFAST: $.95)

A cute café serving typical Lojano food, including breakfasts, lunch, and other traditional treats like humitas, tamales, quimbolitos, bolones and empanadas. Café Real has local Lojano flavor and is a great place to take a break from the day and recharge with a fresh juice and snack. On Miguel Riofrio between Bolivar and Valdivieso.

TOPOLI (SWEETS: $.50-2)

Come to Topoli if you are looking for a quick fix for your sweet tooth. Serving a variety of cakes and ice cream sundaes, along with the best coffee and yogurt in town, this small cafeteria also offers your basic sandwiches and crepes. Service is friendly and the prices are reasonable. Bolivar 13-78 and Riofrio.

GINO GINELLI

This all-in-one pizzeria will satisfy the cravings of anyone. Though a bit dark, a long list of different pizzas, most for $3-4, as well as breakfast, burgers, a variety of ice cream flavors, and a bar downstairs, will cheer the spirits. Address: 14-29 Miguel Riofrio and Bolivar.

DIEGO'S CAFÉ RESTAURANT (ENTREES: $2.50-7)

Hidden away in an old colonial house, Diego's has very elegant upstairs seating overlooking a green courtyard. The menu includes an enormous variety of both typical Lojano and international foods including pastas, ceviches, sandwiches and salads. The breakfasts come with piping hot fresh bread and the service is excellent. Coming to Diego's you feel like you've found one of Loja's most delicious secrets. Colon 14-88 and Sucre, Tel: 593-7-256-0245/593-7-257-5562.

AROUND LOJA
PODOCARPUS NATIONAL PARK

Podocarpus National Park is one of the jewels of Southern Ecuador and is named after the Podocarpus tree, the only native conifer in the Ecuadorian Andes. Spanning 1,462 square kilometers of Andean cloud forest, the park hosts five different microclimates and provides drinking water for Loja, Zamora and a number of smaller towns in the region. The park ranges from 900 to 3,600 meters and is home to toucans, spectacled bears, mountain tapers and pigmy deer; however, 97 percent of the park's fauna is invertebrate.

There are two main access points to the park; from Loja and from Zamora. To access the high zone travel 15 kilometers along the highway between Loja and Vilcabamba until you reach the Cajanuma Ranger Station. From this point head 8.5 kilometers along a smaller road until you reach the administration center. From here there are four main trails: "Oso de Anteojos," 400 meters, moderately steep and easily accessible. "El Bosque Nublado," 750 meters long, and "El Mirador," 1.5 km long are both of medium difficulty. For a day long hike, you can continue along "El Mirador" for 3.5 km, however some parts of this trail are very difficult. The "Lagunas del Compadre Trail" is 15.5 km, one way, and very steep. For this trail you must bring good camping gear and warm waterproof clothes, and for your safety, advise the park that you will be hiking this trail. The access to the low zone is 6.8 km from Zamora. The last 0.8 km you must hike along an easy trail to the Bombuscaro refuge, where there are four different trails. Two lead to waterfalls: "La Chismosa," 200 meters, and "La Poderosa," 450 meters. The other two trails are "La Urraquita," 600 meters, and "Los Higuerones," 3 km. All of these trails are intermediate level. Entrance passes are $10, available at the refuges and are valid for any part of the park and for up to five days. Tel: 593-7-258-5421/593-7-260-5606.

PUYANGO PETRIFIED FOREST

The largest field of exposed petrified wood in the world is found just south of the Ecuadorian city of Loja, not far from the Peruvian border: its name is El Bosque Petrificado de Puyango, or the Puyango Petrified Forest. Massive stone logs, 80 million years old cross the trails, fallen giants from a bygone age. Petrified forests are rare: wood usually decomposes once it dies, and Puyango is considered a very significant source of information by scientists, especially as most of the trees are in the Araucarias family, which are rarely fossilized. There are marine fossils in the park as well, a remnant of a time even before the trees, when the area was a shallow sea. There is more to Puyango then petrified wood. In the local language, Puyango means "dry, dead river," and for good reason. The region is considered a dry tropical forest, a rare ecosystem as most forests in the tropics tend to get a good deal of rain. The area is a protected national park, and features a diverse ecosystem with interesting wildlife. There are more than 130 species of birds that are home there during all or part of the year, and it is also known for being home to many pretty species of butterflies.

For some, the best part will be the fact that Puyango is well off the gringo trail: it's very remote, and the nearest city of any size is Loja, about four hours away. Some facts: The Park is 2569 Hectares, or about 6570 acres. The oldest fossils in the park are marine fossils estimated to be about 500 million years old; the area was once underwater. The tree fossils are considered to be about 65-80 million years old. The park is open from 8 a.m. to 4 p.m. every day. Good local guides are available. Entrance to the park costs $1. The nearest town with any sort of tourist facilities is Alamor. The nearest big city is Loja, about four hours away. It is possible to day trip from Loja, but it's a long day.

From December to May is the rainy season, and the dry season is from June to November. It's preferable to visit during the dry season. Bring water, a hat, light clothes and sunscreen. There are decent trails through the park. It is possible to camp in the park; ask about it at the information center.

SOUTHERN ANDES

VILCABAMBA

Highly publicized as "the valley of eternal youth" for its sprightly 70-and 80-year-old inhabitants, Vilcabamba is also a hotspot on the gringo trail. It is a must for anyone keen to hook up with fellow travelers, or indulge in home-made hippie treats and pamper themselves with a massage or steam bath. For some time, it was thought that residents regularly lived beyond 100 years, however, it is now thought that this is unlikely. At one time a small, isolated village, Vilcabamba is now more of an expat-haven, rich in gringo-run businesses catering to backpackers, than a place equipped to administer a shot of local culture.

Boasting a warm, pleasant climate, set among spectacular scenery and an agreeable atmosphere, Vilcabamba is popular among Lojano weekenders, as well as foreign travelers. This is the place to head for excellent horseback riding, walking, hiking or just plain hanging out. Just outside of town, the scenic Mandango trail makes a great day-hike, while a number of private nature reserves and the famed Podocarpus National Park sit just beyond the village, offering even more opportunities to explore the local landscape and enjoy the pleasant climate. Come between June and September, when the climate is drier and warmer.

GETTING TO AND AWAY

Turn left on the dirt road at the end of Agua de Hierro. Do not cross the first bridge you see, but turn left at the river and walk along the bank (you may have to walk through parts of the river, but it is shallow). Pass the walled-in houses on the left and follow the path to the slanted bridge. Cross the bridge and you will arrive at Rumi Wilco.

ACTIVITIES

HORSEBACK RIDING IN VILCABAMBA

Horseback riding is popular in Vilcabamba, due mostly to the quality of local horses and the absolutely stunning natural beauty of the valley. There are rides for all levels: beginner riders will want to try the four-hour ride around the city. It's pretty easy, and four hours isn't long enough to get too sore. For more advanced riders, there are trips up to Podocarpus Park outside of town. Podocarpus is far enough away from town that horseback riding is the best way to see it: you'll have trouble getting there on foot from town. These trips are longer, go over some very rough terrain, and often involve some hiking. Talk to your outfitter about your level, confidence and what you would like to see and do.

If you go horseback riding in Vilcabamba, wear long sleeves, sunscreen and a hat. Your guide should bring water, but having a small bottle along isn't a bad idea. Carry as little as possible: when the horse starts to run, any cameras, backpacks, fanny packs, etc. will start to bounce up and down, which is very uncomfortable and irritating. Most outfitters will provide rubber boots for you to use while riding: if you have very small or very large feet, you might want to bring your own.

There are several small agencies offering horseback rides in Vilcabamba: just have a look around the main square area and you'll see at least three or four. Two that have good reputations are Caballos Gavilán and La Tasca Tours. A whole-day trip, including lunch, usually runs around $25.

MASSAGE AND BEAUTY CARE

This is the best place in Vilcabamba to treat yourself. Karina offers relaxing full-body massages, facials, reflexology, and reiki, as well as waxing, manicures and pedicures. Located conveniently in the center of town, the salon is always full, so come early to make an appointment for later in the day. Diego Vaca de Vega and Bolivar, Tel: 593-9-326-1944/593-7-264-0295.

LODGING

For a town of its size, Vilcabamba offers a range of places, each varying in style and price, and some of the most scenic and interesting places lie just a short distance (a few kilometers) outside of the town itself. Depending on your tastes and wallet size, you can choose from options as diverse as pampering yourself in a spa, to pitching in on a working farm.

HOSTERIA IZHCAYLUMA (ROOMS: $10-15)

Hosteria Izhcayluma is situated on a hill approximately 2 km outside of Vilcabamba, and enjoys spectacular vistas of the village and surrounding countryside. Guests are housed in beautiful bungalows, set well-spaced within the grounds and decorated in a minimalist style. Balconies and hammocks overlooking the stunning landscape are a very welcome feature of the rooms. The hotel also has a restaurant which serves a delicious mix of both Ecuadorian and Bavarian specialities. Breakfast is included and can be taken at any time during the day. Tel: 593-07-264-0095, E-mail: izhcayluma@yahoo.de, URL: www.izhcayluma.com.

JARDÍN ESCONDIDO

In addition to the sizzling Mexican and international fare offered up at the restaurant, Jardín Escondido has 13 pleasantly appointed rooms, including singles, doubles and family rooms, with private baths. The hotel, as the name would suggest, features a beautiful hidden garden with an inviting pool for taking a dip or lounging about. The owners are friendly and accommodating, a nice match for the warm atmosphere and peaceful grounds. Just off the main square on Sucre, Tel:593-7-264-0281, E-mail: jardinescondido@yahoo.com, URL: www.vilcabamba.org/jardinescondido.

HOTEL LE RENDEZ-VOUS (ROOMS: $9-32)

Rendez-Vous was set up by a French couple who fell in love with and chose to settle in Vilcabamba after traveling extensively throughout South America. The grounds feature eight adobe cabins with private bathrooms and 24-hour hot water. Each has a pretty terrace where you can kick back and relax in your hammock, while enjoying views of the manicured garden below. Before you settle in and swing away, grab a book from the library, which has books in English, French, German and Spanish. Breakfast and taxes are included in the room price. Diego Vaca de la Vega and La Paz, E-mail: rendevousecuador@yahoo.com, URL: www.rendezvousecuador.com.

> *V!VA Member Review-Hotel Le Rendez-Vous*
> *We have been traveling for 5 months, from Mexico. From the 46 hotels we stayed in throughout Latin America, this was the best place: spacious rooms, queen beds, very clean, and the best power shower in South America. And really quiet, the best place to relax. Isabelle, the French owners serves us breakfast on our personal table on the porch with excellent home-made bread. The rate for a double room is good at $9 per person with breakfast included. Don't change anything! 22 March 2007. Switzerland.*

MADRE TIERRA (ROOMS: $39-119)

A highlight of any stay in the Vilcabamba region, for those who wish to shell out a little cash, Madre Tierra offers outstanding accommodation and first-class service. To relax and recharge for a couple of days, head to the health spa and indulge in a luxurious facial or massage, along with more exotic treatments. Set around a landscaped organic garden, each room features its own colorful style. Prices include breakfast and dinner, and veggie-maniacs will be glad to hear that every day features a different veggie option. You do not need to be staying at the hotel to come and hire services at the spa (but you should make reservations). Tel:593-7-264-026, E-mail: madretierra@vilcanet.net, URL: www.madretierra1.com.

RUMI WILCO NATURE RESERVE AND ECOLODGE ($25-$40/PERSON)

Rumi Wilco is only a 10-minute walk from the center of Vilcabamba, but you feel like you are miles away. This nature reserve was created by an Argentinian couple, Alicia and Orlando Falco, in an effort to reverse the environmental degradation caused by slash-and-burn agriculture. The reserve encompasses a beautiful mountainside with plenty of trails for hiking. There is also an ecolodge on the reserve with well-kept rustic adobe cabins with kitchens. A third of what you pay goes toward various management programs on the reserve. Tel:593-7-267-3186, E-mail: rumiwilco@yahoo.com, URL: www.rumiwilco.com

Help other travelers. Publish your favorite places at www.vivatravelguides.com

SACRED SUEÑOS ORGANIC FARM

This organic farm is located in the beautiful mountains that surround Vilcabamba. It is open to anyone interested in organics and willing to help out around the farm. A two- to three-hour hike from Vilcabamba, the farm is a joint effort to improve a degraded mountainside.

There are many projects that need helping hands, including trail building, composting and mulching, animal and tree care, building structures and furniture with local materials, irrigation, and gardening. The hike up to the farm is of medium-difficulty, but the scenery is worth it, as is the peace and quite and amazing views on arrival.

The farm is not a hotel and all visitors are expected to help out with what they can. People are welcome for short stays, and as there is no fee to stay at the farm, they are asked to bring up some food donations. Those who would like to stay for at least two weeks and give advance notice can be met in Vilcabamba—donkey service can be provided from the trailhead for your luggage. There is no electricity at the farm and most people sleep in tents, however there are some beds available. E-mail: sacredsuenos@wildmail.com/infoss@care2.com.

RESTAURANTS

NATURAL YOGURT VILCABAMBA (SNACKS: $1.50-3)

Natural Yogurt Vilcabamba is perhaps the easiest, best find around. Located on the central park, its pleasant outdoor seating area is always filled, due to their delicious yogurt and fruit breakfasts, tasty main meals and exquisite dessert crepes. There are lots of vegetarian options and the food is made with almost all organic ingredients, all for a great price. On Bolivar near the Central Park.

EL PUNTO CAFÉ (ENTREES: $3)

A cute coffee shop on the corner of the central park that caters to the ex-pat residents in Vilcabamba. Serves all types of coffee, teas, cocktails and homemade desserts. Also has sandwiches and pasta, all of which are delicious. Check out the handmade silver jewelry for sale, and if you are in a playful mood, ask to use one of the many table games available. There is nice outdoor seating facing the park, great for people watching. Sucre and Luis Fernando de Vega.

JARDÍN ESCONDIDO

Jardin Escondido is a tranquil restaurant, which is part of the hotel by the same name. The locale, truly a hidden garden, boasts candlelit dining in a lush courtyard, and serves authentic Ecuadorian, Mexican, and international cuisine. Most of the food is organic and homemade. There is live music some Saturday nights. The owner also sells handmade original masks. Sucre and Agua de Hierro.

LAYSECA'S BAKERY (SWEETS: $.25-.75)

A newly opened bakery with a quaint feel, Layseca's is a great place to stop and snack. The Peruvian owner, Leonor, makes you feel right at home, and prides herself on using only organic ingredients. Treats include homemade crepes, waffles, chocolate, cookies, whole grain bread, cakes, marmalade and coffee. Juan Montalvo 114-21 and Bolivar.

SHANTA'S CAFÉ BAR (ENTREES: $2.50-4.50)

A laid-back rustic country café and bar, Shanta's is a place to go if you are looking to relax during the day, or rave during the night. Meals include hamburgers, spaghetti, and pizza, as well as their delicacy of frog's legs. They also have delicious fresh juices and an extensive drink list. Don't miss their specialty, Snake's Juice. A five minute walk from the center, over the bridge heading East on Diego Vaca de la Vega towards Yamburara.

LA TERRAZA (ENTREES: $2-4)

La Terraza is a lovely small restaurant with outdoor seating facing the central plaza. It has striking views of the mountains in the distance. The service is friendly and the menu covers most of the staple meals in Ecuador as well as international fare, such as falafel, sandwiches, Oriental, Mexican and Italian food. On Diego Vaca de Vega and Bolivar.

SOUTHERN ANDES

Photo by Rick Segreda

AMAZON BASIN

The Amazon River Basin, or El Oriente to Ecuadorians, is the biggest region in Ecuador. Ecuador has 2% of the Amazon Rainforest and makes for a convenient jump from major cities. Tourist infrastructure is well developed, and most destinations are less than a day's journey from Quito.

More life hums, buzzes, chatters and bubbles in the Amazon Rainforest than anywhere else on the planet. One Amazonian tree can host more ant species than all of the British Isles put together, one hectare of forest boasts about as many frog species as all of North America and the great expanse of the jungle contains more than twenty percent of the earth's vascular plant species. Here you can find a monkey small enough to sit on your fingertip, an eight-pound toad, a spider that eats birds and the world's largest snake, the 30-foot anaconda.

The Amazon is home to thousands of indigenous inhabitants, who make up nearly 200 distinct nations, including the Siona, Secoya, Cofan, Shuar, Zaparo, Huaorani and Quichua. Having lived there for more than 10,000 years, they know its trees, its animals and its rhythms better than anyone.

A plethora of tour operators based out of Quito, Tena and Baños can help you find a tour that meets your needs, be it a comfy lodge with three-course meals and hot showers, or a mud-up-to-your-knees trekking and camping adventure.

Oil companies are a serious threat to the rainforest today. Even at lodges deep in the jungle, plumes of smoke coming from oil refineries smudge the otherwise untouched horizon day and night. You can learn more about indigenous forest peoples and the rainforest itself joining one of the many community-based ecotourism programs offered in the Ecuadorian Amazon or by becoming a volunteer with one of the many nonprofits working in the region.

AMAZON RAINFOREST LODGES

The Amazon rainforest basin, or El Oriente, is a popular tourist destination, and a number of jungle lodges have sprung up in recent years. Most of them are centered around Tena, Puerto Francisco de Orellana (Coca), or Nueva Loja (Lago Agrio), which are transportation hubs in Ecuador's eastern lowlands. Although each is quite unique, activities and basic features don't vary too much. With a little research on V!VA Travel Guides, you will be able to find the best lodge for you.

Location is the first consideration. The lodges near Tena, such as Cotococha, are more easily accessible than those near Coca or Lago Agrio, but have significantly less wildlife. Getting from Quito to Tena is a relatively easy six-hour bus ride, whereas the buses from Quito to Coca or Lago Agrio can take 10 hours or more. There are also flights to some major launching points in the jungle to and from Quito. Flights to both Coca and Lago Agrio take about 30-40 minutes and cost $120 round trip.

Another consideration is comfort. If your idea of a vacation always includes a pool, a buffet table and hammocks, there are jungle lodges that will provide that. If you're more interested in animals and birds than comfort, you should check out the more remote lodges, such as Sani Lodge and lodges in the Cuyabeno Reserve. If you're willing to pay, there are lodges that offer both comfort and good animal watching. Still other lodges, like Yachana Lodge, offer a closer look at local jungle communities, which can be fascinating as well. See our packing list section for what to pack.

YARINA LODGE

Yarina Lodge is an eco-lodge set in the wilds of the Amazonian jungle near the Yasuní National Park, in the zone reserved for indigenous Quichuas. It was started 7 years ago as an attempt to alert both foreigners and Ecuadorians to the cause of environmentalism in the Amazon. It is now one of the most important environmental centers in the area, in conjunction with Yuturi Lodge. Yarina Lodge contains 20 huts for travelers (single, double, triple and quadruple accommodations), all complete with private bathrooms and showers. The huts are

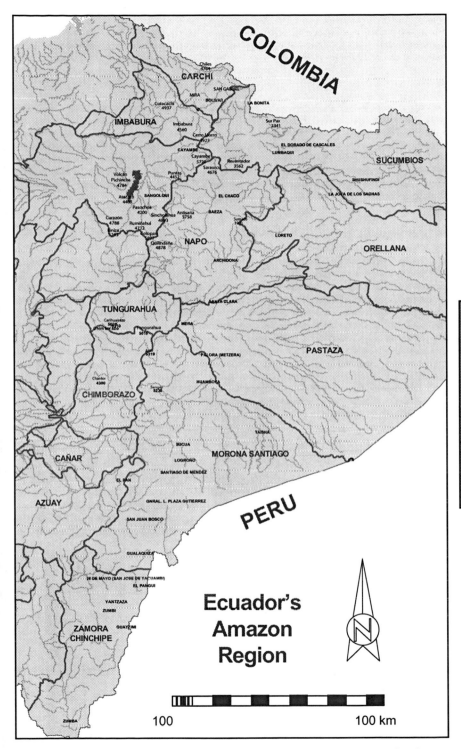

Ecuador's Amazon Region

100   100 km

constructed with materials native to the area. There is a larger meeting place on the resort where travelers can meet to eat, drink and chat about the day's events. The lodge offers a plethora of activities: whether you're interested in fishing for piranhas or visiting a local shaman, you can certainly do it here. Tel: 593-2-250-4037 /250-3225 /254-5179, E-mail: info@yarinalodge.com, URL: www.yarinalodge.com.

HUASQUILA AMAZON LODGE

Only about four hours from Quito (by car), Huasquila Amazon Lodge offers six luxury cabins built with local materials in Quichua Style within the Sumaco Biosphere Reserve. Each cabin has a private bathroom, hot water, wide interior spaces and balcony, from which you can enjoy the fascinating view of the Amazon. Huasquila offers personalized tours and activities (caving, petroglyphs, animal rescue center, jungle walks, visit to Quichua communities, and more!), first class attention in a family atmosphere, delicious national and international dishes, bar service with exotic cocktails and folkloric night show. Good for small groups with individual interests. Tel:593-2-290-8491, Fax: 593-2-290-8491, E-mail: info@huasquila.com, URL: www.huasquila.com.

LA SELVA JUNGLE LODGE

La Selva Jungle Lodge is 60 miles down the Napo river (two and a half hours by canoe) from the town of Coca. Located within Yasuní National Park, it boasts 17 thatched cabins and a dining room with bar/lounge area. Each of the cabins has a private bathroom, mosquito nets, and a hammock for relaxing. One of the more deluxe jungle lodges, each of the cabins has filtered water and hot water in the showers. They also take great pride in their food: the restaurant at La Selva is one of the better ones as jungle lodges go. Remote enough to be located in primary forest, La Selva offers many activities common to jungle lodges. There are various trails, day and night guided hikes, canoe trips and even a 135-foot canopy observation tower. Nearby is a salt lick where parrots and macaws congregate. There is also a butterfly farm. You can visit the home of a local indigenous family, and learn how residents of the rainforest commonly live. If guests wish, they can spend the night out deeper in the wilderness at a camping facility. Native guides are included to show guests the hundreds of species of birds in the park, and it is also common to see monkeys, caimans and a variety of insect life. A four-day / three-night stay at La Selva costs $634 per person, and a five-day / four-night stay costs $756. Prices include transportation to and from Coca, guides, all meals and needs such as rubber boots and rain ponchos. Quito office: San Salvador E7-85 and Carrión, Tel: 593-2-223-2730, E-mail: info@laselvajunglelodge.com, URL: www.laselvajunglelodge.com.

TIPUTINI BIODIVERSITY STATION

Tiputini Biodiversity Station, founded in 1994, is part of the Universidad San Francisco de Quito, or San Francisco University of Quito, one of the premier schools of higher education in Ecuador. It is a complete scientific and research facility, boasting a conference room, lecture facilities, and an air-conditioned computer room. Tiputini owns 650 hectares of rainforest, and the station is within the 1.7 million acre Yasuní National Park, which was recently declared a world bio-

Huasquila Amazon Lodge is your door to Ecuador's Amazon!
Located within the Sumaco Biosphere Reserve between the Andean mountain chain and the Amazon basin. Only a 4 hour drive from Ecuador's capital Quito!!!
"Waterfalls, kichwa communities, jungle walks, petroglyphs, caves, 'El Arca' Rescue Center" kayaking, rafting and so much more!!!

Huasquila Amazon Lodge
242 Amazonas Av. and Veintimilla – Edificio Espinoza 8th floor Of. 801
Quito/ Ecuador
Phone: 00593-2-2908491 Email: info@huasquila.com

sphere reserve. It is on the Tiputini River, which flows into the Napo river (and eventually into the Amazon). The area is home to an astounding number of birds and wildlife, including approximately 540 species of birds, 15 species of primates and five species of cats. They also feature canopy towers for research and bird watching. There are eight rooms, each of which can house two to four guests. A generator provides electricity until 10:00 p.m.. It is eco-friendly, featuring filtered water and recycling programs. Fax: 593-2- 2890-070, E-mail: tbs@mail.usfq.edu.ec.

NAPO WILDLIFE CENTER

The Napo Wildlife Center is located on the Napo river about two hours by motor canoe from Coca. As jungle lodges go, Napo Wildlife Center is one of the more deluxe ones. They boast 10 cabañas, with large, pleasant rooms. Every cabaña has a porch, private bath, ceiling fan, and is well-screened to keep insects out. There is a communal area, with a library, a bar, and a fifty-foot viewing tower attached for those who wish to bird watch from the lodge itself. The Napo Wildlife Center is far enough away from "civilization" that it is possible to see many birds and animals—565 species of bird have been seen in the reserve—and a fortunate tourist can also hope to see monkeys and river otters. It is also near a parrot lick: on a sunny day, hundreds of parrots will visit the lick to get certain nutrients they cannot get elsewhere, making for a memorable experience. Napo Wildlife Center offers package tours through Ecotours. Usual stays are Monday-Friday (five days / four nights) and Friday-Monday (four days / three nights). Their packages are all-inclusive, and include all meals, transportation, park fees, guides, boots, etc. Not included is the flight from Quito to Coca (about $120 round trip), alcoholic beverages, and tips for guides and staff. Tel: 593-2-289-7316, URL: www.napowildlifecenter.com.

V!VA Member Review-Napo Wildlife Center
I was totally in awe and thoroughly amazed at the natural beauty and abundance of wildlife! My trip was most memorable and will forever be a cherished experience. The entire staff at NWC were knowledgeable, enthusiastic, and very accommodating. I would highly recommend this to all bird and nature lovers. NWC should be on everyone's "Things to Do Before I Die" list! 22 February 2006. Placerville, CA.

YUTURI LODGE

Yuturi Lodge is a remote jungle lodge located a four and a half hour canoe trip from Coca. Responsible and modern, Yuturi works closely with the local community who help out as guides and workers. It has 15 huts, each of which can accommodate four guests. The huts are made of local materials, lending an air of authenticity to the experience, and each has

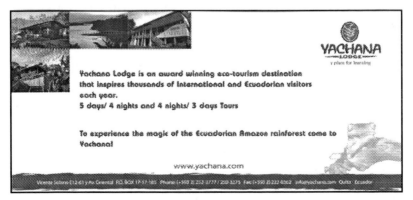

AMAZON BASIN

small, tidy beds and a mosquito net. Each room has a private bath and water 24-hours per day. A generator provides electricity from 6 a.m. to 10 p.m. The main cabin has a restaurant, bar, and a 15-meter observation tower. Yuturi provides hikes, canoe rides, night walks and bird watching. Many tourists have been fortunate enough to glimpse the rare pink river dolphin. Nearby "monkey island" is a protected area where guests can see a family of over 80 monkeys.

Yuturi organizes five day / four night excursions, at $360/person. Yuturi also offers a special, eight-day bird watching trip. If you need a longer or shorter trip, they are available, simply contact Yuturi through their Quito office. Quito office: Amazonas N24-236, between Colon and Cordero Tel:: 593-2-250-4037, E-mail: yuturi@yuturi.com.ec, URL: www.yuturilodge.com.

CUYABENO LODGE

The Cuyabeno Lodge, run by Neotropic Tours, is a popular eco-lodge with minimal impact on the environment. Each cabaña has a thatched roof, with a roughly two-foot space between the wall and roof so you can bird and monkey watch from the comfort of your bed. Mosquitoes are not a serious problem as the rivers are black-water rivers that do not inhabit mosquitoes.

Most tours are four or five days but special arrangements can be made for groups. The cost of a four-day tour is between $200 and $250 depending room type and availability. Three meals a day, free tea, coffee and water and transportation from Lago Agrio to the lodge are all included. A typical tour includes bird watching at dawn, piranha-fishing, dolphin-watching, visit to the community, tours of the rivers by boat, afternoon swims and sunset viewing, and several walks through the rainforest day and night. The guides are all bilingual, certified guide nature specialists accompanied by Siona guides. Open year-round. Between November to March the lagoon could dry up and transportation from the park entrance to the lodge may be difficult. Be sure to ask ahead of time before booking in these months. Quito Office: Pinto E4-340 and Amazonas, Tel: 593-2-252-1212, Fax: 593-2-255-4902, E-mail: info@neotropicturis.com, URL: www.neotropicturis.com.

KAPAWI LODGE

One of the more socially responsible and well-known eco-lodges, Kapawi was founded in 1993 to help the Achuar people who live in the surrounding area. Currently, 70 percent of the workers at Kapawi are Achuar, and in 2011 the entire lodge will be turned over to the Achuar people. The hope is that the Achuar will take to eco-tourism as an alternative to selling their land to oil companies or hunting native wildlife. The lodge is located in Achuar territory, on the Pastaza river near the Peruvian border. The architecture of Kapawi is Achuar-based: the complex boasts several thatched-roof cabins which are quite solid and comfortable. The rooms are attractive and come with balconies, hammocks, private bath and mosquito netting. The lodge can accommodate up to fifty guests in double and triple cabins. There is also an attractive main lodge with bar, library and dining room. It is a true eco-lodge, featuring recycling programs, solar energy and minimal-impact boat motors, to name a few of their ecologically sound practices.There are many activities at Kapawi lodge, including bird-watching (540 different species have been seen in the area), hiking, canoe rides, camping and visits to the Achuar communities. Tel: 593-2-228-0880, E-mail: canodros@canodros.com, URL: www.kapawi.com.

YACHANA LODGE

Yachana Lodge, the only officially certified eco-lodge in Ecuador's Amazon by the Ministry of Tourism, means "a place for learning" in the local language of Quichua. It does a good job of making guests comfortable in its spacious and modern facilities while teaching them about local communities, and the challenges the communities face in the effort to balance rainforest protection, modernization and survival. Unlike many other rainforest lodges, all rooms are fully enclosed with screened-in windows. The bathrooms have 24-hour hot water and potable water from the tap. Paths connect all the buildings, so you never have to set foot even on the grass, if you wish. Activities are all optional and include hikes of varying difficulties through the secondary and primary rainforest as well as visits to communities where activities like basket weaving, pottery-making and traditional ceremonies are offered. The nearby cacao farm, where Yachana Gourmet harvests for their chocolate production, makes for an interesting trip as well. Don't expect to see as many large animals as other Ecuadorian reserves, the area has been highly populated for some time and much of the large wildlife has been hunted or chased deep into the forest. Quito Office: Vicente Solano E12-61 and Oriental Ave, Tel: 593-2-256-6035, 593-2-252-3777, Cell: 593-9-709-9933, E-mail: info@yachana.com, URL: www.yachana.com.

SACHA LODGE

Sacha Lodge, opened in 1991, is located on the Napo river about 2.5 hours from Puerto Francisco de Orellana (Coca) by motor canoe. As jungle lodges go, Sacha has a slightly more academic bent than most: it boasts a butterfly farm and an ornithology research base. There is also a 135-foot canopy observation tower, built around a mighty kapok tree. Lodging is in 10 double cabins, for a maximum occupancy of forty people. The cabins are neat and comfortable, each with private bath and screens to keep the bugs out.Sacha Lodge owns a 3,200 acre private reserve, so good animal viewing is a plus: most guests get to see different species of monkeys in addition to some of the hundreds of species of birds that have been sighted there. Activities include guided hikes, caiman spotting (at night), canoe rides, swimming, night hikes, zip lines and more. Sacha Lodge is affiliated with another jungle lodge, La Casa del Suizo. They share an office in Quito, where you can get information about both lodges. Sacha Lodge sells tours and packages. Current prices for five days / four nights: $956 single occupancy, $735 double. For four days / three nights: $760 single occupancy, $583 double. Prices include all meals, guides, rubber boots, park fees and transportation. Not included is the flight from Quito to Coca ($120 round trip), alcoholic beverages and tips for guides and staff. Quito Office: Julio Zaldumbide 397 and Valladolid, Tel: 593-2-256-6090, E-mail: sachalod@pi.pro.ec, URL: www.sachalodge.com.ec/welc.htm.

BATABURO LODGE

Bataburo Lodge is on the Tiguino River deep in the Amazon rainforest, in the territory of the Huarorani people 7-9 hours by bus and canoe from Coca. The lodge is located in primary rainforest, visitors can expect to see several species of mammals and reptiles, as well as hundreds of species of birds. There are many activities at Bataburo Lodge. Native Huarorani guides, working through interpreters, will take visitors on jungle walks, canoe rides, night walks and visits to local indigenous communities. Many of the walks are intense 4-6 hour hikes through the rainforest. Itineraries are flexible, though. Bataburo is rustic but comfortable. Most rooms have shared baths; two rooms have private baths. Each room is screened in and has mosquito netting. The lodge can accommodate a maximum of 59 guests. There is a central lodge with a lounge and bar area. Bataburo Lodge prides itself on their local food: guests will feast on fish from the river as well as traditional food such as yucca (manioc). Quito Office: Ramirez Dávalos 117 and Amazonas Edificio TurisMundial 1st floor, Tel: 593-2-250-5600, Fax: 593-2-222-6715, E-mail: kempery@kempery.com, URL: www.kempery.com.

> *V!VA Member Review-Bataburo Lodge*
> *Bataburo is a great place to visit, the jungle there is beautiful, no other lodges are around, there are no luxuries but the place is amazing and guides very nice and helpful. 02 April 2007. USA.*

SANI LODGE

Sani is located on a secluded lagoon off of the Napo river on 37,000 hectares (92,500 acres). It is remote: visitors must first get to Coca and from there take a three-hour motor canoe ride to a point on the Napo. If the water is high, smaller canoes can take then guests right to the lodge, otherwise, you may have to hike from the drop-off point off the Napo. In spite of its remoteness, Sani is quite comfortable. Guests are lodged in triple or double cabins, with

AMAZON BASIN

a summer camp sort of feel to them. The cabins are comfortable: they are screened against insects and each bed is equipped with a mosquito net. Each room also has candles, as they only tend to run the generator until about ten o'clock at night. The communal dining room offers hearty, solid fare: meals are done family-style. Sani lodge is 100% owned by the Quichua community, who work in the lodge and serve as guides. Much of the money raised by Sani lodge is returned to the local community in one way or another. Quito Office: Roca E4-49 y Av. Amazonas (pasaje Chantilly), E-mail: info@sanilodge.com, URL: www.sanilodge.com.

COTOCOCHA LODGE
One of the more easily accessible jungle lodge, Cotococha is located in the upper Amazon basin on the Napo river between Tena and Puyo. This is a good location, as it is accessible from both Baños and Quito. It boasts 17 well-built, comfortable bungalows with differing capacities. Each one has a private bath, a balcony, and a hammock. There is a cozy lounge area, with a bar, gardens, social area and an open-air restaurant. Cotococha owns four hectares of rainforest. Quito office: Amazonas N24-03 and Wilson, 2nd Floor, #3, Tel: 593-2-223-4336, E-mail: info@cotococha.com, URL: www.cotococha.com.

LA CASA DEL SUIZO
This jungle lodge is one of the most luxurious, least rustic lodges in Ecuador's Amazon. A short distance from Tena, Casa del Suizo has an outdoor swimming pool, 75 rooms with electricity, ceiling fans, private terraces and hot water. The hotel restaurant serves sprawling buffets of international cuisine and an indoor and pool bar with a full menu of tropical drinks. There is international phone service available for guests, but it is costly. The hotel began as just a lodging house in 1985 and slowly expanded over time to the luxury hotel it is now. Itineraries are flexible and include typical lodge activities like hikes through the rainforest, canoe rides and visits to communities. The rainforest surrounding the lodge is primary forest. The lodge is only 15 minutes from the town of Punta Ahuano, reached by bus or car from Quito. Rates are mid-priced: $70 per person includes all meals, guides and activities. Children pay $49. Prices do not include 22% tax and service charge, tips, alcoholic drinks and souvenirs. Quito Office: Julio Zaldumbide 397 and Valladolid, Tel: 593-2-250-9504, Fax: 593-2-223-6521, E-mail: sachalod@pi.pro.ec, URL:www.casadelsuizo.com.

AMAZON TOURS
There are two basic Ecuadorian tours to the Amazon Rainforest Basin: lodge-based tours and canoe-based tours. In both, you pay a base price at the beginning which includes guides, all meals, transportation from the nearest major town to the launching spot and usually special equipment like boots and rain ponchos. The guides expect tips at the end of your tour. Lodge-based tours tend to be a bit pricier and more comfortable. They are best booked out of Quito, where most have their main offices or arrangements with tour agencies. You can expect a variety of quality and comfort: everything from shared bathrooms with cold water to steamy private baths and gourmet meals. The prices for these tours range right around $60-100 per night.

Canoe tours are great for those willing to rough it. You usually travel by day, stopping to spot flora and fauna along the way and enjoy picnic meals. At night you either camp out or stay in a local community where there will be a small hotel. Sometimes homestays are provided on these tours. Canoe tours can be booked in Quito, or for a discount, plan to book in the towns where your tour will begin. Choose from: Puyo, Tena, Coca or Lago Agrio for trips to the nearby reserves. These tours are significantly cheaper than a lodge-based tour.

IKIAM EXPEDITION
This is not your traditional Amazon tour: Ikiam Expedition is a truly authentic and exceptional travel experience. After traveling from Quito to Puyo to Shell, you depart for Shiona in a 5-passenger Cessna. Upon arrival, you take a 30-minute canoe ride to reach the territory of the Shiwiar, an indigenous community deep in the Ecuadorian jungle. With Ikiam, you become a part of the Shiwiar community, learning and living amongst this community only accessible by air. The Shiwiar are not very westernized, live in a non-monetized society and

continue to practice the rituals and beliefs they have cultivated over thousands of years. Here, there are no expensive meals, no spacious suites: you sleep simply in a traditional house (mosquito net included!) and participate in the daily life of four Shiwiar families, helping to make handicrafts and prepare food. There is no set tour or agenda, you are free to explore the forest, view the amazing diversity of species or swim in the river at your leisure. Only five outsiders are allowed on the site each week. In Shiwiar territory, you are not viewed as a tourist or a client, but as a friend who has come to the jungle to help and to learn. Ikiam Expeditions is pricier than many of the ecotour companies you'll find in Ecuador (around $350 per person per day, including food) but the level of cultural immersion that you are sure to experience should be more than enough to make up for the extra cash. Cell:593-9-832-3637, 593-9-769-2988, E-mail: shiwiarfund@hotmail.com, ikiamp21@hotmail.com, URL: www.ikiam.info

EMERALD FOREST EXPEDITIONS
Emerald Forest Expeditions sells package tours to the Amazon rainforest. The shorter packages—three days, two nights—go to the town of Misahuallí, where travelers stay at Sinchi Runa cabins. From there, guides will lead tourists on jungle hikes, visit the local Quichua community and an animal shelter. Misahuallí is about an hour from Tena, which in turn is about a five to six hour bus ride from Quito.

Pañacocha is a scenic lodge on the Pañayacu river. It is surrounded by primary tropical rainforest, and it is possible to see a number of wild animals there, including monkeys, bats, jaguars and river dolphins. Of course, as with any remote jungle lodge, the birdwatching is phenomenal: toucans, parrots and tanagers are simply a few of the many birds the visitor can expect to see. Guides take tourists on hikes, birdwatching trips, canoe rides and caiman watching expeditions at night. Package prices are all-inclusive: rates include meals, guide, transportation, park fees, rubber boots, etc. What is not covered is alcoholic beverages at the lodge, tips for guides and other hotel staff, and souvenirs. Tel: 593-9-730-1413, URL:www.emeraldexpeditions.com.

PUYO
Until recently, Puyo was nothing more than a stopover on the way into the depths of the Amazon Jungle. However, it now is beginning to earn a reputation as a tourist destination. It is in particular popular with those who either don't want to, or can't, venture deeper into the rainforest. It offers visitors a taste of jungle life in Ecuador, while still slightly in the Andes Mountains.

The city is located relatively near popular tourist destination Baños, which has helped put its name on the map. So much so, in fact, that there have been reports of many business owners from Baños complaining about a reduction of visitors to Baños. This could also be due to the recent activity of the Tungurahua Volcano which is located near Baños. Puyo's increased popularity has lead to a greater selection of good places to stay and eat in the area. There may not be as great of a selection as other tourist towns, but that is part of its appeal: it is more off the beaten track.

GETTING TO AND AWAY
Puyo is often a starting out point to the jungle, and thus there are regular buses to the area. From Quito you often have to go through Ambato, and the total trip time will be around five to seven hours, depending on your wait time in Ambato. There are also regular buses to and from Tena (3.5 hours), Riobamba (5.5 hours) and Baños (2 hours). If you want a little more adventurous trip to Puyo, there is a popular day long bike ride to the city from Baños.

THINGS TO SEE & DO
THE OMAERE PARK
Located about five minutes from the center of Puyo, Omaere Park is a newer addition to the area that proves to be a culturally enriching experience. The park contains an impressive amount of flora, about 15.6 hectares, of which 5 are natural forest that has never experienced human interaction. The park also concentrates on raising awareness of indigenous groups of the area. In the park there are reconstructions of native homes. There is also an area which

explains how many plants are traditionally used in the cultures of the area. Entrance costs $3.00 for the general public. Students get in for $1.50 and it is free for children under 12 years old. Open daily from 8 a.m-5 p.m. Paseo Turístico, El Balneario, Tel: 593-3-288 7656.

PARQUE PEDAGÓGICO ETNOBOTÁNICO OMAERE

If you do not have enough time to go deeper into the jungle, this section of Puyo offers an opportunity to go to a piece of native forest land. The large area of land has many trails weaving through it, so visitors can weave through and take in the nature. There is a two dollar admission fee to enter the park; however the fee includes a guided tour, making it a great value. Open from 8 a.m.-6 p.m. Walk north on 9 de Octubre.

JARDÍN BOTÁNICO LAS ORQUÍDEAS

During your time in Puyo, the Jardín Botánico La Orquideas is a must add to your travel iterary. Located in the suburb of Intipungo, which is about a 15-minute car ride from Puyo, this garden has an unreal selection of flora. What really makes this attraction is its owner, Omar Taeyu, who is always eager to share his love of plants with visitors. Admission costs $5 and includes a two hour tour. Take a cab from Puyo, the fare should be under five bucks. Open from 8 a.m.-6 p.m. Tel: 593-3-228-4855.

LODGING

HOSTAL LAS PALMAS (ROOMS $10)

Hostal Las Palmas is a simple and inexpensive lodging option in Puyo. The rate of ten bucks per night includes taxes, services and breakfast. Definitely not a bad deal at all. All rooms have private bathroom, hot water and cable television. The on-site cafeteria, where breakfast is served, also serves drinks and snacks throughout the day. There are also a couple of social areas with hammocks that are perfect way to relax after a jungle hike. 20 de Julio and 4 de Enero, Tel: 593-3-288-4832, URL: www.laspalmas.pastaza.net/reservas.php.

POSADA REAL (ROOMS $15-20)

The rooms in Posada Real are cozy and tastefully decorated. The beds are comfortable with plush linens and pillows. Its location is near to the main center in Puyo, making for a short walk to restaurants and shopping. On-site there is a dining room, living room, café and internet access. The prices are very reasonable considering the quality of the hotel. 4 de Enero and 9 de Octubre, Tel: 593-3-288-5887, E-mail: posada_real@hotmail.com.

EL JARDÍN (ROOMS $15-25)

One step inside El Jardín it is clear they are trying to achieve a jungle, yet high class feel. Although this can be a hard feat to accomplish, this place seems to have hit it spot on. The rooms are large with dark wood walls and simple, yet nice, linens. There is a lovely balcony with hammocks, which serve as a great place for a nap or to enjoy a good book. There is a restaurant on-site, and internet is offered free to guests. Barrio Obrero, Tel: 593-3-288-5887, E-mail: eljardin_restaurant@yahoo.com.

HOSTERÍA TURINGIA (ROOMS $20-52)

Hostería Turingia, which was named after the German city its owners were born in, is a fine accommodation option in Puyo. This modern hotel has quaint wood paneled bungalows for one, two or three people, all with private bathrooms with hot water. On-site there is a restaurant, bar, pool and sauna. Also all rooms have fans, televisions and telephones. Marin 294 and Orellana, Tel: 593.3-288-5180, Fax: 593-3-288-5384, E-mail: turingia@andinatel.net.

EL PIGUAL (ROOMS $39-118)

For what El Pigual hotel offers its guests, it is a bit overpriced. However, if there is nothing else available, and you have money to spare, it is not a bad place to end up. All rooms have private bathrooms with hot water, cable television, telephones and a mini bar. Most also have personal terraces with hammocks. There is also a restaurant, hot tub and pool on-site. End of the street Tungurahua, Tel: 593-3-288-7972, E-mail: elpigual@hotmail.com.

Restaurants

Rincón de Suecia (Entrees $4-6)

Ricón de Sucia is another one of the places in Puyo that offers more to eat than traditional Ecuadorian food. Instead, this restaurant, dishes up a variety of international favorites, including goulash and curry. It is conveniently located near the park in Puyo, near most of the places to stay in the town. 9 de Octubre.

El Jardín

The El Jardín Restaurant, which is located in the hotel of the same name, is arguably the best place to eat in the area. The chef has won awards, and strives to create dishes that are both traditional and unique. If you would like to sample dishes that are reminiscent of Amazonian cuisine, this is a great place to do so—the food is delicious. Paseo Turístico Tel: 593-3-228-8610.

Pizzeria Buon Giorno (Entrees $4-6)

Pizzería Buon Giorno is a pizza restaurant chain that can be found throughout Ecuador. They are known for their tasty pizzas at decent prices. As far as good places to eat in Puyo, this is one of your best options, especially if you are not in the mood for the Ecuadorian staple of rice and meat. Expect to pay around $6 per person for a dinner with drink. Francisco de Orellana, Tel: 593-3-288-3841.

Baeza

Baeza is a small town about two hours to the east of Quito where most people traveling by land to the Amazon region pass through. Located at the fork in the road that goes to Tena, Baeza features the Napo Province to the South, and Lago Agrio and the Sucumbios Province to the North. It is blessed with the spectacular landscapes of the Quijos River Valley (where there is world class kayaking and rafting). Baeza can be used as a base to explore the surrounding bird-rich cloudforests, Ecuador's highest waterfall San Rafael Falls, Volcan Reventador and Sumaco National Park.

Lodging

The Magic Roundabout (Rooms $5-9)

Perched on a hill in the cloudforest just outside Baeza, the Magic Roundabout is a real gem. Run by a wonderfully eccentric and hospitible British guy, Ali, with his three dogs, it has a warm, homey atmosphere and is a great place to chill out for a few days. The main building features a terrace with hammocks and great views over the cloudforest and river, while inside is a chalet-style open space with huge fall-asleep-in-me armchairs, a bar and a good selection of board games to keep you busy. Most of the accommodation is in the cosy bunkhouse, which sleeps 14, although there is a double room in the main building and one private cabaña (with more on the way). Dinner is a $5 set menu every night (three courses and a vegetarian option) and everyone eats together. Breakfast ($2) is the standard fare—eggs, fruit and bread, and a lunch of soup and bread ($1) is served pretty much whenever you like. During the day, you can take a guided hike through the cloudforest with Ali or, if he's not available, he can point you in the right direction or arrange for a guide (either a birding specialist or a general naturalist guide) to come to the hostel. You can also organize horseriding, rafting and kayaking from here. As credit cards are not accepted, make sure you bring enough cash for your stay (remembering to allow for your drinks) as the nearest bank is in Tena, two-and-a-half hours down the road. Las Palmas, 12 km from Baeza on the road from Quito to Tena. Cell: 593-9-934-5264, URL:www.themagicroundabout.org.

> *V!VA Member Review-Magic Roundabout*
> *Great to be able to have quality time with the owner and really find out about the land, animals (lovely friendly dogs and llamas!)community and area. Fab home-cooked food and cozy fire. Loads of walks to visit waterfalls as well as hang out in home/hostel and play pool. 8 February 2006. Holland.*

NAPO

The Napo Province hosts some breathtaking cloud forests, páramo (grasslands), and one of Ecuador's most beautiful snow-capped volcanoes, Antisana. It is also one of the easiest points to visit the Amazon Basin from Quito. Its capital, Tena, hosts several launch-off points into the rainforest. You can easily plan your jungle trip from Tena along with any number of daytrips like kayaking, rafting, hiking and birdwatching. For travelers with a limited amount of time to see the rainforest, this is your best option. However, if you have at least four days, a more remote tour is recommended. Buses run regularly from Quito and Baños to and from Tena.

TENA

Tena is the quintessential South American jungle town, the kind of place where you would expect to run into Indiana Jones stocking up on supplies before setting out in search of a lost city. Keep that image in your head because if you are in Tena, and that Indiana Jones type is you, then you are in for an adventure.

Five hours southeast of Quito, Tena is the perfect launching point for a jungle trek or a rafting or kayaking trip down one of the countless rivers that pass within reach of town. Once an important colonial trading post in the Amazon, Tena is now the commercial center and capital of the Napo Province. The rainforest surrounding Tena supports a large population of lowland Quichua indigenous. Significant numbers of Quijos and Chibcha Indians live further out in the green expanse that stretches as far as the eye can see. It is possible to visit many of these communities and to observe and sometimes participate in traditional dancing, the preparation of chicha (an alcoholic drink made by masticating maiz, rice or yucca and fermenting the juice), shamanic rituals and blowgun competitions.

CLIMATE

Considering its location in the rainforest, Tena's climate is surprisingly comfortable; it is cooler and drier than most people expect. There is rainfall year-round and the heaviest rains come in June, July and August. Even in this very wet time, it does not necessarily rain every day or all day. The rain is pleasant and warm, like the rain that those of us from the northern hemisphere only get in the sweltering heat of summer.

GETTING TO AND AWAY

Tena is small enough so that you should not have too much trouble getting around. It is divided in two by the rivers Tena and Pano. Two bridges, one for pedestrians and one for automobiles, connect the two halves. There are several sand and pebble beaches on both sides of the river, as well as a number of plazas and parks, the most conspicuous of which is the Parque Amazonica, a botanical garden and zoo located on a small peninsula that is visible from the pedestrian bridge. There is also a nice riverside walkway on the western bank of the river Tena.

The bus terminal is located on Avenida 15 de Noviembre between Calle Montero and Avenida del Chofer. The terminal is unattractive but don't be too quick to judge the rest of the city based on its appearance, the northern part of town is much nicer and boasts and increasing number of interesting shops and decent restaurants.

Most roads that lead to the Amazon are only partially paved and subject to landslides and other delays, especially during the rainy season. The road from Quito to Tena is no exception, though it continues to be improved. There is regular bus service to Tena via Baeza, but you should book in advance as the buses fill up fast, particularly on Fridays and Sundays. There is a small airport outside of Tena but there are no commercial flights, only short flights over the jungle. Small white truck-taxis are abundant in the city. It is a good idea to negotiate your price before getting in because the taxi drivers in Tena sometimes overcharge.

THINGS TO SEE & DO

Tena's claims to fame are the rainforest and its rivers. The jungle, especially if you get outside town 15 or 20 kilometers, is impressive. First-timers will be changed forever after they lay their eyes on a pristine stretch of Amazon. There is no shortage of jungle guides or tour operators, and many have offices at the northern end of town on Avenida 15 de Noviembre.
Tena has reached near legendary status with whitewater enthusiasts and boasts the best rafting and kayaking in Ecuador and, some say, the world. The jungle rivers on the Amazon side of the Andes are bigger and have more consistent flows than their west-Andean counterparts. They are also the cleanest and most scenic rivers in Ecuador.

ISLA PARQUE AMAZÓNICO

Isla Parque Amazónico began in 1996 in an effort to conserve the natural splendor of the Amazon's plants and animals. There are over 135 species of different trees, plants and flowers intermixed in the gardens and waterfalls on the island. There are also many different kinds of birds, monkeys, butterflies, insects, turtles and other animals that you have never seen before. This is an educational day trip that will allow you to enjoy the diverse life of the jungle. Admission for foreingers is $2 and for nationals is $1. Between the Tena and Pano Rivers (just west of the footbridge), Tel: 593-6-288-7597, E-mail: parquelaisla@yahoo.es.

JUMANDY CAVERNAS

Don't let the entrance to the Jumandy Caves deter you from going inside. Yes, you will have to enter through a water park. Yes, you will have to make your way through screaming kids to the café counter to ask for a guide. Yes, it will cost $5 for your guide and flashlight and yes, you will wonder, "What the heck am I doing here?" As soon as you are 100 feet into the cave you will forget what you left behind as you concentrate on working your way deep into the earth without slipping. Your guide will lead you through the creek that has carved out the caves over the years, and at times, you will have to swim through it. You will climb over waterfalls, see sleeping bats and touch stalactites and stalagmites. If you get there early enough and a 45-minute trek through the caves isn't enough for you, there is a cave that takes four hours to get through. Make sure you are comfortable with your guide's knowledge and abilities if you embark on this four-hour adventure. And yes, you will be glad you visited the Jumandy Cavernas. Just outside of Archidona, you can take a $6-8 cab ride from Tena, or hop on a bus in town to get out to the Jumandy Caves. Be sure to mention to the bus driver that you would like to be dropped off there.

LA ISLA DE LOS MONOS

La Isla de los Monos has been declared a protected rescue area for monkeys and other wildlife. Before you even enter, you may hear the competitive cry of the howler monkey from nearly a mile away. In the trees overhead, you can hear many different species of monkeys as they chase each other in an endless game of tag. A few of the friendlier monkeys won't hesitate to drop on down to meet you, tease you and run off with your things if you let them. Besides the playful antics of the monkeys, you can hold a boa constrictor, view brightly colored birds, jungle cats and countless species of birds. There is also a hostería here with comfortable cabins, a tasty restaurant and a bar. There are pools to take a dip in when the sun gets too hot, and there are trails throughout the forest that allow you to get close to nature. The price is $2 for admission. A cab will cost approximately $6 from Tena or you can catch a bus. Be sure to ask the driver if he is going to the Isla de los Monos, and he can let you know where to get off. The ride will take approximately 10-15 minutes. Tel: 593-2-292-0148, E-mail: xmino@orchidsparadise.com, URL: www.orchidsparadise.com.

THE AMAZON SPANISH SCHOOL

The Amazon Spanish School is located along the Tena River, just 1.5 km from the old center. Classes are no larger than four people and are taught by Ecuadorian professionals in English and Spanish to maximize understanding. The program consists of 20 days of classes Monday through Friday from 9 a.m-12 p.m. and 2 p.m.-4 p.m. Prices, which run about $7 per hour, include all lesson materials, trips to waterfalls and caves, a full day of rafting on the Jatun Yacu river (class III) and a certificate of participation. Calle Terere 1, Tel: 593-6-288-6902, E-mail: info@amazonspanishschool.com.

TOURS

Chances are good that if you have ended up in Tena, you are interested in venturing into the jungle. You can do this by canoe, raft, kayak, on foot, pickup, bus or hitchhiking, and there is no shortage of guides willing to take you. It's your responsibility to weed through the travel agencies to find the perfect trip for you, led by certified guides. Be sure to inquire about qualifications. Don't be afraid to compare excursions, ask for reviews other travelers have left and be sure to agree on what exactly is to be provided prior to the trip. The jungle is an incredible place and with a little research, you will take more than a few unbelievable memories home with you.

THE RIVER PEOPLE

Founded by Gary Dent, an Irish transplant who has called Ecuador home for over 10 years, River People Rafting provides exhilirating day and multi-day trips into the jungle for rafting, hiking, kayaking, fun and great food. All guides are certified and bilingual, as well as experts on the twists and turns of Ecuador's wildest rivers. Day trips cost around $65 per person, per day, and they also offer a multi-day kayak school. The day trips can be extended with overnight stays at the Yacuñambi cabins. Additional activities include wilderness hikes, horseback riding, bike riding, mountain climbing and visits to indigenous groups. 15 de Noviembre (across the street from the footbridge), Tel:593-6-288-8349, E-mail: riverpeople03@hotmail.com, URL: www.riverpeopleraftingecuador.com.

AMARONGACHI TOURS

Amarongachi Tours has been specializing in ecological adventures for over 18 years. They have two jungle lodges: the Cabanas Amarongachi that specializes in adrenalin-pumping adventure and Cabanas Shangrila, a place of nature-inspired relaxation. Between the two cabanas, Amarongachi is able to provide multi-day tours that combine the perfect amount of excitement and tranquility. Cabanas are charged at $40 per person per day (though rates are discounted for longer stays). Daytime activities include trekking with indigenous guides, canyoning up waterfalls, plant and animal education and uses, jungle handicrafts, survival skills, panning for gold, swimming in lagoons and river rafting. Day trips are priced at $40 per person per day. Av. 15 de Noviembre 438, Tel: 593-6-288-6372, E-mail:info@amarongachi.com, URL: www.amarongachi.com.

RIOS ECUADOR

Rios Ecuador's team leader and founder is Gynner Coronel Paris. He has over 10 years of experience at an international level on rivers throughout the United States, Ecuador, Costa Rica, Peru and Canada. Rios Ecuador guides are focused on skill and safety and trips are guaranteed to be unforgettable. Rios Ecuador offers rafting trips on the Rio Napo (Class III), the Rio Misahuallí (Class IV) and the Rio Anzu (Class II and III). The Rio Napo is the most popular trip at $55 per person and promises big water and big thrills. The Rio Misahuallí is one of the most challenging day trips offered in Tena and costs $70 per person. The Rio Anzu is a pleasant river with serene views and guarantees a relaxing day. The cost is $55 per person. Rios Ecuador also offers kayak lessons and trips on all class of rapids. The four-day kayak school is taught on the river by professional instructors, costs $250 per person and includes lunches. One day beginners can spend the day learning the basics of the sport for $60 and intermediate-to-expert kayakers can challenge themselves for $60 on some of the most exciting rapids and obstacles in the area. Finally, if you would like to get even deeper into the jungle, Rios Ecuador offers multi-day excursions that include horseback riding, hiking, canoeing, flora and fauna education, swimming, and more. Prices are approximately $40 per person per day. For a more luxurious and packed excursion the cost is approximately $260 total with delicious meals and jungle cabin stays. Tarqui 230 and Días de Pineda, Tel:593-6-288-6727, E-mail: info@riosecuador.com, URL: www.riosecuador.com.

SAPO RUMI TRAVEL AGENCY

Sapo Rumi Travel Agency is run by Misael and Dario Cerda, two Quichua natives who have more than five years of experience. They speak Spanish and tiny bit of English and are friendly and professional. Adventures they offer include jungle trips (day and multi-day), horseback riding, rafting, waterfall viewing, Shaman rituals, cultural exchanges, flora and fauna education, bird and monkey watching, piranha fishing and much more. Prices range from $30-45 per person per day. Augusto Rueda and 12 de Febrero, Tel: 593-288-6367, E-mail: saporumi@yahoo.com.

LODGING

HOSTAL LIMONCOCHA (ROOMS: $5-7)

Even though Hostal Limoncocha is somewhat removed from the footbridge and 'happening end of town' its hard to beat the views. No other hostel in Tena overlooks the town and the surrounding jungle. Its very relaxing to watch the sunset from a hammock on the patio and fall asleep to all the jungle sounds. The rooms are cleaned daily and are spacious and comfortable. Ceiling fans allow for comfortable air circulation and the beds are nice to sleep on. (That is if you can pull yourself out of the hammocks out front!) There are 30 rooms total made up of singles, doubles and matrimonials. Some have shared bathrooms for $5 per person, and the singles/doubles/matrimonials with private bathrooms are $7 / $6 / $6 respectively. The rooms have cable TV and hot showers (although its more of a lukewarm temperature that doesn't change). Breakfast is served for $2. There is a tour agency on-site offering one to multi-day tours for rafting, motor canoeing, museums, jungle expeditions and more. Depending on the river and the level of the river, prices range from $40-50 per day. The agency is certified. ITA Street 533 (300m uphill from the bus station), Tel: 593-6-288-7583, E-mail: limoncocha@salvaselva.net.

HOTEL CARIBE (ROOMS: $6-10)

Hotel Caribe's location is on the southern end of town a few blocks from the bus terminal. It is located near industrial areas on the main street and is far from the footbridge, restaurants and tour companies. The traffic outside can make it difficult to sleep. There are 33 rooms in total made up of doubles, triples and matrimonials. All have a private bathroom with hot water and cable TV. There is also air conditioning. The rooms are pieced together with mismatched furniture and comforters/linens. They do have all the basic comforts and are clean. The restaurant on-site serves breakfast for $1.50, almuerzo for $1.75 and dinner for $1.75. Credit cards are not accepted. Out back, there is a bar and covered area where folkloric dances are often held. Av. 15 de Noviembre, Tel: 593-6-288-6518, E-mail: hotel_caribe@yahoo.es.com.

HOSTAL CANELA (ROOMS: $11.20)

There are 12 rooms at the clean and comfy Hostal Canela. There are doubles, triples and quads available for $11.20 per person (including tax) per night. Large groups are discounted. Rooms have private bathrooms, hot water, cable TV, telephone access and a garage. Rooms are spacious and have everything a worn out traveler might need. Av. Amazonas and Abdon Calderon (corner), Tel: 593-6-288-6081, E-mail: canelahostal@yahoo.com.

A WELCOME BREAK (ROOMS: $5-8/PERSON)

A Welcome Break has a great location just off Tena's main street. The block is quiet and pleasantly mixed into a Quichua area. The hostel is cozy and simple with all the basic amenities. The shared kitchen looks a little run down, but is clean. There is an outdoor patio with hammocks to relax on as well. The rooms are also clean, with private bathrooms and shared bathrooms and hot water. The price is $5 per person for a shared bathroom and $8 for a private bathroom. There is a restaurant on-site called Veronica's Place that serves breakfast only. The restaurant is open 07:30-10:30 a.m. If you are interested in organizing a tour, Lefer Turismo is the on-site travel agency that is certified by the Municipal Gobierno de Tena and the Dirreccion de Turismo and Ambiente. Tours cost between $35 and $45 per person per day and include rafting, motor canoeing and much more. Equipment is included. Rueda 331 and 12 de Febrero Esq., Tel: 593-6 288-6301, E-mail: a_welcome_break@yahoo.com

HOSTAL LOS YUTZOS (ROOMS: $30-55)

The Hostal Los Yutzos is a family-oriented hotel that is located on a quiet street in the middle of the most peaceful residential area of Tena. Many of the rooms overlook the Pano River and guests can hear the soothing sounds of the river just below their balconies. The hostel is pleasant, clean and bright with spacious and comfortable rooms that make for a wonderful stay. All rooms have private bathrooms, hot water, cable TV and telephone. Free internet service is also available. The staff is extra friendly and helpful. Breakfast of juice, fruit, milk or coffee, bread, marmelade and butter is included in the price. Augusto Rueda 190 and 15 de Noviembre, Tel: 593-6-288-6717, 593-6-288-6769, E-mail: yutzos@uchutican.com, URL: www.uchutican.com.

> *V!VA Member Review–Hostal Los Yutzos*
> *Guido, the owner, is a great guy. Can, and will, help you with anything. He's an amazing resource for Ecuador, speaks excellent English and runs a very nice place. Excellent breakfast, too! 18 April 2007. New York.*

ARAJUNO JUNGLE LODGE (PACKAGES FROM $100-$300)

A family-owned jungle lodge located on a private forest reserve next to the Jatun Sacha Biological Field Station on the banks of the Arajuno River offering package stays. Spacious wooden cabins with big screened windows and tiled bathrooms look out over the river. The whole place is runs with environmental conservation in mind, down to an intricate solar electric lighting system. Lots of neat things to do too, from an Ecua-volleyball court to a high canopy lookout tower and rope swing. Cell: 593-9-946-6752, URL: www.arajuno.com.

RESTAURANTS

Most of Tena's eateries are located near the footbridge over the river. Most commonly, you will find Ecuadorian fare, fried meat, pizza and rice. Lots of rice. The restaurants cater to travelers who are have worked up a hearty appetite on the river or in the jungle and prices are cheap for the adventurists. Don't expect to find fancy restaurants in Tena, this is a thrill seeker's town with an appetite for adventure—not award-winning cuisine. That said, food is decent and you'll have no problem refueling for tomorrow's activities.

CHUQUITOS (ENTREES: $3-5)

Chuquitos sits right on the river and is a relaxing restaurant to enjoy an evening cocktail and meal while you compare river-running stories with new found friends. Well, relaxing if you don't mind the dance music on the downstairs patio later in the evening. Chuquitos serves Ecuadorian food, meat and pasta dishes, seafood and more. The food is decent and the atmosphere is fun. Meals cost approximately $3-5 with beers for $1. On García Moreno next to the river and footbridge (by the Plaza).

THE MARQUIS RESTAURANT (ENTREES: $3-15)

The Marquis Restaurant is one of the nicest restaurants to be found in Tena, if not the nicest. This steak house and cocktail lounge serves international contemporary cuisine and is not shy about their fresh grilled seafood. Their cuisine is grilled, and thus a healthier alternative to many other restaurants in Tena. Hours are noon-4 p.m. and 6 p.m.—10 p.m. Salads start at $3, chicken at $5, steaks, seafood and filets at $5-10, and their signature seafood dishes $12-15. Wine runs about $3.50, beer about $2 and sodas are $1. Av. Amazonas 251 and Olmedo, Tel: 593-6-288-6513.

RESTAURANTE SAFARI (ENTREES: $4-6)

Restaurante Safari is located about ten minutes south of the footbridge on Tena's main street. This little restaurant serves Ecuadorian cuisine and has vegetarian options available. The staff is quick and the food is filling. Meals cost approximately $4 and a beer is $1. Open for breakfast, lunch and dinner. Hours are 7 a.m.-10 p.m. Esq. 15 de Noviembre and Federico Monteros, Tel: 593-6-288-8257.

MISAHUALLÍ

Misahuallí is a little port village located on the Napo River, just 45 minutes east of Tena. Despite having lost the bulk of its commercial river trade in the 1980s due to the completion of a road connecting Coca and Tena, Misahuallí has stayed alive thanks to its reputation for ecological tourism.

THINGS TO SEE & DO

Any number of local tour operators and guides sell inexpensive excursions into the rainforests of the Upper Napo River region. This area of the Ecuadorian Amazon has more jungle lodges than anywhere else in the country. There isn't a lot to do after ferreting out your jungle tour, but that's not necessarily a bad thing: take a moment to sip a cold drink while absorbing the sights and sounds of this old Amazon settlement.

BUTTERFLY FARM

If you find yourself with a little free time on your hands and have tired of watching the gang of monkeys run around Misahuallí, be sure to stop in and visit the Butterfly Farm for some interesting information on butterflies and the metamorphosis process. There are some beautiful species of butterflies to observe. The Farm is open from 9 a.m.-4 p.m. and admission is $2. One block north of the Parque Central

LA CASCADA LATAS

If you board a bus headed towards Tena from Misuahallí and ask the driver to drop you off at the Camino de las Cascadas (approximately 15 mins outside of Misuahallí and 25-cent fare depending on the mood of the driver) you'll find yourself on your way to see a pretty waterfall, nice picnic areas and a little swimming hole. The cost is $2 and its a 40-minute hike to the actual falls. Its very slick and muddy at spots so wear good shoes and be sure to go with someone. You will also find yourself wading through the river. The trail can be hard to pinpoint at points and you don't want to find yourself alone and lost in the jungle. El Camino de las Cascadas.

TOURS

There are many guides and travel agencies offering tours up to 12 days into the jungle, including everything (rubber boots, canoe, food, etc.) Be sure to always ask guides for their license and pay half or less of the total cost up front. Pay the balance upon completion. Make sure that everything is included on the trip before signing, or giving away any upfront payment. The average cost per day is between $30 to $70 per person depending on number of tour participants.

TEORUMI TRAVEL AGENCY

Teo Rumi is an indigenous guide specializing in medicinal plants and poisonous snakes. He is licensed through the Ministry of Tourism in Ecuador and offers exciting jungle adventures out of Misahuallí. He offers one, two and three day tours into the surrounding jungle. Activities include motor canoeing to the Shiripuno Com-

Enter photo competitions at www.vivatravelguides.com

munity, typical dances, artisan demos, lunch, jungle walks, forest and waterfall viewings, medicinal explanations and swimming. The multi-day tours also include shaman rituals and visits to the cultural museum and animal rescue shelter. Frente al Parque Central, Tel: 593-6-289-0313, E-mail: teorumiagenciadeviajes@yahoo.es.

SELVA VERDE

Luis Zapata is a super-friendly guide with over 17 years of experience guiding. He has five guides, three that speak English and two that speak Spanish and Quichua who lead adventures into the jungle. Trips are one-day to multi-day and include jungle tours, piranha fishing, birdwatching, canoeing, swimming, rafting, kayaking, butterfly education, gold panning, cultural museums, ceramic and handicraft lessons. Prices range from $40-70 per day depending on the activities and duration of the trip. He also offers day trips canoeing on the river, jungle walks, museum visits and shaman rituals. On the northwest corner of the Parque Central, Tel: 593-6-289-0156, E-mail: salvaverde_sa@yahoo.com.

ECOSELVA

Ecoselva is a reputable tour operator located in Misahuallí, Ecuador. Adventurers can choose from a variety of tours from single-day to 10-day tours (some to the Peruvian border!). There is usually a minimum of five people necessary. Tours include: hikes, night walks, birdwatching, body rafting, swimming, motor canoeing, flora and fauna explanations, piranha fishing, museum visits, cultural activities with native Quichua tribes, overnight stays in jungle cabins, food, water, equipment, waterfalls and much more. Depending on the number of participants, the price can range from $25-70 per person. Ecoselva also participates in volunteer programs associated with working in schools, medical volunteers and the butterfly projects. Guides are licensed and experienced. Opposite the Parque Central de Misahuallí, Tel: 593-6-289-0304, E-mail: ecoselva@yahoo.es.

MANATEE AMAZON EXPLORER

A massive river cruise boat offering four-10 day trips with a variety of itineraries that take passengers through Yasuní National Park, the Terra Firmae Forest, Limonecha Biological Reserve, up the Cuyabeno river, and into various jungle lakes and gorges. El Telégrafo E10 - 63 and Juan Alcántara, Tel: 593-2-244-8985 / 244-7190, E-mail:info@manateeamazonexplorer.com, URL: www.manateeamazonexplorer.com.

LODGING

CASA DE EDUARDO (ROOMS: $5)

The Casa de Eduardo is exactly that, a room in Eduardo's house. Eduardo is friendly guide in the area with experience guiding (but no license or certification) who has opened up his home to guests who need only the bare minimum in accommodations. There is a single, double, triple and quad tucked into his little home with a shared kitchen, electricity and hot water. The upstairs deck looks over a little creek and gets nice breezes. Again, this is the bare minimum in accommodations and tends to be slightly rundown. If you are looking for a place to crash before you head off into the jungle, it will do just fine. Calle Napo, Tel: 593-6-289-0190.

HOSTAL SHAW (ROOMS: $5 +TAX)

Hostal Shaw is a one-stop shop for all of your jungle-getaway needs. Located in the center of the village on the north side of the park, travelers, diners and guests have front row seats to view the antics of the herd of monkeys that affectionately terrorize the community. Rooms are comfortable with private bathrooms, mosquito nets, 24-hour hot water and all your basic needs. The windows are kept locked up tight when nobody is in the room to keep the monkeys from coming in and messing up the bed sheets and tearing down the mosquito nets. Downstairs there is a delicious restaurant that serves up vegetarian and meat dishes in addition to typical Ecuadorian fare. The reputable EcoSelva Travel Agency is also located here and offers tons of activities including nocturnal navigation, night walks, jungle walks, canoeing, swimming, birdwatching, body rafting and can also organize one-10 day trips into the jungle. E-mail: info@ecoselva-jungletours.com, URL: www.ecoselva-jungletours.com.

HOSTAL MARENA INTERNACIONAL ($6 + TAX)

Hostal Marena cannot be missed. Painted bright taffy pink and set against the deep greens of the surrounding jungle, this cheery hostal is on the south side of the main road into Misahuallí. It is just one block from the community's main square. Rooms are also bright with colorful (though peeling) walls and mismatched blankets. The hostal has 35 beds total; 6 doubles, 3 triples, 4 matrimonials and the rest are quads. Each room has a private bathroom, hot water, television and fans. There are areas for lounging outside of the rooms and there is a restaurant that is open when large groups are on-site. In the evening, guests can partake in karaoke in the bar downstairs while drinking cocktails and imported liquors. The hostal also has its own licensed travel agency that can set up jungle tours, visits with nearby Quichua tribes or shaman, rafting, tubing, motor canoe rides and more. Just inquire at reception. Calle Juan Arteaga, Tel: 593-6-289-0085, E-mail: jungle.boyec@yahoo.com.

HOSTAL EL PAISANO (ROOMS: $8/PERSON)

Though a little pricier at $8 per person, Hostal el Paisano could almost be deemed luxurious (jungle standards). It is located just a block off the Parque Central and is clean and fresh. The staff is very friendly and helpful. The hostal has a very open-air feel about it with rooms opening onto an outdoor patio. Generally quiet, the hostal gets noisy when the community's herd of playful monkeys scampers across the tin roof and takes turns pushing each other down the roof. The hostel can accommodate 37 people in double and triple rooms. Each room has a sparkling private bathroom and hot water. Mosquito nets are provided. There is a restaurant on-site serving all meals for cheap prices. Calle Guillermo Rivadeneyra (front of the school), Tel: 593-6-689-0027, E-mail: elpaisano@yahoo.com.

EL ALBERGUE ESPAÑOL (ROOMS: $8-16)

This Spanish-run jungle bunker is situated on a hill overlooking the Río Napo. With views of the river, the location is ideal for a village experience. The hostal sleeps 50 people in rooms with private baths, solar-heated hot water, fans, laundry, internet, parking lot and safe. There's a good restaurant on the first floor to stop off for a meal. Calle Juana Arteaga (a block west of the Parque Central), Tel: 593-6-890-127, E-mail: reservas@albergueespanol.com, URL: www.albergueespanol.com.

MISAHUALLÍ JUNGLE LODGE

The Misahuallí Jungle Lodge was founded by a local pioneer of the Amazon on a beautiful plot of land in the jungle. The lodge can accommodate up to 100 guests in cabanas, doubles, triples and quads. The rooms are cozy and made of natural materials of the region. Each cabana has a private bathroom, hot water, ventilation and 24-hour electricity. The restaurant on-site serves local specialties and international cuisine, all prepared with purified water. Any special requests pertaining to diet can be accommodated. Packages are offered that blend the beauty of the surrounding jungle with adrenalin-pumping activities. Enjoy tranquil hikes, jungle facts, visits with indigenous peoples, shaman rituals, bird-watching and a trip to the rescue center. Follow these activities with rafting, mountain biking, swimming, caving or canoeing. Prices range from $350 to $600 for these multi-day excursions. Quito office: Ramirez Davalos 251 and Paez, Tel: 593-2-252-0043, E-mail: milltour@accessinter.net.

RESTAURANTS

As travelers are drawn to Misahuallí for the adventure, not necessarily the gastronomy, there are just a few options for dining. Fringing the Parque Central are a handful of restaurants and the typical shops selling snacks and ice cream. Almost all of the hostels and lodging in Misahuallí have restaurants or bars on-site and serve standard Ecuadorian fare.

RESTAURANTE DOÑA GLORIA (ENTREES: $1.50-4)

Overlooking the Parque Central, this warm little restaurant is family-owned and serves up Ecuadorian food. The restaurant is clean and has a nice beachy feel to it. Breakfast ranges from $1.50 to $2.25 and includes bread with butter and marmalade, eggs, meat, coffee and juice. Lunch is a set menu of soup, the main course (meat with rice), juice and a dessert for

AMAZON BASIN

$2. Dinner costs $4 and you have your choice of tilapia, chicken, apanados de carne or churrascos (with rice and sides, of course). Drinks range from 50 cents to $1 and a buck will get you a nice cool Pilsener. Calle Juana Arteaga (Parque Central), Tel: ´593-6-289-0100.

EKOKAFE BAR AND RESTAURANTE ($2-4)
EkoKafe Bar and Restaurante is a delicious restaurant that serves up vegetarian and meat dishes in addition to typical Ecuadorian fare. Prices are good with breakfast at approximately $2, main dishes at around $4 and an extensive coffee menu (extensive by Ecuadorian terms). Beers cost $1.25, cocktails average $2.50-4 and wine is $2 per glass or $10 per bottle. Feel free to browse the local native jewelry for sale, pick a movie to watch or a book to read, or simply be entertained by the playful monkeys out front that will try anything to slip into the restaurant for a snack. In front of Parque Central de Misahuallí, Tel: 593-6-289-0304, E-mail: ecoselva@yahoo.es.

MACAS
Macas is located in the eastern part of Ecuador, six hours south of Puyo. This jungle town was founded at the end of the 16th century as a missionary outpost. Today, it serves as a center for exploring the natural and cultural riches of the area. Macas is in the midst of Shuar territory. Once known as the "head-hunting" Jívaro, these indigenous people allow visits to traditional villages only with approved guides, in order to learn about their misunderstood culture. At the confluence of the Kapawari and Pastaza rivers is the Kapawari Ecological Reserve, working in cooperation with the local community. The Achuar-styled complex is set in an area rich in biodiversity, and is reached by plane and canoe.

Tour agencies may arrange short or long treks into the jungle or the Sangay National Park, whitewater rafting on the Río Upano, or other adventures. A few kilometers north, on the Cupueno River, is La Cascada, which offers great swimming, a water slide and a picnic area. Macas offers an alternative route into the cultural and natural richness of the Ecuadorian Oriente. Whether to visit a Shuar community, or merely to gaze upon Sangay glowing on the horizon, a visit to this town promises to be unforgettable.

GETTING TO AND AWAY
It is possible to fly to Macas, a trip that takes 45 minutes. TAME offer flights every day except Saturday at 9:30 a.m., arriving at 10:15 a.m. The return journey leaves on the same days at 5 p.m. and is the same duration. Buses run to Quito a couple of times per day and the journey takes around ten hours. Buses also run to nearby towns such as Sucúa, and some buses head to other parts of the Oriente such as Puyo and Tena.

THINGS TO SEE & DO
MUSEO ARQUEOLÓGICO MUNICIPAL
This small museum has a small collection of artifacts. They are not presented in the most attractive manner, but they are interesting. There is a collection of feather adornment and headdresses, blowpipes, baskets and a replica of a shrunken head. If you happen to be in Parque Recreacional on a weekday it is worth a stop in, after all it is free. Near Parque Recreacional, 8 a.m.-4:30 p.m., closed weekends.

CATHEDRAL
This massive modern church gives its visitors a nice view of the city. The building also features twelve elaborate stained glass windows which depicts the store of the Virgen Purísima de Macas. The cathedral, which was completed in 1992, was constructed to celebrate the 400 year anniversary of this Virgen. At the back of the church one can see the Pio Upano valley, and a number of birds. Near Parque Central

LODGING

HOTEL ESMERALDA (ROOMS: $8.50)

Handily located near the airport terminal, the Esmeralda is still within easy walking distance of the town center. The hotel is pretty basic, but the staff is friendly and helpful. There have been mixed reports about the comfort that the beds offer. Cuenca 612 and Soasti, Tel: 593-7 270-0130.

CASA BLANCA (ROOMS: $11)

The Casa Blanca, is as the name suggests, a white building offering 13 well-appointed rooms set across two floors. The hotel has a fairly decent restaurant, and breakfast is included in the price. There is a garage too. The hotel is centrally positioned and convenient for local eateries and internet cafés. Soasti and Sucre, Tel: 593-7-270-0195, Fax: 593-7-270-1584.

MANZANA REAL (ROOMS: $14)

The Manzana Real or "Real Apple" is located away from the center of things, but is well equipped, including facilities such as hydromassage, sauna, swimming pool and gymnasium. The hotel boasts 26 pleasantly furnished rooms, and also offers internet to guests. You've got it all here—have a swim before dinner, eat in the hotel's restaurant and then dance off the calories in the hotel's discoteca. The hotel also offers parking to guests, which is just as well, given its location. Av. 29 de Mayo and Cap José Villanueva Maldonado, Tel: 593-7-270-0191, Fax: 593-7-270-2728.

HOTEL HELICONIA (ROOMS: $17)

Just one block from the bus terminal, Hotel Heliconia is a decent and convenient choice. The six story building has a bright yellow exterior and a number of the rooms have balconies facing onto the street. The hotel has 23 rooms with hot water and private bathroom. The staff are friendly and helpful, most are able to speak English to some degree. The hotel also offers a number of useful amenities including a restaurant serving regional cuisine, a garage, internet and telephone service. Soasti and 10 de Agosto, Tel: 593-7-270-1956, Fax: 593-7 -270-0441.

COCA

The city of Coca takes its name from its position at the convergence of the Coca, Napo and Payamino Rivers. In the 1980s, with the discovery of petroleum in the surrounding jungle, Coca mutated from a sleepy Amazon outpost into a sprawling oil boomtown. Tourists had no reason to visit Coca during the first two decades of this urban transformation, but in the late 1990s the Municipality began a program to make itself more appealing to travelers. Today, while it's still not the most attractive city, Coca has become an essential hub for the serious eco-tourist. It provides access to a great number of ecological lodges, such as Yachana, Pañacocha, Sani and Yuturi Lodges, as well as Yasuní, a National Park and UNESCO International Biosphere Reserve that encompasses nearly one million hectares of pristine primary rainforest.

GETTING TO AND AWAY

Coca is fairly well-serviced by road and air. The most convenient way to travel to Coca is flying to the Francisco Orellana airport. Flights take around 30 minutes, with both TAME and Icaro offering this service. TAME's flights leave at 8 a.m. Monday through Saturday, 4:30 p.m. Monday through Friday and 2 p.m. on Sundays. Their flights from Coca to Quito leave at 9 a.m. Monday through Saturday, 5:30 p.m. Monday through Friday and 3 p.m. on Sundays. Icaro's flights take 40 minutes and leave frequently throughout the day Monday through Friday, with a couple of flights on Saturdays and Sundays too. Return flights leave with equal frequency. For those prefering a cheaper, more scenic route, buses can be taken from the bus terminal to the north of the town. However, it is possible to pick up many buses from the roadside in the town itself. If you take the bus to Quito, expect to spend at least eight to ten hours on the bus. There are night bus options too. Buses also go to Tena, Lago Agrio, Puyo, Guayaquil, Machala, Santo Domingo and Loja. It is also possible to take a boat to Iquitos in Peru—information regarding this can be obtained at the docks.

THINGS TO SEE & DO

If you have time, you may want to head to the waterfront to see the Municipality's Malecón 2003 Project, which includes a Center for Environmental Education and Tourism that is run by local high school students. The Malecón and the Environmental Education Center overlook the Napo River in front of the Port Authority, known in Spanish as the *Capitanía*. Both initiatives hope to further develop tourism as an alternative to the oil industry, which the Municipality has wisely recognized will not be around forever.

For the adventurous, there is the possibility of traveling by commercial barge down the Napo River to Nuevo Rocafuerte and across the border to Peru. The service is constantly changing, so anybody wishing to try this should check with the Capitanía to find out about current schedules and prices. It should be made clear that such an endeavor is not for the faint of heart; the trip, while surely exhilirating, is fraught with discomfort and perils.

THE LIMONCOCHA NATIONAL RESERVE

The Limoncocha Reserve, located on the north shore of the Napo River between the Coca and Aguarico rivers, is on mostly level ground characterized by the presence of wetlands and swamps. The Limoncocha Reserve is one of the most bio-diverse areas in the world, but its flora and fauna are continually threatened by increasing oil activity. Scientific studies have identified over 450 bird species in the area, and unique trees such as the giant ceibo, cedars, laurel, the balsa and the pambil are common. The Reserve also contains the Laguna Limoncocha, which is famous for being an excellent bird watching site.

Lowland Quichua families live nearby the lagoon and mostly farm for a living. Petroleum activities during the 1980s and 1990s have negatively impacted this region and its people. Therefore, the community is open to ecotourism and other alternative uses of their fragile environment. The best way to access the Reserve from Quito is by taking a plane to Coca or Lago Agrio. Buses also travel to these two destinations as well as directly to the town of Limoncocha. There is also fluvial transportation from Coca to two small ports (Puerto de Palos and Puerto Pompeya).

YASUNÍ NATIONAL PARK

Created in 1979, Yasuní is Ecuador's largest mainland National Park (982,000 hectares). UNESCO declared it an International Biosphere Reserve in the same year of its foundation. This large area in the rainforest protects three types of vegetation ranging from woodlands on dry soil to semi-permanently flooded forest. The main rivers traversing the Park are the Yasuní, Tiputini, Cononaco, Nashiño and the Curaray. The flora and fauna found in the park are varied. Visitors will encounter vegetation such as large cedars, laurel, chonta and sangre de drago, as well as numerous animals including tapirs, harpy eagles and pumas.

Yasuní is mostly uninhabited, except for several Huaorani indigenous families, who have lived within the park boundaries for generations. A large concentration of this indigenous group resides in the Huaorani Reserve, created in 1991. This reserve borders the National Park to the north and serves as a buffer zone helping to maintain conservation efforts. In 1991, the Ecuadorian government gave Conoco, a U.S. based oil company, the right to begin exploitation within the Park but Maxus Oil Consortium and currently YPF of Argentina later replaced it. Since then, a 110-km road has been built into the area for the use of oil workers, locals and researchers. Nevertheless, this area remains remote and relatively difficult to explore. Yasuní is best accessed from Coca via the Napo River, and hiring a tour guide is highly recommended, due to the remote location and difficulty involved with solo travel.

LODGING

HOTEL OASIS (ROOMS: $9)

Located away from the hub of the town center, Hotel Oasis is often used by lodges such as Yuturi and Yarina to accommodate travelers who stay overnight at the begining or end of their stay in the jungle. The hotel is a little worse for wear. Camilo de Torrano and Padre de Vidiana.

HOTEL SAN FERMIN (ROOMS: $10-18)

Centrally located, the Hotel San Fermin is well positioned for travelers staying in Coca. The hotel is tastefully designed from wood and concrete, using vegetation for a more natural finish. The San Fermin offers single, double and triple rooms and cabins with hot water and air conditioning. In case you arrived by car, the hotel also has a large parking lot. There is a living room for chilling out and meeting up with other travelers to talk about jungle adventures. Quito and Bolívar, Tel:593-6-288-1848, 593-6-288-0802, URL:www.wildlifeamazon.com/hotelus.htm.

HOTEL EL AUCA (ROOMS: $15-20)

Long established in Coca, with a good location on the main strip, Hotel El Auca is a reliable traveler's favorite. The staff is pleasant and can provide help to find local guides, or to store baggage. The hotel is well presented and has a rustic charm. It also has a pretty garden courtyard surrounded with interesting looking plants, where you can kick back in the hammocks, while watching the macaws. Rooms are clean and simple and come with a private bathroom and fan. The hotel has a decent restaurant too, serving regional cuisine. Napo and G. Moreno, Tel: 593-6-880127.

HOTEL LA MISIÓN (ROOMS: $17-30)

A popular haunt, Hotel La Misión is situated on the riverside and is a pleasant enough place to lay your head for the night. This hotel is frequently used by tour groups who pass through on their way to or from the lodges. Rooms are well presented, with hot water and private bathrooms. The hotel boasts a swimming pool, perfect for splashing down after a sweaty day on the bus. The food at the restaurant-bar is some of the best that Coca has to offer. Camilo de Torrano, next to the river.

RESTAURANTS

Parrilladas Argentinas, on the corner of Cuenca and Inés, is a good option for dinner. Its menu is limited to steaks and pork chops, nevertheless, the food is surprisingly good. Emerald Forest Blues Bar, on Calle Espejo between Napo and Amazonas, makes a good choice for a sandwich and a beer. There is also Rock Café, on García Moreno between Napo and Amazonas, which is bright and clean and popular among backpackers.

CUYABENO NATIONAL RESERVE

The Cuyabeno Reserve—or Reserva de Producción de Fauna Cuyabeno—is one of Ecuador's largest reserves and part of the Amazon Rainforest basin with over 6,000 sq. kilometers of rainforest. Because of the steep dropoff from the Andes mountains in the sierra region of Ecuador, the basin area is incredibly rich in flora and fauna. An excellent spot for bird lovers, the Cuyabeno reserve has over 500 recorded bird species including the huatzin, which is known to be a direct descendent of prehistoric dinosaurs. Not only does the reserve have species that survived the last ice age, but there is also an abundance of plant species only seen in the Amazon basin, tapirs, occlots, 15 species of monkeys, as well as diverse aquatic wildlife like pink freshwater dolphins, turtles, five species of caiman, anaconda, manatee, giant otters, eels and around 450 species of fish.

There are several lodges to choose from when visiting the Cuyabeno Reserve ranging from rustic to hotel-like. All are reached by boat, usually a hand-carved motorized wooden canoe. A network of lakes and lagoons connect the two main black-water lake systems in the rainy season (April-October) and eventually lead down to the Napo River which leads to the Amazon River. In the dry season (November-March), many of the lodges close down for all but the hardiest tourist who are willing to walk along the dried up river bottom, or what is known as flooded forest, to reach the lodge.

TRANSPORTATION TO AND FROM CUYABENO

Most tour operators will provide transportation from Lago Agrio and from the entrance to the Cuyabeno Reserve to the lodge. Bring your passport. If you take the bus, you will have to get out at a military checkpoint near the border with Colombia.

LODGING

TAPIR LODGE

Tapir Lodge is located in the reserve of Cuyabeno, and has a capacity for 32 guests in double room occupancy, all with private bathrooms, hot water and electricity. Tel: 593-2-254-7275/254-9275, URL: www.tapirlodge.com.

TOURS

Aside from staying in luxurious lodges or eco-retreats, an alternative way to visit the Ecuadorian Amazon is to spend time in a Huaorani community. The Huaorani only came into contact with the outside world in the 1950s, however, they have largely maintained their traditional way of life, living a similar hunter-gatherer lifestyle as they have done for hundreds of years. A few operators offer this type of tour. Their main offices are generally in Quito, so you will need to book in advance.

KEM PERY TOURS

Kem Pery are a provider of tours in Huaorani territory, offering both eight and 15-day tours in this region. Both tours head down the Tiguino river in motorized canoes to Bameno, a Huaorani village. The adventures include learning about medicinal plants, construction, weapon-making and trying your hand at making traditional handicrafts such as necklaces and crowns. There is an option to join the people on a traditional hunt, go fishing, or maybe play a game of soccer against them. The 15-day trip also includes a 4-day expedition with Huaorani guides into the rainforest, building canoes from balsawood and camping in the forest. The tours only leave on certain days of the week, so check in advance. There is a minimum of two people required to run the tour, which costs $720. Quito office: Ramirez Dávalos 117 and Amazonas, Edificio Turis Mundial Oficina 101, Tel: 593-2-250-5599, Fax: 593-2-222-6715, E-mail: Kempery@kempery.com, URL: www.kempery.com.

TROPICAL ECOLOGICAL ADVENTURES

Tropical Ecological Adventures offer tours to experience life with a Huaorani tribe, staying in tents close to the community. The company has been offering this experience since 1994, and there are chances to learn about the Huaorani culture and their practical and spiritual relationship with the forest. Participants can also understand the medicinal properties of plants and learn about the traditional handicrafts that are practised. The experience lasts for six days and starts and ends in Quito. The price of $700 per person includes meals, activities, guides and community entrance costs. This price is based on four travelers. Quito office: Avenida Republica E7-320 and Almagro, Edif. Taurus, Apto. 1-A, Tel: 593-2-223-4594, E-mail: info@tropiceco.com, URL: www.tropiceco.com.

LAGO AGRIO

Lago Agrio (officially Nueva Loja) is seven hours east of Quito by bus or 30 minutes by plane. The town got its unofficial name from Sour Lake, Texas, the original headquarters of Texaco Corporation, which began using it as an outpost for oil exploration in the 1960s. After more than four decades, Lago is a far cry from the lethargic jungle community that Texaco commandeered. Now it's a grimy frontier city that has flattened all greenery for kilometers in every direction to accommodate the oil pipelines that criss-cross the once virgin landscape.

Before the U.S.-backed Plan Colombia took effect in 2000, Lago Agrio, despite being an eyesore, served as the best jumping off point for visiting the Cuyabeno Reserve, a spectacular 603,380-hectare protected area that boasts unparalleled wildlife viewing opportunities. Unfortunately, because of frequent incursions by Marxist rebels and paramilitaries from Colombia as well as the presence of bands of narco-traffickers, there is a certain threat to travelers that can't go unmentioned.

GETTING TO AND AWAY

The quickest and most convenient way to get to Lago Agrio is to fly, which only takes around 30 minutes. The airport is a little way out of town, so you'll need to take a taxi to the center.

TAME offer flights every day except Sunday. On Monday through Saturday they have flights at 10 a.m. that arrive at 10:30 a.m. On Mondays and Fridays, they also have flights leaving at 4 p.m. arriving at 5 p.m. Flights returning from Lago Agrio to Quito operate Monday through Saturday at 11 a.m., and Monday and Friday at 5:30 p.m. Because of the town's importance in the oil industry, flights can get pretty booked up, so reserve early to be sure of flying. If you prefer to take the bus to Quito, the route is very scenic, but expect to be on the bus for about eight hours. Buses also go to Riobamba, Cuenca, Guayaquil, Tena and Puyo. Be aware that there have been increased reports of robberies on buses to and from the jungle in recent months.

LODGING
HOTEL EL COFÁN
Named after a local indigenous group, the El Cofán is well located, close to the center of town. The rooms are decent, with air conditioning, TV, safe box, radio, minibar and satellite TV. The hotel also has a restaurant and bar. Other services the hotel offers includes laundry, parking, money change, room service and a games room. 12 de Febrero and Av. Quito.

HOTEL GRAN COLOMBIA (ROOMS: $11-20)
The Hotel Gran Colombia is centrally positioned and offers reasonable rooms that are fairly good value for money. Rooms come with fans or air conditioning and are clean. The hotel also has a pool table, bar, and restaurant serving up the usual fare. Av. Quito and Pasaje Gonzanamá.

HOTEL D'MARIO (ROOMS: $15-47)
Hotel D'Mario is well located and well established in Lago Agrio. Room facilities vary depending on how much you pay, but the cheapest rooms include a continental breakfast (coffee, water, milk, bread, marmelade, butter) and one hour of internet use. More expensive rooms have a better finish and unlimited internet use. Rooms also have cable TV, telephone and air conditioning. Some rooms have a mini bar. Some deals include hydromassage services in your room. For those who don't have internet included, it costs $1 per hour, and is broadband service. The facilities include a restaurant, gym, swimming pool, sauna, games room, laundry service and car park. The hotel can arrange airport transfers and if you book through their website they will offer you a welcome cocktail on arrival. Prices don't include taxes, and discount rates can be negotiated for groups. They accept Mastercard and Diners credit cards. Av. Quito 2-63 and Pasaje Gonzanamá. Tel: 593-6-283-0172 / 283-0456 / 883-2472, E-mail: info@hoteldmario.com, URL:www.hoteldmario.com.

HOTEL ARAZÁ (ROOMS: $37-47)
A little away from the main hub of hotels and restaurants, Hotel Arazá is long established and a good choice with pleasant, clean rooms. The rooms have hot water and TV, while the hotel itself is well-appointed, boasting a swimming pool and a gym. Av. Quito and Narváez.

RESTAURANTS
PIZZERÍA D'MARIO
Adjoined to the Hotel D'Mario, the restaurant Pizzería D'Mario offers exactly what the name suggests—pizza. In addition, the restaurant offers other simple international options including pasta along with regional specialities. The restaurant is not bad, its offerings are fairly reliable staples. Av. Quito 2-63 and Pasaje Gonzanamá.

THE NORTHERN COAST AND LOWLANDS

Few visitors to Ecuador come solely to visit the coast, understandably so really, as there are more appealing beaches elsewhere in the world. However, those who do have the time to head to the west of Ecuador will find that the coast holds a cultural richness much different from the other regions of Ecuador.

The Northern Coast, which is filled with lush green vegetation, is considerably closer to Quito than the cities of the Southern Coast. The drive to the area also goes through some fascinating cities. One, Mindo, is known for birdwatching, considered by some to be the best in Ecuador. Also on the way is the city of Santo Domingo de los Colorados. The city itself is nothing spectacular, but there are nearby indigenous sites that prove to be very interesting.

Popular desinations on the coast itself include Atacames, which is known for lively nightlife and Canoa, which is know for its chill surfer scene. The larger cities of the area, such as Esmeraldas and Manta are less popular with visitors. Their industrial feel just can't compete with the other beaches of the area.

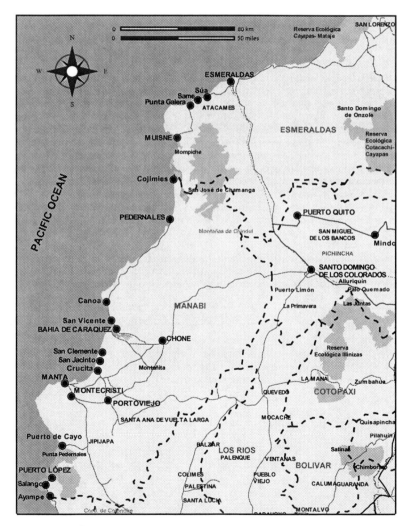

NORTHERN COAST

MINDO

Mindo is set in a breathtaking cloud forest (including 47,444 acres of the nationally protected reserve, Bosque Protector Mindo-Nambillo) teeming with birds. Over 350 species have been identified in the areas around Mindo alone. Tubing is a popular activity on the low-level rapids, there are lots of waterfalls ideal for snapping photos, and you can wade in the nearby pools and jump into the icy waters just below the falls—a 10 m (33 ft) leap!

One of the most ecologically-aware towns in Ecuador, Mindo has recently seen a huge tourist boom. Weekends bring an increase in visitors—make sure you have reservations. Holidays and long weekends will often find the road entering Mindo in bumper-to-bumper traffic. As a result, the town exists almost entirely on tourism. Many private homes will paint a sign "Hostal" and hang it on their fence, offering rooms for around $5 per person. However, a strong local government and an even stronger common awareness of ecology and environmental protection have so far saved Mindo from exploiting this tourist niche too far. Many of the tourist activities work to promote ecologically-aware tourism.

MINDO SEASONS AND WEATHER
Mindo's climate tends to be milder than the weather in Quito, temperatures ranging from about 15°C - 24°C (60°F - 75°F) year-round. Rain storms are common, so bring proper gear. There is no true dry season, but the climate is driest from May - September. As far as the tourist season goes, July - October are the busiest months, but weekends and national holidays throughout the year find Mindo packed to the brim with quiteños dying for some fresh air.

GETTING TO AND AWAY
If you have access to a private car, or don't mind paying up to $45 for one-way private transportation, the drive to Mindo is beautiful, with lots of places to stop along the way, like the Pululahua Volcano, the Bellavista Lodge and nature reserve and a handful of lookout points. However, if you're on a budget, taking a bus to Mindo is a convenient and inexpensive option. The only buses that go directly into the town of Mindo are called Cooperativo Flor de Valle (also known as Cayambe buses, but be sure the bus isn't headed to Cayambe, as this is in the complete wrong direction) and leave from a private station in Quito northwest of El Ejido Park on M Larvea and Asuncion (Tel: 593-2-252-7495). Fare is $2.50 one-way and the trip takes about 2.5 hours.

These buses tend to fill up, so it is smart to get to the station at least 10 minutes early or you might not get a seat. If you miss these buses, buses from the Terminal Terrestre (main bus station in Quito) leave about every 2 hours, headed to the coast by way of Los Bancos. The main companies that run this line are: Cooperativa Kennedy, Cooperativa San Pedro and Cooperativa Aloag. The disadvantage of this option is that you have to request that your bus driver let you off at the turn-off to Mindo. The road into Mindo is all downhill, but is a long hike, so if you aren't in the mood for a good hour of walking, hitchhike or try to hail a cab (good luck!). Several hotels will pick you up (for an extra cost) if you let them know well in advance when you are arriving, so call ahead.

THINGS TO SEE AND DO
Most of the activities in Mindo take advantage of its spectacular natural setting and rich variety of flora and fauna. The Jardín de Orquídeas (Orchid Garden), just across from the sports stadium in town is worth a stroll. The Mariposarío, Butterfly Farm, is 3 km (2 miles) outside of town on the road headed to the waterfall, natural paths and a few hotels. Entrance is $2 per person.

Tubing is a popular sport and involves reclining on several inner tubes tied together with rope down the mellow rapids on Río Mindo ($5-7 per person). The price includes the drive up to the launch point, helmet, guide, life jacket and, of course, the tubes.

NORTHERN COAST

Bike Rental is available at several different spots around town. You can bike to the waterfalls on two different paths—one mostly uphill, and one a little longer but less difficult. Rental is usually about $5 per person per day. Horseback riding can also be done in Mindo, although quality of horses is often questionable.

A ride on the cable car, *tarabito*, from one mountain side to another costs $2 per person. It offers excellent photo opportunities and spectacular views of the cloud forest and river. For a round-trip ride on the cable car and access into the private reserve on the other side, with paths down to the waterfall, the price is $5 per person.

Birdwatchers, nature lovers, and people interested in learning a little more about flora and fauna in the area can rent a local biologist guide either through their hotel (El Monte and Septimo Paraíso provides guides to all guests, Mindo Gardens can rent a guide for guests interested at the cost of $100 per day), or through an international or Quito travel agency when you book. If you choose to rent a guide locally, you probably won't be able to get a bilingual guide, but you will learn a lot about local politics and life.

TOUR OPERATORS
BIRDS TOURS
Located in a beautiful area of Mindo, this company is completely devoted to providing birders with the best possible experience. Leading tours in Mindo and throughout Ecuador, as well as all over South America, Mindo Birds guides are wildlife and birdwatching experts who provide a welcome dose of knowledge to any birding trip. The company is very flexible, able to provide guides and transportation for as little as one person on one day up to large groups for a month. Scheduled tours generally have less than 10 participants. Mindo Birds Tours also offers tours where participants can view rare butterflies in their natural habitats. Casilla Postal 17-17-404, Tel: 1-866-787-9901, E-mail: jlyons@pi.pro.ec, URL: www.mindobirds.com.ec.

VERDECOCHA EXPEDITIONS
Just an hour from Quito on the Non-Mindo road, Verdecocha is a playground for birdwatchers and nature lovers located on a private reserve at the head of the "Paseo del Quinde" route. Verdecocha Expeditions—organized by a foundation of the same name—arranges horseback riding, mountain biking, llama trekking with roundtrip transport from Quito. Incredibly rich biodiversity surrounds trails that loop through waterfalls, thermal baths, prairies and river-beds. Ave. América OE3-236 and Murgeon Corner, Tel: 593-2-255-1508, E-mail: funubesierra@andinanet.net, URL: www.verdecocha.com.

LODGING
Hotels in Mindo have a wide range of quality and price. From a luxury eco-lodge like El Monte—set in an isolated nature reserve and offering full meal service, naturalist

guides, free tubing and cable car rides—to a budget room in a cheap dive in Mindo, Mindo has it all. There are also several hotels just outside of town, which while charging more, will offer an even more remote setting and full services. The tourist season is from July - October, and extends to national holidays. However, because of Mindo's proximity to Quito, the entrance to town can be filled with stop-and-go traffic any weekend of the year, so its not a bad idea to make a reservation in advance.

BUDGET
HOSTAL MELYANG (ROOMS: $5/PERSON)
On the left as you enter Mindo, the Hostal Melyang is a clean, friendly, family-run bargain at $5 per person for a room with private bath. The rustic building boasts an impressive tropical garden sprinkled with tables, chairs and hammocks. Beware: the walls are thin, and the hotel can get quite loud. If you're worried about noisy neighbors, this may not be the place for you. Just on your left as you enter Mindo by bus. From the bus station, backtrack several blocks, across the bridge and up the hill, and it will be on your right, Tel: 593-2-390-0418.

HOSTAL GYPSY (ROOMS: $5/PERSON)
A comfortable budget hostel located with a strip of similar hostels off the main strip (to the right if you are approaching Mindo from the main access road). Family-owned and clean, there is only room for 14 guests, so if you notice the place is looking fairly desolate, you may be able to get a price drop. A community kitchen adds to the convenience. Bring flip flops or slippers, no shoes are allowed inside. Tel: 593-2-390-0446.

POSADA RESTAURANTE EL BIJAO (ROOMS: $5-7.50)
A discount hotel with excellent service. The main building features a restaurant and upstairs lounge and games room with a pool table. This is one of the few budget places in Ecuador that is almost completely handicap accessible. There is a pool, changing area and outdoor lounge. Probably the best feature of this hotel, however, is the service. The owner, Cesar, is an environmental activist in the area and has some great stories about fights with Quito and the government to preserve Mindo's nature reserves from an oil pipeline (which went in anyway) and the current fight to protect Mindo's rivers from being used for potable water in Quito. Av. Quito N° 259, Tel: 593-2-276-5470.

MID-RANGE
EL GALLO DE LA PEÑA HOTEL (ROOMS: $12/PERSON WITH BREAKFAST)
This larger hotel on the edge of the main plaza in Mindo offers lots of extra services at a reasonable price of $12 per person. The hotel includes an outdoor pool, hot tub with views of the surrounding mountains, restaurant and lounge. Each of the rooms has a private bathroom and hot water. With space for 150 guests, this hotel is ideal for big groups or travelers wanting to meet others. Staff can also help you with tours around Mindo, bike rental, etc. Tel: 593-2-276-5469.

CABAÑAS ARMONÍA (ROOMS: $7-14 INCLUDES BREAKFAST)
A friendly family hostel and orchid garden established 10 years ago in the midst of pure tranquility. Cabanas are nestled in a scattering of garden greenery and have various layouts, all with private bath, hot water and a hammock. Tel: 593-2-390-0431 Cell: 593-9-943-5098, E-mail: hugolinoguiacab@hotmail.com, URL: www.orchids-birding.com.

EL DESCANSO (ROOMS: $12-16)
Located off the main drag (to the right if you are entering from the main access road), El Descanso is a little more expensive than its many hotel neighbors, but has clean, fresh rooms with hardwood floors and lofts. An open air café and lounge looks out onto a lovely hummingbird garden, where staff has spotted up to 18 different species of hummingbird. The lounge also has games for guests. Tel: 593-2-390-0443 Cell: 593-9-482-9587, E-mail: info@eldescanso. net, URL: www.eldescanso.net.

MARIPOSAS DE MINDO ($9-22/PERSON + TAX)

A family-run hotel 2 km from Mindo town, which is surrounded by butterfly gardens and dedicated to sustainable tourism and education about the surrounding region. Pleasant rooms and cabanas, with spectacular views of the forest, house up to 26 guests. A pretty restaurant serves up exotic regional dishes, which are included in package rates. Four-night packages run around $70 per person, including meals and gardens. Parroquía de Mindo, Km. 2 Vía Mindo Garden S/N Sector, Tel: 593-2-224-2712 / 593-2-390-0493, E-mail: info@mariposasdemindo.com, URL: www.mariposasdemindo.com.

SACHATAMIA LODGE (ROOMS: $23-65)

A cozy wooden lodge located on a private ecological reserve bordering the protected forest of Mindo-Nambillo, just northwest of Quito. Comfy singles, doubles and triples with rates that can include meals or not. An indoor heated pool and jacuzzi make for a perfect ending to a day of hiking the many magnificent trails that surround the complex. Kilometer 77 via Quito - Calacali - La Independencia. 300 meters before reaching the "Y" of Mindo, Tel: 593-2-390-0907, E-mail: Info@sachatamia.com, URL: www.sachatamia.com.

HOSTERÍA SÉPTIMO PARAÍSO (ROOMS: $55-110)

This hotel is set in a private reserve towards the top of the access road to Mindo closer to the main highway with acres of untouched cloud forest, private paths for bird watching, a hummingbird garden, a lovely open air café and even a jungle gym for kids. The 22 rooms have the feel of a country home and are good for those who like more comfort than most ecolodges of the region offer. Everything is excellent quality and naturalist guides are all bilingual. Tel: 593-2-289-3160, E-mail: info@septimoParaíso.com, URL: www.septimoparaiso.com.

MINDO GARDENS (ROOMS: $35-80)

Mindo Gardens is owned by a huge Ecuadorian corporation. You wouldn't know it with this quiet, isolated hotel, though, which is 2 km past the Butterfly Farm. The hotel complex is set in a 300 hectare (741 acres) private reserve of secondary cloud forest, rivers and waterfalls. Rooms are colorful, clean and comfortable; although punctuated with obnoxiously bright curtains and bed covers. Rooms vary in size depending on the size of your group. The restaurant is spacious and ideal for large groups. The regular menu is quite limited—with a couple of pizzas and traditional Ecuadorian dishes—but for large groups, more food selection is offered. Quito Office: Av. Rep. de El Salvador N35-82 Edif. Twin Tower P.B., Tel: 593-2-225-2488, Fax: 593-2-225-3452, E-mail: info@mindo-garden.com, URL: www.mindo-garden.com.

LUXURY

EL MONTE SUSTAINABLE LODGE ($86/PERSON)

The most ecologically friendly hotel in this incredibly environmentally conscious town, El Monte is a comfortable, full-service lodge with spectacular views. Set in 44 hectares (108 acres) of a private nature reserve, there is rich secondary cloud forest, excellent bird and wildlife watching and a river full of rapids for tubing and waterfalls for cliff jumping. You get a feel for the isolation of El Monte the second you arrive. The only way to reach the lodge is via a wooden swing connected to pulleys and ropes, which carries you across the rushing river to a series of paths leading to the lodge. The place is owned by an American/Ecuadorian couple, who often join guests for meals and make themselves available for conversation, assistance, guiding and transportation. Quito Office: Roca 736 and Amazonas, Tel: 593-2-255-8881, E-mail: mindo@ecnet.ec, URL: www.ecuadorcloudforest.com.

> *VIVA Member Review-El Monte Sustainable Lodge*
> *The food was delicious, the owners were "muy amable" and the place was an isolated experience. If you need your Blackberry 24/7 this place is not for you. 15 April 2007. Washington, USA.*

SAPOS AND RANAS HOTEL ($105-140/PERSON)

A friendly lodge located in the heart of the El Chocó region, a strategic point in the conservation of Mindo's biodiversity with nearly 160 species of birds and surrounded by sub-tropical forests, orchid nurseries, rivers and trails. The charming hotel complex is adorned with over 2000 signature figurines and sculptures of frogs and toads from all over the world. Pretty gardens, thermal pools and a spa make for a relaxing ending to a day of hiking and exploring the natural wonders of the area. On the road toward Las Mercedes, 15 km from Los Bancos, Tel: 593-2-225-1446 / 593-2-224-5871, E-mail:info@saposyranas.com, URL: www.saposyranas.com.

RESTAURANTS

Most restaurants in Mindo are nothing special: offering typical Ecuadorian cuisine as opposed to international. Some of the typical dishes you will find in Mindo are: *tilapía*—a type of fish usually served with rice, salad and patacones, which are fried and smashed plantain chips; *ceviche de palmita*: the typical cold soup made with heart of palm, lime, diced onion, tomato and cilantro; and *trucha al ajillo*: fresh trout in a garlic sauce, usually served with rice, salad and patacones.

If you are craving international cuisine, pizza is probably your best bet. El Rincón del Río, just a block off the main drag before the plaza has excellent thin crust pizza. A personal pizza runs from $4-6 depending on how many ingredients and is served fresh. Pepe Grillo, just up the hill heading out of Mindo is another good Italian option. The only internet café in town is on the main drag, Café Net, and has internet for $1.50/hour.

RESTAURANTE EL BIJAO

A restaurant serving traditional Ecuadorian cuisine at very reasonable prices. The restaurant is in the main building—which also has hotel rooms—and features an upstairs lounge and game room with a pool table, hammocks and a variety of games. This is one of the few budget places in Ecuador that is almost completely handicap accessible. Av. Quito Nº 259, Tel: 593-2-276-5470.

EL GALLO DE LA PENA RESTAURANT

Another one of Mindo's restaurants with all-Ecuadorian cuisine, the benefits of this restaurant are its space—perfect for large groups—relaxed atmosphere, and nice views. Popular dishes are chicken, tilapía and trout. There aren't any veggie options to speak of, unless you don't mind eating a whole lot of *choclo* (corn)! On the main square, Tel: 593-2-276-5469.

HOSTERÍA SÉPTIMO PARAÍSO

If you can't afford to stay at the hotel here (rooms range from $55-110 plus tax and service), it's worth at least lunch or dinner. Located off the main access road to Mindo in the middle of acres of protected cloudforest, the open-air café is lovely. Spend some time walking off your meal on any of the paths around the lodge, playing on the jungle gym, or observing hummingbirds and other rare bird species from the garden. Just off Av. Quito (the main road into Mindo), Tel: 593-2-289-3160, E-mail: info@septimoParaíso.com, URL: www.septimoParaíso.com.

MINDO GARDENS RESTAURANT (ENTREES: $5-10)

Even if you decide not to stay at Mindo Gardens, the restaurant gives you a good excuse to check out this beautiful private reserve full of paths, gardens, birdwatching opportunities and a good portion of the Río Mindo. That said, the food at the restaurant is not amazing. A very limited menu offers a couple of pizzas ranging in price from $4.50-6.50 and some traditional Ecuadorian soups and dishes. Large groups have the advantage of an extended menu and plenty of space to enjoy it. Tel: 593-2-225-2490, Fax: 593-2-225-3452, E-mail: info@mindo-garden.com, URL: www.mindo-garden.com.

NORTHERN COAST

Around Mindo
LODGING AROUND MINDO
BELLAVISTA CLOUD FOREST ($10-69/PERSON; CAMPING AVAILABLE)

Bellavista Cloud forest is one of the few eco-lodges in the Andean cloud forest that has access to primary forest. This is a perfect selection for someone interested in escaping civilization, relaxing, hiking on beautiful cloud forest trails and partaking in excellent bird-watching. Activities like horseback riding are also available for short rides and long distance rides. Bellavista is set 30 minutes off the road from Quito to Mindo. It has over 8 km in trails through the beautiful Tandayapa Valley, which has 330 recorded species of birds; hummingbirds, tanagers and toucans are the most common. Excellent naturalist guides are always on hand to take you on hikes or to hunt for specific birds.

There are five different buildings that offer a range in accommodations from secluded honeymoon suites to rooms with a shared bath in the main domed "Tarzan's lodge". There are also opportunities for independent researchers and volunteers to identify plants and track bird habits. The lodge is about two hours from Quito set about half an hour off the main highway headed to Esmeraldas. Follow signs after the small town of Nanegalito if you are in private transportation. The lodge is not accessible by bus; but they can help arrange for transportation from Quito. Address: Quito Office: Jorge Washington E7-23 y 6 de Diciembre, Lodge Tel: 593-2-290-1539, Quito Tel: 593-2-211-6232, Fax: 593-2-290-3165, E-Mail: info@bellavista-cloudforest.com, URL: www.bellavistacloudforest.com.

MOMOPEHO (ABOUT $20/PERSON DEPENDING ON PACKAGE)

For the traveler seeking a different sort of experience, Momopeho, about two hours from Mindo, offers the life of an Ecuadorian *campesino*. The no-frills living area is only two rooms, with four beds each. There is a ceiling fan in each room, and each room also has its own bathroom. Visitors can experience the tropical humid cloud forest, but the real attraction is working on the farm. Guests are encouraged to assist with daily tasks like milking the cows, feeding the guinea pigs, tending to the horses, etc. Other farm-related activities, such as mending fences or harvesting palm trees for the edible palm hearts are done when necessary. All meals are included, but note that Momopeho cannot guarantee vegetarian or kosher food, or accommodate any other sort of strict diet. Also, handicapped or disabled people are discouraged from going to Momopeho, as the farm work is challenging and there is nothing in the way of facilities for people with special needs. Tel: 593-2-830-9302, E-Mail: momopeho@yahoo.com, URL: www.momopeho.com.

EL ENCANTO RESORT ($24-160/PERSON INCLUDES 3 MEALS AND GUIDES)

El Encanto is a luxurious resort set right on the Equator. It takes advantage of this unique location by showing guests experiments and tricks unique to latitude 0'0'0. The grounds are spacious and beautiful. Guides take guests on hikes of the cloud forest in the area, pointing out orchids growing in their natural habitat, spectacular birds and more. The hotel has a pool and spa with many extra features. 7 via Hacia Valle Hermoso, Tel: 593-2-227-8764, E-Mail: elencantoresort@andinanet.net, URL: www.elencantoresort.com.

TANDAYAPA BIRD LODGE (ROOMS: $90-220)

Self-proclaimed as the 'possibly ultimate birding destination', Tandayapa was built in 1999 on a pasture on the edge of the cloud forest outside of Mindo and has since planted over 30,000 trees to fill in the areas of the cloud forest that had been destroyed. The lodge is stacked with birding gear and viewing equipment and features a viewing deck, extensive trails throughout the forest and full-time guides willing to set out in search of birds at all hours of the day. There are several options for different day trips, each with a list of bird species found in those areas. There are 12 rooms in the main building, all with hot water, private bathrooms and electricity. The price includes three meals, specialized guides, and all taxes. Quito Office: Reina Victoria 1684 y La Pinta Ed. Santiago 1, Dep. 501, Tel: 593-2-222-5180, E-mail: tandayapa@tandayapa.com, URL: www.tandayapa.com.

SANTO DOMINGO DE LOS COLORADOS

Located in the lush central lowland area of northern Ecuador, Santo Domingo de los Colorados is a huge transportation hub, linking Quito and the Sierra to the coastal regions of Ecuador. The city is 129 kilometers from Quito and the area is of great importance to both the banana and palm olive industries, hence the good road links. The city itself is dusty, noisy and polluted, not unlike other coastal lowland towns. However, the surrounding forests offer fabulous opportunities for bird watching as the surroundings are part of the Choco biodiversity region. The population of the town itself is an interesting mix. The area has been a major draw point for Colombian immigrants, migrating south looking for better opportunities. Additionally, the area is famed for its Tsáchila indigenous people, well-known for their use of an achiote dye to color their hair red. In fact the name, "los Colorados" directly translates into Spanish as "the colored" (referring to their hair), a title that the people do not approve of, but nonetheless persists. The people no longer wear their traditional outfits, except for on special occasions.

GETTING TO AND AWAY

The bus terminal is about 1.5 kilometers north of the central part of town, if you head out of town along Avenida de los Tsáchilas. The bus station is actually just off Avenida Abraham Calazacón. For convenience, take a taxi to get into town, especially at night. Due to its central location in Ecuador, getting to and away from Santo Domingo de los Colorados is easy—you can get buses to most other parts of the country from this bus terminal, but it is especially easy to get to coastal towns from here. If you're headed north to Esmeraldas and the beach, the journey takes around three hours. To hit the coast further south of Esmeraldas, you can get a bus to Pedernales (3 hours), or to Bahía de Caráquez (4 hours) or to Manta (6 hours). If you are going to Guayaquil (4 hours), the bus travels via Quevedo. To Quito, the bus takes three hours.

THINGS TO DO

VISIT A TSACHILA COMMUNITY

One really worthwhile trip if you're in the area at a loose end is to head out to a Tsáchilas community to understand a little bit more about the way of life of this group. The group is known for the fact that the men dye their hair red with achiote. A typical visit includes a tour where you are shown the dress, bamboo homes, weapons and you learn more about their history and beliefs, particularly the shamanistic ritualism aspects. Contact a community to find out more. Cell: 593-9-445-5159, URL: www.tsachilas.com.

LODGING

Santo Domingo de los Colorados has many hotels but choose with care as quality varies considerably. Lots of hotels are centered around 29 de Mayo, however, in general these are not recommended as this street is busy and hence very loud. You may find it worthwhile to try to find somewhere off this main strip in order to get a decent night's sleep. However, if you feel compelled to stay in this part of town, try to get a room facing away from the main street.

MILENIO HOTEL

The well presented Milenio Hotel is a bit of a splurge, but perhaps worth it. Spread over five floors, the rooms come with air conditioning which is nice in the humid coastal climate, plus private bathroom and cable TV. In case you didn't watch enough *telenovelas* in your room, there is also a common TV room. If you're done with the TV, head to the Turkish Bath, sauna and hydromassage area, where you can kick back and soak after a long bus journey. The hotel also has a garage and a bar. The hotel restaurant called is called Chelo's and serves an array of meat and seafood options. Vía Quevedo and Juan Pío Montufar, Tel: 593-2-371-0516 / 593-2-371-0517 / 593-2-371-0518, E-mail: info@meleniohotel.com, URL: www.meleniohotel.com/internas/index.html.

HOTEL DEL PACÍFICO (ROOMS: $15-36)

The four star Hotel del Pacífico is centrally located in Santo Domingo de los Colorados, and convenient for just about everything. Because it is on the 29 de Mayo, it can be fairly noisy. Rooms are of a decent size and are comfortable, with private bathrooms and hot water, TV

NORTHERN COAST

and telephone. The hotel has a bar and restaurant, and all guests are given a welcome cocktail. They also provide a laundry service and parking. Prices do not include tax and service charge. Avenida 29 de Mayo # 510 between Ibarra and Latacunga, Tel: 593-2-275-2806 / 276-0373, E-mail: srpacifico@plus.net.ec, URL: www.tsachilas.com/tsachilas.

HOTEL ZARACAY

A fairly reliable choice, Hotel Zaracay is a pleasant hotel located on the road out of town, headed back towards Quito. The hotel has plenty of amenities for your enjoyment, including a pleasant swimming pool which comes in handy in the sweltering heat. There are also areas for playing *fútbol*, basketball, tennis and volleyball. The hotel also boasts a little aviary and a popular casino. There is also a good restaurant serving regional cuisine, and a bar. To get there, head along the Quito road, and the hotel can be found 1.5 kilometers from the center of town. 1639 Av. Quito, Tel: 593-2-275-0316/275-0023, Fax: 593-2-275-4535, E-mail: Hotelzaracay@porta, URL: www.hotelzaracay.com/zaracay.

HOTEL TROPICAL INN

The Tropical hotel was established in 1995 and is modern-looking with decent services. The hotel has 45 clean and well-appointed rooms and a restaurant for the guests' convenience, serving local food. They offer internet use and there is an swimming pool too. The hotel can offer help with organizing rafting trips, a popular pursuit in this area. The hotel can be found 1.5 kilometers outside of the city of Santo Domingo de los Colorados if you take Avenida Quito. Tel: 593-2-276-1771 / -1772 / -1773, E-mail: hotropinn@hotmail.com, URL: www.tsachilas.com/tropical.

TINALANDIA (ROOMS: $40-172)

Built in the 1940s as a farm and later converted for tourism, Tinalandia was one of Ecuador's first eco-lodges. It is located in the cloud forest 2.5 hours from Quito, near Santo Domingo de los Colorados. A modestly sized eco-lodge, Tinalandia has 16 comfortable rooms and capacity for 41 guests. It is world-renowned for bird watching, attracting birdwatchers from around the globe. More than 350 species of birds have been sighted at Tinalandia. Tinalandia is more than just birds, however. The cloud forest is of interest to biologists and hikers, and one of the world's few remaining moss forests is within hiking distance. They can arrange horseback riding, hiking, birdwatching and whitewater rafting trips, and there is even a nine-hole golf course! Tel: 593-2-244-9028, URL: www.tinalandia.com.

PUERTO QUITO

This little town squatting on the shores of the Río Caoni was originally intended to be the capital's port (hence the name). Today, it sits smack dab in the middle of the main circuit to the coast vía Quito, Calacalí and La Independencia. An area of extreme natural beauty, bisected by the Caoni and its tributaries, the lands surrounding Puerto Quito are divided by a number of reserves and dotted with good resorts. Due to its natural resources as well as its growing eco-centric and economic infrastructure, Puerto Quito is ideal for going wild in the wilds: this is the place to clear the mind (and the lungs).

ARASHÁ SPA ($328-619/PERSON)

This internationally recognized resort and spa is located in the heart of Ecuador's tropical forest. The surroundings themselves would be enough to attract travelers, but the sheer luxury and eco-extravagance of this place, with its self-indulgent spas and nature-friendly bungalows, make getting into the woods an ecologically engaging, but undeniably extravagant experience. You won't be roughing it here. Besides lavish accommodation and cuisine to please even the most discerning palate, Arashá offers a number of activity packages, from Wellness Experiences to Eco-Education Expeditions and Family Experiences. Activities range from primary and secondary forest treks (try the nocturnal tour by torch) and trips to nearby cascades and lagoons, to exotic birdwatching and juice-making. 121 de la vía Quito - Calacalí - La Independencia, Cell: 593-9-198-1668 / 593-9-450-4145, Fax: 593-2-390-0009, E-mail: info@arasharesort.com, URL: www.arasharesort.com.

KAONY LODGE

Spread out along the Río Caoni, Kaony Lodge is a private ecological reserve hosting over 30 hectares of tropical forest and a variety of flora and fauna. Cabins are rustic, but cozy and comfortable, and constructed entirely from local materials in order to blend into the surroundings. As well as rest and relaxation, the lodge offers ample opportunity to get out and about in the area. Excursions include swimming, horseback riding and nature walks. After a day of trekking (or lounging in the natural surroundings) make a splash in the nearby natural jacuzzi. Also attached to the grounds is a first class restaurant, specializing in *platos típicos* like local trout and tilapía, as well as a number of international dishes spiced up by the house. Av. 12 de Octubre 2449 and Orellana (Edificio Jerecio), 1st floor, Tel: 593-2-566-719 / 593-2-556-720, Fax: 593-2-527-066, E-mail: info@kaonylodge.com, URL: www.kaonylodge.com.

PROVINCE OF ESMERALDAS

In the northwestern corner of Ecuador, African and indigenous cultures come together amidst jungle, river and sea. The African heritage for many of Esmeraldas' residents comes from the shipwreck of a slave ship off the coast. According to legend, about two-dozen slaves made their way to land and to freedom. You will notice the influence of eastern African dress, music and customs in Esmeraldas. European feet first touched Ecuadorian soil here when the Spanish landed on the Pacific Coast in 1526. The conquistadors were astounded to find Indians bedecked in emeralds awaiting them on shore. Convinced that the region was abundant in the brilliant gems, they named it Esmeraldas.

Photo by Jason Halberstadt

NORTHERN COAST

While today's Esmeraldas harbors few emeralds, it does live up to its other name, the "Green Province." The northernmost of the coastal provinces, Esmeraldas is also the greenest, riddled with estuaries, mangroves and flooded tropical forest. Its wild and remote inland areas, accessible only by canoe, make Esmeraldas the ideal staging ground for a river safari. Gliding past frontier towns that suddenly appear out of the dense green tangle of jungle, you will be reminded of scenes from "The African Queen" and "Heart of Darkness."

If you would rather relax, Esmeraldas also boasts some of the coast's most vibrant beaches with small towns scattered among them. There is a whole range of accommodation here, as it is one of the closest beach areas to Quito and Ibarra and city folk of all income levels love to spend weekends at the beach. If you want to party, check out Atacames. If it's peace and quiet that you're looking for, the sleepy towns of Same, Súa, Tonchigüe or Muisne should be explored. Surfers should head to Mompiche.

CITY OF ESMERALDAS

Despite its rather alluring name, there is nothing much to attract even the most daring adventurer to Esmeraldas. The city is a dirty, depressing industrial port. Part of the blame must reside with a series of mudslides in 1997-1998, which destroyed much of the town and area. Whatever the reason, the city of Esmeraldas is no one's idea of a tourist destination. Oppressive heat and humidity, paired with a reputation for being unsafe, mean the city is more suitable for brief stopovers than longer stays. Dusty streets packed with a mechanical menagerie of buses, cars and taxis crisscross through town, passing street vendors, mom-and-pop stores, fruit and vegetable stalls and a variety of look-alike local restaurants along the way.

Share your travel experiences online at www.vivatravelguides.com

The region, however, is culturally rich, and home to one of Ecuador's earliest communities: La Tolita. La Tolita Island, located to the north, is an important archaeological site. Numerous examples of their ceramic heritage are housed in the Museo del Banco Central (Espejo, between Olmedo and Colon). Afro-Ecuadorian culture is very much alive and well in Esmeraldas, it is best sampled through its marimba music and dance, or local cuisine, which relies heavily on coconut and plantain. If you are stuck in the city, head to Las Palmas, a more upscale beach. Bars and seafood restaurants line the main street, with excellent sea views. This is a good place to grab a meal and cold beer, however, this is not the best place to hang around alone at night.

GETTING TO AND AWAY

A good paved road runs from Esmeraldas to Borbon and San Lorenzo to the north, continuing on to Ibarra in the northern Andes. *Servicio directo* (executive service) buses run to Quito and Guayaquil, and are the best option as they don't stop to pick up passengers along the way, tend to be more comfortable, and are most definitely faster. To Quito, $6 regular, $7 direct, 5-6 hours. Trans-Esmeraldas, 10 de Agosto and Sucre, near the main park, is a good bet. Another station is Sta. Maria 870 and 9 de Octubre, Tel: 593-2-257-2996, www.transesmeraldas.com. Occidental, Aerotaxi, and Panamericana also run buses.

LODGING

Note: a couple of guidebooks recommend Diana as a reliable budget option, unfortunately the once-hostal now only accepts patrons for extended stays of one month or more. Hotels in Esmeraldas are surprisingly clean and friendly considering the general appearance of the city itself. If you can afford to spend a few more dollars, spend the night in the Las Palmas area. While not as classy as it sounds, there is some fairly nice accommodation in this locale.

HOTEL ASIA (ROOMS: $4-20)
This place is a bit of a mixed bag, offering pleasant clean rooms with private baths, or slightly cheaper but much dingier rooms with shared bathrooms and fans. All rooms are located in a large warehouse-like building with an open, well-maintained reception area where you can use the internet ($1/hour) or make international phone calls. Staff wear polo shirts bearing Hotel Asia's name, and the smiles that come with greetings are genuine. This is one of the more professional looking places to stay, though most of the building is in dire need of a re-vamp. More expensive rooms have TV and there is a garage nearby for those with their own wheels. 9 de Octubre 116 and Bolivar.

HOSTAL SULTANA DE LOS ANDES (ROOMS: $7)
Sitting right on the Olmeda drag, this budget hostal is reached via a set of stairs from the street. The walls around the reception area have been painted a cheerful purple color; equally cheerful is the friendly woman waiting to show you available rooms. Rooms are slightly run down, but clean and tidy. Rooms overlooking the street can be noisy, so don't expect a vacationer's retreat. You will get a bed with clean sheets, private bathroom, 24-hour running water, and a relatively safe night's sleep. Av. Olmedo and 9 de Octubre, Tel: 593-6-272-6778.

RESIDENCIAL ZULEMA (ROOMS: $8-14)
Despite its grand appearance this hostel doesn't seem to put its money where its mouth is. The multistoried building with beehive stacked windows has dingy, dark rooms, some with a shared bathroom and a TV. For the price, you're better off staying in one of the other places in town, but the staff does seem friendly if your choices are slim or you're in a rush to get settled. Olmedo and Piedrahita, Tel: 593-6-272-3826 / 593-6-272-3827.

HOSTAL EL CISNE (ROOMS: $10)
Set back from the main road, Hostal El Cisne is a quiet place to rest your head for the night. A large, alarmingly orange concrete building, this hotel lacks the character of smaller hostels but more than makes up for it in value and comfort. Clean, bright rooms come with a big bed, tiled floors, air conditioning, TV and clean cold water showers (private). A parking lot will serve those with cars, and it is conveniently located near the main street. This is probably

one of the best value hotels in Esmeraldas. Most rooms are concrete blocks, with tiny slits for windows at the top of the ceiling, but unless you're one for postcard views of sagging rooftops, there's not much to see in Esmeraldas anyway. 10 de Agosto entre Olmedo and Colon, Tel: 593-6-272-1588 / 593-6-272-3411 / 593-6-271-3627.

HOSTAL ESTEFANÍA (ROOMS: $7-20)
Hostal Estefanía is one of the friendlier and cleaner places to stay in town. Walls adjacent to the staircase bear various brightly colored paintings, and most rooms feature reprints of Ecuador's great master: Guayasamín. Rooms are clean and simple, with private bathrooms, air conditioning and a remarkably safe feel considering the rest of Esmeraldas. The staff is friendly and sure to assist you in anything you need. Sucre and Juan Montalvo, Tel: 593-6-272-3893.

HOTEL ROMA (ROOMS: $10-24)
Located on the ever-busy Olmedo street, Hotel Roma offers very simple but clean accommodation. Rooms are air conditioned, with private bathrooms and 24-hour running water. If you're looking to block out noise from the street below, each room also has cable TV. Though not particularly pleasing on the eyes, this hotel feels reasonably safe and the staff are extremely friendly. The adjacent restaurant is open for breakfast and lunch, and if you need to make a phone call or recharge a cell phone card just head to the shop conveniently located beneath the hostal. Olmedo and Piedrahita, Tel: 593-6-627-11511, Cell: 593-9-422-8782.

HOTEL DEL MAR (ROOMS: $15-25)
Like everything else in Esmeraldas, Hotel del Mar is a bit rough around the edges, but still probably one of the nicer options. Unadorned blue-walled rooms are complemented by private bathrooms, hot water, air conditioning, 24-hour security, cable TV and an oceanside view. A large open restaurant sits adjacent to the hotel and offers an extensive menu (Entrees: $3-6), though the place can seem a bit deserted when lacking clientele. Av. Kennedy, Las Palmas, Tel: 593-6-272-3707 / 593-6-272-3708.

RESTAURANTS
Besides buses and cars, the city is packed with look-alike local eateries, each serving its own special plates and most offering street-side seating. There are a few nicer joints in town, especially if you're in the mood for steak. Head to Las Palmas for seafood.

PANADERÍA AND PASTELERÍA CAFETERÍA COLOMBIANO
Breakfast options are limited in Esmeraldas, unless you're keen for some hearty soup and rice with *platanos* (delicious in its own right, but not what some wake up craving). If you're in search of bread and other baked delights, head down to Cafetería Colombiano. Getting there involves heading down Bolivar towards Las Palmas until it turns into Libertad and crosses Espejo; the bakery sits squat on the corner with a huge red and white sign and an open area with tables and chairs. Really all you have to do is follow your nose; the smell of fresh baked goods wafts on the air for half a block. Corner of Libertad Av. 2DA and El Espejo, towards Malecón.

BAR AND CERVICHERÍA OH! MAR
An open air restaurant facing the sea, this place offers one of the nicest views you'll find in Esmeraldas. Dining is simple and only slightly classier than in town: the plastic tablecloths and glass-top tables are clean and inviting. Specials include the standard range of seafood dishes, but *ceviche*, *langosta* and the regional specialty *encocado* are among the best options. Prices are a tad more expensive than in town, but then none of the inland dives can offer palm tree studded ocean views. Main strip, Las Palmas.

CANTONES INTERNATIONAL RESTAURANT
This sister restaurant to one in Guayaquil of the same name is a traveler's dream in Esmeraldas. Restaurants crammed with people seem a world away from this gem characterized by a quiet, friendly atmosphere set amidst marble floors and tables with bright table cloths. Main entrees are a bit pricey for Esmeraldas standards, but the heaping plates that soon arrive

quickly put your figuring mind at ease. Specialties include Asian-style stir fries and rice and noodle dishes, but the Ecuadorian *Churrasco Cantones* is also sure to please. Perhaps the best service in Esmeraldas. Olmedo 3031 and 10 de Agosto.

PARRILLADAS EL TORO

Parrilladas el Toro is a breath of fresh air. Precisely set tables with wooden-back chairs spread out across the room, astride a classy bar area and walls appointed with Guayasamín reprints. This is the perfect spot for a romantic rendezvous, or to share a bottle of wine and a few drinks with friends. An open-air seating area located towards the back, the centerpiece of which is a lovely fountain, is a great way to breeze through a meal. 9 de Octubre 423 between Olmedo and Colon, Tel: 593-6-272-7925, Cell: 593-9-536-7363.

ATACAMES

Spread across an expansive stretch of fine gray sand, Atacames is a beachside playground for Ecuadorians. Foreigners are more the exception than the norm. Part hustler, part street-side vendor and welcoming hotel owner, Atacames is a town with many faces, which seem to change as the sun moves across the sky. Families can be seen with toddlers lagging along at their sides and young couples walk wrapped in each other's arms. Pods of young Ecuadorian men and women meander through the streets or stake claim to a squat of beach. Volleyball matches and soccer games sporadically appear along the beach where mothers, brothers, sisters, girlfriends and happily single males mingle or lounge across beach chairs.

At sunrise, the beach is practically empty, which seems to draw another crowd: older couples and families with small children. This is the time to stroll the beach strip and enjoy Atacames for its inherent natural beauty: seemingly endless sand set admist rolling green hills that tumble into brown clay cliffs that plunge into the sea. At night, of course, all such attributes disappear beneath a blanket of sky, the only lights being an occasional beach bonfire and the neon glow of Malecón's bouncing bars and hopping restaurants. To taste all of Atacames, you'd have to rise early, party hardy and be prepared to spend a hefty dime or two. Besides over-priced cocktails, the town specializes in *encocado* dishes, *manejar de caco* and ice cream sundaes served in carved out pineapples.

Safety is always an issue, as crowds and money seem to go hand-in-hand with crime and petty theft. Always keep an eye on your bag, never carry anything you'd be sad to lose and stay with the crowds—areas to the far east and west of the Malecón are noticeably less crowded, but also seem to attract more assaults. While hotels run east and west of the main Malecón strip, it's best to stay close to the action if you're in a small group or plan on walking to and from your hotel. Inside the discos, don't accept drinks from unknown people, and beware of pickpockets on crowded dance floors. It is even unwise to drive on the roads near Atacames after dark to nearby towns like Same and Súa, as local thieves have learned that wealthy young quiteños often travel those roads at night on their way back to the posh hotels and resorts in those towns after a night of partying in Atacames.

During Carnival, Quito empties and most quiteños head to the beach. Atacames is the first to fill up: expect hotel rates to at least triple (if you're lucky enough to find one). In the daytime, the beach is so packed, you'll be hard pressed to find a place to lay out a bandanna, let alone a towel.

Tips

Atacames (and most of the other seaside resort areas) has two seasons: *temporada alta* (high season) and *temporada baja* (low season). As you might have guessed, hotel prices tend to rise by at least 10-15 percent during peak season, generally August to December and big holidays like Semana Santa and Carnival. If you're planning a trip during these times, it's best to reserve a room ahead of time, as the best places fill up quickly. Bargaining is always an option; whether you can successfully knock off a few bucks is another question. If you're strapped for cash, there are two ATMs on the Malecón. If you're in search of phone cards, inquire at one of the convenience stores or head to Hotel El Tiburon on the eastern end of Malecón.

GETTING TO AND AWAY

To get to Atacames from Esmeraldas, walk down 10 de Agosto to the Malecón (Esmeraldas), where you'll find the TransCostenita main bus station. Buses leave frequently, tickets can be bought once on the bus. The road to Atacames boasts a network of picturesque green hills frequently interrupted by simple dirt roads or the gross orange-flame bearing pipes marking the site of yet another oil refinery. Beyond the grasp of oil-mongers the picturesque green hills of Esmeraldas roam freely, interrupted only by the white and black colorings of the odd cow. A number of hotels and hosterías (Hostería Pradera) and large eateries (Samanes Restaurant) line the route from Esmeraldas to Atacames, to check them out just walk to the front of the bus and ask them to stop. Buses from Esmeraldas to Atacames cost 50 cents.

THINGS TO DO AND SEE

JARA NET

If you're desperate to send an e-mail home or do some cyber-searching then head to Jara Net (a sign upstairs also says Café Net Kenya, take your pick). Located above the Paco Miller convenience store on the Malecón, the simple, unadorned space has all it needs: air conditioning and a row of computers. Internet is $1.80/hour and you can also make copies here.

MARCO'S PIC-NIC

If you want to do something different in Atacames other than drink and sunbathe, then head to Marco's restaurant on the Malecón and ask to speak with the owner bearing the same name. This outgoing, and genuinely friendly man owns an ecological retreat just outside the town, and a few hours spent strolling the grounds is a fulfilling experience. Marco can arrange guided tours of the grounds, which includes over thirty species of native and non-native plants. This is the perfect opportunity to see the source of all the exotic (and sometimes downright strange) fruit you've tasted or seen in markets around Ecuador. If you're in the mood to camp, there are excellent spots in a clearing beneath the canopy of tropical fruit. Entrance is $2.50 (the same to camp) and the restaurant here has the same menu as Marco's restaurant in Atacames.

LODGING

Accommodation in Atacames runs from cheap backpacker dives offering little more than a bed to more luxurious resorts featuring courtyard pools, air conditioned rooms and on-site restaurants and bars. Budgeters don't necessarily need to suffer through their stay, as a few new places have recently gone up that are reasonably priced and offer brand new, ultra-clean facilities. You're best to scout out the area (and prices) before choosing to throw down your pack. Most places are located on the Malecón, but there are other options further along the beach. Walking the beach alone at night is not recommended—if you plan on bar hopping, stick to the Malecón.

HOTEL GALLERIA (ROOMS: $8-10)

Hotel Galleria has seen better days. The small, dark rooms set in a large, sagging wooden building offer little more than a bathroom, simple bunks and a seems-to-work ceiling fan. Despite appearances, however, the hotel is not without its charms. Balconies feature slivers of seaside views, while the restaurant downstairs has an extensive menu, specializing in pizza and pasta, as well as street-side and ocean views, a perfect spot for sharing a few drinks with friends or just people watching. The package deal is a real steal: room, breakfast, lunch and dinner for $10. You can't beat Hotel Galleria's value. Malecón, Tel: 593-6-273-1149.

HOTEL XIMENA INN (ROOMS: $10/PERSON)

If you plan on hitting Atacames with a group of four or more, then Hostal Ximena is your best bet. Suites include clean, modern rooms with screened windows (a plus considering the mosquitoes) and large tiled bathrooms. Caribbean and coral colors add a splash of flavor to the already appealing hotel, and if you didn't get enough of the beach you can always hang out on the private balconies which come with the rooms. Unfortunately, there is only one matrimonial room so its not the most economical option for less than three or four people. Call ahead for reservations during high season. Malecón, Tel: 593-6-273-1363.

ANDY HOTEL INTERNACIONAL (ROOMS: $8-12)

The concrete building perched above the Malecón strip might be considered an eyesore, but in terms of value for money, travelers will find this place financially appealing. Rooms are simple, with bunks, TV, fan and private bathrooms. Most offer a seaside view through screenless windows (beware of mosquitoes). Bathrooms are nicely tiled and relatively clean, though there's not always hot water. Despite being in need of a good back-breaking once-over clean, the rooms are cozy and tidy and the staff extremely friendly. The hotel is also centrally located, so this is one of the safer options. Malecón, Tel: 593-6-276-0221 / 593-6-276-0228, Cell: 593-9-535-1858 / 593-9-491-5966.

HOTEL EL TIBURÓN (ROOMS: $10-15)

Hotel El Tiburón, located behind a conspicuous purple and white façade, is a friendly and economical option for families and groups of friends. The hospitable staff and central location are a bonus, as are the courtyard restaurant with hammocks and inside pool area. Rooms are nothing to brag about—dated wooden beds and sheets and dark bathrooms—but for the price it's not a bad place to end up for a day or two. Malecón, Tel: 593-6-273-1622 / 593-6-273-1653 / 593-6-273-1623, Cell: 593-9-813-1786, E-mail: antonia_tiburon@hotmail.com.

HOTEL SAN JOSÉ (ROOMS: $10-20)

If you're looking for a place in town but set away from the Malecón's noise, this is an ideal option. You might have to inquire next door at the convenience shop, as the entrance is often unattended. A far cry from four stars, this is a solid place to spend the night: clean sheets, private bathroom, fan and TV. Those with bad backs should probably seek other accommodation, as the beds lack a little give. Rooms are windowless, so don't expect ocean views. Calle las Acacias, turn left at the far west end of Malecón, on the left among a row of other hostels Tel: 593-6-273-1072.

RINCÓN DEL MAR (ROOMS: $10-20)

This sprawling complex located on the beach, behind a gruesome looking chain link fence comes recommended by a couple of guidebooks. However, the hotel seems to have seen better days. Small, shabby looking rooms with a private bathroom and multiple bunks open onto ocean views, while an adobe complex to the back offers more rooms by the pool. The pool appears clean, as do the rooms, but places in town are slightly brighter. If you're traveling alone, consider something closer to town as it's quite a walk down a relatively deserted street or strip of beach to get here. Av. 21 de Noviembre, on the beach, Tel: 593-6-276-0360.

MALECÓN INN (ROOMS: $12.50-25)

Looking like a miniature sky scraper, Malecón Inn has a commanding view of the Malecón strip and beachside. Walk through the glass door and up the stairs and you'll be pleasantly surprised by how clean, modern and safe it feels. Offering simple, but immaculately kept rooms with air conditioning, hot water and TV, this place is certainly one of the best deals in town. Walls and floors look so new you'd think the hotel had just opened. Prices are the same in both high and low season and there's a parking garage nearby. Malecón in front of Mar and Calle Súa, Tel: 593-6-276-1198.

EL MORRO HOTEL (ROOMS: $23)

Located across the street from Hotel Club del Sol, at the quieter western end of Atacames, El Morro Hotel seems to occupy its own peaceful space. Significantly smaller and better maintained than other options nearby this is the perfect place for those in search of a slightly cozier, more intimate place to stay. Rooms are clean and bright with cheerful colored sheets, white tiles, spacious modern bathrooms and secondary amenities like air conditioning, mini-fridge and courtyard pool. Prices include breakfast and tax. The adjacent restaurant features similarly appealing class and tastefulness, but might remain shut when there aren't a lot of people. Western end of Atacames, opposite Hotel Club del Sol, Quito offices: Coruna E-856 and Isabel la Catolica, Tel: Atacames: 593-6-273-1456 / 593-6-273-1272 or Quito: 593-2-250-1174 / 593-2-254-4080.

HOTEL CIELO AZUL (ROOMS: $17-46)

In terms of price, location and facilities, Hotel Cielo Azul is probably one of the best choices on the western side of Atacames. Tucked away from the Malecón's noise and crowds, hotel rooms overlook the beach and a central courtyard appointed with a small, but clean pool. Follow a sandy walkway from the hotel and relax beachside, or mosey on back to the pool area where you can stake claim to a lawn chair and order a drink from the poolside bar. Rooms are clean and bright, with private baths and tiled floors, and the coral hues add to the sub-tropical feel. Av. 21 de Noviembre, on the beach.

HOTEL ORUS (ROOMS: $10-70)

One of the few modern-looking, multistoried hotels in Atacames this place features a terrace-top pool overlooking the sea. Rooms are simple but clean, with private bathrooms and hot water. Unfortunately this otherwise modern hotel lacks air conditioning so you might have to make frequent trips to the terrace for a dip. The hotel also owns Nagiba Bar, on the beachside of Malecón. The entrance is around the corner from the street-facing bakery. Malecón, Tel: 593-6-273-1314.

HOTEL CLUB DEL SOL (ROOMS: $46-88)

This is one of the few places in Atacames offering the distinct feel of a large hotel chain: artwork-adorned walls and precisely made beds with matching nightstands. Besides modern bathrooms and air conditioning, Hotel Club del Sol offers a host of other trademark resort amenities, including a restaurant, bar, pool, and games area. While more expensive than the simple rooms up for grabs on the Malecón, the price is right if you're looking for something private, secure, and upper-scale. West end of beach, past end of Malecón, Quito Offices: Av. Universitaria 550 Oe-284 and 18 de Septiembre, Tel: 593-6-273-1281 / 273-1655 / 276-0660 / -0661 / -0662 / -0663, Cell: 593-9-859-6136, Quito: 593-2-252-9412, 593-2-252-6865, Cell: 593-9-982-0281, E-mail: clubsol@interactive.net.ec, URL: www.hotelclubdelsol.com.

HOTEL JUAN SEBASTIAN (ROOMS: $42-108)

Large and modern, this is one of the classier places in town. A number of options are available, from cabin-like bunks to first class suites. For the price, rooms are a bit shabby but then again the five pools, basketball court, breakfast and friendly staff are also included. Parking is also available. The main pool area is wide open, large, and appointed with palm-thatched huts for picnicking. Malecón, Tel: 593-6-273-1606 / 273-1146 / 273 1607 / 273-1049, Fax: 593-6-224-4874, E-mail: hjsebastian@hotmail.com.

RESTAURANTS

Atacames has its fair share of restaurants, each featuring a unique menu (and prices). Whether you're bustin' for pizza and pasta, or hangin' out for surf and turf, restaurants in this town should satisfy your craving. Like the hotels, most places are easy to find: just take a stroll down the Malecón. Prices from one place to another vary little, so you're more likely to choose a restaurant for its menu and atmosphere rather than how many clams it will set you back.

GABELO'S HELADOS (SNACKS $1-3)

One of the treats in Atacames is *cocada manejar*, something like sweet coconut butter rolled into balls, cut into squares, or served as a spread for toast. Streets are literally filled with vendors, each selling similar looking packets, which Ecuadorians scoop up by the bag. If you're looking for something a bit more unique, or are wary of buying street stuffs then go see Gabriel Ruiz Diaz at Gabelo's Helados. For the past 11 years, Gabriel and his wife have been producing these coconut delights en masse, carefully monitoring each batch for quality and taste. The cocada manejar sold here is more expensive, but softer, richer, and some might say tastier than its street-sold cousins. The shop also sells hot dogs, ice cream, and gigantic ice cream sundaes. Malecón.

PANADERÍA LOOR

The glaring Nescafé sign makes this place an easy spot from the street. Inside you'll find an array of tasty treats, from simple rolls to slightly more extravagant chocolate twist bread.

There's no menu, but if you speak a little Spanish or are good at charades ask for the breakfast, which consists of scrambled eggs, two pieces of bread with butter and jam and a cup of instant coffee, Nescafé of course. There are only three tables and in the mornings there's always a steady stream of people, so be bold and grab a seat. Malecón.

PIZZERÍA NO NAME (ENTREES: $4-8)

A bamboo balcony overlooking the ocean fronts a clean interior decorated with an eclectic collection of art. The chilled out atmosphere is conducive to kicking back, enjoying a meal, and watching the people scurry about on the street below. Whether you're in the mood for pizza, spaghetti, salad, or comida typical, you'll probably find it here. Malecón, Tel: 593-6-276-0457, Cell: 593-9-332-1510.

RESTAURANT PIZZERÍA NARCISS DE JESÚS (ENTREES: $4-7)

Of the places serving pizza in town this is the only one boasting a brick oven. The pizza menu is long and varied and portions are more than enough to fill the belly. Have no fear if pizzas are not your gig, as the menu is as extensive as the pizzas are large. Choose from seafood and meat dishes to salads, sandwiches and pastas. Service is slow but friendly and the balcony-side tables are perfect for catching your breath and grabbing a bite to eat after a day at the beach. This is a great place for families and picky eaters. Malecón.

MARCOS (ENTREES: $4-7)

Caribbean colors and a gurgling fountain greet hungry travelers lucky enough to stumble across Marcos restaurant. An eclectic collection of African-like artwork adorns the white stucco walls, which stretch towards bamboo ceilings and hanging reed-woven lamps. The menu is as delightful as the atmosphere. Specialties include typical Atacames fare: seafood. Unlike other restaurants in town, however, fish dishes are served with flair. Try the whole grilled fish, set amidst an array of vegetables and served still steaming. Besides the food and ambiance, there is a possibility of seeing live folk music on Friday and Saturday nights. Malecón, Tel: 593-6-276-0126, Cell: 593-9-110-6573.

PIZZERÍA DA GIULIO (ENTREES: $3-7)

There are a couple of pizza restaurants in town, but Pizzería Da Giulio is probably the most gourmet. Owner Giulio was born in Italy and spent fourteen years working in Milan; whether or not this is proof of authenticity is something you'll have to decide for yourself. This Italian-Ecuadorian couple goes to great lengths to ensure their ingredients are fresh and true to Italian form, something easier said than done in a country where rice, platanos, and meat are the staples. Cheese is bought from a specialty store in Quito and the mushrooms are hand chopped and marinated in a special mix of olive oil and garlic. Though pizza is the specialty, the restaurant also offers a variety of fish, chicken and meat dishes—all of which can be enjoyed with an ocean view. Malecón, Tel: 593-6-273-1603.

EL TIBURÓN (ENTREES: $3-10)

A popular locals' joint, this restaurant is small but tidy, with colorful decorations and friendly service. The house recommends *Bandeja de Mariscos*, which can be shared between three people. The rest of the menu is pretty typical Atacames fare, with various ceviches and fish, meat and chicken dishes. Those who aren't up for fish or game can treat themselves to a simple spaghetti dish. If you're up early and feeling hungry they also serve breakfasts, but be aware that this party town doesn't get going much before 9 a.m. This is the place to come if you're in the mood to drink, and it's sure to satisfy your seafood cravings as well. Daily 7 a.m - midnight. The restaurant is located at the far end of beach near San Cristobal Cabañas.

DER ALTE FRITZ (ENTREES: $4-6)

Loved by travelers and guidebooks alike, this is a sure win if you're in the mood for something German, something Ecuadorian or simply something a little classier than the rest of Atacames. The menu is extensive, and is written in three languages so almost everyone can understand. If not, ask the stalwart-looking fellow with glasses and long hair: Captain Martin

Einhaus speaks five languages and will most likely be able to answer you back. Seafood is probably fresher than the stuff they serve up beachside, and changes with the season to ensure quality. The menu also features various pastas and special Austrian pancakes. This place boasts some of the most authentic German food in the region. Malecón, Tel: 593-6-273-1610, E-mail: meinhausandina.net, URL: www.deraltefritz-ecuador.com.

EL CUBANO

In Atacames you can take your pick of seafood restaurants, and some of the cheapest and best seafood is found right on the beach. But if you're looking for a place with a bit of atmosphere and a distinctly local feel, El Cubano restaurant is a top-notch establishment. During the day, families and couples drape themselves across the long wooden glass-topped tables and hunker down for a hearty afternoon feed. Orange table cloths complement the colorful seafood dishes that appear in rapid succession from the kitchen. Malecón.

ATACAMES BARS

You guessed correctly if you said Atacames serves up its fair share of drinks. Take your pick of the bamboo and thatched roof bars fronting the beach. Each varies only slightly in style, music played and how the drinks are served, and popularity seems to rotate night-to-night. Early in the evening families can be seen as well as children climbing on the barside swing-seats while night drives another, more rowdy crowd. Prices seem to varies little between bars, and the cocktail list is pretty extensive at all. At the far eastern strip of Malecón, Friends Bar seems to be a popular joint, offering pumping music and weekend Marimba. The guys at Jamaica Bar, a bit further west, know how to make a good cocktail. As with every other place, the juice is fresh-as, but here drinks ($2-4) are artfully prepared and topped off with sliced fruit and tied-napkins. The atmosphere here is chilled out, like the music. At night, on the other side of the street, Tsunami Bar seems to be the most popular Ecuadorian draw.

SAME

Located on a secluded strip of beach away from the blaring bars and packed streets of Atacames, Same is little more than a quiet stretch of exclusive apartment buildings for vacationing quiteños, with the odd hotel squeezed in among them. Although it can feel a bit deserted, it's a nice spot to spend the day. Those prepared to blow a few bucks can head up to Club Casablanca, which spreads out across the adjacent hillside like a white fortress for the wealthy. This is not the place for backpackers and penny-pinchers, but certainly a great getaway for those with means. Back beachside, there are a couple of options for sleeping and eating, though availability seems to depend more on the owner and time of year than physical presence of a room to spare.

GETTING TO AND AWAY

To get to Same from Atacames, head across the footbridge away from the Malecón and walk straight two blocks, bearing left at the fork. Look for people milling about by the moto-taxi stand. Buses run frequently, but without much of a schedule, and usually cost 35 cents. Make sure to be dropped off at Same town and not Casablanca, though a walk up toward the exclusive apartments rewards you with stunning views of turquoise water and rolling green hills.

LODGING

LA TERRAZA ($8-20/PERSON)

This white adobe building is reminiscent of the more expensive versions perched hillside, and the rooms inside are bright, breezy, and a steal for the price. Bathrooms are immaculate and rooms open onto a terrace overlooking the sea. The next door cabins, also part of La Terraza, are slightly more economical but far less attractive. Those in search of food can wander a few steps further to La Terraza restaurant, one of the nicer and more affordable places in Same. The owners Alexandra and Pepo are friendly and helpful and suggest bargaining regardless of the season, though in high season solo travelers would probably have to pay for all the beds in a room. Tel: 593-2-273-3320, Cell: 593-9-732-4405 / 593-9-685-8677.

CASABLANCA BEACH HOTEL AND RESORT (ROOMS: $50-125)

Situated on the beautiful beach of Same, embraced by palm trees and tropical gardens, Casablanca is one of the most luxurious places to stay on the coast. Mediterranean architecture accompanies its already stunning setting by the sea. Relax and unwind amid the outstanding facilities, complete with first-class service and gourmet international cuisine—oh and did we mention the tennis courts and golf course? Quito office: Av. Republica de El Salvador N35-82 and Portugal, Edif. Twin Towers P.B, Tel: 593-2-225-2488 / -2489 / -2490, Fax: 593-2-225-3452, E-mail: info@casablanca.com, URL: www.ccasablanca.com.

RESTAURANTS

BERNABE CERVICHERÍA AND RESTAURANTE (ENTREES: $4-5)

This open, airy restaurant with simple wood floors, seaside views, and a basic menu is a good option, and one of the few in Same. Specialties include Cazuela Mixtos, but you'll also find traditional Ecuadorian seaside fare like rice and fish, and rice and shrimp dishes. If you're up for a splurge, they also serve langosta (lobster) in a variety of ways.

LA TERRAZA RESTAURANT (ENTREES: $5-6.50)

This split level thatched-roof building fronting the beach offers great ocean views and an enticing menu, which includes Italian, Spanish and Ecuadorian fare. There's a bar towards the back and walls bear a sporadically placed collection of 1950s style posters. Owner Alexandria claims all dishes are excellent, but recommends the paella ($8.50/two people) or the encocado mixto ($7.10). A jack of all trades, Alexandra also sells handmade artesanía and beach clothes (boutique located in the restaurant).

SEA FLOWER (ENTREES: $12-25)

Catering mostly to the money-wielding folks vacationing in the high-rise apartment complexes of Same, the Sea Flower offers an expensive menu known for its gastronomic, more than economic appeal. Dishes are carefully prepared and served in style. The restaurant has a unique sea-captain feel, with dark polished wood and a bewildering array of artifacts strewn about the room. Cell: 593-9-245-5038 / 593-9-256-7923.

SÚA

Set in a pleasant cove behind the picturesque green hills, cradling Atacames and separating it from nearby Same, Súa is a slightly—albeit not much—quieter version of its bar-infested big brother to the north. Travelers have mixed reviews about this place: either it's a chilled-out place to throw back a few beers, enjoy the beach and rest your head, or it's a lackluster, lonelier version of Atacames. The town is a bit scruffy, with the same unruly Reggaeton blasting from generic bamboo beachside bars. To give credit where credit's due, the beach is less crowded and surprisingly picturesque, considering the shabby shops and hotels fronting its shores: expanses of fine gray sand stretch towards the sea, curling into a quiet cove at the far end. Head over to the massive cliffs dropping abruptly into the sea on the western side of the bay. Known as Peñón del Suicida (Suicide Rock), the rock is named after Princess Súa and conquistador Captain de León—Ecuador's own Romeo and Juliet—who leapt headlong into the sea after a forbidden love affair gone awry. During the day shrieking pelicans, blue-footed boobies and frigate birds stake out the cliffside, occasionally swooping down on unsuspecting fisherman and their haul. Between June and September, you can catch a boat from here to spot humpback whales off the coast, near Punta Galera (about 40-60 minutes by boat).

LODGING

HOTEL CHAGRA RAMAS ($6/PERSON)

Like everything else in Súa, Hotel Chagra Ramas is a bit rundown and in need of some work. However, its view can't be beat. Rather sad looking cabin-like rooms line the hillside in tiers, while a large open restaurant sits at the bottom—all sections overlook the sea. Bare essential rooms come with dated wooden beds and dark bathrooms.

HOTEL LOS JARDINES ($8-10/PERSON)

Set back from the beach, on the street leading beachside. This hotel is an decent budget option. Bare, but clean rooms surround an appealing pool and attractive garden. Don't be surprised if the entrance is unattended, just knock or say hello and someone is sure to come. This is an option if you're in need of a place to stay and are looking for something slightly better than a bed with sheets. Tel: 593-6-273-4037, 593-6-273-1181.

RESTAURANTS

CHAGRA RAMAS (ENTREES: $3.50-5.50)

The restaurant is oversized and under-nourished; a large seating area appears empty, except for a few patrons and the staff. Meals are cheap and range from stock standard rice, meat, and chicken plates to the only slightly more expensive encocado and ceviche dishes. Main street, occupies entire right side of main street at beach.

KIKE'S RESTAURANT (ENTREES: $4-15)

Set in a large airy room featuring glass-top tables with napkin-bearing cranes, this is one of the cleaner, nicer restaurants in town. The menu is pretty standard seaside fare, but slightly cheaper than the stuff served up in Atacames. Specialties include mariscos and encocado dishes. While the street action outside might feel otherwise, Kike's Restaurant hosts a pleasant family atmosphere. Tel: 593-6-273-4045.

TONCHIGÜE

Tonchigüe is little more than a sleepy fishing village with a modest beach. About 2 kilometers south of town, the road heads west, following the coast towards Punta Galera where it eventually runs into Quingüe, Estero del Plátano, San Francisco and Bunche. Rarely trekked by tourists, this area is abundant in visually arresting and culturally interesting sites, from tiny villages and quiet coastlands to remote forests and hidden waterfalls. Lucky travelers visiting Estero del Plátano between June and September may spot a whale or two breaching the waters offshore. Travelers can also volunteer in nearby communities. Ecotrackers (www.ecotrackers.com) runs a community development program in Estero del Plátano, where you can live with a local family and take part in a variety of projects.

LODGING

PLAYA ESCONDIDA ($5/CAMPING, $10-35/ROOM)

Playa Escondida is located in a beautiful bay, just 10 kilometers from Tonchigüe and six kilometers from Punta Galera. The words "Playa Escondida" mean hideaway beach and, indeed, it is way off the beaten track. The ecological refuge based here is large, covering nearly 100 hectares, and boasts a variety of flora and fauna. As an ecological retreat, Playa Escondida is not just for tourists: it is committed to protecting the surrounding plants and animals from local hunters, logging, cattle and shrimp farming, and commercial tourism. The retreat currently has capacity for thirty people. There is a camping area with plenty of shade and showers. There are no cooking facilities, but small campfires are allowed. For something a bit more private, ask to stay in Casa Wantara, a large house with its own kitchen and private bathroom ($25/person). Tel: 593-6-273-3368, E-mail: judithbarett@hotmail.com, URL: www.ecuadorexplorer.com/playaescondida.

> *V!VA Member Review-Playa Escondida - Ecological Retreat*
> *Swiss Family Robinson atmosphere with Five Star seafood and a casual, indigenous feeling. 12 April 2007. USA.*

NORTHERN COAST

Muisne

Seen boat-side from the Río Muisne, the town appears disappointingly run down compared to the high-heeled hotels and holiday homes located 35 kilometers to the north. Salty sea breezes, strong equatorial sun and high humidity assault the building faces, leaving behind peeling paint and weather-worn wood patched with green mold. Beyond the dock, behind the sagging riverside structures, is an equally lackluster town. Pallid and windowless buildings line the dusty street, where chickens and children roam freely. A single road, Isidro Ayora, stretches away from the docks, past the aging shop fronts, and ends abruptly at the palm-studded stretch of beach at the opposite end of town. It is here, on this quiet strip of clean, bar-less beach, that one begins to understand why travelers make the bumpy overland bus trip and cross-river trek to such a tired little town. Anyone coming from Atacames is sure to appreciate the peace, and even surf and sand snobs will have something positive to say about the beach (though if you're into surfing, Mompiche is a better bet). Stretched out seaside with clear views of beach inhabited only by resident palms, you're bound to breathe easy and let worries wash away like shells with the tide. Although the town and beachfront can feel a bit deserted at times—and it's not recommended to wander away from the main areas alone— Muisne radiates a relaxed "enjoy-today-and-worry-tomorrow" island attitude that can charm even tight-fisted travelers into having just one more beer.

Getting to and Away

A good paved road heading south from Muisne to Pedernales simplifies (to some extent) travel down the entire length of Ecuador's coast. El Salto, a dusty one-horse-type town, is the main hub for bus travel to and from Muisne and places to the south. From El Salto, the road heads 56 kilometers south, before hitting the turn-off for Mompiche and continuing on to Chamanga, a link-up town for buses to Pedernales. From El Salto, grab a bus heading to Muisne. You'll be dropped off at the docks, from which you can hop a boat to Muisne, across the Río Muisne. To get out of Muisne, the earliest boat leaves around 6 a.m., walk up the cement steps and catch a bus to El Salto (50 cents/30 minutes). In El Salto change buses to Chamanga ($1.70), the bus to Chamanga drops you off at the entrance to the road into Mompiche, it's a 3 kilometer walk from here.

Lodging

Don't come here expecting lavish tropical bungalows with king-sized beds and travel-sized shampoos and soaps; what you will find is well-maintained and comfortable accommodation well within range of any backpacker's budget. The salty sea breeze and ocean sounds complement any place fronting the beach.

Hostel Playa Paraíso (Rooms: $5-15)

Small and unassuming from the front, Hostal Playa Paraíso is an undiscovered gem sure to reward anyone who passes through its doors. Rooms are clean and breezy, with bunks and beds featuring bright white sheets (folded down on the corners!), and fluffy pillows and mattresses meant for a good night's sleep. Ask for the rooms towards the front for a seaside view, although most rooms offer the chance to doze off to the sound of breaking waves. Bathrooms are shared, but modern and well-maintained. There are also a few cabins out back, which are (if it's possible) even cleaner and more modern than the front rooms, and these have private bathrooms. A family-run place, Hostal Playa Paraíso is warm and friendly, and the owner and his wife are more than happy to sit and chat—both lived in Texas for years and speak fluent English. On the beach, Tel: 593-6-248-0192, E-mail: byrondhierro@yahoo.com.

San Cristobal Cabañas ($6/person)

This cluster of simple cabins commands a stunning view of the sea, but offers little more than basic lodging with baths. Rooms are simple, but clean and beds are relatively comfy. A good option for small groups and couples looking for something a little more secluded (more rustic retreat than island getaway). Far end of beach, on the right from town, past El Tiburon restaurant, Tel: 593-6-248-0264.

Hotel Galápagos ($8/person)

Certainly the biggest, most hotel-looking joint in Muisne, Hotel Galápagos features large clean rooms organized around a modest central garden. Owner José Miguel Ochoa is an older gentleman, in charge of maintaining the property himself, and he goes great strides to make guests feel comfortable. Originally from Loja, he is also keen to pass an afternoon chatting about local politics, so if you're one for getting the low down on places you visit, pull up a chair. While it may not feature ocean views, the grounds are immaculate and beds comfortable. This is a good spot for families or large groups looking for something a bit more private than hostels on the beach. Calle Manabí, on the way to the beach, Tel: 593-6-248-0289.

Restaurants

Located just off the popular tourist circuit, Muisne maintains its local flavor and is a great spot to try traditional coastal fare like ceviche and *encocado* (dishes steeped in coconut sauce). There are a number of food stalls lining the main street, Isidro Ayora, but the beachside restaurants have a bit more atmosphere and definitely better views. Plates offered and prices vary little from place to place so your decision on where to dine will probably be based more on appearance and atmosphere than anything else. Note that most restaurants operate on beach time, meaning they tend to open and close according to the flow of patrons.

Restaurante Santa Martha (entrees: $3-8)

This place seems to be the local favorite, recommended by motor-taxi drivers and extended-stay tourists. At a glance there is little to set it apart from the other restaurants, except that polished wood has replaced the ever-popular plastic tables and chairs. Inside, owner Martha greets patrons with a broad smile and warm air that makes even the newest islander feel welcome. The food is typical coastal cuisine (seafood served in soup, mixed with rice, or smothered in coconut sauce) but served with a distinct down-home flavor. Martha's ever-chatty husband Lois is a good source of information on the island and more than eager to pass his knowledge on to anyone with an open ear. He can also organize impromptu horseback riding and boat excursions. Cell: 593-9-143-3603.

La Riviera (entrees: $3-15)

An unassuming entryway leads into a small kitchen area where Patricio and his wife Angelica prepare stock-standard coastal fare—try the camaron empanada—for anyone hungry and looking for a meal. Although its name may conjure images of fancy candle-lit dinners and men in striped shirts rowing gondolas, the restaurant bears the family name and dining here is an informal affair, more like eating in than dining out. Even if you're not in the mood for rice and fish it's a good place to just chill out with a beer and watch the beach comings and goings. First on the left as you approach the beach from town.

Mompiche

A well-guarded secret amongst stout-surfers and heavyweight travelers, Mompiche is quite possibly the nicest spot to drop your bags, grab a beer and bum around for a few days. Located in a sheltered bay, on the south side of Ensenada de Mompiche, this once-sleepy fishing village has awakened to a burgeoning tourist industry, so a number of beach bungalows have popped up in recent years. And it's not hard to see why: a backdrop of emerald green hills encircles the stunning seven kilometer stretch of dark sand beach. Surf gurus say this is the best break in Ecuador, but even those who would rather hang out than hang ten will find the surf and sand of Mompiche agreeable.

Considering its mythic status in the travel community, it should come as no surprise that Mompiche harbors a secret of its own: ask around town for boat rides to a nearby, even more remote (and from what we hear, more beautiful) island off the coast. We'd love to tell you more, but travel to such a spot seems to be a rite of passage granted only to those adventurous enough to ask. Lodging options include: Cabañas de Iruna, Hotel Mompiche, Hostal Carolina, Hotel Estrellita, Hostería Gabela and Mompiche Beach Lodge.

NORTHERN COAST

CHAMANGA

Situated south of Muisne and Mompiche, Chamanga is a lively place, featuring houses built on stilts over the estuary. While there is not much going on in town, this is a good piggyback point to more interesting sites nearby, such as the majestic mangroves and good walking trails. The Reserva Ecológica Mache Chindul, managed by the Jatun Sacha Foundation, stretches across the provincial border offering unique flora and fauna. For volunteer opportunities, head to www.jatunsacha.org/ingles/volunteer_ecuador.htm.

MANABÍ

South of Esmeraldas, rests the coastal province of Manabí. The beach cities along the Manabí coast are very popular during holidays and summer months for their mellow surfing towns, big waves and, of course, excellent seafood. The Parque Nacional Machililla is in Manabí and features excellent wildlife, possibly Ecuador's most beautiful beach, Los Frailes, whale watching, kayaking and horseback riding tours, and some beautiful campgrounds. La Isla de la Plata, just off the coast of Puerto López and part of the Parque Machililla, has the nickname of The Poor-Man's Galápagos for its variety in birds also found in Galápagos and great snorkeling and diving. Enjoy excellent whale watching from July to October when humpback whales finish their long trip from as far south as Antarctica. The first whales arrive off the coast of Ecuador in July, when they give birth and spend the summer in the warm currents off the coast of Manabí. The whale watching season ends in late September or October when the humpbacks head south as soon as their babies are big enough to make the long return trip.

GETTING TO AND AWAY

REINA DEL CAMINO

Reina del Camino offers the most direct bus service available from Quito to Manabí and Guayas. Choose between *clase ejecutivo* (first class) and *clase económico*. First class buses usually offer a snack en route, are usually overnight trips and have strict rules for safety and to limit the noise level; no cell phones are permitted on board, most items are stored underneath the bus and passengers are intimately frisked before boarding. Manta Terminal Terrestre - 593-5-262-2474, Guayaquil - 593-4-229-7757, Quito Terminal Terrestre - 593-2-269-7719.

ARAY

One of the two main bus services from Quito to Manabí, Aray has three buses daily along this route which make several stops along the way. The buses are older and not as nice as Reina del Camino, but are cheaper. Unlike Reina del Camino, Aray buses will pick up passengers waiting roadside, which can be more dangerous. Machililla and General Córdova, Puerto López, Tel: 593-4-230-0178.

PARQUE NACIONAL MACHILILLA

Parque Nacional Machililla (136,000 acres) is a nationally protected stretch of beach and dry tropical forest as well as two islands, Isla de la Plata and Isla Salango north of Puerto López and south of Puerto Cayo in the Manabí province. Highlights are the unique wildlife such as blue-footed boobies, sea lions and iguanas that can also be seen in Galápagos. Humpback whales procreate just offshore every year from July to October and can be seen from several inland points and up close on special tours or on your way to and from Isla de la Plata. We recommend skipping the whale watching tours as you get the exact same experience on the Isla de la Plata tour plus you get to see the island!

Other tours in Parque Machililla include horseback riding, kayaking, fishing, snorkeling and diving. If you are planning to visit Isla de la Plata and the mainland areas of Parque Nacional Machililla, buy the combined entrance ticket for the island and the mainland for $20 ($5 for Ecuadorians). Otherwise, entrance to the island is $15 for foreigners and $3.50 for Ecuadorians and entrance to the mainland park areas are $12 and $2 for Ecuadorians. There are also multi-day passes. The park is best during the month of July when the weather is still sunny and the whales are arriving.

There is a small local community 7.5 miles north of Puerto López, three miles off the main highway in the park with ancestors dating back to the Manteña Culture who inhabited the land from 800 to 1532. The Agua Blanca Community and their small museum can be visited with a guide. Tours introduce you to the ancient burial customs, typical dress, and religious practices on a one-mile walk through the forest where you can also bird-watch and see views of the river valley and lagoon.

PEDERNALES

Not much distinguishes Pedernales from other coastal towns. While it features the same bamboo constructed beachside bars as Atacames, it lacks the line of hotels and hostels that might give it more of a welcoming, resort feel. Instead, it remains more of a commercial hub and crossroads for traffic north and south than a desirable destination in itself. That said, the town is not a bad option if you're looking to break up a trip from Esmeraldas, Canoa, Bahía or Manta. The beach, while not spectacular, is certainly picturesque enough to pencil in some time for sand and sun.

GETTING TO AND AWAY

The bus terminal is located on Juan Pereira, just two blocks northeast of the main square. Buses leave every 20 minutes for Santo Domingo, with connections to Quito (5-6 hours). Connections south include Guayaquil ($8, 9 hours) and San Vicente ($3, 2.5 hours).

LODGING

HOTEL YAM YAM (ROOMS: $10-15)

If you're in Pedernales and looking for a place to stay that's convenient to the bus station, this is a good bet. Sitting on a main road, between the station and the beach, Hotel Yam Yam features a modern reception area and clean rooms with private baths. This isn't mint-on-your-pillow, but it's not the worst place to unpack for the night. Av. Gonzáles Suárez and Juan Pereira, Tel: 593-5-268-0566 / 1359, Cell: 593-9-705-2326.

ORION HOTEL (ROOMS: $6-14)

Planted on a hill overlooking the sea, Orion Hotel and its brightly painted blue and white façade are easily spotted from the road leading down from the bus station. One of the more modern-looking joints in town, the hotel features an on-site cafetería, flower adorned terrazas, hot water, private bathrooms, and cable TV. Av. Juan Pereira and Malecón, Tel: 593-5-268-0136, Quito: 593-2-267-8229, Cell: 593-9-879-4408, E-mail: orionecuador@ozu.es.

RESTAURANTS

LA CHOZA (ENTREES: $3-10)

Like most of the coastal towns, Pedernales features its own set of generic beachfront restaurants and bars. In terms of gastronomy, La Choza fits right in; however, its dining area, complete with a collection of wine bottles spread across the back wall, give it a bit more atmosphere than the other seafood dives in town. Calling itself a restaurant of 4 b's—*bueno, bonito, barato* and *bastante*—this place seeks to serve its customers a bit of everything good with a side of better than the rest. The menu includes 50 different plates, so even the picky palates should be able to find something here. Av. Eloy Alfaro and Malecón, beachfront, Tel: 593-2-268-0388.

JAMA

Sitting slightly inland, amid humid pasture-lands, is the unassuming town of Jama. Though this market center offers little in the way of beaches and bars, it does present visitors with the opportunity to experience the rural countryside and its inhabitants. Jama is a great stopover spot for those looking to escape the crowds and get stuck into nature without straying too far from the sand and surf.

NORTHERN COAST

BOSQUE SECO LALO LOOR

Just 20 minutes south of Pedernales (by bus) and a short jaunt north of Jama is a network of recently opened trails winding through unique coastal dry forest, past a stunning variety of flora and fauna and spectacular views of the expansive Pacific Ocean. Bosque Seco Lalo Loor is a great place to get out and about in nature. A number of self-guided trails introduce visitors to dry forest ecology, as well as the area's endemic wildlife, which includes White-Fronted Capuchin monkeys, Mantled Howler monkeys, Red-masked parakeets, Pacific Royal-Flycatchers, boa constrictors, Jaguarundi and a mixed bag of frogs and lizards.

Bird fans and orchid aficionados will also find the area full of interesting sites and sounds. The 45-minute Mariposa Trail begins at the reserve's entrance, winding past tumbling waterfalls, while the Pacífico Trail starts from the Biological Station, eventually climbing a number of ridgelines and presenting visitors with ocean views. Lodging is available in the new Biological Station. Opened in March 2005, the station can accommodate up to 24 people, providing basic lodging for visitors, researchers and volunteers, as well as serving as a research center for reforestation and conservation projects.

To arrange a visit, contact CFTC (Ceiba Foundation for Tropical Conservation). For a few more creature comforts, you can also arrange to stay at Punta Prieta Guest House, just a few kilometers south of the Reserve, or Hacienda Camarones just a 20-minute walk south from the reserve. While in the area, be sure to check out the wave-carved natural monument, El Arco del Amor, located three kilometers south of the reserve, along the coast road towards the town of Tasaste. For maps of the Reserve and its trails head to www.ceiba.org/loormaps.htm. To arrange a visit or to volunteer, contact: CFTC. Eugenio de Santillán N34-248 and Maurián, Casilla Postal 17-12-867, Quito, Tel: 593-2-243-2240, 593-2-243-2246, E-mail: mail@ceiba.org, URL: www.ceiba.org.

LODGING

PUNTA PRIETA GUEST HOUSE (CABINS: $10-30)

A lovely place to pass the time and soak up some Pacific views is Punta Prieta Guest House, located just off the road from Jama, between Pedernales and Canoa. Perched cliff-side overlooking the ocean, this place is as visually pleasing as the beds are comfortable, and salt air and fresh seafood are as ubiquitous as the seaside views. Those on a budget can ask about camping on the beach; for a small fee you can also use the showers and bathrooms. Cabins range in price but beach views are included in the price, as well as kitchens and refrigerators. To sample the local sea fare, head to the on-site restaurant where you can indulge in the catch of the day and enjoy the view. Reservations are recommended. Vía del Pacífico, Km 36 tramo Pedernales-Jama, Cell: 593-9-342-3811, Quito: 593-2-286-2986, Fax: 593-2-286-7910, E-mail: meche14@accessinter.net, URL: www.puntaprieta.com.

CANOA

Mompiche may have the surfer's hearts, and Atacames may have the bars, but Canoa is sure to romance almost anyone into a stupor with its long stretches of white sand, chilled surf, and easy-going town. Whether you like long walks on the beach or lengthy chats in bars, Canoa's spell-binding atmosphere is bound to capture your attention

Photo by Kristi Mohrbacher

NORTHERN COAST

for a day or two, or more; it's not uncommon for travelers to come for the night and stay for a month. Quiet dirt roads crisscross through town, running into the main street and beach front, lined with restaurants and hostels that fill to the brim with foreign and Ecuadorian travelers alike on the weekends. During the week, however, Canoa maintains an unhurried pace which settles nicely with the hushed sound of waves breaking and the palm fronds shifting in the breeze.

LODGING

Canoa is a backpacker haven, geared towards cheap to mid-range accommodation that doesn't skimp on comfy beds and clean sheets (for the most part). Recently, a number of new places have gone up in town, giving most of the older places a run for their money in terms of quality, service and style. Like all places on the coast, Canoa overflows with people on weekends, so you'd be smart to make reservations early. Don't expect to cruise into town on Saturday night and find a place to stay.

HOTEL BAMBU (CAMPING: $2, ROOMS: $7-36)

Commanding a quiet, sandy corner of the main street, Hotel Bambu is a popular traveler hangout and good place to rest your head. Accommodation ranges from cheap to more expensive (by Canoa standards), from a simple hammock and breach breeze to a more elaborate room with private balcony and bathroom, and big comfy bed. Camping spots and private cabins are another option. There is a restaurant and bar, which serves a tempting array of national and international dishes, including salad, crepes, sandwiches and ice cream. Travelers seem to congregate around the beach-like yard, where beach chairs, hammocks, and wooden tables make cozy spots to curl up with a book or catch a bit of shut eye. The sound of waves breaking in the distance, mixed with the hypnotic rustling of wind chimes is bound to lull even the javaholics to sleep. The owner also runs Casa Bambu in Quito and Cabañas Bambusa in Mindo. Main street, far end of beach, Tel: 593-5-261-6370, Cell: 593-9-926-3365, URL: www.ecuadorexplorer.com/bambu.

COCO LOCO (DORM: $5, ROOMS: $12-16)

One of the newest additions to Canoa's beachfront, Hostal Coco Loco is quickly becoming the most popular spot to spend the night. Owners Frans and Rika welcome new arrivals like old friends, quickly winning their hearts with fresh-baked treats, broad smiles, and down-to-earth attitudes. Its easy to spend a morning, afternoon, or evening idling around the kitchen counter, swapping travel stories and shooting the breeze. Of course, this place isn't all talk: newly built and smartly styled rooms bear crisp clean sheets, new mattresses, and high-tech fans, which, when combined with a fresh sea breeze, are certain to relax the limbs and produce droopy eye-lids. Cell: 593-9-397-2884, URL: www.hostalcocoloco.com.

LA POSADA DE DANIEL ($6/PERSON)

A popular Canoa fixture, La Posada de Daniel offers comfortable cabins, perfect for large groups, and equipped with mosquito nets, private bathrooms, fans, and balconies with views of town and a bit of sea. Calm, quiet, and cozy, this place also offers an on-site restaurant, and can organize horseback riding excursions and local tours. The owner, once a slick surfer himself, gives lessons to anyone interested. As if the views weren't enough, this place also has satellite internet, a swimming pool, and vegetarian restaurant. If you're up for a drink head to the hotel-owned Iguana Bar for "crazy" hour from 8 - 9 p.m. 150 meters back from the beach, by the town square, Tel: 593-5-261-6374.

HOSTEL SHELMAR (ROOMS: $6-12)

Located one block from the beach, Hostal ShelMar offers basic, but bright rooms and private bathrooms upstairs and a good, cheap, restaurant downstairs. This isn't the best place in town, but still good value, clean and comfortable. Laundry service is available for both patrons and non-patrons. Active travelers looking to stretch their legs for a while can also rent bikes from here for $1-7.50. One block from the beach, Cell: 593-9-864-4892, E-mail: shelmar3@hotmail.com.

NORTHERN COAST

LA VISTA ($8/PERSON)

A grand, but still beachy-looking hotel fronting the main beach, La Vista is a new place with big new beds, and polished wooden floors which lead towards a private balcony with hammocks and complimented by a stunning sea view. Rooms are open and airy, and emit a chilled out but still classy feel that even the grungiest backpacker will certainly appreciate. Staff is friendly and the bar downstairs serves a variety of hard and soft drinks, a good spot to pull up a stool and contemplate one's luck at finding a place so beautiful and well priced. Main street, next to Coco Loco, Cell: 593-9-919-6000.

CABAÑAS MAR AND PAZ (CABINS: $8-16)

Clusters of modest cabins surround a spacious yard equipped with a volleyball court and picnic tables, making Cabanas Mar and Paz the perfect setting for friendly reunions and family excursions. The ever-amiable owner, Jaime, aims to please, and with notice is happy to organize local tours, and cater for special events, including meals accompanied with live music. Cabins are rustic, but relatively comfortable with simple bunks and wooden floors. A fun, family atmosphere is complimented by plenty of open space and small gardens in which to sit and socialize or challenge a few mates to a friendly match. Cabins fill up quickly during high season and special holidays so it's wise to call ahead and book early. Note: a 50 percent deposit is required with reservation. Tel: 593-5-261-6385, Quito Tel: 593-2-240-9663, Cell: 593-9-895-4458, E-mail: jaimesolisch@yahoo.es, URL: www.cabanasmarypaz.com.

HOTEL SOL AND LUNA ($10/PERSON)

Located at the far south end of the beach, Hotel Sol and Luna is an aging, but good value place built hacienda-style around a courtyard swimming pool which boasts excellent seaside views. A modest garden adds a splash of color to the site, and rooms are big, clean and well-maintained with modern bathrooms. The on-site restaurant serves a range of traditional and international dishes, and paragliding tours can be arranged. Far south end of the beach, Tel: 593-5-261-6363 / 256-2096, Cell: 593-9-805-2275 / 593-9-813-8730.

HOSTERÍA CANOA (ROOMS: $15-64)

Sprawled across its own section of private beach, a few kilometers from town, Hostería Canoa offers a slightly more intimate setting than some of the smaller places in Canoa. Clean, modern, and colorful rooms are set around a courtyard swimming pool and restaurant and bar area offering a spacious, but stylish place for a meal. Cabins are perfect for larger groups, or families, and come with the same well-appointed rooms and modern bathrooms. Pricier than the joints down the road, Hostería Canoa is still a good value considering its facilities and location. Tel: 593-5-261-6380 / 6382, Cell: 593-9-977-4747, E-mail: info@hosteríacanoa.com, URL: www.hosteríacanoa.com.

RESTAURANTS

From fresh fruit salad to fajitas, this little town has got the culinary circuit pretty much covered. And, of course, you'll have no trouble finding typical coastal fare, including ceviches and platos encocados. Prices between places don't vary much, so you're more likely to choose a place based on its menu and atmosphere than by how much cash you'll have to shell out.

ARENA BAR

This is the place to go if you're watching your wallet and aren't looking for anything more complex than a shake and toasted sandwich. Food here may not be first class, and some may consider the atmosphere seriously lacking, but its red leather 1950's style booths face the sea and are more than worthy of sharing a cocktail and a sunset. Of course, you may have to share your moment with the mosquitoes. Malecón Escénico.

SURF SHAK (ENTREES: $.25-4)

A couple of places in town serve up pizza, but none can top the ones coming from the kitchen at Surf Shak, a local fixture made popular by its American-style meals, which in addition to pizza, include staples like spaghetti, cheeseburgers, and french fries. The lasagne comes highly recommended. E-mail: jamesdeanbyrd@yahoo.com.

COMEDOR JIXY (ENTREES: $1.50-4)

This unassuming place set back from the beach is one of the most popular spots to settle the stomach and sample local seafood. Serving good value set meals and cheap mains, Comedor Jixy also knows how to satisfy the budget. There's not much in the way of atmosphere here, but it's hard to argue with the prices, or the sea breeze. Set back from the beach.

RESTAURANTE LA CHOCITA (ENTREES: $2-10)

A simple restaurant serving up excellent local dishes, like fish encocado and langosta a la plancha (a real treat if you've got some cash to spare). Beachy, breezy, and situated away from the main street noise, Restaurante La Chocita is a delightful spot to pull up a chair, order a plate and savor the chilled out atmosphere that is Canoa at its best.

PAPAYA BAR (ENTREES: $2.50-3)

A laid back restaurant just off the main street fronting the beach, Papaya Bar is a family run place serving up traditional coastal fare. But its best kept secret is its huge fruit salad, sprinkled with granola and fresh yogurt, a refreshing snack after a day at the beach. Past Hotel Bambu, on right side of street.

BAR AND RESTAURANT LA CHOZA (ENTREES: $2.50-3.50)

A good hangout if you're in the mood for some coastal cuisine washed down with fresh juice, or a slightly stronger beverage. Atmosphere varies depending on the time of day, with your laid back beach crowd dribbling in during the day and bar hoppers bouncing in at night. Meals are simple, and include ceviche, rice, and fish. The cocktail list is extensive, as well as the juices, and if all else fails you can order the old standby: milkshakes. Cell: 593-9-739-8231.

SHAMROCK DANCE BAR (ENTREES: $3-5, DRINKS: $1.50-3.50)

This hip place on the main street fronting the beach offers a stylish lounge and bar area, perfect for grabbing a drink and chatting with friends, as well as a more formal seating area for taking in a meal. The menu is one of the most diverse in town, offering everything from Chinese and Italian to Mexican and American. This is the place for picky eaters and social drinkers. Owners Diana Castillo and Mark Hamill have worked hard to create a comfortable, but stylish social space, which of course is made all the more enjoyable by great food and an extensive cocktail list. A popular hangout on weekends, the Shamrock also has a downstairs disco, built around a small stage area meant for live local bands (Friday and Saturday night). No worries if you need a refresher after cutting a few shapes; a large bar area stretches across one side of the dance floor. If you're keen to drink without draining your wallet, stop by for happy hour: 7:30 - 9 p.m., drinks two for one. Cell: 593-9-781-2752 / 593-9-485-2613.

RESTAURANTE MARISCOS DEL MAR (ENTREES: $3-5)

A friendly place complimented by wooden picnic tables spread across a sand-covered dining area, Restaurante Mariscos del Mar is a popular seafood joint with a relaxed, beachy atmosphere. When you've eaten your fill and need a place to chill for a while, head to the bamboo hammock hanging out nearby. Traditional Manabí fare is on special, so if you're up for rice and fish or a spicy ceviche then this is the place to come.

CAFÉ FLOR (ENTREES: $3-8)

A cozy little joint set back from the beach in a quiet section of town, Café Flor is a friendly, family-run restaurant that also happens to serve up some of the best plates in town. Pizzas piping hot from the oven and heaped with toppings are a sure win, but the massive salads and spicy burritos aren't a bad bet either. Small tables and chilled out music make the setting notably more intimate than places on the main strip. Whether you come for a romantic rendezvous or to split a meal and share some drinks with friends, you're sure to leave Café Flor feeling satisfied. Owners used to have a restaurant in El Oriente called Chonta Café, but recently relocated to Canoa (probably for the same reasons so many travelers come here). Speak with the owners and you may be able to arrange Spanish lessons ($5/hour).

EL MUELLE UNO (ENTREES: $4-25)

This larger, chain restaurant located on the main road from Canoa to San Vicente is the place for parrilladas, mariscos, and anything else meaty and grilled or from the sea and served with rice. Wash your meal down with any one of many cocktails, select wines, or sangría. Probably the most spacious place in town, El Muelle Uno is also primed for larger groups. Of course, you'll have to share your meal with the chain-restaurant atmosphere. Also located in Bahía de Caráquez. Boasting superb views of the water and San Vicente, El Muello Uno also serves up generous plates of traditional coastal fare, like fish and shrimp. This is a lunch or dinner spot, especially if you've got a hankering for barbecue meat (parrilladas are their specialty). Vegetarian options are available, though nothing too extravagant. Canoa, in front of Colegio Elias Cedeno Jerves, Tel: 593-5-269-2334 / 593-5-269-3147.

BAHÍA DE CARÁQUEZ

This clean and breezy town, sitting on a slender peninsula reaching into the Río Chone, boasts a quiet atmosphere accompanied by tall white-fronted apartment complexes and broad tree-lined avenues. Locals in San Vicente say the best thing about Bahía is the view from San Vicente. To a certain extent, the city does seem a lot more impressive from afar than up-close. Once a holiday haven for high-heeled Ecuadorians, Bahía was tormented by unrelenting El Niño rains in the late 1990s. Severe flooding, coupled with a double earthquake, destroyed buildings and roads, triggered landslides and pretty much washed out tourism in the area. The city has made a brilliant recovery, however, and along with the repaired roads and reconstructed buildings came the growth of a new urban bent: ecotourism.

Navigating the town is relatively easy: the Malecón wraps around the edge of the peninsula, eventually becoming Circunvalación as it approaches the shore. Some of the best and most popular eateries line the riverside, close to the ferry, in an area touted as Malecón 69. For a little culture head to Museo Bahía de Caráquez, which houses an excellent collection of archaeological artifacts from a variety of prehispanic coastal cultures. Casa Velázquez and Casa de la Cultura are also noteworthy.

Although Bahía's beaches are nothing to brag about, the town is lively and friendly on weekends (though a bit deserted during the week) and there are a number of interesting and worthwhile sites located nearby. The Río Chone estuary consists of several islands and mangrove habitats; this unique area is a bird's and a birder's paradise. During mating season, from August to January, visitors can observe the male frigate bird and his characteristic red-puffed chest, among other winged residents, nesting in the mangroves. Lying within striking distance of tropical dry forests, mangrove islands and remote beaches, Bahía is a good place to get down with nature, or just spend a pleasant afternoon meandering along the Malecón.

GETTING TO AND AWAY

Catch one of the buses running along the main road from Canoa to San Vicente (35 cents). From San Vicente take the ferry to Bahía de Caráquez (29 cents), which is located past the gas station and market area towards the right.

LODGING

The choice of hotels in Bahía is not nearly as extensive as in Canoa—and if you like to fall asleep to the sound of waves breaking, you're better off crashing in Canoa and day-tripping to Bahía—but depending on your budget there are a couple of higher-tier hotels that offer a little more luxury than the smaller places in Canoa.

LA QUERENCIA ($5/PERSON)

A large blue and white building fronted by palm trees and a modest garden area, La Querencia offers clean, but dated rooms, some with private baths and good views of the harbor area. Owners are friendly and helpful and meals are available on request. Velasco Ibarra and Eugenio, Santos, Tel: 593-5-269-0009.

HOSTAL BAHÍA BED AND BREAKFAST (ROOMS: $5-8)

A bit of love and affection, and a little artistic flair, infuse an otherwise dark and drab space with life. Climb the sagging wooden stairs from the street entrance and you'll find yourself in a spacious reception area surrounded by walls painted with creeping vines and delicate pink flowers. Clearly, the building has seen better days, but the owners have worked hard to keep it clean, and little touches—like hand-painted walls, clean swept floors, and a hammock-appointed porch area—make aging and run down feel more like old fashioned and unique. The house itself is 120 years old, and the dour faces looking back at you from the walls are members of the owner's family. Very modest, but clean rooms come with bunk beds and either shared or private bathrooms. Spanish classes are also available; ask Jacob or Jairo. The attached restaurant is open for breakfast only. Tel: 593-5-269-0146.

HOTEL PALMA (ROOMS: $5-10)

Cheap to seriously cheap rooms are available at Hotel Palma, but you're better to spend a couple more dollars and stay somewhere else in town. The building is in need of repair and rooms are in desperate for a good cleaning, but the staff is friendly. Tel: 593-5-269-2889.

LA HERRADURA ($10/PERSON, ENTREES: $3.80-8.80)

Aged but atmospheric, La Herradura offers simple rooms set around an attractive Spanish-style building. The front porch and restaurant area face the sea, and vaulted ceilings supported by clean white walls, offer a bright and breezy spot to sit, sip a drink and share a meal with friends. Neatly set tables donning burgundy and white tablecloths and wine glasses add a touch of elegance. Bar Michelangelo is a nice place to pull up a stool and start the night with a drink. Hallways are a bit dark compared to the more spacious front area, but tastefully trimmed with an eclectic collection of art and artifacts. Av. Bolívar and Daniel Hidalgo, Tel: 593-5-269-0266, Fax: 593-5-269-0265.

HOTEL ITALIA (ROOMS: $12-25 / ENTREES: $3-3.50)

Set back from the beach, Hotel Italia is a multi-storied hotel offering clean but dated rooms, which for the price are a bit lackluster. The restaurant downstairs has a modest selection of national and international dishes, and in the morning you can grab a simple breakfast. Av. Bolívar and Calle Checa, Tel: 593-5-269-1137.

HOTEL LA PIEDRA (ROOMS: $48-79)

One of the most lavish places to stay in Bahía de Caraquez, Hotel La Piedra features stunning views and classy modern facilities. A large complex sprawling across the seafront, this place puts on all the airs of a first class hotel, with valet parking, marble-floored reception area, and spacious rooms appointed with double beds, new furniture, and large modern bathrooms. The first floor restaurant, El Faro, is fronted by glass doors that open to a seaside terrace, creating a pleasant, airy place in which to take in a meal and enjoy the local cuisine. Circunvalación Virgilio Ratti 803, in front of the sea, in Quito: Av. Naciones Unidas E6-99 and Shyris, Edificio Banco Bolivariano, 3rd floor, Office 1, Tel: 593-5-269-0780 / 269-0154 / 269-1473, Cell: 593-9-613-3836, Quito phone: 593-2-224-5267 / 224-5268, Fax: 593-2-226-3261, E-mail: piedraturi@easynet.net.ec / cialcotel@cialco.com.

RESTAURANTS

Bahía boasts quite a few options for taking in a meal or two, though the most popular places stick to the same coastal cuisine characteristic of the region. Meat lovers will be glad to hear that there are a number of parrillada joints (just follow your nose). Quite a few places are clustered around the Malecón 69, conveniently located next to the ferry.

TROPHIHELADOS (SNACKS: $1-2)

A small but delicious ice cream parlor located across from Arenabar Pizzeria, Trophihelados is a smart spot to sit and chill. Choose from a variety of flavors, served in a cone or as a shake. If you're feeling really crazy, go for the banana split. Hamburgers, fries, a few other fast food items and some traditional treats are also available. Between Trophihelados and Guacamayo.

HELADERÍA AND CAFETERÍA IL CAPISSIMO (ENTREES: $1.50-9)

For a bite to eat or drink, this modern-looking cafeteria located next to the ferry is your best bet. Their catch phrase, "a little of everything, but much better," isn't far from the truth. A variety of home baked treats—including chocolate cake and scrumptious pies—beckon to unsuspecting street goers from a glass case at the front, and inside you'll find an as-tempting menu boasting a variety of café-style eats. From pancakes and omelettes to hamburgers and chili dogs, this place caters to just about every palate. If you're really hungry (or like a challenge) try the Il Capissimo, a massive feast for almost anyone: four pancakes, three eggs, juice and coffee. Malecón, next to ferry.

RESTAURANTE D'CAMERON (ENTREES: $2-9)

A simple place with a nice view of the sea, Restaurante D'Cameron offers delicious seafood and traditional Ecuadorian dishes, including a long list of ceviches. Glass-topped tables add a little pep to otherwise characterless plastic chairs, and the owners are friendly and helpful. Bolivar and Circunvalación, Cell: 593-9-471-9200.

EL BUEN SABOR (ENTREES: $2-10)

A similar-style restaurant as the others lining the Malecón, El Buen Sabor offers typical meat and seafood dishes, served in an open and airy atmosphere with water views. Service is fairly fast and friendly, and the food is delicious if you're up for traditional meat and seafood plates. Malecón, next to El Muelle Uno, by the ferry, Cell: 593-9-496-7505 / 239-9828.

BRISAS DEL MAR (ENTREES: $2.50-4.50)

Set in a kitty-corner close to the sea, Brisas del Mar is a cozy little place, perfect for sharing a bottle of wine and watching the sun set. Decor consists of plastic chairs tucked under wooden tables and spread across a tiny room colored with a few paintings and randomly placed wine bottles. Atmosphere is more cheap seafood than casual romantic, but the view is bound to romance the unromantic regardless. Av. Virgilio and Daniel Hidalgo, next to Hotel Herradura, Tel: 593-5-269-1511.

LA TERRAZA (ENTREES: $2.50-20)

Inexpensive grilled meat and rice dishes or local seafood plates are offered up at this older, but clean place by the docks. Little sets La Terraza apart from its neighbors—the menu is traditional barbecued meat and Manabí coastal cuisine—but the prices are slightly lower than the other Malecón joints. The set lunch menu is also a fine option for a cheap midday meal. Malecón, next to El Buen Sabor, Tel: 593-5-269-0787.

LA CHOZITA (ENTREES: $3-20)

Specializing in savory parrilladas, La Chozita is a local favorite and fills up at night with the smell of grilling meat and sound of chattering customers. Anyone up for meat eats and a taste of local culture should head here. Malecón, by the ferry.

AROUND BAHÍA

SAIANANDA PARK (ENTRANCE FEE: $2)

Owned by biologist Alfredo Harmsen, Saiananda is a private park situated along the waterfront, just five kilometers from Bahía. In addition to striking views of the sea, the park also features an intriguing menagerie of native and domestic animals and birds. Park residents include itinerant sloths, coatimundi, deer, ostriches, rabbits, macaws, peacocks and geese, all of which freely interact with their human guests. The Japanese bonsai garden, eclectic cactus collection, and variety of other plants are equally worth a day-time gander. The entire area encompasses a spiritual center offering comfortable to out-and-out lavish accommodation and a first class vegetarian restaurant. Spiritual cleansing and relaxation retreats can be organized here, for reservations contact Guacamayo Tours in Bahía. Tel: 593-5-239-8331.

ISLA CORAZÓN

Bumped up against Bahía is Isla Corazón, home to endangered mangroves and numerous bird species. Learn about the local Mangrove Forest and estuary ecosystem, while interacting (and giving back to) the locals. The ever-friendly and outgoing guides Julio and Luciano can point out resident bird species, and explain the importance of this rare Río Chone estuary ecosystem. Tours include an introduction to the area, a boat and boardwalk tour of Isla Corazón and a traditional lunch (usually viche, a peanut-based seafood soup). Come for mating season (August - January) when you can spot the puffed red sacks of male frigate birds and appreciate the age-old search for a suitable (or willing) spouse.

ISLA FRAGATAS

Just a 15-minute boat ride from Bahía, Isla Fragatas is a bird-paradise and mangrove haven. Grab a spot with Guacamayo Tours and you can check out this unique island ecosystem, and take a trip to see La Tortuga Miguelito (the local 93-year old Galápagos turtle and mangrove mascot) and Saiananda Park. A portion of the tour fee is reserved for conservation. One option is to go with Guacamayo Tours.

RÍO MUCHACHO ORGANIC FARM

Situated in the Río Muchacho river valley, just a short distance from the chilled beaches of Canoa and eco-friendly town of Bahía, Río Muchacho Organic Farm focuses on environmental and cultural awareness with a bent towards community development and sustainable tourism. Owners Nicola and Dario have not only created a self-sufficient organic farm based on the practices of permaculture, they have also cultivated a strong relationship with the local community, garnering support for the Bahía Eco-City projects, designing programs for organic recycling (including eco-paper recycling in the city), developing community training eco-camps, and even establishing an environmental primary school such that even the youngest generation is educated on new techniques for sustainable farming, recycling, waste management and reforestation.

Due in part to their hard work and constant toil, the area now has 13 eco-schools, which cater to nearly 900 children. Foreigners, as well as locals, can benefit in uncountable ways from a visit to the farm—whether to volunteer for a couple weeks, or to attend agricultural courses for a few months. A dynamic symbiotic process occurs on Río Muchacho Organic Farm, not just between the land, plants and animals, but between volunteers and the community. It is a unique opportunity to offer up one's time and labor in return for invaluable knowledge and insight into rural Ecuador, its land and its people. From dawn to dusk, this place offers ample opportunity to learn and grow. The farm runs a number of programs and tours, but perhaps the best way to experience the farm is to volunteer for a few weeks.

GUACAMAYO TOURS

In association with the Río Muchacho Organic Farm, Guacaymayo Tours is the main operator in Bahía de Caraquez, offering a variety of exceptional eco-oriented treks and tours. Dedicated to responsible tourism and environmental work, the company is owned by Ecuadorian Dario Proaño and New Zealander Nicola Mears, two individuals who dedicate every waking hour toiling over new ways to facilitate socially and environmentally sustainable tourism in the area. The company offers a variety of educational tours, which not only introduce visitors to the area's best natural attractions, but also bring them face-to-face with the environmental and social issues of the area (and the country). This is the perfect opportunity to learn about fair trade, sustainable development and how even tourists can leave a positive imprint on the places they visit. The main office, fittingly located in the Eco-city of Bahía, also sells local crafts, recycled paper, organic honey and other fair trade products from the fair trade electronic commerce network (www.camari.com). Whether you're an active adventurer or organic guru, Guacamayo Tours will set you up with an exciting, and environmentally-friendly, itinerary.

CRUCITA

About 30 minutes from Manta, Crucita boasts a pleasant ribbon of dark sand beach, and a Malecón with plenty of seafood restaurants. Quiet and relaxed during the week, the town atmosphere shifts on weekends to slightly-noisier and relaxed on weekends. Massive cliffs and good wind conditions are conducive to airborne activities. As such, Crucita has become a popular place to launch paragliding and kite surfing tours. A lovely place with wonderful sunsets, and a few adrenalin-pumping daytime activities, Crucita is a pleasant spot that grows bigger and better year-by-year.

MANTA CITY

Compared to the hippy-haven of Montañita, or peaceful unpopulated beach coasts and coves further north, Manta is only better than average—that is, unless, your idea of a good beach is an overabundance of restaurants and bars backed by skyscraper-like hotels and holiday homes. For the latter, the city is most certainly a beautiful attraction for both nationals and foreigners.

Manta is divided, almost in half by the Río Manta, with the up-market Playa Murciélago to the west and considerably less swanky Playa Tarqui to the east. Running along the coast, and connecting both beaches is the Malecón, Manta's main drag. In general, hotels to the west are more expensive (and the neighborhoods quieter, and safer), but that's not to say you can't find good value, budget-friendly places. The beaches here are OK, but you'll have to share your seaside view with the cranes and hundreds of port boats moored offshore; Manta is an extremely important port in Ecuador and is the second largest port after Guayaquil.

Overlook the eyesore that is maritime Manta, however, and you'll see a vibrant, pulsing city packed with trendy restaurants, bars and upscale hotels. While it's not the most spectacular place to stay, Manta is not without its own unique charms. Spend a day chilling on the beach, then take a stroll along Malecón Escénico, the place to grab a cool beer, or tropical drink, and take in a meal and a sunset at one of the popular seaside-seafood restaurants. History-aholics can spend a few hours poking around the Museo del Banco Central, home to an excellent collection of archaeological pieces, remnants of seven different civilizations that inhabited the coast from 3500 BC to 1530 AD. Market maniacs can meander to the city center, where there are a couple of fruit and vegetable markets. During the day, Tarqui is an interesting place to wander, but you'd be wise to catch a taxi back to your hotel as this is not a safe area at night.

GETTING TO AND AWAY

From Manta most buses head towards the commercial and travel crossroads of Portoviejo and Jipijapa, but an infinitely more appealing option is to find a bus bound for the scenic stretch of road heading south towards San Lorenzo and Puerto Cayo. This paved route features unparalleled views of Ecuador's coast: uninhabited stretches of soft sand bound by turquoise waters and imposing cliffs. Grab a snack at the seafood stalls in Santa Rosa, or trek up to the lighthouse in San Lorenzo. Those looking to avoid the beach crowds can plan a stay at Hostería San Antonio, located near the village of El Aromo.

LODGING

Host to a wide range of hotels and hostals, Manta is bound to suit any traveler's needs, from backpacker dives to 5-star luxury retreats. If you can swing it, find a place in the Oro Verde section of town (named after the lavish hotel of the same name). Situated on a hill in a quiet residential section of Manta, close to Playa Murciélago and Malecón Escénico, the places in this area tend to be safer and more stylish than those located over the Río Manta. And in some cases, staying here is only slightly more expensive than spending the night in Tarqui. If you're really pinching pennies, however, you might be best to start looking in Tarqui. While not considered to be as safe as its western counterpart, this area is full of character and is ready and waiting to greet guests with good budget hotels.

HOSTAL DEL MAR (ROOMS: $5-10)

A dated entrance leads into a dark hallway and upstairs to a modest reception area. Rooms, like the hotel, are aging but offer clean sheets and bathrooms. This is a good no-frills option for budget travelers. Restaurant del Mar, located beneath the hotel, serves good cheap breakfasts and set meals, but don't expect shiny silverware and spotless glasses. Ave. 105 and Calle 104, Tel: 593-5-261-3155.

HOTEL MIAMI (ROOMS: $5-10)

Located at the far end of Tarqui's Malecón, Hotel Miami is a popular spot for young Ecuadorians looking for a cheap place close to the beach. An aging yellow reception leads upstairs to drab, but clean rooms with private bathrooms and cable TV. The pool area could use a little love and attention, but still seems to be a popular retreat from the sun and surf out front. While not always pleasant on the eyes, Hotel Miami doesn't hurt the wallet either. The attached restaurant is convenient and provides solid traditional set meals. Malecón de Tarqui and Calle 108, Tel: 593-5-261-1743.

HOTEL BOULEVARD I (ROOMS: $6-18)

An option if you're really strapped for cash, though you're much better off forking out a few more dollars. Rooms are small, smell a bit musty, and bathrooms are in need of repair. Not the worst place in town, but even those on a budget can do better. Cash only. There are two more hotels of the same name, and same style. Calle 103 and Av. 105, Tel: 593-5-262-5333.

HOTEL PACÍFICO INN ($8-10/PERSON)

Located in an older building with aged facilities, Hotel Pacífico Inn is still good value for those hoping to hang onto their dough. Move beyond the rather drab looking reception area, set in the garage area, and you'll discover bright and clean rooms equipped with air conditioning and cable TV. Beds are spruced up with colorful blankets, and clean white towels hanging on racks in the spacious and spotless bathrooms. Facilities also include a roof-top pool, and hotel guests have access to Complejo El Sol, which has another large pool and sports fields. Considering the price, this is a comfortable option, and seems to be a popular choice among Ecuadorian families. Av. 106 and Calle 101, in front of the beach, Cell: 593-9-910-4259.

HOTEL OLD NAVY (ROOMS: $8-25)

With a modern façade and bright mosaic-tiled reception area that leads to rooms tastefully painted in bright colors and furnished with new beds and bedspreads, tiled floors, modern fixtures and ceiling fans, and clean modern bathrooms, Hotel Old Navy is possibly the best budget option on this side of town. New in 2006, this place has a family-friendly atmosphere and is a comfy place to rest your head—you're sure to sleep soundly on these prices—and the staff is friendly to boot! Calle 104 Ave. 105 and Malecón, Tarqui, Tel: 593-5-262-5295.

HOTEL ARENAMAR (ROOMS: $10-30)

A solid option for those on a budget and looking to stay at the east end of Manta, Hotel ArenaMar presents a professional, modern-looking reception area that leads upstairs to large rooms with cable TV, telephone, surprisingly large modern bathrooms and the capacity to sleep as many as 12 people. Accommodation is tidy, and clean, despite over-washed 1980s style comforters and aged facilities. Calle 101 and Av. 106 and 107, near bridge to Westside, Tel: 593-5-261-2856.

PANORAMA INN AND SU CASCADA SUITE (ROOMS: $8-40)

One of the more modern places to stay in Tarqui, Panorama Inn offers newish rooms overlooking a courtyard pool decked out in an island theme. Ask for the suites across the street, which are even nicer, though a bit steeper, and offer new comforters, small but tidy bathrooms, and doors that open onto the pool deck. Both sections are a popular draw for Ecuadorian families and young couples. An attached cafetería is dated but clean and airy, serving typical Ecuadorian fare. Open daily 7 a.m. - 10 p.m., Entrees: $2-3.50. Av. 105 and Calle 103, Tel: 593-5-261-1552 / 261-2416, E-mail: panoramainn@paginasamarillasec.com.

HOTEL LAS ROCAS (ROOMS: $8-42)

This large hotel facing the sea is, like most of the hotels in Tarqui, in need of a face-lift but still manages to offer clean and comfortable accommodation. Rooms are large and those streetside boast good views of the port. Faded, but clean sheets conceal older beds, which match the Victorian-style dresser drawers. Bathrooms are large and spotless, always a good sign. Air conditioned rooms are slightly nicer, with newer furniture and art on the walls. Las Caraconas, the attached restaurant lacks style but is clean, cool, and offers nicely set tables and good cheap food. Calle 101 and Av. 105, Tel: 593-5-262-0607 / 261-0299, E-mail: lasrocas@manta.telconet.net.

NORTHERN COAST

YARA MARÍA (ROOMS: $10-42)

From the outside, this place seems promising: a small garden area surrounds a quiet court-yard area with colorful hammocks swinging in the breeze. Unless you pay for air condition-ing and ask for one of the nicer rooms, however, you might find yourself squeezed into a very modest room with unscreened windows, scuffed floors, and having to share an outside shower. The location is, however, safer than places to the east in Tarqui, and conveniently located to the west Malecón beach. For the price, there are better places further up the hill. Av. 2 and Calle 20, Tel: 593-5-261-3219, Cell: 593-9-453-1099.

HOSTAL MANAKIN (ROOMS: $15-48)

Previously La Riviera Italian Restaurant, this lovely building, set in a peaceful residential neighborhood, has been renovated and revamped and now houses one of the nicest hostals on this side of town. Modest rooms are tastefully appointed with new beds, bedspreads, and furniture, and brand new gizmos like remote-control air conditioners and TVs. Bathrooms are small, but modern, clean, and equipped with shining sinks and plenty of hot water. When you awake from a solid night's sleep on that brand new mattress, head to the stylish dining area or down to the breezy courtyard where you can start your day with a plate of bread and jam, fruit (fresh from the local market), and coffee. For local travel tips and advice on things to see and do in the area, have a chat with Bret Murphy, Hostal Manakin's manager and in-house expert on Manta. He's particularly knowledgeable about Manta's top dining dives. Calle 20 and Av. 12, Tel: 593-5-262-0413, E-mail: hostalmanakin@hotmail.com, hostalmanakin@yahoo.com.

HOTEL LAS GAVEOTAS (ROOMS: $25-48)

A peeling blue façade leads into a surprisingly professional-looking reception area, where a friendly staff is ready and waiting to help. Rooms are clean and spacious, making Hotel Las Gaveotas one of the better-value options in the area. The attached restaurant, La Barca, maintains a sea-captain theme, with an assortment of sea mariner paraphernalia decorating the walls, and dark polished tables and chairs spread across the floor. Entrees: $2-5. While not the best budget option, it does offer a pool area and nicer views of the beach than other places nearby. Internet available, $2/hour. Malecón 1109, Tel: 593-5-262-0140 / 262-7240, E-mail: hotelgav@aiisat.net.

HOTEL AEROPUERTO (ROOMS: $36-80)

A bright reception area with tiled floors ushers visitors into this older, but immaculately maintained hotel in a quiet residential hillside section of Manta. The friendly staff will show you to your room, which hosts comfy beds adorned with lovely bedspreads, and a large mod-ern bath with steps to the shower. Each room has air conditioning, cable TV and hot water. While not the best place in town, it's good enough for a solid night's sleep. Cuidadela Playa El Murciélago Calle 24 Av. M3 2377, behind KFC and American Deli, Tel: 593-5-262-8040.

HOTEL MANTA IMPERIAL (ROOMS: $38-55)

Located in a prime spot right on the beach, Hotel Manta Imperial is a bit run down but still a good option for those looking to be near the beach. Rooms are sparsely furnished with older furniture, but have clean sheets and scrubbed bathrooms. A large outdoor pool sits in the middle of the complex, overlooking the beach. Prices are a bit inflated, and you could defi-nitely find nicer, better value places on this side of Manta, but again, they've got a monopoly on the beachfront. Malecón beachfront, behind restaurants, Tel: 593-5-622-016 / 612-806 / 621-955.

VISTALMAR CABAÑAS BOUTIQUE (ROOMS: $50-106)

The view itself would be worth its price in gold, but this Manta wonder also offers a unique setting so tranquil even the air seems more relaxed up here, leaving one with the feeling that time might be found just around the corner, relaxing in the bamboo bungalow. Graced with various art and artifacts from around the world (check out the two life-size turquoise horses from Persia), Vistalmar is somewhat of a museum by the sea, as well as peaceful retreat. An ar-chitectural anomaly squeezed between holiday high rises, the delicate cabañas share the same

NORTHERN COAST

ocean view as their lofty neighbors, but offer tasteful rooms designed with local materials and decorated with internationally flavorful art and a Southeast Asian flair. The art and architecture, combined with the well-groomed garden and an infinity pool overlooking the sea, create a luxurious, but intimate setting in which to unwind. For this view and atmosphere, Cabañas Boutique is a steal, and worth the money. Calle M-1 and Ave. 24, Tel: 593-5-262-1671 / 262-1617, Cell: 593-9-319-2775, E-mail: sveraq@hotmail.com, URL: www.vistalmarecuador.com.

HOTEL COSTA DEL SOL (ROOMS: $54-76)

Perched on a high cliff overlooking the sea, the hotel's romantic setting is somewhat marred by the its circus-style construction. Rooms, however, are tasteful and the staff stylish. A modern reception area with marble floors and modern art decorating the walls ushers visitors towards large, modern rooms with all the amenities one might expect from a chain-like hotel: mini-fridge, phone, cable TV, air conditioning and a spacious bathroom with tiled floors and a sliding glass shower door. Relax and unwind in the swimming pool and sauna area, grab a Turkish bath, or make your way directly to the beach. When you get hungry, head to the hotel's bar and restaurant where you can sample traditional Manabí fare, or enjoy more familiar ethnic cuisine. Avenida Malecón 1 and calle 25, Tel: 593-5-262-0025, E-mail: hotel-costadelsol@hotmail.com / hcostadelsol@asetecmanta.com / info@hotelcostadelsol.com.ec, URL: www.hotelcostadelsol.com.ec.

BALANDRIA HOTEL CABAÑAS (ROOMS: $59-115)

A self-sufficient paradise tucked away in a quiet residential neighborhood only 50 meters from Murciélago Beach, Balandria offers stylish and comfortable lodging perfect for families or large groups. The mock-cabin studios topped with green roofs and wooden balconies fronted by plenty of greenery and overlooking a peaceful garden and pool area, are tastefully constructed and mildly reminiscent of a luxury jungle lodge. You won't find monkeys here though, just a friendly staff and smartly decorated bi-level suites. Continuing the classy theme, the hotel's on-site restaurant cooks up a delightful range of dishes, served before peach-colored table cloths, sparkling wine glasses and precisely set cutlery. From the veranda, you can take in stunning sea views while you dine. The menu is extensive, crepes and beef stroganoff even make an appearance, and well priced for the surroundings. Av. 7 and Calle 20, Cordova neighborhood, Tel: 593-5-262-0545, E-mail: balandra@hotelbalandramanta.com, URL: www.hotelbalandramanta.com.

HOTEL ORO VERDE (ROOMS: $95-250)

This large skyscraper-looking building houses the swankiest hotel in Manta. Screaming style and with almost every service imaginable, including an on-site sushi restaurant, spa, and sports facilities, Hotel Oro Verde deserves every one of its five stars. A palatial reception fronts spacious modern rooms with private balconies overlooking the beach and pool area. The bathroom boasts a sliding glass shower door, and sparkling tiled floors, cleaned especially for those pedicured feet. For a bite to eat head to Murciélago Bar, a comfortable space offering exotic seafood and cocktails, or try Buena Vista coffee house and restaurant. The Gourmet Deli, a french bakery and ice cream parlour is good for something fast. Prices are steep, but not when you think about what such facilities might cost back home. Those who can't afford to spend the night can fork out $7 and at least spend the day poolside. Oro Verde Fantasy Casinos, located next door, is a popular night spot for those looking to scratch their itch to gamble. Malecón and Calle 23, P.O. Box 13-05-135, Tel: 593-5-262-9200, Fax: 593-5-262-9210, E-mail: ov_mta@oroverdehotels.com, URL: www.oroverdehotels.com.

RESTAURANTS

Malecón Escénico is the place for seafood and rows of restaurants line the beachfront, each serving similar fare at only slightly varied prices. Over the bridge in Tarqui, you'll find another set of seafood restaurants, without the well-clad customers and fancy fanfare of its neighbors to the west.

EL NOPAL (ENTREES: $1-2.75)

This little joint adds a bit of spice to the restaurant scene, serving up mouth-watering *comida mexicana*. From simple tacos and burritos to harder-to-come-by enchilladas, fajitas, chili con carne, nachos and chalupas, El Nopal is sure to provide your Tex-Mex fix. Owners Jackie and Jose Silva work hard to whip up tasty treats that will fill you up without emptying your wallet. Cell: 593-9-438-8501 / 593-9-453-5197.

DOLCE AND LATTE ICE CREAM (ICE CREAM: $1.50-2)

Despite its name, there's no coffee sold here, just gourmet ice cream, which comes in a variety of flavors. Located in the new and flashy Plaza Jocay, just behind the main restaurants on Malecón west, this is a pleasant pit stop for something cool after a day in the sun.

BASOCA BAR (ENTREES: $1.50-2.50)

A small new place serving up cheap traditional Ecuadorian food, this seems to be a popular local hangout and watering hole. Sip a drink at the long bar area or sit and share a meal with friends at the few tables out back. This is a good place to chill out with funky music and mingle with the young and the hip. Av. 24 Flavio Reyes, Cell: 593-9-154-8190.

RESTAURANT BOULEVARD (ENTREES: $1.50-4)

Located across the street from Old Navy Hotel, in a large open-air complex Restaurant Boulevard is a breezy place to grab breakfast or lunch. The area nearby is under development, with more similar-looking buildings sprouting up alongside. Meals are simple and no-fuss, but cheap.

RESTAURANT KAMIL (ENTREES: $1.80-5)

Owner Kamel Boulhabel and his Japanese wife, Chiyo Ito, run this modest but popular joint fronting the Malecón. Glass topped tables and tiled floors are a refreshing change from the white plastic tables and chairs that occupy other restaurants. Stop by for a bite to eat and a history lesson; Kamel will happily recite his experiences living in Algeria or traveling around Asia. The menu differs only slightly from neighboring restaurants, but the food is decent, service even better, and the Menu del Día a solid value. To really mix things up from standard Manabí fare order a glass of wine and the lasagna—while not Little Italy it is something different. Or go all out and try the chef recommended langosta al BBQ ($12.00). Malecón Escénico Playa Murciélago Local 14, Tel: 593-5-262-4723, Cell: 593-9-448-2128.

BAR TRES PYRAMIDES (ENTREES: $2.50-8)

Located on the terrace of Hotel Costa del Sol, this classy bar offers some of the best views of Manta. From up here life looks good, and with a smooth drink and sumptuous plate of food things only seem to get better. The view is always here so whether you're an early bird looking for breakfast or a night owl just starting out, head here to fuel up and check out the beach bums below. Considering the location, prices are almost as good as the view. Hotel Costa del Sol, Avenida Malecón 1 and Calle 25.

CHEERS RESTAURANT (ENTREES: $2.50-11)

Perhaps the greatest feature of this restaurant is its wiry, gregarious owner Arturo. The self-proclaimed prize fighter, swimmer, and jack of all trades, whips up some of the best ceviche in Manta, in addition to fabulous parrilladas and other traditional fare, all served with a heaping side of Arturo's political and personal opinions—if you get him started. The restaurant is simple, open and airy, and the food is prepared from Arturo's family recipes. Av. Malecón and Calle 19, Tel: 593-5-262-0779.

OCEAN DELIGHT (ENTREES: $3-8)

A slight change from the dominant plastic seating, this place offers neatly arranged wooden tables and chairs, and walls graced with panama hats. From the the outside it looks a slight step up from other places nearby, however, the menu consists of typical Ecuadorian coastal cuisine and prices vary little from those on nearby menus. This is a solid option if you're in the mood for seafood and sea views. Malecón Escénico Playa Murciélago.

LAS VELAS (ENTREES: $3-10)

While differing little in appearance from other places on the Malecón strip, Las Velas is apparently the place to be seen if you're somebody in Manta. At night, well-dressed Ecuadorians chattering beneath the outdoor umbrellas and the sound of clinking glasses is a common occurrence. This is also a good place to come for no-frills continental or americano breakfasts. Malecón Escénico Playa Murciélago.

NEON ARMADILLO (ENTREES: $3-15)

A rather grand entrance leads into a familiar Manta dining scene, with plastic chairs tucked under unadorned tables and hastily decorated walls. In keeping with the professional façade, however, waiters wear blue-collared shirts and bow ties, and take service with a smile seriously. English menus are available, but international dishes are few and far between; the most popular eats consist of fish, chicken, and meat served with a decent portion of rice. This is a good spot to eat if you're looking for something a bit different from the cafeteria style restaurants further west, but expect good rather than gourmet. Malecón Escénico local 10 Playa Murciélago, Cell: 593-9-742-129.

JIREH BAR AND RESTAURANT (ENTREES: $3.50-6.50)

Decked out in simple, but stylish decor, this is one of the more popular places to eat on restaurant row. Open-air seating allows for a cool sea breeze and beach views, and meals are heaping, served still steaming from the kitchen. This is as good a spot as any to try *viche*, a typical Manabí soup, or dig into other traditional Ecuadorian dishes. Anyone indecisive or hoping to try a little of everything can opt for the combo plates, which mix and match culinary creations. Eating here isn't a black tie affair, but the service is fast and friendly and the food delicious. Malecón Escénico Local 11, Tel: 593-5-262-3061, E-mail: jirehale@hotmail.com.

MEDITERRANEO (ENTREES: $4-10.50)

This lovely restaurant distinguishes itself from other Manta eateries, not just by location, but in style and service. While it may not boast beach views, Mediterraneo has bragging rights to the best Spanish and Ecuadorian influenced plates in town, which is no surprise considering owner Martin is from Barcelona, Spain. Meat from Texas is ordered from a specialty shop in town and then matured on-site to ensure each meat dish explodes with flavor. The non-meat dishes are just as flavorful, but then again doesn't everything taste a little better when its served by candlelight? For a romantic night out share a bottle of wine and the tapas, a sure way to melt any heart. Av. Malecón between Calles 16 and 17, Tel: 593-5-262-1804, Cell: 593-9-917-2543 / 593-9-464-8572.

MAMA ROSA BAR AND RESAURANT (ENTREES: $4-11.50)

Somewhat of a local fixture, Mama Rosa restaurant keeps the people coming with over 246 different dishes, top-notch service and an atmosphere that even Italy would find hard to create. Owner Jiorjio carried his culinary secrets with him when he came over from Genova and now Ecuador gets the pleasure of sampling his time-tested and lovingly prepared dishes, including real garlic bread. The atmosphere is almost as delicious as the meals; delicate gravel walkways lead to a terrace-like seating area decorated with flowering plants and miniature street lamps, giving the feeling that you've for a romantic stroll rather than restaurant meal. Wine is served chilled in silver stands and waiters scurry about in black and white uniforms accented by neatly arranged bow ties. A true culinary gem, Mama Rosa's has all the necessary ingredients for a truly pleasurable dining experience. Av. Flavio Reyes and Perimetral, Barrio Umina, Tel: 593-5-262-6076, Cell: 593-9-964-6067.

EL CORMORAN (ENTREES: $4-17)

Laid out like an amusement park, this sprawling restaurant complex is popular with Ecuadorian families and large groups. If the large sign at the entrance doesn't give you a clue, *parrilladas* are the house specialty, among other traditional coastal dishes. You're bound to find something tasty on the menu, that is if you're in the mood for anything surf and turf and served with rice. Picky eaters can make do with the simple pasta dishes, but don't expect

Tuscany. The daring (or anyone searching for a seafood fix) can try the Corvina en Salsa de Mariscos. Av. 24 and Calle M-2, Tel: 593-5-262-9816 / 262-8052.

OH MAR (ENTREES: $5-10)

A seafood chain with a sister restaurant in Salinas, OH Mar is a good choice for standard Ecuadorian meat and seafood dishes. Not the best place if you're looking for character and ambiance, but the space is clean and airy, and in terms of food you can't go wrong. Portions are hearty and prices digestible, at least by Manta standards. Group discounts available. Address: Malecón Escénico Playa El Murciélago Local 9, Tel: 593-5-261-0360, Cell: 593-9-867-2709.

BEACH COMBER (ENTREES: $5-12)

The smell of grilling meat overwhelm even before Beachcomber's flashy neon sign, or thumping music hit the other senses. Good luck finding a place to sit here around dinner time; this is one of the most popular joints in the area and rightfully so. Spectacular food (parrilladas are the house speciality) is served in a lively atmosphere that will lift the spirits of even the most jaded traveler. Calle 20 510 and Av. Flavio Reyes, Tel: 593-5-262-5463 / 262-5244.

AROUND MANTA

SAMAI CENTER

Located on the San José Hill, with views of the sea stretching out 330 feet below, the Samai Center combines holistic healing programs with comfortable accommodation, and is the place to go for a spiritual and emotional breath of fresh air. Natural accommodations with feng shui-oriented architecture compliment the ocean view, while the restaurant offers delicious vegetarian food, so good in fact even carnivores may become converts. In conjunction with Sacred Journeys Inc., owners Ed and Tania Tuttle facilitate Shamanic adventures to the Andes and Amazon, where guests are introduced to indigenous healing techniques using traditional medicinal plants. E15 Km 700 Via del Pacífico, Tel: 593-4-278-0167, Cell: 593-9-462-1316, E-mail: samai@easynet.net.ec.

HOSTERÍA SAN ANTONIO

Rustic meets modern elegance at this lovely coastal retreat. In addition to first-class service and comfortable rooms, this place also features a top-notch restaurant and bar, a zoo (yes, a zoo), and a range of activities, bound to appease both the culture-critic and active adventurer. A stay here offers ample opportunity get out and about, whether on the seat of a mountain bike or saddle of a horse; San Antonio organizes various trips and treks in and around Bosque de Pacoche. Km 576 via Manta-Puerto Cayo, Tel: 593-5-262-2106, Cell: 593-9-413-8284, E-mail: info@sanantoniohotel.com, URL: www.sanantoniohotel.com.ec.

The Southern Coast

The Southern Coast of Ecuador, which is comprised of the Guayas and El Oro provinces, hosts Ecuador's largest city, Guayaquil. Guayaquil is not a very popular tourist destination for foreigners. However, it has become more developed over the last few years. In particular, the Malecón, or boardwalk, has been cleaned up. It is now filled with trendy restaurants and shops. Just three hours north of Guayaquil is the surfer's sweet spot, Montañita. With some of Ecuador's best waves outside of the Galápagos and a lively atmosphere, Montañita is a great place to chill out for a couple of days. The strip of beaches along the Southern Coast is often referred to as the "Ruta Del Sol."

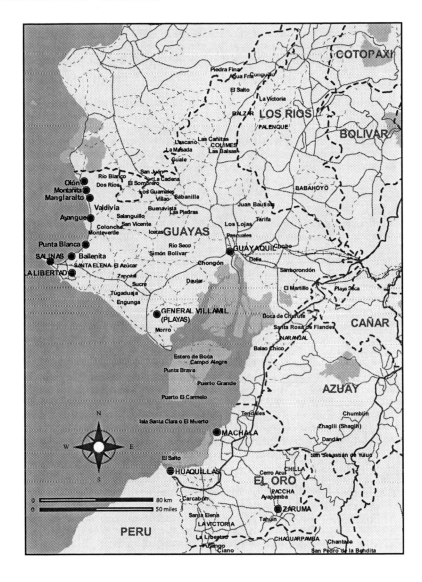

SOUTHERN COAST

LA RUTA DEL SOL

La Ruta del Sol, "The Route of the Sun," is a strip of some of the most popular and nicest beaches in Ecuador, with the best surfing this side of the Galápagos. It is best from December to July, when the sun is shining constantly. However, from September to November, the prices drastically drop, along with the temperatures.

La Ruta del Sol is the section of coastline along highway E15, starting in Manabí at Manta and winding down the best part of the Ecuadorian coast to Salinas in the Guayas province. You could spend months beach-hopping along this practically undiscovered stretch of beaches. However, a shorter trip is also feasible by taking advantage of the rapidly developing tourist infrastructure. The public transportation is fairly extensive and inexpensive. There are also several tour agencies that will offer you package deals to highlighted spots along the Ruta del Sol, although these tend to be overpriced. Places not to miss along the Ruta del Sol from north to south: Los Frailes beach, La Isla de la Plata in the Machililla National Park and Montañita.

PUERTO LÓPEZ

Puerto López is one of the more established cities along the Ruta del Sol and is popular mainly for its close proximity to Isla de la Plata and the Parque Machililla. Although it is one of the cheapest spots to buy tours to Isla de la Plata, to go whale watching and to enter the Parque Machililla, Puerto López is not a great destination in itself. It's a dull, dusty town with just a handful of decent restaurants, bars and hotels. The beach is not nearly as inviting as nearby beaches, like Los Frailes to the north. However, you may find it necessary to stay at least one night here.

LODGING

HOSTERIA ITAPOÂ

Named after the owner's favorite beach in her home country of Brazil, Hostería Itapoâ is about one block from Puerto López's beach and has a comfortable, tranquil atmosphere. When you first enter, it feels a little like you are trespassing into someone's backyard. Press on and you will see three cabanas on the left and rooms in a small building on the right of the main garden and eating area. The cabanas are nicer than the other rooms and have private porches with hammocks. For an extra charge of about $2 a night, you can have unlimited access to the Turkish bath and hot tub. The owner loves to cook and will happily prepare you a meal upon request. During high season, she offers packages which include breakfast and hot tub access. Calle sin nombre and Calle Abdon Calderon, Tel: 593-2-255-1569 / 593-9-984-3042.

HOSTAL TUZCO ($6/PERSON)

The one perk about this hostal is that the $6/person price never changes, high season or low season. Apart from that, however, the hostal is really unimpressive. The rooms are clean, but old and uninteresting. There is a common roof area with hammocks and patio furniture with views of Puerto López and the beach in the distance. It is a fair distance up a hill from the beach and main strip of Puerto López. Other services include a pharmacy, a restaurant in the building across the street, a pool table and games to borrow in the lounge area. General Córdova, east of Av. Machalilla, Tel: 593-2-245-2616 / 593-5-230-0132 / 593-5-230-0120, E-mail: jgsalazar_b@hotmail.com.

MACHILILLA HOTEL

There are two Hotel Machilillas, one in Puerto López, and one about 10 km north of town. You can make reservations in Puerto López for either hotel. In Puerto López, the entrance is dirty and the rooms are ho-hum. The central garden/sitting area is pleasant enough, though. The northern branch is much bigger, in a multi-storied building in need of a paint job right off E15. Internet is $2/hour, which is standard for Puerto López.

SOL INN

Opened in 2001, Sol Inn has a mellow, beach bum atmosphere with a friendly, energetic owner. Relax in the outdoor lounge area, find out information on tours and exchange books.

SOUTHERN COAST

The rooms are clean and creatively painted. There is also availability for camping in the yard at $2 a person. If you are traveling alone, there is an extra charge of about $2 for a private room. Otherwise, you can stay in a dorm room for the same price as those traveling in groups. Juan Montalvo and Eloy Alfaro, E-mail: hostal_solinn@hotmail.com, URL: www.puertoLópez.com/paginas/servicios/solinn.htm.

> *V!VA Member Review-Sol Inn*
> *Friendly, helpful staff. Comfortable rooms, with hammock on balcony. I was backpacking and it more than met my needs. Went for two days, stayed a week. 24 May 2007. USA.*

HOTEL PACÍFICO
A clean and spacious hotel, Hotel Pacífico is the only hotel right in Puerto López with a pool and one of the few places that accepts all credit cards. The rooms with air conditioning are almost double the cost of rooms with a fan, but have great ocean views as well as a common balcony with hammocks and patio furniture. The rooms toward the back of the hotel have fans and are definitely more moist and musty than the rooms facing the beach. The viewless rooms do have the advantage of easy access to the lovely outdoor pool. The price range is generally mid-range, up to $20, but there are also budget rooms with fans and shared baths. Malecón Julio Izurieta and Lascano, Tel: 593-5-230-0147, 593-5-230-0133.

OCEANIC (ROOMS: $50-70)
A beautiful and pleasant resort is surrounded by small hills and an incredible beach. Accommodation in cabins, that are made in part with natural materials. However, you will enjoy of all comfort that you desire. The hostel has a restaurant with a full view of the ocean. A chef prides himself on producing great national and international cuisine. And if you do not like salt water, the hostel offers a relaxing swimming pool. Malecon Julio Izurieta, North area, Tel: 593-9-621-1065, E-mail: registros@oceanic-pl.com, URL: www.oceanic-pl.com.

RESTAURANTS
CARMITA RESTAURANT AND BAR
Restaurant Carmita doesn't offer anything much different than any of the other restaurants along the Malecón with many seafood dishes as well as a few chicken and meat dishes. The one perk is that it is one of the few restaurants that accepts all major credit cards. Malecón Julio Izurieta and General Córdova.

ESPUMA DEL MAR
Located right on the Malecón overlooking the beach, you can't get a better location. There is a porch and plenty of seating as well as tacky, ocean-themed decor. If you are staying at the Hostal Fragata, you can order food from this restaurant to be delivered to your door. Malecón and Eloy Alfaro, Tel: 593-5-230-0187.

HOTEL PACÍFICO RESTAURANTE
The restaurant for the Hotel Pacífico is just south of the entrance to the hotel in an open-air porch overlooking the beach. This is one of the very few restaurants in Puerto López that accepts credit cards. Malecón Julio Izurieta and Lascano, Tel: 593-5-230-0147, E-mail: hpacific@manta.ecua.net.ec, URL: www.hotelycabanaspacifico.com.

SALANGO
A small fishing village just six kilometers south of Puerto López, the main features of Salango are its excellent seafood and a small archaeological museum, Museo Salango. We don't recommend taking a dip in the water—fishers often dump unwanted fish parts in the shallow surf where algae and other scavenger fish flourish on the leftovers. If you are desperate for a swim, just head south to Puerto Rico where there is a great stretch of clean, quiet beach.

SOUTHERN COAST

RESTAURANTS

EL PELÍCANO

IEl Pelícano offers fresh-off-the-boat seafood, at decent prices. Try the *spondylus en salsa de maní*, or any of the fish in the peanut sauce for that matter—you'll be dreaming about it for days. El Pelícano has a very simple atmosphere with thick, wooden picnic tables, benches and boat decor. The highlight is the fresh, deliciously prepared seafood. Calle Principal and La Plaza, Tel: 593-4-278-0295 / 278-3752, E-mail: salango@latinmail.com.

PUERTO RICO

Puerto Rico is still in its early stages of tourist development. Set about 10 km south of Puerto López, along the Ruta del Sol between Salango and Las Tunas, Puerto Rico is very peaceful with a great stretch of beach that you very well may have all to yourself.

LODGING

ALANDALUZ HOSTERÍA AND PUEBLO ECOLÓGICO

Alalandaluz Hostería and Pueblo Ecológico is one of the few true ecologically friendly lodges along the Ruta del Sol. Water is recycled for watering plants and compost is also used for fertilization purposes. The organic garden provides most of the fresh food in the restaurant. You will find several trashcans for organic or un-organic waste spaced around the lodge. Alandaluz also makes an effort to preserve the native culture. With capacity for about 100 guests, Alandaluz has a playful ambiance, with Robinson Crusoe-esque architecture and a clever treehouse play-area for children. Cabanas are divided into tall, wooden structures with rooms for one to four guests each. There is also camping space at $4 per person. Internet is available for emergency use only at $0.50/minute. Km. 12, Puerto López to Salinas, Quito office: Diego Noboa E14-98 and Guanguiltagua, Tel: 593-4-278-0686, Quito office: 593-2-224-8604, E-mail: info@alandaluz.com, Quito office: alandaluz@interactive.net.ec, URL: www.alandaluzhosteria.com, www.alandaluz.com.

LA BARQUITA

The obvious highlight of this hostel is the boat-shaped main building with a common lounge, restaurant, bar and excellent ocean views. Here you can exchange books in four languages, watch satellite TV or shoot pool in the upper decks of the main boat. The boat theme is carried out in the architecture of the cabanas, with porthole mirrors, rounded doors and natural stone locks. Prices are reasonable. The prices listed here are for low season, expect to pay a little more during high season. Laundry service is available at $1/lb. You can also get reasonably priced tours and rental equipment from La Barquita. Kayak rental is $5/hour, as is horse rental. Whale watching tours are $25 per person and tours to Isla de la Plata are $30 per person, plus the park entrance fee of $15. Tel: 593-4-278-0051, E-mail: labarquita@gmail.com, URL: www.labarquita-ec.com.

RESTAURANTS

ALANDALUZ RESTAURANT

The restaurant for the Alandaluz Hosteria is on the second floor of the main building at the end of the main path starting at E15, the Ruta del Sol. The atmosphere is fitting with the eco-lodge, rustic and clean. Open-air seating allows for you to appreciate the natural setting while dining on organic specialties from Alandaluz's own garden and seafood from local fishermen. Km. 12, Puerto López-Salinas, Tel: 593-4-278-0690, 593-4-278-0686, E-mail: info@alandaluz.com, URL: www.alandaluz.com.

LA BARQUITA RESTAURANT

The restaurant for La Barquita is in the main, boat-shaped building. With open-air seating and views overlooking the ocean, it's the next best thing to eating on open water. An obvious specialty is seafood, but Italian food is also highlighted alongside specialty desserts and drinks. Fixed breakfast dishes are between $2 and $3. Tel: 593-4-278-0051, E-mail: info-labarquita@labarquita-ec.com, URL: www.labarquita-ec.com.

LAS TUNAS

Las Tunas is a small beach town between Puerto Rico and Ayampe along the Ruta del Sol, about a 10-minute bus ride south of Puerto López. A very quiet town with a fair stretch of beach, Las Tunas is still in the very developmental stages, as far as tourism goes. If you come for a swim, wear water shoes, as the beach can be fairly rocky.

LODGING

TSAFIKI HOSTERÍA

Tsafiki (or Tsafiky—it is spelled one way on the brochure and another on the main sign) opened in December of 2003, with big plans for future expansion and extended services. In a native Ecuadorian coastal language, Tsafiki means "the toungue of the real man." Tsafiki does a good job of being fairly luxurious without sacrificing personality. Separate cabanas with terraces have fresh flowers, and hypo-allergenic mattresses, pillows and blankets. The main lounge features great ocean views, a pool table, a book exchange in English and Spanish and outdoor restaurant seating. Along with offering tours to nearby hot spots like Isla de la Plata and whale watching excursions, Tsafiki owns 17 horses and offers two different excursions on horseback for $25 per person. Group discounts are offered for parties of more than 12. The discount for children is about half, $10 per child in low season and $15 in high season. The priciest category listed is for suites with space for larger groups. These rooms sleep up to six people and cost $105. Tel: 593-4-278-0557, Cell: 593-9-963-6664, E-mail: info@tsafiki.com, URL: www.tsafiki.com.

RESTAURANTS

TSAFIKI'S WAHOO RESTAURANT

Located on the second floor of the main building in the Tsafiki Hostería with an outdoor porch overlooking the water, Wahoo Restaurant is a great spot to relax and enjoy fresh seafood and other local favorites. There is also a kid's menu for $4.50 and a fairly complete drinks menu. The fixed breakfast menu is $3.50, and lunch and dinners are $7. Items off the menu cost a little more. Tel: 593-4-278-0557, Cell: 593-9-963-6664, E-mail: info@tsafiki.com, URL: www.tsafiki.com.

AYAMPE

Ayampe is a sleepy fishing village just recently being awakened by tourism. Most of the hotels in town must be reached on a dusty path through town, but there are plenty of signs. The beach is clean and rarely crowded, but bring water shoes or grit your teeth, as it is fairly rocky.

LODGING

CABAÑAS LA IGUANA

Cabañas La Iguana has a relaxed atmosphere with a common kitchen area and lounge with hammocks. The owner is a musician with a passion for book collecting. As a result, you will find a collection of CDs, books and musical instruments in the reception area and may be lucky enough to get a personal concert in the evening. The books, in German and Spanish, are available for exchanges; CDs are for sale. There is only hot water in the shared bath. Beach access is through Cabañas La Tortuga just across the way. Prices are per person and children get a great discount, $4/child. Tel: 593-4-278-0725, E-mail: ayampeiguana@hotmail.com, URL: www.designalltag.com/ayampe.

FINCA PUNTA AYAMPE

The location of the lodge, apart from the 20-minute dusty hike to and from the main road, is great. It is set in the middle of the forest south of Ayampe with views of the ocean. There are lovely flowers and plants as you walk around the area. The lodge itself maintains the natural, rustic feeling of the surroundings. However, their claims to be an ecolodge are dubious. With capacity for 26 people, there are two cabanas set apart from the main building. These are more expensive, but worth the privacy and views if you don't mind climbing a moss-covered staircase that is not very well-lit at night. The rooms themselves are really nothing special, and have had reports of bedbugs. The main lounge features satellite TV, a sitting area and a foosball table that looks and plays like an antique. The decorations in the lounge are an eccentrically eclectic mix of the lodge's wholesome natural wood construction. Tel: 593-4-278-0616, Cell: 593-9-970-8329, E-mail: info@fincapuntaayampe.com, URL: www.fincapuntaayampe.com.

CABAÑAS LA TORTUGA

With capacity for 100 people including camping space, Las Cabañas Tortuga is a clean, spacious, interesting and child-friendly spot. A private beach a few steps away from hotel makes a great place to cool off. There is also a games room, a children's area with bikes and cars for kids, a pool table, a ping-pong table, a TV with a satellite dish and a selection of DVDs. Private transportation is available from Guayaquil, Manta and some of the other nearby cities. Ask ahead and be sure to get the price for the trip you need. Internet is available if you are really desperate, for $0.30/minute. There are kayaks for rent at $5. You can make arrangements to go horseback riding for $10/hour or go on a tour of Isla de la Plata for $30 per person plus the $15 entrance fee. Tel: 593-4-278-0613, E-mail: info@latortuga.com.ec, URL: www.latortuga.com.ec.

RESTAURANTS

CABAÑAS LA TORTUGA - RESTAURANT

The restaurant at Cabañas la Tortuga is located in the main building with windows facing the ocean. During low season, you might find the restaurant all but vacated, but they are known for their parilladas and pizzas. Tel: 593-4-278-0613, E-mail: info@latortuga.com.ec, URL: www.latortuga.com.ec.

GUAYAS PROVINCE

Home to Ecuador's largest city, Guayaquil, and to some of Ecuador's sunniest beaches, Guayas is a great spot to beach-hop or soak in culture and nightlife in Guayaquil. Cruise down La Ruta del Sol, enjoying the sand and sun (and a few drinks) on your way to the trendy restaurants and holiday homes of Salinas. From here, zip across the coastal plains towards Guayaquil, Ecuador's main port and commercial crossroads, on your way past the vast tracts of banana plantations and along the coastline south towards Peru. If you're tired of beaching it, make your way inland to the uplands of El Oro, a region suited for trailblazing away from the well-trodden tourist trail. One decent option by which to travel to Guayas is using Reina del Camino buses.

MONTAÑITA

Montañita is a lively beach town with a reputation for its plethora of parties, surfers and hippies. About three and a half hours north of Guayaquil, Montañita is one of the few Ecuadorian beach towns with a great selection of international restaurants and hostels for all budgets. Central Montañita is about ten minutes south (walking) of the best surfing spot, La Punta. There are hostels and restaurants in both places. La Punta tends to be much more quiet at night when parties are raging in the center of town. Likewise, the town becomes ghostlike until the sun is high in the sky while surfers are tearing up the waves at La Punta.

Photo by Lisa Brunetti

Prices skyrocket from December to August, when the weather is the best, as well as on national holidays, when guayaquileños flee the city en-masse. From September to November prices drop, but so does the temperature, as the sun is a rare sight. There is only a limited ability to get cash in Montañita, so bring plenty with you. There is just one, recently installed Banco de

Guayaquil cash machine. Only a few hotels and even fewer restaurants accept credit cards. If you are desperate, and the ATM in Montañita won't work with your card, the closest ATM is in Salinas, about two hours away by bus. Puerto López, one hour to the north, has a Banco del Pichincha, but no ATM. A few places will accept travelers' checks.

LODGING

Hotels in Montañita tend to be ramshackle, unique and inexpensive. A backpacker's paradise, the small town features one inexpensive hostal after another. Prices listed can be extremely flexible: if you're trying to save money, see if you can cut a deal, especially if you're traveling in a good-sized group or staying for a while. If you don't like the look of one place, just keep on walking down the street—there are lots of places to stay in Montañita. There are no luxury hotels in town—no one comes to Montañita to be pampered. They come to surf and have a great time!

HOSTAL PAPAYA (ROOMS: $3-8)

The best rooms at Hostal Papaya are upstairs. There are a few downstairs rooms, one with a shared bath that knocks a few dollars off the price, but the upstairs rooms, especially on the third floor, are more colorful, spacious and some have creatively hidden upper-loft sleeping areas. On the third floor, there is also a pleasant lounge area with hammocks as well as a view of the town and the beach a couple of blocks away. The hotel features a restaurant, hot water and a book exchange. Surfing classes can also be arranged. The staff speaks English, French and Spanish. Rooms are $3-6 with a shared bath, or $5-8 with a private bath. Laundry service is $.60/lb. Cell: 593-9-719-8077, E-mail: info@papayamontanita.com.

HOSTAL DEL AMIGO ($3-10/PERSON)

Hostal del Amigo is tucked away around the corner from the Funky Monkey. The rooms are clean and cheerful and there is a small lounge with a TV. Don't believe the sign out front which advertises a laundromat, internet and a restaurant; there aren't any of those services here. Calle 10 de Agosto and Guido Chiriboga.

THE FUNKY MONKEY ($3-20/PERSON)

The Funky Monkey is fun and fairly cheap. There is a restaurant/bar on the first floor, along with a lounge with TV and a pool table. The rooms are small and musty, but clean and creatively painted. The dorm rooms take up the second floor, and private rooms are above that, with a total space for about 25. Highest prices are during high season, from December to July. Guido Chiriboga and 10 de Agosto, E-mail: francisco_averos@hotmail.com.

EL TURISTA (ROOMS: $3-30)

El Turista is an older hotel, with 12 rooms, including a suite on the top floor that sleeps up to six people and has a small kitchen and living room. There are sad, saggy lounges on each floor and the building is in desperate need of a paint job, but if you split the suite with a big group it can be a very cheap deal, especially during high season. Also, since the hostal is tucked back on a fairly untrod street, you won't be bothered by the noise as much at night. 10 de Agosto and Pompilio Santo, Tel: 593-4-290-1353.

HOTEL TSUNAMI ($4-15/PERSON)

Located on one of the biggest party streets in Montañita, Hotel Tsunami is reasonably priced, with a fun atmosphere. Prices for rooms with a private bath range from $5-15 per person depending on the season. Although you won't get an ocean view, there are rooms for large groups, up to 10 people, with a private bath, colorful decorations and bamboo furniture. Guido Chiriboga north of La Calle Principal, Cell: 593-9-714-7344.

EL CENTRO DEL MUNDO ($4-16/PERSON)

This may just be the cheapest spot to sleep in Ecuador that has ocean views. At the corner where the beach meets the main east-west road, Rocafuerte, you will find El Centro del Mundo, a three story wooden building with dorm space in the attic and plenty of porch space with

SOUTHERN COAST

hammocks to relax. During high tourist season, you won't want to lounge on your pile of mattresses (no real beds in the dorm space) for long; the rooms higher up get quite steamy even without solid walls. There is a bar, restaurant, pool table, common roof lounge and plenty of porches to relax on and enjoy the view. Cell: 593-9-728-2831.

LA CASA BLANCA ($5-10/PERSON)
La Casa Blanca is at the northern end of Guido Chiriboga, about two blocks east of the beach. With capacity for about 50 people and nine years' experience, this hotel has a relaxed, if somewhat old and musty atmosphere. The rooms are pretty standard bunkbed style, some with lofts. Some have ocean views. The hotel staff will help you arrange for a tour to go whale watching from July to October. There is bike rental for $2 an hour and surfboard rental for $5 per day. There is also internet service for $3 an hour. Prices rise up to $15 per person for holidays. Guido Chiriboga and Villafuerte, Tel: 593-4-290-1340, E-mail: lacasablan@hotmail.com.

TIERRA PROMETIDA ($5-20/PERSON)
Run by a young, energetic group of Israeli friends, Tierra Prometida (Promised Land) is hip, new, fun and always changing. The owners have many plans for future improvements including a future internet room, a future mini market downstairs as well as plans for constantly changing decor and paintings. There is a lounge with board games, Play Station II, cable TV and a DVD player with a selection of movies and books. There is a pool table on the balcony upstairs and a few other outdoor balconies for relaxing. The owners encourage young guests as opposed to families. Guests receive a 10 percent discount in the downstairs restaurant, which, among many other things like homemade bread, steak, seafood and breakfasts, serves the only iced cappuccinos for miles. Guido Chiriboga and 10 de Agosto, Cell: 593-9-4575216, 593-9-944-6363, E-mail: hoteltierraprometida@hotmail.com.

CABAÑAS PAKALORO (ROOMS: $6-12)
Pakaloro is a 2-floor wooden structure of beautifully crafted cabanas. The woodwork is inspiring and meticulous. Each room has a spacious balcony with a hammock. The hostal also has a grassy patio and a great reception area to relax and meet other guests. Other bonuses of the hotel besides the aesthetics are: hot water, private baths, clean rooms, private balcony with hammock, ocean and sunset view, kitchen use, access to beach (less than one short block), friendly staff and low rates. Calle Tercera and Guido Chiriboga, Tel: 593-9-741-5413, E-mail: pakaloro2006@hotmail.com, URL:www.pakaloro.com.

PARADISE SOUTH ($7-25/PERSON)
Paradise South is, ironically, just north of Montañita. The hotel features cool, cave-like rooms with stone walls and iron-frame beds. There is also a spacious lawn right on the beach, with a volleyball pit, grill, pool table, ping-pong table and foosball table, shaded by open-air huts. Ask for a room in the cabañas closest to the ocean—they were just installed in July 2004 and are definitely the nicest. Laundry is $1.50 per load, breakfast is included in the price, and the book exchange features books in English, Spanish and some French. If you stay for multiple days, you can negotiate a lower price. Tel: 593-4-290-1185, Cell: 593-9-787-8925, E-mail: paradise_south@hotmail.com.

CASA DEL SOL ($8-15/PERSON)
Run by a Californian surfer, Casa del Sol is relaxing, comfortable and right on the beach. The ambiance is fun, and the restaurant and bar are great. The hotel is set about a ten-minute walk north of the center of Montañita, reached either by beach or by road, right in front of the best surfing spot, La Punta, and away from the noise of central Montañita. Casa del Sol features surfing tours in the Montañita area, the Galápagos, Chile and Peru, all of which can be booked online with any major credit card. Other packages are offered online which include meals and can also be paid for by credit card. Tel: 593-4-290-1302, Cell: 593-9-942-3982, E-mail: info-casasol@casasol.com, URL: www.casasol.com.

CHARO'S HOSTAL (ROOMS: $8-15)

Charo's Hostal has modern rooms with breathtaking ocean views and is right on the board-walk. It is close enough to the center of town (1.5 short blocks), yet at a distance so as to get a restful night's sleep. The rooms are very clean and the staff are friendly. The owners speak English and are very helpful with any general questions you may have. The property is quite large and also has manicured gardens, hammocks, and various plants and trees. At Charo's, you'll also find a restaurant and bar with reasonable prices. The food is excellent and service is much quicker than at other places in the town. There are also rustic economy rooms with two views: street and ocean. All rooms have private bathroom and hot water. Malécon, E-mail: charo117@msn.com, URL: www.charoshostal.com.

HOTEL MONTAÑITA ($8-18/PERSON)

Breaking from Montañita's classic, hippy style, Hotel Montañita is a large, concrete block of rooms with a pool in the central courtyard. During high season, the jacuzzi heats up on a deck overlooking the ocean. With space for 150 guests and eight years of history, the size and age seem to have faded away whatever personality Hotel Montañita could have had. Rooms are fairly cramped and in desperate need of a good airing out, with thin mattresses and concrete bed bases. During high season, breakfast is included in the price. Rooms are always about $3 cheaper during the week. Guido Chiriboga and 10 de Agosto, Tel: 593-4-290-1296 / 593-4-290-1299, E-mail: hmontani@telconet.net.

CABAÑAS ARENA GUADUA ($10-15/PERSON)

With colorful and slightly sandy cabana rooms right on the beach, Cabañas Arena Guadua (Bamboo Sand Cabanas) is a relaxed, quiet spot. Smack between La Punta, where the best waves for surfing are found, and the hub for all-night parties in central Montañita, Arena Guadua is perfect for travelers who want a taste of both worlds. The three cabanas each sleep five. The beach bar serves pizza and burgers and has board games and tables on a patch of private beach. E-mail: arenaguadua@hotmail.com, URL: www.montañita.com/guadua.

HOTEL BAJA MONTAÑITA

A ten-year-old hotel with a large pool and even larger concrete buildings forming a "U" around the pool, Hotel Baja Montañita has a history of financial difficulties. The Ecua-dorian government took over the hotel in 2003 when the owner fell too far behind in loan payments. Under new ownership the hotel is doing better. The best rooms are the cabanas to the north. Cell: 593-9-189-8542, E-mail: mercadeo@bajamontanita.com, URL: www.bajamontanita.com.

RESTAURANTS

CHOCOLATE (ENTREES: $1.50-4)

Tucked off the main tourist drag in the old part of Montañita, Chocolate is a relaxing spot with live music, a coffee selection, a book exchange, games to play at your table and out-door seating with views of the ocean. You will enjoy Chocolate so much, it won't even both-er you that there's nothing chocolate on the menu. Ask for the fixed lunch, which always has a vegetarian option, for between $1.50 and $2.00. Calle Principal Contg. a la Iglesia, Cell: 593-9-951-9692.

BAR-RESTAURANTE EL PUNTO (ENTREES: $2-4)

A mellow beach bar and breakfast spot, Bar-Restaurante El Punto is nowhere near La Punta, but right off the main drag in Montañita. El Punto brings the beach inside with its natural wood tables, coral centerpieces and a pebble floor. In the mornings, travelers flock for the "gigantic breakfasts" and crepes with nutella. At night the bar fills up around the pool table and TV. There is outdoor seating with ocean views. Vicente Rocafuerte and San Isidro.

TIKI LIMBO (ENTREES: $3-5)

Serving up a little bit of everything delicious, Tiki Limbo is the place to go if you're not sure what you want, but know it better be good. The restaurant specializes in a range of culinary

SOUTHERN COAST

creations, from Thai-inspired fusion dishes to oversized salads dripping with dressing and flavor. A quick glance at the menu, or the island-themed furnishing, and you might forget you are in Ecuador. Owners and staff are more than friendly, and take their food seriously: if you like something, be sure to tell them, they love the feedback. Grab a seat upstairs and you can chow down and chit-chat without missing out on the street action below. A good-value hostal is also located upstairs. Malecón, before main intersection to beach.

> *V!VA Member Review-Tiki Limbo*
> *The food in this place is great and the customer service is head and shoulders above the service that you receive elsewhere in Montañita. I would thoroughly recommend this place. 20 February 2007. London, England.*

La Casa Blanca Restaurante (entrees: $3-8)
The restaurant on the first floor of La Casa Blanca features a fair amount of veggie cuisine including the best soy burgers around, burritos, omelets and pancakes. The open air seating is a pleasant way to enjoy your meal and there are board games on hand if you want some time to digest before hitting the surf. Don't visit if you're in a rush, though, because service is often awfully slow. Guido Chiriboga and Villafuerte, Tel: 593-4-290-1340, E-mail: lacasablan@hotmail.com.

Hola Ola Restaurante (entrees: $5-8)
The Hola Ola Restaurante is part of Tierra Prometida. Along with excellent breakfasts, steak, seafood and burger dishes, Hola Ola has the best cappuccinos for miles. Try the iced café with flavoring of your choice. Happy Hour starts at 6 p.m. and goes until closing. Guido Chiriboga and 10 de Agosto, Cell: 593-9-457-5216 / 593-9-944-6363, E-mail: hoteltierraprometida@hotmail.com.

Restaurant Zoociedad (entrees: $6-12)
An Ecuadorian-Italian fusion restaurant with cuisine like nowhere else on the Ecuadorian coast, Zoociedad has delicious food and a great location. With a variety of pastas, salads, seafood and vegetarian options, you can't go wrong. There is an excellent wine bar with several imported Italian wines. Cell: 593-9-787-8910.

Manglaralto
Manglaralto is a coastal town two miles south of Montañita. It is a great escape from the touristy crowd in Montañita and offers a plethora of of natural and cultural experiences. Five minutes from Montanita and 15 minutes away from the bio-diverse Cordillera Chongon Colonche, Manglaralto is an ideal neutral point on this beautiful part of Ecuador's Pacific Coast.

Palmar
South from Manglaralto and Ayangue, La Ruta del Sol continues to hug the coast as it sails towards Salinas. Both Palmar and its neighbor Monteverde have pleasant beaches and popular cafés. Stopping at either town is a good way to break up travels further south, especially if you're keen to stick your feet in the sand and catch some rays for a while.

HOSTERÍA PLAYA ROSADA
Hostería Playa Rosada is located on a remote stretch of Costa del Sol beach, about 3 kilometers north of Palmar, which in turn is located approximately midway between Salinas and Montañita (it is closer to Montañita). The hostería is a retreat of sorts, offering tranquility and a beautiful setting for artists and musicians. They offer meditation and tai chi, as well as massages, snorkeling, archery and adventure travel. To get there, proceed about three kilometers north of Palmar and turn toward the sea when in Pueblo Nuevo at the Santa Paola church. If you have a jeep or other off-road vehicle, you'll be better off, because the road is in bad shape. Proceed to the coast, about 4 kilometers away. Coast, about 3 km north of Palmar, Palmar-Ayangue, Cell: 593-9-482-1171, E-Mail: riz@telconet.net.

SALINAS

A hot spot for the Ecuadorian elite, Salinas is a hopping beach town that most adventurous travelers tend to avoid. However, that's not to say that this modern city by the sea isn't without its charms. The long stretch of white sand beach is nearly empty in the morning, but soon fills up by mid-afternoon with rows of brightly colored umbrellas and family-size tents (rented on the beach). If you don't mind spending an extra couple dollars for a good meal, then the upscale restaurants that line the Malecón are a great place to sample the local gastronomy. Most joints have outside seating, a great place to enjoy the sultry, salty sea breeze and watch the sunglasses-clad people strolling beachside.

While most of the town—behind the retro and very posh hotels, restaurants and holiday high rises—differs little from the characteristic dusty streets and aged concrete buildings of the small coastal towns, its nooks and crannies are full of culture and worth exploring. You won't find the beach-bar huts that clutter Atacames; most of the bars in Salinas are street-side, which means the beach is open, clear and perfect for walkers, runners, bikers and lovers. As the sun sinks behind the high rises and night settles in, the city lights shimmer on the sea and Salinas nightlife really heats up. The laze-by-the-sea attitude that accompanied the day is quickly replaced by an electric-like buzz of the night's prospects: tropical drinks and dance music until the early morning sun sends streaks across the sky and it's time for another day of lounging on the beach.

While this is a great place for young party-goers and hip couples, it is also, amazingly, family friendly. Don't be surprised to find grandmothers and grandfathers or couples with young toddlers in tow, rambling up the Malecón at 10 p.m., ice creams in hand, enjoying the peaceful beachside bliss or checking out the local night markets. Younger or single Salinas inhabitants pour into the restaurants and bars just a few meters away. Salinas probably isn't the best place to spend all your travel time, but it's definitely worth more than a passing glance: stop in and spend a night or two, enjoy the citified beach during the day and lively Malécon restaurants and bars at night. Just remember to bring your wallet.

From July to September, another traveler makes its way to the shores off Salinas: the Humpback Whale. Whale-watching tours can be arranged at offices in Salinas. If you miss whale season, you can also organize fishing and boat tours, water sports activities or city tours. And anyone keen to hang-ten can organize surfing classes with Surfas de Paradise, located (appropriately) on the beach.

NIGHT BUSES DIRECT FROM SALINAS TO QUITO

Take red and white buses from Salinas to La Libertad and ask to be dropped off near the Trans Esmeraldes bus station. Night buses ($9) leave at 7 p.m., 8:30 p.m. and 9:30 p.m.

CITY BUSES

City buses ply up and down the Malecón, but there is also a station if you're looking to catch a bust to La Libertad and can't catch one on the main street. Bus Terminal La Libertad Corner of Av. Luz Gonzalez and Calle Leonardo Aviles.

ATMS

Banco de Guayaquil, on Malecón next to Amazon Restaurant.
Banco del Pichincha Malecón, near Cafetería del Sol.

LODGING

The visitor accustomed to $5 dorm beds and plentiful budget accommodation is in for a bit of shock when they arrive in Salinas. However, there is something available for nearly everybody. True to its reputation as being a favorite destination for some of Ecuador's elite, Salinas boasts some beautiful hotels, featuring almost any amenity a visitor could wish for. Salinas has a fully-functioning casino-hotel, but also has plenty of mid-range options for those looking for something in the $20-50 range. While those looking for a budget option may not find the bottom-of-the-barrel prices available in other cities, the slightly higher hotel prices in Salinas will be accompanied by slightly fancier digs.

HOTEL ORO DEL MAR I, II, AND III ($10/PERSON)
The first Oro Del Mar must have done fairly well, because Salinas now has two others of the same name. Spread out across Salinas, these hotels are a good budget option, offering simple, but clean rooms, with well-maintained private bathrooms and TVs. Air conditioning is also available in some rooms. Reception is friendly and helpful, and compared to some other budget options, the hotels feel relatively safe. Prices are the same for all three hotels. Hotel I: Calle 23 and General Enriquez, Hotel II: Calle 18 and 2da Ave, Hotel III: Av 12 and Calle 38, Tel: Hotel I: 593-4-277-1334, Hotel II: 593-4-277-1389, Hotel III: 593-4-278-6057.

HOSTAL LAS OLAS ($10-12/PERSON)
Previously known as Rachael Hostal, this place has changed owners and seems to have been revamped. A modern entrance leads into a simple, but sparkling, reception area adorned with antique chairs and a few plants. Rooms are standard hostel-style, but clean and equipped with private bathrooms, TV and air conditioning. If you're in Salinas and pinching for pennies, this is your most comfortable (and best value) option. Also included in the price is breakfast and a free 30-minute boat ride. A good place for young travelers and budgeters. Servicio de Lancha Las Olas is affiliated with the hostal and arranges fishing and boat tours, and water sports rentals. To check out what's on offer, head to the beach in front of Costa Bella. Calle Las Palmeras 252, in front of Cevichelandia, Tel: 593-4-277-2501 / 593-4-277-2526, Cell: 593-9-980-7263.

HOTEL YULEE ($10-15/PERSON)
Housed in an old colonial-style building sitting behind glass-faced holiday high rises, Hotel Yulee is a charming architectural throwback. Bright yellow paint enlivens a sagging wooden façade, which leads into a modest, but well-appointed dining area on the first floor and up a flight of stairs towards cathedral ceiling hallways and spacious rooms on the second floor. Accommodation is modest, and perhaps a bit steep considering the aged building and other more modern budget options in town, but the there's no denying this place comes with character. The shuttered windows open to lovely views and at night a soothing breeze blows in from the sea, and you can see the city lights shimming in the distance. Cheaper with shared bath. Be prepared to negotiate with owner. Tel: 593-4-277-2028.

COCOS RESTAURANT AND HOSTAL (ROOMS: $10-25)
Bright and modern, Cocos Restaurant and Hostal is a cheerful place to pass the time. Modern art adorns the walls, themselves colorful enough without the paintings. A patio-like seating area, smartly decorated with green umbrellas and orange and blue tiles, looks past the Malecón and towards the sea and leads upstairs to the hostal, itself as clean and modern as the restaurant below. The glass-top tables and clean table cloths area a welcome change from the dominant white plastic tables and chairs, a common Salinas sight. Breakfast is more extensive than other places, but not much more expensive, which make Cocos a smart place to start off the day. Menu items cover a range of national and international dishes, including pizza and toasted sandwiches, parilladas and pastas—and of course, seafood. For a meal with pizzazz, try the sangria. Almost always full, this is clearly a popular spot and a good choice for travelers looking to meet other travelers. CocosTours also operates from the hostal-restaurant, and can organize a number of activities and excursions, including cultural, ecological and religious tours. Prices depend on the number of people and transport. For information, contact Oton Arboleda, owner of the hostal and restaurant. Malecón and Fidón Tomalá, Tel: 593-4-277-4349 / 593-4-277-2609, Cell: 593-9-977-5337, URL: www.cocoshostal.com.

TRAVEL SUITES (ROOMS: $10-50)
A lovely palm-tree shaded modern building, located away from the main drag, maintains Travel Suites, a set of apartments perfect for longer Salinas stays. Rooms are bright, well-maintained,

modern and spacious, with a small kitchen area fronted by a tiled counter and equipped with a mini-fridge and modest cooking facilities. An outdoor courtyard with a few scattered hammocks provides a peaceful alternative to sand and sun. Facilities and prices are good value compared to other places lining the Malecón, and the atmosphere notably more relaxed. This is definitely a wise option for families or groups of five to six people, or anyone looking to escape the busy beachfront and cook a meal or two. Av. 5ta, between calle 13 and 14, E-mail: maguerra@telconet.net.

Suites Salinas (ROOMS: $25-45)

Black leather couches, glossy floors and a modern reception area greet travelers as they enter Suites Salinas. While not as classy as it sounds, the hotel offers clean and modern rooms with new-looking furniture, beds with clean crisp white sheets bearing the hotel's insignia, as well as smaller details which usually indicate you're staying in a nice place, like miniature soaps and shampoos in the bathroom. If you're only staying the night and have some cash to spare, this is a good option. Compared to other hotels in the same price range, Suites Salinas offers the best bang for your buck. The attached restaurant, Cafetería Gaudua, is good place for coffee and a bite to eat. Gral. Enriquez Gallo and calle 27 esq, Tel: 593-4-277-4267 / 593-4-277-2759 / 593-4-277-1682, E-mail: s_salinas@easynet.net.ec.

El Carruaje Hotel (ROOMS: $30.50-124.44)

One of the nicer places to spend the night in Salinas, El Carruaje Hotel boasts clean, classy rooms with air conditioning and the option for a sea view (if you can afford to spend the extra money). Located on the Malecón, it is conveniently located near the popular Salinas bars, restaurants, and of course, the beach. Another bonus: the restaurant downstairs serves excellent national and international dishes, which come with first class service and a great atmosphere. Prices are a bit steeper than other places, but it's not a bad place to drop a buck. Malecón 517, Tel: 593-4-277-0214, Cell: 593-9-737-5156, E-mail: vrowmaria@hotmail.com.

Hotel Chipipe (ROOMS: $54.90-164.70)

Set back from the busy Malecón in a quiet, but well-kept section of Salinas, Hotel Chipipe is one of the classier hotels in the area. A new addition to the area in the last eight months, the hotel has clean, modern facilities. Uniformed attendants scurry about the professional-looking reception area, collecting bags and directing new arrivals to their rooms, which are modern and bear all the amenities of a nicer hotel. Besides having pleasant rooms with air conditioning and modern private bathrooms, the hotel also offers a lovely pool area and first-class restaurant, complete with fanned napkins and carefully arranged place settings. While not the classiest place in town, it maintains a warm, welcoming atmosphere that some of the larger places lack. Children between 6-11 years pay half price. Calle 12 between Av. 4ta and 5ta, Tel: 593-4-277-0553 / 593-4-277-0554 / 593-4-277-0555, Fax: 593-4-277-0556, E-mail: info@hotelchipipe.com, URL:www.hotelchipipe.com.

Barcelo Colón Miramar

The snazziest (and most expensive) place in Salinas, the Barcelo Colón is where the "who's who of Ecuador" spend the night. If you can afford to throw down a few extra pennies (or dollars), this place is a sure win in class, comfort and style, and certainly worthwhile—even if you're not one for name-dropping. Malecón, between Calle 38 and 40, E-mail: colonmiramar@barcelo.com, URL:www.colonmiramar.com.

RESTAURANTS

Cafetería Roberto

A popular place, almost always packed with hungry patrons, Cafetería Roberto is more a network of outdoor street-stalls than a formal restaurant. But if you're in the mood for something distinctly coastal, this seems to be a popular choice, especially among Ecuadorians, and compared to the Malecón the prices should settle your stomach. Located behind Malecón, near Cevichelandia.

EL TRIUNFO MINI MARKET AND PANADERÍA

A good pit stop for snacks and to stock up on travel items like shampoo and toothpaste. Also has a small selection of fresh breads and fruits. There are a few other markets on the same street. General Enriques Gallo, behind water park.

FAST FOOD TREATS

If you've got a fast food craving, head to the corner of Malecón and Zhumir where you'll find PitStop and Empañadas Milan. These are two good spots for late mid-afternoon snacks and late-night meals. Very cheap.

NICE CREAM HELADERÍA (ICE CREAM: $1-1.50)

This is probably the cheapest place in town to satisfy your frozen-treat cravings. Soft serve is their specialty, including various flavor flurries, twists, and dips that add a little something different to that plain old cup or cone. Malecón, next to Minimarket Kalinka.

YOGURT PERSIA (SNACKS: $1.50-4)

For something to temper the Salinas sun, head to this hole-in-the-wall place, specializing in frozen treats. An Ecuadorian chain, this place specializes in frozen yogurts and various types of *pan de yucca*. You'll can also indulge in cheap (and greasy) fast food fare like pizzas, hamburgers and hot dogs.

BIKING JACK SODA BAR (SNACKS: $1-2.50)

Set back from the upper-crust joints on the Malecón, Biking Jack Soda Bar is a fun and funky place to grab a bite to eat. Besides offering a good, cheap breakfast (including muesli with fresh fruit and yogurt) and real pressed coffee, this café-style restaurant also serves a variety of grilled sandwiches and juices. Prices are budget by Salinas standards, but without skimping on service or smaller details like wooden sugar bowls and chilled out music. While you eat, talk to Jack, the owner, and organize a biking tour for the day. He runs trips, running between $2-10, both in Salinas and along La Ruta del Sol up to Montañita, or to the Chocolatera and nearby cascades. Calle 23 and Malecón, Cell: 593-9-783-2634, E-mail: bikingjack@hotmail.com.

CAFETERÍA GUADUA (ENTREES: $2-5)

Sitting adjacent to Suites Salinas, this little cafetería is a good place to grab a real coffee and a bite to eat. Décor is simple, but stylish, consisting of wooden tables and chairs set in a clean and modern space. The menu is simple, offering a selection of juices, empañadas and sandwiches. If available, try their chocolate cake, which is sure to fix any chocoholic cravings. Large windows occupy two consecutive walls, making this a great place to sit and people watch for a while—the only drawback is there's no sea breeze to accompany your meal. At night there is a small market in the alley behind the restaurant and hotel. Gral. Enriquez Gallo and Calle 27.

RESTAURANT CARLONCHO (ENTREES: $2-7)

Simple but savory Manabí fare is on offer at this popular haunt just off the Malecón. Relatively unassuming-looking during the day, the restaurant kicks into high gear at night when the rows of outside grills overflow with meat, corn and various fried treats, and the tables fill up with hungry families. During peak times, the smell of grilling meat and sound of light-hearted chatter linger in the pleasant outdoor courtyard. You won't find black-and-white clad waiters or sparkling wine glasses that accompany some of the classier joints in Salinas, but the food is hearty and the atmosphere is, like its meat, sizzling. Gral. Enriquez Gallo and Calle 27 esq, across the street from Suites Salinas.

EL MARINERO (ENTREES: $3-5)

This is a no-frills eatery, serving up simple, but cheap, meat and seafood dishes. In the afternoons and at night this place fills up with Ecuadorian families looking for a cheap bite to eat. Meals run the gamut of typical cuisine, from humitas to corvina and a variety of traditional seafood plates.

RESTAURANTE MEDITERRANEO (ENTREES: $3-5)
A simple seafood restaurant on a street lined with similar looking eateries, the Mediterraneo is a slightly cleaner version of its culinary cousins. Lobster napkin holders add a splash of class and color to the plain white plastic tables and chairs, which seem always to be occupied with heaping plates of food and hungry patrons. Tel: 593-4-277-1778, Cell: 593-9-910-3910.

LA BELLA ITALIA (ENTREES: $3-7)
There's no shortage of pricey restaurants in Salinas, but this little culinary gem is worth its price in taste and style. The façade, made to look like a little slice of Italy, leads into a spacious seating area with wooden tables. A large brick oven occupies the front, near a street-side window, so patrons and potential customers alike can watch how the mouth-watering dough dishes are created. Specialties dishes include antipasto, calamare allarabiata, and cannelloni bella Italia—and of course, pizza. We should probably mention that the chef also suggests Pescado en Salsa de Marsicos ($5.50). Second floor seating also has excellent sea and street views, a good place to sip some wine and savor the gastronomical scene. Soccer fans should head here on game nights, when the restaurant fills with patrons proudly sporting their team's colors and all eyes are on the big screen TV in front. Malecón and Calle 17, Tel: 593-4-277-1361 / 593-4-277-2335, Cell: 593-9-807-4129.

OH MAR COMIDA MANABITA (ENTREES: $3-8)
For a taste of traditional Ecuadorian food with a distinct Manabí flair, try this simple seafood restaurant. At night the outside seating area with seaside view fills with people—a testament to its popularity among locals. The menu is fairly extensive and the platos del día combos ($3-4) are pretty good value by Salinas standards. Service is friendly and fast. Owners also have a restaurant by the same name in Manta. Malecón.

CAFETERÍA DEL SOL (ENTREES: $3-12.50)
This classy cafetería is the perfect place to sit and spend some time people watching and enjoying the beach view. An extensive menu is offered, and almost everything coming from the kitchen looks tempting. Come here in the morning and treat yourself to real coffee, whipped up using an authentic cappuccino machine. Lunches and dinners range from traditional meat, chicken and rice dishes, and mariscos, to international delights like tacos and burritos, pizza and hamburgers. Beyond the mains, there is still more on offer, from drinks to desserts (they even have milkshakes!). Just eye the home-baked treats sitting devilishly behind the glass counter and your mouth will water. Prices are standard Salinas expensive, but the atmosphere is certainly more laid back at this end of the Malecón and there's room to breathe.

BRASA CLUB (ENTREES: $3-15)
If you're in the mood for an island getaway, then head to this funky dive opposite La Iglesia. Going for a tropical theme, this restaurant consists of thatch-roof buildings seemingly pulled right off the beach. The menu features 15 different types of broiled meat and paellas, so anyone in the mood for meat should definitely be able to calm their craving here. You'll also find typical coastal cuisine, such as mariscos and various soups. San Lorenzo, diagonal la Iglesia, Tel: 593-4-277-6740 / 593-4-277-9213, E-mail: otonarboleda@yahoo.com.

LA OSTRA NOSTRA (ENTREES: $3.50-12)
Except for its Italian-looking sign out front, this place is pure Ecuadorian. Serving up a variety of traditional coastal fare, from fish and mariscos to meat, rice dishes and soup, La Ostra Nostra is a popular hangout with a flair for anything fried, or served with fish and a side of rice. Almost always packed, the restaurant has a busy fast-food buzz to it, but is a good bet if you're up to trying some local cuisine, and don't want to swallow the Malecón prices. Try the house special, Ostras al Limon. Tel: 593-4-277-4028, Cell: 593-9-413-7736.

RESTAURANT AND BAR VROUW MARÍA (ENTREES: $4-15)
Orange is the color of choice in this pleasant restaurant overlooking the Malecón. Cheerful colors, woven placemats and the almost constant company of a cool sea breeze make Vrouw María

Help other travelers. Publish your favorite places at www.vivatravelguides.com

a popular place to grab a bite. The menu is typical coastal fare and differs little from other Salinas restaurants, except that the seafood here is slightly more expensive than places further back from the beach, like Cevichelandia. But for the extra dollar or two, you get first-class service, and meals served with extras like garlic bread and an assortment of dipping sauces. Malecón.

HOTEL CHIPIPE RESTAURANT (ENTREES: $5.25-14.25)
Located in the classy Chipipe Hotel, this restaurant bears the same style as its commercial neighbor. Tables are carefully set with maroon and white table cloths, fanned napkins and wine glasses. Prices are excellent, considering the atmosphere and facilities, and the menu is extensive. Meals range from traditional chicken, meat, fish and rice dishes to paella and pastas, and a range of desserts and drinks. Calle 12 between Av. 4ta and 5ta, Tel: 593-4-277-0553 / 593-4-277-0554 / 593-4-277-0555.

STEAKHOUSE JIMMY RODEO (ENTREES: $5.25-14.25)
Wild West meets Argentine Gaucho at this meat-lovers dream located just off the Malecón. The restaurant's catch phrase, "steak house and seafood old west-old navy" leaves a lot to the imagination, but is an appropriate introduction to this funky Salinas eatery. Dapper waiters dressed in cowboy hats and boots usher newcomers into an open-air adobe room lined with pine picnic tables sturdy enough to handle the heaps of meat and sides that accompany any meal. Dishes like Texas Burger and Cowboy California City are sure to melt the heart of any carnivore, though Chicken Grill Virginia State and Steak Sandwich New York City would probably also do the job. For something a little less meaty, try the tapas and wine. General Enriquez Gallo and Calle 21, across from Hostal Francisco I, Tel: 593-4-277-0483.

LUV N OVEN
Vegetarians and anyone in search of a decent cup of coffee should head to Luv n Oven, a cozy restaurant on the Malecón. Previously known as Pasquale, this place has changed owners, but still offers a similar menu. While the interior décor is nothing special the outdoor seating with an ocean view is spectacular. Dishes range from traditional coastal cuisine (like mariscos) to lasagna, chicken and a variety of pastas. Vego's will be delighted to find an entire page of the menu dedicated to meat-free dishes like *carne de soya con vegetables* and fifteen other tempting plates. Coffee comes from an espresso machine and is served in colorful ceramic mugs, a nice complement to the already-colorful view. If you've got room for dessert, try the tiramisu or gelato. Cocktails are the popular treat when happy hour kicks off the night's festivities. Malecón, next to La Bella Italia.

JETSET BAR AND DISCOTEC
An unassuming Malecón resident during the day, this place fills up when the sun goes down and remains bumping until the early morning hours. While probably not the most family-friendly place in town, it's a popular haunt for young, hip Ecuadorians looking to drink and dance the night away. Malecón, next to La Bella Italia.

MIS CABINAS ($1/HOUR)
If you're on the Malecón and in search of a place to use the internet or to make an international call, then this is a good bet. This place doesn't put on airs, and there's nothing space age about it, but its air conditioned room is a cool place to surf the net or chat with friends and family. Note, there are only three computers to the back, which is highly contested territory during busy times. It is located in the Malecón, between Mar Bravo Surf Shop and the Alegro store. They charge the going rate of $1/hour.

TOURS
SALINAS AQUA ADVENTURE
If you tire of the beach, but are looking to escape the heat, then head to Salinas Aqua Adventure, the Ecuadorian answer to a modern water park. A network of slides and pools fill with kids and adults alike, and the screams of delight can be heard a block away. Facilities are clean and spacious, though the park tends to get busy in the afternoons. This is a good spot

for some down-home, family fun. Special discount for students and Salinas residents. Credit cards accepted. Av. Sixto Durán Ballén and Eleodora Peña, Tel: 593-4-239-4763, 593-4-277-0660, E-mail: turlatino_aquaadventure@yahoo.com.

PESCA TOURS

Whether or not its an indication of how good they are, Pesca Tours main office is located in Barcelón Mira Mar, the premier hotel in Salinas. Whether you're a landlubber or sea aficianado, you're bound to find something to suit your fancy with this company. It was established in 1958 by Knud Holst Dunn, an avid fishing fan even more determined to turn his favorite hobby into a successful business. Although sport fishing is their specialty (as the name may imply), other popular excursions include city tours, boating trips and whale-watching (June to September only). All-inclusive tours include airport transfers and hotel pick-up and drop-off. If you're keen to keep anything you catch, ask *el capitán* in the office and he can arrange it to be sent to a taxidermist. Malecón 717, next to Café Bar Jetset, Tel: 593-4-240-2504, 593-4-277-2391, E-mail: fishing@pescatours.com.ec, URL: www.pescatours.com.ec.

CAROLTOUR S.A.

This tour company, conveniently located on the Malecón, organizes a range of tours and activities and is a good place to stop by for information on things to see and do in the area. Depending on your time and budget you can choose from simple city tours to trips up La Ruta del Sol and specialized excursions like whale watching (July to September), sports fishing, and water skiing. Those keen to see more of Salinas can take the city tour; this three-hour tour includes visits to Los Marinos, Punto St. Elena, La Chocolatera, Artesenías Genesis and Museo Farallón Dillon (the nautical museum). CarolTours can also make hotel arrangements, organize special events and arrange for customized tours. Malecón, Condominio El Alcazar, first floor, next to El Carruaje hotel, Tel: 593-4-277-0204 / 593-4-277-4914, Cell: 593-9-753-8202 / 593-9-356-6668, E-mail: caroltoursa@hotmail.com.

GUAYAQUIL

Once little more than a commercial hub, frequented more by business visitors than travelers, Ecuador's largest city has recently been swept away in a current of cultural revival. You can easily spend a couple of days strolling along the beachfront boardwalk (Malecón) or visiting museums and trendy restaurants. There are plenty of opportunities to side-trip outside the city. A few highlights include the Bosque Protector Cerro Blanco, Puerto Hondo and Playas, Guayaquil's closest beach.

THINGS TO SEE & DO

GENERAL CEMETERY AND FLOWER MARKET (FREE)

Guayaquil's General Cemetery is among the most elaborate cemeteries in all of the Americas. Boasting neo-classical architecture and sculpture from noted Spanish and Italian artists of the 20th century, each turn through the labyrinth of mausoleums brings surprises and awe. Marble angels weeping or gloriously standing watch frequently decorate graves. The presence of Guayaquil's Masonic influence can also be found while exploring the nooks and crannies. The lavish decoration and expensive materials of the tombs in this area are contrasted by the wooden crosses on the western side of the hill where the practically vertical graves seem to be piled on top of one another. These are the sites where those who cannot afford to pay for a niche in one of the cement mausoleums have snuck their loved ones in during the night to bury them.

Located at the main entrance is the grandiose tomb of Victor Emilio Estrada, former President of the Republic and banker. Legend tells that he made a pact with the devil, exchanging his soul for wealth and power. As a result, his spirit is not at peace and wanders the street near the cemetery at night. Taxi drivers tell of picking up a man walking alone along the street who then requests to be dropped off at the cemetery entrance where his tomb is located. The flower market is in front of this main entrance, where Calle Machala dead-ends into Julián Coronel next to the "salones de velorio." This is where the families of the deceased mourn for 24 hours before

Guayaquil

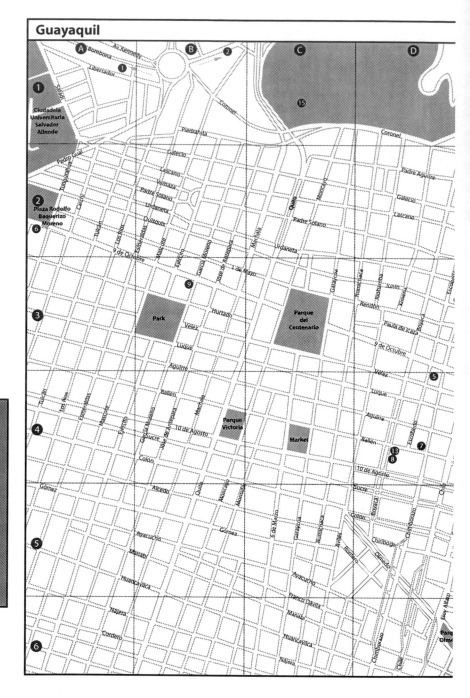

LODGING
1. (A1) DREAMKAPTURE INN
2. (B1) ECUAHOGAR
3. (D3) HOTEL ANDALUZ
4. (E3) HOTEL LA FONTANA
5. (D4) HOTEL LAS PENAS
6. (A2) TANGARA GUEST HOUSE
7. (D4) UNIPARK HOTEL
8. (D4) GRAND HOTEL GUAYAQUIL
9. (B3) HOTEL ORO VERDE

RESTAURANTS
10. (E3) BOPAN - ARTE, CAFE Y PAN
11. (F2) FRUTABAR
12. (E4) LA PARRILLA DEL ÑATO
13. (D4) LA PEPA DE ORO
14. (F4) SWEET & COFFEE

THINGS TO SEE & DO
15. (C1) CEMETARIO GENERAL AND FLOWER MARKET
16. (F3) MALECON 2000

SOUTHERN COAST

carrying loved ones across the footbridge to their final resting places. Flower arrangements are a distinct mixture of roses, orchids and palm fronds. Each booth competes with the next in creating more and more beautiful arrangements. The easiest way to arrive is by taxi. Ask to be taken to the "mercado de flores del cementerio general" (general cemetery flower market). The stairway to the footbridge crossing the street to the main entrance into the cemetery is next to the market. Daily 9 a.m.-6 p.m. Calle Julián Coronel and Calle Machala.

CERRO BLANCO

Cerro Blanco is a great day trip outside the city of Guayaquil. Easily accessible by bus, visitors can take advantage of a self-guided tour along their two self-guided trails or request a trained guide for a more educational experience. Administered by "Fundación Pro-Bosque" (Pro-Forest Foundation), Cerro Blanco protects a section of dry forest that pertains to the Tropical Andes Biodiversity Hotspot, identified by Conservation International as the number one area on the planet in terms of overall number of plant and animal species. In addition to the more than 500 vascular plant species, one of the highlights is seeing the ceibo or kapok trees up-close. Their green, human-like trunks seem to be right out of a Dr. Seuss book.

Despite being bordered by Guayaquil's almost three million inhabitants, the protected forest harbors populations of jaguar, ocelot, agouti, peccary and other mammal species. Birders will be excited by the opportunity to see more than 200 species, of which over twenty are endemic. With almost 10 globally threatened bird species including the guayaquilensis subspecies of the great green macaw (locally called the "Papagayo de Guayaquil"), listed as critically endangered. For those looking to stay for awhile, a camping and picnic area with flush toilets, showers and cooking grills awaits. Or enjoy the comfort of a two-bedroom, sustainably constructed cabin. If interested in getting involved in-depth, contact the very helpful foundation director, Eric Horstman, to find out what kinds of volunteer opportunities he currently has available. Kilometer 16 off the Guayaquil-Salinas Highway, Tel: 593-4-287-4947, 593-4-287-4946, E-mail: bosqueprotector@yahoo.com.

MALECÓN 2000

The Malecón 2000 is a wonderful hub for many activities in downtown Guayaquil. The term "malecón" is commonly found in any city or town that has a street stretching along the waterfront. Since the mid-1800s in Guayaquil, this has been the place where locals and visitors of every social class have spent their evenings looking for a cool breeze off the river, strolling along or visiting with each other on benches. Nowadays, crowds continue to flock for the same reasons.

The same stretch along the river was re-vamped and innaugurated as Malecón 2000 in October 1999. The Southern sector (between Calle Cuenca and 10 de Agosto) is comprised of a shopping center, open-air food courts, an artisan's market and the "Mercado Sur." Hungry visitors can enjoy budget to mid-range seafood dishes while watching the expanse of the Guayas River lazily pass by on its way to the Pacific. The artisan's market is highlighted by the only Pro-Pueblo retailer in the country. Pro-Pueblo represents co-ops of coastal artisans who primarily work from their homes in remote villages to create low-cost products. Their ceramics and tagua nut (vegetable ivory) Christmas decorations are of such an excellent quality that they are sometimes resold in other stores for three times the price. The Mercado Sur, constructed by a contemporary of Eiffel, was home to one of Guayaquil's primary markets until the regeneration project relocated vendors to another part of the city at the end of the 1990s.

The Central sector (between 10 de Agosto and P. Icaza) begins at the Clock Tower, with its Moorish influence, and ends at the "La Rotonda" monument at 9 de Octubre. They became part of the Malecón during the mid-1900s. For the more recent inauguration, architects added monuments to the four elements in this sector. Testaments to the original mangrove forests that flanked the river, thick trees have walkways built around them in this sector.

The Northern sector (between P. Icaza and the Las Peñas neighborhood) hosts exercise and play areas, gardens, an IMAX theater, another food court and the MAAC (Museum of Anthropology and Contemporary Art). The beautifully landscaped gardens decoratively highlight flora from the coastal region and the design includes evidence of the city's long-standing Masonic influence. The MAAC brings in interesting exhibits from all over the world, hosts performances for well-known musicians, and includes a theater that presents both international and national films (one of the only places in the entire world to be able to witness the country's contribution to film). Sargento Vargas 116 and Av. Olmedo (Fundación Malecón 200), Tel: 593-4-252-4530, Fax: 593-4-252-4211, E-mail: info@malecon2000.org.ec, URL: www.malecon2000.com.

PUERTO HONDO
Just a kilometer west of the Cerro Blanco forest reserve entrance is Puerto Hondo, a dry, weatherworn town sitting on the edge of a slender saltwater estuary. Although the village itself is of little interest, the nearby mangrove swamps which spring up around the estuary can be visited via motorized canoes, as part of a tour run by a locally established guide association and the Pro-Bosque foundation. To get there, catch a bus heading towards the Cerro Blanco reserve and ask to be dropped off at the Puerto Hondo turnoff. From here, head south from the highway, about a 5-minute walk.

PLAYAS
The closest place to get beached around Guayaquil is Playas (officially called General Villamil), which has a fairly extensive stretch of beach. On weekends and during the summer, the beach overflows with visitors seeking to escape the scorching city sidewalks. Despite its local attraction, the town remains relatively relaxed, offering little more to see or do than grab a meal, sprawl out on a beach towel, or swim in the sea.

GUAYAQUIL HISTORICAL PARK
Guayaquil Historical Park is a great way to spend day getting to know some of the city's history and a little of the coastal region's culture. The park is separated into three main sections: The Wildlife Zone, The Urban Architectural Zone and The Traditions Zone. The Wildlife Zone consists of elevated paths that have allowed much of the natural plant life to remain intact, while creating areas for exhibit animals such as tapir, caiman, deer and sloths. The Urban Architectural Zone is inspired by the booming construction brought on at the beginning of the 20th century, which also corresponded with Ecuador's cacao boom. The Traditions Zone gives a glimpse at what life is like in rural parts of the coast, where people continue to live in bamboo homes. Walk through an elevated house, built to avoid the floods that affect most of the region during the rainy season, while also providing shelter for animals raised for food or sale. This area also includes the "Granja Urbana Solidaria" program, which promotes community and families working together to grow healthy produce and curative plants. The biggest highlight is the twice-daily theatrical performances presented for audiences. Even those who do not understand Spanish will enjoy the lively shows reenacting traditions and legends from a hundred years ago. Characters might range from a cacao boom plantation owner to a French-educated Ecuadorian heiress to a hoofed devil disguised as a gentleman. Worried about lunch? The kiosks offer a variety of tasty traditional snacks. Av. Esmeraldas and Av. Central Route, Tel: 593-4-283-3807 / 283-2958, E-mail: rramirez@bc.ec.

LODGING
DREAMKAPTURE INN (ROOMS: $8-18)
Dreamkapture is located in a suburban area of Guayaquil, Ecuador, known locally as Alborada. It is mid-range and very secure, offering 16 distinctive guest rooms. There is a small waterfall pool and plenty of hammocks for relaxing. Among other guests and hotel staff you will find, monkeys, parrots and lots more. Alborada Doceava-Benjamin Carrion and Francisco de Orellana, Mz 02, Villa 21, Tel: 593-4-224-2909, E-Mail: info@dreamkapture.com, URL: www.dreamkapture.com.

ECUAHOGAR (ROOMS: $12-30)
For those looking to get out of downtown Guayaquil and into a residential area of the city, or those just looking for a comfortable place to spend the night close to the bus terminal or airport, Ecua-

hogar is an excellent option. This part of the city is a wonderful place to get a feel for a bustling, middle-class neighborhood in a city that never sleeps. All rooms are equipped with air conditioning and a TV, and both private and shared baths have hot water. Extra services include the on-site restaurant called "Mi Tierra," laundry service and staff that speak English, French and German. As a tour operator, they also offer inexpensive shuttle service from the airport or bus terminal for all group sizes and can provide travel advice or arrange itineraries. Escape from the cosmopolitan aspect of Guayaquil that municipal politicians are creating in the renovated downtown area, and get a taste of the warmth for which guayaquileñans are well-known. Sauces 1, Mz F31, Villa 20, Tel: 593-4-224-8341 / 593-4-227-3288, Fax: 593-4-224-8357, E-mail: monfinsa@hotmail.com.

HOTEL ANDALUZ (ROOMS: $18-36)

Located just a few blocks from both the Malecón 2000 and 9 de Octubre, Hotel Andaluz is an excellent deal for travelers looking to be in the middle of everything in downtown Guayaquil. The hotel provides all of the basic amenities: private bath with hot water, air conditioning and a living room area with TV. One of the highlights is the garden-like roof terrace. Decoration is simple with an emphasis on Ecuadorian culture. Rooms off the street may be best for those sensitive to street noise, since the hotel is located on a busy street. No other hotel in this area of downtown Guayaquil is better priced. Junín 842 and Baquerizo Moreno, Tel: 593-4-230-5796, E-mail: hotel_andaluz@yahoo.com.

TANGARA GUEST HOUSE (ROOMS: $20-48)

Located in a residential area on the outskirts of downtown, the Tangara Guest House offers a homey hostel atmosphere not easily found in Guayaquil. If staying awhile, the communal kitchen and gardens make for a pleasant extended visit. At $35 for a single, rooms are not exactly budget, but with a travel buddy, $20 per person (or $15 per person in a triple) including breakfast is a good price, for knowing that guests are taken care of by the staff. The guest house owners also run a tour operator, so they will be able to cater to all of your tourism needs. Ciudadela Bolivariana, Tel: 593-4-228-2828 / 593-4-228-2829 / 593-4-228-4445, Fax: 593-4-228-2829, E-mail: tangara@gye.satnet.net, URL: www.tangara-ecuador.com.

HOTEL LA FONTANA (ROOMS: $45-80)

Situated in Guayaquil's downtown banking district (a.k.a. "a well-guarded area") just three blocks from Malecón 2000 and one block from 9 de Octubre, Hotel La Fontana is the best located hotel in its price range. Considering its central location, the hotel is rather quiet. Just across the street is one of the stops for the Metrovía, which runs from the bus terminal in the North direct to downtown and beyond. Within comfortable walking distance, visitors will find restaurants, bars and nightclubs, as well as our tour operators ready to book Galápagos trips. There are also artisan markets, museums and venues nearby, in addition to the city's oldest churches, parks, plazas and monuments. Rooms have air conditioning, private bath with hot water, TV with cable and a telephone. P. Icaza 404 and Córdova, Tel: 593-4-230-3967 / 593-4-230-7230, E-mail: hlafontana@ecutel.net.

HOTEL LAS PEÑAS (ROOMS: $55-80)

Located above the wonderful bakery "Panadería California" just one block from Av. 9 de Octubre, Hotel Las Peñas is a nice, mid-range option for comfortably staying downtown. Rooms have a hotel-chain feel to them without the hefty price: private bath, air conditioning, mini-bar, TV with cable, telephone and room service. Laundry and private shuttle service are also offered. Light sleepers might want to request an inside room to avoid Guayaquil's street noise. Escobedo 1215 entre Av. 9 de Octubre and Vélez, Tel: 593-4-232-3355, Cell: 593-9-608-6199, E-mail: reservas@hlpgye.com, URL: www.hlpgye.com.

GRAND HOTEL, GUAYAQUIL (ROOMS: $85-150)

The Grand Hotel Guayaquil lives up to its name, featuring a spacious reception area and excellent service. Centrally placed, only four miles from the airport, it shares a block with a beautiful cathedral. The hotel is a great place for those wishing to indulge themselves for a day or two, splashing in the pool, relaxing in the sauna, having a massage or working out in the rooftop gym. Rooms are tastefully decorated and have cable TV, telephones, internet connection, hair dryers, radio alarms and in-room coffee machines (always a nice perk). For a bite to eat, head to La Pepa de Oro the 24-hour coffee shop; alternatives are the 1822 Restaurant, the Turtle Bar and the Barbecue Restaurant. Boyaca between Clemente Ballen and 10 de Agosto, Tel: 593-4-232-7251, E-mail: reservas@grandhotelguayaquil.com, URL: www.grandhotelguayaquil.com.

HOTEL ORO VERDE (ROOMS: $125-190)

Centrally located and only 10 minutes from the airport, the Oro Verde is a plush choice for those with a bit of spare cash. This chain hotel boasts spotless well-furnished rooms, complete with cable TV, internet, radio, telephone, safe and minibar. A couple of days at this hotel would give you just enough time to try out the numerous eateries in the building: El Patio, the Gourmet Deli, La Fondue, Bar El Capitan and the Gourmet Restaurant. The culinary choices are varied enough to satisfy almost anyone's palate, and the buffet breakfast is a delicious way to start the day. Aside from eating, you can get pampered in the beauty parlor or head to Oro Fit, the place to work off that heavy breakfast or lunch. Other services include 24-hour room service, laundry, dry cleaning, currency exchange, airport transfer, valet parking and limousine service. A sister hotel is also located in Manta. If your budget allows this sort of price, and you want to have a relaxing couple of days, this is the perfect place to stay. 9 de Octobre and Garcia Moreno, Tel: 593-4-232-7999, E-mail: reservasgye@oroverdehotels, URL:www.oroverdehotels.com/ingles/gye.

UNIPARK HOTEL

Convenient for a leisurely stroll to the Malecón, this upscale hotel is owned by the Oro Verde chain. Smack in the middle of the central commercial district, the hotel is spread across two towers accommodating 139 rooms, including wheelchair accessible and non-smoking room options. The hotel has several restaurants including the UniCafé, UniBar, the UniDeli and the Sushi Bar, which has an all-you-can-eat promotion on Wednesdays. Rooms are comfortable, pleasant and well-serviced. Airport transfers are available, and there is a casino for those feeling lucky. There is also a small shopping center next door, where it is possible to buy film or hit the Banco de Guayaquil ATM. This is a good option for families because on request the hotel can offer a baby-sitting service, and connecting rooms are also available. Clemente Ballén 406 and Chimborazo, Tel: 593-4-232-7100, E-mail: unipark@oroverdehotels.com, URL: www.oroverdehotels.com.

ECOVITA

An organic farm camping experience located in Pallatanga, two hours from Guayaquil, promoting projects geared toward community efforts and raising awareness about conservation. The name "ecovita" itself means "ecological life," fitting for a place dedicated to agro-tourism and environmental education. Comfortable tents are equipped with mattresses and bug nets, and there are several simple double rooms with baths. Lots of areas for relaxing and play with hammocks, a natural pool, volleyball court, soccer field, pool table, ping-pong tables, mountain bikes and even go-kart racing. Panamericana Sur, Km 139 Guayaquil - Riobamba way, Tel: 593-4-288-8196, Cell: 593-9-908-5226, E-mail: info@vivecovita.com.

RESTAURANTS

SWEET AND COFFEE (DESSERTS: $1-3)

The owners of Sweet and Coffee did not want to leave any doubts about what they serve. Large slices of walnut cake, chocolate Oreo cheesecake and lime meringue pie can be accompanied by a frothy vanilla latte or iced coffee drink. Prices might be a few cents more expensive than other coffee places, but they offer good quality and consistency in their products. Desserts are very well-priced, especially for the portion size. Looking to take home an Ecuadorian coffee blend? Sweet and Coffee also packages and sells its own brand of whole bean or ground coffee. Malecón 2000, Galería C.

BOPÁN'S (ENTREES: $2-9)

If you are looking for a quick stop for a snack and a cool drink, Bopán's corner location facing the Malecón 2000 provides a great place to watch Guayaquil's bustling city life pass by the window. The restaurant holds true to its name by serving real espresso (not always easy to find in Guayaquil) over hand-painted tabletops inspired by tropical flowers, coastal scenes and Ecuadorian culture. The "pan" part is where the restaurant has strayed, when changing

SOUTHERN COAST

owners and becoming a local chain—the bread is not always very fresh. The atmosphere inspires reading a book or journal-writing while sipping a "Frozen" (as the blended, icy juices are called on the menu) and nibbling a "torta de acelga" (chard tart), Spanish omelet or fruity crepes. Bopán also offers breakfast options and lunch specials at reasonable prices. Service is prompt, the place is very clean, and the bathroom is nice. P. Icaza and Malecón (corner).

FRUTABAR (ENTREES: $3-6)
Frutabar feels like a piece of Montañita has been transplanted to the big city. Instead of waves crashing, one might catch a view of the Guayas River slowly drifting by, but surfboards converted into tables definitely inspire a sense of being at the beach. Serving light fare like sandwiches and "humitas" (Ecuador's version of a cheese tamale), the highlight is definitely the huge "batidos" (fruit juice, milk, and ice)! Flavors range from basic strawberry and peach to coconut and mango. Choose from their tried-and-true flavor combinations or create your own. For a kick, try the "borojó"—a dark-brown, endemic fruit paste locally known as an aphrodisiac. Splitting a batido and a "Macombo" sandwich (Ecua-style turkey stuffing on a toasted whole-wheat roll) is refreshing and filling for two on a hot, Guayaquil afternoon. Malecón and Tungurahua (corner), Tel: 593-4-230-0743.

LA PARRILLA DEL ÑATO (ENTREES: $4-20)
La Parrilla del Ñato is an enticing restaurant for a wide variety of travelers looking for a large, satisfying meal. The hungry budget traveler can munch on bread before a $4 foot-long, chicken sandwich arrives. For someone looking to splurge, the challenge will be deciding with which Chilean wine to accompany the many seafood and pasta dishes that are available. Most people come for the "parrillada," or grilled meats, but be careful when ordering from the untranslated menu. Make sure that if you ask for "morcilla" or "chinchulín" that you are ready to eat blood sausage or intestines. Eating with a vegetarian? The ravioli in a rich, four-cheese sauce is to be savored slowly! If there is any room left after dinner, the menu also offers spectacular desserts such as a coconut flan (queso de coco) or an after-dinner sip of "Espíritu del Ecuador" from their full bar. This local chain of restaurants attracts Guayaquil's minor celebrities with excellent quality food and prompt service, but do not expect any frills. Luque and Pichincha (corner), Tel: 593-4-232-1656 / 593-4-232-1649.

LA PEPA DE ORO (ENTREES: $3-9)
With service 24/7, La Pepa de Oro is the perfect place to safely grab a bite to eat in Guayaquil when you have come into town late. Choices range from typical coastal dishes like sea bass "ceviche" or lentils and rice to American options such as a club sandwich or salad bar. Only a few blocks from the Malecón, it also makes a refreshing stop while taking a walking tour of the downtown area on a sunny, Guayaquil afternoon. Enjoy a fresh, tropical fruit salad or a Pilsener under a shady umbrella while you listen to sound of the artificial waterfall tumbling down into the pool—or just stay inside for the air conditioning! On Thursday, Friday and Saturday nights, meals are accompanied by Ecuadorian *pasillos* played on the guitar, but no matter when you go, you will always be welcomed by friendly service. The menu is in English and includes a brief history of the even briefer Ecuadorian cacao boom that inspires the restaurant's décor. Boyacá and Clemente Ballén, Tel: 593-4-232-9690, URL: www.grandhotelguayaquil.com.

TOUR COMPANIES IN GUAYAQUIL
GUAYAQUIL VISION
This company specializes in tours that are a quick, inexpensive and safe way to get to see several parts of the city. The open-top buses are a modern version of the traditional coastal form of transportation, known as a "Chiva," which is still used in some parts of the coast. Currently, they are mostly seen as nightclubs-on-wheels for groups celebrating special occasions. The company offers three regular routes, which include different levels of service and amenities: the Scenic City Tour, Grand Guayaquil Tour, and Noche de Fiesta Tour. Urdesa Central Costanera 1402 and Calle Segunda (corner), Tel: 593-4-288-5800, URL: www.guayaquilvision.com.

EL ORO

El Oro stretches from Guayaquil to the Peruvian border. Considered by many as nothing more than way station between Ecuador and Peru, El Oro can surprise those willing to spend a few days exploring it. The thriving banana and shrimp producing city of Machala divides El Oro's portion of coast in two. While not a beautiful destination in itself, Machala is a great starting point for exploring the mangrove circled town of Puerto Bolívar, the markets of Santa Rosa, the gold-mining community of Zaruma and the peninsula beaches of Jambelí. On the Río Zarumilla, just across the border from Peru, sits Huaquillas, the main immigration point between the two countries. Huaquillas offers little more than a checkpoint and a shopping destination for Peruvians looking for bargains.

UPLANDS OF EL ORO

Head inland from Machala and you'll discover a peaceful corner of the country, devoid of the most commonly spotted species: the tourist. Scenic roads meander through the countryside, winding past quiet colonial cities, and the characteristic gold mines that give this region its name. A network of trails crisscross through the landscape, running into hidden waterfalls and expansive tracts of forests along the way. As a transition zone between the rugged mountains of the Andes and smooth sandy beaches of the coast, this region presents travelers with a unique climate conducive to walking and trekking.

MACHALA

Machala, the capital of El Oro Province, is an important city for Ecuador's banana production. In fact, because of the area's mass banana production and exportation, it is sometimes referred to as the "banana capital of the world." There is even a festival in late September that includes the Banana Queen of Machala contest. Although Machala is an important hub for business in Ecuador, and thus home of a decent amount of conventions and meetings, it is not often frequented by foreigners. Usually it serves as just a stopover for travelers on their way to Peru. Those who do happen to end up in Machala will not be disappointed. It may not have a ton of things to do, but there is a beach, ample hotels and restaurants. There are worse places you could end up for a stopover.

GETTING TO AND AWAY

Although Machala doesn't have a major bus station, all the bus companies have their own small stations which are mostly located in the center of town. In general each company mainly goes to a certain area of town. To get to Guayaquil, take either Rutas Orenas, located at 9 de Octubre and Tarqui, or Ecuatoriano Pullman, located at Colón and 9 de Octubre. To get to Quito take either Panamericana, located at Colón and Bolivar, or Occidental, located at Sucre and Olmedo. To get to other areas of Ecuador, you may have to transfer in a major city, ask around to see if there is a bus going where you need to go.

LODGING

HOTEL INES ($10-20/PERSON)

If you are looking for a place that is budget friendly, Hotel Ines is a good bet. It may not be the fanciest or the newest place, but it is a perfectly acceptable place to stay. Most rooms have air conditioning and cable television. Juan Montalvo 1509 and Pasaje, Tel: 593-4-793-2301, Fax: 593-4-793-1473.

Environmental Tips for Travelers

By Nicola Robinson, Nicola Mears and Heather Ducharme, Río Muchacho Organic Farm

Whilst traveling in a foreign country, it is important to minimize your impact. Here are some tips and information that you should try and remember. We acknowledge that some of this advice may be more difficult to take on board whilst traveling than it would be to incorporate into your daily lives at home. However, even if you only put into practice three or four of our suggestions, be it whilst on the road or whilst at home, it will certainly contribute to reducing our impact on the planet.

Garbage

• Most plastic bottles are not recyclable in Ecuador. Try to use glass bottles (returnable) for sodas etc. Aluminum cans are the next best option as they are at least recyclable. To avoid buying more disposable bottles, carry a water bottle and always check if there is somewhere to fill it up at your hotel/ restaurant (most hotels and restaurants have purified water in large 20 litre bottles called botellones. These places also sell water in small bottles and so they might be reluctant to begin with as they think they are loosing a sale. Of course you will need to pay for the refill also. The concept of reducing garbage is new for Ecua dorians, so don't be surprised if you have to explain it, but if more travelers request it, the more common place it will become. If you have to buy bottles, buy the biggest you can and just refill from there, especially if you plan to be in the same place for a while.

• Consider purifying your own water to avoid creating garbage.

• Try to avoid excessive wrapping and plastic bags which are all too readily dished out for each small purchase. If you can, explain to the shop keeper why you want to give the bag back. If you shop in a local market take your own bag or have them place everything in one large plastic bag instead of numerous small ones.

• You can also reduce the amount of garbage you produce as a result of traveling by using a digital camera instead of using film (the process of developing film can produce a lot of waste - unwanted photos are non recyclable and often end up in the trash).

• Use a re usable container for your soap so that you can use your own and avoid half using the small hotel soaps which come individually wrapped (if you use hotel soap, use one and take the remainder with you! It will just be thrown out.)

• Avoid using excessive cosmetic products e.g. hairspray, mousse, aftershave, perfume and if you must use them, try and find effective environmentally friendly alternatives e.g. biodegradable shampoos, crystal deodorants which last longer etc. (most containers for these products are non recyclable). Avoid using dispos able products e.g. plastic razors, single use contact lenses.

• Try to use re chargeable batteries or eliminate use of batteries entirely e.g. use a wind up or solar torch or radio.

• Where available use recycled paper for letters home, trip diaries, toilet paper.

• Buy in bulk if you are traveling in a large group- this reduces packaging.

• Please remember to recycle whatever you can in the country you are traveling.

However, some products that can not be recycled in the host country can be recycled in your home countries, so please take them home if possible.

FOOD AND HEALTH

• Avoid eating foods that you know are from endangered or threatened species (research these before you come to the country). In Ecuador, lobsters are often caught undersized (the tail should be longer than 8 cm). Buy and eat locally grown and locally processed foods wherever possible, rather than food products shipped from long distances, which use more energy (fossil fuels for transport and generally more packaging).

• Consider using alternative natural medical products for common travelers' illnesses. This may be healthier for you as well as avoids leaving behind pharmaceuticals in the local water and soil (this is becoming a detectable problem in first world countries, thought to affect aquatic organisms like fish and frogs).

NATURE, FLORA AND FAUNA

• Avoid buying souvenirs of local fauna. Many stores sell cases of bright colored butterflies, spiders and insects; these are caught by the hundreds in the Amazon and the sales people will tell you that they are not caught but that they raise them ... it is not true !

• Avoid buying souvenirs that are made with endangered species or species that have to be killed to be made into a craft, support crafts made from renewable resources.

• Don't collect insects, flora and fauna without a permit. Leave them for everyone to enjoy.

• When walking, stay on the trails and close gates behind you.

CAMPING AND WATER

• Use toilets where they exist, if not bury human waste in a hole 20 centimeters deep. Human waste should be buried at least 50 meters from water sources.

• Use biodegradable soaps and detergents. In Ecuador, local "Foca" detergent claims to be biodegradable.

• Don't wash shampoo and detergent off directly in rivers, but rather as far away as you can (4 meters minimum).

• Avoid making fires.

• Use a T-shirt when snorkeling as sunscreen is harmful to the marine life.

TRANSPORT

• Use public rather than private transport (e.g. bus instead of rental car) where possible to reduce fossil fuel use. Share rental cars and taxis with others. If possible, walk or use a bicycle. It not only helps the planet, but it keeps you in shape as well!

ELECTRICITY

• Lights, fans, TVs, radios, or computers: if you are not using it, turn it off!

INDEX

TRAVELING WITH CHILDREN AND BABIES

• Try and teach your child about the local environmental issues. Point out good and bad practices.

• Encourage your child to snack on fruit—this has a biodegradable wrapper!

• If traveling with a baby, why not use cotton nappies? Disposable nappies are becoming a major waste issue in developed countries and are becoming a desirable product in the developing world. Using cotton will set a good example to others and reduce the promotion of disposable nappies.

LOCAL ENVIRONMENTAL ISSUES

• Try and find out what the important environmental issues are in the country. Good environmental practices (e.g. reduce, reuse, recycle!) are often the same in different countries, but the specific issues are often different (e.g. different recycling options, different endangered habitats and species, different laws and policies, etc.)

• Think about where you are eating and staying, and support the more environmentally friendly businesses. If you stay in an ecolodge, talk to the owners / managers, ask how they manage their garbage (including human waste), do they recycle, do they use grey water systems to be able to reuse their water? Where do their building materials, food, and power come from? Do they practice or contribute to conservation? Do they support the local community? Be constructive, rather than critical if you don't get a good response, some people truly think that it can be called an ecolodge if it is built with natural materials.

• Many countries have interesting volunteer opportunities with environmentally oriented organizations. Perhaps support these efforts by volunteering. Research carefully—some volunteer opportunities are not what they say they are. The South American Explorers Club (in Quito) keeps a binder with travelers' comments on Ecotourist volunteer opportunities.

The following is a list of helpful Environmental websites for further information:

WWW.ECOMALL.COM and WWW.GREENHOME.COM are both pages which contain links to places where you can buy all sorts of environmentally friendly products.

WWW.FNATURA.ORG Fundacaión Natura

WWW.AMBIENTE.GOV.EC Ministry of the Environment

WWW.ACCIONECOLOGICA.ORG Fundación Acción Ecologica

WWW.ECOCIENCIA.ORG Fundación Ecociencia

Index

INDEX

Tulcán, 33
Tumbabiro, 230, 232, 234
Tumbaco, 118, 129, 131
Tumipamba, 276
Tungurahua Volcano, 259, 261, 263, 307
Turismo Rural Kushi Waira, 280
TurismoEcuador, 254
Turtle, 109, 124, 177, 182, 194, 196, 212, 218, 355,
Turtle Bar, 385
Turtle Island, 182, 212
Turtle Rock, 183
Tutamanda Bed, 98

U

UNESCO Biosphere Reserve, 143
UNESCO Historical Landmark, 67
UNESCO International Biosphere Reserve, 319
UNESCO World Heritage Cultural, 276
UniGalápagos, 166
Unipark Hotel, 385
Uplands of El Oro, 368, 387
Upper Napo River, 315
Urban Architectural Zone, 383
Urbina Bay, 214, 217

V

Valle de Los Chillos, 129
Valley of Tumbaco, 129
Van Straelen Exhibition Center, 196
Vegan Cuisine, 46
Verde Limon Hostal, 281
Verde Milenio Foundation, 232
Verdecocha Expeditions, 326
Vicente León, 75
Vicente Rocafuerte, 371
Vieja Cuba, 101
Vilcabamba, 296
Villa Colonna Bed, 88
Visa Information, 33
Vista Hermosa, 91
Vistalmar Cabañas Boutique, 358
Volcan Antisana, 255
Volcan Reventador, 309
Volcano Land, 256
Volcanoes, 12, 21, 37, 67, 80, 128, 135, 185, 214, 227, 229, 223, 227, 233, 238, 253, 267, 271, 310,

W

Wahoo Restaurant, 367
Water-skiing, 144, 237
Waterfall of Peguche, 233
Waved Albatross, 12, 40, 169, 171, 207
Western Cordilleras, 37
Western Island Visitor Sites, 214
Whymper Peak, 266
Women Travelers, 42, 58
Wunderbar Café, 284

X

Xocoa, 104
Yachana Lodge, 300, 304

Y

Yarina Lodge, 300
Yasuní National Park, 300, 302, 316, 320
Yasuní Parrot Lick, 40
Yuturi Lodge, 300, 303, 319

Z

Zenith Travel, 72
Zucker Café, 269
Zócalo, 107

PACKING LISTS
(* indicates something that might not be available in Ecuador)

GENERAL PACKING LIST
There are a number of items that every traveler should consider bringing to Ecuador as follows:

- ☐ **Medicines and prescriptions** (Very important. Bringing all relevant medical info and medicines may well save you a lot of grief in Ecuador)
- ☐ **Photocopies of passport** and other relevant ID documents
- ☐ Paperback novels (sometimes you'll be sitting on buses, in airports, or some where else for a long time. Bring some books with you so you're not bored. It is possible to find and/or exchange books in several places in Ecuador, but don't count on much selection)
- ☐ Plug converter (many older buildings in Ecuador have 2-prong outlets only, although the voltage is the same)
- ☐ A good camera (see photography section)
- ☐ Water bottle (bottled water is readily available in Ecuador, but you may want your own bottle)
- ☐ Sunglasses
- ☐ Motion sickness medicine
- ☐ Lip balm
- ☐ *Tampons (difficult to find outside the major cities)
- ☐ Sun hat
- ☐ Condoms and other contraceptives
- ☐ *Foot powder
- ☐ Antacid tablets, such as Rolaids
- ☐ Mild painkillers such as aspirin or ibuprofen
- ☐ *GPS device (especially for hikers)
- ☐ Watch with alarm clock
- ☐ Diarrhea medicine (i.e. Imodium)
- ☐ Warm clothes (Quito and the highlands are cooler than you think).

BACKPACKER PACKING LIST:
- ☐ All of the above, plus,
- ☐ Rain poncho
- ☐ Plastic bags
- ☐ Swiss army knife/leatherman, *
- ☐ Toilet paper
- ☐ Antibacterial hand gel *
- ☐ Small padlock

RAIN FOREST PACKING LIST
- ☐ Rubber boots (most jungle lodges have them, call ahead)
- ☐ *Bug spray (with Deet)
- ☐ Flashlight
- ☐ Waterproof bags
- ☐ Rain poncho
- ☐ First aid kit
- ☐ *Compass
- ☐ Whistle
- ☐ Long-sleeved shirt and pants
- ☐ Malaria/yellow fever medicine
- ☐ Original passport
- ☐ Mosquito net (if your destination does not have one; call ahead)
- ☐ Biodegradable soap

INDEX

GALÁPAGOS PACKING LIST
- ☐ Extra film/camera supplies
- ☐ Waterproof disposable camera for snorkeling
- ☐ Sunscreen
- ☐ Good, wide brimmed hat
- ☐ Long pants, lightweight
- ☐ Long-sleeved shirt, lightweight

ADDITIONAL ITEMS
- ☐ _____
- ☐ _____
- ☐ _____
- ☐ _____
- ☐ _____
- ☐ _____
- ☐ _____
- ☐ _____

ANTI-PACKING LIST: THINGS NOT TO BRING TO ECUADOR
- x   Expensive jewelry. Just leave it home.
- x   Nice watch or sunglasses. Bring a cheap one you can afford to lose.
- x   Go through your wallet: what won't you need? Leave your drivers' license (unless you're planning on driving), business cards, video-club membership cards, 7-11 coffee club card, social security card and anything else you won't need at home. The only thing in your wallet you'll want is a student ID, and if you lose it you'll be gratefull you left the rest at home.
- x   Illegal drugs. You didn't need us to tell you that, did you?
- x   Stickers and little toys for kids. Some tourists like to hand them out, which means the children pester every foreigner they see.
- x   Really nice clothes or shoes, unless you're planning on going to a special event or dining out a lot.

INDEX

Useful Spanish Phrases

Conversational

Hello	Hola
Good morning	Buenos días
Good afternoon	Buenas tardes
Good evening	Buenas noches
Yes	Sí
No	No
Please	Por favor
Thank you	Gracias
It was nothing	De nada
Excuse me	Permiso
See you later	Hasta luego
Bye	Chao
Cool	Chévere
How are you (formal)	¿Cómo está?
" " " (informal)	¿Qué tal?
I don't understand	No entiendo.
Do you speak English?	¿Habla inglés?
I don't speak Spanish.	No hablo español.
I'm from England	Soy de Inglaterra
the USA	Soy de los Estados Unitos.

Food and Drink

Breakfast	Desayuno
Lunch	Almuerzo
Dinner	Cena
Check please	La cuenta por favor.
Main Course	Plato Fuerte
Menu	la carta
Spoon	Cuchara
Fork	Tenedor
Knife	Cuchillo
Bread	pan
Fruit	fruta
Vegetables	verduras
Potatoes	papas
Meat	carne
Chicken	pollo
Beer	cerveza
Wine	vino
Juice	jugo
Coffee	café
Tea	té

Health/Emergency

Call a....	¡Llame a...!
Ambulance	una ambulancia
A doctor	un médico
The police	la policía
It's an emergency.	Es una emergencia.
I'm sick	Estoy enfermo/a
I need a doctor	Necesito un médico.
Where's the hospital?	¿Dónde está el hospital?

I'm allergic to...	Soy alérgico/a a
Antibiotics	los antibióticos.
Nuts	nuez
Penicillin	la penicilina

Getting Around

Where is...?	¿Dónde está...?

The bus station	la estación de bus?
The train station	la estación de tren?
A bank?	¿El banco?
The bathroom?	¿El baño?
Left, right, straight	Izquierda, derecha, recto.
Ticket	Boleto
Where does the bus leave from?	¿De dónde sale el bus?

Accommodation

Where is a hotel?	¿Donde hay un hotel?
I want a room.	Quiero una habitación.
Single / Double / Marriage	Simple / Doble / Matrimonial
How much does it cost per night?	¿Cuanto cuesta por noche?
Does that include breakfast?	¿Incluye el desayuno?
Does that include taxes?	¿Incluye los impuestos?

INDEX

V!VA TRAVEL GUIDES BRINGS YOU A TEAR-OUT LIST OF USEFUL CONTACTS IN ECUADOR.

Feel free to photocopy this sheet for your use, to give to your dog, or to wallpaper your room.

EMERGENCY NUMBERS

All emergencies (Quito only)	911	Police	101 (24 hrs)
Fire	102	Red Cross	131

HOSPITALS / DOCTORS / PHARMACIES

Hospital Vozandes
Villalengua 267 (226 21 42) at 10 de Agosto
Has American and Ecuadorian physicians
24hr emergency room.

Hospital Metropolitano
Mariana de Jesus y Occidental
Tel: 593-2-226-1520
24 hr emergency room

Doctor: Dr John Rosenberg, Med Center Travel Clinic, Foch 476 y Almagro speaks English and German

24 hr Pharmacy: Fybeca – 24hr branches at Amazonas y Tomas de Berlanga and at Centro Comercial El Recreo in the south

ENGLISH SPEAKING LAWYERS IN QUITO (CRIMINAL)

Estudio Juridico Andrade Lara
Asunción 1031 and Canadá
Tel: 593-2-222-4933 Fax: 593-2-255-0782
E-mail: xaviandradec@yahoo.es

Fierro Ruiz Proaño & Co – Bld. Confa Office 203
Grl Vincente Aguiree Oe 121 y Av. 10 de Agosto
Tel: 539-2-250-5620 Fax: 593-2-255-0782
E-mail: chrisfg@ldu.com.ec

TRAVELER GUIDANCE: V!VA Travel Guides: www.vivatravelguides.com

South American Explorers (SAE)
Jorge Washington 311 and Leonidas Plaza
Tel/Fax: 593-2-222-5228
mailto:quitoclub@saexplorers.org
www.saexplorers.org

Ministry of Tourism
Eloy Alfaro N32-300 and Carlos Tobar
Tel: 593-2-250-0719
www.viveecuador.com

POST OFFICE (CORREOS)
Main: Eloy Alfaro 354 y 9 de Octubre
Old Town – Espejo 935 and Guayaquil
Colon y Reina Victoria in Bld.Torres de Almagro

INTERNET CAFES
Papaya Net: Calama and Juan León Mera
Friends: Calama y Diego del Amagro
Zambo Net: Juan León Mera and Pinto

TRANSPORT
Taxis – City-taxi 263 33 33   Occidentaltaxi 249 22 22   and Urgentaxi 222 21 11 offer 24hr service. Usually more expensive than flagging a cab on the street.

Bus Terminal – main bus terminal is Terminal Terrestre in the old city on Maldonado.

Complete the sections below for your convenience:

My Tour Operator:

My Hotel Address:

Taxi Directions to
the hotel:

INDEX

Find more reviews from travelers at www.vivatravelguides.com

AIRLINES:

Aerogal (Ecuadorian)
Amazonas 7797 and Juan Holguin
Tel: 593-2-244-1950

Mon – Fri 09:00 – 13:00 and 14:30 – 18:00
www.aerogal.com.ec

American Airlines (US)
Amazonas and Naciones Unidas First Floor
Tel: 593-2-226-0900
Mon-Fri 09:00-19:00
Sat 10:00–18:00, Sun 10:00–14:00
*Also located in the Hilton Colon and in Mall El Jardin

Avianca (Colombian)
Coruña 1311 y San Ignacio
Tel: 593-2-255-6715
Fax: 593-2-290-3351

Continental Airlines (US)
Av. Naciones Unidas y Rep. de el Salvador
Tel: 593-2-255-7290
Mon – Fri 09:00 – 1800, Sat. 09:00 – 13:00

COPA (Panamanian)
Veintimilla 910 and Juan León Mera
Tel: 593-2-224-9341   Fax: 593-2-227-0445
Mon – Fri 09:00–18:00, Sat 09:00-11:00

Iberia (Spanish)
Eloy Alfaro 939 y Amazonas, Bld. Finandes
566-009 Fax Res: 593-2-255-8033
iberia@pi.pro.ec

Icaro (Ecuadorian)
Amazonas and Calros Endara
Tel: 593-2-299-7400
E-mail: icaro@icaro.com.ec

KLM (Dutch)
12 de Octubre and Abraham Lincoln,
Building Torre 1492
Tel: 593-2-298-6840, Fax: 593-2-298-6640

Lan Chile (Chilean)
Amazonas
Tel: 593-2-256-3003
Mon – Fri 08:30-13:00, Sat 09:00-12:30
*Also located in Quicentro Shopping Center

Taca (El Salvador)
Rep. del Salvador 1033 and Naciones Unidas
www.taca.com.
Mon – Fri 08:30-17:30, Sat 09:00-12:30

TAME (Ecuadorian)
Amazonas 1354 and Colón, 2nd Floor
Tel: 593-2-250-9375 / 593-2-250-9380
For reservations: reservas@tame.com.ec

Varig (Brazilian)
Portugal 794 and República del SalvadorTel: 593-2-
Edificio Porto Lisboa
Tel: 593-2-225-0131

EMBASSIES IN QUITO:

Canada
6 de Diciembre 2816 & Paul Rivet,
Joseuth Gonzales Building, Office 4N
Tel & Fax: 593-2-250-6162 593-2-223-2114

France
Leónidas Plaza 107 and Patria
Tel: 593-2-294-3800 Fax: 593-2-254-6118

Germany
Naciones Unidas and Rep. Del Salvador,
Citiplaza Building, 14th Floor
Tel: 593-2-297-0821

Ireland
Antonio de Ulloa 2651 and Rumipamba
Tel: 593-2-245-1577 Fax: 593-2-226-9862

Italy
Isla 111 and Humberto Albornoz.
Tel: 593-2-256-1077 Fax: 593-2-250-2818

Japan
Juan León Mera 130 and Patria,
Corporación Financiera Bld. 7th Floor

Tel: 593-2-256-1899 Fax: 593-2-250-3670

Netherlands
12 de Octobre 1942 and Cordero,
World Trade Center Building A, 1st Floor
Tel:593-2-222-9229 Fax: 593-2-256-7917

Russia
Reina Victoria 462 and Roca
Tel: 593-2-252-6361 Fax: 593-2-256-5531

Switzerland
Juan Pablo Sanz 120 and Amazonas,
Xerox Building, 2nd Floor
Tel: 593-2-243-4948, Fax: 593-2-244-9314

Spain
La Pinta 455 and Amazonas
Tel: 593-2-256-4373, Fax: 593-2-250-0826

United Kingdom
Naciones Unidas and Rep. del Salvador, Citiplaza Bld
Tel: 593-2-297-0800, Fax: 593-2-297-0809

United States of America
12 de Octubre and Patria
Tel: 593-2-256-2890 Fax: 593-2-250-2052

NOTES:

Printed in the United States
110262LV00001B/60/A